Resource Kit

KT-194-676

Microsoft

WINDOWS

SECURITY

RESOURCE KIT

Ben Smith and Brian Komar
with the Microsoft Security Team

PUBLISHED BY
Microsoft Press
A Division of Microsoft Corporation
One Microsoft Way
Redmond, Washington 98052-6399

Copyright © 2003 by Ben Smith and Brian Komar

All rights reserved. No part of the contents of this book may be reproduced or transmitted in any form or by any means without the written permission of the publisher.

Library of Congress Cataloging-in-Publication Data
Smith, Ben
    Microsoft Windows Security Resource Kit / Ben Smith, Brian Komar.
       p. cm.
    Includes index.
    ISBN 0-7356-1868-2
    1. Computer security. 2. Microsoft Windows (Computer file) I. Komar, Brian. II.
Title.

    QA76.9.A25S63   2003
    005.8--dc21   2002045167

Printed and bound in the United States of America.

1 2 3 4 5 6 7 8 9   QWT   8 7 6 5 4 3

Distributed in Canada by H.B. Fenn and Company Ltd.

A CIP catalogue record for this book is available from the British Library.

Microsoft Press books are available through booksellers and distributors worldwide. For further information about international editions, contact your local Microsoft Corporation office or contact Microsoft Press International directly at fax (425) 936-7329. Visit our Web site at www.microsoft.com/mspress. Send comments to *rkinput@microsoft.com.*

Active Directory, ActiveSync, ActiveX, DirectX, FrontPage, MapPoint, Microsoft, Microsoft Press, MSDN, NetMeeting, Outlook, PowerPoint, SharePoint, Visual Basic, Visual SourceSafe, Visual Studio, Windows, Windows NT, and Win32 are either registered trademarks or trademarks of Microsoft Corporation in the United States and/or other countries. Other product and company names mentioned herein may be the trademarks of their respective owners.

The example companies, organizations, products, domain names, e-mail addresses, logos, people, places, and events depicted herein are fictitious. No association with any real company, organization, product, domain name, e-mail address, logo, person, place, or event is intended or should be inferred.

Acquisitions Editor: Martin DelRe
Project Editor: Julie Miller
Technical Editors: Laura Robinson and Ronald Beekalaar

Body Part No. X09-06385

Table of Contents

Part III   Securing the Core Operating System

7   Securing Permissions   135

8   Securing Services   173

Part VII   Applying Key Principles of Privacy

Foreword

Security is not binary. It is not a switch or even a series of switches. It cannot be expressed in absolute terms. Do not believe anyone who tries to convince you otherwise. Security is relative—there is only more secure and less secure. Furthermore, security is dynamic—people, process, and technology all change. The bottom line is that all of these factors make managing security difficult.

This book has been designed and written to help you increase, assess, and maintain the security of computers running Microsoft Windows 2000 and Microsoft Windows XP. It will also help you better understand how people and process are integral parts of security. By applying the principles, practices, and recommendations detailed in this book, we hope that you are not only better equipped to manage security but also better equipped to think about security!

Good luck!

Ben Smith and Brian Komar
January 2003

Acknowledgments

Although our names are listed on the cover, we are by no means the only people who deserve credit for writing this book. We have been fortunate and honored to be surrounded by some of the very best people in the industry—this book is their creation also.

From the outset, we wanted to create a book that would be readable. Two groups of people shared this goal and were instrumental in making it happen: our technical editors, Laura Robinson and Ronald Beekalaar, and the team at Microsoft Press. Laura did a lot to shape the early part of this book, and Ronald's incredible eye for detail kept us from making many embarrassing errors and contributed countless tips and tricks. Ronald was also the driving force in ensuring that the examples and prose in this book would be clear to non–U.S. residents and non–native English speakers. In the end, however, all errors and omissions are ours.

Readers who know the two of us will realize that Michelle Goodman, the copy editor, had one of the most daunting tasks of producing this book: taming our verbosity! Her attention to detail, memory, and remarkable ability to minimize the number of adverbs used per sentence proved invaluable. Dan Latimer, desktop publisher, and Joel Panchot, artist, did an amazing job of creating a great-looking book—without their contributions, this book would be little more than a pile of Microsoft Word documents. Julie Miller, the project editor, pulled it all together—a truly gargantuan task. Thank you! We also would like to thank the first person who worked on this book—Martin DelRe, the acquisitions editor. Thanks for sticking with it, Martin!

We would like to acknowledge and thank JC Cannon for writing the three chapters on privacy and Jeff Williams for writing the two chapters on incident response. We also would like to thank the following people for reviewing material, answering questions, or otherwise contributing to this book: Jesper Johansson, Andreas Luther, Eric Fitzgerald, Mike Lonergan, David Cross, Joern Wettern, Joe Davies, Laudon Williams, William Dixon, Henry Voight, Rob Trace, Eric Schultze, Aaron Turner, Elliot Lewis, Mike Hintze, and Kristen McCarthy. We would also like to thank Emmanuel Dreux, David Burrell, and Greg Winston who contributed tools they had written to the CD that accompanies this book.

Most important, we would like to thank our wives: Beth Boatright and Krista Kunz. Their support and tolerance is remarkable and much appreciated—more so than we can ever express in words. Thank you.

Ben Smith and Brian Komar
January 2003

Introduction

Welcome to the *Microsoft Windows Security Resource Kit*. This book provides detailed information about security features in Microsoft Windows 2000 and Microsoft Windows XP and explains how to better secure computers running these operating systems. This book also provides information on managing security and privacy on Windows-based computers.

About This Resource Kit

Although you are welcome to read the book from cover to cover, it is divided into seven parts for your convenience. Each part covers a different aspect of Windows 2000 and Windows XP security that you can read in advance of implementing security on computers running these operating systems or as a reference on the job.

The seven parts of this book are:

- **Part 1, "Applying Key Principles of Security,"** provides an overview of thinking about security on a daily basis. Part 1 also introduces some of the fundamental challenges of managing security and provides guidance on how to overcome them.

- **Part 2, "Securing Active Directory,"** provides information on the security of the Active Directory directory service—from handling design issues associated with forests and domains to controlling access to objects and attributes. Part 2 has detailed information on how to secure accounts and authentication—the two central components of security in Windows 2000 and Windows XP. Part 2 also describes how you can use Group Policy to increase the security of networks that use Active Directory.

- **Part 3, "Securing the Core Operating System,"** provides detailed information on how to increase the security of Windows 2000 and Windows XP. Part 3 also discusses how to better secure applications, such as Microsoft Office XP and Microsoft Internet Explorer 6.0, and mobile computers.

- **Part 4, "Securing Common Services,"** describes how to secure common services that run on Microsoft Windows 2000 Server, including Domain Name System (DNS), Dynamic Host Configuration Protocol (DHCP), Windows Internet Name Service (WINS), Terminal Services, Certificate Services, Routing and Remote Access Service (RRAS), and Microsoft Internet Information Services 5.0.

- **Part 5, "Managing Security Updates,"** includes detailed information on the process of managing security updates, including service packs and hotfixes, and discusses strategies for deploying security updates. Part 5 also describes techniques for assessing the security of computers running Windows 2000 and Windows XP.

- **Part 6, "Planning and Performing Security Assessments and Incident Responses,"** provides detailed explanations of security assessments, including vulnerability scanning, IT audits, and penetration testing, and discusses how each can be used to assess the security of your network. Part 6 also provides information about how to design an incident response procedure and introduces methods for investigating security incidents.

- **Part 7, "Applying Key Principles of Privacy,"** provides administrators with an introduction to privacy and how privacy issues impact the collection and storage of both corporate and customer information. Part 7 also includes practical guidance on how administrators can increase the privacy of information.

Resource Kit Companion CD

The *Microsoft Windows Security Resource Kit* companion CD includes a variety of tools and scripts to help you work more efficiently when implementing and managing security on computers running Windows 2000 and Windows XP. Several of these tools are discussed in the book; however, many are not. You can find documentation for each tool in the folder in which the tool is contained. Many of these tools are from the *Microsoft Windows 2000 Server Resource Kit*, Supplement One, so they are designed to be implemented with Windows 2000 operating systems. Specifically, these are the tools found in the root of the Tools folder and the scripts found in the Tools/Scripts/Remote Administration Scripts folder. The companion CD also includes a fully searchable electronic version (eBook).

Resource Kit Support Policy

Microsoft does not support the tools and scripts supplied on the *Microsoft Windows Security Resource Kit* companion CD. Microsoft does not guarantee the performance of the tools or scripting examples, or any bug fixes for these tools and scripts. However, Microsoft Press provides a way for customers who purchase the *Microsoft Windows Security Resource Kit* to report any problems with the software and receive feedback for such issues. To report any issues or problems, send e-mail to rkinput@microsoft.com. This e-mail address is only for issues related to the *Microsoft Windows Security Resource Kit*. Microsoft Press also provides corrections for books and companion CDs through the World Wide Web at: *http://www.microsoft.com/mspress/support/*. To connect directly to the Microsoft Press Knowledge Base and enter a query regarding a question or issue that you may have, go to: *http://www.microsoft.com/mspress/support/ search.as*p. For issues related to the Windows OS, please refer to the support information included with your product.

Part I

Applying Key Principles of Security

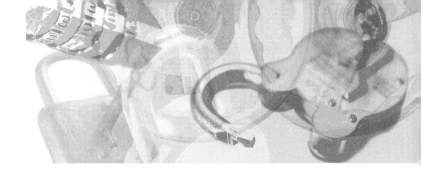

1

Key Principles of Security

Managing information security is difficult. To do it well requires a combination of technical, business, and people skills, many of which are not intuitive. The foundation of information security is risk management. Without a good understanding of risk management, it is impossible to secure any large modern network. More often than not, the failure of network administrators and managers to build a secure network results in the organization's most closely held information being as secure as the lunch menu. Thus, either the lunch menu will be very secure, or the security of important information will be very weak. Neither situation is workable in the long run.

Not every network administrator is a security expert, and most need not be. However, all network administrators must understand the basics of security. There are several key principles that you can follow to secure your networks and applications. By acting on these key principles when completing your day-to-day tasks, you can secure your network—even without being a security expert. And if you are a security specialist or want to become one, you must master these key principles.

Understanding Risk Management

The first key principle of security is that no network is completely secure—information security is really about risk management. In the most basic of terms, the more important the asset is and the more it is exposed to security threats, the more resources you should put into securing it. Thus, it is imperative that you understand how to evaluate an asset's value, the threats to an asset, and the appropriate security measures. In general, without training, administrators respond to a security threat in one of three ways shown on the next page.

- Ignore the threat, or acknowledge it but do nothing to prevent it from occurring.

- Address the threat in an ad hoc fashion.

- Attempt to completely secure all assets to the utmost degree, without regard for usability or manageability.

None of these strategies takes into account what the actual risk is, and all of them will almost certainly lead to long-term failure.

Learning to Manage Risk

Managing security risks can be an incredibly daunting task, especially if you fail to do so in a well-organized and well-planned manner. Risk management often requires experience with financial accounting and budgeting as well as the input of business analysts. Building a risk assessment of an organization's security can take months and generally involves many people from many parts of the company. You can follow this simple process for assessing and managing risk:

1. **Set a scope.**   If you try to assess and manage all security risks in your organization, you are likely to be overwhelmed and certain to miss critical details. Before starting the risk assessment, set the scope of the risk assessment project. This will enable you to better estimate the time and cost required to assess the security risks in the project and to more easily document and track the results.

2. **Identify assets and determine their value.**   The first step in assessing risk is to identify assets and determine their value. When determining an asset's value, take these three factors into account:

    ❑   The financial impact of the asset's compromise or loss

    ❑   The nonfinancial impact of the asset's compromise or loss

    ❑   The value of the asset to your competitors

    The financial impact of an asset's compromise or loss includes revenue and productivity lost because of downtime, costs associated with recovering services, and direct equipment losses. The nonfinancial impact of an asset's compromise or loss includes resources used shaping public perception of a security incident, such as advertising campaigns, and loss of public trust or confidence, known as *goodwill in accounting*. The value of the asset to your organization should be the main factor in determining how you secure the resource. If you do not adequately understand your assets and their value, you might end up securing the lunch menu in the cafeteria as stringently as you secure your trade secrets.

3.   **Predict threats and vulnerabilities to assets.**   The process of predicting threats and vulnerabilities to assets is known as *threat modeling*. Through the exercise of modeling threats, you will likely discover threats and vulnerabilities that you did not know about or had overlooked, and you will document the more well-known threats and vulnerabilities. You can then proactively mitigate risk rather than having to react to it after a security incident.

4.   **Document the security risks.**   After completing the threat model, it is essential that you document the security risks so that they can be reviewed by all relevant people and addressed systematically. When documenting the risks, you might want to rank them. You can rank risks either *quantitatively* or *qualitatively*. Quantitative rankings will use actual and estimated financial data about the assets to assess the severity of the risks. For example, you might determine that a single incident of a security risk will cost your organization $20,000 in financial losses while another will cost the organization only $5,000. Qualitative rankings use a system to assess the relative impact of the risks. For example, a common qualitative system is to rank the product of the probability of the risk occurring and the value of the asset on a 10-point scale. Neither quantitative nor qualitative risk assessment is superior to the other; rather, they complement each other. Quantitative ranking often requires acute accounting skills, while qualitative ranking often requires acute technical skills.

5.   **Determine a risk management strategy.**   After completing the risk assessment, you must determine what general risk management strategy to pursue and what security measures you will implement in support of the risk management strategy. The result from this step is a risk management plan. The risk management plan should clearly state the risk, threat, impact on the organization, risk management strategy, and security measures that will be taken. As a security administrator, you will likely be responsible for or involved in implementing the security measures in the risk management plan.

6.   **Monitor the assets.**   Once the actions defined in the risk management plan have been implemented, you will need to monitor the assets for realization of the security risks. As we've alluded, realization of a security risk is called a *security incident*. You will need to trigger actions defined in contingency plans and start investigating the security incident as soon as possible to limit the damage to your organization.

7.   **Track changes to risks.**   As time progresses, changes to your organization's hardware, software, personnel, and business processes will add and obsolete security risks. Similarly, threats to assets and vulnerabilities will evolve and increase in sophistication. You will need to track these changes and update the risk management plan and the associated security measures regularly.

Risk Management Strategies

Once you have identified an asset and the threats to it, you can begin determining what security measures to implement. The first step is to decide on the appropriate risk management strategy. The rest of this section will examine the four general categories of risk management that you can pursue:

■   Acceptance

■   Mitigation

■   Transference

■   Avoidance

Accepting Risk

By taking no proactive measures, you accept the full exposure and consequences of the security threats to an asset. Accepting risk is an extreme reaction to a threat. You should accept risk only as a last resort when no other reasonable alternatives exist, or when the costs associated with mitigating or transferring the risk are prohibitive or unreasonable. When accepting risk, it is always a good idea to create a contingency plan. A contingency plan details a set of actions that will be taken after the risk is realized and will lessen the impact of the compromise or loss of the asset.

Mitigating Risk

The most common method of securing computers and networks is to mitigate security risks. By taking proactive measures to either reduce an asset's exposure to threats or reduce the organization's dependency on the asset, you are mitigating the security risk. Generally, reducing an organization's dependency on an asset is beyond the scope of a security administrator's control; however, the former is the primary job function of a security administrator. One of the simplest examples of mitigating a security risk is installing antivirus software. By installing and maintaining antivirus software, you greatly reduce a computer's exposure to computer viruses, worms, and Trojan horses. Installing and maintaining antivirus software does not eliminate the possibility of a computer being infected with a virus because there will inevitably be new viruses that the anti-virus software cannot yet protect the computer against. Thus, when a risk is mitigated, you still should create a contingency plan to follow if the risk is realized.

When deciding to mitigate risk, one of the key financial metrics to consider is how much your organization will save because of mitigating the risk, less the cost of implementing the security measure. If the result is a positive number and no other prohibitive factors exist, such as major conflicts with business operations, implementing the security measure is generally a good idea. On occasion, the cost of implementing the security measure will exceed the amount of money saved but will still be worthwhile—for example, when human life is at risk.

Transferring Risk

An increasingly common and important method of addressing security risks is to transfer some of the risk to a third party. You can transfer a security risk to another party to take advantage of economies of scale, such as insurance, or to take advantage of another organization's expertise and services, such as a Web hosting service. With insurance, you are paying a relatively small fee to recuperate or lessen financial losses if the security risk should occur. This is especially important when the financial consequences of your security risk are abnormally large, such as making your organization vulnerable to class action lawsuits. When contracting a company to host your organization's Web site, you stand to gain sophisticated Web security services and a highly trained, Web-savvy staff that your organization might not have afforded otherwise. When you engage in this type of risk transference, the details of the arrangement should be clearly stated in a contract known as a *service level agreement (SLA)*. Always have your organization's legal staff thoroughly investigate all third parties and contracts when transferring risk.

Avoiding Risk

The opposite of accepting risk is to avoid the risk entirely. To avoid risk, you must remove the source of the threat, exposure to the threat, or your organization's reliance on the asset. Generally, you avoid risk when there are little to no possibilities for mitigating or transferring the risk, or when the consequences of realizing the risk far outweigh the benefits gained from undertaking the risk. For example, a law enforcement agency might want to create a database of known informants that officers can access through the Internet. A successful compromise of the database could result in lives being lost. Thus, even though many ways to secure access to the database exist, there is zero tolerance of a security compromise. Therefore, risk must be avoided by not placing the database on the Internet, or perhaps not storing the information electronically at all.

Understanding Security

The most fundamental skill in securing computers and networks is understanding the big picture of security. By understanding the big picture of how to secure computers and networks as well as the limitations of security, you can avoid spending time, money, and energy attempting impossible or impractical security measures. You can also spend less time resecuring assets that have been jeopardized by poorly conceived or ineffective security measures.

Granting the Least Privilege Required

Always think of security in terms of granting the least amount of privileges required to carry out the task. Excess privileges serve no useful business or technical proposes and can lead to users, administrators, or attackers taking advantage of them.

Defending Each Network Layer

Imagine the security of your network as an onion. Each layer you pull away gets you closer to the center, where the critical asset exists. On your network, defend each layer as though the next outer layer is ineffective or nonexistent. The aggregate security of your network will increase exponentially if you defend vigilantly at all levels.

Reducing the Attack Surface

Attackers are functionally unlimited and thus possess unlimited time, while you have limited time and resources. (The concept of being functionally unlimited is detailed in Chapter 2, "Understanding Your Enemy.") An attacker needs to know of only one vulnerability to successfully attack your network, while you must pinpoint all your vulnerabilities to defend your network. The smaller your attack surface, the better chance you have of accounting for all assets and their protection. Attackers will have fewer targets, and you will have less to monitor and maintain.

Avoiding Assumptions

Making assumptions will generally result in you overlooking, prematurely dismissing, or incorrectly assessing critical details. Often these details are not obvious or are buried deep within a process or technology. That is why you must test everything! You might also want to hire a third party to assess the security of your network or applications. Some organizations might even have legal or regulatory compliance statutes that require them to undergo this type of evaluation.

Protecting, Detecting, and Responding

When you think about securing a computer or a network, think about how you can protect the asset proactively, detect attempted security incidents, and respond to security incidents. This is the security life cycle. By looking at security from this perspective, you will be better prepared to handle unpredictable events.

Securing by Design, Default, and Deployment

When you design networks, ensure that the following criteria are met:

- Your design is completed with security as an integral component.

- Your design is secure by default.

- The deployment and ongoing management of the implementation maintains the security of the network.

By accomplishing these three goals, you can address security proactively and natively rather than reactively and artificially.

The 10 Immutable Laws of Security

In 2000, Scott Culp of the Microsoft Security Response Center published the article "The Ten Immutable Laws of Security" on the Microsoft Web site, which you can read at *http://www.microsoft.com/technet/treeview/default.asp?url=/technet/columns/security/essays/10imlaws.asp*. Despite that the Internet and computer security are changing at a staggering rate, these laws remain true. These 10 laws do an excellent job of describing some of the limitations of security:

1. **If a bad guy can persuade you to run his program on your computer, it's not your computer anymore.**   Often attackers attempt to encourage the user to install software on the attacker's behalf. Many viruses and Trojan horse applications operate this way. For example, the ILOVEYOU virus succeeded only because unwitting users ran the script when it arrived in an e-mail message. Another emerging class of applications that attackers prompt a user to install are spyware applications. Once installed, spyware monitors a user's activities on his computer and reports the results to the attacker.

2. **If a bad guy can alter the operating system on your computer, it's not your computer anymore.**   A securely installed operating system and the securely procured hardware that it is installed on is referred to as a *Trusted Computing Base (TCB)*. If an attacker can replace or modify any of the operating system files or certain components of the system's hardware, the TCB can no longer be trusted. For example, an attacker might replace the file Passfilt.dll, which is used to enforce password complexity with a version of the file that also records all passwords used on the system. If an operating system has been comprised or you cannot prove that it has not been compromised, you should no longer trust the operating system.

3. **If a bad guy has unrestricted physical access to your computer, it's not your computer anymore.**   Once an attacker possesses physical access to a computer, you can do little to prevent the attacker from gaining administrator privileges on the operating system. With administrator privilege compromised, nearly all persistently stored data is at risk of being exposed. Similarly, an attacker with physical access could install hardware or software to monitor and record keystrokes that is completely transparent to the user. If a computer has been physically compromised or you cannot prove otherwise, you should not trust the computer.

4. **If you allow a bad guy to upload programs to your Web site, it's not your Web site any more.**   An attacker who can execute applications or modify code on your Web site can take full control of the Web site. The most obvious symptom of this is an attacker defacing an organization's Web site. A corollary to this law is that if a Web site requests input from the user, attackers will use bad input. For example, you might have a form that asks for a number between 1 and 100. While normal users will enter numbers within the specified data range, an attacker will try to use any data input he feels will break the back-end application.

5. **Weak passwords trump strong security.**   Even if a network design is thoroughly secure, if users and administrators use blank, default, or otherwise simple passwords, the security will be rendered ineffective once an attacker cracks the password.

6. **A machine is only as secure as the administrator is trustworthy.**   One constant on all networks is that you must trust the network administrators. The more administrative privileges an administrator account has, the more the administrator must be trusted. In other words, if you do not trust someone, do not give him administrator privileges.

7. **Encrypted data is only as secure as the decryption key.**   No encryption algorithm will protect the ciphertext from an attacker if she possesses or can gain possession of the decryption key. Encryption alone is not a solution to a business problem unless there is a strong component of key management and unless users and administrators are vigilant in protecting their keys or key material.

8. **An out-of-date virus scanner is only marginally better than no virus scanner at all.**   New computer viruses, worms, and Trojan horses are always emerging and existing ones evolving. Consequently, antivirus software can become outdated quickly. As new or modified viruses are released, antivirus software is updated. Antivirus software that is not updated to recognize a given virus will not be able to prevent it.

9. **Absolute anonymity isn't practical, in real life or on the Web.**   Two issues related to security that are often confused are *privacy* and *anonymity*. Anonymity means that your identity and details about your identity are completely unknown and untraceable, while privacy means that your identity and details about your identity are not disclosed. Privacy is essential, and technology and laws make achieving it possible. On the other hand, anonymity is not possible or practical when on the Internet, or when using computers in general.

10. **Technology is not a panacea.**   Although technology can secure computers and computer networks, it is not—and will never be—a solution in and of itself. You must combine technology with people and processes to create a secure computing environment.

The 10 Immutable Laws of Security Administration

As a follow-up to his article on security, Microsoft's Scott Culp wrote "The Ten Immutable Laws of Security Administration," which you can find at *http://www.microsoft.com/technet/treeview/default.asp?url=/technet/columns/security/essays/10salaws.asp*. These 10 laws address the security issues that network administrators must contend with, issues entirely separate from the day-to-day security concerns of users:

1. **Nobody believes anything bad can happen to them, until it does.**   Because attacks on computer networks often cannot be seen, felt, or heard, it is easy for users and administrators to place them out of their minds. With attacks far from one's mind, it is difficult to see the need for security. Unfortunately, after a security incident takes place, the need for security is frequently still dismissed and the

breach regarded as a one-time incident. Attackers *will* attempt to compromise the security of your network. It is not a question of if or when—it is a question of how frequently. You must protect your networks against attackers, detect their attempts to compromise your network, and respond when security incidents do occur.

2. **Security only works if the secure way also happens to be the easy way.**   For most users and administrators, the more difficult or invasive a security measure is, the more likely they are to ignore it, forget it, or subvert it. Ideally, security should be transparent to users and administrators. When the security measure requires a user or an administrator to change his behavior, you should create clear and easy-to-follow procedures for completing the task in question and explain your rationale for implementing the security measure.

3. **If you don't keep up with security fixes, your network won't be yours for long.**   After a security update is announced and the vulnerability is explained, a race begins between attackers attempting to exploit the vulnerability and administrators attempting to apply the security update. If you do not keep up with applying security updates, an attacker will exploit one of the known vulnerabilities on your network.

4. **It doesn't do much good to install security fixes on a computer that was never secure to begin with.**   Although installing security updates will prevent exposure to newly discovered vulnerabilities, installing security updates in and of itself will not result in a secure computer. For a computer to be secure, it is essential that the base operating system be securely configured.

5. **Eternal vigilance is the price of security.**   Security is an ongoing effort. The security administrator must remain vigilant to attacks and attackers who constantly strive to increase the level of sophistication of their attacks. An infinite number of potential attackers exist, and they have infinite time on their hands to crack your network. Attackers have little to lose and need to know only one exploit. Security administrators, on the other hand, have a finite amount of time and resources to defend their organization's network. A security administrator is defeated when a single attack is successful against the network.

6. **There really is someone out there trying to guess your passwords.** Because of the mythic qualities surrounding attackers—much like the monster under the bed—it is easy to push the possibility of attackers out of one's mind. Unlike the monster under the bed, attackers do exist and they do attack networks. In movies, attackers break powerful encryption algorithms; in real life, they guess simple passwords and exploit mundane, known vulnerabilities.

7. **The most secure network is a well-administered one.** Although a security expert can secure a network, it will not remain secure if it is not well managed—from the CIO, to the security administrator, to the end user.

8. **The difficulty of defending a network is directly proportional to its complexity.** The more complex a network is, the greater the chance for administrators to misconfigure computers, lose track of the configuration of computers, and fail to understand how the network really works. When in doubt, keep it simple.

9. **Security isn't about risk avoidance; it's about risk management.** You will never avoid all security risks. It would be too costly and impractical. Claims of unbreakable security stem from ignorance or arrogance.

10. **Technology is not a panacea.** Although it is essential to ensure the bits and bytes on your network are configured securely, doing so will not prevent rogue administrators, poor processes, careless users, or apathetic managers.

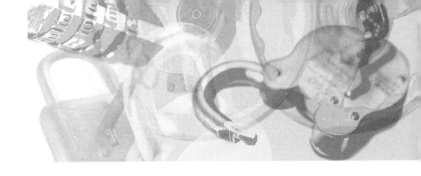

2

Understanding Your Enemy

"If you know the enemy and know yourself, you need not fear the result of a hundred battles. If you know yourself but not the enemy, for every victory gained you will also suffer a defeat. If you know neither the enemy nor yourself, you will succumb in every battle."

—*The Art of War*, Sun Tzu

Although Sun Tzu's classic military-strategy text, *The Art of War*, was written more than 2000 years before computers were invented, many of the statements are relevant to computer security. Figure 2-1 expresses the principle of battle in a binary decision table.

	Know your enemy	Do not know your enemy
You know yourself	You will generally succeed	You will succeed sometimes
Do not know yourself	You will succeed sometimes	You will never succeed

Figure 2-1   Decision table of knowing your enemy and yourself

Knowing Yourself

In respect to information security, knowing yourself and your enemy is not necessarily a straightforward endeavor—if it were, networks would be much more secure than they are today. To know yourself, you must do the following:

- Accurately assess your own skills.

- Possess detailed documentation of your network.

- Understand the level of organizational support you receive.

Accurately Assessing Your Own Skills

The skill set of a network administrator should include formal training on operating systems and applications; experience designing, installing, and configuring networks and network services; and the ability to predict problems before they occur and solve them when they do. To prevent design and configuration mistakes that can lead to security breaches, you must be able to accurately assess your network management skill set. Overestimating your knowledge of a network, operating system, or application can easily lead to vulnerabilities that attackers can exploit. Accurately assessing your skill set enables you to be proactive in obtaining training and acquiring the services of experienced consultants if the situation requires it.

For example, you might be asked to install and configure an Internet Web server for customers to access their order history on a Web application that your organization is deploying. Although you might be an experienced MCSE who has installed and configured intranet Web servers, you might not have any knowledge or experience with Internet Web applications or configuring servers that have direct Internet connectivity. By not accurately assessing your skills, you could easily and unwittingly expose customer information to attackers and not realize it until the information has already been compromised.

Possessing Detailed Documentation of Your Network

A key requirement of securing your organization's network is maintaining detailed documentation about the physical infrastructure of your network, complete and up-to-date network diagrams, documentation of the configuration of computers, applications, and the audit log. Without this documentation, network administrators might overlook resources that must be secured, and the network will almost certainly be inconsistent in its level of security. Without baseline performance and security information, it is difficult to detect attacks, regardless of whether they are successful. For example, your network might have a direct connection to the Internet that is no longer used but is still connected to a router. Over time, a router's access control list (ACL) can become outdated and can present a significant security risk. This is because the outdated ACL can enable an attacker to compromise your organization's network by using tactics that did not exist when the router was secure and was monitored. Although such situations might seem obscure, they are quite common for organizations that have grown by being acquired by another organization. When consolidating IT resources, you can easily overlook these types of details. Similarly, it often takes such organizations a long time to create detailed documentation on their newly formed networks.

Understanding the Level of Organizational Support You Receive

The level of support that you receive from your organization—from management to your end users—greatly determines how you will secure network resources. This is often called your organization's *security position* or *security posture*. The security position of your organization includes the level of executive sponsorship for security policies and procedures, security requirements mandated by industry or government regulations, end user compliance with security policies and procedures, and training for end users and administrators. Your organization's security policies and procedures are central to the level of organizational support that you have.

In general, the completeness and clarity of an organization's security policies and procedures can indicate the support network administrators will receive for securing a network. Failing to understand your organization's security position can result in you oversecuring network resources to the point that end users will work around security measures and cause security vulnerabilities. For example, your organization might create policies that greatly restrict the types of Web applications that can be installed on a Web server, causing departments to purchase and deploy their own Web servers. Because the IT department does not know of the rogue Web servers, it cannot manage the application of security updates and services packs to those servers.

Identifying Your Attacker

Knowing your enemy is as complicated as knowing yourself—maybe even more so. Too often, network administrators know their enemies only through stereotypes of attackers, and like most stereotypes, these are generally not accurate and rely on fear. For example, when you see movies that portray computer crime, more often then not, the penetration of the computer systems involves breaking an encryption key. The movie attacker fiercely pounds at his keyboard to break the encryption key by guessing it, which usually happens within a matter of seconds. Or he quickly writes a program with a well-designed user interface featuring big numbers that crack each character in the encryption key one by one. Although both attacks add drama to these movies, they are not only mathematically absurd and impossible, they also are not an accurate depiction of how networks are attacked. If this is all you know about the people who will attack your network, your network will be compromised.

In reality, breaking an industry-standard encryption key such as the 25-year-old Data Encryption Standard (DES) algorithm takes special hardware, significant computer programming skills, and plenty of time. To prove the insecurity of the DES algorithm, the Electronic Frontier Foundation (EFF) spent more than a year building a computer, using custom-built hardware and software, that could crack a 56-bit DES key. It took three days to crack the key.

You could design and build a network more secure then a government currency vault, but it would take only one computer that does not have the latest service pack installed for an attacker to compromise the network. A computer network looks very different from the attacker's point of view than from your viewpoint, as the defender. For example, you might think applying a security update for a known vulnerability to all but one computer on your network will be successful. To the attacker, this lone computer without the security update is the key to compromising the network.

By understanding (or "knowing") the attacker, you can think like an attacker when designing security for your network. For example, many organizations complete vulnerability assessments on their networks. But you might want to consider training members of your organization's IT staff or hiring external experts to attempt to break into the network from the outside. We describe this process in detail in Chapter 25, "Assessing the Security of a Network." In fact, there are those in the field of computer security who boldly assert that you cannot secure a computer network without being able to attack one.

When most people think about attackers, or "hackers," they generally think of a know-it-all, 14-year-old boy who wears a black T-shirt every day and is pale as a vampire as a result of all the hours he spends in front of his computer or video game console. Although this stereotypical attacker certainly exists, he represents only a small portion of the attacker population. For convenience, we'll group attackers into two general categories: external attackers (those outside your organization) and internal attackers (those within it).

Understanding External Attackers

The majority of attackers that you hear about in the media work outside the organizations they attack. These attackers include everyone from teenagers to professional hackers employed by governments and rogue nations. In addition to the attackers who are outright malicious, there exist groups of self-styled "white hat," or nonmalicious, attackers. Although these attackers might not have malicious intentions, they present significant dangers to networks too. For example, a "harmless" attacker might break into a network for the challenge, but while attempting to compromise a server, might render it inoperable, resulting in a denial-of-service condition. When examining attackers, it can be helpful to think about the dangers they present in terms of their skill level—be it novice, intermediate, or advanced.

Novice Attackers

Novice attackers generally possess only rudimentary programming skills and basic knowledge of the inner workings of operating systems and applications. These attackers represent the majority of attackers. Although this group of attackers might not possess significant skills, they are a threat to networks primarily because of the number of them out there and the knowledge they lack. For example, a novice attacker is much more apt to destroy information (either intentionally or accidentally) even though it will reveal her compromise of the network and quite possibly result in her apprehension. Although secure networks will rarely be compromised by novice attackers, networks that are not vigilantly secured are extremely vulnerable to this type of attacker because of the sheer number of them. Novice attackers exploit known vulnerabilities with tools created by more experienced attackers, and thus are often called *script kiddies*. They also present a serious threat to obvious security vulnerabilities, such as weak passwords. Novice attackers who are also employees (making them internal attackers) often present the same level of danger as external attackers because they already posses valid network credentials from which they can launch attacks and they have access to network documentation.

Intermediate Attackers

Attackers with intermediate skills are less numerous than novice attackers but generally possess programming skills that enable them to automate attacks and better exploit known vulnerabilities in operating systems and applications. This group of attackers is capable of penetrating most networks if given enough time, but they might not be able to do so without being detected. These attackers frequently port attacks from other operating systems and conduct more sophisticated attacks than novice attackers. Attackers with an intermediate skill level often launch such attacks as an attempt to increase their notoriety or boost their skill level by creating tools to attack networks and publishing information that helps other attackers break into networks.

Advanced Attackers

Attackers with advanced skills usually are not only accomplished programmers but also have experience breaking into networks and applications. These attackers discover vulnerabilities in operating systems and applications and create tools to exploit previously unknown vulnerabilities. Advanced attackers are generally capable of compromising most networks without being detected, unless those networks are extremely secure and have well-established incident response procedures.

Understanding Internal Attackers

Contrary to what you might hear in the media, the majority of attacks on networks are conducted by attackers who have company badges—in other words, your fellow employees. Attackers who are employees of the organization they're attacking present a unique danger to networks for several reasons. Such attackers have the following in their favor:

- Higher levels of trust
- Physical access to network resources
- Human resources protections

Higher Levels of Trust

Almost all networks place a much higher level of trust in users and computers accessing resources on the local area network (LAN) than on publicly available network resources, such as servers connected to the Internet. Many networks allow authentication methods and unencrypted data transmissions on LANs that they would never consider using on the Internet. It is also much easier for attackers to enumerate information about the configuration of computers and applications when they have valid credentials on the network. Employees have valid credentials to the network, which also gives them greater initial access to network resources than external attackers might initially have. It can be very difficult to discern whether an employee is using her credentials legitimately or illegitimately—especially when she is a network administrator.

Physical Access to Network Resources

Employees have much greater physical access to network resources—namely, the computers of their coworkers. In general, when an attacker has physical control of a computer, that computer can no longer be protected from the attacker; rather, it is only a matter of time and computing power before the attacker can recover all data on the computer. Similarly, employees have much greater access to documentation on the network, which can be a critical resource for attacking it.

Human Resources Protections

Employees, even those who attack network resources, are often protected by employment laws and HR policies that can greatly hinder their employer from detecting them or preventing them from doing further damage once detected. For example, local laws might prohibit an organization from inspecting the Internet usage of its employees without a court order. An employee could take advantage of this by attacking internal Web resources.

What Motivates Attackers?

Attackers attempt to break into computer networks for many reasons. Although all attackers present a clear and present danger to networks, the motivation of the attacker will greatly determine the actual threat posed. By understanding what might motivate potential attackers to attempt to compromise your organization's network, you can predict what type of threats the network faces. Armed with this knowledge, once you detect an attack, you might be more able to prevent further damage or better equipped to identify who the attacker is.

Many attackers are motivated by more than one factor. Here are the reasons that attackers attempt to break into computer networks, in ascending order of the danger they present:

- Notoriety, acceptance, and ego
- Financial gain
- Challenge
- Activism

- Revenge

- Espionage

- Information warfare

Notoriety, Acceptance, and Ego

An attacker's quest for notoriety, desire for acceptance, and ego comprise one of the most common motivations for attempts to break into computer networks and applications. Attackers motivated by notoriety often are naturally introverted and seeking a way to gain acceptance in the electronic hacker community; thus, their exploits are very public. Examples of such attacks include defacing Web sites and creating computer viruses and worms.

By breaking into a network of a major company or government agency and defacing its Web site, an attacker is virtually guaranteed national and international publicity and enshrined in the electronic hacker community. For example, Attrition.org runs a Web site that catalogs nearly all Web site defacements in recent years. Querying any major search engine for the phrase *Web site defacement* invariably returns thousands of accounts of an organization's Web site being defaced, including those of most major corporations and government agencies.

Although not normally regarded as attackers, people who create and release computer viruses and worms cause billions of dollars of damage each year. In 1991, the Michelangelo virus opened a Pandora's box of sorts for computer viruses. Although the Michelangelo virus did little actual damage, the coverage that it received in the mainstream media, including newspapers, magazines, and television news, brought computer viruses into the popular consciousness and opened the door for other malicious publicity seekers. Since then, many other computer viruses have created similar media frenzies, such as Fun Love, I Love You, Melissa, and most recently, Code Red and NIMDA.

Popular media and antiauthoritarian romanticism transformed outlaws of the United States' western frontier—such as Jesse James and Billy the Kid—from common criminals who robbed banks and murdered people into cult heroes. Similarly, several attackers have gained cult hero status in the hearts and minds of computer geeks. Two recent examples include Kevin Mitnick and Adrian Lamo. Other attackers and prospective attackers seek the attention of the media and hacker communities that Mitnick and Lamo received and are envious, if not worshipful. The cult following of these two hacker legends is particularly strong with impressionable teenagers who have not fully developed their own sense of morality and rarely understand the true consequences their actions have on business continuity and information technology.

In all these examples and in many similar incidents, the exploits of the attackers received international publicity. Attackers motivated by notoriety, acceptance, and ego look at these incidents as proof that they too can become famous. You can probably imagine the sense of accomplishment an attacker might feel, seeing his handiwork in the headlines of major newspapers and discussed on television news programs by political pundits. Often attackers know that their actions are illegal but consider their behavior harmless because there is no clear victim, no one physically harmed, and no tangible goods stolen or destroyed. Thus, in the minds of many attackers, they are not doing anything discernibly wrong. Certainly this is not the case. For example, although the direct financial consequences of Web site defacements are often low, the loss of public confidence in how well the organization can ensure the confidentiality and privacy of their employee, business partner, and customer information can be severe. This can result in indirect financial losses from customer distrust and defection.

Financial Gain

We can separate attackers motivated by monetary gain into two categories: those motivated by direct financial gain, and those motivated by indirect financial gain.

Attackers motivated by direct financial gain are little more than common criminals, akin to bank robbers with computer skills. These attackers break into computer networks or applications to steal money or information. In the past few years, there have been several high-profile thefts of credit card information from the databases of companies that conduct online commerce. These attackers did one of three things with the credit card information that they stole: they used the credit cards to purchase products or make cash withdrawals, sold the credit card numbers to other criminals, or attempted to extort money from the companies from which they stole the credit cards. In nearly every case, the attacker was apprehended, but not before causing significant damage. For example, in 1994, a Russian attacker broke into Citibank and transferred roughly $10 million to accounts in several countries. He was captured, and all but $400,000 was recovered. But the real damage to Citibank was in their customers' loss of trust because of Citibank's inability to secure their customers' bank accounts. The attacker was sentenced to three years in prison and fined $240,000, whereas U.S. Federal Sentencing Guidelines call for a minimum 6–10 year sentence for someone with no prior criminal record who robs a bank in person.

Another way that attackers seek financial gain from attacking networks and applications is to successfully break into an organization's network and then offer to help the organization secure the network. Although many of these attackers maintain the position that they are "good guys" wanting only to help the target organization, in reality, they are little more than extortionists demanding "protection money," like a 1920s gangster in cyberspace.

Some attackers are motivated by financial gain but in an indirect manner. A researcher or computer security company might make a large effort to discover vulnerabilities in commercial software applications and operating systems, and then use their discovery and the publication of such previously unknown vulnerabilities as a marketing tool for their own security assessment services. The publicity that a company or individual receives from unearthing a serious vulnerability in a commercial software application, especially a widely used application, can be priceless. For example, most significant vulnerabilities discovered in a widely used software application will be reported on the front page of major news and computer industry Web sites and in the technology or business sections of major newspapers. The discoverer of such a vulnerability might even receive airtime on the cable news television networks. For most small computer consulting companies, obtaining this type of publicity normally would be out of the question.

There is a critical point in the process of discovering commercial software vulnerabilities when one leaves the realm of ethical behavior and becomes an attacker: the reporting of that vulnerability to the general public without the software company's knowledge or consent. Most commercial software companies are more than willing to work with researchers who have discovered security vulnerabilities to ensure that a software patch is available before the vulnerability is announced. Many software companies will also give credit to the person and company that discovers the vulnerability, thus balancing the interests of their software users with the public recognition earned by the person and company reporting the vulnerability. However, many researchers not only publish the vulnerability without notifying the software vendor, they also create code to exploit the vulnerability. Further complicating this issue are laws such as the 1998 Digital Millennium Copyright Act (DMCA), which prohibits individuals from exposing vulnerabilities in certain software and hardware encryption techniques used for digital rights management. The bottom line is this: although discovering vulnerabilities for indirect financial gain can be done illegitimately via extortion, it can also be done legitimately to advance the mutual business goal of software vendors and researchers—protecting consumers.

Challenge

Many attackers initially attempt to break into networks for the mere challenge. In many ways, attackers view networks as a game of chess—a battle of minds that combines strategic and tactical thinking, patience, and mental strength. However, chess has precisely defined rules, and attackers clearly operate outside the rules. Attackers motivated by the challenge of breaking into networks often do not even comprehend their actions as criminal or wrong. Attackers motivated by the challenge are often indifferent to which network they attack; thus, they will attack everything from military installations to home networks. These attackers are unpredictable, both in their skill level and dedication.

Activism

One newer type of attacker is the *hactivist*, an attacker who breaks into networks as part of a political movement or cause. This type of attacker might break into a Web site and change the content to voice his own message. The "Free Kevin Mitnick" hactivists frequently did this in an attempt to get Mitnick released from U.S. federal custody after he was arrested on multiple counts of computer crime. Attackers motivated by a specific cause might also publish intellectual property that does not belong to them, such as pirated software or music. They might carry out sophisticated denial-of-service attacks, called *virtual sit-ins*, on major Web sites to call attention to a particular cause.

Revenge

Attackers motivated by revenge are often former employees who feel they were wrongfully terminated or hold ill will toward their former employers. These attackers can be particularly dangerous because they focus on a single target and—being former employees—often have intricate knowledge of the security of the networks. For example, on July 30, 1996, employees of Omega Engineering arrived at work to discover that they could no longer log on to their computers. Later they discovered that nearly all their mission-critical software had been deleted. The attack was linked to a logic bomb planted by an administrator who had been fired three weeks earlier. The attack resulted in more than $10 million in losses, prompting the layoff of 80 employees. In early 2002, the former administrator was sentenced to 41 months in prison, which pales in comparison to the financial and human damages that he caused.

Espionage

Some attackers break into networks to steal secret information for a third party. Attackers who engage in espionage are generally very skilled and can be well funded. Two types of espionage exist: industrial and international. A company might pay its own employees to break into the networks of its competitors or business partners, or the company might hire someone else to do this. Because of the negative publicity associated with such attacks, successful acts of industrial espionage are underreported by the victimized companies and law enforcement agencies. A widely publicized industrial espionage incident using computers recently took place in Japan. In December 2001, an engineer at Japan's NEC Toshiba Space Systems broke into the network of the National Space Development Agency of Japan. This engineer illegally accessed the antenna designs for a high-speed Internet satellite made by Mitsubishi in an attempt to help NEC gain business from the space agency. As a result, the Japan Space Agency prohibited NEC from bidding on new contracts for two months, but no criminal charges were filed.

Attackers who engage in international espionage attempt to break into computer networks run by governments, or they work for governments and rogue nations to steal secret information from other governments or corporations. The most famous case of computer-related international espionage is documented in Cliff Stoll's book *The Cuckoo's Egg: Tracking a Spy Through the Maze of Computer Espionage* (Pocket Books, 2000). In 1986, Stoll, an astronomer by trade, was working as a computer operator at Lawrence Berkeley Lab when he discovered a 75-cent discrepancy in an accounting log from the mainframe computer. One thing led to another, and eventually Stoll discovered that German attackers being paid by the KGB were breaking into both military and nonmilitary computers to steal secret information.

Information Warfare

Information warfare is another motivation for attacking computer networks that is becoming increasingly dangerous as people around the world rely on them for mission-critical services. Major wars have been marked by the evolution of weapons systems—the machine gun changed the nature of combat in World War I, the tank changed the nature of combat in World War II, and airpower changed the nature of combat in Vietnam. Behind the scenes, each war also marked the evolution of electronic combat. From intercepted telegrams broken by hand, to radar jamming, to satellite transmissions that could be broken only by stealing the encryption keys (despite the power of many supercomputers)—electronic combat and intelligence has become a deciding factor in modern warfare. Although no widely reported incidents of cyber-terrorism exist, you can be certain that these attempts have been made. There is evidence of information warfare in China, Israel, Pakistan, India, and the United States. The U.S. President's Critical Infrastructure Protection Board was formed in 2001 specifically to address countering the threat of cyber-terrorism and information warfare against the United States.

Why Defending Networks Is Difficult

In traditional combat, defenders enjoy a distinct advantage over their attackers. However, in information technology, several factors give attackers the advantage:

- Attackers have unlimited resources.

- Attackers need to master only one attack.

- Defenders cannot take the offensive.

- Defenders must serve business goals.

- Defenders must win all the time.

Attackers Have Unlimited Resources

At any given time, defenders must protect their network against both attackers around the globe and their own employees. This accumulation of attackers, as a group, limits a defender's resources. Many attackers can spend all day systematically attempting to break into your network. Attackers can collaborate to develop new and more sophisticated attacks. As a network administrator, you have other duties besides defending the network, and unlike attackers, you go home at night, take sick days, and go on vacations. Over time, some attackers will cease attempting to break into your network, but new ones will take their place. Defending networks against unrelenting hoards of attackers with much more time than you gives attackers an advantage.

Attackers Need to Master Only One Attack

As a network administrator, you have to secure many servers and applications. You must learn how all your operating systems, applications, and network devices work, as well as how to secure and manage them. You must determine the threats to each component of your network and keep current with newly reported vulnerabilities. Attackers, on the other hand, need to master attacking only a single application or operating system feature in order to compromise it and break into your network.

Defenders Cannot Take the Offensive

Although attackers can attack networks with a certain amount of impunity, defenders can retaliate only through litigation, which is expensive and time-consuming. Attacking an attacker is not only illegal in most countries, it is impractical. This is because attackers often use previously compromised third-party computers, called *zombie systems*, or many zombie systems acting in unison to attack networks. By using zombie systems to carry out or amplify an attack, an attacker can protect her identity. Frequently attackers use the networks of colleges and universities as an attack vector because of their openness, computing power, and bandwidth. An attack can also originate from another legitimate organization whose employee has attacked your network, or whose network has already been compromised by an intruder. In any of these cases, retaliating against an intruder can result in your organization illegally attacking an unwitting individual, company, or organization. Thus, legally and practically, you cannot retaliate against attackers.

Defenders Must Serve Business Goals

Although network administrators are responsible for securing their organizations' networks, they also must install and configure operating systems and applications that help employees meet the goals of the business. In some situations the pursuit of company business goals conflicts with maintaining the security of the network.

For example, company executives might travel with laptops that contain sensitive information about the company. The executives might be unwilling to comply with security policies that require long and complex passwords. Knowing this, a network administrator might supply the executives with smart cards that they must use to access their laptops. This security measure will better protect the information on the laptop, but it also introduces other potential problems, such as the loss or misplacement of smart cards. To mitigate this situation, a network administrator might decide to create a second account for local computer users that could be used without the protection of a smart card, granting certain trusted employees the new account password, which could result in a serious security vulnerability. Another situation in which the pursuit of business goals can interfere with the protection of the network occurs when your organization has a business rule that conflicts with the security of the network. For example, your organization might have a business rule that requires network traffic to the payroll server to be encrypted. This security measure will make data transmission of employee compensation secure, but makes it impossible for you to monitor network traffic to determine whether traffic is legitimate or illegitimate. It also prevents you from using any type of network intrusion detection software. In both scenarios, having to serve business goals jeopardizes your ability to protect the network.

Defenders Must Win All the Time

An attacker needs only one successful attack to comprise a network, while a network administrator must prevent *all* attacks to succeed in his role. These are ominous odds for ill-equipped or under-resourced network administrators. Given all the other problems defenders of networks face, it is inevitable that the security of your network will be compromised at some point. As a network administrator, you must ensure that these compromises are detected early and happen infrequently.

Is defending a network impossible? Not at all. But one thing is certain: it is impossible to defend a network without trained, skilled, and knowledgeable network administrators. By applying the key principles of security outlined in Chapter 1 to the information this book presents on securing computers running Windows 2000 and Windows XP, you can build a strong foundation for defending your networks.

Part II

Securing Active Directory

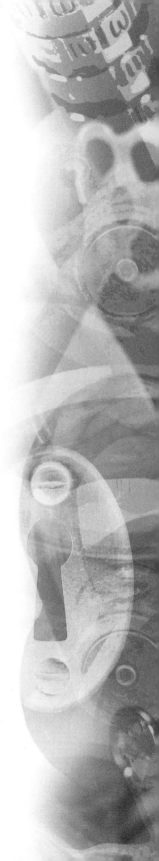

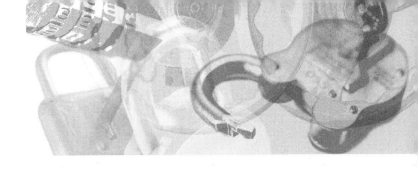

3

Securing User Accounts and Passwords

The account is the central unit of security on Microsoft Windows NT, Windows 2000, and Windows XP computers and the applications that run on them. Rights and permissions are assigned to accounts and checked by a resource such as a file or a folder at the time of access. It is important to understand that a user and a user account are different entities. Anyone who possesses the credentials associated with a user account can use that account, despite the name on it. A computer can secure and audit access to resources based on user accounts only, not on the identity of the person using the account.

For example, you might be asked to restrict access to a certain file to your organization's payroll managers, while in reality, you are restricting access to the file to the user account that the payroll managers use. Thus, you must protect the credentials used to validate that the person attempting to use the account is the person the account was issued to. By default, the credentials needed to use an account are the account name and password.

Securing Accounts

Each user, computer, or group account is a security principal in Windows NT, Windows 2000, and Windows XP. Security principals receive permissions to access resources such as files and folders. User rights, such as interactive logons, are granted or denied to accounts directly or via membership in a group. The accumulation of these permissions and rights define what security principals can and cannot do when working on the network.

User accounts are either domain or local in scope. In Windows 2000, domain accounts are stored in the Active Directory directory service on domain controllers, while local accounts are stored in individual Security Accounts Manager (SAM) databases on the hard drives of workstations and member servers. In Windows NT, domain accounts are stored in a SAM database that is synchronized to all domain controllers in the domain by the primary domain controller (PDC), which holds the only writable copy of the database. Domain accounts can be used to authenticate to any machine in the forest and any domains that trust logons performed by the domain where the account exists, while local accounts are used to authenticate to the local computer only.

Understanding Security Identifiers

While users reference their accounts by the user name or universal principal name (UPN), the operating system internally references accounts by their security identifiers (SIDs). For domain accounts, the SID of a security principal is created by concatenating the SID of the domain with a relative identifier (RID) for the account. SIDs are unique within their scope (domain or local) and are never reused. This is an example of a SID:

S-1-5-21-833815213-1531848612-156796815-1105

SIDs have several components:

- **Revision**   This value indicates the version of the SID structure used in a particular SID. The revision value is 1 in Windows NT, Windows 2000, and Windows XP.

- **Identifier authority**   This value identifies the highest level of authority that can issue SIDs for this particular type of security principal. The identifier authority value in the SID for an account or group in Windows NT, Windows 2000, and Windows XP is 5 for the NT Authority.

- **Subauthorities**   The most important information in a SID is contained in a series of one or more subauthority values. All values up to but not including the last value in the series collectively identify a domain in an enterprise. This part of the series is known as the *domain identifier*. The last value in the series identifies a particular account or group relative to a domain. This value is the RID. In the example just given, this value is 1105.

By default, several security principals are created during installation of the operating system or domain; the SIDs for these accounts are called *well-known SIDs*. Table 3-1 lists the well-known SIDs for Windows NT, Windows 2000, and Windows XP.

Table 3-1   Well-Known SIDs

Security Principal	SID
S-1-0	Null Authority
S-1-0-0	Nobody
S-1-1	World Authority
S-1-1-0	Everyone
S-1-2	Local Authority
S-1-3	Creator Authority
S-1-3-0	Creator Owner
S-1-3-1	Creator Group
S-1-3-2	Creator Owner Server (Windows NT only)
S-1-3-3	Creator Group Server (Windows NT only)
S-1-4	Nonunique Authority
S-1-5	NT Authority
S-1-5-1	Dialup
S-1-5-2	Network
S-1-5-3	Batch
S-1-5-4	Interactive
S-1-5-5-*X-Y*	Logon Session (X and Y values uniquely identify the logon session)
S-1-5-6	Service
S-1-5-7	Anonymous
S-1-5-9	Enterprise Controllers
S-1-5-10	Principal Self (or Self)
S-1-5-11	Authenticated Users
S-1-5-12	Restricted Code (Windows XP only)
S-1-5-13	Terminal Server Users (Windows 2000 only)
S-1-5-18	Local System
S-1-5-<*domain SID*>-500	Administrator
S-1-5-<*domain SID*>-501	Guest
S-1-5-<*domain SID*>-502	KRBTGT (Windows 2000 only)
S-1-5-<*domain SID*>-512	Domain Admins
S-1-5-<*domain SID*>-513	Domain Users
S-1-5-<*domain SID*>-514	Domain Guests

(continued)

Table 3-1   Well-Known SIDs   *(continued)*

Security Principal	SID
S-1-5-<*domain SID*>-515	Domain Computers
S-1-5-<*domainSID*>-516	Domain Controllers (Windows 2000 only)
S-1-5-<*domain SID*>-517	Cert Publishers (Windows 2000 only)
S-1-5-<root domain SID>-518	Schema Admins (Windows 2000 only)
S-1-5-<root domain SID>-519	Enterprise Admins (Windows 2000 only)
S-1-5-<*domain SID*>-520	Group Policy Creators (Windows 2000 only)
S-1-5-<*domain SID*>-553	RAS and IAS Servers (Windows 2000 only)
S-1-5-32-544	Administrators
S-1-5-32-545	Users
S-1-5-32-546	Guests
S-1-5-32-547	Power Users
S-1-5-32-548	Account Operators
S-1-5-32-549	Server Operators
S-1-5-32-550	Print Operators
S-1-5-32-551	Backup Operators
S-1-5-32-552	Replicators (Windows NT only)

Understanding Access Tokens

When a user successfully logs on to the network, an access token is created. A copy of the access token is attached to every process and thread that executes on the user's behalf. The access token is used by the computer to determine whether the user has the appropriate authority to access information or to perform an action or operation. The contents of an access token include the following:

- **Account SID**   The SID for the account.

- **Group SIDs**   A list of SIDs for security groups that include the account. In a Windows 2000 native mode domain, this list also includes the SID that is stored in the account's SID-History attribute.

- **Rights**   A list of rights and logon privileges that the accounts possess directly or through security group membership.

- **Owner**   The SID for the user or security group who, by default, becomes the owner of any object that the user either creates or takes ownership of.

■ **Primary group**   The SID for the user's primary security group. This information is used by the POSIX subsystem when using the File Server for Macintosh or Print Server for Macintosh services to provide file and print services from Windows NT 4.0 or later servers to Macintosh clients. (For information on File Server for Macintosh and Print Server for Macintosh, see Chapter 8, "Securing Services.")

■ **Source**   The process that caused the access token to be created, such as the Session Manager, LAN Manager, or remote procedure call (RPC) Server process.

■ **Type**   A value indicating whether the access token is a *primary token* or an *impersonation token*. A primary token is an access token that represents the security context of a process. An impersonation token is an access token that a thread within a service process can use to temporarily adopt a different security context, such as the security context for a client of the service.

■ **Impersonation level**   A value that indicates to what extent a service can adopt the security context of a client represented by this access token.

■ **Statistics**   Information about the access token itself. The operating system uses this information internally.

■ **Restricted SIDs**   An optional list of SIDs added to an access token by a process with authority to create a restricted token. Restricting SIDs can limit a thread's access to a level lower than that allowed to the user.

■ **Session ID**   A value that indicates whether the access token is associated with the Terminal Services client session.

You can see the details of your access token by using the Whoami.exe utility. Figure 3-1 shows the contents of an access token using Whoami.exe.

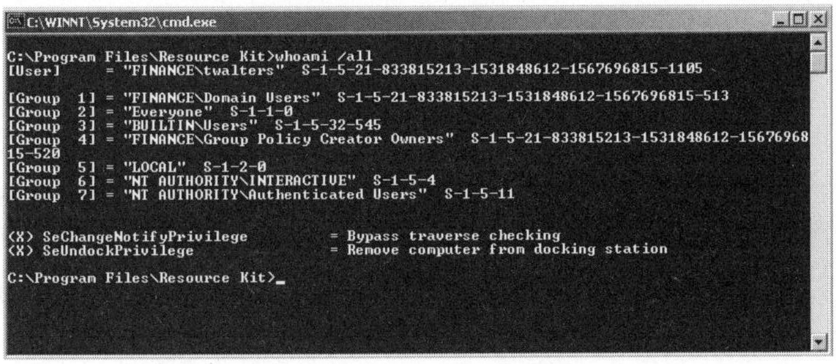

Figure 3-1   Viewing the contents of an access token using Whoami.exe

> **On the CD**   Whoami.exe is located in the Tools folder on the CD included with this book.

Configuring Account Security Options

User accounts are a core unit of network security. Consequently, you might want to secure user accounts to a greater degree than the default settings provide. Active Directory enables you to secure individual user accounts in several ways, including these options:

- **Logon Hours**   Determines the days and times of the week, in one-hour periods, when a user can log on to the network. Group Policy provides a setting to forcibly log a user off the network when the allowed logon hours have expired.

- **Logon Workstation**   Restricts accounts to interactively logging on to only certain computers on the network, specified by the computers' NetBIOS name(s).

- **User Must Change Password At Next Logon**   Forces the user to change his password at the next interactive logon.

- **User Cannot Change Password**   This setting prevents users from changing their own passwords. This option is commonly used with shared accounts, such as those used on a kiosk PC.

- **Password Never Expires**   Exempts the password from domain password expiration policy restrictions. You should use this option only when you have a clear business reason, such as for accounts that are not used interactively and thus would not receive a password expiration notification, including service accounts that must run in the domain context.

- **Store Password Using Reversible Encryption**   Stores the password in such a way that it can be decrypted by the operating system to be compared with a plaintext password. This option is required when using legacy protocols such as Challenge Handshake Authentication Protocol (CHAP) or Shiva Password Authentication Protocol (SPAP) for authentication. When this option is selected, the next time the user changes his password, the new password will be stored using a reversible hash of the password that will be created. This hash is sent across the network for authentication purposes, then decrypted and matched to the plaintext copy of the password. You should set this option only for accounts that require the plaintext of the password to be known by the domain controller, such as those used in Microsoft Internet Information Services (IIS) digest authentication and authentication from Macintosh computers.

Important   You cannot set the following account options on the built-in Administrator account:

- Password Never Expires
- Store Password Using Reversible Encryption
- Account Is Disabled
- Smart Card Is Required For Interactive Logon
- Account Is Trusted For Delegation
- Account Is Sensitive And Cannot Be Delegated
- Use DES Encryption Types For This Account
- Do Not Require Kerberos Preauthentication

- **Account Is Disabled**   Prevents the account from being used, but does not delete the account. You commonly set this option when a user has been terminated, but items associated with user account might still be required, such as private keys or mailbox access.

- **Smart Card Is Required For Interactive Logon**   Requires that a smart card be used for interactive logons, which include Terminal Services logons. Users with this option set on their accounts will not be allowed to log on interactively by using their user names and passwords. In Windows 2000, the password that was previously used for the account before setting this option is preserved. If you enable this setting, you should set the password to a random value to prevent the account from being used for other types of logons, such as network logons.

- **Account Is Trusted For Delegation**   Enables the account to be used by processes and threads on the account's behalf. This option is available on both computer and user accounts and is commonly used with applications that run on Web servers, as well as on SQL and COM servers. You should set this option only if you know that it is required for proper functionality of a distributed application, such as on Web server accounts running applications that use Kerberos and Windows Integrated Security with IIS 5.0. Additionally, for users to use the encrypting file system (EFS) to encrypt files on remote servers, the server's account must be trusted for delegation so that it can retrieve the user's keys via Kerberos delegation and store them locally.

- **Account Is Sensitive And Cannot Be Delegated**   Prevents an account from being delegated. If both the Account Is Trusted For Delegation and Account Is Sensitive And Cannot Be Delegated options are set, the latter will apply.

- **Use DES Encryption Types For This Account**   Enables the account to use DES encryption, which supports multiple levels of encryption, for interoperability with Unix-based Kerberos realms, rather than the RC4 algorithm used by default in Windows 2000.

- **Do Not Require Kerberos Preauthentication**   Disables Kerberos preauthentication, which is employed by default, for interoperability with MIT Kerberos v4 realms.

- **Account Expiration**   Automatically disables an account on a specified date in the future. Often organizations will synchronize this setting with the employment duration of temporary, vendor, or intern employees to ensure that they do not have continued access to the network after their employment ends.

You can control Remote Access permissions for each user account by granting or allowing Remote Access privileges, as well as setting caller ID, callback, static IP addresses, and routes. Once you have converted your domain to native mode, you can configure Remote Access policies to control Remote Access permissions. Remote Access policies allow for much greater granular control of Remote Access permissions and are discussed in depth in Chapter 19, "Implementing Security for Routing and Remote Access." You can also determine whether a user can use Terminal Services and how the terminal server session can be used by configuring Environment, Sessions, Remote Control, and Terminal Services Profile settings on a user account in Active Directory.

Securing Administrative Accounts

Regardless of the security deployed on a network, you will always have one collection of user accounts that are inherently trusted administrators. Administrators are granted rights and permissions that allow them to subvert nearly any security mechanism, through their innate rights, by elevation of privileges, or through physical compromise of the hardware. Although you might have thoroughly vetted administrators during the hiring process, the administrator account on most networks is only a password away. Once compromised, an administrator account is a passport to the entire network and all the data on it. Therefore, it is paramount to secure administrator accounts. In addition to applying account security options, consider the following best practices for administrator accounts:

- **Minimize the number of accounts that are granted Administrator access.**   Windows 2000 enables you to delegate authority over nearly every object in Active Directory and the file system. Additionally, most services install special management groups. For example, when you install the Domain Name System (DNS) or Dynamic Host Configuration Protocol (DHCP) on Windows 2000, a domain local group is automatically created with permissions to manage the respective services. These built-in administrative groups are discussed later in this section in "Built-In Domain Groups."

- **Use Restricted Groups to control membership in administrative groups.**   Restricted Groups in Windows 2000 Group Policy enable you to control group membership automatically. Domain controllers refresh Group Policy every 5 minutes by default; thus, every 5 minutes, accounts that are not defined in the Restricted Groups policy settings are removed from the security group. If you audit account management events, enforcement of this policy will log an event to the security event log under the event ID 637. The Caller field in the error message will list the computer name of the domain controller computer that the change was made on instead of the user account name.

- **Require multiple factor authentication.**   You can require smart card or other multiple factor authentications for accounts with administrative access, especially members of the Enterprise group or the Domain Administrators group. By doing this, you can avoid the risks associated with passwords and add an element of physical security to using administrator accounts. You can also require smart cards for Terminal Services logons.

- **Restrict the use of administrator accounts to specific computers.**   Doing this can create management inconveniences. However, for high security requirements, you can use the Logon Workstation account option to restrict the interactive logon to certain computers for administrator accounts. By combining this setting with good physical security of the computers the account is restricted to, you greatly increase the security of the Administrator account.

■ **Do not use administrative accounts for routine activities.** By not using administrative accounts for routine activities such as browsing the Internet, you can limit the damage that a virus or Trojan horse could do to a computer if compromised. Instead, use the secondary logon (RunAs) service. See the following sidebar for details of this service.

Using the RunAs Service

Windows 2000 and Windows XP include the RunAs service, although in Windows XP it is called the Secondary Logon service. This service allows an interactive user to use a different security context to run applications and utilities. You can use the RunAs service at the command line by pressing the Shift key while right-clicking on an application, or by creating a shortcut to an application and selecting the option to automatically invoke the Secondary Logon service. RunAs is not scriptable by any method other than keystroke passing utilities because the service requires that the password be typed interactively. If you are logging on to the RunAs service in Windows XP by using a privileged security context such as an Administrator account, you can create a restricted token for the secondary logon session. An access token will be created for the logged-on user that eliminates all users rights except Bypass Traverse Checking and restricts rights received by membership in the local Administrators group by creating a deny DACL, or discretionary access control list, on the access token for this group. Because Whoami.exe does not display deny DACLs, you will not see the Administrators group membership denied when inspecting a restricted token. In Windows XP, you can also use the RunAs service with smart cards.

■ **Do not allow users to be local administrators.** Unless you have a clear business or technical reason for doing so, you should prohibit users from having local administrative privileges. Users who have local administrative privileges can reconfigure the computer and have unrestricted access to the operating system and registry. Not only could this lead to information disclosure if a user shares confidential data without proper security, but many virus and Trojan horses rely on this level of access to infect computers and spread to other machines. Additionally, users with local administrative access can exempt their machines from Group Policy and otherwise manipulate their computers to render security measures ineffective.

- **Vet employees before granting them administrative access.** You should work with your organization's HR department to evaluate network administrators during the hiring process to prevent granting access to potentially malicious or overly careless administrators.

- **Lock servers and workstations.**   Locking unattended servers and workstations is especially important when using accounts with administrative access. An attacker might need only a few seconds at a computer that is logged on with administrative privileges to compromise the system. You can require smart cards for interactive logons, implement Group Policy to set the smart card removal behavior to lock the workstation when the smart card is removed, and require your administrators to carry their smart cards with them at all times.

Implementing Password Security

By default, the only protection accounts are given are user-chosen passwords. Users—and for that matter, administrators—historically have been poor generators of random passwords and even worse at keeping passwords secret. Your organization might have near-perfect security, but one weak password can cause the exposure of company secrets, be used to launch a successful denial-of-service attack, or sabotage the network. Unless you employ multifactor authentication methods for all users on your network, you should implement password security settings.

In Windows 2000, you can create password policies at the domain level for all domain accounts though Group Policy, or at the OU level for local accounts on Windows 2000 and Windows XP member computers. Table 3-2 lists password policies in Active Directory that you can set for all accounts in the domain. We will describe each of these policies momentarily.

Table 3-2   Default Password Policy Settings in Windows 2000 and Windows XP

Setting	Default Value	Range
Enforce Password History	One password remembered	0 to 24
Maximum Password Age	42 days	0 to 999
Minimum Password Age	0 days	0 to 999
Minimum Password Length	0 characters	0 to 14
Password Must Meet Complexity Requirements	Disabled	Enabled or disabled
Store Password Using Reversible Encryption For All Users In The Domain	Disabled	Enabled or disabled

Enforce Password History

You can force users to vary their passwords by setting the Enforce Password History option. When configuring this setting, you must define how many passwords will be retained in history. If you do not configure this setting, the user can reuse a password, even if it has expired, simply by changing the password to the previous password. Set this value to 24, the maximum.

Maximum Password Age

You can also configure how long users can use a password by configuring the Maximum Password Age setting. Users are forced to change their password when the password expires. By enabling this setting, you can avoid a situation in which a user or administrator uses the same password indefinitely. However, configuring passwords to expire too frequently can result in users incrementing passwords in an unsophisticated manner, such as changing **WeakPass1** to **WeakPass2**, or writing the password in an obvious place, such as on a sticky note on their monitor.

Tip   The maximum length of time that a user can use a password should be in accordance with the time it would take to successfully issue a brute force attack against the password offline. Unfortunately, no magic calculation exists for this, given the continuing improvements in the hardware and software used to carry out these attacks.

Password Never Expires

The Maximum Password Age setting can be overridden on individual domain and local user accounts by setting the Password Never Expires option on the account. This is commonly used for service accounts, for which no interactive logon exists. Thus, no notification that the password is about to expire is needed.

Minimum Password Age

The Minimum Password Age setting prevents users from circumventing the enforcement of password history and password expiration. For example, if a minimum password age is not configured, at the expiration date of a password, a user could simply change her password to dummy values a sufficient number of times to reuse her previous password. This value should be set to at least two days to prevent users from utilizing this technique.

Minimum Password Length

The Minimum Password Length setting determines the minimum number of characters a user must use in his password. The longer a password is, the more difficult it generally is to compromise. However, one of the side effects of requiring long passwords is that users will choose passwords that are easy to guess or they will write them down. Part of the problem with users' conception of passwords is the very word *password*, which implies that the secret information should be a single word. When implementing a long minimum password length (10 characters or more), it is essential to educate users on how to create good passwords.

> **Tip**   A password of 20 or more characters can actually be set so that it is easier for a user to remember than an 8-character password. The following is a 36-character password: **Thelastgoodbooklboughtcost$59.99**, for example. It might be simpler for a user to remember a phrase such as this than to remember a shorter password such as **P@sSw0rd**.

Password Complexity Issues

Windows 2000 provides a built-in filter, Passfilt.dll, that requires passwords to contain characters of different types. By enabling this filter, you will increase the total keyspace for passwords. For example, without creating a password filter, a user could use only lowercase Roman letters in his password. The *keyspace*, or pool of available keys, for lowercase Roman letters is 26. Thus, a password of 8 characters would have 26^8 or 208,827,064,576 (2.089×10^{11}) possible combinations. On the surface, this might seem a mind-boggling number. However, at 1,000,000 attempts per second, a capability of many password-cracking utilities, it would take only 59 hours to try all possible passwords. If the keyspace included lowercase Roman letters, uppercase Roman letters, and numbers, it would contain 62 characters. An 8-character password would now have 218,340,105,584,896 (2.18×10^{14}) possible combinations. At 1,000,000 attempts per second, it would take 6.9 years to cycle through all possible permutations.

In practice, password keyspaces do not completely apply because humans rarely create passwords with a random distribution of characters. Brute force attacks and modified dictionary attacks often employ sophisticated logic to exploit known characteristics of human-created passwords, such as using the number *1* much more frequently than any other number or adding a number to a dictionary word. Although these calculations are important, you must use them carefully and underestimate the time that you think it will take to successfully perform a brute force attack on a password.

The built-in password complexity filter requires all passwords to be at least eight characters in length and include characters from three of these four categories:

- English uppercase letters (A, B, C, ... Z)
- English lowercase letters (a, b, c, ... z)
- Westernized Arabic numerals (0, 1, 2, ... 9)
- Nonalphanumeric characters (`~!@#$%^&*_-+=|\{}[]:;"'<>,.?/)

You also can use other ASCII characters in passwords, such as é and ½ (Alt+233 and Alt+189). Additionally, if your organization has its own password security requirements, you can create a custom password filter and install it on each domain controller. Creating your own password filter requires advanced knowledge of C++ programming and familiarity writing programs using Windows APIs.

> **On the CD**   Altchar.vbs is located in the Tools\Scripts folder on the CD included with this book that will display the character for an ASCII decimal value from the command line.

Store Passwords Using Reversible Encryption For All Users In The Domain

The setting to store passwords using reversible encryption for all users in the domain is required if the domain controller needs the ability to quickly decrypt the password to a plaintext form for use with certain authentication methods, including CHAP, and for use with some Macintosh computers. Setting this option greatly weakens the security of passwords and should be done only if required for the entire domain. This option can be set on individual user accounts rather than at the domain level if only some passwords need to be stored reversibly.

Although you will need to adjust the settings in Table 3-3 for your own organization, at a minimum, you should configure the password policy detailed in the table.

Table 3-3   Recommended Minimum Password Policy Settings

Setting	Value
Enforce Password History	24 passwords remembered
Maximum Password Age	42 days
Minimum Password Age	2 days
Minimum Password Length	8 characters
Password Must Meet Complexity Requirements	Enabled
Store Password Using Reversible Encryption For All Users In The Domain	Disabled

> **Tip**   As a best practice, accounts with high levels of access, such as enterprise or domain administrators, should use passwords with at least 15 characters. This will prevent a LAN Manager password hash from being created. LAN Manager password hashes are explained later in this chapter, in the "Securing Passwords" section.

You can also set account lockout policies for the entire domain or for local accounts on individual computers by using security policies. You must configure three settings when implementing an account lockout policy, as Table 3-4 shows.

Table 3-4   Default Account Lockout Settings in Windows 2000 and Windows XP

Setting	Default Value	Range
Account Lockout Threshold	Not applicable	1–99,999 minutes (A value of 0 will never reset the number of failed attempts tracked in a given attempt to log on.)
Account Lockout Duration	0 attempts (disabled)	1–999 attempts
Reset Account Lockout Counter After	Not applicable	1–99,999 minutes (A value of 0 will require an administrator to unlock the account.)

Although account lockout settings are common, often they are the cause of numerous support calls to the help desk. If passwords are appropriate in length and complexity, this setting provides little additional security. On a similar—albeit much more sinister—note, an attacker could easily exploit an account lockout policy to carry out a denial-of-service attack by locking out all users. A better security approach is to educate users and administrators on how to create strong passwords, enable auditing of account logon events, and actively review audit log files for excessive failed logon attempts that might indicate a brute force or dictionary attack on an account. Doing this not only can greatly improve your security, it also can decrease your organization's support costs.

> **Note**   In Windows 2000, members of the Domain Administrators group are not affected by account lockout settings.

Creating stringent requirements for password length and complexity does not necessarily translate into users and administrators using strong passwords. For example, **IceCream!** meets the technical complexity requirements for a password defined by the system, but anyone who looks at the password can see that there is nothing complex about it. By knowing the person who created this password, you might be able to guess his password based on his favorite food. One strategy for educating users on choosing strong passwords is to create a poster describing poor passwords and display it in common areas, such as near the water fountain or copy machine. Guidelines for creating strong passwords include the following:

- Avoid using words, common or clever misspellings of words, and foreign words.

- Avoid incrementing passwords with a digit.

- Avoid using passwords that others can easily guess by looking at your desk (such as names of pets, sports teams, and family members).

- Avoid using words from popular culture.

- Avoid thinking of passwords as *words* per se—think secret codes.

- Use passwords that require you to type with both hands on the keyboard.

- Use uppercase and lowercase letters, numbers, and symbols in all passwords.

- Use mnemonics, such as taking the first letter from each word in a sentence that only you would know. For example, "I drink 10 cups of coffee every morning, before noon," becomes **Id10coceAM,b12:00**.

- Use space characters and characters that can be produced only by pressing the Alt key.

> **Warning**   In general, it is a good practice to regularly audit passwords to ensure that users and administrators are creating strong passwords. Before performing any type of audit on user passwords, you must get formal approval from your company's HR and legal departments. Privacy laws vary greatly from country to country—and many countries and states specifically prohibit accessing this type of information.

Granting Rights and Permissions Using Groups

In Windows NT, Windows 2000, and Windows XP, the capabilities granted to accounts are comprised of two areas: *rights* and *permissions*. Rights are actions or operations that an account can or cannot perform. Permissions define which resources accounts can access and the level of access they have. Resources include Active Directory objects, file system objects, and registry keys. Although accounts are the central unit of security in Windows NT, Windows 2000, and Windows XP, assigning rights and permissions directly to accounts is difficult to manage and troubleshoot and frequently leads to misapplication of rights and permissions. Consequently, rights and permissions should not be assigned directly to accounts; rather, they should be assigned to groups, and accounts should be placed into groups. Creating a structure of groups to assign rights and permissions is an essential part of securing Windows NT, Windows 2000, and Windows XP.

User Rights and Permissions

The actions an account can perform and the degree to which a user can access information are primarily determined by user rights and permissions. Accounts receive rights and permissions either by having the right or permission assigned directly to the account, or through membership in a group that has been granted the right or permission.

User Rights

Administrators can assign specific rights to group accounts or to individual user accounts. These rights authorize users to perform specific actions, such as logging on to a system or backing up files and directories. User rights are different than permissions: user rights apply to accounts, and permissions are attached to objects (such as printers or folders). Two types of user rights exist:

- **Privileges** A right assigned to an account and specifying allowable actions on the network. An example of a privilege is the right to back up files and directories.

- **Logon rights** A right assigned to an account and specifying the ways in which the account can log on to a system. An example of a logon right is the right to log on to a system locally.

Privileges Some privileges can override permissions set on an object. For example, a user logged on to a domain account as a member of the Backup Operators group has the right to perform backup operations for all domain servers. However, this requires the ability to read all files on those servers, even files whose owners have set permissions that explicitly deny access to all users, including members of the Backup Operators group. A user right—in this case, the right to perform a backup—takes precedence over all file and directory permissions. The following list shows the privileges that can be granted to an account by assigning user rights. These privileges can be managed with the user rights policy settings in Group Policy.

- **Act As Part Of The Operating System**   Allows a process to authenticate as any user, and therefore gain access to resources under any user identity. Only low-level authentication services should require this privilege. The user or process that is granted this privilege might create security tokens that grant more rights than their normal security contexts provide. This could include granting the user or process access as an anonymous user, which defeats attempts to audit the identity of the token's user. Do not grant this privilege unless you are certain it is needed.

- **Add Workstations To A Domain**   Allows the user to add computers to a specific domain, beyond the default limit of 10 in Active Directory and the default limit of 0 in Windows NT.

- **Back Up Files And Directories**   Allows the user to circumvent file and directory permissions to back up the system. Specifically, this privilege is similar to granting the following permissions on all files and folders on the local computer: Traverse Folder/Execute File, List Folder/Read Data, Read Attributes, Read Extended Attributes, and Read Permissions.

- **Bypass Traverse Checking**   Allows the user to pass through directories to which she otherwise has no access, while navigating an object path in any Windows file system or in the registry. This privilege does not allow the user to list the contents of a directory, only to traverse directories, which is often needed to successfully browse Web sites or file shares.

- **Change The System Time**   Allows the user to set the time in the internal clock of the computer.

- **Create A Token Object**   Allows a process to create a token that it can then use to gain access to local resources when the process uses *NtCreateToken()* or other token-creation APIs.

- **Create Permanent Shared Objects**   Allows a process to create a directory object in the Windows 2000 Object Manager. This privilege is useful to kernel-mode components that plan to extend the Windows 2000 object namespace. Because components running in kernel mode already have this privilege assigned to them, it is not necessary to specifically assign this privilege.

- **Create A Pagefile**   Allows the user to create and change the size of a pagefile. This is done by specifying a paging file size for a given drive in the Performance Options dialog box, which is accessible through the System Properties dialog box.

- **Debug Programs**   Allows the user to attach a debugger to any process. Without this privilege, you can still debug programs that you own. This privilege provides powerful access to sensitive and critical system operating components—you should not grant this permission to anyone unless you have clear business reasons to do so.

- **Enable Trusted For Delegation On User And Computer Accounts**   Allows the user to select the Trusted For Delegation setting on a user or computer object. The user or object that is granted this privilege must have Write access to the account control flags on the user or computer object. A server process either running on a computer that is trusted for delegation or being run by a user who is trusted for delegation can access resources on another computer. The process uses a client's delegated credentials, as long as the client account does not have the Account Cannot Be Delegated account control flag set. Misuse of this privilege or of the Trusted For Delegation settings might make the network vulnerable to sophisticated attacks using Trojan horse programs that impersonate incoming clients and use their credentials to gain access to network resources.

- **Force Shutdown Of A Remote System**   Allows a user to shut down a computer from a remote location on the network.

- **Generate Security Audits**   Allows a process to generate entries in the security log for auditing of object access. The process can also generate other security audits. The security log is used to trace unauthorized system access.

- **Increase Quotas**   Allows a process with Write access to another process to increase the processor quota assigned to that other process. This privilege is useful for system tuning but can be abused in a denial-of-service attack.

- **Increase Scheduling Priority**   Allows a process with Write access to another process to increase the execution priority of that other process. A user with this privilege can change the scheduling priority of a process through the Task Manager.

- **Load And Unload Device Drivers**   Allows a user to install and uninstall Plug and Play device drivers. Device drivers that are not

Plug and Play are not affected by this privilege and can be installed only by administrators. Because device drivers run as trusted (highly privileged) programs, this privilege can be misused to install hostile programs and give these programs destructive access to resources.

■ **Lock Pages In Memory**   Allows a process to keep data in physical memory, preventing the system from paging the data to virtual memory on disk. Exercising this privilege might significantly affect system performance. This privilege is obsolete and is therefore never used by default.

■ **Manage Auditing And Security Log**   Allows a user to specify object access auditing options for individual resources such as files, Active Directory objects, and registry keys. Object access auditing is not performed unless you have enabled the audit policy settings that enable object auditing. A user with this privilege can also view and clear the security log from the Event Viewer.

■ **Modify Firmware Environment Values**   Allows modification of the system environment variables, either by a process or by a user through the System Properties dialog box.

■ **Profile A Single Process**   Allows a user to use Windows NT and Windows 2000 performance-monitoring tools to monitor nonsystem processes.

■ **Profile System Performance**   Allows a user to use Windows NT and Windows 2000 performance-monitoring tools to monitor system processes.

■ **Remove A Computer From Docking Station**   Allows a user to undock a portable computer through the user interface.

■ **Replace A Process-Level Token**   Allows a process to replace the default token associated with a subprocess that has been started.

■ **Restore Files And Directories**   Allows a user to circumvent file and directory permissions when restoring backed up files and directories, and to set any valid security principal as the owner of an object.

■ **Shut Down The System**   Allows a user to shut down the local computer.

■ **Take Ownership Of Files Or Other Objects**   Allows a user to take ownership of any securable object in the system, including Active Directory objects, files and folders, printers, registry keys, processes, and threads.

Logon Rights   Logon rights are assigned to users and specify the ways in which a user can log on to a system. The following list describes the various logon rights:

- **Access This Computer From A Network**   Allows a user to connect to the computer over the network. By default, this privilege is granted to the Administrators, Everyone, and Power Users groups.

- **Deny Access To This Computer**   Denies a user the ability to connect to the computer over the network. By default, this privilege is not granted to anyone. Use caution when setting this privilege because it is possible to lock yourself out of the system.

- **Log On As A Batch Job**   Allows a user to log on using a batch-queue facility. By default, this privilege is granted only to Administrators.

- **Deny Logon As A Batch Job**   Denies a user the ability to log on using a batch-queue facility. By default, this privilege is granted to no one.

- **Log On As A Service**   Allows a security principal to log on as a service to establish a security context. The LocalSystem account always retains the right to log on as a service. Any service that runs under a separate account must be granted this right. By default, this right is not granted to anyone.

- **Deny Logon As A Service**   Denies a security principal the ability to log on as a service to establish a security context. The LocalSystem account always retains the right to log on as a service. Any service that runs under the security context of a user account must be granted this right. By default, this right is not granted to any accounts.

- **Log On Locally**   Allows a user to log on at the computer's keyboard via a Terminal Services session and through IIS. By default, this right is granted to the Administrators, Account Operators, Backup Operators, Print Operators, and Server Operators groups. Use caution when setting this privilege because it is possible to lock yourself out of the system.

- **Deny Logon Locally**   Denies a user the ability to log on at the computer's keyboard. By default, this right is granted to no one. Use caution when setting this privilege because it is possible to lock yourself out of the system.

Active Directory, File, and Registry Permissions

Active Directory, file, and registry permissions are granted by using discretionary access control lists, or DACLs. You grant permissions to objects by creating an access control entry (ACE) for the account, or for a group that the account is a member of. File and registry permissions are discussed in depth in Chapter 7, "Securing Permissions."

Group Types and Scope

Windows NT, Windows 2000, and Windows XP enable you to organize users and other domain objects into groups to manage rights and permissions. Defining security groups is a major requirement for securing a distributed network.

You can assign the same security permissions to large numbers of accounts in one operation by using security groups. This ensures consistent rights and permissions for all members of a group. Using security groups to assign rights and permissions also means that the access control lists (ACLs) on resources will remain fairly static and will be much easier to control and audit. User accounts that require access to a specific resource are added or removed from the appropriate security groups as needed so that the ACLs change infrequently, are smaller, and are easier to interpret.

Special Groups

There are some groups whose membership even administrators cannot manage—these groups are called *special groups*. Membership in a special group is granted to accounts automatically, as a result of their activity on the machine or network. It is essential that you understand how these groups function because they are often misused and can seriously impact your network's security if not properly implemented. This next list describes all the special groups in Windows NT, Windows 2000, and Windows XP:

- **Anonymous Logon**   Used for network logons for which credentials are not provided. Anonymous logons cannot be used interactively.

- **Authenticated Users**   Any account, with the exception of the Guest and Anonymous accounts, that has been authenticated by a trusted domain controller or the local computer. This identity provides accounts with the rights necessary to operate the system as an end user.

- **Creator Group**   Used as a placeholder in an inheritable ACE. When the ACE is inherited, the system replaces this SID with the SID for the primary group of the object's current owner.

- **Creator Owner**   Used as a placeholder in an inheritable ACE. When the ACE is inherited, the system replaces this SID with the SID of the object's current owner.

- **Dialup**   Used for accounts connected to the computer over a dial-up connection.

- **Everyone**   Contains all users who access the computer, including Guests and Users from other domains. In Windows NT and Windows 2000, the Everyone group includes Authenticated Users, Guests, and Anonymous logons. In Windows XP, the Everyone group does not include Anonymous logons.

- **Interactive**   Used for accounts that have logged on at console through Terminal Services or through IIS.

- **Network**   Used for accounts that have logged on over the network.

- **Remote Interactive Logon (Windows XP only)**   Used for users who have logged on to the computer by using a Remote Desktop connection.

- **Terminal Server User**   Used for users who have logged on to the computer by using a terminal server session.

- **Batch**   Batch processes that are accessing resources on the computer.

- **Local Service (Windows XP only)**   Services that are local to the computer have no need for extensive local privileges and do not need authenticated network access. A service running as Local Service has significantly less authority than a service running as System (discussed in a moment), both locally and on the network. When services running as Local Service access local resources, they do so as members of the local Users group. When they access network resources, they do so as Anonymous users.

- **Network Service (Windows XP only)**   Services that have no need for extensive local privileges but do need authenticated network access. A service running as Network Service has the same network access as a service running as System, but has significantly reduced local access. When services running as Network Service access local resources, they do so as members of the local Users group. When they access network resources, they do so using the SID assigned to the computer.

- **Service**   Used by services.

- **System**   Used to represent the operating system itself.

- **Enterprise Domain Controllers (Windows 2000 only)**   All domain controllers in the forest.

- **Restricted (Windows XP only)**   Used by a process that is executing in a restricted security context, such as running an application with the RunAs service. When code executes at the restricted security level, the Restricted SID is added to the user's access token.

- **Self**   A placeholder in an ACE on a user, group, or computer object in Active Directory. When you grant permissions to Self, you grant these permissions to the security principal represented by the object. During an access check, the operating system replaces the SID for Self with the SID for the security principal represented by the object.

Special groups are used to manage the rights and restrictions that apply to users based on the type of logon session they have initiated. For example, suppose you want a user named Alice to have access to a certain file or share—but only when she is logged on interactively. You can accomplish this by allowing Alice access to the resource but denying access to requests accompanied by access tokens that include the Dialup security principal.

Computer Local Groups

Computer local groups are security groups that are specific to a computer and are not recognized elsewhere in the domain or on other computers. These groups are a primary means of managing rights and permissions to resources on a local computer. Several types of built-in local groups exist by default on Windows NT, Windows 2000, and Windows XP computers. Figure 3-2 shows local accounts in the Computer Management Microsoft Management Console (MMC) in Windows 2000 Server.

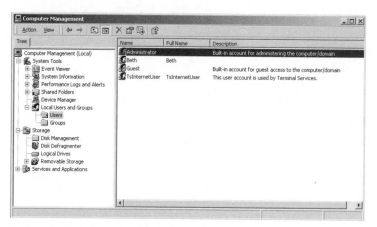

Figure 3-2   Local accounts

> **Tip**   No local accounts on domain controllers exist in Windows NT 4.0 and Windows 2000. Windows 2000 has a local administrator account called the Directory Services Restore Administrator. This account is stored in a normally inaccessible local SAM and can be viewed, used, and managed only when the computer is interactively booted into Directory Services Restore Mode.

The computer local groups follow:

■ **Administrators**   The built-in Administrator account is the only default member of this group. If the computer is added to a domain, the Domain Admins group is added to the local Administrators group, making all members of the Domain Admins group local administrators on all computers in the domain. Local administrators have complete control over all local resources, including accounts and files. Membership in the local Administrators groups should be limited to only those accounts that require this level of access.

■ **Backup Operators**   Members of the Backup Operators group can back up and restore files on the local computer, regardless of the permissions that protect those files, including files and folders encrypted using the EFS. Members of this group can also log on to the computer interactively and shut it down. However, Backup Operators cannot change security settings. By default, the Backup Operators group has no members.

- **Guests**   By default, members of the Guests group are denied access to the application and system event logs. Otherwise, members of the Guests group have the same access rights as members of the Users group. Members of the Guests group can also shut down the computer on Windows 2000 and Windows XP client computers. By default, the only member of this group is the built-in Guest account, which is disabled by default.

- **Power Users**   Although members of the Power Users group have less system access than Administrators but more than Users, they should be considered Administrators for security purposes because they can generally elevate their privileges to become Administrators.

   The default Windows 2000 and later security settings for Power Users are backward compatible with the default security settings for Users in the Windows NT 4.0 operating system. This allows Power Users to run legacy applications that are not certified for Windows 2000 and Windows XP Professional and therefore cannot be run under the more secure Users context. In a secure environment, you should investigate how to run applications under the Users context, rather than making all users members of the Power Users group. Power users can perform many systemwide operations, such as changing system time and display settings, and creating user accounts and shares. Power users also have Modify access to the following:

  ❏   HKEY_LOCAL_MACHINE \Software

  ❏   Program files

  ❏   %windir%

  ❏   %windir%\system32

  > **Warning**   If nonadministrators gain permissions to modify files in the %windir%\system32 folder, they can take control of the operating system by replacing the operating system files with malicious files. This is one reason that members of the Power Users group must be considered local administrators for all intents and purposes.

- **Replicator**   Members of the Replicator group are allowed to replicate files across a domain. This group is not used in Windows 2000 and Windows XP. By default, this group contains no members.

■   **Users**   Members of the Users group have limited access on the system. By default, members of the Users group have Read/Write permissions only to their own profiles. User security settings are designed to prohibit members of the Users group from compromising the security and integrity of the operating system and installed applications. Users cannot modify computerwide registry settings, operating system files, or program files, and they cannot install applications that can be run by other users. As a result, the Users group is secure to the extent that members cannot run viruses or Trojan horse applications that affect the operating system or other users of the operating system.

■   **HelpServicesGroup (Windows XP only)**   Members of the HelpServicesGroup group can use helper applications to diagnose system problems. This group, in conjunction with the Support and HelpAssistant accounts (whose names are appended with a random number to ensure their uniqueness on each computer), can be used by members of Microsoft Help and Support Center to access the computer from the network and to log on locally. The built-in Support account is the only default member of this group.

■   **Network Configuration Operators (Windows XP only)**   Members of the Network Configuration Operators group have limited administrative privileges that allow them to configure networking features, such as IP address configuration of the machine's network adapters. By default, this group contains no members.

■   **Remote Desktop Users (Windows XP only)**   The Remote Desktop Users group enables members to log on remotely by using Remote Desktop Services. By default, this group contains no members.

In addition to the built-in groups, you can create additional computer local groups that fit the security needs of your organization. You can add global groups from any trusted domain to local groups to grant rights and permissions to local resources. You cannot add computer local groups from one computer to computer local groups on another computer.

More Info   See *Writing Secure Code, Second Edition* by Michael Howard and David LeBlanc (Microsoft Press, 2003) for more information on determining the rights and permissions required to run applications.

Built-In Domain Groups

Just as built-in computer local groups exist on all computers, built-in groups also exist in Active Directory and Windows NT 4.0 domains. These built-in groups have predelegated rights and permissions. These are the built-in domain groups:

- **Administrators**   Just as the computer local group Administrators has complete control over local resources, members of the built-in domain group Administrators have complete control over all resources in the domain. The Domain Admins global group (discussed momentarily) gets its rights and permissions by having membership in this group. When a computer joins the domain, the Domain Admins group is automatically added to this group. Similarly, in Windows 2000, the Enterprise Admins global group (also discussed momentarily) gets much of its authority because it is a member of this group on every domain controller in the forest.

- **Backup Operators**   Members of the domain built-in Backup Operators group can back up and restore files and folders, regardless of permissions and encryption, on computers throughout the domain. Backup Operators can also log on locally and shut down servers, including domain controllers.

- **Server Operators**   Members of the Server Operators group can manage resources on the local server, and they have the ability to perform the following tasks:

  - ❏   Log on locally and lock, unlock, and shut down the server

  - ❏   Create, manage, and delete shared folders

  - ❏   Create, manage, and delete printers

  - ❏   Back up and restore files and folders

- **Account Operators**   Members of the Account Operators group can manage user accounts and groups but cannot manage accounts that are members of Administrators, Domain Admins, Server Operators, Backup Operators, Print Operators, and Account Operators. Nor can they change the membership of these groups. Account Operators can also log in locally and shut down servers, including domain controllers.

> **Important**   Because of the ability to delegate authority on a granular level in Active Directory, the Server Operators and Account Operators groups should be used only for compatibility with Windows NT.

- **Print Operators**   Members of the Print Operators group can manage printers and print jobs. Print Operators can also log in locally and shut down servers, including domain controllers.

- **Pre-Windows 2000 Compatible Group (Windows 2000 only)** The Pre-Windows 2000 Compatible group is granted permissions in ACLs on objects in Active Directory. When the first domain controller for each domain is promoted, the DCPROMO Wizard asks whether you want to use this group. If you enable pre-Windows 2000 compatibility, the Everyone group will be made a member of the Pre-Windows 2000 Compatible group. This setting is particularly relevant to a domain operating in mixed mode with Windows NT 4.0 backup domain controllers (BDCs) that are also Remote Access Service (RAS) servers. You should not place any members in this group unless you have a clear business or technical requirement to do so.

The domain built-in groups Replicator, Guests, and Users also exist in Active Directory and Windows NT 4.0 domains and function just as their computer local built-in groups, but with a scope that includes all computers in the domain.

Domain Local Groups

Domain local groups exist in the Windows 2000 domains group after the domain has been converted to native mode. These groups can contain members from anywhere in the forest, trusted forests, or a trusted pre-Windows 2000 domain. Domain local groups can be used only to grant permissions to resources on machines that are members of the domain in which they exist.

Global Groups

Global groups in Windows 2000 and Windows NT 4.0 domains can contain accounts from their own domain and can be used to populate ACLs in all trusted domains. In Windows 2000, once a domain is converted to native mode, global groups can be nested—that is, they can contain other global groups from the same domain. Global groups never contain accounts or global groups from other domains, regardless of whether the domain is in mixed mode or native mode. Active Directory and Windows NT domains contain several built-in global groups:

- **Domain Admins**   Members of the Domain Admins group have complete control over all objects in the domain. The Domain Admins group is also a member of the local Administrators group on all computers in the domain. Membership in this group should be kept to a minimum.

- **Enterprise Admins (Windows 2000 only)**   Members of the Enterprise Admins group have complete control of all objects in the forest. Enterprise Admins are members of all the built-in domain local Administrators groups in each domain in the forest. Enterprise Admins can also manage all objects not associated with any single domain, such as the objects in the Configuration container. Membership in the Enterprise Admins group on most networks will contain from zero to five accounts. The Enterprise Admins group is changed from a global group to a universal group when the forest root domain is converted to native mode.

- **Schema Admins (Windows 2000 only)**   Members of the Schema Admins group can create classes and attributes in the schema as well as manage the schema master flexible single-master operation (FSMO). By default, the Schema Admins group contains no members. Only members of the Enterprise Admins group can add and remove accounts from the Schema Admins group. The Schema Admins group is changed from a global group to a universal group when the forest root domain is converted to native mode.

- **RAS and IAS Servers (Windows 2000 only)**   Members of the RAS and IAS Servers group can manage Remote Access policies, Routing and Remote Access Server (RRAS), and Internet Authentication Service (IAS) on all RRAS servers in the domain. By default, this group contains no members.

- **Group Policy Creator Owners**   Members of the Group Policy Creator Owners group can fully manage all group policy in the domain. Because this group can control security policies by deploying or removing the deployment of Group Policy objects (GPOs), membership should be minimal to nonexistent. By default, this group contains no members.

Universal Groups

Once you convert an Active Directory domain to native mode, you can use universal security groups. As with global groups, you can use universal groups in any trusted domain. However, universal groups can have members from any domain in the forest. Because of this forestwide scope, membership in universal groups is stored in the Global Catalog. The Global Catalog is fully replicated throughout the forest, which means that universal group membership should be kept fairly static, especially on forests where convergence does not occur quickly.

Implementing Role-Based Security in Windows 2000

All rights and permissions in Windows NT, Windows 2000, and Windows XP are granted on a discretionary basis—meaning that any account with Full Control, Change Permissions, or Take Ownership permissions can grant or deny permissions on the object to other security principals. In order to create a secure network, you should create a structure for granting rights and permissions that is scalable, flexible, manageable, and above all else, secure. By using a role-based structure for granting rights and permissions, you can control access to information in this manner. In a role-based structure, rights and permissions are never granted or denied to specific accounts, but instead to groups based on job roles or functions.

To implement role-based security for access control, each type of group is used for a specific purpose to create a discrete separation of the account and the assignment of permissions, based on the job function or role of the user. Create domain local groups or local groups, and assign them permissions to resources. Create global groups based on job function or role. Place the global groups in the appropriate domain local groups or local groups, and place users in the appropriate global group. This process is shown in Figure 3-3. A convenient way to remember this process is by using the mnemonic A-G-DL-P. Accounts are placed into global groups, global groups are placed into domain local groups, and permissions are assigned to domain local groups.

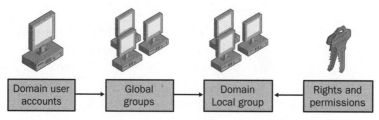

Figure 3-3   Implementing role-based security in Windows 2000

Domain local groups and local groups are assigned permissions to resources based on the permission needed on the resource. For example, a payroll server can use the following group payroll folders:

■   Payroll_data_Read

■   Payroll_data_Modify

■   Payroll_data_FC

> **Tip**   Because the icon for domain local, local, and global groups is the same in the user interface, you need to use a meaningful naming convention for group names. Often, lowercase letters are used for domain local group names and local group names, and uppercase letters are used for global group names. Another strategy is to preface each group name with its type, such as DL_*groupname* and GG_*groupname*. Doing this will arrange the groups by type when they are alphabetized in the user interface.

Global groups are created based on job functions or roles. In Windows 2000, after converting to native mode, global groups can be placed in other global groups to further stratify the A-G-DL-P model into A-G-G-DL-P. For example, a payroll department could contain the following global groups:

■   PAYROLL_MGRS

■   PAYROLL_ADMINS

■   PAYROLL_USERS

Now suppose all payroll managers require Modify rights on the payroll data. After ensuring that payroll managers are members of the PAYROLL_MGRS group, place the group in the Payroll_Modify domain local group. All payroll managers will have Modify access on the payroll information.

Universal Groups vs. Global Groups

Once in native mode, Active Directory adds the ability to use universal groups. When should you use universal groups for security purposes?

First, you can use universal groups when two resources with the same security needs exist in many domains in the forest and users for these resources exist in many domains in the forest. You cannot gracefully achieve this many-to-many mapping without using universal groups. For example, suppose a forest has an empty root domain and four child domains. Each of these domains has a payroll server for the payroll department that uses domain local groups to assign permission to payroll data. Each domain has a global group for payroll managers containing all the payroll managers from the domain. Instead of adding all four payroll manager groups to servers in all four domains, you create a universal group called All_Payroll_Managers and add the payroll managers global group from each domain into it. Place this group in the appropriate domain local groups on the payroll servers. By doing this, you will have significantly fewer groups to manage and simpler ACLs on resources. When using universal groups, the role-based security structure is A-G-U-DL-P.

Second, you can use universal groups when assigning permissions to Active Directory objects in a multiple domain forest. The role-based security structure to use in this scenario is A-G-U-P, or simply, A-U-P. You will need to do this because objects either will need to move between domains or will not be owned by any specific domain, such as objects in the Configuration container.

The benefits of using a role-based security structure include the following:

- Groups are segmented in discrete areas. Only domain local groups or local groups have permissions assigned to them and contain only global groups or universal groups. Moreover, global groups contain only accounts or other groups.

- Permissions are close to the resources, not the account. This enables resource administrators to be able to control security over the resource, without significant access to accounts.

- When users transfer jobs or are terminated, permissions are not tied to their user accounts, making permission reassignment or removal simpler.

- Permissions can be mapped and traced easily.

- Permissions are controlled by group management, not by changing permissions on resources, making audit logs much easier to read and manage.

- Permissions scale as the number of users increases and the frequency of changes to user accounts increases.

- Authorization can be implemented by assigning the resource owners the sole management of domain local groups or local groups with permission to the resources that they manage.

Securing Passwords

Historically, user passwords are the biggest security risk to networks. This risk includes the creation of passwords, the way users protects their passwords, how the operating system stores these passwords, and how the passwords are transmitted across the network.

Understanding Authentication

The operating system is responsible for securely storing and transmitting credentials (user names and passwords) for accounts. Windows 2000 and Windows XP support a variety of protocols to transmit credentials across the network to authenticate accounts, including user accounts, computer accounts, and service accounts. The operating system also stores credentials in a variety of formats.

When a user logs on to Windows NT, Windows 2000, or Windows XP by using the Windows Logon dialog box, several components work together to securely authenticate her credentials. Figure 3-4 shows the information flow of authentication.

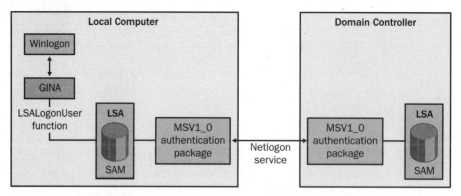

Figure 3-4   Authentication in Windows NT, Windows 2000, and Windows XP

Windows NT, Windows 2000, and Windows XP support authentication using the LAN Manager (LM), NT LAN Manager (NTLM), and NT LAN Manager version 2 (NTLMv2) protocols. Windows 2000 and Windows XP use Kerberos v5 as the default authentication protocol. Because few networks use a single operating system version or applications that use the same authentication APIs, Windows NT, Windows 2000, and Windows XP support current and legacy authentication methods to preserve compatibility with downlevel operating systems.

LAN Manager

LAN Manager authentication is supported in Windows NT, Windows 2000, and Windows XP to support legacy applications. LM passwords are limited to 14 characters. With LM, passwords themselves are not stored by the operating system. Instead, the passwords are encrypted with the LAN Manager one-way function (OWF), which is formed by converting the password to uppercase characters, breaking the 14-character password into 7-character halves, adding padding for passwords with less than 14 characters, and encrypting a constant with the 7-character halves by using the DES encryption algorithm. This process is illustrated in Figure 3-5.

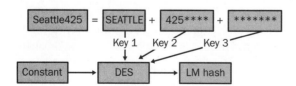

Figure 3-5   LM password storage

When a user authenticates a password by using the LM authentication protocol, the authentication is done with a simple challenge/response from the authenticating domain controller or computer. Figure 3-6 shows the process of authenticating an account by using LM.

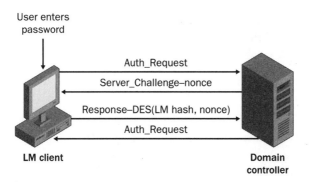

Figure 3-6   LM authentication

In Figure 3-6, the client sends an authentication request to the logon server. The server returns a challenge, which is comprised of a random number, or *nonce*. The client then uses the LM password hash to encrypt the nonce by using the DES encryption algorithm. Next, the server decrypts the encrypted nonce from the client by using the LM password it has stored in the accounts database. If the nonce matches the nonce sent to the client, the client's credentials are validated.

By reducing the keyspace for letters to include only uppercase letters, limiting passwords to 14 characters, and separating passwords into 7-character pieces, you make LM password hashes especially vulnerable to brute force and dictionary attacks. Many tools available on the Internet can easily crack most LM password hashes given enough computer power and time. Windows 2000 Service Pack 2 adds functionality that enables you to remove LM password hashes from Active Directory or local computer SAM databases. The following table shows the registry key and value to add to the registry in order to remove LM password hashes. You can also add a custom registry modification to Windows 2000 security templates and deploy the change by using Group Policy.

Location	HKLM\SYSTEM\CurrentControlSet\Control\Lsa
Type	DWORD
Key	NoLMHash
Default value	0
Recommended value	1 (removed LM password hashes)

You must implement this registry change on all domain controllers in the domain to fully prevent the creation of LM password hashes. Additionally, this change will not take place until users change their passwords the first time after the registry has been changed. You can also prevent the LM authentication protocol from being used by a Windows NT, Windows 2000, or Windows XP computer by setting the LM compatibility to a level greater than 0. We will discuss LM compatibility levels in further detail momentarily, when we examine NTLMv2.

NTLM

NT LAN Manager, also known as NTLM, first shipped with Windows NT and is an improvement over the LM authentication protocol. Unlike LM passwords, NTLM passwords are based on the Unicode character set, are case sensitive, and can be up to 128 characters long. As with LM, the operating system does not actually store the password; rather, it stores a representation of the password by using the NTLM OWF. The NTLM OWF is computed by using the MD4 hash function, which computes a 16-byte hash, or *digest*, of a variable-length string of text, which in this case is the user's password.

> **Note** A hash function takes a variable-length binary input and produces a fixed-length binary output that is irreversible. No two binary inputs will produce the same binary output, and no two binary outputs will match the same binary inputs. Common hash functions include MD4, MD5, and SHA1.

Another difference between NTLM and LM is that NTLM passwords are not broken into smaller pieces before having their hash algorithm computed. NTLM uses the same challenge/response process for authentication as LM does. NTLM is the default authentication provider in Windows NT and Windows 2000 (when the Windows 2000 machine is not a member of an Active Directory domain).

NTLMv2

NTLMv2, the second version of the NTLM protocol, was first available in Windows NT 4.0 Service Pack 4 and is included in Windows 2000. NTLMv2 passwords follow the same rules as NTLM passwords; however, NTLMv2 uses a slightly different process to compute the password hash and a different process for authentication. NTLMv2 also requires that the clocks of clients and servers be within 30 minutes of each other.

NTLMv2 uses a keyspace for password-derived keys of 128 bits. This makes brute force attacks difficult. If both the client and the server support NTLMv2, enhanced session security is negotiated. This enhanced security provides separate keys for message integrity and confidentiality, provides client input into the challenge to prevent chosen plaintext attacks, and uses the HMAC-MD5 algorithm for message integrity checking. Because the datagram variant of NTLM does not have a negotiation step, use of otherwise negotiated options (such as NTLMv2 session security and 128-bit encryption for message confidentiality) must be configured. This next table lists the registry key for setting NTLM negotiation options:

Type	DWORD
Location	HKLM\SYSTEM\CurrentControlSet\Control\Lsa\MSV1_0\
Key	NtlmMinServerSec
Default value	0x00000000

The following table lists the registry key for configuring the levels of NTLMv2 support:

Type	DWORD
Location	HKLM\SYSTEM\CurrentControlSet\Control\Lsa\MSV1_0\
Key	NtlmMinClientSec
Default value	0x00000000

Table 3-5 lists the values for the client negotiation options just described.

Table 3-5   Values for Setting NTLMv2 Client Negotiation Options

Value	Description
0x00000010	Message integrity
0x00000020	Message confidentiality
0x00080000	NTLMv2 session security
0x20000000	128-bit encryption

Tip   You can combine multiple NTLMv2 options by performing a logical OR on the settings in Table 3-5.

Enable NTLMv2 by setting the LM compatibility level by using Group Policy. The six LM compatibility settings are described in Table 3-6.

Table 3-6 LM Compatibility Levels

Level	Description	Details
Level 0	Send LM and NTLM response and never use NTLMv2 session security.	Clients will use LM and NTLM authentication and never use NTLMv2 session security. Domain controllers will accept LM, NTLM, and NTLMv2 authentication.
Level 1	Use NTLMv2 session security if negotiated.	Clients will use LM and NTLM authentication and use NTLMv2 session security if the server supports it. Domain controllers will accept LM, NTLM, and NTLMv2 authentication.
Level 2	Send NTLM response only.	Clients will use only NTLM authentication and will use NTLMv2 session security if the server supports it. Domain controllers will accept LM, NTLM, and NTLMv2 authentication.
Level 3	Send NTLMv2 response only.	Clients will use NTLMv2 authentication and use NTLMv2 session security if the server supports it. Domain controllers will accept LM, NTLM, and NTLMv2 authentication.
Level 4	Domain controllers refuse LM responses.	Clients will use NTLM authentication and use NTLM 2 session security if the server supports it. Domain controllers will accept only NTLM and NTLMv2 authentication; they will refuse LM authentication.
Level 5	Domain controllers refuse LM and NTLM responses.	Clients use NTLMv2 authentication and use NTLMv2 session security if the server supports it. Domain controllers will accept only NTLMv2 authentication; they will refuse NTLM and LM authentication.

When setting LM compatibility levels on your network, you will need to ensure that the levels are consistently set on both clients and servers. Setting LM compatibility to Level 4 or higher on servers might cause authentication issues with some applications. The registry key for setting LM compatibility levels is shown in the following table. You can also set this option using Group Policy.

Type	DWORD
Location	HKLM\SYSTEM\CurrentControlSet\Control\Lsa
Key	LMCompatibilityLevel
Default value	0

On the CD   SetImcompat.vbs is located in the Tools\Scripts folder on the CD included with this book. This tool will configure the LAN Manager compatibility level on a computer running Windows NT 4.0 or later operating systems.

Kerberos

The default authentication protocol in Windows 2000 and Windows XP is Kerberos v5. Windows operating systems prior to Windows 2000 do not support the use of Kerberos. The implementation of Kerberos in Windows 2000 is compliant with RFC 1510 and is interoperable with other Kerberos v5 realms that are RFC 1510 compliant. Kerberos provides the following benefits:

- **Mutual authentication**   Kerberos enables the client to verify a server's identity, one server to verify the identity of another, and the client to verify its identity to the server.

- **Secure transmission over the wire**   Kerberos messages are encrypted with a variety of encryption keys to ensure no one can tamper with the client's ticket or with other data in a Kerberos message. Furthermore, the actual password—and any derivation of it— can never be sent across the network when using Kerberos.

- **Prevention of replay of authentication packets**   Kerberos minimizes the possibility of someone obtaining and reusing a Kerberos authentication packet by using timestamps as an authenticator. By default in Windows 2000, all clocks must be synchronized to within 5 minutes of each other for Kerberos authentication to function.

- **Delegated authentication**   Windows services impersonate clients when accessing resources on their behalf. Kerberos includes a proxy mechanism that allows a service to impersonate its client when connecting to other services.

The following four components allow Kerberos v5 authentication between Windows 2000 clients and Windows 2000 domain controllers:

■ **Key distribution center (KDC)**   The network service that supplies both ticket-granting tickets (TGTs) and service tickets to users and computers on the network. The KDC manages the exchange of shared secrets between a user and a server when they authenticate with each other. The KDC contains two services: the Authentication Service and the Ticket Granting Service. The Authentication Service provides the initial authentication of the user on the network and provides the user with a TGT. Whenever users request access to a network service, they supply their TGT to the Ticket Granting Service. The Ticket Granting Service then provides the user with a service ticket for authentication with the target network service. In a Windows 2000 network, the KDC service runs on all Windows 2000 domain controllers.

■ **Ticket-granting ticket (TGT)**   Provided to users the first time they authenticate with the KDC. The TGT is a service ticket for the KDC. Whenever the user needs to request a service ticket for a network service, she presents the TGT to the KDC to validate that she has already authenticated with the network. For additional security, Windows 2000 verifies, by default, that the user account is still active every time a TGT is presented to the KDC. In other words, the KDC verifies that the account has not been disabled. If the account has been disabled, the KDC will not issue any new service tickets to the user.

■ **Service ticket**   Provided by a user whenever he connects to a service on the network. The user acquires the service ticket by presenting the TGT to the KDC and requesting a service ticket for the target network service. The service ticket contains the target server's copy of a session key and contains information about the user who is connecting. This information is used to verify that the user is authorized to access the desired network service by comparing the authentication information—namely, the user's SID and his group SIDs—against the DACL for the object that he is attempting to access. The service ticket is encrypted using the key that is shared between the KDC and the target server. This ensures that the target server is authenticated because only the target server can decrypt the session key.

■ **Referral ticket**   Issued anytime a user attempts to connect to a target server that is a member of a different domain. The referral ticket is actually a TGT to the domain where the resource is located. The referral ticket is encrypted using an interdomain key between the initial domain and the target domain that is exchanged as part of the establishment of transitive trust relationships.

All Kerberos authentication transactions will be composed of some combination of these three message exchanges:

- **Authentication Service Exchange**   Used by the KDC to provide a user with a logon session key and a TGT for future service ticket requests. The Authentication Service Exchange is comprised of a Kerberos Authentication Service Request (*KRB_AS_REQ*) sent from the user to the KDC and a Kerberos Authentication Service Reply (*KRB_AS_REP*) returned by the KDC to the user.

- **Ticket-Granting Service Exchange**   Used by the KDC to distribute service session keys and service tickets. The service ticket that is returned is encrypted using the master key shared by the KDC and the target server so that only the target server can decrypt the service ticket. A Ticket-Granting Service Exchange is comprised of a Kerberos Ticket-Granting Service Request (*KRB_TGS_REQ*) sent from the user to the KDC and a Kerberos Ticket-Granting Service Reply (*KRB_TGS_REP*) returned by the KDC to the user.

- **Client/Server Authentication Exchange**   Used by a user when presenting a service ticket to a target service on the network. The message exchange is comprised of a Kerberos Application Request (*KRB_AP_REQ*) sent from the user to the server and a Kerberos Application Response (*KRB_AP_REP*) returned by the target server to the user.

To use the Client/Server Authentication Exchange, the user enters her login name, password, and domain in the Windows Logon dialog box. The client computer then locates a KDC by querying DNS server. Next, the user's computer sends a Kerberos Authentication Service Request (*KRB_AS_REQ*) to the domain controller. The user's account information and the current computer time are encoded by using the long-term key shared between the user's account and the KDC. Finally, the authentication service at the KDC authenticates the user, generates a TGT for her, and sends the TGT to her in a Kerberos Authentication Service Response (*KRB_AS_REP*) message.

When a user authenticates himself by using Kerberos, a series of packets are exchanged to complete the validation of his credentials. Figure 3-7 illustrates this process. In the figure, the user sends a Ticket-Granting Service Exchange Request (*KRB_TGS_REQ*) to the KDC to acquire a service ticket for his computer.

The *KRB_TGS_REQ* contains an authenticator and the TGT that was issued to the user. The Ticket-Granting Service of the KDC checks the TGT and the authenticator. If both are valid, the Ticket-Granting Service generates a service ticket and sends it back to the user via a Ticket-Granting Service Response (*KRB_TGS_REP*). At the client computer, the service ticket is presented to the Local Security Authority, which will create an access token for the user. (We will discuss the Local Security Authority in a moment.) From then on, any process acting on behalf of the user can access the local machine's resources.

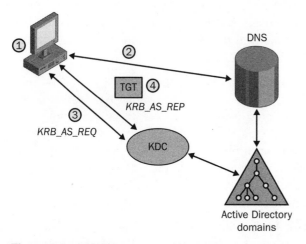

Figure 3-7   Initial Kerberos authentication

This sequence provides the user with the proper TGT. If the user is using a Windows 2000–based computer, he must now acquire a service ticket for that computer. The following steps and Figure 3-8 explain how the service ticket for the computer is acquired.

1.   The user sends a Ticket-Granting Service Request (*KRB_TGS_REQ*) to the KDC to acquire a service ticket for the target computer. The *KRB_TGS_REQ* includes the TGT and an authenticator.

2.   The Ticket-Granting Service of the KDC checks the authenticator and the TGT, generates a new service ticket, and sends it back to the user via a Kerberos Ticket-Granting Service Response (*KRB_TGS_REP*). The service ticket is encrypted by using the target service's long-term key, which is known only by the KDC and the target service.

3.   The user sends the service ticket and an authenticator to the target server by using a Kerberos Application Request (*KRB_AP_REQ*).

4.   The target server verifies the ticket with the authenticator, decrypts

the session key by using the master key that is shared with the KDC, and sends back an authenticator to the user in a Kerberos Application Response (*KRB_AP_REP*). This provides mutual authentication of the user and server.

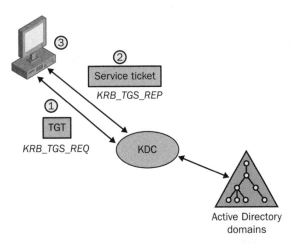

Figure 3-8   Obtaining a Kerberos session ticket

You can view the Kerberos tickets that have been issued to your user and computer accounts by using either Klist.exe, a command-line tool, or Kerbtray.exe, a GUI tool. Both of these utilities not only display the tickets, but also all their properties and expiration dates.

After initially authenticated with the network, the user must authenticate with other computers as he accesses resources on them. Every time the user connects to a resource or service on a remote computer, he has to perform a network authentication.

Storing Secrets in Windows

In addition to storing passwords in Active Directory or SAM databases, Windows NT, Windows 2000, and Windows XP store passwords and other secrets in other locations for a variety of purposes.

LSA Secrets

The Local Security Authority (LSA) maintains information about all aspects of local operating system security. The LSA performs the following tasks:

■   Authenticating users

■   Managing local security policy

- Managing audit policy and settings

- Generating access tokens

In addition, the LSA stores information secretly used by the operating system, known as *LSA secrets*. LSA secrets include items such as persistently stored RAS information; trust relationship passwords; user names, passwords, and account names; and passwords for services that run under a user account context. LSA secrets can be revealed locally by accounts with the Debug Programs user right. Consequently, you should be careful about the information applications have stored in LSA secrets. Attackers who physically compromise the computer can easily gain access to the information stored as LSA secrets if no other precautions are taken, such as using the System Key (Syskey.exe).

> **More Info**   *Writing Secure Code, Second Edition* by Michael Howard and David LeBlanc (Microsoft Press, 2003) contains detailed information and code sample of how to retrieve LSA secrets. Additionally, you can view most LSA secrets by using LSADUMP2.exe from BindView. The tool is available at *http://razor.bindview.com/tools/*.

Using System Key (Syskey.exe)

The System Key utility was first available in Windows NT 4.0 Service Pack 2 and is enabled by default in Windows 2000 and Windows XP. You can configure the System Key utility by typing **syskey** at the command prompt. Only members of the Administrators group can run Syskey.exe to initialize or change the System Key. The System Key is the "master key" used to protect the password encryption key; therefore, protection of the System Key is a critical system security operation. You have three options for managing the System Key:

- **Level 1**   Uses a machine-generated random key as the System Key and stores the key on the local system. Because the key is stored on the operating system, it allows for unattended system restart. By default, System Key Level 1 is enabled on all computers running Windows 2000 and Windows XP.

- **Level 2**   Uses a machine-generated random key and stores the key on a floppy disk. The floppy disk with the System Key is required for the system to start before the system is available for users to log on. Because the System Key is stored on the floppy disk, the operating system is vulnerable to destruction of the floppy disk, which would render the operating system unable to boot.

- **Level 3**   Uses a password chosen by the administrator to derive the System Key. The operating system will prompt for the System Key password when the system begins the initial startup sequence, before the system is available for users to log on. The System Key password is not stored anywhere on the system; instead, an MD5 hash of the password is used as the master key to protect the password encryption key. If the password is forgotten, the operating system will be rendered unable to boot.

Setting the System Key to Level 2 or Level 3 will greatly increase the security of the operating system and the secrets it contains (such as contents of the SAM database and LSA secrets) in the event an attacker physically compromises the computer. However, the Level 2 and Level 3 settings can be difficult to manage because you cannot recover forgotten or lost keys. If a key is lost, the computer will not be able to boot. You should develop a secure method of archiving System Keys if you decide to implement System Key Level 2 or Level 3 on your network.

DPAPI

The Data Protection API (DPAPI) enables secrets to be stored securely by applications by using a key derived from the user's password. The encryption of secrets can only be done locally, unless unencrypted roaming profiles are used. If the user's password is reset, the key used for DPAPI will be lost unless it is archived. DPAPI is available only on Windows 2000 and Windows XP.

Cached Credentials

By default, Windows NT, Windows 2000, and Windows XP cache the credentials of domain accounts used to log on to the network at the local computer. The credentials include the user's user name, password, and domain. Rather than storing the actual credential information, the information is stored in an irreversibly encrypted form and on the local computer. After a user has successfully logged on to the network from the computer once, he can use his domain credentials, even if the computer is not attached to the network or if no domain controllers are available. This functionality is critical to laptop users and users in branch offices without local domain controllers. You can control the number of credentials stored on a computer at any time by setting the registry key shown in this table:

Location	HKEY_LOCAL_MACHINE\Software\Microsoft\ Windows NT\Current Version\Winlogon\
Key	CachedLogonsCount
Type	REG_SZ
Default value	10
Recommended value	0–50, depending on your security needs

In high security networks, you might want to set the number of cached credentials to 0. This setting requires all users of the computer to have their domain account credentials validated by a domain controller. This prevents a user who has been terminated from disconnecting her computer from the network, logging on by using cached credentials, and destroying information. When you implement this setting, laptop users can log on only when connected to the network, greatly limiting their mobility.

Credential Manager

Windows XP introduced a new method of managing credentials as well as the credentials of a user who is logged on. This functionality is provided by the Credential Manager, labeled Stored User Names And Passwords in the Windows XP user interface. The Credential Manager dynamically and manually creates credential sets (a user name and password) for resources that are available in the user interface and from the command line. You can manage the following types of credentials with the Credential Manager:

■ User names and passwords

■ X.509 certificates, including smart cards

■ Passport accounts

Best Practices

■ **Protect administrative accounts.** Avoid using administrative accounts for routine computing needs, minimize the number of administrators, and avoid giving users administrative access.

■ **Use multiple factor authentication.** Using multiple factor authentication such as smart cards for administrative accounts and

Remote Access assists in validating that the user is who she claims to be when security requirements are high or physical identity cannot be established.

■ **Physically secure computers with sensitive information.** Always physically secure domain controllers and servers with sensitive information, and consider using System Key Level 2 or Level 3 to protect account information and LSA secrets stored on computers.

■ **Use security groups.** By using security groups correctly (A-G-G-U-DL-P), you can implement a role-based security model for granting permissions.

■ **Apply least privilege.** Assign users and administrators the least privilege they need to complete their job tasks.

■ **Create password policies that reflect organizational culture.** Create policies to enforce the use of passwords that balance complexity, randomness, and length.

■ **Educate users and other administrators on how to create strong passwords.** Despite enabling password policies that enforce the use of technically strong passwords, users make many common mistakes when creating passwords, mistakes that can undermine a well-planned policy.

■ **Remove LM hashes.** If LAN Manager authentication is not used on your network, remove the LM password hashes from all domain controllers and local computers.

■ **Configure LM compatibility.** Set the LM compatibility to the highest level that applications on your network will support.

Additional Information

■ 147706: How to Disable LM Authentication on Windows NT"

■ 299656: New Registry Key to Remove LM Hashes from Active Directory and Security Account Manager"

■ 239869: How to Enable NTLM 2 Authentication for Windows 95/98/2000 and NT"

■ 102716: User Authentication with Windows NT"

- 175641: "LMCompatibilityLevel and Its Effects"

- 266280: Changing User Rights from a Batch File or Command Line"

> **Note**   The six articles above can be accessed through the Microsoft Knowledge Base. Go to *http://support.microsoft.com* and enter the article number in the Search The Knowledge Base text box.

- RFC 1510: The Kerberos Network Authentication Service (v5)"

- RFC 3244: "Microsoft Windows 2000 Kerberos Change Password and Set Password Protocols"

> **Note**   The two articles above can be accessed through the Request for Comments repository. Go to *http://ietf.org/rfc.html* and enter the RFC number in the FFC Number text box.

- "Windows 2000 Kerberos Authentication" white paper (*http://www.microsoft.com/TechNet/prodtechnol/windows2000serv/deploy/kerberos.asp*)

- "Data Protection and Recovery in Windows XP" white paper (*http://www.microsoft.com/technet/prodtechnol/winxppro/support/DataProt.asp*)

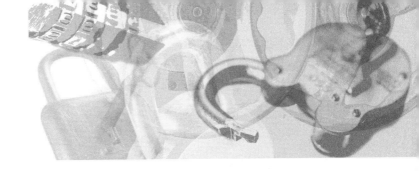

4

Securing Active Directory Objects and Attributes

All objects and attributes in the Active Directory directory service are individually secured though the use of discretionary access control lists. Although the default security on Active Directory might be suitable for your organization, you might need to adjust the security of objects or attributes to increase the overall security of Active Directory. You also might need to delegate authority over objects or attributes, or create custom objects and attributes that need to have security defined for them. For each of these situations, you must know how Active Directory objects are secured by default and how you can configure permissions.

Understanding the Active Directory Schema

All the objects that you can create in Active Directory and all their properties are defined in the Active Directory Schema. In Microsoft Windows 2000, the only copy of the schema is hosted by the domain controller that holds the schema flexible single-master operation (FSMO) role, which by default is the first domain controller in the forest. The schema is replicated from the schema master to all domain controllers in the forest through normal Active Directory replication. In the schema, objects and properties are defined as object classes and attributes. Once an object class has been defined and attributes assigned to it, you can instantiate, or create, objects of that class.

Attributes

The attributes defined in the schema represent the possible properties that can be used in object classes. Attributes are defined in the schema only one time and are reused for each object class with which they are associated. For example, nearly every object class includes the attribute *cn*, which will be populated with the common name of the object in the Lightweight Directory Access Protocol (LDAP) naming convention. Table 4-1 lists the contents of an attribute.

Table 4-1   Contents of an Attribute

Contents	Description
Common name	LDAP display name of the attribute.
Description	Description of the attribute.
X.500 object ID (OID)	Object identifier for the attribute.
Globally unique identifier (GUID)	128-bit randomly generated number that uniquely identifies the attribute.
Syntax	Data type of the attribute.
Range	Range of values for the attribute. For integers, range defines the minimum and maximum value; for strings, range defines the minimum and maximum length.
Multi/single value	Defines whether the attribute will contain one value or more than one value.
Index	Determines whether the attribute is indexed.
Global Catalog	Determines whether the attribute is replicated to the Global Catalog for all objects that use it.
Security descriptor	Defines the base security for the attribute.
Metadata	Data used by Active Directory for internal processing, such as replication metadata.

Members of the Schema Admins group can add attributes to the schema of a forest. Attributes cannot be deleted; however, they can de deactivated, which prohibits them from being used in object classes.

Classes

Object classes are collections of attributes that can be instantiated to create objects. Active Directory is based on the X.500 1993 specification for directory services that defines the hierarchal structure of classes. X.509 requires that object classes be assigned to one of three categories:

- **Structural classes**   Structural classes are the only kind of class from which you can create objects in Active Directory. A structural class can be used in defining the structure of the directory and is derived from either an abstract class or another structural class. A structural class can include any number of auxiliary classes in its definition. For example, *user* and *organizationalUnit* are structural object classes.

- **Abstract classes**   Abstract classes are templates that are used only to derive new structural classes. Abstract classes cannot be instantiated in the directory. This means that no object can belong to an abstract class only; each object of an abstract class must also belong to some nonabstract subclass. A new abstract class can be derived from an existing abstract class. Classes of the abstract category exist for the sole purpose of providing attributes for subordinate classes, referred to as *subclasses*. A subclass contains all mandatory and optional attributes of the class from which it is derived, known as its *superclass*, in addition to those attributes specific to the class itself. Likewise, a subclass of a subclass contains all attributes of both its superclasses, and so forth.

- **Auxiliary classes**   Auxiliary classes are similar to include files in the C programming language; they contain a list of attributes. Adding the auxiliary class to the definition of a structural or abstract class adds the auxiliary class's attributes to the definition. An auxiliary class cannot be instantiated in the directory, but new auxiliary classes can be derived from existing auxiliary classes. For example, the *securityPrincipal* class is an auxiliary class, and it derives its attributes from the parent abstract class named *top*. Although you cannot create a security principal object in the directory (because auxiliary classes cannot have instances), you can create an object of the structural class *user*, which has the *securityPrincipal* class as an auxiliary. The attributes of the *securityPrincipal* class contribute to making the *user* object recognizable to the system as a security account. Similarly, the *group* class has *securityPrincipal* as an auxiliary class.

An object class is defined by the attributes that are tagged as either mandatory or optional. Mandatory attributes must be populated with values when an object is created, while optional attributes can have null values.

Security on the Active Directory Schema

Before viewing the Active Directory Schema, you must register the schema management .dll file. You can do this by typing **regsvr32 schmmgmt.dll** at the command prompt or in the Run command and then adding the Active Directory Schema Microsoft Management Console (MMC) snap-in to a blank MMC. You can also automatically register the schema management .dll file and all other management .dll files by installing the Windows 2000 Adminstrator's Pack. You do this by running Adminpak.msi from any Windows 2000 server or from the Windows 2000 Server CD.

The schema FSMO is read-only by default. Only members of the Schema Admins group can mark the schema as writeable. Once the changes to the schema have been made, the schema must replicate to all domain controllers in the forest.

Because modifications to the schema in Windows 2000 are irreversible, you should exercise extreme caution when making modifications or extensions to the schema. You should also ensure that the Schema Admins group has no members unless the schema is in the process of being modified or extended. Only members of the Enterprise Administrators group, which includes Domain Admins from the forest root domain, can manage membership in the Schema Admins group.

Configuring DACLs to Secure Active Directory Objects

All objects and their properties in Active Directory have security descriptors to control access to the object and the values of the object's attributes. As with NTFS file system objects, the Active Directory object's security descriptor includes a discretionary access control list (DACL) and a system access control list (SACL) in addition to the object's ownership data. Figure 4-1 shows a security descriptor.

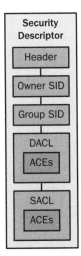

Figure 4-1   Contents of a security descriptor for Active Directory objects and attributes

What Are DACLs?

Discretionary access control lists can be configured at the discretion of any account that possesses the appropriate permissions to modify the configuration, including Take Ownership, Change Permissions, or Full Control permissions. DACLs consist of several elements, as described in this list:

■ **Header**   Metadata pertaining to the access control entries (ACEs) associated with the DACL.

■ **SID (user)**   The security identifier of the owner of the object.

■ **SID (group)**   The security identifier of the built-in Administrators or Domain Admins group if the account that owns the object is a member of either of these groups.

■ **Generic deny ACEs**   Access control entries that deny access to an account or security group based on their SIDs. These ACEs can be inherited from the object's parent or assigned directly to the object, and they are specific to the object and child objects of the same class, based on the security settings defined in the object class in the schema.

■ **Generic allow ACEs**   Access control entries that allow access to child objects to an account or security group based on their SIDs. These ACEs can be inherited from the object's parent or assigned directly to the object, and they are specific to the object and child objects of the same class.

■ **Object-specific deny ACEs**   Access control entries that deny access to child objects to an account or security group based on their SIDs. These ACEs can be inherited from the object's parent or assigned directly to the object, and they apply to specific classes of child objects.

■ **Object-specific ACEs**   Access control entries that deny access to an account or security group based on their SIDs. These ACEs can be inherited from the object's parent or assigned directly to the object, and they apply to specific classes of child objects.

Table 4-2 shows the settings of an example DACL an organizational unit (OU) might have.

Table 4-2   Example of a DACL

Group	Permissions	Scope
Enterprise Admins	Full Control	This object and all child objects
Authenticated Users	Read	This object
Security Managers	Reset Password	User objects

Figure 4-2 offers a visual depiction of these settings, and Figure 4-3 displays the user interface for this DACL.

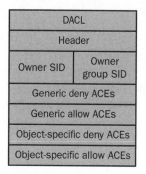

Figure 4-2   Elements of DACL example shown in Table 4-2

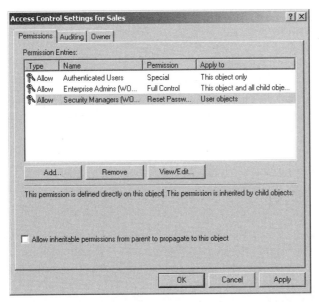

Figure 4-3   User interface view of DACL example shown in Table 4-2

Generic ACEs offer limited control over the kinds of child objects that can inherit them. Generic ACEs distinguish between objects that can contain other objects, such as group and organization unit objects and objects that cannot contain other objects, such as user objects. For example, the DACL on an organizational unit object can include a generic ACE that allows a member of a group object the permissions to delete members of other group objects in the OU. Because this ACE can be performed only on container objects and child objects of the same class, it will not be inherited by noncontainer objects, such as user objects.

Object-specific ACEs offer greater granularity of control over the types of child objects that can inherit them. For example, an organizational unit object's DACL can have an object-specific ACE that is marked for inheritance only by user objects. Other types of objects, such as computer objects, will not inherit the ACE. This capability is the crux of object-specific ACEs: their inheritance can be limited to specific object classes of child objects.

These two categories of ACEs control access to objects in a somewhat similar fashion. Generic ACEs apply to an entire object. If a generic ACE gives a particular user Read access, the user can read all information associated with the object—both data and properties.

Object-specific ACEs can apply to any individual property of an object or to a set of properties. These ACE types are used only in ACLs for Active Directory objects, which, unlike other object types, store most of their information in properties. It is often desirable to place independent controls on each property of an Active Directory object, and object-specific ACEs make that possible. For example, when you define permissions for a user object, you can use one object-specific ACE to allow Principal Self (the user) Write access to the Phone-Home-Primary property (*homePhone*). You also can use other object-specific ACEs to deny Principal Self access to the Logon-Hours property (*logonHours*) and other properties that set restrictions on the user account.

How DACLs Work

When access is requested to an Active Directory object, the Local Security Authority (LSA) compares the access token of the account requesting access to the object to the DACL. The security subsystem checks the object's DACL, looking for ACEs that apply to the user and group SIDs referenced in the thread's access token. The security subsystem then steps through the DACL until it finds any ACEs that either allow or deny access to the user or one of the user's groups. The subsystem does this by first examining ACEs that have been explicitly assigned to the object and then examining ones that have been inherited by the object.

If an explicit deny is found, access is denied. Explicit deny ACE entries are always applied, even if conflicting explicit allow ACEs exist. Explicit allow ACEs are examined, as are inherited deny and allow ACEs. The ACEs that apply to the user are accumulated. Inherited deny ACEs overrule inherited allow ACEs, but are overruled themselves by explicit allow permissions. If none of the user or groups SIDs in the access token match the DACL, the user is denied access implicitly. Figure 4-4 shows the process of evaluating access token contents against a DACL.

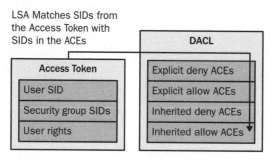

Figure 4-4   Access control in Active Directory

> **Tip**   Accounts with Full Control, Modify Permissions, or Modify Owner permissions can change the DACL and SACL on the object.

Securing Active Directory Objects and Attributes

In Active Directory, all attributes of all objects and the objects themselves have permissions that can be defined when the object is created or after it has been created. You must be able to examine these permissions and secure them according to your organization's security policy. This is especially true if your organization is planning on extending the Active Directory Schema to include additional attributes or objects.

You can secure Active Directory objects at their creation globally for all newly created objects of a given object class by modifying the default security descriptor for the object class in the schema. You can also secure objects after their creation by creating an object-specific ACE on the parent container that the object will be created in or by configuring the DACL on the object directly.

The method used to build a DACL for a new Active Directory object differs slightly from the method used to build DACLs for other object types. Two key differences exist. First, when building a DACL for a new Active Directory object, each object class defined in the schema has a default DACL that is applied to all objects when they are created. Second, the rules for creating a DACL distinguish between generic inheritable ACEs and object-specific inheritable ACEs in the parent object's security descriptor. Generic inheritable ACEs can be inherited by all types of child objects. Object-specific inheritable ACEs can be inherited only by the type of child object to which they apply. Other objects that have DACLs, such as files, do not have object-specific ACEs.

Configuring Default DACLs on Objects and Attributes

You can configure the default DACL on object classes by modifying the schema. To modify the schema, you must be a member of the Schema Admins security group and the schema FSMO must be marked as writeable. To configure a default DACL on an object class, perform the following steps:

1. Open a blank MMC from the command prompt by typing **MMC**.

2. Add the Active Directory Schema MMC snap-in to the blank MMC.

3. Right-click the object class that you want to modify. Then select Properties and click the Security tab of the object class.

4.   Configure the default DACL and close the open windows.

> **Important**   The schema partition of Active Directory will need to fully replicate throughout the forest before all new objects will receive the new default security as defined on the default DACL.

Figure 4-5 shows a custom security group named Security Managers being granted Full Control permissions over all new user objects in the forest. Because a single schema exists for the entire forest, the DACL that you modify will be applied to all new objects of that object class created in any domain in the forest. Consequently, if you are assigning permissions to a new security group rather than modifying the existing permissions, you should use universal groups to ensure that the permissions are applicable throughout the Active Directory forest. You can then make the appropriate global groups members of the universal group.

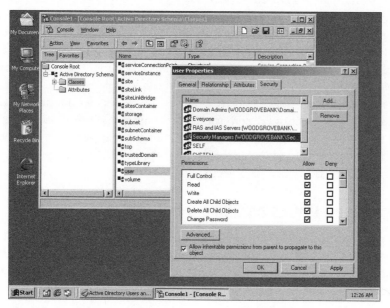

Figure 4-5   Adding a security group to an object class default DACL

The new default DACL only applies to new objects. Existing objects of the object class that you have modified the default DACL of will not be affected. The change will affect only objects created after the schema has replicated to the domain controller where the new object is created. Settings in the default DACL remain with the object even if they are moved to a different container.

Securing Objects After Being Created

Setting the default DACL on an object class is an effective way to configure the security of Active Directory objects during their creation because the change is forestwide in scope and affects only newly created objects. However, you might want to configure an object-specific ACE on the parent object, such as an OU. The object-specific ACE will be applied to the object when the object is created or when objects are moved into the parent object. For example, rather than assigning the Security Managers security group full control of all newly created user objects in the forest, you might want to only grant them full control over all user objects in an OU. You can do this by editing the DACL for the organizational unit. The following steps explain how to do this:

1. Open Active Directory Users and Computers.

2. Right-click the OU, click Properties, and select the Security tab.

3. Click the Advanced button.

4. Click Add and add the appropriate security groups to the DACL. Then click OK.

5. In the Apply Onto drop-down box, ensure that the correct object class is chosen.

6. Configure the new access that you are granting or denying.

7. Close all windows.

> **Tip**   You must enable the Advanced view in Active Directory Users and Computers to expose the Security tab on objects.

Figure 4-6 shows the creation of an object-specific ACE granting full control over user objects to the Security Managers custom security group.

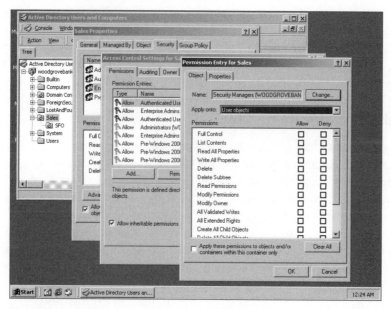

Figure 4-6 Adding an object-specific ACE to an OU

When adding an object-specific ACE to an OU, the OU (or any other type of parent object) will propagate the immediate inheritance of the permissions to all objects of that object class in the OU and in all child OUs. Similarly, when objects of that object class are moved into the OU, the permissions will be inherited by the object. If the object-specific ACEs are removed from the OU, the permissions will be immediately removed from the objects of that object class in the OU and all child OUs. If an object of that object class is moved to a new parent container, the ACE will be removed from the object.

Active Directory not only enables you to configure security on objects but also to configure security on individual properties. Setting security on properties entails the same process as setting permissions on objects.

Configuring DACLs from the Command Line

Although configuring DACLs by using the MMC is convenient, you might want to set permissions from the command line. In Windows 2000, you can do this in one of two ways: though Active Directory Services Interface (ADSI) scripts, or by using the Support Tools utility Dsacls.exe. You can install Support Tools from the Windows 2000 Server CD, from the Support\Tools directory.

> **More Info**   Writing custom ADSI programs is beyond the scope of this book. The MSDN Library provides detailed information on controlling access to objects in Active Directory using ADSI at *http://msdn.microsoft.com/library/en-us/netdir/ad/controlling_access_to_active_directory_objects.asp*.

Dsacls.exe is the command-line equivalent of the Security tab in the Properties dialog box for an Active Directory object in Active Directory tools, such as Active Directory Users and Computers. You can display all permissions on a given object in Active Directory by typing **dsacls "ou=sales.dc=woodgrovebank,dc=com"**. Another convenient feature of Dsacls.exe is its ability to reset the security on an object or set of objects to the default DACL of the object's object class in the schema. To reset the security on an object, type **dsacls "ou=sales.dc=woodgrovebank,dc=com" /S**. This is a common use of Dsacls.exe in a test environment when evaluating changing permissions on Active Directory objects. The complete syntax of Dsacls.exe can be referenced in the Support Tools Help file.

Another important tool for managing DACLs on Active Directory objects is Acldiag.exe, which you can also obtain from Support Tools. Acldiag.exe enables you to do the following:

- Compare the current DACL on the object against the default DACL on the object's class. For example, typing **acldiag "cn=jobrown,ou=sales,dc=woodgrovebank,dc=com" /schema** would compare the DACL of the user object *Jo Brown* to the default DACL on the object class user.

- Determine the effective permissions that a user or group has to an object. Typing **acldiag "cn=jobrown,ou=sales,dc=woodgrovebank,dc=com" /geteffective:*** would retrieve the effective permissions for the user object *Jo Brown* and all the properties of the object and then print them to the console.

- Export the permissions to a comma-delimited or tab-delimited file. By using the switches /cdo or /tdo at the end of an Acldiag command, you can format the output in comma-delimited or tab-delimited format. This is especially useful if you want to import the permissions into a spreadsheet or database.

> **Tip** You can direct the output of any command-line program to a text file or local printer by using the standard redirector in the operating system. To direct the output to a file, append the command string with **>*filename***. To direct the output to a local printer, append the command string with **>lpt1**. For example, **acldiag "cn=jobrown,ou=sales,dc=woodgrovebank,dc=com" /geteffective:* /cdo >joDACL.csv** will compile the effective permissions for all users on the user object *Jo Brown* on a comma-separated file named JoDACL.csv.

Best Practices

- **Always apply the theory of least privilege.** Whenever you are configuring security on Active Directory object, assign only the least permissions needed by the users to complete their job function.

- **Use a consistent model for assigning permissions.** Do not assign permissions to individual users; rather, use a well-defined model for assigning permissions to security groups and placing user accounts into the security groups.

- **Avoid assigning permissions to domain local groups.** Domain local security groups are valid only in the domain; thus, permissions replication to the Global Catalog will not be applied as expected. Assign forestwide permissions by using universal groups. This is one of the only exceptions to assigning permissions using the A-G-DL-P model. (For more on this model, see the "Implementing Role-Based Security in Windows 2000" section in Chapter 3, "Securing User Accounts and Passwords.")

- **Document changes made to DACLs.** Be certain to record changes that you make to Active Directory object DACLs. This will simplify troubleshooting in the event of an error arising from the new permissions.

- **Remove users from the Schema Admins security group.** When the schema is not in the process of being extended or altered, remove users from the Schema Admins security group to ensure that the schema is not unintentionally altered and ensure that the schema is not write-enabled.

- **Use Restricted Groups.**   Use Restricted Groups in Group Policy to limit membership in the Schema Admins security group.

Additional Information

- 218596: How to Assign Access Control Permissions on the Properties of an Active Directory Object"

- 292304: How to Prevent Windows 2000 Users from Changing Personal Detail Information"

> **Note**   The preceding two articles can be accessed through the Microsoft Knowledge Base. Go to *http://support.microsoft.com* and enter the article number in the Search The Knowledge Base text box.

- MSDN Library, "Active Directory Programmer's Guide" (*http://msdn.microsoft.com/library/en-us/netdir/adsi/active_directory.asp*)

- MSDN Library, "Controlling Access to Active Directory Objects" (*http://msdn.microsoft.com/library/en-us/netdir/ad/controlling_access_to_active_directory_objects.asp*)

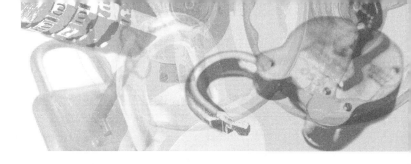

5

Implementing Group Policy

One of the most powerful and useful security features in Microsoft Windows 2000 is Group Policy. Group Policy enables administrators to manage large numbers of users and computers running Windows 2000 and Windows XP centrally, in the Active Directory directory service. Unlike system policies in Windows NT, group policies do not make permanent changes, or "tattoo" the registry—rather, computers can easily have policies added or removed. Group policies also differ from system policies in that they are applied dynamically. Furthermore, nearly all Group Policy settings are applied without requiring a reboot of the operating system.

Understanding Group Policy

Group policies have two types of application: those that apply to the computer, and those that apply to the user. Computer-related group policies are always applied, regardless of what user account is used to log on to the computer. The user-related group policies apply to specific users. Security policies are applied to the computer and thus will apply to all users of the computer, including members of the Administrators group. By default, a local security policy is stored on and applied to each computer running Windows 2000 or Windows XP. In addition, you can implement Group Policy settings on a local computer, although local group policies are not stored in and enforced by Active Directory. Group policies are associated with site, domain, and OU containers in Active Directory in the form of Group Policy objects (GPOs).

A GPO can be associated with any site, domain, or OU, and the GPO can be linked to multiple sites, domains, or OUs. Conversely, a given site, domain, or OU can have multiple GPOs linked to it. In the event that multiple GPOs are linked to a particular site, domain, or OU, you can prioritize the order in which these GPOs are applied.

By linking GPOs to Active Directory sites, domains, and OUs, you can implement Group Policy settings for as broad or narrow a portion of the organization as you require, including the following:

■   A GPO linked to a site applies to all users and computers in the site.

■   A GPO applied to a domain applies to all users and computers in the domain, even if the users and computers are located within OUs in the domain. GPOs associated with parent domains are not inherited by child domains.

■   A GPO applied to an OU applies to all users and computers located directly in the OU and, by inheritance, to all users and computers in child OUs.

The accumulation of GPO settings from site, domain, and OUs are applied. GPOs are stored on a per-domain basis. You can link a site, domain, or OU to a Group Policy object in another trusted domain, but this is not generally recommended for performance reasons. GPOs associated only with a site are stored in the forest root domain, and those policies will be retrieved from a domain controller in the forest root domain. Group Policy objects are applied in a hierarchical arrangement. By default, GPOs are cumulative and processed in the following order:

1.   The local Group Policy object (LGPO) is applied.

2.   GPOs linked to sites are processed.

3.   GPOs linked to domains are processed.

4.   GPOs linked to OUs are processed. In the case of nested OUs, GPOs associated with parent OUs are processed prior to GPOs associated with child OUs.

Computer-Related Group Policies

Computer-related group policies are specific to the computer and apply to all users of the computer. Computer-related group policies are applied during the startup phase of the operating system and are fully applied by default before the Windows Logon dialog box appears. Table 5-1 lists the types of computer-related Group Policy settings.

Table 5-1   Computer-Related Group Policy Settings

Group	Description
Software Installation	Enables software to be installed on nondomain controllers
Windows Settings	Enables security templates to be deployed and computer startup and shutdown scripts to be executed
Administrative Templates	Enables computer-related registry changes to be made

By using software installation policies, you can ensure that security-related software is installed on all computers on the network. For example, you might want to use a Group Policy object to assign antivirus software to all desktop and laptop computers in your organization.

You can import security templates into the computer configuration portion of Group Policy to deploy uniform security to computers on your organization's network. Table 5-2 describes the security settings in Group Policy.

Table 5-2   Security Options in Group Policy

Area	Description
Account Policies	Password policies, account lockout policies, and Kerberos policies
Local Policies	Audit policy, user rights assignment, security options
Event Log Settings	Application, system, and security event log settings
Restricted Groups	Membership of security-sensitive groups
System Services	Startup parameters and permissions for system services
Registry	Permissions for default registry keys
File System	Permissions for folders and files

You can use Windows settings to run scripts at the startup or shutdown of a computer. Startup scripts execute before the Security dialog box appears, and shutdown scripts run after the user has logged off but before services cease.

Administrative templates are settings that configure the Windows 2000 and Windows XP registries. In addition to the administrative templates included by default, you can import custom settings by creating and importing .adm files. In contrast with using Windows NT system policies, when you use Group Policy, policy settings made through administrative templates do not tattoo the registry and are applied immediately, rather than after one or more reboots.

> **More Info**   Security templates are discussed in detail in Chapter 11, "Configuring Security Templates."

Preferences vs. Policies

Registry policy or .adm templates take the form of *policies* (registry entries under the special keys) or *preferences* (registry keys anywhere else). The .adm files are used to apply policies or preferences. We recommend you use policies rather than preferences. Policies do not tattoo the registry. If you use a GPO to deploy policies and preferences, when the GPO is removed, the policies will be removed. However, the preferences will remain. Preferences are not refreshed unless the GPO changes. Users can change their preferences, and these preferences will not be restored until Group Policy changes and the GPOs are reapplied. Policies, on the other hand, are given an access control list (ACL) in the registry so that users cannot change them.

If you must use preferences, you need to add them via the .adm file. By default, if nothing changes at the GPO, nothing will be applied to the client computer (assuming the client has received the policy in the past).

Computer-related policy settings are stored in the registry hive HKEY_LOCAL_MACHINE (HKLM), and user-related policy settings are stored in the registry hive HKEY_CURRENT_USER (HKCU). In each of these registry hives, Group Policy settings are stored in these two registry keys:

■   \Software\Policies (preferred location)

■   \Software\Microsoft\Windows\CurrentVersion\Policies

User-Related Group Policies

In addition to the computer-related group policies applied to the computer a user logs on to, user-related group polices are applied to specific users. By default, user-related group policies are applied immediately after the user's credentials are successfully authenticated but before the user gains control of the Windows Explorer shell. Table 5-3 describes the various types of user-related group policies.

Table 5-3   **User-Related Group Policy Settings**

Group	Description
Software Installation	Enables software to be assigned or published to a user
Windows Settings	Enables security templates to be deployed and user logon and logoff scripts to be executed
Administrative Templates	Enables registry changes to be made for the user

Software can be deployed to users in two ways: they can be *assigned*, or they can be *published*. Software packages assigned to a user will be advertised in the Start menu and will be installed on the computer only if the user chooses to use the application or invokes the application by attempting to open a file with the default file type that the application uses (if this option is enabled in the policy). Software can also be published to the user. Published software will appear in the Control Panel under Add/Remove Programs. Published software can also be installed by document-based invocation, if enabled.

Important   Applications installed by using Group Policy Software Installation policies will only install the application's core files once per computer if multiple users of the computer have the same application assigned or published to them. The application information unique to each user will be written to the Application Data folder in the user profile or the HKEY_USER (HKU) registry hive for the user.

The Windows Settings for users contains options for configuring logon and logoff scripts, folder redirection behavior, Microsoft Internet Explorer settings, Public Key Infrastructure (PKI) enterprise trusts, and Remote Installation Services (RIS) settings. The Administrative Templates settings for users function similarly to the settings for computers.

> **Important**   Before deploying Group Policy objects, you should test the settings in a test environment to ensure that the GPOs do not prevent users from completing tasks required by their job function. If possible, you should also conduct a pilot deployment in the production environment.

Using Group Policy Containers

All computers running Windows 2000 and Windows XP have a local GPO that defines the default configuration of the computer. The local GPO applies to all users of the computer. In addition, if the computers are members of an Active Directory domain, you can deploy GPOs to all computers in a site, domain, or OU.

The Local Group Policy Object

You can configure a local Group Policy for any computer, regardless of whether it is a member of Active Directory. To configure the local Group Policy object (LGPO), use the Group Policy MMC snap-in and select to focus on the local computer. The local Group Policy editor is shown in Figure 5-1.

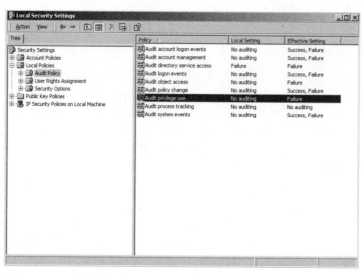

Figure 5-1   Configuring the LGPO

Group Policy is processed in this order:

1.   Local Group Policy object

2.   Site GPOs

3. Domain GPOs

4. Organizational unit GPOs

5. Nested organizational unit GPOs

The LGPO cannot be filtered by a user account. Unlike Group Policy objects in Active Directory, there is no discretionary access control list (DACL) permission named Apply Group Policy; there is only the Read permission. User accounts need the Read permission to either read the Group Policy object settings or have them apply to the logon session. The Apply Group Policy permission is checked during Group Policy processing. If the user has this permission on the Group Policy object, it will be processed.

Site Group Policy Objects

Group Policy objects that are linked to site containers affect all computers or users in a forest of domains that have membership in the site. Computers running Windows 2000 and Windows XP are automatically members of the Default-First-Site-Name site unless other sites and subnet objects have been defined. Site information replicates to all domain controllers in the forest. Therefore, any Group Policy object that is linked to a site container is applied to all computers in that site, regardless of the domain. This enables a single GPO to span multiple domains but also results in cross-domain authentication because domain controllers must retrieve the policy from the domain in which it is stored. Because site GPOs can affect multiple domains, you must either be a member of the Enterprise Admins group or have been specifically delegated control to manage site GPOs.

Site GPOs are effective for managing settings that apply a group of computers that exist on the same high-speed communications channel. For example, you might want to assign Proxy Server settings in Internet Explorer by site or install antivirus software from a server on the same network as the computer.

Domain Group Policy Objects

Group Policy objects that are linked to a domain affect all computers or users in the domain. By default, two GPOs exist in each Active Directory domain:

- Default Domain Policy
- Default Domain Controllers Policy

The Default Domain Policy contains the default security policy for all computers in the domain and the account policies for domain accounts. The Default Domain Controllers Policy contains the default security policy for domain controllers and augments the security policy of the Default Domain Policy. For example, the Default Domain Controllers Policy prohibits nonadministrators from logging on interactively.

OU Group Policy Objects

One of the primary purposes of OU containers is to facilitate the deployment of Group Policy objects to users and computers. Unlike domains, OUs are flexible: objects, including security principals, can easily be moved between OUs, and OUs can be created and deleted without much consequence. You can create OUs that facilitate the application of GPOs based on the security needs of the users or computers. The domain controller's OU is the only OU created by default in each domain. Its purpose is to facilitate the deployment of the Default Domain Controllers GPO.

Processing Group Policy Objects

Group policies are processed and applied initially when the computer starts up and when the user logs on. After the initial application, group policies are processed and applied at regular intervals. By default, during the refresh interval, the client computer retrieves the Group Policy objects only if the GPO version stored in Active Directory is incremented. You can change this behavior in the Group Policy settings that affect group policies. In addition, you can manually refresh Group Policy settings.

Initial Group Policy Application

GPOs are processed when the computer is started and when the user logs on via the Security dialog box. When a computer boots up, settings from the LGPO are applied, if present. Then, the computer retrieves all the settings from the site, if present. If two or more GPOs are linked to a container, they are processed starting with those of the lowest precedence, which appear lower in the user interface. Domain GPOs are then retrieved and processed, as are OU Group Policy objects (if present), beginning with the root OU and continuing to the computer's parent object.

Settings in Group Policy objects are cumulative; however, if the settings conflict with each other, the policy processed later will override the previous setting. For example, suppose that at the domain level, a software package is assigned and the number of previously cached logons is set to five. Now suppose that a policy at the OU level defines a startup script and sets the number of cached logons to two. The resultant settings will include installation of the software package, application of the startup script, and caching of two logons.

When the user logs on, the GPOs are processed in the same order that the computer-related group policies are applied. If a setting creates a conflict between the computer-related Group Policy applied and the user-related group applied (such as conflicting Task Scheduler Administrative Templates settings), the computer-related Group Policy setting will generally apply.

Group Policy Refresh

Group Policy is processed periodically, according to a defined interval. By default, for nondomain controllers, this occurs every 90 minutes with a randomized offset of up to 30 minutes. For domain controllers, Group Policy is refreshed every 5 minutes. You can change these default values by using a Group Policy setting in Administrative Templates. Setting the value to 0 minutes causes the refresh rate to be set to 7 seconds. While most changes made to GPOs or settings in new GPOs will be enforced during the refresh cycles, the following settings will not be enforced:

■   Computer-related group policies for Software Installation

■   User-related group policies for Software Installation

■   User-related group policies for Folder Redirection

These settings are refreshed the next time that the computer is restarted or the user interactively logs on.

> **Note**   Security settings in a computer-related Group Policy are refreshed every 16 hours, regardless of whether a change in Group Policy is detected by the client.

On-Demand Processing

You can also trigger a background refresh of Group Policy on demand from the client. However, the application of Group Policy cannot be pushed to clients on demand from the server. To refresh Group Policy manually on Windows 2000 computers, use the Secedit command as follows:

Computer-related group policies	Type **secedit /refreshpolicy machine_policy /enforce** at the command prompt.
User-related group policies	Type **secedit /refreshpolicy user_policy /enforce** at the command prompt.

To refresh Group Policy manually on Windows XP computers, use the Gpupdate command as follows:

Computer-related group policies	Type **gpupdate target:computer /force** at the command prompt.
User-related group policies	Type **gpupdate target:user /force** at the command prompt.
Both computer-related and user-related group policies	Type **gpupdate /force** at the command prompt.

Altering Group Policy Application

When you create Group Policy structure in your organization, you might need to alter the default processing of GPOs. Group Policy provides four options for doing this:

■   Block Inheritance

■   No Override

■   Group Policy Object Filtering

■   Loopback Mode Processing

Block Inheritance

You might have a situation in which a subcontainer such as an OU should not receive GPOs from parent objects. For example, suppose you have configured a GPO and linked it to the domain container, thus applying it to all computers. But what if you want to ensure that computers in a specific OU containing computers do not inherit the domain Group Policy settings? In this case, you can implement Block Inheritance on the OU container, which will prevent all GPOs from the parent container from being processed, and therefore, from being applied to the computer or user. Note that you cannot block the inheritance of individual GPOs with this setting. Blocking inheritance will block all GPOs from a higher level in the processing hierarchy.

No Override

You might be the administrator of GPOs linked to the domain and need to ensure that certain policies are applied, even if an OU has the Block Inheritance option configured or a GPO configured with an opposite or conflicting setting. In this case, you can mark the individual GPO as "No Override". A GPO with the No Override option set on a parent object will be applied even if the Block Inheritance option is configured on the child object. Unlike Block Inheritance, No Override is specified on individual GPOs.

Group Policy Object Filtering

When a Group Policy object is applied to a container, it applies to all computer and user objects in the container and all subcontainers. You might need to have some computers or users exempted by the GPO. Rather than create a special container and use a series of No Override and Block Inheritance restrictions, you can filter Group Policy by using the DACLs on the GPO.

You can view and modify the security settings from the Security tab on the Properties page of the specific GPO. The Security tab for a GPO is accessible by right-clicking the root node in the Group Policy snap-in, clicking Properties, and then clicking Security. Alternately, from the Properties page of a given site, domain, or OU, you can select the Group Policy tab, right-click the appropriate GPO in the Group Policy Object list, select Properties, and then click Security.

For the GPO to be applied to a computer or user, the computer and user objects in Active Directory must have both Read and Apply Group Policy permissions on the GPO. By default, members of the Authenticated Users group are granted both Apply Group Policy and Read permissions. Computer and user accounts automatically receive membership in the Authenticated Users group after the successful validation of their credentials, which occurs before Group Policy is processed. Therefore, the default behavior is for every GPO to apply to Authenticated Users. By default, domain administrators, enterprise administrators, and the local system have Full Control permissions, without the Apply Group Policy access control entry (ACE). However, administrators are members of Authenticated Users, which means that they will receive the settings in the GPO by default.

Preventing Group Policy from applying to a specified group requires removal of the Apply Group Policy ACE from that group. If you remove the Apply Group Policy ACE (clear the Allow check box) for Authenticated Users, you can explicitly grant this permission to individual security groups that should receive the policy settings. Alternatively, you could set Apply Group Policy to Deny for certain security groups that should not have the policy applied. Because an explicit deny permission always overrides an allow permission, the computer or user accounts on the security group will not process the GPO.

Note   Group Policy administrators also need the Read permission to manage the GPO. Use caution when altering the default assignment of Read for the Authenticated Users group.

Loopback Mode Processing

Another scenario in which you might need to alter the default processing of Group Policy is when you have computer and user object in different containers in Active Directory. The OU that holds the user object has restrictive GPO settings activated, such as preventing users from altering network settings, removing Control Panel applets, and preventing certain applications from running. When a user logs on to her workstation, the GPO policies act to protect the network and standardize the desktop configuration; however, the user can also manage a Windows 2000 file and print server. When the user logs on to the server, the Group Policy settings prevent her from completing the management task she is required to do. Rather than create a separate account for the user to use when managing the server, you can implement Group Policy loopback mode.

Group Policy loopback mode is itself a Group Policy setting that you can enable in the Computer Configuration section of Group Policy. Group Policy loopback mode has two settings:

- **Replace**   When you enable Group Policy loopback mode using this setting, the GPO that applies to the user object will not be processed. Hence, the only settings that apply to the logon session are computer-related Group Policy settings. This setting is commonly used to resolve the scenario just described.

- **Merge**   When you use this setting, user configuration settings from the computer object location will be applied after the user configuration settings from the location of the user object. This results in the computer location's user settings combining with the user location's user settings and overriding them in the event of conflicts.

You can set the Group Policy loopback mode by enabling User Group Policy Loopback Processing Mode policy in the Computer Configuration section of Group Policy\Administrative settings\System\Group Policy.

Managing Group Policy

One GPO can be used to configure the security on all computers in a site, domain, or OU. This makes securing the management of Group Policy itself very important. For example, an administrator of an OU could exempt computers and users in the OU from receiving Group Policy settings configured at the domain level if that administrator has the ability to manage Group Policy. When implementing security in your forest, you must consider the management of Group Policy.

Default Group Policy Permissions

By default, several groups have administrative authority over Group Policy. These settings may or may not be appropriate for your organization. Table 5-4 describes the permissions for managing Group Policy.

Table 5-4   Group Policy Permissions

Permission	Object	Description
Full Control	GPO	Gives full control over the GPO to the user account or security group
Write	GPO	Enables the user account or security group to modify the settings in the GPO
Read	GPO	Enables the user account or security group to read the setting in the GPO
Apply Group Policy	GPO	Enables the user account or security group to have the GPO processed during the initial logon or refresh cycle
Link Group Policy (gPLink)	Container	Enables the user account or security group to link a GPOs to the container
Read Group Policy Options (gPOptions)	Container	Enables the user account or security group to block the inheritance of GPOs to the container

By default, the groups Domain Admins, Enterprise Admins, Creator Owner, and Local System have Full Control permissions over all GPOs linked to domains and OUs. The groups Enterprise Admins and Authenticated Users have Read and Apply Group Policy permissions. The groups Enterprise Admins, Creator Owners, and Local System have Full Control permissions over GPOs linked to a site.

Delegating Group Policy Management

In Active Directory, you can delegate the permissions to manage Group Policy either by using the Delegation of Authority Wizard or by using the Security tab of the Properties dialog box of a GPO or container object. Delegation of authority in Active Directory is flexible enough to allow you to grant administrative control over GPOs according to the security requirements of your organization.

Adding Users to the Group Policy Creator Owners Group

By default, members of the Domain Admins and Group Policy Creator Owners security groups can create new GPOs in their home domain. Although members the Group Policy Creator Owners security group can create new GPOs, they do not have the permission to link the GPO to a container. After a member of the Group Policy Creator Owners security group has created a GPO and it has been linked to a container, that user account retains the explicit permissions to modify the GPO. Other members of the Group Policy Creator Owners security group do not have any permissions on GPOs created by other members of the group.

gPLink Permission

User accounts that have the Write gPLink permission can link existing GPOs to the container for which they possess this permission. User accounts that have been granted Write or Full Control permissions over a domain or OU container possess this permission by default. This permission does not allow the user account to create new GPOs.

gPOptions Permission

User accounts that have the Write gPOptions permission can enable the Block Inheritance option of a domain or OU container. User accounts that have been granted Write or Full Control permissions over a domain or OU container possess this permission by default. Possessing this permission does not grant the user account any additional permissions on GPOs.

Best Practices

- **Use Group Policy for security.**   Use Group Policy to secure Windows 2000 and Windows XP computers. Because GPOs are dynamic and are refreshed frequently, they are an excellent method of ensuring a base or additional level of security on your network.

- **Use caution when delegating authority over Group Policy.** Administrators who manage Group Policy can easily compromise the security of your network by maliciously or accidentally deploying security templates or security-related settings that weaken or remove the base security of Windows 2000 and Windows XP computers.

- **Use Block Inheritance, No Override, and Group Policy Object Filtering sparingly.**   Use these methods of altering the default behavior of Group Policy only when required and when no reasonable design workarounds exist. Using these options will greatly increase the difficulty of troubleshooting Group Policy, and the resulting confusion could lead to the misapplication of Group Policy.

Additional Information

- "Windows 2000 Group Policy" white paper (*http://www.microsoft.com/ windows2000/techinfo/howitworks/management/grouppolwp.asp*)

- "Step-by-Step Guide to Understanding the Group Policy Feature Set" (*http://www.microsoft.com/windows2000/techinfo/planning/ management/groupsteps.asp*)

- *Microsoft Windows 2000 Resource Kit*, "Group Policy" section (*http:// www.microsoft.com/windows2000/techinfo/reskit/samplechapters/ dsec/dsec_pol_zbgy.asp*)

- "Implementing Registry-Based Group Policy" white paper (*http:// www.microsoft.com/WINDOWS2000/techinfo/howitworks/management/ rbppaper.asp*)

- "Implementing Common Desktop Management Scenarios" white paper (*http://www.microsoft.com/windows2000/techinfo/howitworks/ management/grouppolicy.asp*)

- "Microsoft Platform SDK Documentation: Group Policy" (*http:// msdn.microsoft.com/library/en-us/policy/policy/ group_policy_start_page.asp*)

- "Group Policy Registry Table" (*http://www.microsoft.com/ windows2000/techinfo/reskit/en-us/default.asp?url=/windows2000/ techinfo/reskit/en-us/gp/gpref.asp*)

- "Best Practices for System Policies in Windows 2000 Networks" (*http://www.microsoft.com/technet/tcevents/itevents/network/ tnq10107.asp*)

- 275715: "How to Delegate Administration of Group Policies"

- 221577: "How to Delegate Authority for Editing a Group Policy Object (GPO)"

- 294777: "How to Delegate Group Policy Control to Users in Trusted Domain"

- 315676: "How to Delegate Administrative Authority in Windows 2000"

- 321476: "How to Change the Default Permissions on Group Policy Objects in Windows 2000"

> **Note**   The preceding five articles can be accessed through the Microsoft Knowledge Base. Go to *http://support.microsoft.com* and enter the article number in the Search The Knowledge Base text box.

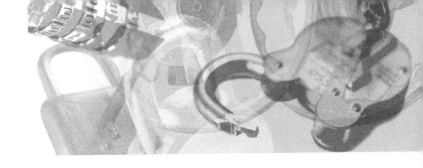

6

Designing Active Directory Forests and Domains for Security

The security of your network hinges on the design of the Active Directory directory service. While no one "right" way of designing Active Directory exists, many ways of designing Active Directory will put your organization at risk. The technology is flexible enough to be deployed according to the business requirements of any organization. However, an Active Directory implementation has several important security considerations. This chapter is by no means an exhaustive text on how to design Active Directory. But it will provide guidance on designing Active Directory forests and domains with security in mind.

Autonomy and Isolation in Active Directory

In Microsoft Windows NT, members of the Domain Admins group have complete control over all objects in their own domain but no inherent control over any objects in a trusting domain. Similarly, changes made to one domain do not affect trusting or trusted domains. Furthermore, within the domain, the primary domain controller (PDC) owns the only writeable copy of the Security Accounts Manager (SAM). For these reasons, domains are considered discrete security boundaries in Windows NT.

Unlike Windows NT, Active Directory domains are not security boundaries because they are not fully autonomous and isolated from each other.

Understanding how this affects an Active Directory forest is a key stepping-stone to designing and deploying a secure Active Directory. When discussing autonomy and isolation, we need to separate the rights and permissions of two types of administrative capabilities: Active Directory service administrators and Active Directory data administrators.

Active Directory service administrators are responsible for the configuration and management of the directory service itself. This includes tasks such as maintaining domain controller servers and managing directorywide configuration settings. Active Directory service administrators are also generally data administrators because of the rights and permissions required to allow them to be Active Directory service administrators.

Active Directory data administrators are responsible for managing data stored in Active Directory objects or on computers joined to Active Directory, but they have no authority over the configuration or management of the directory service itself. Active Directory data administrator roles include the following functions:

- The management of a subset of objects in Active Directory, such as user accounts in a specific OU

- The management of data that is stored on computers joined to the domain

When designing Active Directory, you must consider your organization's security requirements for autonomy and isolation of authority in relation to Active Directory services and Active Directory data management. Your security requirements will have a significant effect on how you design Active Directory to facilitate delegation of authority and administrative responsibility.

Autonomy of authority means that Active Directory services and data administrators can independently manage all or part of the resources over which they have authority. Isolation of authority means that accounts and people not authorized for Active Directory services and Active Directory data management are prevented from controlling or interfering with service management (services management isolation), or from controlling or viewing a subset of data in the directory or on member computers joined to the directory (data management isolation).

Designing Forests for Active Directory Security

The forest is the largest management unit of Active Directory as well as the ultimate unit of autonomy and isolation of authority. Active Directory design begins with answering the question, "How many forests will my organization require?" The answer to this question is based on security considerations for autonomy and isolation of authority. Characteristics of forests and security considerations that can affect your design include the following:

- Enterprise administration boundaries
- Default permissions and schema control
- Global Catalog boundaries
- Domain trust requirements
- Domain controller isolation
- Protection of the forest root domain

Enterprise Administration Boundaries and Isolation of Authority

The forest is the boundary of enterprise administration. The built-in Administrator account in the forest root domain is the forest owner because this account, along with members of the Enterprise Admins and the forest root Domain Admins security groups, has ultimate authority over all objects in all domains in the forest. Collectively, members of the Enterprise Admins and forest root Domain Admins groups are known as *enterprise administrators*. Enterprise administrators control the Active Directory objects in the configuration container that do not belong to any one domain, including Enterprise Certification Authority objects and other configuration data that affects all domains in the forest. Needless to say, these accounts have high security requirements.

Because enterprise administrators have authority over all domains in the forest, the domain administrators in each domain must trust the enterprise administrators. You cannot truly restrict enterprise administrators from managing objects in any domain in the forest. Enterprise administrators can always regain control over objects. Some organizations with political challenges, such as those frequently encountered in mergers and acquisitions, might find the scope of this enterprise authority too great and require more than one forest. If your organization requires strict isolation of authority between domains, you will need to deploy multiple forests with manually created trusts between domains in the different forests. These are similar to the structures commonly used in Windows NT domains.

Default Permissions and Schema Control

Each Active Directory forest has one collection of object classes and attributes defined in the Active Directory Schema container and used as templates for objects created in the directory. Object classes in the schema can be instantiated in any domain in the forest. The default permissions on all objects created in the forest are derived from the schema. Thus, alterations or extensions to the schema affect the security of the entire forest, and permissions to make changes to the schema must be restricted. The only user accounts that can make changes to the schema of a forest are members of the Schema Admins security group, which is created by default in the forest root domain and contains only the built-in Administrator account for the forest root domain. Only enterprise administrators (members of the forest root domain Administrators, Domain Admins, and Enterprise Admins groups) can modify membership in the Schema Admins group. If your organization employs multiple groups that require autonomy and isolation of object classes or default security on objects, you will need to create multiple forests.

Global Catalog Boundaries

The Global Catalog contains a read-only listing of all objects and a subset of attributes from every object in every domain in the forest. The Global Catalog is used by applications to locate objects and look up attributes of objects. The Global Catalog also provides a boundary of searchable objects that can be accessed by all security principals in the forest. Therefore, if objects that should not be universally searchable exist, your organization will require multiple forests. Similarly, Microsoft Exchange 2000 Server uses the Global Catalog to populate the global address list (GAL) for internal e-mail recipients, with a single Exchange organization mapping to a single forest. Thus, creating multiple forests impacts your organization's Exchange design as well.

Domain Trust Requirements

In Active Directory, all domains are connected by Kerberos trusts. Kerberos trusts are two-way and transitive in nature. This differs from Windows NT–style trusts, which are one-way and intransitive. Each child domain trusts its parent domain, and each tree root trusts the forest root domain. Thus, the forest root domain is the key to transitive trust in the forest. Removal of the Kerberos trusts between domains in the forest will destroy Active Directory functionality. In Windows NT, it was common to create a domain that trusted logons from another domain that itself did not trust logons from the trusted domain—in other words, implementing one-way trust relationships was common.

In Active Directory, however, all Kerberos key distribution centers (KDCs) in the forest are trusted equally and implicitly. Therefore, credentials from a compromised KDC and a legitimate KDC are indistinguishable by other KDCs and will be implicitly accepted. If your organization's security requirements dictate that domains must have only one-way trusts with other domains in your organization or isolation of Kerberos KDCs, the domains must be created in separate forests. The only external Kerberos trust relationships that can be created in Windows 2000 are trusts between a Windows 2000 domain and an MIT Kerberos realm. You can create Windows NT–style trusts between Active Directory domains in a different forest, but those trusts cannot be used by other domains in either forest. If you require trusts between multiple domains in different Windows 2000 forests, each trust must be created manually between each of the domain pairs.

Domain Controller Isolation

In Active Directory, each domain controller holds replicas of at least three logical partitions in the Active Directory database: the schema container, the configuration container, and the domain naming context for the domain controller's domain. The first two containers are replicated among all domain controllers in the forest, and the latter is replicated among all domain controllers for the same domain. Because all domain controllers' replicas of the Active Directory database are writeable and can replicate shared information to domain controllers in other domains, compromise of a single domain controller can affect the entire forest.

For example, it is possible for an attacker who has physical access to any domain controller to view or manipulate data stored anywhere in the forest or on any computer in the forest. That attacker can even make offline changes to forestwide partitions in the directory database, thus compromising the entire implementation. Consequently, physical access to all domain controllers must be restricted to trusted personnel. Similarly, any account with Active Directory service administrator privileges in a domain can potentially hijack a domain controller under its control to compromise the entire forest, either by data manipulation or denial-of-service attack. If your organization requires complete isolation of domains, even from other domain administrators—as is commonly seen in large holding corporations or hosting solutions—you must deploy multiple forests.

Protection of the Forest Root Domain

Regardless of how many forests your organization implements, you must protect the forest root domain. This is because compromise of this domain could have catastrophic effects on your network. You must protect the two main components of a forest root domain shown on the following page.

■   Enterprise administrative accounts

■   Physical security of forest root domain controllers

Enterprise Administrator Accounts

The forest root domain contains the built-in Administrator account for the root, which by default is the only member of the Enterprise Admins, Schema Admins, and Administrators security groups. If an attacker compromises this account or any accounts placed into these groups, the attacker can gain complete control over the entire forest. You can build several safeguards into your Active Directory design to protect these accounts and security groups. The following list describes these safeguards:

■   **Limit the number of enterprise administrators.**   Make only the accounts that require enterprise authority members of the Enterprise Admins, Domain Admins, and Schema Admins security groups. In most organizations, this should amount to less than five people. You should use these accounts only when absolutely necessary.

■   **Use Restricted Groups.**   You can use Restricted Groups in the Group Policy security settings to limit membership in built-in Administrators, Enterprise Admins, Domain Admins, and Schema Admins security groups. Restricted Groups, by default, are enforced every 5 minutes on each domain controller.

■   **Perform all administration locally.**   Restrict the enterprise administrator accounts to logging on interactively to forest root domain controllers. This will prevent enterprise administrator accounts from being attacked on nondomain controllers.

■   **Use smart cards.**   For accounts that require enterprise administrator rights or permissions, require the use of smart cards for interactive logon and enable the smart card removal behavior to lock the computer if the smart card is removed from the reader. Before enabling the option to require a smart card for interactive logon, be sure to change the password on the account to a strong password. Ideally, this password should be random and longer than 50 characters to prevent brute force attacks.

■   **Use strong passwords.**   For the built-in Administrator account, which cannot be disabled or required to use smart card logon, create a password with a minimum of 15 characters. This will prevent a LAN Manager (LM) password hash from being created. Ideally, use a longer password.

■ **Provide physical security over the forest root domain controllers.** If the physical security of a forest root domain controller is compromised, all accounts in the forest root domain are vulnerable, including enterprise administrative accounts. Remember, even if strong passwords are employed, any password can be broken, given adequate hardware resources and time.

Physical Security of Forest Root Domain Controllers

In a multiple domain forest, the forest cannot function without the presence of the forest root domain. For example, suppose your organization houses all the domain controllers from the forest root domain in a single facility and that facility is destroyed by a natural disaster such as a tornado or hurricane. If the forest root domain cannot be recovered by using backup media, your organization's Active Directory must be completely rebuilt. Similarly, the physical compromise of a domain controller can lead to the exposure of Active Directory account password hashes. The password hashes can then be attacked offline.

As previously discussed, the physical compromise of a domain controller can compromise the entire forest if an attacker exploits a domain controller's ability to write data to other domain controllers in the forest, or if the attacker utilizes implicit and equal trust given to all KDCs by other KDCs to attack other domains. You must design Active Directory with the location and physical security of domain controllers in mind, and you might need to implement multiple forests to isolate sensitive accounts or operations.

Designing Domains for Active Directory Security

After your organization decides whether to require more than one forest, you should design the domain structure for your organization. The forest is the ultimate security boundary in Active Directory. Domains, on the other hand, are limited security boundaries with respect to the autonomy of domain accounts and administration, although the forest root domain is a special case in domain security. As previously mentioned, the forest root domain is central to the forestwide Kerberos trusts and houses the enterprise administrative groups and accounts.

With the exception of the forest root domain, the Domain Admins security group has autonomous authority over all objects in the domain but has only user access outside its own domain. Members of the Domain Admins security group in the forest root domain can manipulate the membership of the Enterprise Admin and Schema Admins security groups and thus can control all objects in the forest. You might have trusted administrators who require domainwide administrative privileges for some part of their duties but not forestwide administrative capabilities. By creating a separate domain, you avoid having to place these administrators into the Domain Admins group of the forest root domain.

All Active Directory service administrators in domains—including Domain Admins, Server Operators, and the other built-in domain administrator security groups—must be highly trusted because they have the ability to jeopardize forest security via domain controller compromise. If your organization's administrators do not meet this isolation criteria, you must decide on one of the following:

- Accepting the risk and using a single forest

- Mitigating the risk by not granting administrators who are not as trusted as other administrators membership in Active Directory service administrator groups

- Avoiding the risk by creating separate forests

If you build two domains in your forest, each containing resources and accounts, you need to consider that the domain administrators in the forest root domain will also be domain administrators in the other domain. This is because all members of the Administrators group in the root domain have enterprise administration rights. In this situation, which is generally true for multiple domain scenarios, you might consider deploying an empty root forest design. In this design, the forest root is used only to contain the enterprise administrative accounts; all production resources and user accounts reside in child domains. By employing an empty root design, you can preserve the ability to centrally manage the forest and use a single Global Catalog, while enabling autonomy and limited isolation between domains.

Although enterprise administrators can create Group Policy objects (GPOs) at the site level, the domain is also the unit of isolation for domain account policies. This is because domain account policies do not flow from parent domain to child domain and cannot be set in a more granular way than in a domain, such as by an OU. These settings apply to all computer and user accounts in the domain and are not inherited by child domains. Account policies include the following:

- **Password policy**   Determine the password composition and validating rules that must be met, such as password length and complexity requirements

- **Account lockout policy**   Define thresholds for the automatic locking of accounts

- **Kerberos ticket policy**   Determine the lifetime of Kerberos tickets, as well as parameters relating to renewal of existing Kerberos tickets

> **More Info**   Account policies are discussed in depth in Chapter 3, "Securing User Accounts and Passwords."

The account policy for the domain is configured, by default, in the default domain policy GPO. Although you can configure account policies on GPOs linked to OUs, those settings affect only local computer SAM databases, not domain accounts. If your organization consists of business units that require different account policies, you must create multiple domains.

Because domain administrators can create data administrators by delegating control over all domain resources to other user accounts, including Group Policy, you should limit the number of domain administrators in your organization. The Domain Admins security group is automatically added to the local Administrators security group on all computers that are members of the domain. Because this gives domain administrators full control over all computers in the domain, including servers, domain administrators are also data administrators for all computers, accounts, and information in the domain. If possible, you should apply the same security thresholds for domain administrators as enterprise administrators because these accounts are inherently powerful in a manner similar to enterprise administrative accounts.

Designing DNS for Active Directory Security

The successful operation of Active Directory depends on the successful operation of the Domain Name System (DNS). After your organization has designed its forest and domain plan, you must design the DNS infrastructure to support Active Directory. DNS provides three crucial functions for Active Directory in Windows 2000:

- **Name resolution**   DNS resolves host names to IP addresses and vice versa. DNS is the default location mechanism in Windows 2000.

- **Service locator**   Windows 2000 and Windows XP computers use DNS to locate services (represented by SRV records) such as the Global Catalog and Kerberos Key Distribution Centers, as well as domain controllers, domains, and site information.

- **Namespace definition**   DNS establishes the namespace used to define Active Directory.

Tip   You do not have to use a Windows 2000 DNS server to support an Active Directory implementation. At minimum, the DNS server that you use must support the use of SRV records. Microsoft also strongly recommends that your DNS server support incremental zone transfers (IXFRs) and dynamic updates. Window 2000 DNS provides all these features.

Several common designs for DNS support Active Directory. Each of these models has security benefits and drawbacks, and other valid designs are possible. These are the common designs:

- Single namespace
- Delegated namespace
- Internal namespace
- Segmented namespace

Regardless of which DNS model you adopt for Active Directory, you must ensure the security of the DNS server and services because the compromise of DNS services can lead to a denial-of-service attack or the disclosure of information. An attacker or rogue administrator could compromise your DNS server and erase Service resource records (also known as SRV records), causing Active Directory replication to fail and client logons to be rejected. An attacker or rogue administrator could also change SRV record information to redirect replication and logon traffic to illegitimate servers to retrieve information from the packets. This process is known as *DNS poisoning*.

More Info   See Chapter 15, "Implementing Security for DNS Servers," for in-depth information on how to secure Windows 2000 DNS Servers.

Single Namespace

In a single namespace Active Directory, SRV records are intermingled with all the other resource records for your organization. Although this is the simplest design, you risk the external exposure of your namespace and SRV records, which could prove useful to an attacker. Also, a single namespace will require a potentially complex set of permissions to update and manage the DNS zone information.

Delegated Namespace

In a delegated namespace, a subzone of your public namespace is delegated to support Active Directory. This allows you to segregate your Active Directory SRV records from your publicly available records, such as your Web presence. This design also enables your Active Directory administrators to manage a specific portion of DNS, while the current DNS administrators can continue to maintain their portion of DNS.

Internal Namespace

You might want to use an internal namespace for Active Directory. For example, you can create a DNS namespace for Active Directory named *woodgrove-bank.corp*. Although using a nonpublic domain can add security to your Active Directory installation and alleviates any concerns over who would manage the portion of DNS that supports Active Directory, this DNS design can hamper the scalability of Active Directory. Alternatively, you might want to register a public DNS namespace and only use it internally for Active Directory.

Segmented Namespace

You might want to use the same namespace for Active Directory as you use for your public presence but not use the same DNS infrastructure. For example, your organization's ISP could host your public DNS namespace, but you could host a parallel namespace internally to support Active Directory. If you choose this configuration, you can isolate your Active Directory DNS infrastructure, while preserving the possibility of public scalability for later. If you select this DNS design, you more than likely will have to manually replicate some entries from your public DNS infrastructure to your internal DNS infrastructure.

Active Directory Integrated Zones and Security

In addition to standard primary and secondary zones, Windows 2000 supports Active Directory integrated zones. Active Directory integrated zones improve on the security of standard zones by doing the following:

- **Allowing DNS records to be dynamically updated securely**   In Windows 2000, primary zones have a Boolean dynamic update permission—the zone either accepts or denies dynamic updates. Active Directory integrated zones add a third option: to allow only secure dynamic updates. If you choose this option, when a computer attempts to update or create a resource record in DNS, the DNS server will forward the attempt to Active Directory. There, the change will be compared to the discretionary access control list (DACL) on the zone object and to the resource record, if it exists. The change will occur only if the computer has the necessary permissions.

- **Enabling DNS records to be secured as Active Directory objects**   Because resource records are stored as objects in Active Directory objects, security on those objects can be configured as your organization requires.

- **Securing the DNS records during zone transfer**   In a default standard zone transfer, records are sent as clear text, which means that securing the connection between DNS servers for zone transfers requires additional configuration. However, when DNS zones are stored as Active Directory integrated objects, Active Directory replication is used to facilitate the transfer of zone updates. This replication is automatically encrypted by using remote procedure call (RPC) encryption without additional configuration.

Active Directory integrated zones can be hosted only on DNS servers that are also domain controllers. Thus, Active Directory integrated zones are appropriate only for internal use or for use in an isolated forest with exposure to public networks, as is common with perimeter network (also known as DMZ, demilitarized zone, and screened subnet) Active Directory installations.

Designing the Delegation of Authority

Rather than granting all administrators the rights and permissions of Active Directory service administrators by making them members of the Domain

Admins or other Active Directory service administrator security groups, as was commonly done in Windows NT domains, Active Directory enables you to place accounts and resources into OUs and delegate an appropriate level of authority over those objects to administrative staff. By doing this, you can create data management administrators who have autonomous or semiautonomous authority over Active Directory objects, domain member computers, and data. The simplest way to do this in Active Directory is to create OUs based on management requirements and to delegate authority over the OU (or objects in the OU) to specific data administrator security groups. Consequently, OUs are the primary management unit in Active Directory. By delegating limited control over objects in a domain, you can minimize the number of Active Directory service administrators while ensuring that data administrators have only the rights and permissions they require to complete their job tasks.

Delegation of administration allows you to create custom administrative security groups that administer the users, computers, or other objects in an OU, OU tree, or domain. To accomplish this, you must first design an effective OU structure. When designing an OU structure, consider three things: Group Policy, delegation of authority, and your organization's management model. Place all objects with similar administrative and security requirements in an OU or OU tree. Then create the custom security groups, and delegate administration of the OUs (or objects in OUs) to the appropriate groups. Windows 2000 offers granular control over the administrative tasks that can be delegated. On an OU, you can delegate authority over the following:

- The OU

- The OU and all child OUs

- Specific types of objects in the OU

- Specific attributes of specific objects in an OU

- Tasks that affect specific types of objects in an OU

You can delegate authority either by setting the permissions on the container by using the object's Security tab, by using command-line utilities such as Dsacls.exe, or by using the Delegation of Control Wizard in the Microsoft Management Console (MMC). The Delegation of Control Wizard might not expose all the permissions you want to modify on an object, so you might need to use the Security tab or even ADSIEdit from the Windows 2000 Support Tools to directly edit the DACL of the object. In some cases, you will need to make further modifications to Windows 2000 to delegate the necessary authority—for example, when delegating the ability to unlock accounts.

When delegating authority to objects in Active Directory, you will need to consider how the administrators will manage the objects over which you have given them authority. Several administrative interfaces are available in Windows 2000:

■   **Server Console**   Performing local administration of a Windows 2000 environment while physically seated at a server is a significant security risk and should be avoided whenever possible. To log on locally to a domain controller, administrative staff must be granted the right to log on locally to the server.

■   **Terminal Services**   Consider utilizing Terminal Services in remote administration mode for administrative tasks, which requires that you delegate to the user performing the administration the right to connect to the server via a remote administration terminal session, as described in 253831, "Remote Administration of Terminal Services by Non-Administrators Accounts". (You can access this article through the Microsoft Knowledge Base at *http://support.microsoft.com*.) Terminal Services is considered by the system to be an interactive logon, so its users will need the right to log on locally to the server. Because the system does not differentiate between a terminal services "local" logon and a physical "local" logon, you must ensure that your servers are secured against physical access by users who have been granted the right to log on locally to facilitate terminal session management.

■   **MMC**   You can install Windows 2000 Administrative Tools on any Windows 2000 computer by installing Adminpak.msi from the Windows 2000 Server CD or from the System32 directory on any Windows 2000 server installation. By installing these tools on the workstations of administrative staff, you provide them with the interfaces needed to remotely manage servers without granting them local logon rights on those servers. You can limit which MMC snap-ins the administrator can use by implementing the appropriate settings in Group Policy.

Best Practices

■   **Use multiple forests if you require discrete isolation.**   If your security policy calls for discrete isolation of control between domains, use separate forests.

- **Physically secure domain controllers.**   If an attacker or rogue administrator can physically compromise domain controllers, he not only can gain access to the information stored on the domain controller, but he can potentially compromise information on the domain controller to jeopardize the entire forest.

- **Train administrators.**   Once you have delegated authority to a user over a set of objects, you have created an administrator of some degree. You should, at a minimum, provide training to make the administrator aware of the capabilities and limits of her account, the ways she can protect her account, and the techniques she can use to complete the tasks for which you have given her responsibility.

- **Perform audits.**   You should always audit delegated objects to ensure that the administrator is completing the tasks he has been assigned and to provide an audit trail to detect misuse of administrative authority.

- **Complete background checks.**   Work with your organization's HR department to complete background checks on all enterprise and domain administrators. Also carefully consider the employees to whom you delegate authority and the level of responsibility and accountability you require of them.

- **Minimize the number of Active Directory service administrators.**   The fewer accounts with Active Directory service administration rights and permissions—especially membership in the Enterprise or Domain Admins security groups—the more secure they generally will be.

- **Control membership in security groups with high security requirements.**   Use Restricted Groups in Group Policy to control membership in security groups such as Active Directory service administrators and other custom security groups that have high security requirements. Allow only other service administrator groups to modify the membership of service administrator groups. Do not include users or groups from external trusted forests in Active Directory service administrator groups in your forest, unless the Active Directory service administrators from the external forest are as trusted as your forest's Active Directory service administrators.

■ **Isolate the management of computers on which Active Directory service accounts are used.** Allow only Active Directory service administrator groups to manage workstations used by Active Directory service administrators. For example, a rogue administrator or attacker could install Trojan horse software such as keystroke logging applications to retrieve passwords. After an administrator logs on to the computer using an enterprise administrator account or a domain administrator account, the rogue administrator could retrieve her password.

■ **Use smart cards.** Require the use of smart cards for accounts with high security requirements—preferably all administrative accounts in the forest.

■ **Delegate control over OUs or objects within OUs.** Use OUs as your primary unit of management. Delegate authority over OU containers or objects within an OU to administrators.

■ **Use Active Directory integrated DNS.** Use Active Directory integrated zones to take advantage of security enhancements offered by Active Directory over standard zone files.

■ **Document delegated permissions.** When delegating authority, be sure to document the permissions you grant to users. Active Directory does not differentiate between permissions that have been delegated and those that are default permissions.

Additional Information

■ Microsoft Official Curriculum, course 1561: "Designing Microsoft Windows 2000 Directory Services Infrastructure" (*http://www.microsoft.com/traincert/syllabi/1561bfinal.asp*)

■ "Best Practice Active Directory Design for Managing Windows Networks" (*http://www.microsoft.com/windows2000/techinfo/planning/activedirectory/bpaddsgn.asp*)

■ "Windows 2000 Domain Architecture: Design Alternatives" (*http://www.microsoft.com/technet/prodtechnol/ad/windows2000/plan/w2kdomar.asp*)

■ "Design Considerations for Delegation of Administration in Active Directory" (*http://www.microsoft.com/technet/prodtechnol/ad/windows2000/plan/addeladm.asp*)

- 315676: "How to Delegate Administrative Authority in Windows 2000"

- 221577: "How to Delegate Authority for Editing a Group Policy Object (GPO)"

- 235531: "Default Security Concerns in Active Directory Delegation"

- 279723: "How to Grant Help Desk Personnel the Specific Right to Unlock Locked User Accounts"

- 301191: "How to Integrate DNS with Existing DNS Infrastructure If Active Directory Is Enabled in Windows 2000"

- 274438: "Cannot Use Kerberos Trust Relationships Between Two Forests in Windows 2000"

- 253831: "Remote Administration of Terminal Services by Non-Administrators Accounts"

> **Note**   The seven articles above can be accessed through the Microsoft Knowledge Base. Go to *http://support.microsoft.com* and enter the article number in the Search The Knowledge Base text box.

Part III

Securing the Core Operating System

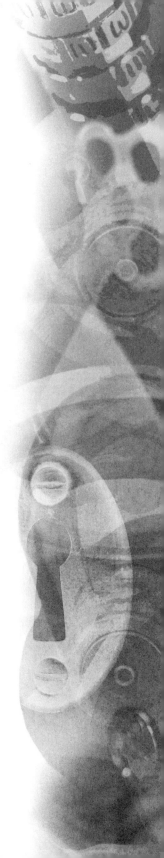

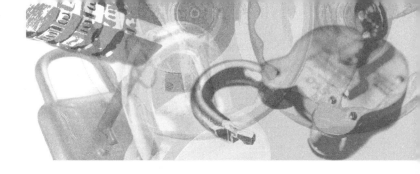

7

Securing Permissions

In Microsoft Windows 2000 and Windows XP, a security principal's level of access to files and folders is determined by NTFS file system and share permissions. These permissions are discretionary: anyone with ownership of a file or folder, Change Permissions, or Full Control permissions can assign access control at his discretion. When freshly installed, Window 2000 and Windows XP assign default permission structures to operating system files and folders, but you might need to alter these permissions to meet your security requirements.

Securing File and Folder Permissions

All file and folder objects stored on an NTFS volume have security descriptors to control access to the object. The security descriptor includes a discretionary access control list (DACL) and a system access control list (SACL), in addition to information that identifies the object's owner. Figure 7-1 shows the contents of a security descriptor.

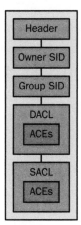

Figure 7-1 Contents of a security descriptor   **135**

DACLs owe their name to the fact that they can be configured at the discretion of any account that possesses Take Ownership, Change Permissions, or Full Control permissions to the file system object. DACLs consist of several elements, which are described in Table 7-1 and shown in Figure 7-2.

Table 7-1   Elements of a DACL

Element	Description
Header	Metadata pertaining to the access control entries (ACEs) associated with the DACL.
SID (user)	The security identifier (SID) of the owner of the object.
SID (group)	The SID of the built-in Administrators or Domain Admins group if the account that owns the object is a member of either group.
Generic deny ACEs	ACEs that deny access to an account or security group based on that group's SIDs. These ACEs can be inherited from the object's parent or assigned directly to the object.
Generic allow ACEs	ACEs that allow access to child objects to an account or security group based on that group's SIDs. These ACEs can be inherited from the object's parent or assigned directly to the object.

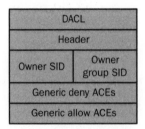

Figure 7-2   Composition of a DACL

Tip   You can see the ACEs for files and folders, as well as other types of objects, by using Subinacl.exe. Type **subinacl /verbose=2 /objecttype objectname**, where *objecttype* is the type of object and *objectname* is the name of the object.

What Does Owning a Resource Mean?

The owner of a resource, such as a file or folder, is the account that ultimately determines the access control over a resource. The owner has complete control over the resource, including the ability to assign permissions to other accounts. Even if the owner is explicitly denied access to a resource, the owner changes the permissions on the resource to restore her access. File ownership is also used by the quota system in Windows 2000 and Windows XP to calculate the amount of disk space used by each tracked account, if disk quotas are enabled. The default owner of files and folders in Windows 2000 and Windows XP installations is the built-in Administrators group, although a user who creates a file or folder is the owner of anything she creates.

Members of the Administrators group can always take ownership of files and folders on the local computer—even if NTFS permissions prohibit administrators from accessing the resource. This ensures that files can be recovered by an administrator in the event that a user leaves the company or permissions are incorrectly configured and must be corrected. When a member of the Administrators group takes ownership of a resource, the ownership is granted to the Administrators group. However, the SID of the individual administrator is also recorded and stored in the DACL for accountability reasons. When a user who is not a member of the Administrators group takes ownership of a resource, ownership is associated with her account's SID.

Although the user interface prevents you from assigning ownership of an object to another user account, you can complete this action from the command line if you are a member of the Administrators group on the computer using the command-line tool Subinacl.exe. The syntax for replacing the owner of a file using Subinacl.exe follows:

Subinacl /onlyfile *filename.ext* /setowner=*domain\newowner*

You can use Subinacl.exe to configure permissions on:

- Files
- Folders
- Registry keys
- Services
- Printers
- Kernel objects

(continued)

What Does Owning a Resource Mean?   *(continued)*

■   Shares

■   Metabases

Subinacl.exe is a low-level utility and should be used with caution. For routine permission changes on files and folders, other tools such as Xcacls.exe and Cacls.exe are easier to use.

You can define NTFS permissions at either the folder or file level. For folders, you can assign the following standard permissions in the Security tab of the folder's Properties dialog box:

■   Full Control

■   Modify.

■   Read & Execute

■   List Folder Contents

■   Read

■   Write

For individual files, these are the standard permissions:

■   Full Control

■   Modify

■   Read & Execute

■   Read

■   Write

Standard NTFS permissions are compilations of several special permissions, including these:

■   **Traverse Folder/Execute File**   Traverse Folder allows or denies navigating through folders, even though the user does not have permissions to access files or folders within that folder. This permission applies to folders only. Execute File allows or denies running program files and applies to files only. Setting the Traverse Folder permission will not automatically set the Execute File permission on the files in the folder. Additionally, by default the Everyone group is assigned the Bypass Traverse Checking user right, which prevents the Traverse Folder permissions from being assessed when a resource is accessed.

■ **List Folder/Read Data**   List Folder allows or denies viewing file names and subfolder names within the folder and applies to folders only. Read Data allows or denies viewing data in files and applies to files only.

■ **Read Attributes**   Allows or denies viewing the attributes of a file or folder, such as Read-Only and Hidden attributes.

■ **Read Extended Attributes**   Allows or denies viewing the extended attributes of a file or folder. Specific programs define the extended attributes.

■ **Create Files/Write Data**   Create Files allows or denies creating files within a folder. Write Data allows or denies making changes to a file and overwriting existing content.

■ **Create Folders/Append Data**   Create Folders allows or denies creating folders within a folder. Append Data allows or denies making changes to the end of the file but not changing, deleting, or overwriting any existing data in the file.

■ **Write Attributes**   Allows or denies changing the attributes of a file or folder, such as Read-Only and Hidden attributes.

■ **Write Extended Attributes**   Allows or denies viewing the extended attributes of a file or folder. The extended attributes are defined by specific programs.

■ **Delete Subfolders and Files**   Allows or denies deleting subfolders and files when applied at a parent folder, even if the Delete permission has not been granted on the specific subfolder or file.

■ **Delete**   Allows or denies the deletion of a file or folder.

■ **Read Permissions**   Allows or denies reading permissions assigned to a file or folder.

■ **Change Permissions**   Allows or denies modification of the permissions assigned to a file or folder.

■ **Take Ownership**   Allows or denies taking ownership of the file or folder.

Table 7-2 displays how, in Windows 2000, the special permissions map to the basic permissions.

Table 7-2 File and Folder Permissions Mapping in Windows 2000

Special Permissions	Basic Permissions					
	Full Control	**Modify**	**Read & Execute**	**List Folder Contents (Permissions apply to folder objects only)**	**Read**	**Write**
Traverse Folder/ Execute File	X	X	X	X		
List Folder/Read Data	X	X	X	X	X	
Read Attributes	X	X	X	X	X	
Read Extended Attributes	X	X	X	X	X	
Create Files/Write Data	X	X				X
Create Folders/ Append Data	X	X				X
Write Attributes	X	X				X
Write Extended Attributes	X	X				X
Delete Subfolders and Files	X					
Delete	X	X				
Read Permissions	X	X	X	X	X	X
Change Permissions	X					
Take Ownership	X					

How DACLs Work

When a user attempts to access a file or folder on an NTFS partition, the user's access token is compared with the DACL of the file or folder. If no ACEs correspond to a SID in the user's access token, the user is implicitly denied access to the resource. If ACEs correspond to the user's access token, the ACEs are applied in the following order:

■ **Explicit deny** An ACE applied directly to the resource that denies access. An explicit deny will always override all other permissions.

- **Explicit allow**   An ACE applied directly to the resource that grants access. An explicit allow will always override an inherited deny but will always be overridden by explicit deny ACEs.

- **Inherited deny**   An ACE inherited from the resource's parent object. An inherited deny ACE will override an inherited allow permission but will be overridden by an explicit allow.

- **Inherited allow**   An ACE inherited from the resource's parent object.

ACEs that apply to the user are cumulative, meaning that the user will receive the sum of the ACEs that apply to his user account and groups of which he is a member. For example, if an access control list (ACL) contains two allow ACEs that apply to the user, one for Read access and the other for Write access, the user will receive Read and Write access.

> **Caution**   Because explicit allow ACEs override inherited deny ACEs, you should assign explicit permissions with caution. For example, if the Sales_Managers group has been denied the Write permission on all file and folders in the d:\finance_audit folder but a user named Tom is granted Write permissions to the d:\finance_audit\review\Excel1.xls file, Tom will be able to modify the Excel1.xls file—even if he is a member of the Sales_Managers group, which is denied Write permissions by inheritance.

Assigning DACLs at Creation

When a file or folder is created, it inherits from its parent object the permissions that are applicable to its type of object. This includes both permissions that are inherited by the parent object and permissions that are explicitly assigned to the parent object. Once created, you can augment the inherited permissions by adding ACEs to the newly created resource.

In Windows 2000 and Windows XP, each file and folder has a property enabled by default that stipulates that the object will Allow Inheritable Permissions From The Parent Object To Propagate To This Object. By default, if you alter the permissions on the parent object, the permission change will automatically flow to the child object. If you want to modify this behavior, you need to decide whether you want to remove the inherited permissions or copy them to the object. If you choose to remove the inherited permissions, the only permissions that will remain are those explicitly granted to the object. If you choose to copy the permissions, the object will have the same permissions as it had previously, but the formerly inherited permissions will instead be explicitly assigned to the object.

> **Note**   In the Windows 2000 and Windows XP user interfaces, explicit permissions are displayed with a check in a white check box and inherited permissions are displayed with a check in a gray check box. Gray check boxes cannot be directly modified unless the permissions are made explicit, which changes the check boxes to white to indicate explicit assignment.

How DACLs Are Handled When Files and Folders Are Copied or Moved

The way DACLs are handled for files and folders that are moved and copied into other locations can be confusing. If you are responsible for securing files and folders, you must understand several intricacies of copying and moving files and folders, or you might unwittingly create a security risk.

The first thing you need to know is that creating a copy of a file on the same partition actually creates a new file in the destination container. Thus, all permissions are inherited from the new parent object. The original object's permissions are unchanged. This action creates a potential security risk because two copies of the same file that have different security settings can exist.

Second, when a file is moved on the same partition, it is not physically relocated to a different address on the disk—instead, the reference to the object in the file system hierarchy is updated. When the ACL on a parent object or an object itself is changed, the permissions structures are updated, but moving an object on the same partition does not trigger a refresh of ACLs. Therefore, all previously inherited and explicit permissions on the moved object *initially* remain unchanged. The Security tab for the object will indicate that the permissions are inherited from its parent object, but until the ACL is refreshed, the Security tab shows inherited permissions from the object's previous parent, along with any permissions assigned directly to the object. The next time that the ACLs for the object itself or for any parent object in the inheritance hierarchy are changed, the inherited permissions on the object will be received from the object's new location in the file system hierarchy. However, the moved object will retain any explicitly assigned permission.

This behavior is a departure from the way that permissions on moved file system objects functioned in Windows NT, where objects that were moved within the same partition retained all permissions. If you want to achieve Windows NT–style retention of all permissions on an object you move within the same partition, before moving the object, you must deselect the inheritance attribute on the object and copy the existing inherited permissions so that they become explicit permissions. Or you must remove existing inherited permissions altogether and assign any desired explicit permissions. You can then move the object and reenable permissions inheritance, which will refresh the ACL on the object. When the ACL is refreshed in this manner, the moved object will retain its explicit permissions but will receive new inherited permissions from its new parent.

Finally, when you move a file or folder to a different partition or computer, the operation is actually a copy-and-delete process. The file is copied in the new location, thus creating a new file system object, and upon successful creation of the new object, the original is deleted. Creating a copy of a file system object—regardless of whether the copy is created on the same partition or on a different partition or computer—always creates a new instance of the object in the destination location. Therefore, all permissions on the object are inherited from the new parent. Original copies of the object are either deleted (in a move operation across partitions or computers) or unaffected (in a copy operation). Therefore, you should exercise caution when moving or copying files and folders to different partitions or computers. This is because the permissions on the newly created object might not be consistent with the permissions on the original object.

Command-Line Tools

In Windows 2000 and Windows XP, the Xcopy.exe command can be used to preserve the permissions and ownership of file and folders when they are copied. Additionally, you can use several command-line tools to control the file and folder permissions:

- Cacls.exe

- Xcacls.exe

- Subinacl.exe

- Robocopy.exe

> **On the CD**   Robocopy.exe, Xcacls.exe, and Subinacl.exe are located in the Tools folder on the CD included with this book. Cacls.exe is included in the default installation of Windows 2000 and Windows XP.

Cacls.exe

Cacls.exe is a command-line utility that enables basic management of file and folder permissions. The usage for Cacls.exe follows:

CACLS *filename* [/T] [/E] [/C] [/G *user:perm*] [/R *user* [...]] [/P *user:perm* [...]] [/D *user* [...]]

Table 7-3 shows the command-line options for Cacls.exe. You can also use wildcard characters to specify more than one file in a command.

Table 7-3   Command-Line Options for Cacls.exe

Option	Description
filename	Placeholder for the name of the file. Running Cacls.exe with just the file name will display the DACL of the file or folder.
/T	Changes DACLs of specified files in the current directory and all sub-directories.
/E	Edits the existing DACL instead of replacing it.
/C	Continues processing even if an access denied error occurs.
/G *user:perm*	Grants the specified user access rights to the file or folder using explicit permissions.
user	Domain and user name that you are modifying permissions for. You can specify more than one user in a command.
perm	R for Read, W for Write, C for Change (Write), F for Full Control, N for None.
/R *user*	Revokes all the specified user's access rights (valid only with /E).
/P *user:perm*	Replaces the specified user's access rights.
/D *user*	Denies the specified user access to the file or folder.

> **Tip**   You can redirect console output from the command line by using a standard redirection character. For example, to redirect output from the Cacls.exe tool to a file, type **Calcs.exe *filename.ext*>output.txt**. The results of running the command will be written to the Output.txt file rather than to the console.

Xcacls.exe

Xcacls.exe is a more robust version of Cacls.exe. Not only does Xcacls.exe give you greater control over the special permissions, it is scriptable: unlike Cacls.exe, Xcacls.exe allows you to suppress message prompts. The usage for Xcacls.exe follows:

xcacls *filename* [/T] [/E] [/C] [/G *user:perm;spec*] [/R *user*] [/P *user:perm;spec* [...]] [/D *user* [...]] [/Y]

Table 7-4 shows the command-line options for Xcacls.exe.

Table 7-4   Command-Line Options for Xcacls.exe

Option	Description
filename	Placeholder for the name of the file. Running Xcacls.exe with just the file name will display the DACL of the file or folder.
/T	Recursively walks through the current directory and all its subdirectories, applying the chosen access rights to the matching files or directories.
/E	Edits the existing DACL instead of replacing it.
/C	Causes Xcacls.exe to continue if an "access denied" error occurs.
/G *user:perm;spec*	Grants access to the user to the matching file or directory. The *perm* variable applies the specified access right to files.
perm	R for Read, C for Change (Write), F for Full Control, P for Change Permissions, O for Take Ownership, X for Execute, E for Read, W for Write, D for Delete.
/R *user*	Revokes all access rights for the specified user.
/P *user:perm;spec*	Replaces access rights for the user.
/D *user*	Denies the user access to the file or directory.
/Y	Disables confirmation when replacing user access rights. By default, Xcacls.exe prompts for confirmation, and when used in a batch routine, causes the routine to stop responding until the confirmation is entered. The /Y option was introduced to avoid this confirmation so that Xcacls.exe can be used in batch mode.

On the CD   Xcacls.exe is located in the Tools folder of the CD that is included with this book. Xcacls.vbs, a Microsoft Visual Basic script, is also included on the CD in the Tools\Scripts\XCACLS VBS folder. You can use Xcacls.vbs to assign permissions in a similar way that you do with Xcacls.exe, albeit from a script. Xcacls.exe is designed to be used at the command-line or in batch files; Xcacls.vbs is designed to be used in a scripting environment, where better automation and error handling are required. In addition, you can edit Xcacls.vbs by using any text editor to add custom functionality, such as logging permission changes to a file.

Subinacl.exe

Subinacl.exe is a low-level utility for managing DACLs on many types of objects, including files and folders. The syntax for using Subinacl.exe follows:

subinacl [view_mode] [/test_mode] *object_type object_name* [action[=*parameter*]] [action[=*parameter*]] ... [/playfile *file_name*] [/help [/full] [keyword]]

The options you can use with Subinacl.exe are explained in Table 7-5.

Table 7-5 Command-Line Options for Subinacl.exe

Option	Description
view_mode	Defines the level of detail in the output of Subinacl.exe. You can use the following switches with this option:
	■ /noverbose
	■ /verbose (defaults to /verbose=2)
	■ /verbose=1
	■ /verbose=2
/test_mode	When this option is specified, changes are not actually made to the object's security descriptor. This option enables you to view what the results of the command would be without actually making the changes.
object_type	Specifies the type of object on which you are modifying the permissions. You can use these types of objects:
	■ /file
	■ /subdirectories
	■ /onlyfile
	■ /share
	■ /clustershare
	■ /keyreg
	■ /subkeyreg
	■ /service
	■ /printer
	■ /kernelobject

Table 7-5   Command-Line Options for Subinacl.exe   *(continued)*

Option	Description
object_name	Defines the name of an object on which you are viewing or modifying the permissions.
Action	Sets the action that you are attempting to carry out on the object. The Action switches include:

- /display (default)
- /setowner=*owner*
- /replace=[*DomainName*\]*OldAccount*=[*DomainName*\]*NewAccount*
- /changedomain=*OldDomainName*=*NewDomainName*
- /migratetodomain=*SourceDomain*=*DestDomain*
- /findsid=[DomainName\]*Account*[=stop]
- /suppresssid=[*DomainName*\]*Account*
- /confirm
- /perm
- /audit
- /ifchangecontinue
- /cleandeletedsidsfrom=*DomainName*
- /accesscheck=[*DomainName*\]*UserName*
- /setprimarygroup=[*DomainName*\]*Group*
- /grant=[*DomainName*\]*UserName*[=*Access*]
- /deny=[*DomainName*\]*UserName*[=*Access*]
- /revoke=[*DomainName*\]*UserName*
- /playfile *filename*

Robocopy.exe

Robocopy.exe is a 32-bit Windows command-line application that simplifies the task of maintaining an identical copy of a folder tree in multiple locations, either on the same computer or in separate network locations. Robocopy is robust—it retries operations after network errors and efficiently copies only changed files. Robocopy is flexible—you can copy a single folder or walk a directory tree, specifying multiple file names and wildcard characters for source files. For detailed information on using Robocopy, see the Robocopy.doc file on the CD included with this book.

Default File and Folder Permissions

In Windows 2000 and Windows XP, file and folder permissions are automatically inherited from their parent objects. Therefore, understanding the default permission on files and folders is important in planning directory structures. You might need to change the default permissions to meet your organization's security policy. Table 7-6 provides a legend to the various Windows 2000, Windows XP, and Windows NT default permissions.

Table 7-6   Default Permissions Legend

Abbreviation	Description
CI (Container Inherit)	The ACE will be applied to the current directory and inherited by subdirectories.
OI (Object Inherit)	The ACE will be applied to files in the directory and inherited by files in subdirectories.
IO (Inherit Only)	The ACE will not be applied to the current folder or file but will be inherited by child folders.
NI (Not Inherited)	The ACE is not propagated to any child objects.

Recommended Permissions for Windows 2000 and Windows XP

In Windows 2000 and Windows XP the default permissions on files and folders are configured during setup when you choose to format a partition with NTFS. Unfortunately, for most organizations, the default permissions do not provide enough security for information stored on the computer. Table 7-7 contains the recommended permissions for files and folders in Windows 2000 and Windows XP. Unless otherwise stated, the permissions listed in the table apply to the folder mentioned in the leftmost column, as well as all of its subfolders and files.

> **On the CD**   The security template MWSRK_NTFS.inf is located in the Tools\Template folder on the CD included with this book. You can use this template on computers with Windows 2000 and Windows XP newly installed to configure the permissions listed in Table 7-7. Applying this template to an existing installation could cause applications to cease to function.

Table 7-7   Recommended Permissions for Windows 2000 and Windows XP

File/Folder	Administrators	System	Creator Owner	Users	Power Users
%programfiles%	Full Control	Full Control	Full Control (subfolders and files only)	Read & Execute, List Folder Contents, Read	Modify
%system drive%\ IO.SYS	Full Control (this folder only)	Full Control (this folder only)			Read & Execute (this folder only)
%systemdrive%	Full Control	Full Control	Full Control (subfolders and files only)	Read & Execute, List Folder Contents, Read (this folder, subfolders, and files) Create Files (subfolders only) Create Folders (this folder and subfolders only)	Modify (subfolders and files only)
%systemdrive%\ autoexec.bat	Full Control	Full Control			Read & Execute (this folder only)
%systemdrive%\ boot.ini	Full Control	Full Control			Read & Execute (this folder only)
%systemdrive%\ config.sys	Full Control	Full Control			Read & Execute (this folder only)
%systemdrive%\ Documents and Settings	Full Control	Full Control	Full Control (subfolders and files only)	Traverse Folder/ Execute File, List Folder Contents (this folder only)	Traverse Folder/Execute File, List Folder Contents (this folder only)
%systemdrive%\ Documents and Settings\Administrator	Full Control	Full Control			

(continued)

Table 7-7   Recommended Permissions for Windows 2000 and Windows XP *(continued)*

File/Folder	Administrators	System	Creator Owner	Users	Power Users
%systemdrive%\ Documents and Settings\All Users	Full Control	Full Control		Read & Execute, List Folder Contents, Read	Read & Execute, List Folder Contents, Read
%systemdrive%\ Documents and Settings\Default User	Full Control	Full Control		Read and Execute, List Folder Contents, Read	Read and Execute, List Folder Contents, Read
%systemdrive%\ MSDOS.SYS	Full Control (this folder only)	Full Control (this folder only)			Read & Execute (this folder only)
%systemdrive%\ ntbootdd.sys	Full Control (this folder only)	Full Control (this folder only)			Read & Execute (this folder only)
%systemdrive%\ ntdetect.com	Full Control (this folder only)	Full Control (this folder only)			Read & Execute (this folder only)
%systemdrive%\ ntldr	Full Control (this folder only)	Full Control (this folder only)			Read & Execute (this folder only)
%systemdrive%\ Temp	Full Control	Full Control	Full Control (subfolders and files only)	Traverse Folder/ Execute File, Create Files/ Write Data, Create Folders/ Append Data (this folder and subfolders only)	Traverse Folder/Execute File, Create Files/ Write Data, Create Folders/Append Data (this folder and subfolders only)
%systemdrive%\ addins	Full Control	Full Control	Full Control (subfolders and files only)	Read & Execute, List Folder Contents, Read	Read & Execute, List Folder Contents, Read (this folder, subfolders, and files) Modify (this folder and subfolders only)

Table 7-7   Recommended Permissions for Windows 2000 and Windows XP   *(continued)*

File/Folder	Administrators	System	Creator Owner	Users	Power Users
%systemroot%	Full Control	Full Control	Full Control (subfolders and files only)	Read & Execute, List Folder Contents, Read (this folder, subfolders, and files) Create Files (subfolders only) Create Folders (this folder and subfolders only)	Modify (subfolders and files only)
%systemroot%\ $NtServicePack-Uninstall$	Full Control	Full Control			
%systemroot%\ Application Compatibility Scripts	Full Control	Full Control			Read & Execute, List Folder Contents, Read
%systemroot%\ AppPatch	Full Control	Full Control			Read & Execute, List Folder Contents, Read
%systemroot%\ Cluster	Full Control	Full Control			
%systemroot%\ Config	Full Control	Full Control			Read & Execute, List Folder Contents, Read
%systemroot%\ Connection Wizard	Full Control	Full Control			Read & Execute, List Folder Contents, Read
%systemroot%\ Connection Wizard	Full Control	Full Control			Read & Execute, List Folder Contents, Read
%systemroot%\ CSC	Full Control	Full Control			

(continued)

Table 7-7   Recommended Permissions for Windows 2000 and Windows XP   *(continued)*

File/Folder	Administrators	System	Creator Owner	Users	Power Users
%systemroot%\ debug	Full Control	Full Control	Full Control (subfolders and files only)	Read & Execute, List Folder Contents, Read	Read & Execute, List Folder Contents, Read
%systemroot%\ Debug\User-Mode	Full Control	Full Control		Traverse Folder/ Execute File, List Folder/Read Data, Create Files/Write Data (this folder only) Create Files/ Write Data, Create Folders/ Append Data (files only)	Traverse Folder/Execute File, List Folder/Read Data, Create Files/Write Data (this folder only) Create Files/ Write Data, Create Folders/Append Data (files only)
%systemroot%\ Driver Cache	Full Control	Full Control		Read & Execute, List Folder Contents, Read	Read & Execute, List Folder Contents, Read
%systemroot%\ Help	Full Control	Full Control			
%systemroot%\ inf	Full Control	Full Control		Read & Execute, List Folder Contents, Read	Read & Execute, List Folder Contents, Read
%systemroot%\ installer	Full Control	Full Control			Read & Execute, List Folder Contents, Read
%systemroot%\ java	Full Control	Full Control	Full Control	Read & Execute, List Folder Contents, Read	Read & Execute, List Folder Contents, Read (this folder, subfolders, and files) Modify (subfolders and files only)

Table 7-7   Recommended Permissions for Windows 2000 and Windows XP   *(continued)*

File/Folder	Administrators	System	Creator Owner	Users	Power Users
%systemroot%\ media	Full Control	Full Control		Read & Execute, List Folder Contents, Read	Read & Execute, List Folder Contents, Read
%systemroot%\ msagent	Full Control	Full Control		Read & Execute, List Folder Contents, Read	Read & Execute, List Folder Contents, Read
%systemroot%\ Registration	Full Control	Full Control		Read	Read
%systemroot%\ repair	Full Control	Full Control		List contents (this folder only)	Modify
%systemroot%\ security	Full Control	Full Control		Read & Execute, List Folder Contents, Read	Read & Execute, List Folder Contents, Read
%systemroot%\ ServicePackFiles	Full Control	Full Control			
%systemroot%\ system32\	Full Control	Full Control	Full Control (subfolders and files only)	Read & Execute, List Folder Contents, Read	Read & Execute, List Folder Contents, Read
%systemroot%\ system32\ appmgmt	Full Control	Full Control		Read & Execute, List Folder Contents, Read	
%systemroot%\ system32\ Netmon	Full Control	Full Control			
%systemroot%\ system32\Group Policy	Full Control	Full Control		Read & Execute, List Folder Contents, Read	Read & Execute, List Folder Contents, Read
%systemroot%\ system32\ias	Full Control	Full Control	Full Control (subfolders and files only)		

(continued)

Table 7-7 Recommended Permissions for Windows 2000 and Windows XP *(continued)*

File/Folder	Administrators	System	Creator Owner	Users	Power Users
%systemroot%\system32\config	Full Control	Full Control	Full Control (subfolders and files only)	Read & Execute (this folder and subfolders only)	Read & Execute (this folder and subfolders only)
%systemroot%\system32\NTMSData	Full Control	Full Control			
%systemroot%\system32\spool\printers	Full Control	Full Control	Full Control (subfolders and files only)	Traverse Folder/Execute File, Read Attributes, Read Extended Attributes, Create Folders/Append Data (this folder and subfolders only)	Traverse Folder/Execute File, Read Attributes, Read Extended Attributes, Create Folders/Append Data (this folder and subfolders only)
%systemroot%\Temp	Full Control	Full Control	Full Control (subfolders and files only)	Traverse Folder/Execute File, Create Files/Write Data, Create Folders/Append Data (this folder and subfolders only)	Traverse Folder/Execute File, Create Files/Write Data, Create Folders/Append Data (this folder and subfolders only)
c:\autoexec.bat	Full Control (this folder only)	Full Control (this folder only)			Read & Execute (this folder only)
c:\boot.ini	Full Control (this folder only)	Full Control (this folder only)			Read & Execute (this folder only)

Table 7-7   Recommended Permissions for Windows 2000 and Windows XP   *(continued)*

File/Folder	Administrators	System	Creator Owner	Users	Power Users
c:\config.sys	Full Control (this folder only)	Full Control (this folder only)			Read & Execute (this folder only)
c:\ntbootdd.sys	Full Control (this folder only)	Full Control (this folder only)			Read & Execute (this folder only)
c:\ntdetect.com	Full Control (this folder only)	Full Control (this folder only)			Read & Execute (this folder only)
c:\ntldr	Full Control (this folder only)	Full Control (this folder only)			Read & Execute (this folder)

> **Tip**   You can apply the built-in security template Rootsec.inf to restore the permissions to the default inheritance hierarchies. Applying this template will not affect explicit permissions or nondefault folders.

Note that the first time that a user logs on to a Windows XP computer causes a profile for her to be created in the %systemroot%\Documents and Settings directory. The operating system applies the permissions Administrators, System, and User accounts Full Control OI, CI, rather than inheriting the permissions from the Documents and Settings folder.

Securing Files and Folder Access by Using Share Permissions

NTFS permissions always apply to files and folders, regardless of whether they are accessed locally or over the network through a file share. When you share a folder, the share and its contents are accessed via the server service running on the machine on which the share is created. Share permissions differ from NTFS permissions in that they apply only when the share is accessed via the network and they do not offer the level of granularity provided by NTFS permissions. Table 7-8 explains the permissions that you can assign to a share.

Table 7-8   Share Permissions

Permissions	Description
Full Control	Full control over all folders and files in the share
Change	Read and Write permissions to files and folders
Read	Read permission for files and folders

By default in Windows 2000 and Windows XP, when a share is created, the share permissions are set to Everyone Full Control. Like NTFS permissions, share permissions are cumulative. Furthermore, deny permissions override allow permissions.

When a user attempts to access a file or folder on a share, cumulative share permissions as well as the cumulative NTFS permissions are calculated. The user accessing the share receives the more restrictive set of these two sets of permissions. For example, if the share permissions are left to the default setting of Everyone Full Control and the user has only Read and Execute rights on the files and folders in the share, the user will have only Read and Execute access.

Although share permissions are not nearly as granular as NTFS permissions, they are still useful if implemented correctly. For example, you can achieve a higher degree of security on a share's contents by removing the default share permissions and granting members of the Everyone group Change permissions. This will prevent the changing of permissions on the files and folders in the share remotely, through the network redirector. This is particularly important because the user who creates a file owns that file and can reassign permissions in a manner that compromises security. When you remove the Everyone Full Control share permission, the owner of a file can modify only permissions via an interactive logon session, either at the server console or through Terminal Services.

Using the Encrypting File System

Although properly configured DACLs will protect data, sometimes you need a greater degree of protection. Your organization might have some data that must be kept confidential from administrators, even those who have Full Control permissions on the files. Also, your organization might have data that is stored temporarily on laptops issued to employees and needs to remain confidential even if the physical security of the laptop is compromised. The encrypting file system (EFS) allow users and administrators to encrypt files and folders to extend file and folder security beyond NTFS permissions.

EFS combines asymmetric and symmetric encryption to encrypt files and manage the encryption keys. EFS uses symmetric encryption—either the DES-X algorithm or the 3DES algorithm (Windows XP only)—to encrypt the data and asymmetric encryption to manage the symmetric encryption keys. The default configuration of EFS allows users to encrypt files without any configuration by an administrator. When a user encrypts a file, EFS automatically generates a public-key pair for the user and either obtains a digital certificate by requesting one from a Certification Authority (CA) or self-creates a certificate if no CA is available to issue certificates.

File encryption and decryption is supported on a per-file or entire-directory basis. Directory encryption is transparently enforced. All files (and subdirectories) created in a directory marked for encryption are automatically encrypted. Each file has a unique encryption key, making it safe for rename operations. If you move a file from an encrypted directory to an unencrypted directory on the same volume, the file remains encrypted because the move operation does not actually change the location or structure of the file on disk. Encryption and decryption can be set using the properties of the file or folder in Windows Explorer. Additionally, command-line tools and administrative interfaces are provided for advanced users and recovery agents to ease management of encrypted files.

A file need not be decrypted before use; encryption and decryption is done transparently when bytes travel to and from the disk. EFS will automatically detect an encrypted file and locate the user's certificate and associated private key to decrypt the file.

How EFS Works

EFS works differently depending on whether a computer is a member of a domain or it is a stand-alone computer. The following description explains how EFS works in a domain environment.

When a user chooses to encrypt a file, the file is loaded into protected memory and the user's computer generates a random encryption key known as a file encryption key (FEK). The computer uses a symmetric encryption algorithm—either DES-X in Windows 2000 or Windows XP, or 3DES in Windows XP only—to encrypt the file using the FEK as the key, as Figure 7-3 shows.

Figure 7-3   Encrypting the contents of a file using EFS

Next, the computer retrieves the user's EFS certificate from the user's pro-file and extracts the user's public key. If the user does not have an EFS certifi-cate, the computer generates an EFS certificate based on the user's account information, including the user's password. The FEK is encrypted using the RSA algorithm with the public key from the user's EFS certificate and added to the header of the file in the data decryption field (DDF). This process is shown in Figure 7-4.

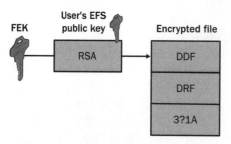

Figure 7-4   Encrypting the FEK of a file using the EFS public key of the user account

The final step in encrypting the file is accomplished by the computer retrieving the certificate for each EFS recovery agent. For each EFS recovery agent certificate, the computer extracts the public key and encrypts the FEK by using the RSA encryption algorithm and stores the encrypted FEK in the data recovery field (DRF) located in the file's header. This process is shown in Figure 7-5.

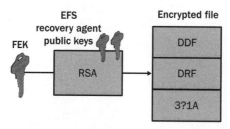

Figure 7-5   Encrypting the FEK of a file using the EFS recovery agent's public key

The only users who can view the information in the file are those who encrypted the file and anyone who possesses a recovery agent's private key. Even another user with Full Control permissions on the file will not be able to read it. When a user attempts to open the file, the user's private key is retrieved and used to decrypt the FEK. The decrypted FEK is then used to decrypt the file. Files secured with EFS are not paged out of volatile memory when decrypted, preventing data from the file from being stored in the page file. When the user saves the file, a new FEK is generated and the process of creating the EFS header is repeated.

If the user opens the file and moves it to a non-NTFS partition or to a remote server, the file will be transparently decrypted. Users with Back Up Files And Folders user rights on a computer containing encrypted files will be able to back up the files. However, if the backup is restored to a non-NTFS partition, the contents of the files will be unintelligible.

EFS Command-Line Tools

In addition to configuring EFS in the Explorer interface, you can use two command-line tools to get information about EFS encrypted files or manipulate EFS encryption: Efsinfo.exe and Cipher.exe.

> **On the CD**   Efsinfo.exe is located in the Tools folder on the CD included with this book. Cipher.exe is available in Windows XP Professional and Windows 2000 Service Pack 3 or higher.

Efsinfo.exe

Efsinfo.exe is a command-line tool that allows you to retrieve information from the EFS header of a file encrypted with EFS. You must have the permission to read the attributes of the file to retrieve the information from the file you specify. The syntax for using Efsinfo.exe follows:

EFSINFO [/U] [/R] [/C] [/I] [/Y] [/S:*dir*] [*pathname* [...]]

The options for using Efsinfo.exe are decribed in Table 7-9.

Table 7-9   Efsinfo.exe Options

Option	Description
/U	Displays user information from the DDF.
/R	Displays recovery agent information from the DRF.
/C	Displays certificate thumbprint information for the user account that encrypted the file. You access the properties of a certificate by double-clicking an issued certificate in the certificate's Microsoft Manangement Console (MMC).

(continued)

Table 7-9   Efsinfo.exe Options   *(continued)*

Option	Description
/I	Forces the utility to continue the specified operation even after errors have occurred. By default, Efsinfo.exe stops when an error is encountered.
/Y	Displays your current EFS certificate thumbprint on the local PC.
/S:*dir*	Performs the specified operation on directories in the given directory and all subdirectories.

Cipher.exe

Cipher.exe enables you to manipulate EFS-encrypted files from the command prompt. The versions of Cipher.exe in Windows 2000 and Windows XP are different and cannot be interchanged. In Windows 2000, the syntax of the Cipher.exe command is this:

CIPHER [/E | /D] [/S:*dir*] [/P:*keyfile*] [/K:*keyfile*] [/L:*keyfile*] [/I] [/F] [/Q] [*filename* [...]]

Table 7-10 describes the options available when using Cipher.exe in Windows 2000.

Table 7-10   Cipher.exe Options in Windows 2000

Option	Description
/E	Encrypts the specified files. Directories will be marked so that files added afterward will be encrypted.
/D	Decrypts the specified files. Directories will be marked so that files added afterward will not be encrypted.
/S	Performs the specified operation on files in the given directory and all subdirectories.
/A	Encrypts files and the folders they are stored in.
/I	Forces the computer to continue performing the specified operation even after errors have occurred. By default, Cipher.exe stops when an error is encountered.
/F	Forces the encryption operation on all specified files, even those already encrypted. For files that have already been encrypted, a new FEK will be generated and the EFS header re-created. Files already encrypted are skipped by default when using the /F option.

Table 7-10   Cipher.exe Options in Windows 2000   *(continued)*

Option	Description
/K	Forces the computer to generate and use a new FEK for all files. When this option is specified, the computer attempts to update the user's EFS certificate. This option is useful after deploying EFS certificates from your Public Key Infrastructure (PKI).
/Q	Reports only the most essential information.

Used without parameters, Cipher.exe displays the encryption state of the current directory and any files it contains. You can use multiple file names and wildcards. You must put spaces between multiple parameters.

> **Important**   The Cipher.exe command was replaced in Windows 2000 Service Pack 3 with a version that adds the /W option. The /W option permanently deletes, or wipes, all deleted data from a directory. This removes all artifacts of files that have been deleted but not necessarily removed from the hard drive. It also removes all NTFS mount and junction points.

The Windows XP version of Cipher.exe includes all the options that the Windows 2000 version does as well as the options described in Table 7-11.

Table 7-11   Cipher.exe Options in Windows XP

Option	Description
/R	Generatates a .pfx file and a .cer file. You can use the certificate in the .cer file as the recovery agent and export the .pfx file (which contains the private key and the certificate) for archival. You can store these files in a secure offline location until they are needed to recover encrypted files. By removing the EFS recovery agent (RA) from the local computer, you prevent an attacker from using the RA account to gain access to encrypted files and folders.
/U	Updates the FEK and recovery agent on all encrypted files. The only other option that works with /U is /N.
/N	Works only in combination with /U. When used with /U, /N supresses the updating of the FEK and recovery agent. This option is used to locate encrypted files on a hard drive.

Using EFS with Local Accounts in Windows 2000 and Windows XP

When EFS is used with local accounts by default, the EFS certificate used by default is self-generated based on the user's logon credentials on the local computer. In Windows 2000, this leaves encrypted files vulnerable if the physical security of the computer is compromised because there are a number of tools that enable an attacker to reset the password on local accounts. Once the password is reset, the attacker can then log on to the computer as the user and decrypt the files. This is because the attacker will have access to the EFS private key stored in the user profile.

In Windows XP, the EFS private key is stored by using the Data Protection API (DPAPI), which encrypts secrets by using an encryption key based on the user's password. If the password is reset administratively, the DPAPI encryption key will no longer be valid. Thus, resetting the password causes the derived EFS private key to be inaccessible forever. Furthermore, the encrypted files would remain confidential. Windows XP issues a warning when an administrator attempts to reset the password of a local user. To prevent losing data with encrypted files, always ensure that you have an exported data recovery agent stored in a secure location. If you are using Windows 2000 and EFS with local accounts, you can increase the protection of the local account database by enabling the System Key (Syskey.exe) in either mode 2 or mode 3. By default, if the Administrator account is used to encrypt files and folders, no RA exists.

Additional EFS Features in Windows XP

Windows XP makes several improvements to EFS. These features are built on the features of EFS in Windows 2000 but add support for additional functionality and security. The main improvements include these:

- Encryption of offline files
- Remote encryption of files using WebDAV (discussed momentarily)
- Sharing of encrypted files

Encryption of Offline Files

Windows XP enables offline files and folders to be encrypted using EFS. Offline folders use a common database on the local computer to store all offline files, and they limit access to those files through explicit DACLs. The database displays the files to the user in a manner that hides the database structure and format and appears as a normal folder to the user. Other users' files and folders are not displayed and are not available to other users. Because the offline folders directory is in the %systemroot% folder, no individual user can encrypt its contents. Thus, the entire database is encrypted by the System account.

One limitation of encrypting the offline files database is that files and folders will not be displayed in an alternate color when the user is working offline. The remote server can contain copies of the files that have been individually encrypted on the server, and when the user is online and working with server-based copies of those files, they can display in an alternate color. Although the files are encrypted, this might seem an inconsistency to the user.

> **Important** The offline folders feature, also known as the *client-side caching (CSC)* feature, runs as a System process and therefore can be accessed by any user or process that can run as System. This includes administrators on the local machine. Therefore, when sensitive data is stored in offline folders, administrative access should be restricted to users and the System Key should be used in mode 2 or mode 3.

Remote Encryption of Files Using WebDAV

Windows XP supports a new method for encrypting files on remote servers through a protocol known as Web-Based Distributed Authoring and Versioning (WebDAV). When the Windows XP client maps a drive to a WebDAV access point on a remote server, files can be encrypted locally on the client and then transmitted as raw encrypted files to the WebDAV server by using an HTTP PUT command. Similarly, encrypted files downloaded to a Windows XP client are transmitted as raw encrypted files and decrypted locally on the client by using an HTTP GET command. The Temporary Internet Files directory is used for intermediate transfer of the files by using HTTP where the WebDAV detects and sets the encrypted file attribute for Windows XP. Therefore, only public-key pairs and private-key pairs on the client are used to encrypt files, even though the files are stored on a remote server.

The WebDAV redirector is a new mini-redirector that supports the WebDAV protocol for remote document sharing by using HTTP. The WebDAV redirector supports the use of existing applications, and it allows file sharing across the Internet (through firewalls, routers, and so on) to HTTP servers. Both Microsoft Internet Information Server 5.0 (Windows 2000) and IIS 5.1 (Windows XP) support WebDAV folders, known as *Web folders*. The WebDAV redirector does have some limitations on the files that can be transmitted using the WebDAV protocol. The actual limitation varies depending on the amount of virtual memory available, but in general, only files of less than 400 megabytes can be transferred in Windows XP with EFS over WebDAV. Files and folders, when encrypted using a WebDAV share, will appear as unencrypted if a user or administrator logs on to the server locally. Once a file has been encrypted using WebDAV, that file should be accessed and decrypted only by using WebDAV. This unique behavior does not affect the ability to back up and restore the server by using Ntbackup.exe or the Windows NT backup API set.

Administrators and users should not encrypt files locally on a volume that hosts a WebDAV share. All administration should be done through the WebDAV share only. You can create a WebDAV folder in Windows 2000 or Windows XP by enabling Web Sharing on the properties of any folder. Note that if a user does not have a key to decrypt the file on a WebDAV share, she will receive an "access denied" error if she attempts to modify the advanced EFS attributes of the file.

Sharing of Encrypted Files

In Windows XP, EFS supports the sharing of files between multiple users on a per-file basis. However, users must be specified individually instead of by security group, and multiple encryption accounts are not supported on folders. Once a file has been encrypted, you can add users to the list of those who can decrypt the encrypted file by selecting the Advanced Properties dialog box of an encrypted file and clicking the details button. Individual users can add other users (but not groups) from the local machine or from the Active Directory directory service, provided the user has a valid EFS certificate and keys. Figure 7-6 shows this process.

Figure 7-6 Sharing files encrypted with EFS in Windows XP

Introduction to Designing a Data Recovery Agent Policy

When utilizing EFS, you must ensure that files can be recovered if a user's EFS private key is lost or if the files need to be retrieved for legal reasons. The data recovery agent (DRA) private key can decrypt files and can remove the encryption attribute on those files.

> **More Info**   Establishing a data recovery policy requires in-depth knowledge of PKI and thus is outside the scope of this book. For more information on designing a data recovery policy, see the "Data Protection and Recovery in Windows XP" white paper at *http://www.microsoft.com/ technet/prodtechnol/winxppro/support/dataprot.asp*.

EFS automatically enforces a recovery policy that requires a recovery agent be available for files to be encrypted. The recovery policy is a type of public-key policy that provides user accounts to be designated as DRAs. A default recovery policy is automatically established when the Administrator account logs on to the system for the first time, making the administrator the recovery agent.

The default recovery policy is configured locally for workgroup computers. For computers that are part of an Active Directory–based domain, the recovery policy is configured in a domain OU Group Policy object (GPO). If no recovery agent policy is created, the computer's local recovery agent policy is used. Recovery certificates are issued by a certificate authority, or CA, and managed by using the MMC Certificates snap-in or by using the Cipher.exe /r command in Windows XP.

In a network environment, the domain administrator controls how EFS is implemented in the recovery policy for all users and computers in the scope of influence. In a default Windows 2000 or Windows XP installation, when the first domain controller is set up, the domain administrator is the specified recovery agent for the domain. The way the domain administrator configures the recovery policy determines how EFS is implemented for users on their local machines. Administrators can define one of three types of policy:

- **Recovery agent policy**   When an administrator adds one or more recovery agents, a recovery agent policy is in effect. These agents are responsible for recovering any encrypted data within their scope of administration. This is the most common type of recovery policy. You can ensure all recovery agents are available to all Windows 2000 and Windows XP computers by using Group Policy.

- **Empty recovery policy**   When an administrator deletes all recovery agents and their public-key certificates, an empty recovery policy is in effect. An empty recovery policy means that no recovery agent exists, and if the client operating system is Windows 2000, EFS is disabled altogether. Only the Windows XP client supports EFS with an empty DRA policy.

- **No-recovery policy**   When an administrator deletes the private keys associated with a given recovery policy, a no-recovery policy is in effect. Because no private key is available, there is no way to use a recovery agent and recovery will not be possible. This policy is useful for organizations with a mixed environment of Windows 2000 and Windows XP clients where no data recovery is desired.

In a Windows 2000 environment, if an administrator attempts to configure an EFS recovery policy with no recovery agent certificates, EFS is automatically disabled. In a Windows XP Professional environment, the same action enables users to encrypt files without a DRA.

Warning   In a mixed environment, an empty EFS recovery policy turns off EFS on Windows 2000 computers but only eliminates the requirement for a DRA on Windows XP Professional computers.

When a domain user logs on at a domain computer that is within the scope of the EFS recovery policy, all DRA certificates are cached in the computer's certificate store. This means that EFS on every domain computer can easily access and use the DRA's public key (or multiple public keys, if multiple DRAs are designated). On computers where an EFS recovery policy is in effect, every encrypted file contains at least one data recovery field in which the file's FEK is encrypted by using the DRA's public key and stored. By using the associated private key, any designated DRA can decrypt any encrypted file within the scope of the EFS recovery policy.

Securing Registry Permissions

The registry is a dynamic, hierarchical database that contains values of variables for the operating system and applications. The operating system and other programs also store data about users and about the current configuration of the system and its components in the registry. Because the registry is available whenever the system is running, programs that start and stop can keep persistent data in the registry and the settings will be saved when the system shuts down. The registry is constructed of six hives that are used for different purposes, as described in Table 7-12.

Table 7-12   Default Registry Hives

Hive	Abbreviation	Description
HKEY_CURRENT_USER	HKCU	Stores information about the profile of the currently logged-on user that is persistently stored in HKU
HKEY_USERS	HKU	Contains subkeys for all local user profiles
HKEY_CLASSES_ROOT	HKCR	Contains file association and COM registration information
HKEY_LOCAL_MACHINE	HKLM	Contains entries for the configuration of the operating system and applications.
HKEY_CURRENT_CONFIG	HKCC	Contains the current hardware profile that is persistently stored in HKLM\SYSTEM\CurrentControlSet\Hardware Profiles\Current
HKEY_PERFORMANCE_DATA	HKPD	Contains information about performance counters

When the computer is running, the registry is loaded in memory and active. When the computer is powered down, the persistent information stored in the registry is written to the hard drive. Table 7-13 lists the storage location for some common registry hives.

Table 7-13   Default Storage Locations of Common Hives

Hive	Storage Location
HKEY_LOCAL_MACHINE\SYSTEM	%systemroot%\system32\Config\System
HKEY_LOCAL_MACHINE\SAM	%systemroot%\system32\Config\Sam
HKEY_LOCAL_MACHINE\SECURITY	%systemroot%\system32\Config\Security
HKEY_LOCAL_MACHINE\SOFTWARE	%systemroot%\system32\Config\Software
HKEY_USERS	%systemdrive%\Documents and Settings\<username>\Ntuser.dat
HKEY_USERS	%systemdrive%\Documents and Settings\<username>\Local Settings\Application Data\Microsoft\Windows\Usrclass.dat
HKEY_USERS\DEFAULT	%systemroot%\system32\Config\Default

When you use an administrative tool to change the configuration of a system feature or service, the change usually takes effect immediately or soon thereafter. However, if you make the same change by editing the registry, you might need to log off and log on again, restart the service, or restart. In general, if you change the value of any entry in HKLM\Services\System\CurrentControlSet, you must restart the computer for the changes to take effect. Also, if you use a registry editor to change values for most entries in HKEY_CURRENT_USER, you must log off and log on again for the changes to take effect.

> **More Info**   For detailed information on the structure of the registry and the specifics of the data stored in the registry, see the Technical Reference to the Registry eBook (Regentry.chm) in the *Microsoft Windows 2000 Server Resource Kit*, Supplement One (Microsoft Press, 2000).

Configuring Registry Permissions

As with files and folders stored on NTFS partitions, the registry is secured by using DACLs. Unlike NTFS permissions, registry permissions are assigned to container objects only. An individual registry value inherits its security from its parent object. A registry key has two basic permissions: Full Control and Read. The Full Control permission includes all of the special permissions in Table 7-14. The Read permission is comprised of the following special permissions: Read Control, Query Value, Notify, and Enumerate Subkeys. Table 7-14 lists the special permissions on registry keys.

Table 7-14   Special Registry Permissions

Permissions	Description
Query Value	Allows the value of the registry key to be read
Set Value	Allows the value of an existing key to be written
Create Subkey	Allows the creation of subkeys
Enumerate Subkeys	Allows the enumeration of subkeys
Notify	Required to request change notifications for a registry key or for subkeys of a registry key
Create Link	Reserved for use by the operating system

Table 7-14 **Special Registry Permissions**   *(continued)*

Permissions	Description
Delete	Allows the key to be deleted
Write DACL	Allows the modification of the DACL
Write Owner	Allows the modification of the owner
Read Control	Allows the SACL to be read

In Windows 2000 and Windows XP, you can use Regedt32.exe to alter registry permissions from the user interface or you can use the Subinacl.exe command-line tool. Changing permissions on registry values requires the same techniques as modifying NTFS permissions.

Best Practices

- **Use least privilege.** Whenever assigning permissions, assign the least privilege the user needs to complete her job function.

- **Assign permissions at the highest possible point in a hierarchy.** Always assign permissions at the highest point in the container hierarchy and allow them to be inherited by child object to simplify their application.

- **Assign permissions to security groups, not users.** Assigning permission to security groups by using a structured model will make assigning permissions scalable and flexible. This is helpful when users and files change.

- **Use caution when encrypting files.** Always archive the DRA when encrypting files with EFS to prevent files from being irreversibly encrypted.

Additional Information

- "Data Protection and Recovery in Windows XP" (*http://www.microsoft.com/technet/prodtechnol/winxppro/support/dataprot.asp*)

- "New Security Tool for Encrypting File System" (*http://www.microsoft.com/technet/security/tools/tools/cipher.asp*)

- "Encrypting File System for Windows 2000" white paper (*http://www.microsoft.com/technet/treeview/default.asp?url=/TechNet/prodtechnol/windows2000serv/deploy/confeat/nt5efs.asp*)

- "Third-Party Certification Authority Support for Encrypting File System" (*http://support.microsoft.com/default.aspx?scid=kb;en-us;Q273856&sd=tech*)

- "Default Access Control Settings" white paper (*http://www.microsoft.com/windows2000/techinfo/planning/security/secdefs.asp*)

- Access Control Lists (ACLs) on MSDN (*http://msdn.microsoft.com/library/en-us/security/security/access_control_lists_acls_.asp*)

- 243756: "How to Use Encrypting File System (EFS) with Internet Information Services"

- 222022: "How to Disable EFS for All Computers in a Windows 2000–Based Domain"

- 223338: "Using a Certificate Authority for the Encrypting File Service"

- 241201: "How to Back Up Your Encrypting File System Private Key"

- 242296: "How to Restore an Encrypting File System Private Key for Encrypted Data Recovery in Windows 2000"

- 243026: "Using Efsinfo.exe to Determine Information About Encrypted Files"

- 243035: "How to Disable/Enable EFS on a Stand-Alone Windows 2000–Based Computer"

- 255742: "Methods for Recovering Encrypted Data Files"

- 273856: "Third-Party Certificate Authority Support for Encrypting File System"

- 230520: "How to Encrypt Data Using EFS in Windows 2000"

- 222054: "Encrypting Files in Windows 2000"

- 221997: "Cannot Gain Access to Previously Encrypted Files on Windows 2000"

- 227825: "Backup Tool Backs Up Files to Which You Do Not Have Read Access"

- 230490: "The Encrypted Data Recovery Policy for Encrypting File System"

- 257705: "How to Reinitialize the EDRP on a Workgroup Computer Running Windows 2000"

- 216899: "Best Practice Methods for Windows 2000 Domain Controller Setup"

- 223093: "Encrypted Files Cannot Be Compressed"

- 223178: "Transferring Encrypted Files That Need to Be Recovered"

- 223316: "Best Practices for Encrypting File System"

- 223448: "Cannot Use Shared Encrypted Files in Windows 2000"

- 254156: "Encrypted Files Made Available Offline Not Encrypted on the Client"

- 272279: "How to Troubleshoot the File Replication Service and the Distributed File System"

- 283223: "Recovery of Encrypted Files on a Server"

- 248723: "Info: Understanding Encrypted Directories"

> **Note**   The 24 articles above can be accessed through the Microsoft Knowledge Base. Go to *http:// support.microsoft.com* and enter the article number in the Search The Knowledge Base text box.

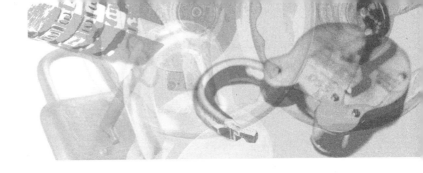

8

Securing Services

In Microsoft Windows 2000 and Windows XP, several applications run independent of any user and regardless of whether a user is logged on to the computer. These applications are registered as *services,* or more specifically, *Service Control Programs (SCP)*. Services are controlled by the Service Control Manager (SCM), which runs as Services.exe. The configuration of services is stored in the registry, under the key HKLM\System\CurrentControlSet\Services. You can use the Srvany.exe utility to cause an executable to run as a service.

> **On the CD**   Srvany.exe is located in the Tools folder on the CD included with this book.

Managing Service Permissions

To view or manipulate services, you must have appropriate access to the SCM. Rights to the SCM cannot be altered, although rights over specific services can be modified. Tables 8-1 and 8-2 list the default rights for the SCM in Windows 2000 and Windows XP, respectively. To view or manage the permissions on services, you must use either the Subinacl.exe tool or the Local Security Policy Microsoft Management Console (MMC) snap-in. These services are not exposed in a human-readable format in the registry.

Table 8-1   SCM Permissions in Windows 2000

Group	Permissions Granted
Everyone	■ Connect to the SCM ■ Enumerate services ■ Query the status of services ■ Read the permissions on services
LocalSystem	■ Connect to the SCM ■ Enumerate services ■ Query the status of services ■ Read the permissions on services ■ Change the permissions on services
Administrators	Full Control

Table 8-2   SCM Permissions in Windows XP

Group	Permissions Granted
Authenticated Users	■ Connect to the SCM ■ Enumerate services ■ Query the status of services ■ Read the permissions on services
LocalSystem	■ Connect to the SCM ■ Enumerate services ■ Query the status of services ■ Read the permissions on services ■ Change the permissions on services
Administrators	Full Control

You can control services by using the Services MMC snap-in under Administrative Tools, by typing **services.msc** at the command prompt or Run command, or by editing the registry directly. Security configuration of services includes the ability to do the following:

■ Configure the startup behavior for each service

■ Stop, start, pause, and resume services

■ Configure the security context under which the service runs

■ Configure the discretionary access control list (DACL) for the service

Configuring the Startup Value for a Service

When the computer starts, the SCM retrieves service startup and dependency information from the registry and starts SCPs accordingly. Table 8-3 lists the startup values that can be assigned to services.

Table 8-3 **Startup Values for Services**

Startup Value	Registry Value	Description
Boot Start	0x0	Ntldr or Osloader preloads the driver so that it is in memory during system boot. This value is used only for kernel-mode drivers, which are generally not manageable by administrators. This value can be set only in the registry.
System Start	0x1	The driver loads and initializes after Boot Start drivers have initialized. The Boot Start drivers are loaded before the Starting Windows screen appears. This value can be set only in the registry.
Automatic	0x2	The SCM starts services with an automatic startup value during the boot process when the Starting Windows screen appears. The progress bar indicates the loading and starting of services. Some services are not loaded until after the network devices have been initialized.
Manual	0x3	The SCM starts the service when prompted by another application or a user with the necessary permissions. Often services will start dependant services only when they are needed.
Disabled	0x4	The SCM will not permit the service to be started.

When a service is started, it runs in the Services.exe process, the Lsass.exe process, its own instance, or an instance of Svchost.exe. To view the process in which a service is running, you can use the Tlist.exe command from Windows 2000 Support Tools. Type **tlist –s** at the command prompt. Figure 8-1 shows the output of running Tlist –s on Windows 2000.

You should configure services to start up automatically or manually only if they are necessary for the operation of the computer or applications that run on the computer. By setting unused services to Disabled, you can decrease the potential attack surface of the computer. You can set a service startup value to Disabled in the Services MMC snap-in, through Security Templates, or by manually setting the registry startup value to 4.

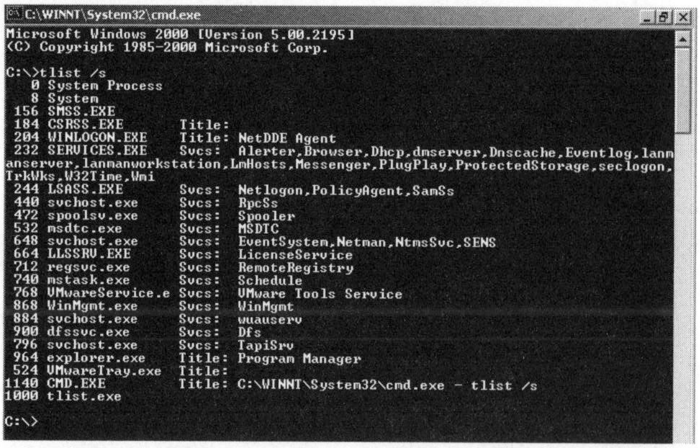

Figure 8-1   Using the Tlist command to map services to processes

Stopping, Starting, Pausing, and Resuming Services

You can control the operating status of services by using the Services MMC snap-in. You can also do so from the command line by using the Net command if you have permissions to do so. In Windows 2000 and Windows XP, you generally must have local administrative privileges to stop or pause services, unless you have been granted appropriate permissions for those services. You can use the following commands from the command line or in a batch file to control services:

- **Net start *servicename***   Starts a stopped service

- **Net stop *servicename***   Stops a started service

- **Net pause *servicename***   Pauses a started service

- **Net continue *servicename***   Continues a paused service

> **Note**   You either can use a service's name or its display name with the Net command. If the display name of the service has a space embedded in it, place the service name within quotes. You can also suppress the prompt by appending */Y* to the Net command. This is useful when configuring batch files.

When a service is stopped, it will no longer respond to or initiate requests. Each service responds differently to being paused; you should research how a service will respond to being paused before pausing it. As mentioned, you must have the appropriate permissions to stop and start a service.

Configuring the Security Context of Services

Each service runs under a security context. The security context in which a service runs determines its rights and permissions. In Windows 2000, most services run under the LocalSystem account. This account has full control over all resources on the computer. Services that run in the LocalSystem account security context not only have membership in the local Administrators group, but they also have rights not normally assigned to any user account, such as process manipulation rights. Thus, you might not want to run a service under the Local-System account. In Windows XP, services can run under the LocalSystem account, or under either the Local Service account or the Network Service account—both of which have limited rights and permissions on the local computer.

In Windows 2000 and Windows XP, you can also run a service in the security context of a user account. If you run a service under the security context of a user account, the password for the account will be stored as a local security authority (LSA) secret. If a computer is compromised and the attacker gains Administrator or System access, the attacker can retrieve LSA secrets, including the user names and passwords of service accounts. Therefore, if you run services under the security context of a user account, always use a local user account. If the computer should be compromised and the LSA secrets exposed, the attacker will not gain domain credentials—this will significantly minimize the impact of the security incident. This is especially true of service accounts that require elevated privileges. In addition, do not use the same password for all service accounts because the compromise of one of the accounts could lead to a greater network compromise.

> **Warning**   Microsoft strongly recommends that services that run in an elevated security context, such as System, not run as interactive services. For the Windows user interface, the desktop is the security boundary. Any application running on the interactive desktop can interact with any window on the interactive desktop, even if that window is not displayed on the desktop. This is true for every application, regardless of the security context of the application that creates the window and the security context of the application running on the desktop. The Windows message system does not allow an application to determine the source of a window message. Because of these design features, any service that opens a window on the interactive desktop exposes itself to applications that are executed by the logged-on user. If the service tries to use window messages to control its functionality, the logged-on user can disrupt that functionality by using malicious messages.

Configuring the DACL for the Service

Each service has a DACL that determines the permissions that users have over the service. The DACL for services is not exposed in the UI. You can view the DACL on a service by using Subinacl.exe or exporting the security configuration of a computer into a security template and viewing the service's DACL by using the Security Templates MMC snap-in. The basic permissions for services are listed in Table 8-4.

Table 8-4   Service Permissions

Permissions	Full Name	Description
Full Control	*SERVICE_ALL_ACCESS*	Grants full control over the service
Query Template	*SERVICE_QUERY_CONFIG*	Allows the service configuration to be viewed
Change Template	*SERVICE_CHANGE_CONFIG*	Allows the service configuration to be modified
Query Status	*SERVICE_QUERY_STATUS*	Allows the SCM to be queried for the status of a service
Enumerate Dependents	*SERVICE_ENUMERATE_DEPENDENTS*	Allows the dependent services to be displayed

Table 8-4 **Service Permissions** *(continued)*

Permissions	Full Name	Description
Start	*SERVICE_START*	Allows the service to be started
Stop	*SERVICE_STOP*	Allows the service to be stopped
Pause And Continue	*SERVICE_PAUSE_CONTINUE*	Allows the service to be paused and resumed
Interrogate	*SERVICE_INTERROGATE*	Allows the service to respond to status queries
User Defined Control	*SERVICE_USER_DEFINED_CONTROL*	Allows for special instructions to be given to the service
Delete	*DELETE*	Allows for the deletion of the service
Read Permissions	*READ_CONTROL*	Allows the DACL of the service to be viewed
Change Permissions	*WRITE_DACL*	Allows the DACL of the service to be modified
Take Ownership	*WRITE_OWNER*	Allows the owner of the service to be modified

You must know the full name of the service to read the permissions for it when using the Subinacl.exe command. The following listing shows how to use Subinacl.exe to read permissions on a service in Windows XP:

```
===================
+Service netlogon
===================
/owner               =system
/primary group       =system
/audit ace count     =1
/aace =everyone                SYSTEM_AUDIT_ACE_TYPE-0x2
     FAILED_ACCESS_ACE_FLAG-0x80    FAILED_ACCESS_ACE_FLAG-0x0x80
     SERVICE_ALL_ACCESS
/perm. ace count     =4
/pace =authenticated users     ACCESS_ALLOWED_ACE_TYPE-0x0
     SERVICE_QUERY_CONFIG-0x1    SERVICE_QUERY_STATUS-
     0x4SERVICE_ENUMERATE_DEPEND-0x8   SERVICE_INTERROGATE-
     0x80READ_CONTROL-0x20000           SERVICE_USER_DEFINED_CONTROL-0x0100
/pace =builtin\power users     ACCESS_ALLOWED_ACE_TYPE-0x0
     SERVICE_QUERY_CONFIG-0x1       SERVICE_QUERY_STATUS-0x4
     SERVICE_ENUMERATE_DEPEND-0x8   SERVICE_START-0x10
     SERVICE_INTERROGATE-0x80       READ_CONTROL-0x20000
     SERVICE_USER_DEFINED_CONTROL-0x0100
/pace =builtin\administrators    ACCESS_ALLOWED_ACE_TYPE-0x0
```

(continued)

```
       SERVICE_ALL_ACCESS
/pace =system                        ACCESS_ALLOWED_ACE_TYPE-0x0
     SERVICE_QUERY_CONFIG-0x1          SERVICE_QUERY_STATUS-0x4
     SERVICE_ENUMERATE_DEPEND-0x8          SERVICE_START-0x10
     SERVICE_STOP-0x20SERVICE_PAUSE_CONTINUE-0x40
     SERVICE_INTERROGATE-0x80
READ_CONTROL-0x20000          SERVICE_USER_DEFINED_CONTROL-0x0100
```

You can also use the Security Template MMC snap-in to view and configure the permissions on services. Figure 8-2 shows the permissions for the Help and Support service in Windows XP using the Security Templates MMC snap-in.

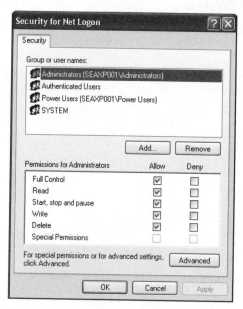

Figure 8-2 Managing service permissions with the Security Templates MMC snap-in

Default Services in Windows 2000 and Windows XP

In Windows 2000 and Windows XP, many services are installed by default with the OS. Each service is configured according to different security needs. You should evaluate each service to determine whether the service is required by computers on your network and whether you need to change the permissions on the startup value, change the startup value itself, or change the permissions for the service. The following list describes each of these default services.

> **Note**   Unless otherwise noted, all services are installed by default on both Windows 2000 and Windows XP.

- **Alerter**   Notifies selected users and computers of administrative alerts. If this service is turned off, the computer will not be able to receive administrative alerts, such as those from the Messenger service or Performance Monitor. This service should be disabled unless you use administrative alerts.

- **Application Layer Gateway**   Provides support for third-party plug-ins to Windows XP Internet Connection Sharing (ICS) and Internet Connection Firewall (ICF). Stopping or disabling this service will prevent ICS or ICF from working. You should set this service to start manually.

- **Application Management**   Provides software installation services, such as Assign, Publish, and Remove. This service processes requests to enumerate, install, and remove applications deployed via a corporate network. This service is called when you use Add/Remove Programs in Control Panel to install or remove an application. If the service is disabled, users will be unable to install, remove, or enumerate applications deployed by using Group Policy. This service should be set to Manual. The service is started by the first call made to it—it does not terminate until you stop it manually or restart the computer.

- **Automatic Updates**   Enables the download and installation of critical Windows updates. If the service is disabled, the OS can be manually updated at the Windows Update Web site (*http://windowsupdate.microsoft.com*) or via a Software Updates Services server. Automatic Updates is a default service in Windows XP and is added to Windows 2000 computers during the application of Windows 2000 Service Pack 3. You should enable this service to start automatically unless you have your own security update management solution. You can configure Automatic Updates in the system Control Panel applet or by using Group Policy.

- **Background Intelligent Transfer Service**   Uses idle network bandwidth to transfer data to avoid interfering with other network connections. This service is available only in Windows XP and should be set to either Disabled or Manual depending on your organization's security requirements.

- **Boot Information Negotiation Layer (BINL)**   Enables you to install Windows 2000 and Windows XP on computers equipped with preexecution-compatible network interface cards. The BINL service is the primary component of Remote Installation Services (RIS). If BINL is no longer needed on the system, you can discontinue its use via the Add/Remove Windows option in Control Panel to remove the RIS component. If turned off, RIS will not allow client machines to install the OS remotely. This service is available on Windows 2000 Server only when RIS is installed.

- **Certificate Services**   Creates, manages, and removes X.509 certificates and is installed on Windows 2000 Server. You can remove this service via Add/Remove Programs in Control Panel.

- **ClipBook**   Enables the ClipBook Viewer to create and share "pages" of data to be viewed by a remote computer via NetDDE, which is described later in this chapter. This service is turned off by default, and it is started only when a user starts the ClipBook. If you disable or remove the service, the remote features of ClipBook will be disabled, but the ClipBook will still function properly on the local computer. You should disable this service.

- **Cluster Service**   Operates the two types of cluster solutions in the Windows platform that support different application styles: Server Clusters and Network Load Balancing (NLB) Clusters. This service is available only on Windows 2000 Advanced Server and Datacenter Server with clustering or NLB installed. You can remove this service by removing Clustering by using Add/Remove Programs in Control Panel.

- **COM+ Event System**   Provides automatic distribution of events to subscribing COM components. If the service is turned off, the System Event Notification System (SENS) stops working—COM+ login and logoff notifications will not occur. Other COM+ Inbox applications, such as the Volume Snapshot service, will not work correctly. You should set this service to Manual, unless your COM+ components are installed on the computer.

- **COM+ System Application**   Manages the configuration and tracking of COM+-based components. If the service is stopped, most COM+-based components will not function properly. If this service is disabled, a COM+ application installed on the computer will not start. This service is available only in Windows XP and should be set to start manually, unless COM+ applications are installed on the computer.

- **Computer Browser**   Maintains an up-to-date list of computers on your network and supplies the list to programs that request it. The Computer Browser service is used by Windows-based computers that need to view network domains and resources. If you disable this service, the computer will no longer participate in browser elections and will not maintain a server list. You can safely disable this service on most clients and servers on networks that use only Windows 2000–based and later computers.

- **Cryptographic Services**   Provides three management services: Catalog Database Service, which confirms the signatures of Windows files and Microsoft ActiveX components; Protected Root Service, which adds and removes Trusted Root Certification Authority certificates from the computer; and Key Service, which helps enroll the computer for certificates. If Cryptographic Services is stopped, the three management services will not function properly. You should set this service to start automatically. This service is available only in Windows XP.

- **DHCP Client**   Manages network configuration by registering and updating IP addresses if the computer has network adapters configured to use the Dynamic Host Configuration Protocol (DHCP) to obtain TCP/IP information. You should set this service to start automatically, unless you have statically configured IP addresses and information.

- **DHCP Server**   Uses DHCP to allocate IP addresses and allow the advanced configuration of network settings—such as Domain Name System (DNS) servers and Windows Internet Name Service (WINS) servers—to DHCP clients automatically. If the DHCP Server service is turned off, DHCP clients will not receive IP addresses or network settings automatically. This service is available only on Windows 2000 Server when the DCHP service is installed. You can remove this service by using Add/Remove Programs in Control Panel.

- **Distributed File System (DFS)**   Manages logical volumes distributed across a local area network (LAN) or wide area network (WAN). DFS is a distributed service that integrates disparate file shares into a single logical namespace. This service is available only on Windows 2000 Server when DFS is installed. You can remove this service by using Add/Remove Programs in Control Panel.

- **Distributed Link Tracking (DLT) Client** Maintains links between the NTFS file system files within a computer or across computers in a network domain. The DLT Client service ensures that shortcuts and object linking and embedding (OLE) links continue to work after the target file is renamed or moved. If the DLT Client service is disabled, you will not be able to track links. Likewise, users on other computers will not be able to track links for documents on your computer. In a workgroup, you should disable this service because it is not used frequently. In a domain environment, you should use this service only if you frequently move files and folders on NTFS volumes.

- **Distributed Link Tracking (DLT) Server** Stores information so that files moved between volumes can be tracked for each volume in the domain. The DLT Server service runs on each domain controller in a domain. This service enables the DLT Client service to track linked documents that have been moved to a location in another NTFS v5 (the version of NTFS used in Windows 2000 and later) volume in the same domain. If the DLT Server service is disabled, links maintained by the DLT Client service might be less reliable.

- **Distributed Transaction Coordinator** Coordinates transactions that are distributed across multiple computer systems and/or resource managers, such as databases, message queues, file systems, or other transaction-protected resource managers. The Distributed Transaction Coordinator is necessary if transactional components will be configured through COM+. This service is also required for transactional queues in Microsoft Message Queuing (MSMQ) and Microsoft SQL Server operations that span multiple systems. Disabling this service prevents these transactions from occurring. You should set this service to Manual unless you are using it.

- **DNS Client** Resolves and caches Domain Name System (DNS) names. The DNS Client service must be running on every computer that will perform DNS name resolution. An ability to resolve DNS names is crucial for locating domain controllers in Active Directory domains. Running the DNS Client service is also critical for enabling location of the devices identified by using DNS names. If the DNS Client service is disabled, your computers might not be able to locate the domain controllers of the Active Directory domains and Internet connections. You should set this service to start automatically, unless you are certain that the computer will not require any hostname resolution services.

- **DNS Server**   Enables DNS name resolution by answering queries and update requests for Domain Name System (DNS) names. This service is available only on Windows 2000 Server when DNS is installed. You can remove this service by using Add/Remove Programs in Control Panel.

- **Event Log**   Logs event messages issued by programs and Windows. Event Log reports contain information that can be useful in diagnosing problems. Reports are viewed in Event Viewer. The Event Log service writes to log files the events sent by applications, services, and the OS. If the Event Log service is disabled, you will not be able to track events, which reduces your ability to quickly diagnose problems with your system. In addition, you will not be able to audit security events. You cannot disable this service through the user interface.

- **Event Reporting**   In Windows XP, by default, when an application crashes the user is prompted to report the incident, along with the crash dump information. This information is sent to Microsoft for analysis. You can configure this service in the System applet in Control Panel. For example, you can define which applications should and should not send crash-dump information. To prevent this service from running, you must set it to Disabled. You should always set this service to Disabled, unless you are having difficulty with an application.

- **Fast-User Switching Compatibility**   Enables Windows XP computers in a workgroup to use the fast-user switching feature of Windows XP. This feature does not work when the computer is a member of a domain. You should disable this service.

- **Fax Service**   Enables you to send and receive faxes. This service is not installed by default and can be added and removed by using Add/Remove Programs in Control Panel.

- **File Replication**   Maintains file synchronization of file directory contents among multiple servers. File Replication is the automatic file replication service in Windows 2000. It is used to copy and maintain files on multiple servers simultaneously and to replicate the Windows 2000 system volume (SYSVOL) on all domain controllers. In addition, this service can be configured to replicate files among alternate targets associated with the fault-tolerant DFS. If this service is disabled, file replication will not occur and server data will not be synchronized. Stopping the File Replication service can seriously impair a domain controller's ability to function.

- **File Server for Macintosh**   Enables Macintosh-based computers to store and access files on a Windows server machine. If this service is turned off, Macintosh-based clients will not be able to view any NTFS shares. This service is not installed by default and can be removed by using Add/Remove Programs in Control Panel. You should remove this service if you are not sharing files with Macintosh-based clients.

- **FTP Publishing Service**   Provides FTP connectivity and administration through the Microsoft Internet Information Services (IIS) snap-in. Features include bandwidth throttling, use of security accounts, and extensible logging. You should remove this service if you are not running an FTP site. You can do so by using Add/Remove Programs in Control Panel.

- **Help and Support**   Enables the Help and Support application in Windows XP to provide dynamic help to users. If disabled, the Help and Support service will still function with local Help files but will not pull in help from the Internet. You should disable this service on computers in managed environments that have an IT support staff to help users with support requests.

- **Human Interface Devices**   Enables generic input access to the Human Interface Devices (HID) service, which activates and maintains the use of predefined hot buttons on keyboards, remote controls, and other multimedia devices. If this service is stopped, the hot buttons it controls will no longer function. You should set this service to Disabled, unless you use a custom keyboard or other input device for hotkey mappings. This service exists only in Windows XP.

- **IIS Admin Service**   Allows administration of IIS. If this service is not running, you will not be able to run Web, FTP, Network News Transfer Protocol (NNTP), or Simple Mail Transfer Protocol (SMTP) sites, and you will not be able to configure IIS. You should remove or disable this service if you will not be using the IIS Admin Web site when running IIS on a computer. You can remove this service by using Add/Remove Programs in Control Panel.

- **IMAPI CD-Burning COM Services**   Enables Windows XP computers equipped with a CD-ROM to create CDs. You should disable this service on computers that do not have a CD-R or CD-RW drive and set the service to start manually on computers that do. This service will start when you send files to a CD-R or CD-RW drive.

■ **Indexing Service**   Indexes contents and properties of files on local and remote computers and provides rapid access to files through a flexible querying language. The Indexing Service also enables quick searching of documents on local and remote computers as well as a search index for content shared on the Web. If this service is either stopped or disabled, all search functionality will be provided by traversing the folder hierarchy and scanning each file for the requested string. When the service is turned off, search response is typically much slower. You should remove this service if you do not need to build or maintain indices for searchable content. You can remove this service by using Add/Remove Programs in Control Panel.

■ **Internet Authentication Service (IAS)**   Performs centralized authentication, authorization, auditing, and accounting of users who are connecting to a network (LAN or remote) by using virtual private network (VPN) equipment, Remote Access Service (RAS), or 802.1x Wireless and Ethernet/Switch Access Points. IAS implements the Internet Engineering Task Force (IETF) standard Remote Authentication Dial-In User Service (RADIUS) protocol. If IAS is disabled or stopped, authentication requests will failover to a backup IAS server, if one is available. If none of the other backup IAS servers are available, users will not be able to connect. This service is available only with Windows 2000 Server when IAS is installed. You should remove this service on computers that are not RADIUS servers, proxies, or clients by using Add/Remove Programs in Control Panel.

■ **Internet Connection Firewall (ICF)/Internet Connection Sharing (ICS)**   Provides personal firewall and Internet connection sharing in Windows XP. You should configure this service to start automatically on computers that will be using ICF or ICS, but disable it on computers that will not be using either of these services.

■ **Internet Connection Sharing (ICS)**   Provides network address translation (NAT), addressing, and name resolution services for all computers on your home or small-office network through a dial-up or broadband connection in Windows 2000. This service is available only in Windows 2000 and should be disabled unless the computer will be used as a gateway to another network.

■ **Intersite Messaging (ISM)**   Allows the sending and receiving of messages between Windows Server sites. This service is used for mail-based replication between sites. Active Directory directory service includes support for replication between sites by using SMTP over IP transport. If you are not using the SMTP service in IIS, you should remove this service by using Add/Remove Programs in Control Panel.

- **IPSec Policy Agent (IPSec Services in XP)**   Manages IP Security (IPSec) policy, starts the Internet Key Exchange (IKE), and coordinates IPSec policy settings with the IP security driver. If you know you will not be using IPSec, you should set this service to manual startup. Otherwise, you should set this service to start automatically.

- **Kerberos Key Distribution Center**   Enables users to log on to the network using the Kerberos v5 authentication protocol. If this service is stopped on a domain controller, users will be unable to log on to the domain and access services when using that domain controller for authentication. This service exists only on Windows 2000 Active Directory domain controllers.

- **License Logging Service**   Tracks Client Access License usage for server products, such as IIS, Terminal Services, and file and print services, as well as products such as SQL Server and Microsoft Exchange Server. If this service is disabled, licensing for these programs will work properly, but usage will no longer be tracked. This service is available only in Windows 2000 Server and should be disabled unless you are tracking license usage.

- **Logical Disk Manager**   Watches Plug and Play events for new drives to be detected and passes volume and/or disk information to the Logical Disk Manager Administrative Service to be configured. If disabled, the Disk Management MMC snap-in display will not change when disks are added or removed. This service should not be disabled if dynamic disks are in the system. You should set this service to start manually.

- **Logical Disk Manager Administrative Service**   Performs administrative services for disk management requests. This service is started only when you configure a drive or partition, or when a new drive is detected. This service does not run by default, but it is activated whenever dynamic disk configuration changes occur or when the Disk Management MMC snap-in is open. The service starts, completes the configuration operation, and then exits. You should set this service to start manually.

- **Message Queuing**   A messaging infrastructure and development tool for creating distributed messaging applications for Windows. Microsoft Message Queuing (MSMQ) provides guaranteed message delivery, efficient routing, security, support for sending messages within transactions, and priority-based messaging. Disabling MSMQ affects a number of other services, including COM+ Queued Component (QC) functionality, some parts of Windows Management Instrumentation (WMI), and the MSMQ Triggers service. If you are not using a message queue on the computer, you should remove the MSMQ service by using Add/Remove Programs in Control Panel.

- **Messenger**   Sends messages to or receives them from users and computers. This service also sends and receives messages transmitted by administrators or the Alerter service. If disabled, Messenger notifications cannot be sent to or received from the computer or from users currently logged on, and the NET SEND and NET NAME commands will no longer function. You should disable this service unless you have applications that send administrative alerts, such as uninterruptible power supply (UPS) software or print notifications.

- **MS Software Shadow Copy Provider**   Manages software-based volume shadow copies taken by the Volume Shadow Copy service in Windows XP. If this service is stopped, software-based volume shadow copies cannot be managed. You should disable this service unless you are using volume shadow copies to archive data.

- **Net Logon**   Supports pass-through authentication of account logon events for computers in a domain. This service is started automatically when the computer is a member of a domain. It is used to maintain a secure channel to a domain controller for use by the computer in the authentication of users and services running on the computer. In the case of a domain controller, the Net Logon service handles the registration of the computer's DNS names specific to domain controller locator discoveries. On domain controllers, the service enables pass-through authentication for other domain controllers by forwarding pass-through authentication requests to the destination domain controller, where the logon credentials are validated. If this service is turned off, the computer will not operate properly in a domain. Specifically, it can deny NTLM authentication requests and, in the case of a domain controller, will not be discoverable by client machines. You should set this service to start automatically.

■ **NetMeeting Remote Desktop Sharing**   Allows authorized users to remotely access your Windows desktop from another PC over a corporate intranet by using Microsoft NetMeeting. The service must be explicitly enabled by NetMeeting and can be disabled in NetMeeting or shut down via a Windows tray icon. Disabling the service unloads the NetMeeting display driver used for application sharing. You should disable this service unless you are using NetMeeting for business needs.

■ **Network Connections**   Manages objects in the Network and Dial-Up Connections folder, in which you can view both network and remote connections. This service takes care of network configuration (client side) and displays the status in the notification area on the desktop (the area on the taskbar to the right of the taskbar buttons). You can also access configuration parameters through this service. Disabling this service will prevent you from configuring your LAN settings and group policies with undefined behavior. You should set this service to start manually.

■ **Network DDE**   Provides network transport and security for dynamic data exchange (DDE) by applications running on the same computer or on different computers. This service is turned off by default, and it is started only when invoked by an application that uses Network DDE (NetDDE), such as Clipbrd.exe or DDEshare.exe. If you disable the service, any application that depends on NetDDE will time out when it tries to start the service. You should disable this service unless you use NetDDE-enabled applications. This is one of the few services that the User group can start and stop.

■ **Network DDE DSDM**   Manages shared dynamic data exchange and is used only by Network DDE to manage shared DDE conversations. You should disable this service unless you use NetDDE-enabled applications. This is one of the few services that the User group can start and stop.

■ **Network Location Awareness**   Collects and stores network configuration and location information and notifies applications when this information changes. Disabling this service will prevent the Windows XP Internet Connection Firewall from working. You should set this service to start manually.

■ **Network News Transfer Protocol (NNTP)**   Creates an NNTP-enabled news server. If the service is off, client computers will not be able to connect and read or retrieve posts. You should remove this service if you are not running an NNTP server by using Add/Remove Programs in Control Panel.

■   **NT LM Security Support Provider**   Enables users and applications to log on to the network by using the NTLM authentication protocol called through the NLTM SSP. If this service is stopped, users will not be able to log on to the domain when the NTLM SSP is called. Most applications do not call this Security Support Provider (SSP) directly. You should set this service to start manually.

■   **Performance Logs and Alerts**   Configures performance logs and alerts. This service is used to collect performance data automatically from local or remote computers that have been configured by using the Performance Logs and Alerts snap-in. If the service is stopped by a user, all currently running data collections will terminate and no scheduled collections will occur. You should set this service to Disabled unless you are monitoring the performance of a server.

■   **Plug and Play**   Enables a computer to recognize and adapt to hardware changes with little or no user input. With Plug and Play, a user can add or remove devices without any intricate knowledge of computer hardware and without being forced to manually configure hardware or the OS. Stopping or disabling this service will result in system instability. You should set this service to start automatically.

■   **Portable Music Serial Number**   Enables a Windows XP computer to retrieve information about portable music players attached to the computer as part of the Digital Rights Management (DRM) features in Windows XP. You should disable this service on computers that will be used with portable music devices, such as MP3 players.

■   **Print Server for Macintosh**   Enables Macintosh clients to route printing to a print spooler located on a computer running Windows 2000 Server. If this service is stopped, printing will be unavailable to Macintosh clients. If the computer does not have a printer used by Macintosh-based clients, you should remove this service by using Add/Remove Programs in Control Panel.

■   **Print Spooler**   Queues and manages print jobs locally and remotely. The print spooler is the heart of the Windows printing subsystem and controls all printing jobs. This service manages the print queues on the system and communicates with printer drivers and I/O components. If the Print Spooler service is disabled, you will not be able to print and other users will not be able to print to a printer attached to your computer. You should set this service to Manual, unless you are certain that no one will be printing to or from the computer.

■ **Protected Storage**   Provides protected storage for sensitive data, such as private keys, to prevent access by unauthorized services, processes, or users. Protected Storage (P-Store) is a set of software libraries that allows applications to fetch and retrieve security and other information from a personal storage location, hiding the implementation and details of the storage itself. The storage location provided by this service is secure and protected from modification. P-Store uses the Hash-Based Message Authentication Code (HMAC) and the SHA1 cryptographic hash function to encrypt the user's master key. This component requires no configuration. Disabling it will make information protected with this service inaccessible to you. P-Store is an earlier service that has been supplanted by the Data Protection API (DPAPI), which is currently the preferred service for protected storage. Unlike DPAPI, the interface to P-Store is not publicly exposed. You should set this service to start automatically.

■ **QoS Admission Control (RSVP)**   Provides network signaling and local traffic-control setup functionality for Quality of Service–aware programs and control applets. You should set this service to start manually.

■ **QoS RSVP**   Invoked when an application uses the Generic Quality of Service (GQoS) API requesting a specific quality of service on the end-to-end connection it uses. If disabled, QoS is not guaranteed to the application. The application must then decide whether to accept best-effort data transmission or refuse to run. You should set this service to start manually.

■ **Remote Access Auto Connection Manager**   Creates a connection to a remote network whenever a program references a remote DNS or NetBIOS name or address. This service detects an attempt to resolve the name of a remote computer or share, or an unsuccessful attempt to send packets to a remote computer or share. The service brings up a dialog box that offers to make a dial-up or VPN connection to the remote computer. Disabling the service has no effect on the rest of the OS. You should disable this service unless you have a specific reason to use it.

- **Remote Access Connection Manager**   Creates a network connection. This service manages the actual work of connecting, maintaining, and disconnecting dial-up and VPN connections from your computer to the Internet or other remote networks. Double-clicking a connection in the Network and Dial-Up Connections folder and selecting the Dial button generates a work request for this service that is queued with other requests for creating or destroying connections. This service will unload itself when no requests are pending. But in practice, the Network and Dial-Up Connections folder calls on this service to enumerate the set of connections and to display the status of each one. So unless the Network and Dial-Up Connections folder contains no connections, the service will always be running. The service cannot be disabled without breaking other portions of the OS, such as the Network and Dial-Up Connections folder. You should set this service to Manual, unless you are certain that you will not be using remote access connections, in which case you should disable the service.

- **Remote Desktop Help Sessions Manager**   Manages and controls the Remote Assistance feature of Windows XP. If this service is stopped or disabled, Remote Assistance will be unavailable. You should disable this service unless your organization uses the Remote Assistance feature, in which case you should set the service to start manually.

- **Remote Procedure Call (RPC)**   Provides the RPC endpoint mapper and other miscellaneous RPC services. If this service is turned off, the computer will not boot. You should set this service to start automatically.

- **Remote Procedure Call (RPC) Locator**   Provides the name services for RPC clients. This service helps locate RPC servers that support a given interface (also known as an *RPC named service*) within an enterprise. This service is turned off by default. Note that no OS component uses this service, although some applications might. You should set this service to start manually.

- **Remote Registry Service**   Allows remote registry manipulation. This service lets users connect to a remote registry and read and/or write keys to it—provided they have the required permissions. This service is usually used by remote administrators and performance monitor counters. If disabled, the service doesn't affect registry operations on the computer on which it runs; therefore, the local system will run in the same manner. Other computers or devices will no longer be able to connect to this computer's registry. You must be running this service in order to use some patch management tools, such as HFNetChk and MBSA. You should set this service to start manually.

- **Remote Storage Engine**   Migrates infrequently used data to tape. This service leaves a marker on disk, allowing the data to be recalled automatically from tape if you attempt to access the file. If you are not using the remote storage feature of Windows 2000 or Windows XP, you should disable this service. Otherwise, you should set it to start up manually.

- **Remote Storage File**   Manages operations on remotely stored files. If you are not using the remote storage feature of Windows 2000, you should disable this service.

- **Remote Storage Media**   Controls the media used to store data remotely. If you are not using the remote storage feature of Windows 2000, you should disable this service.

- **Remote Storage Notification**   Enables Remote Storage to notify you when you have accessed an offline file. Because it takes longer to access a file that has been moved to tape, Remote Storage will notify you if you are attempting to read a file that has been migrated and will allow you to cancel the request. If this service is turned off, you will not receive any additional notification when you try to open offline files. Nor will you be able to cancel an operation that involves an offline file. If you are not using the remote storage feature of Windows 2000, you should disable this service.

- **Removable Storage**   Manages removable media drives and libraries. This service maintains a catalog of identifying information for removable media used by a system, including tapes, CDs, and so on. This service is used by features such as Backup and Remote Storage to handle media cataloging and automation. This service stops itself when there is no work to do. If you are not using the remote storage feature of Windows 2000, you should disable this service.

- **Routing and Remote Access**   Offers routing services in LAN and WAN environments, including VPN services. If this service is turned off, incoming remote access and VPN connections, dial-on-demand connections, and routing protocols will not be available. In a routing context, Routing and Remote Access Service (RRAS) drives the TCP/IP stack-forwarding engine. The forwarding code can be enabled outside the service for various reasons, most notably Internet Connection Sharing (ICS). You should set this service to start manually.

■ **RunAs Service**   Allows you to run specific tools and programs with different permissions than your current logon provides. This service is called the *Secondary Logon Service* in Windows XP. You should set this service to start automatically.

■ **Security Accounts Manager**   Startup of this service signals to other services that the Security Accounts Manager (SAM) subsystem is ready to accept requests. This service should not be disabled. Doing so will prevent other services in the system from being notified when the SAM is ready, which can in turn cause those services to not start correctly.

■ **Server**   Provides RPC support, file print sharing, and named pipe sharing over the network. The Server service allows the sharing of your local resources (such as disks and printers) so that other users on the network can access them. It also allows named pipe communication between applications running on other computers and your computer, which is used for RPC. You should set this service to start automatically. Disabling this service results in the following:

❑ An inability to share files and printers on your computer with other computers on the network

❑ An inability of your computer to service RPC requests

❑ An inability to communicate between machines via named pipes

■ **Simple Mail Transfer Protocol (SMTP)**   Transports e-mail across the network. The SMTP service is used as an e-mail submission and relay agent. It can accept and queue e-mail for remote destinations and retry at specified intervals. Windows domain controllers use the SMTP service for intersite e-mail-based replication. The Collaboration Data Objects (CDO) for Windows 2000 COM components can use the SMTP service to submit and queue outbound e-mail. If you are not using this service, you should remove it by using Add/Remove Programs in Control Panel.

- **Single Instance Storage (SIS) Groveler** An integral component of Remote Installation Services (RIS). Although the SIS Groveler is installed by default in Windows server installations, it is set to Disabled unless you either add the RIS component from Add/Remove Windows Components in Control Panel or select it when initially installing the OS. If the service is turned off, RIS installation images will expand to their full image size and you will not be able to conserve space on the hard drive. You should remove the RIS service by using Add/Remove Programs in Control Panel if the computer is not a RIS server.

- **Site Server ILS Service** As part of IIS, this service scans TCP/IP stacks and updates directories with the most current user information. Windows 2000 is the last version of the OS to support the Site Server Internet Locator Service (ILS). You should remove this service by using Add/Remove Programs in Control Panel if you are not using it on your Web server.

- **Smart Card** Manages and controls access to a smart card inserted into a smart card reader attached to the computer. The smart card subsystem is based on personal computer/smart card (PC/SC) consortium standards for accessing information on smart card devices. Disabling the smart card subsystem will result in a loss of smart card support in the system. You should set this service to Disabled unless the computer uses smart cards for authentication, in which case, you should set the service to start manually.

- **Smart Card Helper** Provides support for earlier smart card readers attached to the computer. This component is designed to provide enumeration services for the smart card subsystem so that earlier non–Plug and Play smart card reader devices can be supported. Turning off this service will remove support for non–Plug and Play readers. You should set this service to Disabled unless the computer uses smart cards for authentication, in which case, you should set the service to start manually.

- **SNMP Service** Allows incoming Simple Network Management Protocol (SNMP) requests to be serviced by the local computer. SNMP includes agents that monitor activity in network devices and report to the network console workstation. If the service is turned off, the computer no longer responds to SNMP requests. If the computer is being monitored by network management tools, the tools will not be able to collect data from the computer or control its functionality via SNMP. If you are not monitoring the computer with SNMP, you should remove this service by using Add/Remove Programs in Control Panel.

- **SNMP Trap Service**   Receives SNMP trap messages generated by local or remote SNMP agents and forwards the messages to SNMP management programs running on the computer. If the service is turned off, SNMP applications will not receive SNMP traps that they are registered to receive. If you are using a computer to monitor network devices or server applications via SNMP traps, you might miss significant system occurrences. If you are not monitoring the computer with SNMP, you should remove this service by using Add/Remove Programs in Control Panel.

- **SSPD Discovery Services**   Enables the discovery of Universal Plug and Play (UPnP) devices in Windows XP. You should set this service to Disabled, unless you actively use UPnP devices on your network.

- **Still Image Service**   Loads necessary drivers for imaging devices (such as scanners and digital still-image cameras), manages events for those devices and associated applications, and maintains device state. The service is needed to capture events generated by imaging devices (such as button presses and connections). If the service is not running, events from the imaging devices connected to the computer will not be captured and processed.

- **System Event Notification (SENS)**   Tracks system events, such as Windows logon network events and power events, and notifies COM+ Event System subscribers of these events. SENS is an AutoStarted service that depends on COM+ Event System service. Disabling this service has the following effects:

    ❏ The Win32 APIs *IsNetworkAlive()* and *IsDestinationReachable()* will not work well. These APIs are mostly used by mobile applications and portable computers.

    ❏ SENS interfaces do not work properly. In particular, SENS's Logon/Logoff notifications will not work.

    ❏ Microsoft Internet Explorer 5.0 or later uses SENS on portable computers to trigger when the user goes offline or online (by triggering the Work Offline prompt).

    ❏ SyncMgr (Mobsync.exe) will not work properly. SyncMgr depends on connectivity information and Network Connect/Disconnect and Logon/Logoff notifications from SENS.

    ❏ COM+ Event System will try to notify SENS of some events but will not be able to.

■   **System Restore Service**   Performs the automatic system restore (ASR) function in Windows XP. ASR is configured in the System applet in Control Panel. You should set this service to start manually, unless you are certain that you will not be using it.

■   **Task Scheduler**   Enables a program to run at a designated time. This service allows you to perform automated tasks on a chosen computer. Task Scheduler is started each time the OS is started. If Task Scheduler is disabled, jobs that are scheduled to run will not run at their designated time or interval. You should set this service to start manually.

■   **TCP/IP NetBIOS Helper Service**   Enables support for the NetBIOS over TCP/IP (NetBT) service and NetBIOS name resolution. This service is an extension of the kernel mode NetBT. It should be considered an integral part of NetBT, rather than a normal service. This service does two things for NetBT, which you cannot do in kernel mode:

❑   Performs DNS name resolution

❑   Pings a set of IP addresses and returns a list of reachable IP addresses

If this service is disabled, NetBT's clients—including the Workstation, Server, Netlogon, and Messenger services—could stop responding. As a result, you might not be able to share files and printers, you might not be able to log on, and Group Policy will no longer be applied. You should set this service to start automatically.

■   **Telephony**   Provides Telephony API (TAPI) support for programs that control telephony devices and IP-based voice connections on the local computer and through the LAN on servers that are running the service. The telephony service cannot be stopped if another dependent service such as Remote Access Service (RAS) is active. If no other dependent service is running and you stop the telephony service, it will be restarted when any application makes an initialization call to the TAPI interface. If the service is disabled, any program that depends upon it, including modem support and Internet Connection Firewall (ICF), will not be able to run. You should set this service to start manually.

- **Telnet**   Allows a remote user to log on to the system and run console programs by using the command line. A computer running the Telnet service can support connections from various TCP/IP telnet clients. You should disable this service unless you use the Telnet service to manage your computer.

- **Terminal Services**   Provides a multisession environment that allows client devices to access a virtual interactive logon to a Windows XP or Windows 2000 Server. Terminal Services allows multiple users to be connected interactively to the computer in their own isolated session. You should set this service to start automatically unless you are certain that you will not be using Windows Terminal Services, Remote Desktop, Fast-User Switching, or Remote Assistance, in which case you can disable this service.

- **Terminal Services Licensing**   Installs a license server and provides registered client licenses when connecting to a Windows 2000 terminal server. If this service is turned off, the server will be unavailable to issue terminal server licenses to clients when they are requested. If another license server is discoverable on a domain controller in the forest, the requesting terminal server will attempt to use it. You should remove this service by using Add/Remove Programs in Control Panel.

- **Themes**   Provides management themes in the Windows XP user interface. You should set this service to start automatically.

- **Trivial FTP Daemon**   Trivial File Transfer Protocol (TFTP) is an integral part of Remote Installation Services. To disable this service, uninstall RIS. Disabling the Trivial FTP Daemon service directly will cause RIS to malfunction. You should remove RIS by using Add/Remove Programs in Control Panel if the computer is not a RIS server.

- **Uninterruptible Power Supply**   Manages communications with an uninterruptible power supply (UPS) connected to the computer by a serial port. If this service is turned off, communications with the UPS will be lost. You should disable this service unless you have a UPS device connection to the computer.

- **Universal Plug and Play Device Host**   Manages the operation of UPnP devices on the local computer. Disabling this service will prevent the use of UPnP devices; however, regular Plug and Play devices will continue to function normally. You should disable this service unless your network actively uses UPnP devices.

- **Upload Manager**   Manages synchronous and asynchronous file transfers on Windows XP computers between clients and servers on the network. If this service is stopped, synchronous and asynchronous file transfers between clients and servers on the network will not occur.

- **Utility Manager**   Starts and configures accessibility tools from one window. Utility Manager allows faster access to some accessibility tools and displays the status of the tools or devices that it controls. This service saves users time because an administrator can designate that certain features start when Windows 2000 starts. Utility Manager includes three built-in accessibility tools: Magnifier, Narrator, and On-Screen Keyboard.

- **Web Client**   Enables Windows XP computers to modify Internet-based or intranet-based files, including Web-Based Distributed Authoring and Versioning (WebDAV) extensions for HTTP. You should set this service to start manually.

- **Windows Audio**   Enables Windows XP to manage audio devices. You cannot disable this service.

- **Windows Image Acquisition**   Manages the retrieval of images from digital cameras and scanners from devices attached to Windows XP computers. You should set this service to Disabled unless you use these devices on computers.

- **Windows Installer**   Installs, repairs, or removes software according to instructions contained in .msi files provided with the applications. If disabled, the installation, removal, repair, and modification of applications that make use of the Windows Installer will fail. You should set this service to start manually.

- **Windows Internet Name Service (WINS)**   Enables NetBIOS name resolution. Presence of the WINS server(s) is crucial for locating the network resources identified by using NetBIOS names. WINS servers are required unless all domains have been upgraded to Active Directory and all computers on the network are running Windows 2000. If you are not running a WINS server on the computer, you should remove this service by using Add/Remove Programs in Control Panel.

- **Windows Management Instrumentation (WMI)**   Provides system management information. WMI is an infrastructure for building management applications and instrumentation. WMI provides access to the management data through a number of interfaces, including COM API, scripts, and command-line interfaces. If this service is turned off, WMI information will be unavailable.

- **Windows Management Instrumentation Driver Extensions** Tracks all the drivers that have registered Windows Management Instrumentation (WMI) information to publish. If the service is turned off, clients cannot access the WMI information published by drivers. However, if the WMI APIs detect that the service is not running, the APIs will attempt to restart the service.

- **Windows Time Service (W32Time)**   Sets the computer clock. W32Time maintains date and time synchronization on all computers running on a Microsoft Windows network. It uses the Network Time Protocol (NTP) to synchronize computer clocks so that an accurate clock value, or timestamp, can be assigned to network validation and resource access requests. The implementation of NTP and the integration of time providers make W32Time a reliable and scalable time service for enterprise administrators. For computers not joined to a domain, W32Time can be configured to synchronize time with an external time source. If this service is turned off, the time setting for local computers will not be synchronized with any time service in the Windows domain or with an externally configured time service. You should set this service to start automatically.

- **Wireless Zero Configuration**   Provides the automatic configuration of supported 802.11 wireless network adapters in Windows XP. You should set this service to start automatically, unless you will not be using wireless network adapters on the computer, in which case, you should disable the service.

- **Workstation**   Provides network connections and communications. The Workstation service is a user-mode wrapper for the Microsoft Networks redirector. The service loads and performs configuration functions for the redirector, provides support for making network connections to remote servers, provides support for the Windows Network (WNet) APIs, and furnishes redirector statistics. If this service is turned off, no network connections can be made to remote computers using Microsoft Networks.

- **World Wide Web Publishing Service**   Provides HTTP services for applications on the Windows platform. The service depends on the IIS administration service and kernel TCP/IP support. If this service is turned off, the OS will no longer be able to act as a Web server. See also the "IIS Admin Service" entry in this list.

Best Practices

■   **Disable unused services.**   For Windows 2000 and Windows XP computers, carefully evaluate which services are required to support your organization's software applications. Disable any services you are certain you will not need in order to minimize the potential attack surface of the computer.

These are the recommended minimum services to run:

Service	Setting
COM+ Event System	Manual
DHCP Client	Automatic (if needed)
DNS Client	Automatic
Event Log	Automatic
Logical Disk Manager	Automatic
Logical Disk Manager Administrative Service	Manual
Net Logon	Automatic
Network Connections	Manual
Performance Logs and Alerts	Manual
Plug and Play	Automatic
Protected Storage	Automatic
Remote Procedure Call (RPC)	Automatic
Remote Registry Service	Automatic (required for Microsoft Baseline Security Analyzer)
Security Accounts Manager	Automatic
Server	Automatic
System Event Notification (SENS)	Automatic
TCP/IP NetBIOS Helper Service	Automatic
Windows Management Instrumentation Driver Extensions	Manual
Windows Time Service (W32Time)	Automatic
Workstation	Automatic

Domain Controllers require these additional services:

Service	Setting
Distributed File System (DFS)	Automatic
DNS Server	Automatic
File Replication	Automatic
Kerberos Key Distribution Center	Automatic
NTLM Security Support Provider	Automatic
Remote Procedure Call (RPC) Locator	Automatic

Additional Information

■ *Inside Microsoft Windows 2000, Third Edition* (Microsoft Press, 2000)

■ Services on MSDN (*http://msdn.microsoft.com/library/en-us/dllproc/base/services.asp*)

■ 288129: "How to Grant Users Rights to Manage Services in Windows 2000"

■ 327618: "Security, Services, and the Interactive Desktop"

> **Note**   The previous two articles can be accessed through the Microsoft Knowledge Base. Go to *http://support.microsoft.com* and enter the article number in the Search The Knowledge Base text box.

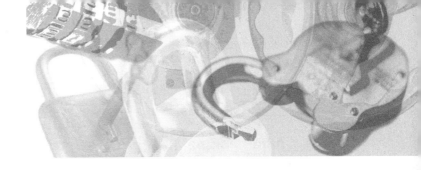

9

Implementing TCP/IP Security

TCP/IP is an industry-standard suite of protocols designed to facilitate communication between computers on large networks. TCP/IP was developed in 1969 by the U.S. Department of Defense Advanced Research Projects Agency (DARPA), as the result of a resource-sharing experiment called ARPANET (Advanced Research Projects Agency Network). Since 1969, ARPANET has grown into a worldwide community of networks known as the Internet, and TCP/IP has become the primary protocol used on all networks. Unfortunately, TCP/IP was not designed with security in mind and thus has very few security components by default. Consequently, it is often a source of network vulnerabilities. On your Microsoft Windows 2000 and Windows XP computers, you can secure the TCP/IP protocol in several ways, which include securing the TCP/IP stack itself and using IP Security (IPSec). We will examine both techniques in this chapter.

Securing TCP/IP

You cannot successfully secure computer networks without knowing how TCP/IP works. Nearly all computers today use TCP/IP as their primary network communication protocol. Thus, without physical access to a computer, an attacker must use TCP/IP to attack it. Consequently, TCP/IP security is often your first line of defense against attackers attempting to compromise your organization's network and therefore should be part of any defense-in-depth strategy for securing networks. You can secure the TCP/IP protocol in Windows 2000 and Windows XP to protect a computer against common attacks, such as denial-of-service attacks, and to help prevent attacks on applications that use the TCP/IP protocol.

Understanding Internet Layer Protocols

TCP/IP primarily operates at two levels in the OSI model: the Internet layer and the transport layer. The Internet layer is responsible for addressing, packaging, and routing functions. The core protocols of the Internet layer include the Internet Protocol (IP), Address Resolution Protocol (ARP), and Internet Control Message Protocol (ICMP):

- **IP**   A routable protocol responsible for logical addressing, routing, and the fragmentation and reassembly of packets

- **ARP**   Resolves IP addresses to Media Access Control (MAC) addresses and vice versa

- **ICMP**   Provides diagnostic functions and reporting errors for unsuccessful delivery of IP packets

The TCP/IP protocol suite includes a series of interconnected protocols called the *core protocols*. All other applications and protocols in the TCP/IP protocol suite rely on the basic services provided by several protocols, including IP, ARP, and ICMP.

IP

IP is a connectionless, unreliable datagram protocol primarily responsible for addressing and routing packets between hosts. *Connectionless* means that a session is not established to manage the exchange data. *Unreliable* means that delivery is not guaranteed. IP always makes a best-effort attempt to deliver a packet. An IP packet might be lost, delivered out of sequence, duplicated, or delayed. IP does not attempt to recover from these types of errors. The acknowledgment of packets delivered and the recovery of lost packets is the responsibility of a higher-layer protocol, such as TCP. IP is defined in RFC 791.

An IP packet consists of an IP header and an IP payload. The IP header contains information about the IP packet itself, and the IP payload is the data being encapsulated by the IP protocol to be transmitted to the receiving host. The following list describes the key fields in the IP header:

- **Source IP Address**   The IP address of the source of the IP datagram.

- **Destination IP Address**   The IP address of the destination of the IP datagram.

■   **Identification**   Used to identify a specific IP datagram and all fragments of a specific IP datagram if fragmentation occurs.

■   **Protocol**   Informs IP at the destination host whether to pass the packet up to TCP, UDP, ICMP, or other protocols.

■   **Checksum**   A simple mathematical computation used to verify the integrity of the IP header. If the IP header does not match the checksum, the receiving host will disregard the packet. This checksum does not include any information outside the IP header.

■   **Time To Live (TTL)**   Designates the number of networks on which the datagram is allowed to travel before being discarded by a router. The TTL is set by the sending host and used to prevent packets from endlessly circulating on an IP network. When forwarding an IP packet, routers decrease the TTL by at least one.

■   **Fragmentation And Reassembly**   If a router receives an IP packet that is too large for the network to which the packet is being forwarded, IP fragments the original packet into smaller packets that fit on the downstream network. When the packets arrive at their final destination, IP on the destination host reassembles the fragments into the original payload. This process is referred to as fragmentation and reassembly. Fragmentation can occur in environments that have a mix of networking technologies, such as Ethernet and Token Ring. The fragmentation and reassembly works as follows:

1.   When an IP packet is sent, the sending host places a unique value in the Identification field.

2.   The IP packet is received at the router. If the router determines that the Maximum Transmission Unit (MTU) of the network onto which the packet is to be forwarded is smaller than the size of the IP packet, the router fragments the original IP payload into multiple packets, each of which is smaller than the receiving network's MTU size. Each fragment is sent with its own IP header that contains the following:

The original Identification field, which identifies all fragments that belong together.

The More Fragments flag, which indicates that other fragments follow. The More Fragments flag is not set on the last fragment because no other fragments follow it.

The Fragment Offset field, which indicates the position of the fragment relative to the original IP payload.

3. When the fragments are received by the destination host, they are identified by the Identification field as belonging together. The Fragment Offset field is then used to reassemble the fragments into the original IP payload.

ARP

Address Resolution Protocol performs IP address–to–MAC address resolution for outgoing packets. As each outgoing addressed IP datagram is encapsulated in a frame, source and destination MAC addresses must be added. Determining the destination MAC address for each frame is the responsibility of ARP. ARP is defined in RFC 826.

ICMP

Internet Control Message Protocol provides troubleshooting facilities and error reporting for packets that are undeliverable. For example, if IP is unable to deliver a packet to the destination host, ICMP sends a Destination Unreachable message to the source host. Table 9-1 shows the most common ICMP messages.

Table 9-1 Common ICMP Messages

Message	Description
Echo Request	Troubleshooting message used to check IP connectivity to a desired host. The Ping utility sends ICMP Echo Request messages.
Echo Reply	Response to an ICMP Echo Request.
Redirect	Sent by a router to inform a sending host of a better route to a destination IP address.
Source Quench	Sent by a router to inform a sending host that its IP datagrams are being dropped because of congestion at the router. The sending host then lowers its transmission rate.
Destination Unreachable	Sent by a router or the destination host to inform the sending host that the datagram cannot be delivered.

When the result of an ICMP request is a Destination Unreachable message, a specific message is returned to the requestor detailing why the Destination Unreachable ICMP message was sent. Table 9-2 describes the most common of these messages.

Table 9-2   Common ICMP Destination Unreachable Messages

Unreachable Message	Description
Host Unreachable	Sent by an IP router when a route to the destination IP address cannot be found
Protocol Unreachable	Sent by the destination IP node when the Protocol field in the IP header cannot be matched with an IP client protocol currently loaded
Port Unreachable	Sent by the destination IP node when the destination port in the UDP header cannot be matched with a process using that port
Fragmentation Needed and DF Set	Sent by an IP router when fragmentation must occur but is not allowed because of the source node setting the Don't Fragment (DF) flag in the IP header

ICMP does not make IP a reliable protocol. ICMP attempts to report errors and provide feedback on specific conditions. ICMP messages are carried as unacknowledged IP datagrams and are themselves unreliable. ICMP is defined in RFC 792.

Understanding Transport Layer Protocols

The transport layer is responsible for providing session and datagram communication services over the IP protocol. The two core protocols of the transport layer are the Transmission Control Protocol (TCP) and User Datagram Protocol (UDP):

■   **TCP**   Provides a one-to-one, connection-oriented, reliable communications service. TCP is responsible for the establishment of a TCP connection, the sequencing and acknowledgment of packets sent, and the recovery of packets lost during transmission.

■   **UDP**   Provides a one-to-one or one-to-many, connectionless, unreliable communications service. UDP is used when the amount of data to be transferred is small (such as data that fits into a single packet), when the overhead of establishing a TCP connection is not desired, or when the applications or upper layer protocols provide reliable delivery.

How TCP Communication Works

When two computers communicate using TCP, the computer that initiates the communication is known as the client, regardless of whether it is running a client or server OS, and the responding computer is known as the host. If the client and host are on the same network segment, the client computer first uses ARP to resolve the host's MAC address by sending a broadcast for the IP address of the host. Once the client has the MAC address of the host, it can commence communication to the port on the host by using the transport layer protocol specified by the application. There are 65,535 TCP and UDP ports, beginning with 0. Ports 1023 and below are regarded as well-known ports for legacy reasons, and ports above 1023 are known as high ports. Functionally, no difference exists between the well-known ports and the high ports. On the host, an application is bound to a certain port it specifies and is initialized in a listening state, where it waits for requests from a client. When the client initiates a connection to a TCP port, a defined series of packets, known as a *three-way handshake* and illustrated in Figure 9-1, constructs a session for reliable packet transmission. The steps for establishing connections follow:

1.   The client sends the host a synchronization (SYN) message that contains the host's port and the client's Initial Sequence Number (ISN). TCP sequence numbers are 32 bits in length and used to ensure session reliability by facilitating out-of-order packet reconstruction.

2.   The host receives the message and sends back its own SYN message and an acknowledgement (ACK) message, which includes the host's ISN and the client's ISN incremented by 1.

3.   The client receives the host's response and sends an ACK, which includes the ISN from the host incremented by 1. After the host receives the packet, the TCP session is established.

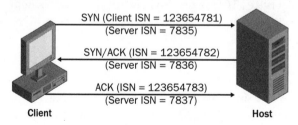

Figure 9-1   Three-way TCP handshake

When the communication between the client and host is complete, the session is closed once the following steps occur:

1.   The client sends a finalization (FIN) message to the host. The session is now *half closed*. The client no longer sends data but can still receive data from the host. Upon receiving this FIN message, the host enters a passive closed state.

2.   The host sends an ACK message, which includes the client's sequence number augmented by 1:

3.   The server sends its own FIN message. The client receives the FIN message and returns an ACK message that includes the host's sequence number augmented by 1.

4.   Upon receiving this ACK message, the host closes the connection and releases the memory the connection was using.

The Netstat.exe Command

To see port activity on your Windows 2000 or Windows XP computers, you can use the Netstat.exe command. Netstat.exe will also show the status of TCP ports. The syntax for using Netstat.exe follows, and Table 9-3 describes the options available when using this command.

```
NETSTAT [-a] [-e] [-n] [-o] [-s] [-p proto] [-r] [interval]
```

Table 9-3   Netstat.exe Options

Option	Description
-a	Displays all connections and listening ports.
-e	Displays Ethernet statistics. This can be combined with the -s option.
-n	Displays addresses and port numbers in numerical form.
-o	Displays the owning process ID (PID) associated with each connection. This option exists in Windows XP only.
-p *protocol*	Shows connections for the protocol specified by *protocol*, which can be TCP, UDP, TCPv6, or UDPv6. If used with the -s option to display per-protocol statistics, the value for protocol can be IP, ICMP, TCP, or UDP.
-r	Displays the routing table.
-s	Displays per-protocol statistics. By default, statistics are shown for IP, ICMP, TCP, and UDP.
interval	Determines the refresh interval for the data displayed by Netstat.

> **Tip**   To find the process associated with a given active port in Windows XP, you can locate the PID associated with the port by typing **netstat –aon**. You can then find the process associated with the PID by typing **tasklist –FI "PID eq *XX*"**, where *XX* is the PID of the process.
>
>   As mentioned in Table 9-3, the -o option of Netstat.exe is not available in Windows 2000; however, you can download utilities from the Internet that have similar functionality and will run on Windows 2000.

Common Threats to TCP/IP

Several types of threats to TCP/IP can either compromise network security or lead to information disclosure. Although these attacks are more prevalent on the Internet, you should be concerned about them on internal computers as well. These common threats include:

- Port scanning

- Spoofing

- Denial of service

Port Scanning

In order to communicate with TCP/IP, applications running on host computers must listen for incoming TCP or UDP connections, and host operating systems must listen for broadcast and other network maintenance traffic. By scanning a computer to see what ports a host is listening for and what protocols it uses, an attacker might be able to locate weaknesses in the host that he can later use to attack the computer. Attackers often perform port scans to reveal this information. Several types of port scans exist:

- **Ping sweeps**   An attacker might use an automated tool to send ICMP Echo Request packets to entire networks or subnets. By default, all active hosts will respond. This lets the attacker know that the host exists and is active. An attacker can also analyze the structure of the ICMP packet to determine the OS running on the host.

- **Port enumeration**   At attacker might want to enumerate all the services running on a host computer. Because hosts must respond to client computers to carry out legitimate operations, attackers can exploit this behavior to obtain critical information.

Tip   You can download a command-line port-scanning tool from Microsoft called Portqry.exe. This tool, found at *http:// www.microsoft.com/downloads/release.asp?ReleaseID=37344*, tests the security of hosts and performs network diagnostics. In addition, many free utilities that can perform port scans are available on the Internet.

■   **Banner grabbing**   Many common services respond with banners when sessions are initiated or requested. These banners contain basic information on the service or server. For example, by using Telnet to connect to port 25 of a Windows 2000 server running the default Simple Mail Transfer Protocol (SMTP) service, you can retrieve this banner:

```
220 SFOFS001.finance.woodgrovebank.com Microsoft ESMTP MAIL Service,
    Version: 5.0.2195.5329 ready at Sat, 12 Oct 2002 16:18:44 -0800
```

From interpreting this banner, you can determine that the target server is named SFOFS001. SFOFS001 is probably a file server running Windows 2000 with Service Pack 3 installed and is physically located in the Pacific Time zone—most likely in San Francisco. The server is running a built-in instance of the SMTP service, which is installed as part of Microsoft Internet Information Services (IIS) 5.0. Knowing that IIS is installed by default in Windows 2000 and that this server does not appear to be a Web server, it is likely that the server has a default installation of Windows 2000.

Important   Changing service banners can also break applications that rely on them for information about the server they are communicating with. Furthermore, changing banners can break an application running on the computer that uses the information from service banners from other services running on the computer.

■   **Half scan**   This type of port scanning does not follow the precise TCP three-way handshake protocol and leaves TCP connections half open. Because most host system logs do not log packets until the host receives the final ACK, half scans can enable an attack to gain information about a host without being detected.

Spoofing

Attackers might want to spoof, or mimic, a legitimate TCP/IP packets to attack a computer or network. Usually spoofing a packet requires that the attacker handcraft a TCP/IP packet and send it to either the host he wants to attack or a third party host that he has previously compromised in order to attack the targeted host or network. Many types of spoofing attacks exist. These following three are among the most well-known:

- **Land attack**   Takes advantage of security flaws in the many implementations of TCP/IP. To carry out a land attack, an attacker opens a legitimate TCP session by sending a SYN packet but spoofs the packet so that the source address and port and the destination address and port match the host IP address and the port the packet is being sent to.

  For example, to carry out a land attack on an e-mail server with the IP address 192.168.183.200, an attacker can create a packet with the source address of 192.168.183.200 and the source port of 25, rather than using the source address and port of his own computer. Now the source and destination addresses will be the same, as will the source and destination ports. If not patched to protect against the land attack, the e-mail will continually attempt to make a connection with itself on its own port 25, resulting in a denial-of-service situation.

- **Smurf attack**   Uses a third-party network to carry out a denial-of-service attack on a host system by spoofing an ICMP Echo Request packet. The attacker obtains the host IP address and creates a forged ICMP Echo Request packet that looks like it came from the host IP address. The attacker sends thousands of copies of the spoofed packet to the broadcast address on an improperly secured third-party network. This results in every computer in the third-party network responding to each spoofed packet by sending an ICMP Echo Reply packet to the host system. The amount of ICMP traffic that is generated by this attack will deny legitimate traffic from reaching the target host.

- **Session hijacking**   Takes advantage of flaws in many implementations of the TCP/IP protocol by anticipating TCP sequence numbers to hijack a session with a host. To hijack a TCP/IP session, the attacker creates a legitimate TCP session to the targeted host, records the TCP sequence numbers used by the host, and then computes the round-trip time (RTT). This step often takes many exchanges in sequence. Using the stored sequence numbers and the RTT, the attacker can potentially predict future TCP sequence numbers. The attacker can then send a spoofed packet to another host, using the targeted host IP address as the source address and the next sequence number. If successful, the second host system will believe the packet originated from the targeted system and accept packets from the attacker. This type of attack is particularly effective when the second host trusts the targeted host.

More Info   IP spoofing by predicting TCP/IP sequence numbers was the basis for the famous Christmas 1994 attack on Tsutomu Shimomura by Kevin Mitnick. The attack is chronicled in the book *Takedown: The Pursuit and Capture of Kevin Mitnick, America's Most Wanted Computer Outlaw—By The Man Who Did It* (Hyperion, 1996).

Denial of Service

Denial-of-service attackers attempt to exploit the way the TCP/IP protocol works to prevent legitimate traffic from reaching the host system. One of the most common types of denial-of-service attacks is a SYN flood. A SYN flood attempts to create a situation in which the host system's maximum TCP connection pool is locked in a half-open state, thus denying legitimate traffic to and from the host. To carry out a SYN flood, the attacker creates a spoofed IP packet with an unreachable IP address for a source address, or she clips the receive wire on the Ethernet cable she is using. When the host receives the packet, it responds by sending a SYN/ACK response and waits for the final ACK in the TCP three-way handshake, which never comes. The session will remain in the half-open state until the predefined time-out is reached. This process is repeated until no more TCP sessions are allowed by the host system, which then cannot create any new sessions.

Configuring TCP/IP Security in Windows 2000 and Windows XP

The remainder of this section presents several ways you can secure your Windows 2000 and Windows XP computers against attacks on TCP/IP, including basic TCP/IP binding configurations, custom registry settings, and TCP/IP filtering.

Implementing Basic TCP/IP Security

Three basic settings, outlined in the following list, will increase the security of TCP/IP for each network adapter in Windows 2000 and Windows XP. You will need to ensure that each of these settings is compatible with your network and the applications that either run on the computer or must be accessible from the computer.

- **File And Printer Sharing For Microsoft Networks** By default, File and Printer Sharing for Microsoft Networks is bound on all network interfaces. The File and Printer Sharing for Microsoft Networks component enables other computers on a network to access resources on your computer. By removing the binding to File and Printer Sharing for Microsoft Networks from a network interface, you can prevent other computers from enumerating or connecting to files and printers that have been shared through that network interface. After removing this binding from a network interface, the computer will no longer listen for direct Server Message Block (SMB) connections on TCP ports 139 or 445 of that interface. Removing this setting will not interfere with the computer's ability to connect to other shared files or printers. You can unbind File and Printer Sharing for Microsoft Networks in the Network And Dial-Up Connections Control Panel applet or on the properties of the network interface.

- **NetBIOS Over TCP/IP** Windows 2000 and Windows XP support file and printer sharing traffic by using the SMB protocol directly hosted on TCP. This differs from earlier operating systems, in which SMB traffic requires the NetBIOS over TCP/IP (NetBT) protocol to work on a TCP/IP transport. If both the direct hosted and NetBT interfaces are enabled, both methods are tried at the same time and the first to respond is used. This allows Windows to function properly with operating systems that do not support direct hosting of SMB traffic. NetBIOS over TCP/IP traditionally uses the following ports:

NetBIOS name	137/UDP
NetBIOS name	137/TCP
NetBIOS datagram	138/UDP
NetBIOS session	139/TCP

> **Note**   Direct hosted "NetBIOS-less" SMB traffic uses port 445 (TCP and UDP). If you disable NetBIOS Over TCP/IP (NetBT) and unbind File And Printer Sharing For Microsoft Networks, the computer will no longer respond to any NetBIOS requests. Applications and services that depend on NetBT will no longer function once NetBT is disabled. Therefore, verify that your clients and applications no longer need NetBT support before you disable it.

■ **DNS Registration**   By default, Windows 2000 and Windows XP computers attempt to automatically register their host names and IP address mappings in the Domain Name System (DNS) for each adapter. If your computer is using a public DNS server or cannot reach the DNS server, as is often seen when the computer resides in a screened subnet, you should remove this behavior on each adapter.

Configuring Registry Settings

Denial-of-service attacks are network attacks aimed at making a computer or a particular service on a computer unavailable to network users. Denial-of-service attacks can be difficult to defend against. To help prevent denial-of-service attacks, you can harden the TCP/IP protocol stack on Windows 2000 and Windows XP computers. You should harden the TCP/IP stack against denial-of-service attacks, even on internal networks, to prevent denial-of-service attacks that originate from inside the network as well as on computers attached to public networks. You can harden the TCP/IP stack on a Windows 2000 or Windows XP computer by customizing these registry values, which are stored in the registry key HKLM\System\CurrentControlSet\Services\Tcpip\Parameters\:

■ **EnableICMPRedirect**   When ICMP redirects are disabled (by setting the value to 0), attackers cannot carry out attacks that require a host to redirect the ICMP-based attack to a third party.

■ **SynAttackProtect**   Enables SYN flood protection in Windows 2000 and Windows XP. You can set this value to 0, 1, or 2. The default setting, 0, provides no protection. Setting the value to 1 will activate SYN/ACK protection contained in the TCPMaxPortsExhausted, TCP-MaxHalfOpen, and TCPMaxHalfOpenRetried values. Setting the value to 2 will protect against SYN/ACK attacks by more aggressively timing out open and half-open connections.

- **TCPMaxConnectResponseRetransmissions**   Determines how many times TCP retransmits an unanswered SYN/ACK message. TCP retransmits acknowledgments until the number of retransmissions specified by this value is reached.

- **TCPMaxHalfOpen**   Determines how many connections the server can maintain in the half-open state before TCP/IP initiates SYN flooding attack protection. This entry is used only when SYN flooding attack protection is enabled on this server—that is, when the value of the SynAttackProtect entry is 1 or 2 and the value of the TCPMaxConnectResponseRetransmissions entry is at least 2.

- **TCPMaxHalfOpenRetired**   Determines how many connections the server can maintain in the half-open state even after a connection request has been retransmitted. If the number of connections exceeds the value of this entry, TCP/IP initiates SYN flooding attack protection. This entry is used only when SYN flooding attack protection is enabled on this server—that is, when the value of the SynAttackProtect entry is 1 and the value of the TCPMaxConnectResponseRetransmissions entry is at least 2.

- **TCPMaxPortsExhausted**   Determines how many connection requests the system can refuse before TCP/IP initiates SYN flooding attack protection. The system must refuse all connection requests when its reserve of open connection ports runs out. This entry is used only when SYN flooding attack protection is enabled on this server—that is, when the value of the SynAttackProtect entry is 1, and the value of the TCPMaxConnectResponseRetransmissions entry is at least 2.

- **TCPMaxDataRetransmissions**   Determines how many times TCP retransmits an unacknowledged data segment on an existing connection. TCP retransmits data segments until they are acknowledged or until the number of retransmissions specified by this value is reached.

- **EnableDeadGWDetect**   Determines whether the computer will attempt to detect dead gateways. When dead gateway detection is enabled (by setting this value to 1), TCP might ask IP to change to a backup gateway if a number of connections are experiencing difficulty. Backup gateways are defined in the TCP/IP configuration dialog box in Network Control Panel for each adapter. When you leave this setting enabled, it is possible for an attacker to redirect the server to a gateway of his choosing.

- **EnablePMTUDiscovery**   Determines whether path MTU discovery is enabled (1), in which TCP attempts to discover the largest packet size over the path to a remote host. When path MTU discovery is disabled (0), the path MTU for all TCP connections will be fixed at 576 bytes.

- **DisableIPSourceRouting**   Determines whether a computer allows clients to predetermine the route that packets take to their destination. When this value is set to 2, the computer will disable source routing for IP packets.

- **NoNameReleaseOnDemand**   Determines whether the computer will release its NetBIOS name if requested by another computer or a malicious packet attempting to hijack the computer's NetBIOS name.

- **PerformRouterDiscovery**   Determines whether the computer performs router discovery on this interface. Router discovery solicits router information from the network and adds the information retrieved to the route table. Setting this value to 0 will prevent the interface from performing router discovery.

Table 9-4 lists the registry entries that you can make to harden the TCP/IP stack on your Windows 2000 and Windows XP computers.

Table 9-4   Registry Settings to Harden TCP/IP

Value	Data (DWORD)
EnableICMPRedirect	0
SynAttackProtect	2
TCPMaxConnectResponseRetransmissions	2
TCPMaxHalfOpen	500
TCPMaxHalfOpenRetired	400
TCPMaxPortsExhausted	5
TCPMaxDataRetransmissions	3
EnableDeadGWDetect	0
EnablePMTUDiscovery	0
DisableIPSourceRouting	2
NoNameReleaseOnDemand	1
PerformRouterDiscovery	0

> **On the CD**   Tcpip_sec.vbs automatically configures the registry in Windows 2000 and Windows XP to use the settings for securing TCP/IP shown in Table 9-4. This file is located in the Tools\Scripts folder on the CD included with this book.

Additionally, you can secure the TCP/IP stack for Windows Sockets (Winsock) applications such as FTP servers and Web servers. The driver Afd.sys is responsible for connection attempts to Winsock applications. Afd.sys has been modified in Windows 2000 and Windows XP to support large numbers of connections in the half-open state without denying access to legitimate clients. Afd.sys can use dynamic backlog, which is configurable, rather than a static backlog. You can configure four parameters for the dynamic backlog:

- **EnableDynamicBacklog**   Switches between using a static backlog and a dynamic backlog. By default, this parameter is set to 0, which enables the static backlog. You should enable the dynamic backlog for better security on Winsock.

- **MinimumDynamicBacklog**   Controls the minimum number of free connections allowed on a listening Winsock endpoint. If the number of free connections drops below this value, a thread is queued to create additional free connections. Making this value too large (setting it to a number greater than 100) will degrade the performance of the computer.

- **MaximumDynamicBacklog**   Controls the maximum number of half-open and free connections to Winsock endpoints. If this value is reached, no additional free connections will be made.

- **DynamicBacklogGrowthDelta**   Controls the number of Winsock endpoints in each allocation pool requested by the computer. Setting this value too high can cause system resources to be unnecessarily occupied.

Each of these values must be added to the registry key HKLM\System\CurrentControlSet\Services\AFD\Parameters. Table 9-5 lists the parameters and the recommended levels of protection.

Table 9-5   Registry Settings to Harden Winsock

Value	Data (DWORD)
DynamicBacklogGrowthDelta	10
EnableDynamicBacklog	1
MinimumDynamicBacklog	20
MaximumDynamicBacklog	20,000

On the CD   Winsock_sec.vbs automatically configures the registry in Windows 2000 and Windows XP to use the settings for securing Winsock shown in Table 9-5. This file is located in the Tools\Scripts folder on the CD included with this book.

Using TCP/IP Filtering

Windows 2000 and Windows XP include support for TCP/IP filtering, a feature known as TCP/IP Security in Windows NT 4.0. TCP/IP filtering allows you to specify which types of inbound local host IP traffic are processed for all interfaces. This feature prevents traffic from being processed by the computer in the absence of other TCP/IP filtering, such as that provided by Routing and Remote Access (RRAS), Internet Connection Firewall (on Windows XP), and other TCP/IP applications or services. TCP/IP filtering is disabled by default.

When configuring TCP/IP filtering, you can permit either all or only specific ports or protocols listed for TCP ports, UDP ports, or IP protocols. Packets destined for the host are accepted for processing if they meet one of the following criteria:

- The destination TCP port matches the list of TCP ports.

- The destination UDP port matches the list of UDP ports.

- The IP protocol matches the list of IP protocols.

- The packet is an ICMP packet.

> **Note**   TCP/IP port filtering applies to all interfaces on the computer and cannot be applied on a per-adapter basis. However, you can configure allowed ports and protocols on a per-adapter basis.

In addition to being able to configure TCP/IP filtering on the Options tab of the TCP/IP advanced properties in the user interface, you can apply the settings directly to the registry. Table 9-6 lists the registry values to configure TCP/IP filtering. TCP/IP filtering is set in the key HKLM\SYSTEM\CurrentControlSet\Services\Tcpip\Parameters, while the specific settings for each interface are configured in the key HKLM\SYSTEM\CurrentControlSet\Services\Tcpip\Parameters\Interfaces*Interface_GUID*.

Table 9-6   Registry Values for TCP/IP Filtering

Setting	Type	Description
EnableSecurityFilters	DWORD	1 enables TCP/IP filtering; 0 disables TCP/IP filtering.
UdpAllowedPorts	MULTI_SZ	0 allows all UDP ports; an empty (null) value blocks all UDP ports; otherwise, the specific allowed UDP ports are listed.
TCPAllowedPorts	MULTI_SZ	0 allows all TCP ports; an empty (null) value blocks all TCP ports; otherwise, the specific allowed TCP ports are listed.
RawIpAllowedProtocols	MULTI_SZ	0 allows all IP protocols; an empty (null) value blocks all IP protocols; otherwise, the specific allowed IP protocols are listed.

Using Internet Connection Firewall in Windows XP

Windows XP includes a personal firewall called Internet Connection Firewall (ICF). ICF is a stateful firewall—it monitors all aspects of the communications between the Windows XP computer and other hosts, and it inspects the source and destination address of each message that it handles. To prevent unsolicited traffic from the public side of the connection from entering the private side, ICF keeps a table of all communications that have originated from the ICF computer. When used in conjunction with Internet Connection Sharing (ICS), ICF creates a table for tracking all traffic originated from the ICF/ICS computer and all traffic originated from private network computers. Inbound Internet traffic is allowed to reach the computers in your network only when a matching entry in the table shows that the communication exchange originated within your computer or private network. You can enable ICF on a per-interface basis on the Advanced tab of the interface.

You can configure services to allow unsolicited traffic from the Internet to be forwarded by the ICF computer to the private network. For example, if you are hosting an HTTP Web server service and have enabled the HTTP service on your ICF computer, unsolicited HTTP traffic will be forwarded by the ICF computer to the HTTP Web server. A set of operational information, known as a *service definition*, is required by ICF to allow the unsolicited Internet traffic to be forwarded to the Web server on your private network. The Services tab of ICF is shown in Figure 9-2.

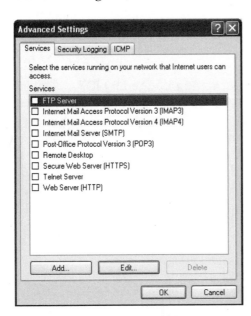

Figure 9-2   Services tab of ICF

In addition, you can add custom services to the Services tab of ICF. ICF can also perform port translation for incoming connections. When you create a custom service, you will need to specify the following:

■ **Description of service**   Determines how the service is displayed on the Services tab

■ **Name or IP address**   Determines the host name or IP address of the computer offering the service if the service is not hosted on the local computer

- **External port**   Defines the TCP or UDP port on the ICF computer that will listen to inbound traffic to the service

- **Internal port**   Defines the TCP or UDP port to which the ICF computer will forward the inbound traffic to the computer defined in the Name Or IP Address field

Communications that originate from a source outside the ICF computer, such as the Internet, are dropped by the firewall unless an entry in the Services tab is made to allow passage. ICF silently discards unsolicited communications, preventing common attacks, such as port scanning and NetBIOS enumeration. ICF can create a security log so you can view the activity that is tracked by the firewall. You can choose whether to log dropped, successful, or dropped and successful packets. By default, packets are logged to c:\windows\pfirewall.log. The log file has a default maximum size of 4098 KB. Table 9-7 describes the fields in the packet log file.

Table 9-7   Description of Information Logged by ICF

Field	Description
Date	Specifies date that the recorded transactions occurred in the format YY-MM-DD.
Time	Specifies time that the recorded transaction occurred in the format HH:MM:SS.
Action	Specifies which operation was observed by the firewall. The options available to the firewall are OPEN, CLOSE, DROP, and INFO-EVENTS-LOST. An INFO-EVENTS-LOST action indicates the number of events that happened but were not placed in the log.
Protocol	Specifies which IP protocol was used for the communication.
Src-ip	Specifies the source IP address of the computer attempting to establish communications.
Dst-ip	Specifies the destination IP address of the communication attempt.
Src-port	Specifies the source port number of the sending computer. Only TCP and UDP will return a valid src-port entry.
Dst-port	Specifies the port of the destination computer. Only TCP and UDP will return a valid dst-port entry.
Size	Specifies the packet size in bytes.

Table 9-7   Description of Information Logged by ICF   *(continued)*

Field	Description
Tcpflags	Specifies the TCP control flags found in the TCP header of an IP packet: ■ **ACK** Acknowledgment field significant ■ **FIN** No more data from sender ■ **PSH** Push function ■ **RST** Reset the connection ■ **SYN** Synchronize sequence numbers ■ **URG** Urgent Pointer field
Tcpsyn	Specifies the TCP synchronization number in the packet.
Tcpack	Specifies the TCP acknowledgment number in the packet.
Tcpwin	Specifies the TCP window size in bytes in the packet.
Icmptype	Specifies a number that represents the Type field of the ICMP message.
Icmpcode	Specifies a number that represents the Code field of the ICMP message.
Info	Specifies an information entry that depends on the type of action that occurred. For example, an INFO-EVENTS-LOST action will create an entry of the number of events that happened but were not placed in the log since the last occurrence of this event type.

Using IPSec

By its design, TCP/IP is an open protocol created to connect heterogeneous computing environments with the least amount of overhead possible. As is often the case, interoperability and performance design goals do not generally result in security—and TCP/IP is no exception to this. TCP/IP provides no native mechanism for the confidentiality or integrity of packets. To secure TCP/IP, you can implement IP Security. IPSec implements encryption and authenticity at a lower level in the TCP/IP stack than application-layer protocols such as Secure Sockets Layer (SSL) and Transport Layer Security (TLS). Because the protection process takes place lower in the TCP/IP stack, IPSec protection is transparent to applications. IPSec is a well-defined, standards-driven technology.

The IPSec process encrypts the payload after it leaves the application at the client and then decrypts the payload before it reaches the application at the server. An application does not have to be IPSec aware because the data transferred between the client and the server is normally transmitted in plaintext.

IPSec is comprised of two protocols that operate in two modes with three different authentication methods. IPSec is policy driven and can be deployed centrally by using Group Policy. To deploy IPSec, you must determine the

- Protocol
- Mode
- Authentication methods
- Policies

Securing Data Transmission with IPSec Protocols

As mentioned, IPSec is comprised of two protocols: IPSec Authentication Header (AH) and IPSec Encapsulating Security Payload (ESP). Each protocol provides different services; AH primarily provides packet integrity services, while ESP provides packet confidentiality services. IPSec provides mutual authentication services between clients and hosts, regardless of whether AH or ESP is being used.

Using AH

IPSec AH provides authentication, integrity, and anti-replay protection for the entire packet, including the IP header and the payload. AH does not provide confidentiality. When packets are secured with AH, the IPSec driver computes an Integrity Check Value (ICV) after the packet has been constructed but before it is sent to the computer. With Windows 2000 and Windows XP, you can use either the HMAC SHA1 or HMAC MD5 algorithm to compute the ICV. Figure 9-3 shows how AH modifies an IP packet.

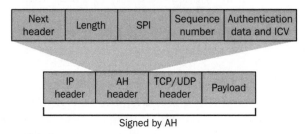

Figure 9-3   AH modifications to an IP packet

The fields in an AH packet include these:

- **Next Header**   Indicates the protocol ID for the header that follows the AH header. For example, if the encrypted data is transmitted using TCP, the next header value would be 6, which is the protocol ID for TCP.

■   **Length**   Contains the total length of the AH.

■   **Security Parameters Index (SPI)**   Identifies the security association (the IPSec agreement between two computers) that was negotiated in the Internet Key Exchange (IKE) protocol exchange between the source computer and the destination computer.

■   **Sequence Number**   Protects the AH-protected packet from replay attacks in which an attacker attempts to resend a packet that he has previously intercepted, such as an authentication packet, to another computer. For each packet issued for a specific security association (SA), the sequence number is incremented by 1 to ensure that each packet is assigned a unique sequence number. The recipient computer verifies each packet to ensure that a sequence number has not been reused. The sequence number prevents an attacker from capturing packets, modifying them, and then retransmitting them later.

■   **Authentication Data**   Contains the ICV created against the signed portion of the AH packet by using either HMAC SHA1 or HMAC MD5. The recipient performs the same integrity algorithm and compares the result of the hash algorithm with the result stored within the Authentication Data field to ensure that the signed portion of the AH packet has not been altered in transit. Because the TTL, Type of Service (TOS), Flags, Fragment Offset, and Header Checksum fields are not used in the ICV, packets secured with IPSec AH can cross routers, which can change these fields.

Using ESP

ESP packets are used to provide encryption services to transmitted data. In addition, ESP provides authentication, integrity, and antireplay services. When packets are sent using ESP, the payload of the packet is encrypted and authenticated. In Windows 2000 and Windows XP, the encryption is done with either Data Encryption Standard (DES) or 3DES, and the ICV calculation is done with either HMAC SHA1 or HMAC MD5.

> **Tip**   When designing an IPSec solution, you can combine AH and ESP protocols in a single IPSec SA. Although both AH and ESP provide integrity protection to transmitted data, AH protects the entire packet from modification, while ESP protects only the IP payload from modification.

ESP encrypts the TCP or UDP header and the application data included within an IP packet. It does not include the original IP header unless IPSec tunnel mode is used. Figure 9-4 shows how ESP modifies an IP packet.

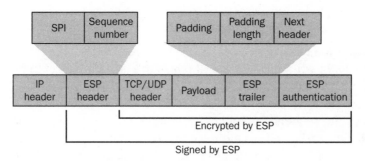

Figure 9-4 ESP modifications to an IP packet

The ESP header has two fields that are inserted between the original IP header and the TCP or UDP header from the original packet:

- **Security Parameters Index (SPI)**   Identifies the SA that was negotiated between the source computer and the destination computer for IPSec communication. The combination of the SPI, the IPSec protocol (AH or ESP), and the source and destination IP addresses identifies the SA used for the IPSec transmission within the ESP packet.

- **Sequence Number**   Protects the SA from replay attacks. This field is incremented by 1 to ensure that packets are never received more than once. If a packet is received with a previous sequence number, that packet is dropped.

The ESP trailer is inserted after the application data from the original packet and includes the following fields:

- **Padding**   A variable length from 0–255 bytes that brings the length of the application data and ESP trailer to a length divisible by 32 bits so that they match the required size for the cipher algorithm.

- **Padding Length**   Indicates the length of the Padding field. After the packet is decrypted, this field is used to determine the length of the Padding field.

- **Next Header**   Identifies the protocol used for the transmission of the data, such as TCP or UDP.

Following the ESP trailer, the ESP protocol adds an ESP authentication trailer to the end of the packet. The ESP authentication trailer contains a single field:

■ **Authentication Data**   Contains the ICV, which verifies the originating host that sent the message and ensures that the packet was not modified in transit. The ICV uses the defined integrity algorithm to calculate the ICV. The integrity algorithm is applied to the ESP header, the TCP/UDP header, the application data, and the ESP trailer.

ESP provides integrity protection for the ESP header, the TCP/UDP header, the application data, and the ESP trailer. ESP also provides inspection protection by encrypting the TCP/UDP header, the application data, and the ESP trailer.

Choosing Between IPSec Modes

IPSec operates in two modes: transport mode and tunnel mode. IPSec transport mode is used for host-to-host connections, and IPSec tunnel mode is used for network-to-network or host-to-network connections.

Using IPSec Transport Mode

IPSec transport mode is fully routable, as long as the connection does not cross a network address translation (NAT) interface, which would invalidate the ICV. Used this way, IPSec must be supported on both hosts, and each host must support the same authentication protocols and have compatible IPSec filters configured and assigned. IPSec transport mode is used to secure traffic from clients to hosts for connections where sensitive data is passed.

Using IPSec Tunnel Mode

IPSec tunnel mode is used for network-to-network connections (IPSec tunnels between routers) or host-to-network connections (IPSec tunnels between a host and a router). Used this way, IPSec must be supported on both endpoints, and each endpoint must support the same authentication protocols and have compatible IPSec filters configured and assigned. IPSec tunnel mode is commonly used for site-to-site connections that cross public networks, such as the Internet.

Selecting an IPSec Authentication Method

During the initial construction of the IPSec session—also known as the Internet Key Exchange, or IKE—each host or endpoint authenticates the other host or endpoint. When configuring IPSec, you must ensure that each host or endpoint supports the same authentication methods. IPSec supports three authentication methods:

- Kerberos
- X.509 certificates
- Preshared key

Authenticating with Kerberos

In Windows 2000 and Windows XP, Kerberos is used for the IPSec mutual authentication by default. For Kerberos to be used as the authentication protocol, both hosts or endpoints must receive Kerberos tickets from the same Active Directory directory service forest. Thus, you should choose Kerberos for IPSec authentication only when both hosts or endpoints are within you own organization. Kerberos is an excellent authentication method for IPSec because it requires no additional configuration or network infrastructure.

> **Important**   Some types of traffic are exempted by default from being secured by IPSec, even when the IPSec policy specifies that all IP traffic should be secured. The IPSec exemptions apply to Broadcast, Multicast, Resource Reservation Setup Protocol (RSVP), IKE, and Kerberos traffic. Kerberos is a security protocol itself, can be used by IPSec for IKE authentication, and was not originally designed to be secured by IPSec. Therefore, Kerberos is exempt from IPSec filtering.
>
> To remove the exemption for Kerberos and RSVP, set the value *NoDefaultExempt* to 1 in the registry key HKEY_LOCAL_MACHINE\SYSTEM\CurrentControlSet\Services\IPSEC, or use the Nodefaultexempt.vbs script located in the Tools\Scripts folder on the CD included with this book.

Authenticating with X.509 Certificates

You can use X.509 certificates for IPSec mutual authentication of hosts or endpoints. Certificates allow you to create IPSec secured sessions with hosts or endpoints outside your Active Directory forests, such as business partners in extranet scenarios. You also must use certificates when using IPSec to secure VPN connections made by using Layer Two Tunneling Protocol (L2TP). To use certificates, the hosts must be able to validate that the other's certificate is valid.

Authenticating with Preshared Key

You can use a preshared key, which is a simple, case-sensitive text string, to authenticate hosts or endpoints. Preshared key authentication should be used only when testing or troubleshooting IPSec connectivity because the preshared key is not stored in a secure fashion by hosts or endpoints.

Creating IPSec Policies

IPSec is a policy-driven technology. In Windows 2000 and Windows XP, you can have only one IPSec policy assigned at a time. IPSec policies are dynamic, meaning that you do not have to stop and start the IPSec service or restart the computer when assigning or unassigning IPSec policies. You can also use Group Policy to deploy IPSec policies to Windows 2000 and Windows XP clients. Windows 2000 and Windows XP include three precreated IPSec policies:

- **Client (Respond Only)** A computer configured with the Client policy will use IPSec if the host it is communicating with requests using IPSec and supports Kerberos authentication.

- **Server (Request Security)** A computer configured with the Server policy will always attempt to negotiate IPSec but will permit unsecured communication with hosts that do not support IPSec. The Server policy permits unsecured ICMP traffic.

- **Secure Server (Require Security)** A computer configured with the Secure Server policy will request that IPSec be used for all inbound and outbound connections. The computer will accept unencrypted packets but will always respond by using IPSec secured packets. The Secure Server policy permits unsecured ICMP traffic.

In addition to the built-in policies, you can create custom IPSec policies. When creating your own IPSec policies, you must configure rules that include the following settings:

- IP Filter List
- Tunnel Settings
- Filter Actions

- Authentication Methods

- Connection Types

IPSec rules determine what types of network traffic will initiate IPSec between the computer and the host or endpoint it is communicating with. A computer can have any number of IPSec filters. You should ensure that only one rule is created for each type of traffic. If multiple filters apply to a given type of traffic, the most specific filter will be processed first.

IP Filter List

The IP filter list defines the types of network traffic that the IPSec rule applies to. You must define the following details for each entry in the filter list:

- **Source address** Can be a specific IP address, a specific IP subnet address, or any address.

- **Destination address** Can be a specific IP address, a specific IP subnet address, or any address.

- **Protocol** The protocol ID or transport protocol used by the protocol. For example, Point-to-Point Tunneling Protocol (PPTP) uses Generic Routing Encapsulation (GRE) packets. GRE packets are identified by their protocol ID, which is protocol ID 47. Telnet, on the other hand, uses TCP as its transport protocol, so an IPSec filter for Telnet would only define the protocol type as TCP.

- **Source port** If the protocol were to use TCP or UDP, the source port could be defined for the protected connection. The source port is set to a specific port or to a random port, depending on the protocol being defined. Most protocols use a random port for the source port.

- **Destination port** If the protocol uses TCP or UDP, the protocol uses a specific port at the server to accept transmissions. For example, Telnet configures the server to listen for connections on TCP port 23.

When configuring IP filter lists for transport mode connections, you should always choose to have the IPSec rule mirrored to secure the return communication defined in the rule. For tunnel mode connections, you must manually specify both the inbound and outbound filter list.

Tunnel Settings

The tunnel setting determines whether IPSec operates in transport or tunnel mode. If you want IPSec to operate in transport mode, select This Rule Does

Not Specify A Tunnel when creating an IPSec rule using the Security Rule Wizard. If you want the filter to operate in tunnel mode, you must specify the IP address of the endpoint of the tunnel.

Filter Actions

For each filter rule, you must choose a filter action. The filter action defines how the traffic defined in the IP filter will be handled by the filter rule. The three filter actions are listed here and shown in Figure 9-5.

- **Permit**   Allows packets to be transmitted without IPSec protection. For example, Simple Network Management Protocol (SNMP) includes support for devices that might not be IPSec aware. Enabling IPSec for SNMP would cause a loss of network management capabilities for these devices. In a highly secure network, you could create an IPSec filter for SNMP and set the IPSec action to Permit to allow SNMP packets to be transmitted without IPSec protection.

- **Block**   Discards packets. If the associated IPSec filter is matched, all packets with the block action defined are discarded.

- **Negotiate Security**   Allows an administrator to define the desired encryption and integrity algorithms to secure data transmissions if an IPSec filter is matched.

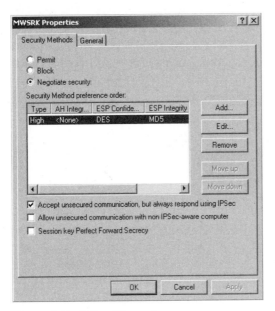

Figure 9-5   IPSec filter actions

In addition to these three basic actions, you can define settings that indicate how the Windows 2000–based computer will react if non-IPSec protected data is received and how frequently new session keys are defined to protect the IPSec data. Options include the following:

- **Accept Unsecured Communication, But Always Respond Using IPSec** You use this option when the IPSec protection is enforced only at the servers, not at the clients. In a typical IPSec deployment, clients are configured to use IPSec if requested by the server but to never initiate an IPSec SA. This setting allows the initial packet to be received by the server, which then starts the IKE process to negotiate an SA between the client and the server. Although it is riskier to have the initial packet of a data transmission accepted by using plaintext, the response packet sent from the server will not be transmitted until an SA is established.

- **Allow Unsecured Communication—With Non-IPSec-Aware Computers** In a mixed network, this option allows non-IPSec aware clients to connect to the server. Windows 2000 clients, if configured to do so, will connect to the server and negotiate IPSec protection. Non-IPSec-aware clients will still be allowed to connect by using unprotected data streams.

- **Session Key Perfect Forward Secrecy** Using Perfect Forward Secrecy will ensure that an existing key is never used as the foundation of a new key. When you use Perfect Forward Secrecy, all keys will be generated without using existing keys. This reduces the risk of continual data exposure should a key be compromised because previous keys cannot be used to determine future keys.

Authentication Methods

For each filter rule, you must choose an authentication method. You can enable multiple authentication methods for each rule and determine their order of precedence by editing the filter rule after it has been created.

Connection Types

You must specify what type of interfaces each filter rule applies to. In Windows 2000 and Windows XP, you can choose to have the rule apply to the following:

- All network connections

- Local area network (LAN) connections

- Remote access connections

> **Note**   You can create IPSec policies by using Ipsecpol.exe from the command line or from batch files and scripts, in addition to using the user interface.

How IPSec Works

IPSec can be initiated by either the sending host or the receiving host. The two hosts or endpoints enter into a negotiation that will determine how the communication will be protected. The negotiation is completed in the IKE, and the resulting agreement is a set of security associations, or SAs.

IKE has two modes of operation, main mode and quick mode. We will examine each mode momentarily. IKE also serves two functions:

- Centralizes SA management, reducing connection time

- Generates and manages the authenticated keys used to secure the information

The SA is used until the two hosts or endpoints cease communication, even though the keys used might change. A computer can have many SAs. The SA for each packet is tracked using the SPI.

Main Mode

During the main mode negotiation, the two computers establish a secure, authenticated channel—the main mode SA. IKE automatically provides the necessary identity protection during this exchange. This ensures no identity information is sent without encryption between the communicating computers, thus enabling total privacy. Following are the steps in a main mode negotiation:

1. **Policy negotiation**   These four mandatory parameters are negotiated as part of the main mode SA:

   ❑ The encryption algorithm (DES or 3DES)

   ❑ The hash algorithm (MD5 or SHA1)

   ❑ The authentication method (certificate, preshared key, or Kerberos v5 authentication)

   ❑ The Diffie-Hellman (DH) group to be used for the base keying material

If certificates or preshared keys are used for authentication, the computer identity is protected. However, if Kerberos v5 authentication is used, the computer identity is unencrypted until encryption of the entire identity payload takes place during authentication.

2. **DH exchange (of public values)**   At no time are actual keys exchanged; only the base information needed by DH to generate the shared, secret key is exchanged. After this exchange, the IKE service on each computer generates the master key used to protect the final step: authentication.

3. **Authentication**   The computers attempt to authenticate the DH exchange. Without successful authentication, communication cannot proceed. The master key is used, in conjunction with the negotiation algorithms and methods, to authenticate identities. The entire identity payload—including the identity type, port, and protocol—is hashed and encrypted by using the keys generated from the DH exchange in the second step. The identity payload, regardless of which authentication method is used, is protected from both modification and interpretation.

    After the hosts have mutually authenticated each other, the host that initiated the negotiation presents an offer for a potential SA to the receiving host. The responder cannot modify the offer. Should the offer be modified, the initiator rejects the responder's message. The responder sends either a reply accepting the offer or a reply with alternatives. After the hosts agree on an SA, quick mode negotiation begins.

Quick Mode

In this mode, SAs are negotiated on behalf of the IPSec service. The following are the steps in quick mode negotiation:

1. **Policy negotiation**   The IPSec computers exchange their requirements for securing the data transfer:

    ❑   The hash algorithm for integrity and authentication (MD5 or SHA1)

    ❑   The algorithm for encryption, if requested (3DES or DES)

    ❑   A description of the traffic to protect

2. **Session key material refresh or exchange**   IKE refreshes the keying material, and new, shared, or secret keys are generated for authentication and encryption (if negotiated) of the packets. If a rekey is required, a second DH exchange takes place or a refresh of the original DH exchange occurs.

3. **SA exchange**   The SAs and keys are passed to the IPSec driver, along with the SPI.

   A common agreement is reached, and two SAs are established: one for inbound communication, and one for outbound communication.

During the quick mode negotiation of shared policy and keying material, the information is protected by the SA negotiated during main mode. As mentioned in step 3, quick mode results in a pair of SAs: one for inbound communication and one for outbound communication, each having its own SPI and key. Figure 9-6 shows a summary of what is negotiated during main mode and quick mode.

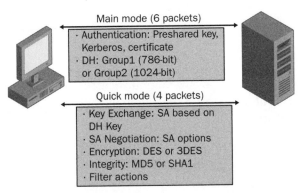

Figure 9-6   Main mode and quick mode negotiation

IPSec, Routers, and NAT

IPSec creates a new IP header for a packet that can be routed as normal IP traffic. Routers and switches in the data path between the communicating hosts simply forward the packets to their destination. However, when a firewall or gateway lies in the data path, you must enable IP forwarding at the firewall for the following IP protocols and UDP ports:

(continued)

IPSec, Routers, and NAT   *(continued)*

- **IP protocol ID 50**   Create inbound and outbound filters to allow ESP traffic to be forwarded.

- **IP protocol ID 51**   Create inbound and outbound filters to allow AH traffic to be forwarded.

- **UDP port 500**   Create inbound and outbound filters to allow IKE traffic to be forwarded.

    Because of the nature of the NAT and port address translation (PAT) technologies, which require that packets be altered to change IP address and port information, IPSec is not compatible with NAT. IPSec does not allow manipulation of packets during transfer. The IPSec endpoint will discard packets that have been altered by NAT because the ICVs will not match. At the time of the printing of this book, research into encapsulating IPSec packets in UDP packets so that they can pass through NAT devices is under way.

Monitoring IPSec

You can monitor IPSec in Windows 2000 with IPSecmon.exe and in Windows XP the IP Security Monitor Microsoft Management Console (MMC) snap-in. In addition, you can create log files in both Windows 2000 and Windows XP to view IPSec negotiations.

Using IPSecmon in Windows 2000

In Windows 2000, you can view the status of IPSec SAs and basic information on IPSec sessions by running IPSecmon from the Run prompt. IPSecmon displays information about each SA and the overall statistics of IPSec and IKE sessions. Figure 9-7 shows IPSecmon in Windows 2000. The built-in Server IPSec policy is applied to the Windows 2000 computer named SFOFS001. The SFOFS001 computer has attempted to negotiate IPSec with three other computers: SEADC001, SFODC001, and SFOXP001. However, SFOFS001 has successfully negotiated an SA with SFOXP001 only. The IPSec session with SFPXP001 uses the IPSec protocol ESP with 3DES as the encrypting algorithm and HMAC SHA1 as the authentication algorithm.

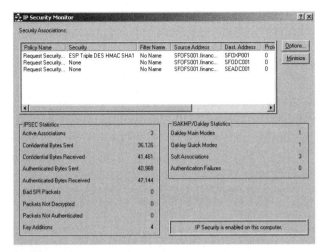

Figure 9-7   Using IPSecmon in Windows 2000

Using the IP Security Monitor MMC Snap-In

In Windows XP, IPSecmon has been replaced with an MMC snap-in that provides all the information that IPSecmon did in Windows 2000, only in much greater detail. You can use the IP Security Monitor MMC snap-in to view details of each SA, whereas in Windows 2000, you could view only the basic details of an SA. Figure 9-8 shows the IP Security Monitor MMC snap-in in Windows XP, which enables you to view the exact SA details negotiated during both main mode and quick mode.

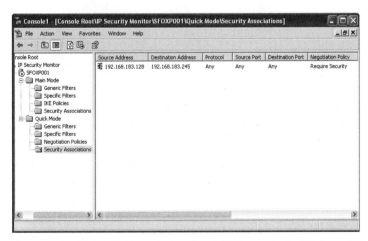

Figure 9-8   Using IP Security Monitor MMC snap-in in Windows XP

Using IPSec Logs in Windows 2000 and Windows XP

In both Windows 2000 and Windows XP, you can have IPSec log the IKE exchanges to a log file on the hard drive for troubleshooting or monitoring needs. To have your computer log IKE exchanges, you must create a registry value named *EnableLogging* in the registry key HKLM\System\CurrentControlSet\Services\PolicyAgent\Oakley. To enable logging, set the value to 1 and restart the IPSec services. The log file will be written to the file %systemroot%\debug\oakley.log. Ipseclog.vbs automatically configures the registry in Windows 2000 and Windows XP to enable IPSec logging. This file is located in the Tools\Scripts folder on the CD included with this book.

Note Although the IPSec log file will contain more detailed information than a network capture made with Network Monitor, you can also use Network Monitor to determine how IPSec SA negotiations function in relation to the other traffic on the network.

Best Practices

- **Create a TCP/IP hardening policy.** Ensure that the TCP/IP stack on your Windows 2000 and Windows XP computers is appropriately secure, based on the threats to it. This is especially true of any computer directly connected to the Internet or in screened subnets.

- **Use ICF for mobile and home computers running Windows XP.** ICF provides an excellent degree of protection for mobile clients and home computers. Be certain to provide training to users on how to enable and disable ICF.

- **Use IPSec hardware accelerators when possible.** By using IPSec hardware accelerators on computers that will have many IPSec sessions at a time, such as servers, you can prevent the computer's CPU performance from being overly taxed.

Additional Information

- Internet Assigned Numbers Authority's (IANA) TCP and UDP port number assignment list (*http://www.iana.org/assignments/port-numbers*)

- IANA's IP protocol ID number list (*http://www.iana.org/assignments/protocol-numbers*)

- "5-Minute Security Advisor—Essential Security Tools for Home Office Users" (*http://www.microsoft.com/technet/columns/security/5min/5min-105.asp*)

- Internet Connection Firewall Overview—Windows XP Help File (*http://www.microsoft.com/windowsxp/home/using/productdoc/en/hnw_understanding_firewall.asp*)

- "IPSec Architecture" white paper (*http://www.microsoft.com/technet/security/prodtech/network/ipsecarc.asp*)

- "IPSec Implementation" white paper (*http://www.microsoft.com/technet/security/prodtech/network/ipsecimp.asp*)

- "Security Considerations for Network Attacks" white paper (*http://www.microsoft.com/technet/security/prodtech/network/secdeny.asp*)

- "Best Practices for Preventing DoS/Denial of Service Attacks" white paper (*http://www.microsoft.com/technet/security/bestprac/dosatack.asp*)

- 309798: "How to Configure TCP/IP Filtering in Windows 2000"

> **Note**   The previous article can be accessed through the Microsoft Knowledge Base. Go to *http://support.microsoft.com* and enter the article number in the Search The Knowledge Base text box.

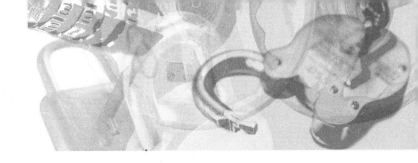

10

Securing Microsoft Internet Explorer 6 and Microsoft Office XP

Most organizations that use Microsoft operating systems also use Microsoft Internet Explorer and Microsoft Office. In fact, browsing the Internet and exchanging documents and spreadsheets have become mission-critical business activities; however, they also can provide attackers with a direct avenue into the corporate network. Consequently, when securing computers on your network, you should also consider how you will secure these applications.

Security Settings in Internet Explorer 6

The Web browser has become a mission-critical application for nearly all organizations. Unfortunately, browsing Web sites on the Internet also can be a major security risk because Web browsers provide attackers with direct access to an organization's local area network (LAN). Fortunately, Internet Explorer enables administrators to easily configure privacy and security settings, and enables knowledgeable users to view privacy and security information to make decisions on whether to trust specific Web sites.

Privacy Settings

In April 2002, the World Wide Web Consortium (W3C)—found at *http://www.w3c.org*—ratified the Platform for Privacy Preferences Project (P3P), an industry standard providing a simple, automated way for users to gain more control over the use of their personal information on Web sites they visit. Internet Explorer 6 fully supports P3P version 1.0. P3P helps protect the privacy of users' personal information on the Internet by making it easier for users to decide whether and under which circumstances personal information is disclosed to Web sites.

In Internet Explorer 6, users can define their privacy preferences for disclosing personal information. When users browse Web sites, Internet Explorer determines whether those sites abide by the P3P privacy standards. If the Web site does support P3P standards, Internet Explorer compares the user's privacy preferences to the Web site's privacy policy information. To be P3P compliant, a Web site must provide a clear definition of its privacy policies, including these:

- The organization that is collecting information about users

- The type of information that is being collected

- What the information will be used for

- Whether the information will be shared with other organizations

- Whether users can access the information about them and change how the organization will use that information

- The method for resolving disputes between users and the organization

- How the organization will retain the collected information

- Where the organization publicly maintains detailed information that users can read about their privacy policies

Internet Explorer 6 includes a new Privacy Report option on its View menu. This option enables users to view P3P privacy information known as a *privacy report* on P3P-compliant Web sites. For example, to view the privacy report for the Microsoft Web site, follow these steps:

1. Open Internet Explorer.

2. In the Address box, type **http://www.microsoft.com**.

3. Click View, and then click Privacy Report.

4. From the Web Sites With Content On The Current Page box, select *http://www.microsoft.com* and then click Summary.

Figure 10-1 shows the privacy report for the Microsoft Web site.

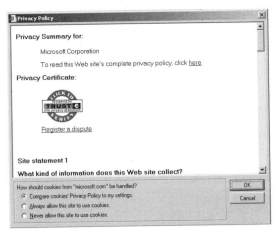

Figure 10-1   P3P privacy report for Microsoft.com

In addition to viewing P3P-compliant Web site privacy reports, Internet Explorer 6 enables P3P support for user cookie management. A *cookie* is a small file that an individual Web site stores on your computer. Web sites can use cookies to maintain information and settings, such as your customization preferences. Two types of cookies exist: *persistent cookies* and *session cookies*. Persistent cookies include an expiration date that identifies when the browser can delete them. Session cookies do not have an expiration date; they are deleted when the user closes the browser.

Internet Explorer 6 includes advanced cookie management capabilities that determine whether cookies can be stored on a user's computer. When you configure your privacy preferences, you can configure Internet Explorer to handle cookies in the following ways:

■ **Prevent all cookies from being stored on your computer.**   This setting might prevent you from viewing certain Web sites, such as e-commerce Web sites that save shopping cart information in cookies.

■ **Block or restrict first-party cookies.**   First-party cookies originate in the same domain as the Web site being visited. This setting blocks those cookies.

■ **Block or restrict third-party cookies.**   Third-party cookies do not originate in the same domain as the Web site being visited and therefore are not covered by that Web site's privacy policy. For example, many Web sites contain advertising from third-party sites that use cookies. This setting blocks those cookies.

- **Use the Allow option.**   Enabling this option permits Web sites to place cookies on your computer without notifying you. Previous versions of Internet Explorer included a similar option.

- **Use the Prompt option.**   This option enables you to determine on a cookie-by-cookie basis whether to allow the cookie to be placed on your hard drive.

An additional option enables you to always allow session cookies. Figure 10-2 shows the Advanced Privacy Settings user interface on which you can configure cookie management in Internet Explorer 6.

Figure 10-2   Advanced Privacy Settings user interface in Internet Explorer 6

For convenience, Internet Explorer 6 offers six predefined privacy configurations and an option to create a custom configuration. By default, Internet Explorer 6 is set to Medium for sites in the Internet zone. (We will discuss the Internet zone on page 251.) In addition to the predefined configurations, you can override the settings for individual Web sites on the Privacy tab of the Internet Options menu item (from the Tools menu). These are the predefined privacy configurations:

- **Block All Cookies**   Prevents all Web sites from storing cookies on your computer, and Web sites cannot read existing cookies on your computer. Per-site privacy actions do not override these settings. This setting can prevent some Web sites from being viewed or Web applications from working correctly.

- **High**   Prevents Web sites from storing cookies that do not have a compact privacy policy—a condensed, computer-readable P3P privacy statement. The browser prevents Web sites from storing cookies that use personally identifiable information without your explicit consent. Per-site privacy actions override these settings.

- **Medium High**   Prevents Web sites from storing third-party cookies that do not have a compact privacy policy or that use personally identifiable information without your explicit consent. The browser prevents Web sites from storing first-party cookies that use personally identifiable information without your implicit consent. The browser also restricts access to first-party cookies that do not have a compact privacy policy so that they can be read only in the first-party context. Per-site privacy actions override these settings.

- **Medium (default)**   Prevents Web sites from storing third-party cookies that do not have a compact privacy policy or that use personally identifiable information without your implicit consent. The browser allows first-party cookies that use personally identifiable information without your implicit consent but deletes these cookies from your computer when you close the browser. The browser also restricts access to first-party cookies that do not have a compact privacy policy so that they can be read only in the first-party context. Per-site privacy actions override these settings.

- **Low**   Allows Web sites to store cookies on your computer, including third-party cookies that do not have a compact privacy policy or that use personally identifiable information without your implicit consent. However, closing the browser deletes these third-party cookies from your computer. The browser also restricts access to first-party cookies that do not have a compact privacy policy so that they can be read only in the first-party context. Per-site privacy actions override these settings.

- **Accept All Cookies**   Allows all Web sites to store cookies on your computer, and allows Web sites that create cookies on your computer to read them. Per-site privacy actions do not override these settings.

Security Zones

On most networks, the Web browser on a user's computer is an open communication channel from the Internet directly to the computer and the local network the computer is attached to. A malicious attacker can embed scripts in a Web site that, when viewed, attack the computer or the local network of the user browsing that Web site. To prevent attacks delivered through Web sites, you can use

Internet Explorer security settings, which are configured by using security zones. Security zones in Internet Explorer are flexible and customizable, enabling you to configure browser security while maintaining Web site functionality.

Security zones group Web sites into categories based on levels of trust. When using Internet Explorer to browse Web sites, the security zone of the Web is displayed in the lower right-hand corner of the Internet Explorer System bar, as shown in Figure 10-3.

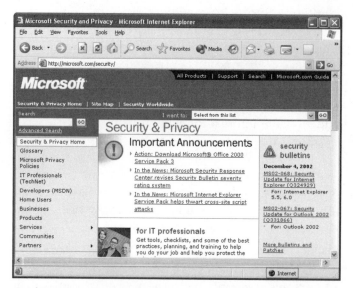

Figure 10-3   Viewing the current security zone in Internet Explorer

You can use four predefined levels of security with these security zones:

- **High**   Greatly restricts what you can do when browsing Web sites, including disabling all Microsoft ActiveX and Java content. This security setting disables Active Scripting. (We will discuss Active Scripting later in this section.)

- **Medium**   Provides a moderate level of protection, including preventing unsigned ActiveX controls from being downloaded and prompting users for confirmation when downloading any ActiveX content. Active Scripting is enabled in this security setting. This level sets Java security to High.

- **Medium-Low**   Provides the same level of protection for non-Java content that the Medium security level does, without prompting the user for as many of the security options. This level sets Java security to Medium.

- ■ **Low**   Provides little to no security control over Web site content. This level sets Java security to Low. You should not use this security level.

Table 10-1 shows the security configuration of the predefined security zones in Internet Explorer 6. We will discuss these security options in more detail momentarily. In addition to the predefined security levels, as mentioned earlier, you can create a custom level of security and assign it to a security zone.

Table 10-1   Default Security Zones in Internet Explorer 6

Security Option	Low	Medium-Low	Medium	High
Download Signed ActiveX Controls	Enable	Prompt	Prompt	Disable
Download Unsigned ActiveX Controls	Prompt	Disable	Disable	Disable
Initialize And Script ActiveX Controls Not Marked As Safe	Prompt	Disable	Disable	Disable
Run ActiveX Controls And Plug-Ins	Enable	Enable	Enable	Disable
Script ActiveX Controls Marked Safe For Scripting	Enable	Enable	Enable	Disable
File Download	Enable	Enable	Enable	Disable
Font Download	Enable	Enable	Enable	Prompt
Microsoft VM Java Permissions	Low safety	Medium safety	High safety	Disable Java
Access Data Sources Across Domains	Enable	Prompt	Disable	Disable
Allow META REFRESH	Enable	Enable	Enable	Disable
Display Mixed Content	Prompt	Prompt	Prompt	Prompt

(continued)

Table 10-1   Default Security Zones in Internet Explorer 6   *(continued)*

Security Option	Low	Medium-Low	Medium	High
Don't Prompt For Client Certificate Selection When No Certificates Or Only One Certificate Exists	Enable	Enable	Disable	Disable
Drag And Drop Or Copy And Paste Files	Enable	Enable	Enable	Prompt
Installation Of Desktop Items	Enable	Prompt	Prompt	Disable
Launching Programs And Files In An IFRAME	Enable	Prompt	Prompt	Disable
Navigate Subframes Across Different Domains	Enable	Enable	Enable	Disable
Software Channel Permissions	Low safety	Medium safety	Medium safety	High safety
Submit Nonencrypted Form Data	Enable	Enable	Prompt	Prompt
Userdata Persistence	Enable	Enable	Enable	Disable
Active Scripting	Enable	Enable	Enable	Disable
Allow Paste Operations Via Script	Enable	Enable	Enable	Disable
Scripting Of Java Applets	Enable	Enable	Enable	Disable
User Authentication	Automatic logon only in Intranet zone	Automatic logon only in Intranet zone	Automatic logon with current user name and password	Prompt for user name and password

When configuring security zones, you must remember that although security zones are configured and maintained in Internet Explorer, they also apply to other applications, such as Office XP; Microsoft Outlook Express and Microsoft Outlook Preview Pane and HTML messages; and HTML Help applications. These are the default security zones in Internet Explorer:

- **Local Intranet**   The Local Intranet zone applies to all local Internet domains, Web sites that bypass the proxy server, dotless IP addresses, and all Universal Naming Convention (UNC) paths. Internet domains are considered local based on the domains listed in the Domain Name System (DNS) suffix search order in the TCP/IP properties. The Web sites that bypass the proxy server are defined as local on the Connections tab of Internet Options, which is often configured by the proxy server or firewall. By default, the security on this zone is set to Medium-Low. In addition, you can add sites to the Local Intranet zone this way:

  1. Open Internet Explorer.

  2. Open the Tools menu and then select Internet Options.

  3. Click the Security tab of the Internet Options window; then click the Local Intranet zone icon.

  4. Click Sites; then click Advanced.

  5. Enter the name of the site to add to the Local Intranet zone in the Local Intranet window. Click OK and close all open windows.

- **Trusted Sites**   The Trusted Sites zone applies only to Web sites added to it. By default, all Web sites placed in this zone must use *https://*, meaning that they are protected by Secure Sockets Layer (SSL) or Transport Layer Security (TLS), to verify the confidentiality and integrity of the data coming from the Web site as well as to authenticate the Web site itself. You can remove this restriction but should do so only if absolutely required. The security on this zone is set to Low by default and contains no Web sites.

- **Restricted Sites**   The Restricted Sites zone applies only to Web sites added to it. The security level on this zone is set to High by default. Sites in this zone are given little trust.

- **Internet**   The Internet zone applies to all Web sites not defined in any other security zone. By default, the security on this zone is set to Medium—only a limited amount of trust is given to Web sites in this zone. You should configure the security on this zone to meet your organization's business and technical needs.

> **Note** In addition to the four default security zones in Internet Explorer 5 and 6, a hidden security zone called My Computer contains security settings for unsigned ActiveX controls on the local computer. You can unhide the My Computer security zone by setting the registry value HKEY_CURRENT_USER\SOFTWARE\Microsoft\Windows\ CurrentVersion\Internet Settings\Zones\0\Flags to 0x47 or by running the Showallseczones.vbs tool located in the Tools\Scripts folder on the CD included with this book.

The security settings in Internet Explorer are divided into the following categories:

- ActiveX controls and plug-ins
- Downloads
- Microsoft VM
- Miscellaneous
- Scripting
- User authentication

Unfortunately, no one correct implementation of these settings exists for all users or all organizations. You must analyze the business and technical requirements of your organization to configure these security settings in Internet Explorer.

ActiveX Controls and Plug-Ins

ActiveX controls enable Web sites to deliver interactive context to users through Internet Explorer. The ActiveX controls and plug-ins section of Internet Explorer 6 security includes settings for how Internet Explorer approves, downloads, runs, and scripts ActiveX controls. If a user downloads an ActiveX control that is hosted on a Web site that belongs to a different security zone from the page on which it is used, Internet Explorer applies the more restrictive of the two sites' security zone settings. These are the ActiveX security settings:

- **Download Signed ActiveX Controls** This option determines whether users can download signed ActiveX controls from a page in the specified security zone. You can choose from the following settings:

❑   **Disable**   Prevents all signed controls from downloading. Although this setting will greatly enhance the security of Internet Explorer, it can prevent users from accessing Internet resources they need to use to complete their job functions.

❑   **Enable**   Downloads valid signed controls without user intervention and prompts users to choose whether to download signed controls that have been revoked or have expired.

❑   **Prompt**   Prompts users to choose whether to download controls signed by publishers who are not trusted. Controls signed by trusted publishers are silently downloaded even if this option is selected.

■   **Download Unsigned ActiveX Controls**   Determines whether users can download unsigned ActiveX controls from the zone. Unsigned controls are potentially harmful, especially when they come from an untrusted Web site. You can choose from the following settings:

❑   **Disable**   Prevents unsigned controls from running. You should always disable the downloading of unsigned ActiveX controls.

❑   **Enable**   Runs unsigned controls without user intervention.

❑   **Prompt**   Prompts users to choose whether to allow the unsigned control to run. You should enable this setting only for the Trusted Sites or My Computer zone when you have a specific reason, such as testing an ActiveX control in the development process.

■   **Initialize And Script ActiveX Controls Not Marked As Safe**   ActiveX controls are classified as either *trusted* or *untrusted*. This option controls whether a script can interact with untrusted controls in the security zone. Untrusted controls are not meant for use on Internet pages, but some Web sites might require them. Object safety should be enforced unless you can trust all ActiveX controls and scripts on pages in the zone. You can set this option to one of the following:

❑   **Disable**   Enforces object safety for untrusted data or scripts. ActiveX controls that cannot be trusted are not loaded with parameters or scripted.

❑ **Enable** Overrides object safety. ActiveX controls are run, loaded with parameters, and scripted without setting object safety for untrusted data or scripts. This setting is not recommended, except for secure and administered zones. This setting causes Internet Explorer to initialize and script both untrusted and trusted controls and to ignore the Script ActiveX Controls Marked Safe For Scripting option, thus removing all security for controls not marked as safe.

❑ **Prompt** Attempts to enforce object safety. However, if ActiveX controls cannot be made safe for untrusted data or scripts, users are given the option of allowing the control to be loaded with parameters or to be scripted.

■ **Run ActiveX Controls And Plug-Ins** This option determines whether Internet Explorer can run ActiveX controls and plug-ins from pages in the security zone. You can set this option to the following:

❑ **Administrator Approved** Runs only those controls and plug-ins that you have approved for your users. To select the list of approved controls and plug-ins, use Internet Explorer System Policies And Restrictions. The Control Management category of policies enables you to manage these controls.

❑ **Disable** Prevents controls and plug-ins from running.

❑ **Enable** Runs controls and plug-ins without user intervention.

❑ **Prompt** Prompts users to choose whether to allow the controls or plug-ins to run.

■ **Script ActiveX Controls Marked Safe For Scripting** This option determines whether an ActiveX control that is marked safe for scripting can interact with a script. This option affects only controls that are loaded with *<param>* tags. You can choose from the following settings:

❑ **Disable** Prevents script interaction

❑ **Enable** Allows script interaction without user intervention

❑ **Prompt** Prompts users to choose whether to allow script interaction

Download Options

The Download options specify how Internet Explorer downloads files and fonts. These are the two options:

- **File Download**   Controls whether file downloads are permitted based on the security zone of the Web page that contains the download link, not the zone from which the file originated. You can set this option to the following:

    □ **Disable**   Prevents files from being downloaded from the zone

    □ **Enable**   Allows files to be downloaded from the zone

- **Font Download**   Determines whether Web pages within the zone can download HTML fonts. You can set this option to the following:

    □ **Disable**   Prevents HTML fonts from being downloaded

    □ **Enable**   Downloads HTML fonts without user intervention

    □ **Prompt**   Prompts users to choose whether to allow the download of HTML font

Microsoft VM Options

The Microsoft virtual machine (VM) options enable you to configure security for Microsoft VM, which is compatible with Java applets and libraries. In Windows XP, this section is available only after you download and install the Java Virtual Machine. Unless you have Java applications that users access through Internet Explorer, you should set the Java security to the Disable Java option. You can set the Microsoft VM security level to one of the following options:

- **Custom**   Enables you to control permissions manually

- **Disable Java**   Prevents any Java applets from running

- **High Safety**   Enables Java applets to run in their respective sandbox, which is an insolated place in memory.

- **Low Safety**   Enables Java applets to perform all operations

- **Medium Safety**   Enables applets to run in their respective sandbox and gives the applets other capabilities, such as access to scratch space and user-controlled file input and output

Miscellaneous Options

The Miscellaneous options control whether users can access data sources across domains, submit data by using nonencrypted forms, launch applications and files from *IFRAME* elements, install desktop items, drag and drop files, copy and paste files, and access software channel features from this zone. These are the options:

- **Access Data Sources Across Domains**   Specifies whether components that connect to data sources should be allowed to connect to a different server to obtain data. You can set this option to the following:

  - ❑ **Disable**   Allows database access only in the same domain as the Web page

  - ❑ **Enable**   Allows database access to any source, including other domains

  - ❑ **Prompt**   Prompts users before allowing database access to any source in other domains

- **Allow META REFRESH**   Specifies whether Web pages can use meta-refreshes to reload pages after a preset delay. You can set this option to the following:

  - ❑ **Disable**   Prevents Web pages from using meta-refreshes

  - ❑ **Enable**   Allows Web pages to use meta-refreshes

- **Display Mixed Content**   Specifies whether Web pages can display content from both secure and nonsecure servers. You can set this option to one of the following:

  - ❑ **Disable**   Prevents Web pages from displaying nonsecure content.

  - ❑ **Enable**   Allows Web pages to display both secure and nonsecure content.

  - ❑ **Prompt**   Prompts users before allowing Web pages to display both secure and nonsecure content. You should set this option to prompt you when not everything on the Web site you are viewing is secured by SSL or TLS.

- **Don't Prompt For Client Certificate Selection When No Certificates Or Only One Certificate Exists**   Specifies whether users are prompted to select a certificate when no trusted certificate or only one trusted certificate has been installed on the computer. You can choose from the following settings:

❑   **Disable**   Allows users to be prompted for a certificate

❑   **Enable**   Prevents users from being prompted for a certificate

■   **Drag And Drop Or Copy And Paste Files**   Controls whether users can drag and drop files, or copy and paste them, from Web pages within the zone. You can set this option to one of these:

❑   **Disable**   Prevents users from dragging and dropping files, or copying and pasting them, from the security zone

❑   **Enable**   Enables users to drag and drop files, or copy and paste them, from the security zone without being prompted

❑   **Prompt**   Prompts users to choose whether they can drag and drop files, or copy and paste them, from the security zone

■   **Installation Of Desktop Items**   Controls whether users can install desktop items from Web pages within the zone. You can choose one of these settings:

❑   **Disable**   Prevents users from installing desktop items from this zone

❑   **Enable**   Enables users to install desktop items from this zone without being prompted

❑   **Prompt**   Prompts users to choose whether they can install desktop items from this zone

■   **Launching Programs And Files In An IFRAME**   Controls whether users can launch programs and files from an *IFRAME* element (containing a directory or folder reference) in Web pages within the zone. You can choose from these settings:

❑   **Disable**   Prevents programs from running and files from downloading from *IFRAME* elements on Web pages in the zone

❑   **Enable**   Runs programs and downloads files from *IFRAME* elements on Web pages in the zone without user intervention

❑   **Prompt**   Prompts users to choose whether to run programs and download files from *IFRAME* elements on Web pages in the zone

■   **Navigate Subframes Across Different Domains**   Controls whether readers of a Web page can navigate the subframe of a window with a top-level document that resides in a different domain. You can set this option to one of the following choices:

❑ **Disable**   Allows users to navigate only among Web page sub-frames that reside in the same domain

❑ **Enable**   Allows users to navigate among all Web page sub-frames, regardless of the domain, without being prompted

❑ **Prompt**   Prompts users to choose whether to navigate among Web page subframes that reside in different domains

■ **Software Channel Permissions**   Controls the permissions given to software distribution channels. You can set this option to any of the following:

❑ **High Safety**   Prevents users from being notified about software updates by e-mail, prevents software packages from being automatically downloaded to users' computers, and prevents software packages from being automatically installed on users' computers.

❑ **Medium Safety**   Notifies users about software updates by e-mail, and allows software packages to be automatically downloaded to (but not installed on) users' computers. The software packages must be validly signed; users are not prompted about the download.

❑ **Low Safety**   Notifies users about software updates by e-mail, allows software packages to be automatically downloaded to users' computers, and allows software packages to be automatically installed on users' computers.

■ **Submit Nonencrypted Form Data**   Determines whether HTML pages in the zone can submit forms to or accept them from servers in the zone. Forms sent with SSL encryption are always allowed; this setting affects only data that is submitted by non-SSL forms. You can choose from the following settings:

❑ **Disable**   Prevents information from forms on HTML pages in the zone from being submitted

❑ **Enable**   Allows information from forms on HTML pages in the zone to be submitted without user intervention

❑ **Prompt**   Prompts users to choose whether to allow information from forms on HTML pages in the zone to be submitted

■ **Userdata Persistence**   Determines whether a Web page can save a small file of personal information associated with the page to the computer. You can set this option to the following:

❑ **Disable**   Prevents a Web page from saving a small file of personal information to the computer

❑ **Enable**   Allows a Web page to save a small file of personal information to the computer

Scripting Options

The Scripting options specify how Internet Explorer handles scripts embedded in Web pages:

■ **Active Scripting**   Determines whether Internet Explorer can run script code on Web pages in the zone. You can set this option to one of the following:

❑ **Disable**   Prevents scripts from running

❑ **Enable**   Runs scripts without user intervention

❑ **Prompt**   Prompts users about whether to allow the scripts to run

■ **Allow Paste Operations Via Script**   Determines whether a Web page can cut, copy, and paste information from the Clipboard. You can choose one of the following settings:

❑ **Disable**   Prevents a Web page from cutting, copying, and pasting information from the Clipboard

❑ **Enable**   Allows a Web page to cut, copy, and paste information from the Clipboard without user intervention

❑ **Prompt**   Prompts users about whether to allow a Web page to cut, copy, or paste information from the Clipboard

■ **Scripting Of Java Applets**   Determines whether scripts within the zone can use objects that exist within Java applets. This capability allows a script on a Web page to interact with a Java applet. You can set this option to one of these:

❑ **Disable**   Prevents scripts from accessing applets

❑ **Enable**   Allows scripts to access applets without user intervention

❑ **Prompt**   Prompts users about whether to allow scripts to access applets

The User Authentication Option

Only one User Authentication option exists: the Logon option. This option controls how HTTP user authentication is handled. Logon has the following settings:

■ **Anonymous Logon**   Disables HTTP authentication and uses the guest account only for authentication by using the Common Internet File System (CIFS) protocol.

■ **Automatic Logon Only In Intranet Zone**   Prompts users for user IDs and passwords in other security zones. After users are prompted, these values can be used for the remainder of the session without user interaction.

■ **Automatic Logon With Current User Name And Password**   Attempts logon by using NT LAN Manager (NTLM) authentication. If NTLM is supported by the server, the logon uses the network user name and password for logon. If the server does not support NTLM, users are prompted to provide their user names and passwords. You should use this setting only for sites in the Intranet zone.

■ **Prompt For User Name And Password**   Always prompts users for user IDs and passwords. User names and passwords are cached for the remainder of the session.

In addition to the security settings in security zones, some global security settings apply to all security zones when using Internet Explorer. You can configure these global options on the Advanced tab of Internet Options. Here are the security settings on the Advanced tab and their default values:

■ **Check For Publisher's Certificate Revocation**   Internet Explorer will check the certificate revocation list (CRL) for the status of a software publisher's certificate when downloading ActiveX controls. This option is enabled by default.

■ **Check For Server Certificate Revocation**   Internet Explorer will check the CRL for Web sites that require SSL or TLS. Enabling this option might cause a slight delay in connecting to secure Web sites but adds to the security of browsing the Internet. This option is disabled by default.

- **Check For Signatures On Downloaded Programs**   Internet Explorer will verify the digital signatures on ActiveX controls. This option is disabled by default.

- **Do Not Save Encrypted Pages To Disk**   No Web pages or parts of Web pages viewed in a secure session will be saved in the Temporary Internet Files folder. This option should be enabled on all public computers or computers with high security requirements. This option is disabled by default.

- **Empty Temporary Internet Files Folder When Browser Is Closed**   Deletes the contents of the Temporary Internet Files folder each time the Web browser is closed. This option should be enabled on all public computers or computers with high security requirements. This option is disabled by default.

- **Enable Integrated Windows Authentication**   Only NTLM-based authentication methods will be used to authenticate users if prompted by the Web server. This option is disabled by default.

- **Enable Profile Assistant**   Allows you to use the Profile Assistant to store and maintain personal information. This option is disabled by default.

- **Use SSL 2.0**   Allows the use of SSL 2.0 for connections over secure channels. This option is enabled by default.

- **Use SSL 3.0**   Allows the use of SSL 3.0 for connections over secure channels. This option is enabled by default.

- **Use TLS 1.0**   Allows the use of TLS 1.0 for connections over secure channels. This option is disabled by default.

- **Warn About Invalid Site Certificates**   Presents a message box to users, warning them that the secure Web site they are connecting to is using a certificate that is no longer valid. This option is enabled by default.

- **Warn If Changing Between Secure And Not Secure Methods**   Presents a message box to users, warning them that they are moving between Web sites that either are secure or not secure. This option is enabled by default.

- **Warn If Forms Submittal Is Being Redirected**   Presents a message box to users, warning them that Internet Explorer is being redirected to another Web site or location to retrieve content. This option is enabled by default.

Configuring Privacy and Security Settings in Internet Explorer 6

You can configure privacy and security settings in Internet Explorer manually though Internet Options from the Tools menu, during installation with the Internet Explorer Administration Kit (IEAK), or by using Group Policy. If you plan to deploy Internet Explorer in your organization, you should consider using the IEAK.

> **More Info** The IEAK is beyond the scope of this book, but you can get more information about it from the IEAK Web site at *http://www.microsoft.com/windows/ieak/default.asp.*

You can use Group Policy to manage the privacy and security settings in Internet Explorer on a per-user basis and control whether users can change settings on a per-user basis or a per-computer basis.

Group Policy in Windows 2000 enables you to centrally configure and manage Internet Explorer security on a per-user basis. To configure Internet Explorer privacy and security settings through Group Policy, open the Microsoft Management Console (MMC) on a computer running Windows XP and add the Group Policy snap-in. If you create a Group Policy object (GPO) on Windows 2000, you might not be able to configure the privacy settings unless you have Internet Explorer 6.0 or later installed.

After importing the security zones and privacy settings from the computer you are editing the GPO on, you can modify the settings and apply the GPO to a site, domain, or OU containing the user accounts that should be subject to the privacy and security settings. You can also export the settings into .ins and .cab files for use with the IEAK.

In addition to configuring the privacy and security zone settings, as a network administrator, you can configure whether the user can modify Internet Explorer security settings. You can configure the following settings in the user-related portion of Group Policy by selecting the Administrative Templates menu option, then Windows Components, and then Internet Explorer:

■ **Disable Changing Connection Settings** Users will be prevented from changing how Internet Explorer connects to the Internet.

■ **Disable Changing Proxy Settings** Users will not be able to change the proxy server settings used by Internet Explorer.

■ **Disable Changing Profile Assistant Settings** Users will not be able to change the Profile Assistant settings.

- **Do Not Allow AutoComplete To Save Passwords**   Users will not be given the option to have Web site passwords saved by Internet Explorer.

- **Internet Control Panel/Disable The Security Page**   The Security page in Internet Options will not appear. Thus, users will not be able to change the security zones on the computer.

- **Internet Control Panel/Disable The Advanced Page**   The Advanced page in Internet Options will not appear. Thus, users will not be able to change the advanced security settings on the computer.

You also can make four Group Policy settings in the computer-related Internet Explorer security options. These settings will apply to all users of the computer.

- **Security Zones: Use Only Machine Settings**   Internet Explorer will use only the security zones configured on the computer, rather than configuring them on a per-user basis according to the user-related Group Policy settings.

- **Security Zones: Do Not Allow Users To Change Policies**   Users will be prevented from making changes to the security zones on the computer.

- **Security Zones: Do Not Allow Users To Add/Delete Sites**   Users will not be able to add or remove sites from the Trusted Sites or Restricted Sites zones.

- **Disable Automatic Install Of Internet Explorer Components**   Internet Explorer will not automatically download and install ActiveX components when a user visits a Web site where these components are used.

Security Settings in Office XP

Office XP provides several methods for managing application and document security. A basic understanding of how the Office XP security features work can help you create a secure environment for your users' applications and data. The primary areas for Office XP security are ActiveX and macros security.

Configuring ActiveX and Macros Security

Office XP enables you to configure security for ActiveX controls and macros that are signed using Microsoft Authenticode. Office XP verifies that the control or macro code remains unchanged after being signed with a digital certificate. Signing controls and macros also provides assurance that they originated from the signer.

ActiveX controls are used to add dynamic or interactive content and functionality to Office XP documents. When the ActiveX security controls are active or when a user attempts to load an unregistered ActiveX control, the Office XP application checks to see whether the control has been digitally signed.

Macros are used to complete a series of application commands and instructions that are grouped together as a single command to accomplish a task automatically. Many of the viruses that are active on the Internet today attempt to exploit the macro features of Microsoft Office applications. Thus, you must consider the level of macro security configured on your network.

Signing macros allows you to exercise control over the macros users can run. You can specify that unsigned macros may or may not run. You can also control which certificates will be trusted by Office XP for signing macros. Because the digital certificates that you create yourself are not issued by a formal Certification Authority (CA), macro projects signed by using such a certificate are referred to as *self-signed projects*. Certificates you create yourself are considered unauthenticated and generate warning messages if the security level is set to High or Medium.

You can configure how Office XP applications handle ActiveX controls and macros by configuring the level of macro security in Office XP. Three levels of macro security exist:

■   **High Security**   ActiveX controls not signed by a trusted authority will not run.

■   **Medium Security**   Users are prompted to accept or reject the digital signature of the control. If the signature is accepted, the control is loaded and run.

■   **Low Security**   Digital signatures are ignored and the ActiveX controls are run without user intervention. You should configure this setting only if you have specific technical reasons for doing so.

Note   After the control is registered on the user's system, the control no longer displays code-signing dialog boxes asking the user whether the control should be allowed to run. Once a control is installed, it is considered safe, even if it did not have a digital signature when it was installed.

The Office XP Trusted Sources feature enables you to specify that executables must be digitally signed to run on users' computers and that only executables from a list of trusted providers can be executed. Using the Trusted Sources feature requires that a digital certificate be used to sign each executable. The digital signature identifies the source, providing assurance to the user that the code is safe to run.

With Office XP, you can turn the Trusted Sources feature off or create a list of trusted sources as a default. When the use of trusted sources is enabled, any installable code (such as COM add-ins, applets, and executables) is automatically copied to, or run from, the user's computer on the condition that the signature on the code indicates that it came from a trusted source.

You can configure Office XP and Office 2000 security settings on Windows 2000 and Windows XP computers by using Group Policy. To add the Administrative Template files for Office XP or Office 2000 to Group Policy, follow the instructions in 307732: "How to Add a Windows 2000 ADM Template to a Group Policy Snap-In in Office XP." (You can access this article by going to *http://support.microsoft.com* and entering the article number in the Search The Knowledge Base text box.) Figure 10-4 shows the computer-related security settings in Group Policy for Office XP.

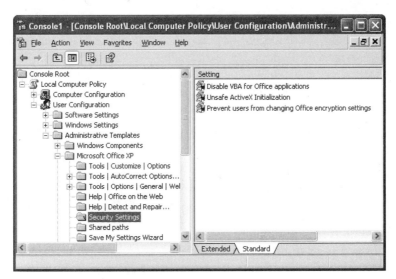

Figure 10-4   Computer-related security settings for Office XP in Group Policy

Configuring Security for Outlook 2002

Arguably, the biggest security threats to most computers are e-mail viruses and Web viruses. Although user education and antivirus software are the best defenses against these viruses, you can also configure the security in Outlook 2002 to help prevent these threats. Default settings for security can be created during deployment by using the Custom Installation Wizard (CIW). After the deployment, the security settings can be maintained and updated by using the Custom Maintenance Wizard (CMW). However, the CIW and CMW do not provide any policy enforcement. For policy enforcement, you can use Group Policy.

Attachment Security

Code attached to e-mail messages can contain worms or viruses. After one machine is infected with a worm or virus, the nature of networked e-mail systems allows these rogue applications to propagate themselves rapidly. To protect against virus infection, Outlook checks the file type of each message attachment against an internally maintained list of attachment file types. Administrators can also specify a list in a Microsoft Exchange public folder so that specific Outlook clients in an organization have a custom list. Each file type on the list is assigned one of these levels:

- **Level 1**   File types, such as .bat, .exe, .vbs, and .js, are blocked by Outlook, and users cannot view or execute the attachment. A message is displayed to the user, letting her know about the blocked attachments. In addition, when you send an attachment that has a Level 1 file type extension, a message displays to warn you that Outlook recipients might not be able to access this type of attachment.

- **Level 2**   This level applies to all other file types. Level 2 attachments let you see the icon for the attachment. When you double-click this icon, you are prompted to save the attachment to your hard disk, but you cannot run the file directly from its location. After you have saved the attachment, you can decide how to handle it.

Protecting HTML Messages

To protect against viruses that might be contained in HTML messages you receive, you can use the default security zone in Outlook 2002: Restricted Sites. When you use this security zone, scripts in HTML-formatted e-mail messages will not run and ActiveX controls will be deactivated. You also should consider turning off JavaScript to protect against malicious exploits that are based on JavaScript. However, note that doing so can reduce some mail functionality when you are reading mail sent by users or organizations that depend on embedded

JavaScript. You can turn off JavaScript by customizing the security options in the Restricted Sites zone by disabling JavaScript or by prompting users to choose Active Scripting.

Best Practices

■ **Educate users.** The best defense against e-mail viruses and Web viruses is to educate users about how to safely use the Internet. You should teach users how to answer common prompts relating to ActiveX controls and macros.

■ **Install and maintain antivirus software.** By keeping antivirus software up to date you will be protected from nearly all known attacks on Office applications and documents.

■ **Apply security updates.** Always apply the latest security updates to any application that you use on your network, including Internet Explorer and Office.

■ **Implement secure default settings.** Use the IEAK and the CIW to install security default settings for Internet Explorer and Office XP.

■ **Use Group Policy to manage security settings.** Import the Administrative Templates included with the *Microsoft Office XP Resource Kit* (Microsoft Press, 2001) into Group Policy and configure the security settings for Office applications that users work with on your network.

■ **Do not install software that will not be used.** Do not install applications on computers if they will not used. For example, if a user will be using only Microsoft Word and Outlook, do not install Microsoft PowerPoint and Microsoft Excel on his computer. This will increase the potential attack surface of the computer.

Additional Information

■ Internet Explorer Administration Kit (IEAK) home page (*http://www.microsoft.com/windows/ieak/default.asp*)

■ Microsoft Office XP Resource Kit/Toolbox, including downloadable deployment and maintenance tools (*http://www.microsoft.com/office/ork/xp/appndx/appa00.htm*)

- 182569: "Description of Internet Explorer Security Zones Registry Entries"

- 296287: "Port Numbers Are Missing from URL of Web Sites Assigned to Security Zones"

- 308983: "How to Specify Trusted Sources for Digital Certificates in Excel 2002, PowerPoint 2002, and Word 2002"

- 283185: "How to Manage Cookies in Internet Explorer 6"

- 300443: "A Description of the Changes to the Security Settings of the Web Content Zones in Internet Explorer 6"

- 287567: "Considerations for Disabling VBA in Office XP"

- 249972: "How Outlook Renders HTML"

- 233396: "How to Reduce the Chances of Macro Virus Infection"

- 211607: "Frequently Asked Questions About Word Macro Viruses"

> **Note**   The previous nine articles can be accessed through the Microsoft Knowledge Base. Go to *http://support.microsoft.com* and enter the article number in the Search The Knowledge Base text box.

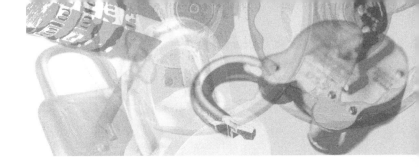

11

Configuring Security Templates

Security templates are files that contain settings for securing your Microsoft Windows 2000 and Microsoft Windows XP computers. You can apply security templates to the local computer or import them into a Group Policy object (GPO) in the Active Directory directory service. When you import a security template into a GPO, Group Policy processes the template and makes the corresponding settings to the computers affected by the GPO. You can use security templates to apply consistent security settings to a large group of computers when you cannot use Group Policy. Windows 2000 provides a set of precreated security templates for you to use in specific scenarios but also gives you the ability to create custom security templates.

Using Security Template Settings

Security templates offer seven categories of security settings. Additionally, in the Security Settings section of computer-related section Group Policy, two additional categories of security settings exist. You use each category to apply specific computer-based security settings. The categories of security settings follow:

- **Account Policies** Define password policies, account lockout policies, and Kerberos policies

> **Important**   Account policy settings applied at the OU level affect the local Security Accounts Manager (SAM) databases but not the user accounts in Active Directory. The account policies for domain accounts can be configured only at the domain-level Group Policy.

- **Local Policies**   Define audit policy, user rights assignment, and security option settings for computers

- **Event Log**   Defines the properties of the application, security, and system logs

- **Restricted Groups**   Define and enforce membership in security groups

- **System Services**   Define settings for services installed on a computer

- **Registry**   Defines security and auditing permissions for registry keys and their subtrees

- **File System**   Defines NTFS file system security and auditing settings for any files and folders included within this policy

- **Public Key Policies**   Define settings for enterprise Certification Authority (CA) trust lists, encrypting file system (EFS) data recovery agents, trusted root CAs, and automatic certificate renewal settings

- **IP Security Policies**   Define the IP Security (IPSec) policy that is assigned to the computer

Account Policies

Account policies define security on domain and local accounts. Account policy settings for domain accounts must be configured at the domain level. When you define individual account policy settings for a specific OU, the account policies apply to local accounts on the computers that are affected by the group policy. Account policies contain three subcategories of configuration:

- Password Policy
- Account Lockout Policy
- Kerberos Policy

Table 11-1 describes the policy settings for each category.

Table 11-1   Account Policy Settings

Setting	Subcategory	Description
Enforce Password History	Password Policy	Determines the number of unique new passwords that have to be associated with a user account before an old password can be reused. The value must be set to a number of passwords between 0 and 24.
Maximum Password Age	Password Policy	Determines the number of days that a password can be used before the system requires the user to change it. You can set passwords to expire after a number of days between 1 and 999, or you can specify that passwords never expire by setting the number of days to 0.
Minimum Password Age	Password Policy	Determines the number of days that a password must be used before the user can change it. You can set values to a number of days between 1 and 999, or you can allow changes immediately by setting the number of days to 0.
Minimum Password Length	Password Policy	Determines the least number of characters a user account's password can contain. You can set values to a number of characters between 1 and 14. Setting this value to 0 will allow users to use a blank password.
Password Must Meet Complexity Requirements	Password Policy	Determines whether passwords must meet complexity requirements, which require a password to have at least six characters from three of these four sets: ■ English uppercase letters ■ English lowercase letters ■ Base 10 digits ■ Nonalphanumeric symbols, such as !, $, #, and %
Store Password Using Reversible Encryption For All Users In The Domain	Password Policy	Determines whether Windows 2000 will store passwords by using reversible encryption in the account database.

(continued)

Table 11-1 Account Policy Settings   *(continued)*

Setting	Subcategory	Description
Account Lockout Threshold	Account Lock-out Policy	Determines the number of failed logon attempts that will cause a user account to be locked out. You can set values to a number of failed logon attempts between 1 and 999, or you can specify that the account will never be locked out by setting the value to 0.
Account Lockout Duration	Account Lock-out Policy	Determines the number of minutes a locked-out account remains locked out before automatically becoming unlocked. The range is 1–99,999 minutes. You can specify that the account will be locked out until an administrator explicitly unlocks it by setting the value to 0.
Reset Account Lockout After	Account Lock-out Policy	Determines the number of minutes that must elapse after a failed logon attempt before the bad logon attempt counter is reset to 0. The range is 1–99,999 minutes.
Enforce User Logon Restrictions	Kerberos Policy	Determines whether the key distribution center (KDC) validates that the user possesses the Log On Locally or Access The Computer From The Network user rights for every session ticket request.
Maximum Lifetime For Service Ticket	Kerberos Policy	Determines the maximum number of minutes that a granted session ticket can be used. The setting must be greater than 10 minutes.
Maximum Lifetime For User Ticket	Kerberos Policy	Determines the maximum number of hours that a user's ticket-granting ticket (TGT) can be used before it is renewed or a new one is requested.
Maximum Lifetime For User Ticket Renewal	Kerberos Policy	Determines the number of days during which a user's TGT can be renewed.
Maximum Tolerance For Computer Clock Synchronization	Kerberos Policy	Determines the maximum number of minutes that Kerberos will tolerate between the time on a client's system clock and the time on a server's system clock when issuing and using Kerberos tickets. This is to prevent replay attacks on authentication packets.

> **More Info**   Account policies are discussed in depth in Chapter 3,
> "Securing User Accounts and Passwords," of this book.

Local Policies

Local policies determine security settings on the local computer. These policies
are separated into three subcategories:

- Audit Policy
- User Rights Assignment
- Security Options

Table 11-2 describes the policy settings for each category.

Table 11-2   Local Policy Settings

Setting	Subcategory	Description
Audit Account Logon Events	Audit Policy	Determines whether to audit each instance of a user logging on or logging off of another computer that was used to validate the account.
Audit Account Management Events	Audit Policy	Determines whether to audit each event in which an account is created, modified, or deleted on a computer.
Audit Directory Service Access	Audit Policy	Determines whether to audit the event of a user accessing an Active Directory object that has its own system access control list (SACL) specified.
Audit Logon Events	Audit Policy	Determines whether to audit each instance of a user logging on, logging off, or making a network connection to this computer
Audit Object Access	Audit Policy	Determines whether to audit the event of a user accessing a file, folder, registry key, or printer object that has its own SACL specified.
Audit Policy Change	Audit Policy	Determines whether to audit every instance of a change to user rights assignment policies, audit policies, or trust policies.

(continued)

Table 11-2 Local Policy Settings *(continued)*

Setting	Subcategory	Description
Audit Privilege Use	Audit Policy	Determines whether to audit each instance of a user exercising a user right with the exception of the Bypass Traverse Checking, Debug Programs, Create A Token Object, Replace Process Level Token, Generate Security Audits, Backup Files And Directories, and Restore Files And Directories user rights.
Audit Process Tracking	Audit Policy	Determines whether to audit detailed tracking information for events such as program activation, process exit, handle duplication, and indirect access of system objects.
Audit System Events	Audit Policy	Determines whether to audit when a user restarts or shuts down the computer, or when an event occurs that affects either the system security or the security log.
Access This Computer From The Network	User Rights Assignment	Determines which users and groups are allowed to connect to the computer over the network.
Act As Part Of The Operating System	User Rights Assignment	Allows a process to authenticate as any user and therefore gain access to the same resources under the security context of that user. Only low-level authentication services should require this privilege.
Add Workstations To Domain	User Rights Assignment	Determines which groups or users can add workstations to a domain. This policy is valid only on domain controllers. By default, any authenticated user has this right and can create up to 10 computer accounts in the domain with this right.
Allow Logon Through Terminal Services	User Rights Assignment	Determines which groups or users can log on using Remote Desktop Services. This right applies to Windows XP computers only.
Back Up Files And Directories	User Rights Assignment	Determines which groups and users can run processes to back up files and folders without regard to NTFS permissions.

Table 11-2   Local Policy Settings   *(continued)*

Setting	Subcategory	Description
Bypass Traverse Checking	User Rights Assignment	Determines which groups and users can traverse directory trees even though the user might not have permissions on the traversed directory.
Change The System Time	User Rights Assignment	Determines which groups and users can change the time and date on the system clock of the computer.
Create A Pagefile	User Rights Assignment	Determines which users and groups can create and change the size of a pagefile.
Create A Token Object	User Rights Assignment	Determines which accounts can be used by processes to create a token that can then be used to gain access to any local resources when the process uses *NtCreateToken()* or other token-creation APIs.
Create Permanent Shared Objects	User Rights Assignment	Determines which accounts can be used by processes to create a directory object in the Windows 2000 Object Manager. By default, only kernel-mode components, which run under the security context of LocalSystem, possess this right.
Debug Programs	User Rights Assignment	Determines which users can attach a debugger to any process. This privilege provides powerful access to sensitive and critical OS components.
Deny Access To This Computer From The Network	User Rights Assignment	Determines which users are prevented from accessing a computer over the network. This policy setting supercedes the Access This Computer From The Network policy setting if a user account is subject to both policies.
Deny Logon As A Batch Job	User Rights Assignment	Determines which accounts are prevented from logging on as a batch job. This policy setting supercedes the Log On As A Batch Job policy setting if a user account is subject to both policies.
Deny Logon As A Service	User Rights Assignment	Determines which service accounts are prevented from registering a process as a service. This policy setting supercedes the Log On As A Service policy setting if an account is subject to both policies.

(continued)

Table 11-2   Local Policy Settings   *(continued)*

Setting	Subcategory	Description
Deny Logon Locally	User Rights Assignment	Determines which users are prevented from logging on at the computer. This policy setting supercedes the Log On Locally policy setting if an account is subject to both policies.
Deny Logon Through Terminal Services	User Rights Assignment	Determines which groups or users cannot log on using Remote Desktop Services. This right applies to Windows XP computers only.
Enable Computer And User Accounts To Be Trusted For Delegation	User Rights Assignment	Determines which users can set the Trusted For Delegation setting on a user or computer object.
Force Shutdown From A Remote System	User Rights Assignment	Determines which users are allowed to shut down a computer from a remote location on the network.
Generate Security Audits	User Rights Assignment	Determines which accounts a process can use to add entries to the security log. By default, only LocalSystem has this right.
Increase Quotas	User Rights Assignment	Determines which users or groups can use a process with Write access to another process to increase the processor quota assigned to the other process. This setting has nothing to do with disk quotas. In Windows XP, this setting has been renamed to Adjust Memory Quotas.
Increase Scheduling Priority	User Rights Assignment	Determines which accounts can use a process with Write access to another process to increase the execution priority assigned to the other process. A user with this privilege can change the scheduling priority of a process by using the Task Manager.
Load And Unload Device Drivers	User Rights Assignment	Determines which users can dynamically load and unload device drivers. This right is necessary for installing drivers for Plug and Play devices.
Lock Pages In Memory	User Rights Assignment	This right is obsolete and therefore is never checked.

Table 11-2   Local Policy Settings   *(continued)*

Setting	Subcategory	Description
Log On As A Batch Job	User Rights Assignment	Determines which groups or users can log on using a batch-queue application such as the Task Scheduler.
Log On As A Service	User Rights Assignment	Determines which service accounts can register a process as a service.
Log On Locally	User Rights Assignment	Determines which users can log on at the computer interactively by using the Windows Logon dialog box, Terminal Services, or Internet Information Services (IIS).
Manage Auditing And Security Log	User Rights Assignment	Determines which users can specify object access auditing options for individual resources such as files, Active Directory objects, and registry keys.
Modify Firmware Environment Values	User Rights Assignment	Determines which groups or users can modify systemwide environment variables.
Perform Volume Maintenance Tasks	User Rights Assignment	Determines which users and groups have the authority to run volume maintenance tools, such as Disk Cleanup and Disk Defragmenter. This right applies to Windows XP computers only.
Profile Single Process	User Rights Assignment	Determines which users can use performance monitoring tools to monitor the performance of nonsystem processes.
Profile System Performance	User Rights Assignment	Determines which users can use performance monitoring tools to monitor the performance of system processes.
Remove Computer From Docking Station	User Rights Assignment	Determines which users can undock a laptop computer from its docking station. This right applies only to computers that have been upgraded from Microsoft Windows NT.
Replace A Process Level Token	User Rights Assignment	Determines which user accounts can initiate a process to replace the default token associated with a launched subprocess. Only LocalSystem possesses this right.

(continued)

Table 11-2   Local Policy Settings   *(continued)*

Setting	Subcategory	Description
Restore Files And Directories	User Rights Assignment	Determines which groups and users can run processes to restore files and folders without regard to NTFS permissions. Users with this permission can also reassign ownership of files and folders.
Shut Down The System	User Rights Assignment	Determines which users logged on locally to the computer can shut down the OS.
Synchronize Directory Service Data	User Rights Assignment	This right is not used in Windows 2000 or Windows XP.
Take Ownership Of Files Or Other Objects	User Rights Assignment	Determines which users can take ownership of system objects, including Active Directory objects, files and folders, printers, registry keys, processes, and threads.
Additional Restrictions For Anonymous Connections	Security Options	Determines the security level on anonymous NetBIOS enumeration by configuring the HKEY_LOCAL_MACHINE\SYSTEM\CurrentControlSet\Control\LSA\RestrictAnonymous registry value. You can change this setting to one of the following: ■ None. Rely On Default Permissions Allows null credentials ■ Do Not Allow Enumeration Of SAM Accounts And Shares Replaces Everyone with Authenticated Users in the security permissions for resources ■ No Access Without Explicit Anonymous Permissions Removes Everyone and Network from the anonymous users token, thus requiring that Anonymous be given explicit access to any required resources
Allow Server Operators To Schedule Tasks (Domain Controllers Only)	Security Options	Determines whether Server Operators are allowed to submit scheduled tasks using the Task Scheduler on domain controllers.

Table 11-2 **Local Policy Settings**   *(continued)*

Setting	Subcategory	Description
Allow System To Be Shut Down Without Having To Log On	Security Options	Determines whether a computer can be shut down without the user having to log on to the OS. Unless you have a specific reason for allowing anyone with physical access to the computer to shut down the computer, you should not enable this option.
Allowed To Eject Removable NTFS Media	Security Options	Determines who is allowed to eject removable NTFS media from the computer.
Amount Of Idle Time Required Before Disconnecting Session	Security Options	Determines the number of minutes that must pass in a Server Message Block (SMB) session before the session is disconnected because of inactivity. After an SMB connection is disconnected, the user or computer account must be reauthenticated. The default value for this setting is 15 minutes.
Audit The Access Of Global System Objects	Security Options	Determines whether access of global system objects that have SACLs configured (for example, mutexes and semaphores) will be audited. You should enable this option only if you are troubleshooting OS internal operations.
Audit Use Of Backup And Restore Privilege	Security Options	Determines whether the Audit Privileged Use audit policy should include use of the Backup/Restore privilege.
Automatically Log Off Users When Logon Time Expires	Security Options	Determines whether to disconnect users from SMB resources that are connected to the local machine outside the user account's valid logon hours for all computers in the domain. You should enable this setting if you have users whose logon times are restricted.
Automatically Log Off Users When Logon Time Expires (Local)	Security Options	Determines whether to disconnect users from SMB resources that are connected to the local machine outside the user account's valid logon hours.

(continued)

Table 11-2 Local Policy Settings   *(continued)*

Setting	Subcategory	Description
Clear Virtual Memory Pagefile When System Shuts Down	Security Options	Determines whether the virtual memory data stored in the pagefile should be cleared before the computer is shut down. On servers with large amounts of RAM, enabling this setting could result in lengthy shutdown and restart times.
Digitally Sign Client Communications (Always)	Security Options	Determines whether the computer will always digitally sign SMB communications by using SMB signing when connecting to SMB resources on other computers.
Digitally Sign Client Communications (When Possible)	Security Options	Determines whether the computer will, when requested, digitally sign SMB communications by using SMB signing. Otherwise, the computer will communicate normally when connecting to SMB resources.
Digitally Sign Server Communications (Always)	Security Options	Determines whether the computer will require digital signing for connections to local SMB resources from remote computers. Computers that do not digitally sign client communications will not be able to connect to computers with this setting enabled. Enabling this setting on heavily used computers, such as domain controllers, file servers, or print servers, can cause CPU performance degradation.
Digitally Sign Server Communications (When Possible)	Security Options	Determines whether the computer will request digital signing for connections to local SMB resources from remote computers that digitally sign SMB communications.
Disable Ctrl+Alt+Del Requirement For Logon	Security Options	Determines whether a user must press Ctrl+Alt+Del to invoke the Windows Logon dialog box. You should enable this setting only if you have users with special accessibility requirements.

Table 11-2 Local Policy Settings   *(continued)*

Setting	Subcategory	Description
Do Not Display Last User Name In Logon Screen	Security Options	Determines whether the user name of the last logged-on user appears in the Windows Logon dialog box when the next user attempts to log on. Consider enabling this setting on computers in public areas to prevent user account names and their home domain name from being disclosed.
LAN Manager Authentication Level	Security Options	Determines the value of the HKEY_LOCAL_MACHINE\System\CurrentControlSet\Control\LSA\LMCompatibility registry key, which controls how the LAN Manager (LM), NT LAN Manager (NTLM), and NT LAN Manager version 2 (NTLMv2) authentication protocols are used. See Chapter 3 for more information on LM compatibility levels.
Message Text For Users Attempting To Log On	Security Options	Determines the text in the message box that a user must agree to before the Windows Logon dialog box appears. You must also configure the message title for this option to take effect. You should consult your organization's legal department about what text should be used in this warning.
Message Title For Users Attempting To Log On	Security Options	Determines the title of the message box that a user must agree to before the Windows Logon dialog box appears. You must also configure the message text for this option to take effect.
Number Of Previous Logons To Cache (In Case Domain Controller Is Not Available)	Security Options	Determines the number of previous logon sessions to cache as cached credentials. Cached credentials can be used on the computer to log on when no domain controllers are reachable. You can set this to a value between 0 and 50. If you set this option to 0, users will not be able to log on unless a domain controller is available to validate their credentials. Setting the value to 10, which is the default, will cache the logon credentials from the last 10 users to log on to the computer.

(continued)

Table 11-2   Local Policy Settings   *(continued)*

Setting	Subcategory	Description
Prevent System Maintenance Of Computer Account Password	Security Options	Determines whether the computer account password should be prevented from being reset every 30 days automatically. Do not enable this setting unless you have a specific technical reason.
Prevent Users From Installing Printer Drivers	Security Options	Determines whether members of the Users group are prevented from installing print drivers. This setting is enabled by default.
Prompt User To Change Password Before Expiration	Security Options	Determines how far in advance to warn users that their password will expire. This setting is 14 days by default.
Recovery Console: Allow Automatic Administrative Logon	Security Options	Determines whether the Recovery Console will require a password or whether it will log on automatically. You should enable this setting only on computers that have strong physical security.
Recovery Console: Allow Floppy Copy And Access To All Drives And All Folders	Security Options	Determines the behavior of copying files when operating in the Recovery Console.
Rename Administrator Account	Security Options	Determines whether a different account name will be associated with the security identifier (SID) for the built-in Administrator account. After changing the display name of the Administrator account, you can monitor audit logs to look for attackers attempting to use the new name for this account. If an attacker attempts to use the renamed account, you will know that he has some level of knowledge and skill in compromising networks. In addition to configuring this option, you must also manually change the description of this account. Otherwise, the default description will still be displayed.

Table 11-2   Local Policy Settings   *(continued)*

Setting	Subcategory	Description
Rename Guest Account	Security Options	Determines whether a different account name will be associated with the SID for the built-in Guest account. In addition to configuring this option, you must also manually change the description of this account. Otherwise, the default description will still be displayed.
Restrict CD-ROM Access To Locally Logged-On User Only	Security Options	Determines whether users not logged on interactively can access CD-ROM drives on the local computer when an interactive user is using the CD-ROM.
Restrict Floppy Access To Locally Logged-On User Only	Security Options	Determines whether users not logged on interactively can access floppy drives on the local computer when an interactive user is using the floppy drive.
Secure Channel: Digitally Encrypt Or Sign Secure Channel Data (Always)	Security Options	Determines whether secure channels require encryption or signing. Secure channels are used by the Netlogon service during authentication.
Secure Channel: Digitally Encrypt Secure Channel Data (When Possible)	Security Options	Determines whether secure channels will be encrypted if requested. Secure channels are used by the Netlogon service during authentication.
Secure Channel: Digitally Sign Secure Channel Data (When Possible)	Security Options	Determines whether secure channels will be signed when requested. Secure channels are used by the Netlogon service during authentication.
Secure Channel: Require Strong (Windows 2000 Or Later) Session Key	Security Options	Determines whether strong (128-bit) session keys are used for encrypting or signing secure channel traffic.
Send Unencrypted Password To Connect To Third-Party SMB Servers	Security Options	Determines whether the computer is allowed to send passwords in plaintext to SMB servers that do not support encryption.

(continued)

Table 11-2 Local Policy Settings   *(continued)*

Setting	Subcategory	Description
Shut Down System Immediately If Unable To Log Security Audits	Security Options	Determines whether the system will stop if security events cannot be logged. If this setting is enabled and security events cannot be logged, the computer will display a stop error (blue screen) and only the built-in Administrator account can log on to reset the *Crash-OnAuditFail* registry value to 1.
Smart Card Removal Behavior	Security Options	Determines what should happen when the smart card for a logged-on user is removed from the smart card reader. You can set this to No Action, Lock Workstation, or Force Logoff.
Strengthen Default Permissions Of Global System Objects (e.g. Symbolic Links)	Security Options	Determines the strength of the default discretionary access control lists (DACLs) on system objects such as mutexes and semaphores.
Unsigned Driver Installation Behavior	Security Options	Determines what should happen when an attempt is made to install a device driver that has not been certified by the Windows Hardware Quality Lab (WHQL). You can set this to Silently Succeed, Warn But Allow Installation, or Do Not Allow Installation.
Unsigned Non Driver Installation Behavior	Security Options	Determines what should happen when an attempt is made to install any nondevice driver software that has not been certified. You can set this to Silently Succeed, Warn But Allow Installation, or Do Not Allow Installation.
Accounts: Administrator Account Status	Security Options	Determines whether the built-in Administrator account is enabled or disabled in Windows XP.
Accounts: Guest Account Status	Security Options	Determines whether the built-in Guest account is enabled or disabled in Windows XP.
Accounts: Limit Local Account Use Of Blank Passwords To Console Logon Only	Security Options	Determines whether accounts with blank passwords are restricted to console interactive logons in Windows XP.

Table 11-2 **Local Policy Settings** *(continued)*

Setting	Subcategory	Description
Devices: Allow Undock Without Having To Log On	Security Options	Determines whether a laptop computer can be removed from the docking station that has a mechanical release by a Windows XP user who has not logged on.
Domain Controller: LDAP Server Signing Requirements	Security Options	Determines whether a domain controller will request or require Lightweight Directory Access Protocol (LDAP) packets to be digitally signed. By default, domain controllers do not request LDAP signing.
Domain Controller: Refuse Machine Account Password Changes	Security Options	Determines whether the computer account password will be changed according to the computer account expiration interval, which is 30 days by default. You might enable this setting if a computer will be disconnected from the network for more than 30 days.
Interactive Logon: Require Domain Controller Authentication To Unlock Workstation	Security Option	Determine whether accounts are revalidated by a domain controller rather than being validated by using the cached credentials when the computer running Windows XP is unlocked.
Network Access: Allow Anonymous SID/Name Translation	Security Options	Determines whether an anonymous user can request SID attributes for another user.
Network Access: Do not Allow Storage Of Credentials Or .NET Passports For Network Authentication	Security Options	Determines whether the passwords or credentials are stored for later use in Windows XP.
Network Access: Let Everyone Permissions Apply To Anonymous Users	Security Options	Determines which anonymous connections receive rights and permissions assigned to the Everyone group on the computer.

(continued)

Table 11-2 Local Policy Settings   *(continued)*

Setting	Subcategory	Description
Network Access: Do Not Allow Storage Of Credentials Or .NET Passports For Network Authentication	Security Options	Determines how network logons that use local accounts are authenticated. If this option is set to Classic, network logons that use local account credentials authenticate by using those credentials. If this option is set to Guest Only, network logons that use local accounts are automatically mapped to the Guest account. This option is available in Windows XP only.
Network Access: Named Pipes That Can Be Accessed Anonymously	Security Options	Determines which communication sessions (pipes) will have attributes and permissions that allow anonymous access.
Network Access: Remotely Accessible Registry Paths	Security Options	Determines which registry paths will be accessible remotely.
Network Access: Shares That Can Be Accessed Anonymously	Security Options	Determines which network shares can accessed by anonymous users.
Network Access: Sharing And Security Model For Local Accounts	Security Options	Determines how network logons that use local accounts are authenticated. If this option is set to Classic, network logons that use local account credentials authenticate by using those credentials. If this option is set to Guest Only, network logons that use local accounts are automatically mapped to the Guest account. The Classic model allows fine control over access to resources. By using the Classic model, you can grant different types of access to different users for the same resource. When you use the Guest Only model, all users will be treated equally. All users authenticate as Guest and receive the same level of access to a given resource, which can be either Read Only or Modify.

Table 11-2 Local Policy Settings   *(continued)*

Setting	Subcategory	Description
Network Security: Do Not Store LAN Manager Hash Values For Passwords	Security Options	Determines whether LM password hashes are created for user accounts. This setting does not take effect until the next time the user changes her password.
Network Security: Minimum Session Security For NTLM SSP Based (Including Secure RPC) Clients	Security Options	Determines the minimum security standards for NTLM authentication of client connections.
Network Security: Minimum Session Security For NTLM SSP Based (Including Secure RPC) Servers	Security Options	Determines the minimum security standards for NTLM authentication of server connections.
Network Security: LDAP Client Signing Requirements	Security Options	Determines whether your computer's communications with an LDAP server must be digitally signed.
System Cryptography: Use FIPS Compliant Algorithms For Encryption, Signing, and Hashing	Security Options	Determines whether 3DES is used for EFS and Transport Layer Security (TLS) in Windows XP.
System Objects: Default Owner For Objects Created By Members Of The Administrators Group	Security Options	Determines whether the Administrators group or the object creator is the default owner of any system objects that are created.
System Objects: Require Case Insensitivity For Non-Windows Subsystems	Security Options	Determines whether the POSIX and OS/2 subsystems require case insensitivity for file names.
System Objects: Strengthen Default Permissions Of Internal System Objects (e.g. Symbolic Links)	Security Options	Determines the strength of the default DACL for objects. If this policy is enabled, the default DACL is stronger, allowing users who are not administrators to read shared objects but not allowing these users to modify shared objects that they did not create.

> **More Info**   Audit policies are discussed in depth in Chapter 12, "Auditing Microsoft Windows Security Events," of this book, and user rights assignments are discussed in depth in Chapter 3.

Event Log

You can control the behavior of Windows 2000 and Windows XP event logs by using security templates. Table 11-3 describes the event log policy settings.

Table 11-3   Event Log Policy Settings

Setting	Description
Maximum Application Log Size	Determines maximum size of the application log before the retention policy setting takes effect.
Maximum Security Log Size	Determines maximum size of the security log before the retention policy setting takes effect.
Maximum System Log Size	Determines maximum size of the system log before the retention policy setting takes effect.
Prevent Local Guests Group From Accessing Application Log	Determines whether guests can read the application log.
Prevent Local Guests group from accessing security log	Determines whether guests can read the security log.
Prevent Local Guests Group From Accessing System Log	Determines whether guests can read the system log.
Retain Application Log	Determines the number of days' worth of events that should be retained for the application log if this log is set to retain events by an age.
Retain Security Log	Determines the number of days' worth of events that should be retained for the security log if this log is set to retain events by an age.
Retain System Log	Determines the number of days' worth of events that should be retained for the system log if this log is set to retain events by an age.

Table 11-3 **Event Log Policy Settings**   *(continued)*

Setting	Description
Retention Method For Application Log	Determines the retention method for the application log. You can set this to Overwrite Events As Needed, Overwrite Events By Days, or Do Not Overwrite Events. This option requires that the log be cleared manually. When the maximum log size is reached, new events will be discarded.
Retention Method For Security Log	Determines the retention method for the security log. You can set this to Overwrite Events As Needed, Overwrite Events By Days, or Do Not Overwrite Events. This option requires that the log be cleared manually. When the maximum log size is reached, new events will be discarded.
Retention Method For System Log	Determines the retention method for the system log. You can set this to Overwrite Events As Needed, Overwrite Events By Days, or Do Not Overwrite Events. This option requires that the log be cleared manually. When the maximum log size is reached, new events will be discarded.

Restricted Groups

Restricted groups enable you to control the Members and Member Of properties security groups. You can control which accounts have membership to a group by defining the Members list. You can define which groups the restricted group is a member of by defining the Member Of list. When the security template is enforced by Group Policy, any current member of a restricted security group that is not on the Members list is removed from the security group. Any user on the Members list who is not currently a member of the restricted group is added to the security group.

System Services

You can use system services policies to configure the default startup behavior of services and the permissions to those services. By using system services policies, you can prevent users and power users from stopping or starting services that they have default rights to. You can also disable services that are not used on your network from starting.

Registry

You can use registry policies to control the DACL and SACL of registry keys. By using registry policies, you can increase security on registry keys, or you can decrease the security, which is sometimes needed to run applications under user security contexts.

File System

You can use file system policies to control the DACL and SACL of NTFS files and folders. By using file system policies, you can increase the security of files and folders, or you can decrease their security, which is sometimes needed to run applications under user security contexts.

Public Key Policies

Public key policies are available only in the computer-related section of Group Policy. You can use public key policies to define settings for the following:

- **Automatic Enrollment For Computer Certificates** You can specify automatic enrollment and renewal for computer certificates. When auto-enrollment is configured, the specified certificate types are issued automatically to all computers within the scope of the public-key Group Policy. Computer certificates that are issued by auto-enrollment are renewed automatically from the issuing CA. Auto-enrollment does not function unless at least one enterprise CA is online to process certificate requests.

- **Add Trusted Root Certificates For Groups Of Computers** When you install an enterprise root CA or a stand-alone root CA, the certificate of the CA is added automatically to the Trusted Root Certification Authority Group Policy for the domain. You also can add certificates for other root CAs to Trusted Root Certification Authority Group Policy. The root CA certificates that you add become trusted root CAs for computers within the scope of the Group Policy. For example, if you want to use a third-party CA as a root CA in a certification hierarchy, you must add the certificate for the third-party CA to the Trusted Root Certification Authority Group Policy.

- **Create Certificate Trust Lists (CTLs) For Computers And Users** You can create CTLs to trust specific CAs and to restrict the uses of certificates issued by the CAs. For example, you might use a CTL to trust certificates that are issued by a commercial CA and restrict the permitted uses for those certificates. You might also use CTLs to control trust on an extranet for certificates that are issued by CAs that are managed by your business partners. You can configure CTLs for computers and for users. Before you can create CTLs, you must have a valid trust list signing certificate, such as the Administrator certificate or the Trust List Signing certificate that have been issued by enterprise CAs.

■ **Designate EFS Recovery Agent Accounts**   You can use the Group Policy console to designate alternative EFS recovery agents by adding the EFS recovery agent certificates into public-key Group Policy, which means you must first issue EFS recovery agent certificates to designated recovery agent user accounts on local computers. When you are configuring the EFS recovery settings, you have two choices: You can add recovery agent certificates that are published in Active Directory, or you can add recovery agent certificates from a file located on a disk or in a shared folder that is available on the computer from which you are configuring public-key settings. If you add recovery agent certificates from files, you must first export the appropriate certificates to the disk or shared folder that will be used to add the files during the EFS recovery Group Policy configuration process.

IP Security Policies

You can assign IPSec policy by using the security settings to computers that are members of the domain. By assigning IPSec policies through Group Policy, you can ensure the integrity of the confidentiality of data transmission.

How Security Templates Work

All computers that run Windows 2000 or Windows XP have a local GPO that includes security settings and is applied when the computer starts up. You can also configure security templates by using Group Policy at the site, domain, and OU levels.

Applying Security Templates to a Local Computer

The local security template provides the base security for Windows 2000 and Windows XP computers. A local security template is applied to all Windows 2000 and Windows XP computers when they are upgraded from Windows NT or during installation. Windows 2000 and Windows XP computers include the Security Templates Microsoft Management Console (MMC) snap-in, which enables you optimize the baseline security of a local computer. The Security Templates MMC snap-in allows you to create security templates—text-based files that contain security settings—for all the security areas supported by the Security Configuration Toolset. The Security Configuration Toolset includes the following:

- Security Templates MMC snap-in

- Security Configuration and Analysis MMC snap-in

- Secedit.exe command-line utility

Tip   NTFS system and boot partitions that are converted by using the Convert.exe command do not have the same default DACLs as system and boot volumes that use native NTFS formatting. To resolve this issue with converted partitions, see 237399, "The Default NTFS Permissions Not Applied to a Converted Boot Partition." You can access this article at the Microsoft Knowledge Base (*http://support.microsoft.com*).

Security Templates MMC Snap-In

The Security Templates MMC snap-in enables you to create and modify security templates. By default, the Security Templates MMC snap-in lists all the templates in the %windir%\security\templates folder, which includes the built-in security templates. Figure 11-1 shows the Security Templates MMC snap-in in Windows XP.

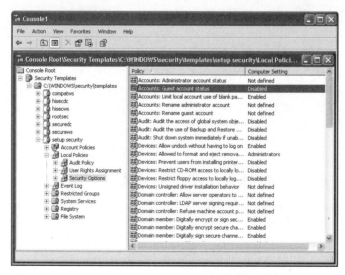

Figure 11-1   Security Templates MMC snap-in in Windows XP

You can create a blank security template by right-clicking the Security Template store and selecting New Template. You can then populate the settings. When a setting in the security template is marked as Not Configured, the computer's setting will not change.

> **Tip**   Read the wording of the security settings carefully. Many settings disable a certain behavior; configuring some settings as Disabled will enable the behavior.

Security Configuration and Analysis MMC Snap-In

You can use the Security Configuration and Analysis MMC snap-in to complete two different tasks: analyze the security settings of the local computer, and configure the security settings on the local computer by using security templates.

Because the security settings configured when the local computer security policy was applied can change because of security settings in Group Policy or by installing applications, you might want to periodically review and verify the security settings on a Windows 2000 or Windows XP computer. The Security Configuration and Analysis MMC snap-in enables you to quickly perform a security analysis and review the differences between the current settings on a computer and the settings contained in a security template.

The Security Configuration and Analysis MMC snap-in performs security analysis by comparing the current state of system security against an analysis database. During creation, the analysis database uses at least one security template. If you choose to import more than one security template, the database will merge the various templates and create one composite template. The database resolves conflicts in order of import—the last template that is imported takes precedence.

To analyze the current security settings of a local computer by using the Security Configuration and Analysis MMC snap-in, follow these steps:

1. Open a blank MMC and add the Security Configuration and Analysis MMC snap-in to it.

2. In the console tree, right-click Security Configuration and Analysis and click Open Database.

3. In Open Database, create a new database by entering a name for the database in the File Name field and click Open.

4. In the Import Template window, select the Setup Security template and click Open.

5.   In the details pane, right-click Security Configuration and Analysis and then click Analyze Computer Now.

6.   In the Error Log file path, click OK to create a log file in the default location.

For example, you might want to analyze a Windows XP computer to compare its security settings to the default policy that gets applied during installation. Figure 11-2 shows the results of comparing a Windows XP computer's security settings with the Setup Security template.

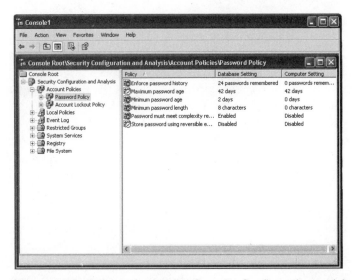

Figure 11-2   Output of using the Security Configuration and Analysis MMC snap-in

You can use the output of the analysis to perform a side-by-side comparison of the security settings. The Security Configuration and Analysis MMC snap-in displays the result of the analysis by using the icons described in Table 11-4.

Table 11-4   Using the Output of the Security Configuration and Analysis MMC Snap-In

Icon	Description
Red X	The entry is defined in the analysis database and on the system, but the security setting values do not match.
Green check	The entry is defined in the analysis database and on the system, and the setting values match.

Table 11-4   Using the Output of the Security Configuration and Analysis MMC Snap-In   *(continued)*

Icon	Description
Question mark	The entry is not defined in the analysis database and therefore was not analyzed. This occurs when a setting was not defined in the analysis database or when the user running the analysis did not have sufficient permissions.
Exclamation point	This item is defined in the analysis database but does not exist on the actual system.
No highlight	The item is not defined in the analysis database or on the system.

You can also use the Security Configuration and Analysis MMC snap-in to directly configure local system security. You can import security templates that have been created with the Security Templates MMC snap-in and apply these templates to the local computer. This immediately configures the system security with the levels specified in the template. To use the snap-in to configure the security settings on a local computer, follow the steps to analyze security outlined earlier—only instead of choosing to analyze the security of the computer, choose to configure security on the computer.

Secedit.exe Command-Line Utility

The Secedit.exe command includes all the functionality of the Security Configuration and Analysis MMC snap-in and has the ability to force a refresh of Group Policy in Windows 2000. In Windows XP, you must use the Gpupdate.exe command-line utility to force a refresh of Group Policy. By calling the Secedit.exe command-line tool from a batch file or automatic task scheduler, you can use it to automatically apply templates and analyze system security. You can view the options for how to use Secedit.exe by typing **secedit** at the command prompt.

Applying Security Templates by Using Group Policy

In addition to the local security policy, you can use Group Policy to deploy the settings in security templates to provide incremental security. Security settings are deployed by the same rules that apply to other Group Policy settings, except that they are not as volatile as other Administrative Template settings. You can place all client computers that have the same security requirements into an OU and create a GPO that contains security settings to deploy the new security settings to the computers.

You can import a previously created and tested security template into a GPO by right-clicking Security Settings in the computer-related configuration section of a GPO. When you do this, the settings from the template are applied in an incremental fashion. If you import more than one template and you have conflicting settings, the settings from the last imported security template will take precedence. To completely clear the security settings in the GPO before importing the security template, ensure that you select the option to clear the database before importing when you select the security template that you want to import.

Default Security Templates

Windows 2000 and Windows XP include several built-in security templates that you can use as a baseline for creating your own templates or for resetting the security on a computer. The built-in templates include the following:

- **Basic** The Basic security templates apply the Windows 2000 default access control settings. You can use the Basic templates on Windows NT computers that have been upgraded to Windows 2000. This will bring the upgraded computer in line with the new Windows 2000 default security settings that are applied only to a newly installed computer. The Basic templates can also be used to revert back to the defaults after making any undesirable changes. There are Basic templates for Windows 2000 Professional computers, Windows 2000 Server computers, and Windows 2000 Active Directory domain controllers.

- **Optional Component File Security** The Optional Component File Security templates apply default security to optional component files that might be installed during or after Windows 2000 Setup. The Optional Component File Security templates should be used in conjunction with the Basic templates to restore default security to Windows 2000 system files that are installed as optional components.

- **Compatible** Some customers might not want their users to be Power Users group members in order to run applications that are not compliant with the Windows 2000 application specification. This is because Power Users have additional capabilities (such as the ability to create shares) that go beyond the more liberal access control settings necessary to run legacy applications. For customers who do not want their end users to be Power Users, the Compatible template opens up the default access control policy for the Users group in a manner that is consistent with the requirements of legacy applications such as Microsoft Office 97. A computer that is configured with the Compatible template is not considered a secure installation. One Compatible template exists for Windows 2000 Professional computers, and one exists for Windows 2000 Server computers.

- **Secure**   The Secure template focuses on making OS and network behavior more secure by making changes, such as removing all members of the Power Users group and requiring more secure passwords. The Secure template does not focus on securing application behavior. This template does not modify permissions, so users with the proper permissions can still use legacy applications, even though all members are removed from the Power Users group by defining the Power Users group as a restricted group. Secure templates exist for Windows 2000 Professional, Windows 2000 Server, and Windows 2000 domain controllers.

- **High Secure**   The High Secure template increases the security defined by several of the parameters in the Secure template. For example, the Secure template might enable SMB packet signing, but the High Secure template requires SMB packet signing. Furthermore, the Secure template might warn about the installation of unsigned drivers, while the High Secure template blocks the installation of unsigned drivers. In short, the High Secure template configures many operational parameters to their extreme values without regard for performance, operational ease of use, or connectivity with clients using third-party or earlier versions of NTLM. The High Secure template also changes the default access permissions for Power Users to match those assigned to Users. This allows administrators to grant Users privileges reserved for Power Users, such as the ability to create shares, without having to give those Users unnecessary access to the registry or file system. The High Secure template is primarily designed for use in an all–Windows 2000 network because the settings require Windows 2000 technology. Using High Secure templates in an environment with Windows 98 or Windows NT can cause problems. High Secure templates exist for Windows 2000 Professional, Windows 2000 Server, and Windows 2000 domain controllers.

- **No Terminal Server User SID**   The default file system and registry access control lists that are on servers grant permissions to a terminal server SID. The terminal server SID is used only when terminal server is running in application compatibility mode. If terminal server is not being used, this template can be applied to remove the unnecessary terminal server SIDs from the file system and registry locations. However, removing the access control entry for the terminal server SID from these default file system and registry locations does not increase the security of the system. Instead of removing the terminal server SID, simply run terminal server in full security mode. When the computer is running in full security mode, the terminal server SID is not used.

■ **System Root Security** Rootsec.inf specifies the new root permissions introduced with Windows XP. By default, Rootsec.inf defines these permissions for the root of the system drive. This template can be used to reapply the root directory permissions if they are inadvertently changed, or the template can be modified to apply the same root permissions to other volumes. As specified, the template does not overwrite explicit permissions that are defined on child objects; it propagates only the permissions that are inherited by child objects.

■ **Default Security** Setup Security.inf is a computer-specific template that represents the default security settings that are applied during the installation of Windows 2000 or Windows XP, including the file permissions for the root of the system drive. You can use this template or portions of it for disaster recovery purposes. Setup Security.inf should never be applied by using Group Policy.

Creating Custom Security Templates

You might want to add more security settings to security templates to meet your organization's security requirements. Windows 2000 and Windows XP enable you to add settings to a security template by directly editing the security template file, or in the case of system services, configuring the security template on a computer that has the desired services installed.

Adding Registry Entries to Security Options

You might want to add a security-related registry configuration to a security template that you will be deploying on many computers in your organization. By using security templates, the registry value will be dynamically applied and enforced by Group Policy each time the security settings are refreshed, by default every 16 hours.

You can customize the list of registry values exposed in the Security Options section of security templates by modifying and then registering the information in the Sceregvl.inf file located in the %windir%\inf folder. Although you must register the Sceregvl.inf file on the computers on which you will view and modify security templates, you do not have to register it on every computer to which the security template will be applied. Once the Sceregvl.inf file has been modified and registered, your custom registry values are exposed in the security templates on that computer. You can then create security templates or policies that define your new registry values and apply them to local computers or through Group Policy.

To add a registry value to a security template, follow these steps:

1. Open the Sceregv1.inf file from %windir%\inf by using Notepad.exe or another text editor.

2. Add the registry value and security template settings to the [Register Registry Values] section using the information shown on the next page, in Table 11-5.

3. Add a display value for the value in the security template in the [Strings] section.

4. Save the Sceregvl.inf file. Then right-click the file in Windows Explorer and select Install The File.

5. Reregister the Scecli.dll file by typing **regsvr32 scecli.dll** at the command prompt.

For example, you might want to add policy that prevents CDs from playing automatically. The registry value for this setting is named Autorun and is written to the key HKEY_LOCAL_MACHINE\System\CurrentControlSet\Services\CDRom. To add this setting to security templates, you need to add the following section to the Sceregvl.inf file:

```
[Register Registry Values]
MACHINE\System\CurrentControlSet\Services\CDRom\Autorun,4,%Autorun%,0
[Strings]
Autorun = Prevents CD-ROMs from auto-playing CDs
```

This is the syntax for the registry value section:

RegistryPath,RegistryType,DisplayName,DisplayType,Options

Table 11-5 describes each of the fields.

Table 11-5 Syntax for the Registry Values in *Sceregvl.inf*

Field	Description
RegistryPath	Defines the full path of the registry key and value that you want to add to the security templates. Only values that exist in the HKEY_LOCAL_MACHINE hive can be configured, and this hive is referenced by the keyword MACHINE.
RegistryType	This is a number that defines the type of the registry value, as follows: ■ **1** REG_SZ ■ **2** REG_EXPAND_SZ ■ **3** REG_BINARY ■ **4** REG_DWORD ■ **7** REG_MULTI_SZ
DisplayName	Defines the variable for the string that is displayed in the security templates.
DisplayType	Specifies the type of dialog box the security template will render to allow the user to define the setting for the registry value. Supported *DisplayTypes* include the following: ■ **0; Boolean** Enables you to enable or disable the registry value. If Enabled is selected, the registry value is set to 1. If Disabled is selected, the registry value is set to 0. ■ **1; numeric** Enables you to set the value to a numeric value from 0 to 99,999. Numeric display types can specify "unit" strings such as "minutes" and "seconds" in the Options field. ■ **2; string** Causes the UI to render a text box. The registry value is set to the string entered by the user. ■ **3; list** Enables you to select one of several options from a list box. The registry value is set to the numeric value associated with the option. The options presented in the Security template are defined in the Options field. ■ **4; multivalued (available on Windows XP only)** Enables you to enter multiple lines of text. This display type should be used to define values for MULTI_SZ types. The registry value is set to the strings entered by the user, where each line is separated by a null byte. ■ **5; bitmask (available on Windows XP only)** Enables you to select from a series of check boxes, where each check box corresponds to a numeric value defined in the Options field.

Table 11-5   Syntax for the Registry Values in *Sceregvl.inf*   *(continued)*

Field	Description
Options	Qualifies different *DisplayTypes*, as follows:

- If *DisplayType*=1 (numeric), the Options field might contain a string that defines the units for the numeric value. The "unit" string has no impact on the value set in the registry.
- If *DisplayType*=3 (list), the Options field defines the list options. Each option consists of a numeric value separated by the pipe character (|), followed by the text for the choice. The registry value is set to the numeric value associated with the choice made by the user. See the LMCompatibilityLevel entry in Sceregvl.inf for an example of a registry value that allows the user to select from one of five possible values.
- If *DisplayType*=5 (bitmask), the Options field defines the choices that are available. Each choice consists of a numeric value separated by the pipe character (|), followed by the text for the choice. The registry value is set to the bitwise OR of the choices selected by the user. See the NTLMMinClientSec entry in Sceregvl.inf for an example of a registry value of this type.

Adding Services, Registry Values, and Files to Security Templates

You can manage the security of services, registry values, and files by using security templates. By default, all the services, registry values, and files that are in the base installation of Windows 2000 or Windows XP are manageable in security templates. You can manage the startup behavior and the permissions on the service by using security templates. For registry values and files, you can manage the DACL and SACL. If you have a service, registry value, or file that is not in the default installation, such as a service that is added by an application, you can edit the security template on a Windows 2000 or Windows XP computer that does have the service, registry value, or file that you want to manage. When you save this template, it will automatically update the newly added resource.

Best Practices

- **Use templates properly.** Never edit the built-in security templates, especially templates such as Setup Security.inf, which gives you the option to reapply the default security settings. Instead of just modifying a predefined template, customize the predefined template and then save the changes under a different template name.

■   **Monitor the size of security templates when using Group Policy.**   Security templates can become very large if many settings are made. For example, the Setup Security.inf template is 770 KB. Security templates this large could cause network performance degradation when applied by using Group Policy.

■   **Create templates for specific computer roles.**   Because security templates are easy to create and customize, they can easily be created to fit the security requirements of computers in different roles. For example, your Web server might have different security requirements than a domain controller.

■   **Test security templates.**   Always test security templates in a nonproduction environment to ensure that the settings do not prevent legitimate uses of the computer. Furthermore, it is possible to prevent all accounts from accessing a computer using settings in security templates.

Additional Information

■   313434: "How to Define Security Templates in Security Templates Snap-In in Windows 2000"

■   309689: "How to Apply Predefined Security Templates in Windows 2000"

■   321679: "How to Manage Security Templates in Windows 2000 Server"

■   214752: "How to Add Custom Registry Settings to Security Configuration Editor"

■   238965: "Removing Additional Permissions Granted to Terminal Services Users"

■   246261: "How to Use the RestrictAnonymous Registry Value in Windows 2000"

■   321470: "Unexpected Results Occur If You Set File Security by Using Either Group Policy or Security Templates"

■   313222: "How to Reset Security Settings Back to the Defaults"

■   314834: "How to Clear the Windows Paging File at Shutdown"

■   237399: "The Default NTFS Permissions Are Not Applied to a Converted Boot Partition"

Note   The previous 10 articles can be accessed through the Microsoft Knowledge Base. Go to *http://support.microsoft.com* and enter the article number in the Search The Knowledge Base text box.

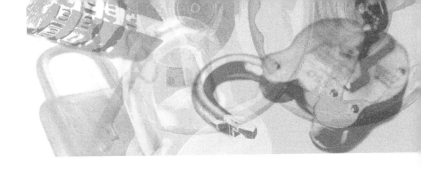

12

Auditing Microsoft Windows Security Events

No security strategy is complete without a comprehensive auditing strategy. More often than not, organizations learn this the hard way—only after they have experienced a security incident. Without an audit trail of actions made by the intruder, it is almost impossible to successfully investigate a security incident. As part of your overall security strategy, you must determine which events you need to audit, the level of auditing appropriate for your environment, how the audited events will be collected, and how they will be reviewed. There are several reasons to enable auditing and monitor audit logs:

- To create a baseline for normal network and computer operations

- To detect attempts to break into the network or computer

- To determine which systems and data have been compromised during or after a security incident

In addition, by regularly monitoring audit logs, especially by using automatic event monitoring software, you can help prevent further damage to networks or computers once an attacker has penetrated the network but has not yet inflicted widespread damage.

Your organization might be subject to industry or government regulations that not only dictate that certain events must be audited but also specify how audit logs are handled and how long they are archived. Check with your organization's legal representatives to ensure that your strategy for auditing is in compliance with these regulations, if applicable.

Determining Which Events to Audit

The first step in creating a strategy for auditing the OS is to determine the type of actions or operations to record. Which OS events should you audit? The easy answer to this question is *all of them*. Unfortunately, auditing all OS events would require enormous system resources and could negatively affect system performance. Bear in mind that the more you audit, the more events you generate and the more difficult it can be to spot critical events. If you plan to monitor the audited events manually or if you do not have a clear understanding of how to read audit logs, it can be extremely difficult to isolate potential malicious events from innocuous ones. You will need to work with other security specialists—ideally those who specialize in forensics or computer crime investigations—and IT decision makers to determine the OS events to audit. Audit only those events that you believe will be useful for later reference. Although this is certainly easier said than done, many of these events will be readily apparent. For example, you should audit account management and account logon events.

If your organization does not have a security policy for auditing, an effective way to begin determining which events to audit is to gather all the relevant people in your organization in a room and brainstorm. Determine the following:

- The actions or operations you want to track

- The systems on which you want these events tracked

For example:

- We want to track all domain and local logon events to all computers.

- We want to track the use of all files in the payroll folder on the HR server.

You can later match these audit statements to the audit policies and settings in the OS.

In Microsoft Windows NT, Microsoft Windows 2000, and Microsoft Windows XP, audit events can be split into two categories: *success events* and *failure events*. A success event indicates that the action or operation has been successfully completed by the OS, whereas a failure event shows that the action or operation was attempted but did not succeed. Failure events are useful in tracking attempted attacks on your environment; success events are much more difficult to interpret. Although the vast majority of successful audit events are simply indications of normal activity, an attacker who manages to gain access to a system will also generate a success event. Often, a pattern of events is as important as the events themselves. For example, a series of failures followed by a success might indicate an attempted attack that was eventually successful. Similarly, the deviation from a pattern might also indicate suspicious activity. For example, suppose the audit logs show that a user at your company logs on every workday between 8 A.M. and 10 P.M., but suddenly you see that this user is logging on to the network at 3 A.M. Although this behavior might be innocuous, it should be investigated.

Managing the Event Viewer

All OS security events in Windows NT, Windows 2000, and Windows XP are recorded in the Event Viewer security log. In addition, security-related events might be recorded in the application log and system log.

Before you enable audit policies, you must evaluate whether the default configuration of the log files in the Event Viewer are set properly for your organization. The default settings for the security event log are shown in Figure 12-1.

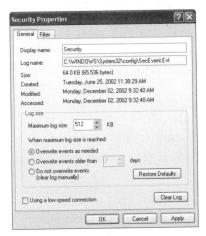

Figure 12-1   Security event log default settings

For each event log, you must determine the

■   Storage location

■   Maximum log file size

■   Overwrite behavior

Determining the Storage Location

By default, the security event log is stored in the %systemroot%\system32\config\ directory in a file named SecEventevt. In Windows XP, you can change the log file location in the Properties dialog box. In Windows NT 4.0 and Windows 2000, you must edit the registry to change the storage location of each log file. The path and file name for the security log is stored in the registry value HKEY_LOCAL_MACHINE\SYSTEM\CurrentControlSet\Services\Eventlog\Security.

By default, only the System account and the Administrators group have access to the security event log to ensure that nonadministrators do not have access to read, write, or delete security events. If you move the log to a new location, ensure that the new file has the correct NTFS file system permissions. Because the Event Log service cannot be stopped, changes to this setting will not take place until after the server is rebooted.

Determining the Maximum Log File Size

By default, the maximum size that the security event log can reach before the overwrite behavior is initiated is 512 KB. Because hard disk space is more readily available now than in the past, you will likely want to increase this setting. How much you increase this setting depends on your overwrite behavior, but a general guideline is to set the maximum size to at least 50 MB. The maximum size that you should set an event log to is 300 MB. Each security event is 350–500 bytes, so a 10-MB event log will contain approximately 20,000–25,000 security events.

You can change the maximum size of the log file on individual computers in the security event log Properties dialog box or by editing the registry. You can also change the maximum log file size on many computers by using Group Policy security templates . The maximum size for the security event log is stored in the registry value HKEY_LOCAL_MACHINE\SYSTEM\CurrentControlSet\Services\Eventlog\Security\MaxSize.

Configuring the Overwrite Behavior

When configuring the security event log settings, you must define what will happen when the maximum log file size is reached—also known as the *overwrite behavior*. Windows NT 4.0 and later versions have three overwrite behavior settings:

■   **Overwrite Events As Needed**   New events will continue to be written when the log is full. Each new event replaces the oldest event in the log.

- **Overwrite Events Older Than [*x*] Days**   Retain events in the log for the number of days you specify before overwriting events. The default is 7 days.

- **Do Not Overwrite Events**   New events will not be recorded, and the event log will need to be cleared manually.

In addition, you can configure the OS to shut down if security events cannot be written to the security audit log file. When this setting is enabled and events cannot be written to the security event log, the computer will initiate a stop error, commonly known as the *Blue Screen of Death*, with the following error message:

```
STOP: C0000244 {Audit Failed}
An attempt to generate a security audit failed
```

After this stop error has occurred, only members of the local Administrators group will be allowed to log on, to troubleshoot why the events cannot be written to the event log. Until events can be written to the event log, the computer will not operate normally. This is an important setting for high-security environments because it ensures that all security events are recorded. However, a large number of security events generated by an attacker or network problem could cause a denial-of-service condition. Similarly, shutting down the server might not necessarily be in accordance with availability service level agreements (SLAs). If your organization has high security needs and high availability needs, you should implement a method of removing auditing events from the system programmatically.

> **Note**   You can configure Windows NT 4.0 and later versions to shut down if security events cannot be logged, by setting the registry value HKEY_LOCAL_MACHINE\SYSTEM\CurrentControlSet\Control\Lsa\ CrashOnAuditFail to 1.

Unless you have a centralized auditing system, such as the Microsoft Operations Manager or the Microsoft Auditing Control System, you will need to carefully evaluate which overwrite behavior settings are best for your organization. In general, you will want to ensure that the security event log size is large enough to record all events that occur between the archival of events.

Configuring Audit Policies

Windows NT 4.0, Windows 2000, and Windows XP provide several categories of auditing for security events. When designing your enterprise audit strategy, you will need to decide whether to include success and failure events for the following categories of security audit events:

- Account logon events

- Account management events

- Directory service access

- Logon events

- Object access

- Policy change

- Privilege use

- Process tracking

- System events

You can see the current status of auditing for each area by looking in the Local Security Policy Microsoft Management Console (MMC) in Windows 2000 or Windows XP or in the User Manager in Windows NT 4.0. Figure 12-2 shows how the audit policy settings are displayed in Windows 2000.

Figure 12-2 Viewing audit policy settings in the Local Security Policy MMC in Windows 2000

Auditing Account Logon Events

When a user logs on to a domain, the logon is processed at a domain controller. When you audit account logon events on all domain controllers, domain logon attempts will be recorded on the domain controller that validates the account. Account logon events are created when an authentication package validates—successfully or not—a user's or computer's credentials. When domain credentials are used, account logon events are generated only in domain controllers' event logs. If the credentials presented are local computer credentials, the account logon events are created in the server's or workstation's local security event log.

> **Tip**   Because an account logon event can be recorded at any valid domain controller in the domain, you must ensure that you consolidate the security log across domain controllers to analyze all account logon events in the domain.

If you define this policy setting, you can specify whether to audit successes or audit failures. Success audits generate an audit entry when an account logon attempt succeeds. Failure audits generate an audit entry when an account logon attempt fails.

Auditing successful account logon events will provide you with a record of users' and computers' successful logons to a domain or local computer. By auditing failed account logon attempts, you might be able to detect attempts to attack the network by compromising an account. For example, you might notice that hundreds or thousands of failed logon attempts for a given user account within the span of a few seconds. This can be a sign of a brute force attack on the user account's password.

By examining successful and failed logon attempts, you not only can determine the account—or the security identifier (SID) of the account—whose logon succeeded or failed, you also can detect the following information:

- Name of the computer on which the logon attempt originated. Attackers often use *unprintable characters*—those from the extended character set—in their computer names to mask their identity from the Event Viewer.

- Domain or computer name for the account being used from a workgroup computer attempting an attack.

■   Type of logon attempt, which can be one of the following:

Logon Type	Name	Description
2	Interactive	Includes both logons from terminal service users and users who are physically at the computer
3	Network	Generally for file and print access
4	Batch	Initiated by a process with batch logon rights
5	Service	Initiated by services using the logon as a service right
6	Proxy	Has never been implemented by any version of Windows
7	Unlock Workstation Logon	Recorded when the console of a computer is unlocked
8	NetworkCleartext	Reserved for cleartext logons over the network
9	NewCredentials	Initiated by using the Runas command with the /netonly switch
10	RemoteInteractive	Recorded for Terminal Services logons
11	CachedInteractive	Recorded when cached credentials are used to log on locally to a computer

■   The process that originated the logon, which can be one of the following:

❑   **Advapi**   For API calls to LogonUser

❑   **Microsoft Internet Information Services (IIS)**   For logons using the Anonymous account or logon attempts using basic or digest authentication

- ❑ **LAN Manager Workstation Service** For logon attempts using the LAN Manager (LM) protocol

- ❑ **Kerberos** For calls from the Kerberos Security Support Provider (SSP)

- ❑ *KSecDD* For network connections

- ❑ *MS.RActive* **DirectoryIU** For logon attempts from the Microsoft Internet Authentication Service (IAS)

- ❑ **NT LAN Manager** (NTLM) or NTLM Security Support Provider (NtLmSsp) For logon attempts using the NTLM protocol

- ❑ **Service Control Manager (SCMgr)** For service logon attempts

- ❑ **Seclogon** For logon attempts using the Runas command

- ❑ **User32 or WinLogon\MSGina** For interactive logon attempts

- ■ The authentication package used for the logon attempt, which can be one of the following:

  - ❑ Kerberos

  - ❑ Negotiate

  - ❑ NTLM

  - ❑ Microsoft_Authentication_Package_v10

Always audit both account logon success events and account logon failure events. Success events are critical in building a baseline of user behavior and can be important information in a security investigation. Failure events can be a sign of an attacker attempting to penetrate the network. By proactively monitoring failure events, you might prevent attacks in which the attacker does significant damage to the network. Table 12-1 describes common account logon events.

Table 12-1 Common Account Logon Events

Event ID	Description
672	An Authentication Service ticket was successfully issued and validated.
673	A Ticket Granting Service ticket was granted.
674	A security principal renewed an Authentication Service ticket or Ticket Granting Service ticket.
675	Kerberos preauthentication failed.

(continued)

Table 12-1 Common Account Logon Events *(continued)*

Event ID	Description
676	Authentication ticket request failed.
677	A Ticket Granting Service ticket was not granted.
678	An account was successfully mapped to a domain account.
679	An account failed to map to a domain account.
680	Identifies the account used for the successful logon attempt. This event also indicates the authentication package used to authenticate the account.
681	A failed domain account logon was attempted.
682	A user has reconnected to a disconnected Terminal Services session.
683	A user disconnected from a Terminal Services session without logging off. Terminal Services sessions can be left in a connected state that allows processes to continue running after the session ends. Event ID 683 indicates when a user does not log off from the Terminal Services session, and event ID 682 indicates when a connection to a previously disconnected session has occurred.

In addition, if the logon attempt should fail, an event ID 681 will be recorded. This event will also contain code that gives the reason the authentication attempt failed. This reason code will appear in a decimal value. Table 12-2 contains a list of the failure codes in both decimal and hexadecimal format, along with a description of each code.

Table 12-2 Event 681 Failure Reason Codes

Decimal Value	Hexadecimal Value	Reason
3221225572	C0000064	User logged on with a misspelled or bad user account
3221225578	C000006A	User logged on with a misspelled or bad password
3221225583	C000006F	User logged on outside authorized hours
3221225584	C0000070	User logged on from unauthorized workstation
3221225585	C0000071	User logged on with an expired password
3221225586	C0000072	User logged on to an account disabled by the administrator
3221225875	C0000193	User logged on with an expired account
3221226020	C0000224	User logged on with Change Password At Next Logon flagged
3221226036	C0000234	User logged on with the account locked

Auditing Account Management Events

Because anyone with access to an administrative account has the authority to grant other accounts increased rights and permissions and create additional accounts, auditing account management events is an essential part of any network security design and implementation. Unless sophisticated biometrics or similar high-security measures are employed, it might be difficult or even impossible to guarantee that the person using the administrative account is the user that the account was issued to. Similarly, auditing is one of the ways organizations can hold administrators accountable for their actions.

By enabling the auditing of account management events, you will be able to record events such as these:

- A user account or group is created, changed, or deleted.

- A user account is renamed, disabled, or enabled.

- A password is set or changed.

- A computer's security policy is changed.

Although changes to user rights appear as account management events on the surface, they are actually policy change events. If both audit policies are disabled, a rogue administrator might be able to subvert the security of a network without an audit trail. For example, if an administrator made the user account Sally a member of the Backup Operators group, an account management event would be recorded. However, if the same administrator directly granted Sally's account the Back Up Files And Folders advanced user right, an account management event would not be recorded. Changes to a computer's security policy are also recorded under account management auditing. Unexpected changes to security policy can be a prelude to the compromise or destruction of data. For example, an attacker might weaken the security policy on a computer to carry out a specific attack that requires a resource that has been disabled.

You should enable the auditing of both success and failure account management events. Success audits generate an audit entry when any account management event succeeds. Failure audits generate an audit entry when any account management event fails. Although successful account management events are more often than not completely innocuous, they provide an invaluable record of activities when a network has been compromised. For example, you can see which accounts were modified and created by the attacker. Account management failure events often indicate that a lower-level administrator (or an attacker who has compromised a lower-level administrator account) might be attempting to elevate his privilege. For example, you might see an account used for the backup service try to grant itself or another account

Domain Administrator group membership. Hence, monitoring account management failures is critical. Table 12-3 contains descriptions of common account management events.

Table 12-3 Common Account Management Events

Event ID	Description
624	A user account was created.
627	A Password Change Attempted; this event records both successful and failed attempts.
632	A security-enabled global group member was added.
633	A security-enabled global group member was removed.
634	A security-enabled global group was deleted.
635	A security-disabled local group was created.
636	A security-enabled local group member was added.
637	A security-enabled local group member was removed.
638	A security-enabled local group was deleted.
639	A security-enabled local group was changed.
641	A security-enabled global group was changed.
642	A user account was changed.
643	A domain policy was changed.
644	A user account was locked out; when an account is locked out, two events will be logged at the primary domain controller (PDC) emulator operations master. A 644 event will occur, indicating that the account name was locked out. Then a 642 event will be recorded, indicating that the user account is now locked out. This event is logged only at the PDC emulator.
645	A computer account was created.
646	A computer account was changed.
647	A computer account was deleted.
648	A local security group with security disabled was created.
649	A local security group with security disabled was changed.
650	A member was added to a security-disabled local security group.
651	A member was removed from a security-disabled local security group.
652	A security-disabled local group was deleted.
653	A security-disabled global group was created.
654	A security-disabled global group was changed.
655	A member was added to a security-disabled global group.

Table 12-3   Common Account Management Events   *(continued)*

Event ID	Description
656	A member was removed from a security-disabled global group.
657	A security-disabled global group was deleted.
658	A security-enabled universal group was created.
659	A security-enabled universal group was changed.
660	A member was added to a security-enabled universal group.
661	A member was removed from a security-enabled universal group.
662	A security-enabled universal group was deleted.
663	A security-disabled universal group was created.
664	A security-disabled universal group was changed.
665	A member was added to a security-disabled universal group.
666	A member was removed from a security-disabled universal group.
667	A security-disabled universal group was deleted.
668	A group type was changed.
684	Set the security descriptor of members of administrative groups.
685	A name of an account was changed.

Auditing Directory Service Access

You can audit changes to the Active Directory directory service by enabling directory service auditing. Although enabling auditing of account management events will record changes to user, computer, and group objects, you might need to track changes to other objects or attributes in Active Directory. For example, you might want to record changes to Active Directory infrastructure components, such as site objects, or changes to the Active Directory schema. Another common set of objects to audit in Active Directory are the enterprise Certification Authority (CA) objects stored in the configuration container when you install a Windows 2000 enterprise public-key infrastructure (PKI).

To audit successful or failed changes to Active Directory objects or attributes, you not only must enable directory services auditing on all domain controllers, but you must also configure the system access control list (SACL) for each object or attribute you want to audit. In addition to recording changes to Active Directory objects and attributes, directory service auditing also records Active Directory events such as replication. Consequently, enabling directory service auditing for successful events will greatly increase the number of events recorded in the security event log. Besides resulting in an increase in log file size, this will also make it more difficult to locate meaningful events without the assistance of sophisticated tools to parse the security event log.

If you define this policy setting, you can specify whether to audit successes or failures. Success audits generate an audit entry when a user successfully accesses an Active Directory object that has a SACL specified. Failure audits generate an audit entry when a user unsuccessfully attempts to access an Active Directory object that has a SACL specified.

> **Tip**   Because Active Directory is a multiple master database, meaning that changes can be written on any domain controller, you must ensure that you enable directory service auditing on all domain controllers. The best way to ensure this is to create an audit policy Group Policy object (GPO) at the domain level.

All directory service events, both successful and failed, will have the event ID 565 in the security event log. You will have to examine the details of each 565 event to see if it was successfully or not successfully completed.

Auditing Logon Events

By enabling the auditing of logon events, you can track every time a user logs on or logs off a computer. The event will be recorded in the security event log of the computer where the logon attempt occurs. Similarly, when a user or computer connects to a remote computer, a logon event is generated in the security event log of the remote computer for the network logon. Logon events are created when the logon session and token are created or destroyed.

> **Note**   Because Terminal Services logons are treated as interactive logons, creating a terminal server session remotely will cause a logon event to be recorded. If you enable logon events on a computer running Terminal Services, you will need to differentiate between console logons and Terminal Services logons.

Logon events audit logon attempts from users as well as those from computers. You will see separate security event log entries for both the computer account and the user account if a network connection is attempted from a Windows NT, Windows 2000, or Windows XP computer.

Note   Only the user account logon event is recorded when a user logs on to the domain from a Microsoft Windows 95 or Microsoft Windows 98 computer. Windows 95 and Windows 98 computers do not have computer accounts in the directory and consequently do not generate computer logon event entries for network logon events.

Logon events can be useful for tracking attempts to log on interactively at servers or to investigate attacks launched from a particular computer. Success audits generate an audit entry when a logon attempt succeeds. Failure audits generate an audit entry when a logon attempt fails.

A subtle but very important difference between auditing account logon events and logon events exists. Account logon events are recorded on the computer that authenticates the account, whereas logon events are created where the account is used. For example, if a user uses her domain account to log on to the network on a computer that is part of the domain, an account logon event will be recorded on the domain controller that performed the authentication of the account and a logon event will be recorded on the computer the user used to log on to the network.

On domain controllers that have logon events audited, only interactive and network logon attempts to the domain controller itself generate logon events—computer logon attempts are not audited. Success audits generate an audit entry when a logon attempt succeeds. Failure audits generate an audit entry when a logon attempt fails.

You should always enable both successful and failed logon attempts. Successful logon attempts will provide a baseline record of a user's logon behavior that can be useful in identifying suspicious behavior. Similarly, a record of successful logon events is essential evidence in any computer investigation. By tracking failed logon events, your organization might be able to prevent network attacks or further damage to a network by proactively responding to suspicious behavior. For example, suppose that in a weekly review of a server's audit logs you notice many failed logon attempts with various user accounts. Upon further investigation, you notice that even though the server is located in a physically secure area, the logon attempts have been made at the console of the server. In this situation, you can respond proactively to the suspicious behavior, prevent damage to information, and start an investigation into the possible compromise of physical security. Table 12-4 contains descriptions of common logon events.

Table 12-4 Common Logon Events

Event ID	Description
528	A user successfully logged on to a computer.
529	The logon attempt was made with an unknown user name or a known user name with a bad password.
530	The user account tried to log on outside the allowed time.
531	A logon attempt was made by using a disabled account.
532	A logon attempt was made by using an expired account.
533	The user is not allowed to log on at this computer.
534	The user attempted to log on with a logon type that is not allowed, such as network, interactive, batch, service, or remote interactive.
535	The password for the specified account has expired.
536	The Netlogon service is not active.
537	The logon attempt failed for other reasons.
538	A user logged off.
539	The account was locked out at the time the logon attempt was made. This event is logged when a user or computer attempts to authenticate with an account that has been previously locked out.
540	Network logon succeeded.
682	A user has reconnected to a disconnected Terminal Services session.
683	A user disconnected a Terminal Services session without logging off.

Auditing Object Access

When you enable object auditing, called File And Object Auditing in Windows NT, you can track successful and failed attempts at accessing file, print, and registry resources. As with directory services auditing, when you enable object auditing, you will also need to configure the SACL for each resource you want to audit. Figure 12-3 displays where auditing is enabled on a file in Windows XP.

A SACL is comprised of access control entries (ACEs). Each ACE contains three pieces of information:

■ The security principal (user, computer, or group) to be audited

■ The specific access type to be audited, called an *access mask*

■ A flag to indicate whether to audit failed access events, successful access events, or both

If your organization has clear business reasons for recording access attempts on files, registry keys, or printers, you should enable object auditing and create the appropriate SACL on the resource. When configuring file auditing, you should decide in advance what types of actions on a file you want to track. For example, opening a text file, changing one line, and saving the file will create more than 30 events in the security event log in Windows XP when all actions are logged. (This occurs when you select to audit Full Control on a file.)

Figure 12-3   Configuring auditing on a file in Windows XP

> **Tip**   Exercise caution when auditing Read & Execute permissions on executable files because this type of auditing will cause a large amount of events to be logged. Antivirus software will cause thousands of object access events each time the system is scanned if Full Control auditing is enabled.

You should define only the actions you want enabled when configuring SACLs. For example, you might want to enable Write and Append Data auditing on executable files to track the replacement or changes to those files, which computer viruses, worms, and Trojan horses commonly do. Similarly, you might want to track changes or even the reading of sensitive documents.

> **Tip**   Before implementing the auditing of files, registry keys, and printers, you should ensure auditing the resource does not impact the performance of the server and the resource in such a way that it disrupts business processes.

By enabling the auditing of object access, you can record the successful and failed attempts at accessing files, folders, registry keys, and printers. Success audits generate an audit entry when a user successfully accesses an object that has a SACL specified. Failure audits generate an audit entry when a user unsuccessfully attempts to access an object that has a SACL specified. Table 12-5 contains descriptions of common object access events.

Table 12-5   Common Object Access Events

Event ID	Description
560	Access was granted to an already existing object.
561	A handle to an object was allocated.
562	A handle to an object was closed.
563	An attempt was made to open an object with the intent to delete it.
564	A protected object was deleted.
565	Access was granted to an already existing object type.

Auditing Policy Change

Auditing policy changes will enable you to track changes in three areas:

- User rights assignment
- Audit policies
- Domain trust relationships

Although the name *audit policy change* implies that this event records the security policy of computers, this event is recorded when account management auditing is enabled with event ID 643. Changes to the assignment of user rights are recorded when policy changes are audited. An attacker can elevate her own privileges or those of another account—for example, by adding the Debug privilege or the Back Up Files And Folders privilege. Policy change auditing also includes making changes to the audit policy itself as well as changes to trust relationships.

You should enable the auditing of both successful and failed policy changes to track the granting and removal of user rights and changes to the audit policy. Successful and failed attempts generate an audit entry when an attempt to change to security policies, user rights assignment policies, audit policies, or trust policies is successful. Table 12-6 contains descriptions of common policy change events.

Table 12-6   Common Policy Change Events

Event ID	Description
608	A user right was assigned.
609	A user right was removed.
610	A trust relationship with another domain was created.
611	A trust relationship with another domain was removed.
612	An audit policy was changed.
671	Security policy was changed or refreshed. ("--" in the Changes Made field means that no changes were made during the refresh.)
768	A collision was detected between a namespace element in one forest and a namespace element in another forest.

Auditing Privilege Use

By enabling privilege use auditing, which is called Use Of User Rights in Windows NT 4.0, you can record when user and service accounts use one of the user rights to carry out a procedure, with the exception of a few user rights that are not audited. These rights are the exceptions:

- Bypass Traverse Checking
- Debug Programs
- Create A Token Object
- Replace Process Level Token
- Generate Security Audits
- Back Up Files And Directories
- Restore Files And Directories

Windows 2000 and Windows XP have a Group Policy setting under Security Options named Audit Use Of Backup And Restore Privilege, which enables you to audit the use of the Back Up And Restore Files And Folders privilege.

Privilege use auditing will detect events associated with many common attacks. These types of events include the following:

■ Shutting down a local or remote system

■ Loading and unloading device drivers

■ Viewing the security event log

■ Taking ownership of objects

■ Acting as part of the OS

> **Tip**   In Windows NT 4.0, only the local use of the Take Ownership right is audited. If you need to enable the use of the Take Ownership right for remote objects, you will need to enable object auditing on the remote computers. Windows 2000 and Windows XP do this automatically.

You should enable the logging of failed privilege use events at a minimum. Failed use of a user right is an indicator of a general network problem and often can be a sign of an attempted security breach. You should enable the success use of privileges if you have a specific business reason do so. Success audits generate an audit entry when exercising a user right succeeds. Failure audits generate an audit entry when exercising a user right fails. Table 12-7 describes common privilege use events.

Table 12-7   Common Privilege Use Events

Event ID	Description
576	Specified privileges were added to a user's access token. (This event is generated when the user logs on.)
577	A user attempted to perform a privileged system service operation.
578	Privileges were used on an already open handle to a protected object.

Auditing Process Tracking

Process tracking auditing enables you to have a detailed record of the execution of processes, including program activation, process exit, handle duplication, and indirect object access. Process tracking, at a minimum, will generate an event for the activation and exit of every process. Thus, by enabling the auditing of success events, a large number of events will be recorded in the security Event Viewer.

Enabling process tracking is excellent for troubleshooting applications and learning about how applications work; however, you should enable process tracking only if you have a clear business reason. You will also likely need an automated method of parsing event logs to successfully analyze log files where process tracking has been enabled. Success audits generate an audit entry when the process being tracked succeeds. Failure audits generate an audit entry when the process being tracked fails. Table 12-8 contains descriptions of common process tracking events.

Table 12-8   Common Process Tracking Events

Event ID	Description
592	A new process was created.
593	A process exited.
594	A handle to an object was duplicated.
595	Indirect access to an object was obtained.

Auditing System Events

By enabling the auditing of system events, you can track when a user or process alters aspects of the computer environment. Common system events include clearing the security event log of events, shutting down the local computer, and making changes to the authentication packages operating on the computer.

You should enable the successful auditing of system events to record system restarts. An unexpected system reboot might be an indicator that a security compromise has occurred and generally will be a sign of some sort of problem, security related or not. Success audits generate an audit entry when a system event is executed successfully. Failure audits generate an audit entry when a system event is attempted unsuccessfully.

Successful attempts at clearing the security event log are recorded regardless of whether system event auditing is enabled. Table 12-9 contains descriptions of common system events.

Table 12-9   Common System Events

Event ID	Description
512	Windows is starting up.
513	Windows is shutting down.
514	An authentication package was loaded by the Local Security Authority (LSA).
515	A trusted logon process has registered with the LSA.
516	Internal resources allocated for the queuing of security event messages have been exhausted, leading to the loss of some security event messages.
517	The security log was cleared.
518	A notification package was loaded by the Security Accounts Manager (SAM).

How to Enable Audit Policies

You can enable audit policies in Windows 2000 and Windows XP locally by using the Local Security Policy MMC or by applying security templates. You can also apply audit policies to Windows 2000 and Windows XP computers remotely by using Group Policy. The following steps explain how to enable an audit policy locally by using the Local Security Policy MMC, and Figure 12-4 shows what you will see onscreen when doing so. To enable an audit policy in Windows XP, follow these steps:

1. Open the Local Security Policy MMC.

2. Double-click Local Policies to expand it, and then double-click Audit Policy.

3. In the right pane, double-click the policy that you want to enable or disable.

4. Click the Success and Fail check boxes to designate which the audit policies you want to enable.

5. Close the MMC.

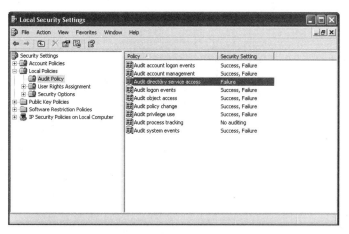

Figure 12-4   Configuring the audit policy by using the Local Security Policy MMC

Table 12-10 contains the audit policies that you should enable to track security events. For object access and directory service events, you will also need to configure the SACL on the objects or on the attributes of each object that you want to track operations on.

Table 12-10   Baseline Audit Policy

Audit Policy	Events to Audit
Audit Account Logon Events	Success, Failure
Audit Account Management Events	Success, Failure
Audit Directory Service Access	Success, Failure
Audit Logon Events	Success, Failure
Audit Object Access	Success, Failure
Audit Policy Change	Success, Failure
Audit Privilege Use	Failure
Audit Process Tracking	None
Audit System Events	Success, Failure

> **More Info**   For detailed information on configuring audit policies by
> using security templates and Group Policy, see Chapter 11, "Configur-
> ing Security Templates."

Monitoring Audited Events

A number of methods exist for monitoring events written to the security event
log. These methods range from reading the events manually by using the Event
Viewer to using powerful automated event-consolidating and event-monitoring
software such as Microsoft Operations Manager. Each method serves a specific
purpose; you will need to select a method that is most appropriate for your
environment and particular situation. These are the four primary methods for
monitoring events:

- Event Viewer
- Custom scripts
- Event Comb
- Fully automated tools, such as Microsoft Operations Manager

The discussion of fully automated event monitoring tools is outside the scope of
this book. This section will cover the other three methods.

Using the Event Viewer

The simplest method for monitoring the OS for security events is to use the
Event Viewer. The Event Viewer allows you perform the following:

- View event details
- Sort events by type, audit policy, and time
- Search for events by using common fields
- Filter events by common fields
- Export event logs to an .evt, .csv, or .txt format
- Connect to remote computers to view and manage the event log

The Event Viewer does not allow for the consolidation of events. Thus, it
might be difficult to monitor events that are recorded on many servers, such as
account logon events, which are recorded on the authenticating domain control

for domain accounts. The Event Viewer also does not allow for the searching of event details. By exporting the events to a file, you can import them into a database or run custom scripts on the exported files from many computers.

Using Custom Scripts

Several scripts are available for managing events. A few of them are:

- **Dumpel.exe**   Also known as the Dump Event Log, this script is a command-line tool that will dump an event log for a local or remote system into a tab-separated text file. This file can then be imported into a spreadsheet or database for further investigation. Dumpel.exe can also be used to filter for or filter out certain event types. (Dumpel.exe is located in the Tools folder on the CD included with this book.)

- **Eventlog.pl**   This Perl script clears and copies log files, and it displays and changes the properties of log files on local and remote computers that are running Windows 2000. You can use this script tool to perform the following event log management tasks:

    - ❏   Change the properties of event logs

    - ❏   Back up (save) event logs

    - ❏   Export event lists to text files

    - ❏   Clear (delete) all events from event logs

    - ❏   Query the properties of event logs

- **Eventquery.pl**   This Perl script displays events from the Event Viewer logs on local and remote computers running Windows 2000 and offers a wide range of filters to help you find specific events.

> **Note**   Eventlog.pl and Eventquery.pl are included on the *Microsoft Windows 2000 Server Resource Kit*, Supplement One (Microsoft Press, 2000).

Using Event Comb

Event Comb parses event logs from many servers at the same time, spawning a separate thread of execution for each server that is included in the search criteria. With Event Comb, you can collect events from many computers running

Windows NT 4.0, Windows 2000, and Windows XP. You can also search for occurrences of events by any field in the event record in the collected log files. Event Comb can also search archived log files.

On the CD Event Comb (EventcombMT.exe) is located in the Tools\ EventComb folder on the CD included with this book.

Event Comb enables you to do the following:

- **Define either a single event ID or multiple event IDs to search for.** You can include a single event ID, or multiple event IDs separated by spaces.

- **Define a range of event IDs to search for.** The endpoints are inclusive. For example, if you want to search for all events from event ID 528 through event ID 540, you would define the range as 528 < ID < 540. This feature is useful because most applications that write to the event log use a sequential range of events.

- **Limit the search to specific event logs.** You can choose to search the system, application, and security logs. If executed locally at a domain controller, you can also choose to search the file replication service (FRS), Domain Name System (DNS), and Active Directory event logs in addition to the application, security, and system logs.

- **Limit the search to specific event message types.** You can choose to limit the search to error, informational, warning, success audit, failure audit, or success events.

- **Limit the search to specific event sources.** Choosing to limit the search to events from specific event sources to increase the speed of the search.

- **Search for specific text within an event description.** With each event, you can search for specific text. This is useful if you are trying to track specific users or groups.

- **Define specific time intervals to scan back from the current date and time.** This allows you to limit your search to events in the past day, week, or month.

The first thing you must do when using Event Comb is select the computers you want to search for events. To add computers to the search list in Event Comb, follow these steps:

1.   In the Event Comb utility, ensure that the correct domain is autodetected in the Domain box. If you want to search event logs in a different domain, manually type the new domain name in the Domain box.

2.   To add computers to the search list, right-click the box below Select To Search/Right Click To Add. The following options are available:

   ❑   **Get DCs In Domain**   Adds all domain controllers for the current domain to the listing.

   ❑   **Add Single Server**   Allows you to add a server or workstation by name to the listing.

   ❑   **Add All GCs In This Domain**   Allows you to add all domain controllers in the selected domain that are configured to be Global Catalog servers.

   ❑   **Get All Servers**   Adds all servers found in the domain using the browser service. The servers exclude all domain controllers.

   ❑   **Get Servers From File**   Allows you to import a file that lists all servers to be included in the search scope. Each server should be entered on a separate line in the text file.

3.   Once the servers are added to the list, you must select which servers to perform the search against. When selected, the server will appear highlighted in the list. You can choose multiple servers by holding down the Ctrl key and clicking each server to select it.

Once you have selected the servers to be included in your event log search, you can narrow the scope of the search by selecting the event logs and event types to include. You can select the event log, the type of event, and other important search criteria. Event Comb also enables you to save your searches and reload them later. This can be useful if you frequently use Event Comb to search for the same event. Search criteria are saved in the registry under HKLM\Software\Microsoft\EventCombMT.

The results of the search are saved to the C:\Temp folder by default. Because the permissions on many computers allow users to read files from this folder to support legacy applications, you should consider changing this path. The results include a summary file named EventCombMT.txt. For each computer included in the event log search, a separate text file named *Computer-Name-EventLogName*_LOG.txt is generated. These individual text files contain all the events extracted from the event logs that match your search criteria.

You can use Event Comb to search for events that are recorded in a distributed fashion, such as account logons. To do so, follow these steps:

1. In the Event Comb tool, ensure that the domain is configured to the correct domain name.

2. In the Select To Search/Right Click To Add box below the domain name, right-click the box and then click Get DCs In Domain.

> **Note** When searching for events such as account logon and account management, ensure that you search all domain controllers. Because Windows 2000 uses a multiple master model for account management, an account can be added, modified, or deleted at any domain controller in the domain. Likewise, authentication can be validated by any domain controller in the domain. Because of this, you cannot be sure where the specific update or authentication attempt takes place.

After you have retrieved the events from all the computers you want to search, you can specify the type of event you want to see displayed. For example, you might want to search for all account logon failures for domain accounts (event ID 681), as shown in Figure 12-5. The following procedure shows how to search all servers from which events have been collected for 681 events:

1. From the File menu, select Open Log Directory.

2. Right-click the Select To Search/Right Click To Add box, and then click Select All Servers In List.

3. Select Security under Choose Log Files To Search.

4. Select Success Audit and Failure Audit under Event Types.

5. In the Event IDs box, type the following event ID: **681**.

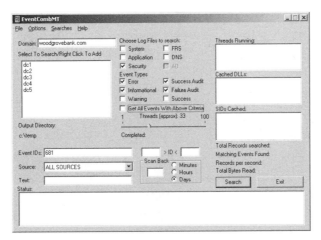

Figure 12-5   Searching for event ID 681 on all domain controllers

When the search is complete, the results can be viewed in the log directory, which should open automatically. In the C:\Temp folder, double-click the output file for a domain controller to view the specific events logged by the Event Comb tool.

Best Practices

■ **Determine which events should be recorded.**   Work with business and technical decision makers to ensure that all actions and operations that should be audited are audited. Because auditing does result in performance degradation, you should audit only for events that you believe you might need to refer to in the future.

■ **Synchronize the time on all computers and network devices.** To correlate events that take place on different computers and network devices, you must ensure that the time is synchronized. Ideally, all computers and devices should be synchronized with the same time source.

■ **Create a baseline of events.**   Create a baseline of security events under normal conditions that can be used later for comparisons with possible suspicious behavior. Without being able to refer to a baseline log file, it is often difficult to distinguish between events that are innocuous and those that are malicious.

■ **Monitor log files for suspicious behavior.**   For auditing to be an effective security measure, you must monitor the audit log files for suspicious behavior. You might also want to use a test environment to stage common attacks and analyze the audit log files. This will enable you to better detect common attacks on the production environment. You should consider using automated software or writing custom scripts to parse event files for common events that indicate suspicious behavior.

Additional Information

■ 300549: "How to Enable and Apply Security Auditing in Windows 2000"

■ 314955: "How to Audit Active Directory Objects in Windows 2000"

■ 246120: "How To Determine Audit Policies from the Registry"

■ 232714: "How to Enable Auditing of Directory Service Access"

■ 299475: "Windows 2000 Security Event Descriptions (Part 1 of 2)"

■ 301677: "Windows 2000 Security Event Descriptions (Part 2 of 2)"

■ 174074: "Security Event Descriptions" (for Windows NT 4.0)

> **Note**   The previous seven articles can be accessed through the Microsoft Knowledge Base. Go to *http://support.microsoft.com* and enter the article number in the Search The Knowledge Base text box.

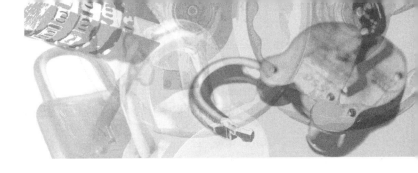

13

Securing Mobile Computers

Mobile computers present a special security risk because of their portability and small size. They are at much greater risk of physical compromise and are much more difficult to manage. Often, when people hear the term *mobile computers*, they think it applies to only laptop computers. But mobile computers also include Microsoft Tablet PCs, PDAs, Microsoft Pocket PCs, and wireless phones. Each of these devices can carry secret information, such as passwords, or information that could be used to break into their respective networks.

Understanding Mobile Computers

Mobile computers face all the threats that desktop computers do, but they also face additional threats. These vulnerabilities include the following:

- Increase in the possibility of being lost or stolen
- Difficulty in applying security updates
- Exposure to untrusted networks
- Eavesdropping on wireless connectivity

Increase in the Possibility of Being Lost or Stolen

Laptops and other mobile devices have a much greater chance of being stolen because of their mobility and small size. A thief could easily hide a laptop in a briefcase or under a coat. Even organizations that have tight physical security are susceptible to this type of theft. For example, in February 2000, a laptop belonging to a U.S. State Department employee and containing top-secret information was stolen from a conference room inside the State Department.

Furthermore, although some laptops will always remain within the boundaries of company facilities, most users will work on their laptops away from the office. Consequently, the network security of such laptop computers is enforced by those organizations' corporate security and IT departments. But the users themselves are responsible for the physical security of their laptops. Users take their laptops home, on business and personal trips, and to school, and they sometimes leave their laptops in their cars—unattended and in plain view—during those stops. In July 2000, a commander in the British Royal Navy had his laptop stolen from his car, which was parked outside his house. His laptop was reported to hold top-secret information.

Thieves target laptops because they are small, high-value items that can easily be sold. If a thief is sufficiently computer-savvy or sells the laptop to an attacker, he can potentially retrieve all the information from the laptop. This information includes cached passwords for network accounts; cached personal information from Microsoft Internet Explorer; personal information, such as names, addresses, and birthdates for people in address books; and the actual company data on the laptop. An attacker can use this information to attack the organization's network or steal the identity of the user or her friends and family. Furthermore, the stolen laptop might contain information that is confidential or secret. An information leak resulting from a stolen laptop could have a tremendous impact on your organization if that information falls into the wrong hands. This might sound alarmist, but several high-profile incidents of laptop theft have occurred in the past few years, including those government incidents mentioned earlier.

The corporate world has not been immune to such incidents of laptop theft. In 2000, the laptop belonging to the CEO of Qualcomm was stolen after he delivered a presentation at an industry conference. According to the media, the CEO was less than 30 feet away when his laptop was stolen from the podium from which he had been speaking. Because the CEO had been using his laptop to give the presentation, it is likely that he left it unlocked when he walked off the podium, rendering many types of data protection, such as encrypting file system (EFS), useless. Although the thieves in the cases we have mentioned so far might not have been targeting the organizations whose laptops they stole or the information on those laptops, no evidence to the contrary exists.

Some organizations face a greater threat of their having laptops stolen. For example, hardware and software companies might be targeted by attackers hoping to steal the companies' latest and greatest inventions. And law enforcement and government agencies might be targeted by attackers hoping to gain access to the secret information contained on their networks.

Mobile telephone devices also have a high incidence of theft and loss. At the very least, a thief can use a stolen phone to make long-distance and international phone calls, creating very expensive phone bills for the owner. A thief can also retrieve contact information from a phone's address book, potentially subjecting the phone owner's friends and family to identity theft. A more serious vulnerability, however, is that many mobile phones have Internet access, or even full computing power, such as the Pocket PC Phone Edition devices. Such devices can have confidential information stored on them, such as passwords and private e-mail messages. Other types of devices in this category include handheld e-mail devices such as the BlackBerry, PDA devices such as Palm Pilots, and handheld PCs such as the Compaq iPAQ. Because it is often difficult for users to input data into these devices, perhaps because they must use an onscreen keyboard or handwriting recognition software, users of these devices frequently store network credentials, such as passwords, persistently. An attacker could retrieve these credentials to later attack the network of the device user's organization. These mobile devices also have the capability to store files, which an attacker could retrieve from the device if stolen.

Laptop computers and mobile devices often have accessories and add-ons that might hold confidential information. Such accessories include conventional removable media, such as floppy disks and CDs. Another class of removable media includes high-capacity, solid-state devices, such as CompactFlash cards, Secure Digital (SD) cards, smart cards, and Subscriber Identity Module (SIM) cards for cellular and wireless phones. Smart cards and SIM cards, in particular, can contain data such as private keys and personal information that could be used to attack the network of the device user's organization, if they fall into the wrong hands.

Difficulty in Applying Security Updates

Unlike desktop computers, which have a somewhat static place in the network infrastructure, laptop computers often roam among many subnets and networks, not to mention leaving the local area network (LAN) altogether. The mobility of laptop computers makes them much more difficult to manage centrally, which greatly increases the difficulty in applying security updates, including hotfixes, service packs, and virus definition files. This mobility also increases the difficulty in assessing how current the security updates are. Traditional methods of applying security updates, including manual application and the use of network management software such as Microsoft Systems Management Server (SMS), are often ineffective with laptop computers. This is because these methods depend on computers being in a static physical location as well as a logical one on the network.

This issue is especially problematic for laptop computers that rarely or never are connected to the LAN. When these computers do connect to the network, they often do so through low-bandwidth connections, such as modems. For all intents and purposes, these computers are self-managed by their users, making these users responsible for knowing how to locate and apply security updates themselves. If security updates are not installed, the laptop computer will be vulnerable to known exploits, which is particularly alarming because these computers are often directly connected to untrusted networks.

Exposure to Untrusted Networks

Desktop computers are always connected to the LAN on which their security settings can be managed and are protected from the Internet and other untrusted networks by firewalls. On the other hand, network administrators cannot be sure which networks laptop users will connect to. When at home or in hotels, a laptop user will connect directly to the Internet without any protection—and the machine will be exposed to the legions of attackers scanning for vulnerable computers connected to the Internet. A user might also connect her laptop to the networks of her business partners and the semipublic networks at industry conventions, where confidential information can be exposed to anyone who succeeds in breaking into the laptop. Once the user connects her computer to such an untrusted network, a network administrator can do little to protect the machine from attacks that can be launched against it. For example, enabling Internet Connection Firewall (ICF) in Microsoft Windows XP will provide excellent protection against attacks attempted over the organization's network when a user is connected to untrusted networks; however, when the user is connected to the corporate network, ICF will prevent the application of Group Policy.

Eavesdropping on Wireless Connectivity

Many laptops and mobile devices are now equipped with 802.11b or Bluetooth wireless network interfaces. Many users do not realize that connecting their laptop or mobile device to a wireless network that is not secure is similar to having a sensitive conversation in a crowded restaurant or subway—anyone who wants to listen in can. Public and private wireless networks are becoming more common in public areas, such as airport terminals and cafes. Users might be temped to connect their laptop or mobile device to these networks for the convenience it affords, not realizing that the information they are sending and receiving might be traveling via an untrusted network.

Many home computer users and businesses are installing 802.11b wireless networks these days. Unfortunately, the built-in security measure of these networks—Wired Equivalent Privacy (WEP)—has an inherent security vulnerability. When exploited by an attacker, this vulnerability can enable the attacker to connect to the wireless network directly. In addition, many users and administrators are lulled into a false sense of security by the signal strength of their wireless access points. These users and administrators assume that their laptops can achieve this maximum signal strength, but in reality, attackers can build or purchase inexpensive wireless antennas to intercept wireless network transmissions from more than half a mile to a mile away.

Implementing Additional Security for Laptop Computers

Mobile computers are one of the most difficult IT assets to secure because network administrators must rely on users to be responsible for the security of their computers on a daily basis. To secure mobile computers, you not only must implement technology-based security, you must ensure that users understand the threats to their mobile computers and can make appropriate judgments about using their machines so that they do not jeopardize the security of information on their mobile computers or the network itself.

When implementing security for laptop computers beyond the baseline configuration, you should have two goals in mind: to secure the information on the laptop, and to prevent a compromise of the laptop from leading to the compromise of the network. To accomplish these goals you must address the following areas:

- Hardware protection

- Boot protection

- Data protection

- User education

Hardware Protection

The first area of additional security for laptop computers is protecting the laptop itself. To help prevent a laptop from being stolen when left unattended, you can use hardware locks. Several types of hardware locks exist, and they vary in cost and degree of protection. The most basic type of lock is a passive cable lock. Passive cable locks use a cable connected to the security slot on a laptop that wraps around an unmovable object. For example, a user storing a laptop in the trunk of a car could wrap the cable around the frame of the car. Typically, these locks use a key or combination lock and have cables that cannot be easily cut with handheld cable cutters. To circumvent a passive hardware lock, an attacker must pick the lock, cut the cable, or figure out a way to move the object the laptop is attached to. Some passive cable locks have alarms built into them. When the cable is looped around an object and reattached to the cable lock base, the lock creates a weak electric circuit that passes through the cable. If the circuit is broken because the cable is cut, the alarm sounds. These alarms are typically loud enough to be heard clearly from 100 yards or more. The alarm will continue to sound until the lock is unlocked or the internal battery runs out.

The effectiveness of a cable lock is dependent on the laptop user using the lock properly. Two common mistakes that users make with cable locks are leaving the key to the lock in an obvious location and attaching the cable to an object that is not secure. For example, users might leave the key to the lock in their laptop carrying case and place the case on the floor near the locked laptop, or they might loop the cable around the leg of a table, which could easily be picked up. Thus, if you implement hardware locks, you must train users in how to properly use them; otherwise, the locks can be ineffective. Hardware locks are by no means undefeatable, but if properly used, they can deter would-be thieves. The addition of an alarm to such a lock increases the likelihood of capturing the thief immediately after he steals the laptop.

Instead of (or in addition to) using passive cable locks, you can use active security systems. The most common types of active security systems use a hardware token that detects unusual motion of the laptop and sounds an alarm. If an unusual amount of motion is detected, the security system will activate. In the event of unusual motion—depending on the computer you are protecting—the security system might prevent the computer from being booted without the deactivation code, encrypt sensitive information (including data already encrypted by the OS, such as passwords), and sound an alarm. Some active security systems use proximity switches instead of motion detectors. These hardware protection systems prevent computers from leaving a confined area, such as an office building or a particular floor in the building. Active security systems typically cost two to three times more than passive cable locks.

In addition to using locks, alarms, and countermeasures to protect laptops that have highly confidential information, you might consider using a hardware tracking system. Such a system enables you to locate the laptop after it has been stolen and thereby catch the thief (and have her arrested). Hardware tracking systems for laptops or desktops typically rely on one of two mechanisms: an Internet tracking system, or a Global Positioning System (GPS). The client-side tracking agent is installed in protected areas on the computer's hard drive or in hardware tokens installed inside the laptop's case. The agent contacts the tracking service periodically with information about where the computer is located, on the Internet or physically. If the computer is reported stolen, the tracking service can wait for the device to contact it. When contacted by the agent running on the device, the tracking service can retrieve the information about the location of the device. You can then give this information to law enforcement officials to attempt to track the stolen computer. Obviously, not all laptops need this degree of protection. This type of protection is very expensive. You might want to consider hardware tracking services on laptops that you know could hold information that, if compromised, might result in the loss of human life. For example, such hardware tracking services might be more appropriate for laptops that are used by government agencies, law enforcement agencies, or mission-critical assets, such as offline root Certification Authorities (CAs).

One other type of hardware protection for computers that you should consider is to remove removable media drives from the laptop. One of the most common methods of breaking into a computer running Microsoft Windows NT 4.0 or later is to boot the computer by using a bootable floppy disk or CD. Although this is by no means a foolproof security measure, by removing these drives, you make compromising the laptop computer much more difficult and time-consuming. If you remove the floppy disk and CD-ROM drives from a computer, you should also disable the use of USB ports in the BIOS. Otherwise, the attacker might be able to attach a USB floppy or CD-ROM drive to the computer and use it as a boot device.

Boot Protection

One way that you can protect information contained on a laptop and protect account information stored on the laptop from being used to attack your organization's network if the computer is stolen is to prevent the OS from loading. You can do this by using BIOS passwords or the Windows System Key feature (Syskey).

Although different BIOS versions have different names for passwords, most BIOS versions on laptop computers have two types of passwords that you can install: *boot passwords* and *setup passwords*. Both password types are configured in the BIOS. A boot password prevents the BIOS from transferring control to the OS installed on the hard drive or any other type of media, including bootable floppy disks and CDs, without entering the password. A boot password does not prevent a user or attacker from entering the BIOS configuration; however, in newer BIOS versions, you must enter the existing password to change the boot password. BIOS setup passwords prevent a user or attacker from entering the BIOS configuration and changing information stored in the BIOS, such as the boot password or the order of precedence for boot devices.

There are only two ways to reset the BIOS setup password and boot password: by entering the existing password, or by clearing the CMOS. To clear the CMOS memory on a laptop, you must disassemble the laptop and remove the CMOS battery, which completely clears the BIOS settings. Although BIOS passwords will not completely prevent an attacker from booting the computer, under most conditions, these passwords will buy network administrators enough time to disable the user's user account and any other accounts that need to be disabled. The use of BIOS passwords also gives the user enough time to change any Web site account passwords that have been persistently stored on the laptop.

You can also use the Windows System Key utility to prevent the OS from being loaded by unauthorized people. To do so, set System Key to use Mode 2 or Mode 3 (explained in the following list). You can configure System Key by typing **syskey** at the command prompt. Only members of the Administrators group can initialize or change the system key level. The system key is the *master key* used to protect the password database encryption key. System keys have three modes:

■ **Mode 1**   Uses a machine-generated random key as the system key and stores the key on the local system. Because the key is stored on the OS, it allows for unattended system restart. By default, System Key Mode 1 is enabled during installation on all computers running Microsoft Windows 2000 and Windows XP.

■ **Mode 2**   Uses a machine-generated random key and stores the key on a floppy disk. The floppy disk with the system key is required for the system to start before the system is available for users to log on. The OS will not load unless the floppy disk is in the floppy drive. When System Key is enabled in Mode 2, the OS will never be able to be loaded if the floppy disk is damaged or lost, unless you have previously created a repair disk.

■   **Mode 3**   Uses a password chosen by the administrator to derive the system key. The OS will prompt for the system key password when the system begins the initial startup sequence, before the system is available for users to log on. The system key password is not stored anywhere on the system; instead, an MD5 hash of the password is used as the master key to protect the password encryption key. If the password is forgotten, the OS will be rendered unbootable.

Setting the System Key to Mode 2 or Mode 3 will greatly increase the security of the OS and the password-based keys it contains, such as the contents of the Security Accounts Manager (SAM) database and local security authority (LSA) secrets.

Caution   Because there is no way to recover from a damaged or lost floppy disk or a forgotten System Key password, you should implement System Key Mode 2 or Mode 3 with great caution. Develop a secure method of archiving system keys if you decide to implement System Key Mode 2 or Mode 3 on your network.

Data Protection

Regardless of whether you use hardware alarms or boot protection mechanisms, you should implement protection for data that is stored on a laptop computer. On network servers, discretionary access control lists (DACLs) are the primary method of protecting files. Unfortunately, access control lists (ACLs) are of little use when a computer is in the possession of an attacker. Unlike network servers, whose physical security can be protected by network administrators, laptop computers can be easily stolen. An attacker can remove the hard drive from a laptop and install it in a computer that they are the administrator of. The attacker can take ownership of the files and folders on the laptop computer's hard drive and read the files and folders.

To lessen this risk, you can use the EFS to secure the information on a laptop. When you use EFS properly, the only way to retrieve the information contained in the files is by performing a brute force attack on the encryption algorithm. In Windows 2000 and Windows XP, EFS uses the 56-bit DESX algorithm. Although computationally feasible, this algorithm is difficult to break. Windows XP also allows you to use the 3DES algorithm, which is computationally infeasible and thereby makes performing a brute force attack virtually impossible, given current hardware constraints.

> **More Info**   EFS is covered in detail in Chapter 7, "Securing Permissions," of this book.

The other data protection issue to address with laptop computers is the logical security of the laptop. Unlike desktop computers, which are protected from untrusted networks by firewalls and routers, laptop computers might be connected to untrusted networks on a regular basis. For example, a user might use the high-speed connection in her hotel room to create a virtual private network (VPN) connection to the corporate network. By doing this, the user creates a relatively unprotected, authenticated route to the corporate network from the Internet, not to mention placing the data stored locally on her laptop in danger. To prevent this situation, users can use personal firewall applications, such as Internet Connection Firewall, or ICF, in Windows XP.

> **More Info**   ICF is covered in detail in Chapter 9, "Implementing TCP/IP Security," of this book.

You might have certain users in your organization who have especially high security requirements, such as those needed to safeguard information that, if disclosed, could lead to the loss of life. You should avoid storing any important information persistently on the laptops of these users. You should also require these users to create a VPN connection to the corporate network and then use Terminal Services to connect to a computer on the network to access information. Furthermore, you should disable the option of storing cached credentials by setting the number of cached credentials to 0 in Group Policy or in the local Group Policy object (GPO) if the laptop is not a member of a domain. When you prevent credentials from being cached on the laptop, the user will not be able to log on to his laptop when a domain controller cannot be located to authenticate his credentials. You also should not install any applications locally on the laptop. This means the laptop will have little functionality other than acting as a remote access point to the network, but it will not place precious data or the network in danger.

Securing Mobile Devices

Securing mobile devices, such as Pocket PCs and Pocket PC Phone Edition devices, is similar to securing laptop computers. Mobile devices should have user passwords to prevent unauthorized users and attackers from accessing them. For example, Pocket PC 2002 supports both four-digit passwords and alphanumeric passwords for protecting access to the device. Each time an incorrect password is attempted, a time delay is activated before the logon screen will reappear. The delay increases exponentially upon each successive incorrect attempt.

In addition, if the mobile device will be connecting to the Internet or untrusted networks, such as public 802.11b wireless networks, you should ensure that the computer securely transmits authentication packets and data. For example, Pocket PC 2002 supports connecting to Web sites that have Secure Sockets Layer (SSL) connections enabled and wireless networks that use WEP.

Although no viruses or Trojan horses that specifically attack the Pocket PC platform or other types of mobile devices have been reported, as with laptop computers, you must install and maintain antivirus software on mobile devices and ensure that all security updates are applied as soon as they are released.

User Education

All the security measures discussed so far are completely dependent on the user properly protecting his laptop. Consequently, you must train users in the potential threats to their laptops and the measures they must take to secure their computers. Although most of the measures users must take to protect their laptops might seem obvious to you—such as not leaving a laptop in the car while buying groceries, or at least using a hardware lock to secure the laptop inside the trunk—they might not be obvious to your users. As with any type of training, it's best to be creative in how you get your message across to users in a way that they will understand. For example, when explaining to users the level of attention they should give to protecting their laptops, you can use this analogy: tell them to secure their laptops as though they were $2000 bundles of cash. Few people would ever consider locking $2000 in a car or leaving it on a table in a restaurant while they used the restroom. Posters, wallet cards, and e-mail reminders containing laptop security tips are also particularly effective in helping train users.

Securing Wireless Networking in Windows XP

Windows XP natively supports automatic configuration for the IEEE 802.11 standard for wireless networks, which minimizes the configuration that is required to access wireless networks. Users can roam between different wireless networks without the need to reconfigure the network connection settings on their computer for each location. When a user moves from one wireless network to another, Windows XP searches for available wireless networks and connects to them or prompts the user to select a wireless network to connect to. From a usability standpoint, the automatic—and even transparent—configuration of wireless networking in Windows XP is great. From a security standpoint, it presents some serious problems. Not all wireless networks are secure, and thus, a user could unwittingly endanger his laptop computer or even the corporate network.

Using Wireless Zero Configuration in Windows XP

The Wireless Zero Configuration service in Windows XP enables automatic connection to the following:

- **Infrastructure networks** Computers and devices connect to wireless access points. Access points function as network bridges between the wireless clients and a wired network infrastructure. When a user enters the transmission area of an infrastructure network, where the access points broadcast their service set identifier (SSID), Windows XP will automatically attempt to connect to the access point it gets the strongest signal from. For example, your organization might have more than one building equipped with a wireless network. When a user moves between buildings, Windows XP will always connect to the wireless network without intervention from the user.

> **Tip** Enable wireless access points to broadcast their SSID only if you intend the network to be public. Consider disabling the broadcasting of SSIDs for networks connected to your corporate network to prevent potential attackers from gaining valuable information about your network. This will, however, prevent the use of the Wireless Zero Configuration functionality.

- **Ad hoc networks**   Ad hoc networks are formed when computers and devices with wireless network connectivity connect directly to each other, instead of connecting to access points. Unlike infrastructure networks, which operate as network bridges to other networks, ad hoc networks only allow you to access resources on the computer or devices that you connect to.

By default, Windows XP connects to both infrastructure networks and ad hoc networks, even those that the computer has not connected to before. For security purposes, you might not want the laptop computers in your organization to connect to untrusted networks automatically. You can define how Windows XP connects to wireless networks in the advanced wireless network connection properties. To increase the security of Windows XP laptops with wireless network cards, you should select to connect to only infrastructure networks and deselect the option to automatically connect to *nonpreferred networks*, which are networks that are not stored as preferred networks in the wireless network configuration utility (shown in Figure 13-1).

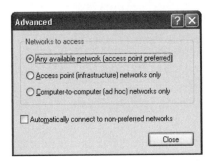

Figure 13-1   Advanced wireless network connection properties

Configuring Security for 802.11 Wireless Network Connectivity

The most basic type of security for 802.11 wireless networks is Wired Equivalent Privacy, or WEP. WEP provides for authentication and data transmission security for wireless clients to protect against unauthorized access and eavesdropping. Unlike Windows XP, Windows 2000 does not have integrated wireless network management features. In Windows XP, you can configure the network key that is used for WEP. The key is used for authentication to the wireless network. In addition, the data encryption is enabled, which means a shared encryption key is generated to encrypt the data transmission between the computer and the wireless access point. In Windows 2000, 802.11 configuration must be done in the application provided by the wireless network interface vendor.

Configuring 802.11 Security with WEP

802.11 supports two subtypes of network authentication service: open system and shared key. When open system authentication is used, any computer or device can request authentication for the access point, and consequently, any computer or device can connect to the network. Using open system authentication does not prevent data transmission encryption. Unlike open system authentication, shared key authentication requires that the client computer or device have knowledge of a secret key that is shared by the wireless access point and all other wireless clients.

When using shared key authentication, the access point generates a random 64-bit or 128-bit number that is used as a challenge. The wireless client returns the challenge, which is encrypted with the WEP shared key. The encryption process involves using the RC4 stream cipher to perform an exclusive or (XOR) binary operation on the plaintext payload. The RC4 keystream is generated by using a random number generator (RNG). The seed of the RNG is the result of concatenating the 40-bit or 104-bit WEP key with a 24-bit initialization vector. The encrypted payload and the initialization vector are sent to the access point. The access point concatenates the WEP key with the initialization vector to seed the keystream for RC4 to perform an XOR binary operation on the encrypted payload to reveal the plaintext payload.

Unfortunately, an attacker who captures these frames possesses the plaintext challenge, the ciphertext challenge, and the initialization vector. Because of the way that XOR operations work, the attacker will now know the keystream that was used, which is the concatenated initialization vector and the WEP key. Although the attacker still does not know the WEP key, she can attempt to authenticate to the access point and use the keystream derived from the captured packets to encrypt the challenge and retransmit the captured initialization vector.

> **Note**   Several utilities available on the Internet automate this process of compromising shared key authentication.

How XOR Operations Work

To understand how an attacker can compromise WEP security, you must know how the binary XOR operation works. An XOR takes two binary numbers of equal length and performs a comparison of each bit, yielding a result of bits that is equal to the two numbers. The following list shows the result of XOR operations:

```
0 XOR 0 = 1
0 XOR 1 = 0
1 XOR 0 = 0
1 XOR 1 = 1
```

The XOR is frequently used by stream ciphers to encrypt data. For example, the name *BEN* can be represented in ASCII as 0x42 0x45 0x4E and converted to the binary. The RC4 algorithm might generate the keystream shown next. You then perform an XOR on the plaintext with the keystream. The result is the ciphertext.

```
Plaintext            01000010    01000101    01001110
Keystream     XOR    01101100    00010111    01101111
Ciphertext           11010001    10101101    11011110
```

If you convert the ciphertext back to ASCII characters, you get the following: Þ -Ñ. The problem with using XOR for encryption is that if you know any two of the three elements, you can determine the one you do not know. For example, if you can intercept the plaintext and the ciphertext, you can determine the keystream by performing an XOR on the plaintext with the ciphertext:

```
Plaintext            01000010    01000101    01001110
Ciphertext    XOR    11010001    10101101    11011110
Keystream            01101100    00010111    01101111
```

Although shared key authentication is not completely secure, it does provide more protection than Open System authentication. Thus, when combined with Media Access Control (MAC) address filtering, implementing shared key authentication provides a base level of security for wireless networks against novice attackers. If your organization issues laptops to users with wireless network cards, the users will likely install a home wireless network. To ensure that employees do not expose information contained on their laptops to potential attackers, you should create guidelines for installing home wireless networks, and these guidelines should include enabling shared key authentication.

WEP also provides data encrypted services by using the same process as defined for shared key authentication. Because only 2^24 (roughly 16 million) initialization vectors exist, if you assume that each packet uses a new initialization vector, the probability is that one initialization vector will be repeated after about 4500 packets have been transmitted. This is an example of a birthday attack on a cryptography algorithm. Thus, if an attacker can get the access point to send known plaintext (such as ping packets) and then capture all encrypted packets, he will be able to compute the keystream by performing an XOR on the plaintext with the ciphertext. The attacker could then place the keystream in a database organized by the initialization vector. The next time that the attacker intercepts a packet with that initialization vector, he can look up the keystream in the database and decrypt the packet.

In addition, a known vulnerability exists in the scheduling algorithm in RC4, meaning that a small subset of initialization vectors will be weak. Researchers at AT&T labs estimate that this vulnerability could be exploited by intercepting as few as 1,000,000 packets. By exploiting this vulnerability, an attacker could retrieve the static WEP key. If the attacker knows what the WEP key is, he can decrypt any packet he wants to view. Most newer, enterprise-oriented access points and wireless network cards are programmed not to use these weak initialization vectors. You can protect your wireless clients that use Windows XP by using 802.1x.

Configuring 802.11 Security with 802.1x

At the time of the printing of this book, IEEE 802.1x is a draft standard for port-based network access control, which provides authenticated network access to 802.11 wireless networks and to wired networks. Port-based network access control uses the physical characteristics of a switched LAN infrastructure to authenticate devices that are attached to a LAN port and to prevent access to that port in cases where the authentication process fails.

During a port-based network access control interaction, a LAN port adopts one of two roles: *authenticator* or *supplicant*. In the role of authenticator, a LAN port enforces authentication before it allows user access to the services that can be accessed through that port. In the role of supplicant, a LAN port requests access to the services that can be accessed through the authenticator's port. An authentication server, which either can be a separate entity or an entity colocated with the authenticator, checks the supplicant's credentials on behalf of the authenticator. The authentication server then responds to the authenticator, indicating whether the supplicant is authorized to access the authenticator's services.

The authenticator's port-based network access control defines two logical access points to the LAN, through one physical LAN port. The first logical access point, the *uncontrolled port*, allows data exchange between the authenticator and other computers on the LAN, regardless of the computer's authorization state. The second logical access point, the *controlled port*, allows data exchange between an authenticated LAN user and the authenticator.

IEEE 802.1x uses standard security protocols, such as Remote Authentication Dial-In User Service (RADIUS), to provide centralized user identification, authentication, dynamic WEP management, and accounting. In Windows XP, you can use X.509 certificates or the Protected Extensible Authentication Protocol (PEAP) with Microsoft Challenge Handshake Authentication Protocol version 2 (MS-CHAPv2) to authenticate clients on the Authentication tab on the profile of a preferred wireless network connection, as shown in Figure 13-2.

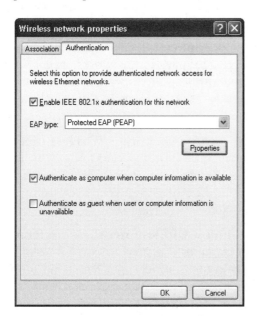

Figure 13-2   Configuring 802.1x authentication for wireless connections in Windows XP

The PEAP authentication has two phases. First, an encrypted TLS channel is established to the RADIUS server using a PEAP exchange. Second, MS-CHAPv2 is used to authenticate the wireless client to the network. After the wireless user and computer have been authenticated, encryption keys can be exchanged.

Best Practices

- **Educate your users.** Ultimately, the security of information stored on laptop computers and mobile devices will rest with how seriously users take securing these assets and how well users follow guidelines and security polices for protecting their laptops. Although you can use technology to secure these devices to a certain extent, you must train users to do their part in securing laptop computers and mobile devices.

- **Use hardware locks for laptop computers.** If the risk to your organization from supplying users with laptop computers is high enough, consider using hardware locking devices.

- **Use BIOS or System Key passwords.** Passwords that prevent an attacker from booting a laptop computer, even temporarily, will increase the security of your network and the information stored on a stolen computer.

- **Install personal firewall applications for mobile users.** For users that will be connecting to untrusted networks, install Windows XP or a personal firewall application to prevent an attacker from compromising the computer. Be sure to show the user how to use the application.

- **Implement 802.1x to secure corporate wireless networks.** The security provided by WEP is not strong enough to prevent knowledgeable and skilled attackers from compromising data sent on wireless networks. 802.1x provides secure authentication, dynamic key exchanges, and data transmission security.

- **Create guidelines for home wireless network configuration.** To protect information on laptops issued to employees who will install wireless networks in their homes, create guidelines on what wireless access point to install and how to implement basic security measures, such as disabling SSID broadcasting, enabling WEP with shared key authentication, and MAC address filtering.

Additional Information

- "Overview of Mobile Information Server Security" white paper (*http://www.microsoft.com/technet/prodtechnol/mis/evaluate/security.asp*)

■ "Enterprise Deployment of IEEE 802.11 Using Windows XP and Windows 2000 Internet Authentication Service" white paper, which covers 802.1x (*http://www.microsoft.com/windowsxp/pro/ techinfo/deployment/wireless/default.asp*)

■ "RADIUS Protocol Security and Best Practices" white paper (*http:// www.microsoft.com/windows2000/techinfo/administration/ radius.asp*)

■ "5-Minute Security Advisor: The Road Warrior's Guide to Laptop Protection" (*http://www.microsoft.com/technet/columns/security/5min/ 5min-205.asp*)

■ 314647: "How to Increase Information Security on the Pocket PC"

■ 143475: "Windows NT System Key Permits Strong Encryption of the SAM"

Note   The previous two articles can be accessed through the Microsoft Knowledge Base. Go to *http://support.microsoft.com* and enter the article number in the Search The Knowledge Base text box.

Part IV

Securing Common Services

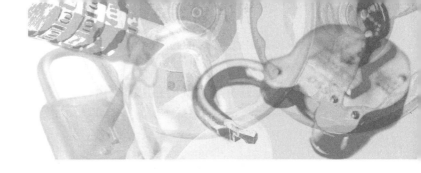

14

Implementing Security for Domain Controllers

Microsoft Windows 2000 domain controllers provide the Active Directory directory service to Windows 2000 forests. The domain controllers maintain the Active Directory database and must be secure to prevent the compromise of the Active Directory database and the objects stored within the database. This chapter looks at the security measures you must take to protect domain controllers and to ensure that the Active Directory database is secure.

Threats to Domain Controllers

Windows 2000 domain controllers are likely targets of attacks that attempt to compromise user and computer accounts, as well as other objects stored within Active Directory. Specifically, Windows 2000 domain controllers face the following threats:

- Modification of Active Directory objects
- Password attacks
- Denial-of-service attacks
- Replication prevention attacks
- Exploitation of known vulnerabilities

Modification of Active Directory Objects

If attackers can compromise a domain controller, they can effectively make any changes they want to Active Directory. This includes the deletion or modification of existing objects and the creation of new objects in Active Directory. For example, attackers who gain administrative access to a domain controller can create a user account for their purposes, as well as add that user account to any number of administrative accounts in the domain.

Password Attacks

If attackers can gain access to a domain controller, they can back up the Active Directory database by performing a System State backup or by copying the Active Directory database and logs to another computer by booting the domain controller into another OS. This backup of the domain controller can be restored to a remote computer and used to mount an offline password attack. The advantage to the attacker is that the password attack is not taking place against the production network, but on a computer that is removed from the network.

Denial-of-Service Attacks

Attackers can prevent users from performing authentication by performing denial-of-service attacks against domain controllers. Denial-of-service attacks typically take advantage of unpatched Windows 2000 security flaws. Denial-of-service attacks can also be launched against Domain Name System (DNS) servers, preventing clients from finding domain controllers. Clients find domain controllers by requesting a Service (SRV) resource record from a DNS server. If the DNS server is unable to respond, clients will not be able to find a domain controller for their domain.

Replication Prevention Attacks

If attackers are able to disrupt replication between domain controllers, they might be able to prevent the application of Group Policy objects (GPOs), which lock down domain controllers. For example, if you modify the GPO applied to all domain controllers and the GPO is not replicated to all domain controllers, some of the domain controllers will not have the new security settings applied.

Attackers can prevent replication between domain controllers by performing a number of attacks. If DNS resource records are modified or deleted, a domain controller might not be able to find its replication partners. Likewise, if wide area network (WAN) links are blocked, replication traffic might not be able to reach domain controllers at remote sites.

Exploitation of Known Vulnerabilities

Attackers might be able to compromise a domain controller that is not kept up to date with the latest service packs and security updates. For example, if the latest service packs are not applied to a domain controller, attackers might be able to disable it by performing a buffer overflow attack that prevents the OS from responding to any network requests. In the worst case scenario, a buffer overflow might allow attackers to modify configuration and take control of a domain controller.

Implementing Security on Domain Controllers

To prevent attacks against Windows 2000 domain controllers, you must implement security measures that lessen the vulnerabilities. These security measures range from physically securing domain controllers in order to prevent direct access by attackers, to logically configuring domain controllers to reduce threats. Specifically, you must take the following security measures to secure Windows 2000 domain controllers:

- Provide physical security.

- Increase the security of stored passwords.

- Eliminate nonessential services.

- Apply security settings by using Group Policy.

- Protect against the failure of a domain controller.

- Implement Syskey.

- Secure built-in accounts and groups.

- Enable auditing.

- Secure Active Directory communications.

Providing Physical Security

A physical compromise of a domain controller can easily lead to the compromise of the Active Directory database copy stored at the domain controller. You must protect domain controllers by storing them in physically secure locations, such as a server room that requires card-key access.

For example, if attackers gain physical access to a domain controller, they can boot the computer with a third-party boot disk. Once attackers have administrator access, they can back up Active Directory by performing a System State backup, restore Active Directory to another server, and run any number of offline password attacks against the Active Directory database.

Increasing the Security of Stored Passwords

To protect passwords stored in Active Directory, enable the following configuration options:

■ Do not implement protocols that require passwords to be stored in a reversibly encrypted format, such as Challenge Handshake Authentication Protocol (CHAP) or digest authentication for Web applications. A password stored in this format is more susceptible to password attacks if attackers gain physical access to a domain controller. A password attack can easily decrypt passwords if they are stored in this format.

> **Note**   A password cracker can still crack passwords stored in Active Directory that are not reversibly encrypted. The difference is that cracking a normally stored password takes much longer.

■ Disable LAN Manager (LM) hash values in the Active Directory database. A password stored in an LM hash value is more susceptible to password attacks. You can disable the storage of passwords in this format by enabling the Network Security: Do Not Store LAN Manager Hash Values On Next Password Change Group Policy setting in Security Options. This security option is available only when you modify the GPO from a Microsoft Windows XP computer. Group Policy is applicable to Windows 2000 computers with Service Pack 2 or later, or to Windows XP.

> **Caution**   Ensure that no client computers that use LM authentication exist on the network. For Microsoft Windows 95 and Windows 98 clients, install the Directory Services Client software from the Windows 2000 Server CD. This client software ensures that Windows 95 and Windows 98 computers authenticate by using NT LAN Manager version 2 (NTLMv2) authentication.

■   Enable password complexity at the domain. When the Password Must Meet Complexity Requirements group policy is enabled, passwords must be at least six characters in length and consist of at least three of the following four forms:

English uppercase letters	A, B, C, ... Z
English lowercase letters	a, b, c, ... z
Westernized Arabic numerals	1, 2, ... 9
Nonalphanumeric characters	!, @, #, and so on

Eliminating Nonessential Services

A domain controller should not run nonrequired services. In its most secure configuration, a domain controller does not run any services other than the DNS service to allow for Active Directory–integrated zones.

The "Security Operations Guide for Windows 2000 Server" recommends that only specific services be enabled at a Windows 2000 domain controller. Table 14-1 shows the recommended startup configuration for services required by a Windows 2000 domain controller.

Table 14-1   Windows 2000 Domain Controller Services

Service	Manual	Automatic
COM+ Event System	X	
DHCP Client		X
Distributed File System		X
Distributed Link Tracking Client		X
DNS Server		X
DNS Client		X
Event Log		X
File Replication Service		X
Kerberos Key Distribution Center		X
Logical Disk Manager	X	
Logical Disk Manager Administrative Service		X
Net Logon		X
Network Connections	X	
NT LM Security Support Provider		X

(continued)

Table 14-1   Windows 2000 Domain Controller Services   *(continued)*

Service	Manual	Automatic
Performance Logs and Alerts	X	
Plug and Play		X
Protected Storage		X
Remote Procedure Call (RPC)		X
Remote Procedure Call (RPC) Locator		X
Remote Registry Service		X
Security Accounts Manager		X
Server		X
System Event Notification		X
TCP/IP Net BIOS Helper Service		X
Windows Management Instrumentation Driver Extensions	X	
Windows Time		X
Workstation		X

In addition to the services listed in Table 14-1, a Windows 2000 domain controller might require other services, depending on your network's configuration. These services include the following:

■ **Simple Mail Transport Protocol (SMTP)**   This service is required if your intersite replication topology implements SMTP replication.

■ **Intersite Messaging**   If your replication topology implements SMTP replication, you must start this service in order to direct inbound and outbound intersite messages to the appropriate replication protocol: remote procedure calls or SMTP.

■ **IIS Admin Service**   If you implement the SMTP service, you must load the IIS Admin Service to manage the SMTP service. In addition, the SMTP service is dependent on the IIS Admin Service to start.

■ **Distributed Link Tracking Server Service**   If you implement the Distributed Link Tracking Client Service, you must start the Distributed Link Tracking Server Service so that clients can contact the server service when tracking files on NTFS file system volumes.

Applying Security Settings by Using Group Policy

The simplest way to ensure consistent security settings across all domain controllers is to create a security template that defines the required settings and to apply the template by using Group Policy. When defining Group Policy settings, remember the following guidelines:

■ Define account policy settings in the default domain policy. The account policy settings include the domain's password policy, account lockout policy, and Kerberos policy. These settings must be defined at the domain—rather than at individual OUs—because they are attributes related to the Security Accounts Manager (SAM). Also, the domain is the only Group Policy container that ensures that every domain controller has a uniform account policy defined if domain controller computer accounts are moved from the Domain Controllers OU.

■ Review the recommended security settings for domain controllers presented in the BaselineDC.inf security template included in the "Security Operations Guide for Windows 2000 Server" and the U.S. National Security Agency's (NSA) W2kdc.inf security template.

> **Note** Use these recommended security templates as the starting point for your company's domain controller security configuration. You should modify these security templates to enforce your company's security policy.

Protecting Against the Failure of a Domain Controller

You can protect against the failure of a domain controller in two ways: by performing regular backups of your domain controller and by implementing at least two domain controllers for each domain.

By performing regular backups of your company's domain controllers, you ensure that the domain controllers can be quickly recovered in the event of hardware failure or data corruption on the hard disk. To back up Active Directory, you must include the System State, which comprises the Active Directory database and log files, in your backup set. The backup strategy should make certain that backups are performed at regular intervals and are periodically tested by performing test restores, which ensure that disaster recovery will work in the event of a domain controller failure.

In addition to performing regular backups, you should make sure that at least two domain controllers exist in each domain in your forest. Doing so ensures that if a single domain controller fails, an additional domain controller can service authentication requests and maintain the Active Directory database.

Implementing Syskey

Windows 2000, by default, implements strong encryption of the account information stored in Active Directory. This information is protected by the System Key. The level of protection offered by the System Key is configured by using the Syskey.exe utility. When you run the Syskey.exe utility, you can choose to protect the System Key by using one of three methods:

- **A machine-generated random key stored on the local system by using a complex encryption algorithm**   This is the default configuration of Syskey.exe, and it provides strong encryption of password information in the registry. Because the System Key is stored on the local system, this method allows for unattended system restarts.

- **A machine-generated random key stored on a floppy disk**   The floppy disk with the System Key is required for the system to start. This disk must be inserted when Windows 2000 prompts you for it after beginning the startup sequence, but before the system is available for users to log on.

- **An administrator-chosen password to derive the System Key**   Windows 2000 will prompt you for the System Key password when the system is in the initial startup sequence, but before the system is available for users to log on. An MD5 digest of the password is used as the System Key to protect the password encryption key.

The method you use to protect the System Key will depend on your company's security policy. Although storing the System Key on a floppy disk or requiring a password to start the computer increases the security of the Active Directory database, both of these methods remove the possibility of an unattended domain controller startup.

Securing Built-In Accounts and Groups

Several built-in groups and user accounts must be protected in an Active Directory environment. These users and groups are assigned specific permissions and user rights that allow them to manage Active Directory. Specifically, you should manage the membership of the following user and group accounts:

- **Administrator**   The Administrator account in each domain is a built-in user account that is a member of the Domain Admins and Administrators groups in each domain. In the forest root domain, this account is also a member of the Schema Admins and Enterprise Admins groups. To secure this group, consider renaming the Administrator account and changing the description of the user account because it is a well-known description.

> **Tip**   Consider creating another account named Administrator with the description "Built-In Account For Administering The Computer/Domain." This user account should be tracked to determine whether anyone is attempting to connect to the account with the user's credentials. Verify that this account is only a member of the Domain Guests global group to ensure that the group is assigned minimum network privileges.

- **Administrators**   The Administrators built-in local group is assigned administrative permissions and user rights for a domain. Members of this group can manage all aspects of the Active Directory domain in which the Administrators group exists.

- **Domain Admins**   In each domain, the Domain Admins global group is a member of the Administrators built-in local group. Through this membership, the group can modify the membership of the Administrators group and has full administrative privileges for the domain. In the forest root domain, members of this group can modify the membership of the Enterprise Admins and Schema Admins groups.

- **Enterprise Admins**   The Enterprise Admins group can administer all domains in the forest and is assigned permissions to manage several objects stored in the configuration-naming context. For example, members of the Enterprise Admins group can add enterprise Certification Authorities (CAs) to the forest.

- **Schema Admins**   The members of the Schema Admins group can modify the schema by defining new attributes and classes in the Active Directory schema.

You can manage the membership of these groups by using the restricted groups group policy. The restricted groups group policy prevents the addition and deletion of user accounts and groups from a group defined in this policy.

> **More Info**   For more information on implementing restricted groups, please see 320045, "How to Restrict Group Membership By Using Group Policy in Windows 2000."

Enabling Auditing

To ensure that attacks against domain controllers are detected, enable auditing in the default domain controllers policy. Auditing will record events to the Windows 2000 Security Log that can aid in detecting intrusion attempts and attacks against the domain controller. Table 14-2 outlines the recommended auditing settings for a domain controller.

Table 14-2   Windows 2000 Domain Controller Audit Settings

Audit Policy	Prescribed Setting
Audit account logon events	Success, Failure
Audit account management	Success, Failure
Audit directory service access	Failure
Audit logon events	Success, Failure
Audit object access	Success, Failure
Audit policy change	Success, Failure
Audit privilege use	Failure
Audit system events	Success, Failure

> **More Info**   For more details on configuring auditing in a Windows 2000 network environment, see Chapter 12, "Auditing Microsoft Windows Security Events."

Securing Active Directory Communications

You can increase the security of data transmitted to and from domain controllers by implementing different strategies. These strategies include restricting which users and computers can connect to the domain controller and protecting the data as it is transmitted to and from domain controllers.

Implementing SMB Signing

You can restrict which users and computers can connect to a domain controller by implementing Server Message Block (SMB) signing or IP Security (IPSec) by using Authentication Headers (AHs). Both solutions provide mutual authentication of the client and the server and protect the data against modification during transmission.

To implement SMB signing, you must implement the Digitally Sign Server Communications (Always) security option in a GPO applied to the domain controller's OU. To ensure that client computers also implement SMB signing, you must implement the Digitally Sign Client Communications (Always) security option in a GPO linked to the domain. This GPO will affect only Windows 2000 and Windows XP computers.

More Info   If you need to enable SMB signing for Windows 98 or Microsoft Windows NT computers, see 230545, "How to Enable SMB Signing in Windows 98," and 161372, "How to Enable SMB Signing in Windows NT."

Disabling Anonymous Connections

In some cases, you might want to prevent anonymous access to resources on a domain controller. You can do this by configuring the RestrictAnonymous registry key at each domain controller. You can implement this in a GPO by configuring the Additional Restrictions For Anonymous Connections policy under Security Options.

To ensure the highest level of security, you can define Group Policy to be set to No Access Without Explicit Anonymous Permissions (a registry value of 2). This registry value ensures that the access token built for nonauthenticated users does not include the security identifier (SID) of the Everyone group. This effectively restricts anonymous users to accessing resources that explicitly allow access by anonymous users.

Enable the RestrictAnonymous registry entry only if your domain does not include downlevel member workstations, servers, or Windows NT 4.0 backup domain controllers. When you enable this option, the following conditions will be in effect:

- Windows 95, Windows 98, and Windows NT 4.0 member workstations or servers cannot set up a Netlogon secure channel.

- Windows NT 4.0 domain controllers in trusting domains cannot set up a Netlogon secure channel.

- Macintosh users cannot change their passwords at all.

- The Browser service cannot retrieve domain lists or server lists from backup browsers, master browsers, or domain master browsers that have the RestrictAnonymous registry key set to a value of 2.

Implementing IPSec Encryption

To protect data transmitted to and from domain controllers from inspection, you can implement IPSec encryption. Because communications with domain controllers might also require communications with other services, such as DNS, you typically will implement IPSec encryption for all network traffic.

> **Warning**   To implement IPSec encryption for all network traffic, all network clients must be running Windows 2000 or Windows XP as the OS. IPSec encryption is not available to previous versions of the Microsoft OS.

If you want to implement IPSec to protect all data transmitted to and from a domain controller, you must first ensure that all other computers in the domain are configured to implement IPSec, if required to do so. You can accomplish this by assigning the default Client (Respond Only) IPSec policy at the domain. This policy will allow any client computer to use IPSec to protect data if requested to do so by a Windows 2000 server.

> **Note**   The Client (Respond Only) IPSec policy assumes that a server protected by IPSec has the Accept Unsecured Communications, But Always Respond Using IPSec option enabled. If this option is not enabled, the Client (Respond Only) IPSec policy will not work because IPSec is implemented only if the server requests IPSec. Because the client always initiates communications with the server, all communications will fail if this option is not enabled.

To ensure that IPSec is used to protect data transmitted to and from domain controllers, assign the Secure Server (Require Security) IPSec policy in a GPO linked to the domain controller's OU. This IPSec policy ensures that all network traffic is encrypted by using Encapsulating Security Payload (ESP). The actual encryption and integrity algorithms are negotiated between the client and the server during the Internet Key Exchange (IKE) negotiations.

> **Note**   Do not implement IPSec if the data that is transmitted between any clients on the network to the domain controllers must pass through network devices that perform network address translation (NAT). Currently, IPSec is unable to pass through NAT devices. Microsoft is considering implementing the Internet Engineering Task Force (IETF) Draft entitled "UDP Encapsulation of IPSec Packets," which will allow IPSec to pass through NAT devices in a future service pack or security update.

Best Practices

- **Physically secure domain controllers.**   All domain controllers should be stored in network server rooms secure from nonauthorized personnel. A domain controller should not be used as a desktop computer. The domain controllers ideally should be stored in a card-key-access room where access is restricted to network administrators.

- **Leave domain controller computer accounts in the Domain Controllers OU.**   Domain controllers should have consistent application of security settings. You can ensure that the same security settings are applied to domain controllers by keeping all domain controllers in a common OU. The Domain Controllers OU is defined by default as the Active Directory storage location for domain controller computer accounts. Ensure that the domain controller computer accounts remain in this default OU.

- **Develop the baseline domain controller settings in a security template.**   Defining the security settings in a security template ensures that the security settings are reproducible. You can import the security template into a GPO linked to the Domain Controllers OU to ensure consistent application. In addition, the security template provides documentation of the security settings defined by your company for domain controllers.

- **Apply the security template in a separate GPO linked to the Domain Controllers OU.**   By applying the security template in a GPO other than the default domain controllers policy, you allow users to disable the security template settings by either unlinking the GPO from the Domain Controllers OU or deleting the GPO entirely. If the security template is imported into the Domain Controllers OU, it will be more difficult to modify changes and reverse the settings of the security template.

- **Enable auditing and increase log setting.**   Auditing should be defined in a GPO applied at the domain controller's OU to ensure that the Security Log contains relevant information about potential attacks against your company's domain controllers.

- **Store baseline security templates in a central, secure location.**   To ensure that version control is maintained, maintain a single store for all security templates or use version control software such as Microsoft Visual SourceSafe. Version control ensures that a single "master" version of the security template is maintained and applied to computers.

- **Restrict who can manage and link GPOs.**   You can protect domain controllers from incorrect security settings by restricting who is delegated permissions to modify the GPO that applies the security settings. In addition, you can restrict which users and groups can link GPOs to the Domain Controllers OU.

- **Install more than one domain controller in each domain.**   By installing two or more domain controllers in each domain, you ensure that at least one domain controller exists for the domain in case a domain controller fails. The second domain controller ensures that a domain controller is available to handle authentication requests and modifications to Active Directory objects in the event of a domain controller failure.

Additional Information

- "UDP Encapsulation of IPSec Packets" IETF Draft (*http://www.ietf.org/ internet-drafts/draft-ietf-ipsec-udp-encaps-04.txt*)

- "Security Operations Guide for Windows 2000 Server" (*http:// www.microsoft.com/downloads/release.asp?releaseid=37123*)

- "Security Operations Guide for Windows 2000 Server—Tools and Scripts" (*http://www.microsoft.com/downloads/release.asp?releaseid=36834*)

- "Step-by-Step Guide to Using the Delegation of Control Wizard" (*http://www.microsoft.com/technet/prodtechnol/windows2000serv/howto/delestep.asp*)

- U.S. National Security Agency's "Guide to Securing Microsoft Windows 2000 Active Directory" (*http://www.nsa.gov/snac/win2k/guides/w2k-5.pdf*)

- U.S. National Security Agency's baseline domain controller security template (*http://www.nsa.gov/snac/win2k/guides/inf/w2k_dc.inf*)

- 259576: "Group Policy Application Rules for Domain Controllers"

- 143475: "Windows NT System Key Permits Strong Encryption of the SAM"

- 320045: "How to Restrict Group Membership By Using Group Policy in Windows 2000"

- 230545: "How to Enable SMB Signing in Windows 98"

- 161372: "How to Enable SMB Signing in Windows NT"

- 246261: "How to Use the RestrictAnonymous Registry Value in Windows 2000"

- 299656: "New Registry Key to Remove LM Hashes from Active Directory and Security Account Manager"

> **Note**   The previous seven articles can be accessed through the Microsoft Knowledge Base. Go to *http://support.microsoft.com* and enter the article number in the Search The Knowledge Base text box.

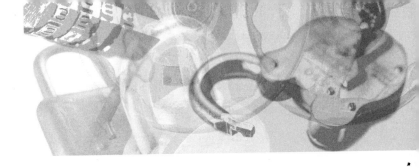

15

Implementing Security for DNS Servers

A Domain Name System (DNS) server provides resolution of DNS names to Internet Protocol (IP) addresses and resolution of IP address to DNS names. The Active Directory directory service is dependent on DNS and uses DNS as its default name resolution service. The Microsoft Windows 2000 DNS service provides new features to ease administration and configuration of DNS. The new features introduced since the DNS service of Microsoft Windows NT 4.0 include the following:

- **Dynamic DNS updates** A Windows 2000 DNS server can accept dynamic updates from DNS clients that support the dynamic update protocols described in RFC 2136, "Dynamic Updates in the Domain Name System (DNS UPDATE)."

- **Secure DNS updates** To protect the DNS server against unauthorized updates, Windows 2000 can enforce DNS client authentication for updates. DNS clients must authenticate with the Windows 2000 DNS server by using the Generic Security Service Application Program Interface (GSS-API), as described in the RFC draft "GSS Algorithm for TSIG (GSS-TSIG)."

- **Active Directory–integrated zones** The security of DNS zone data is ensured by storing each DNS resource record as an individual Active Directory object. Each DNS resource record has its own discretionary access control list (DACL) that determines which security principals can modify the resource records.

- **Service (SRV) resource records** Windows 2000 advertises its Active Directory services in DNS by using SRV resource records. SRV resource records identify the host name of the servers that host Active Directory services so that a DNS client can connect to the required Active Directory service. This is the format of the SRV resource record:

```
_ldap._tcp.example.com. 600 SRV 0 100 389 dc1.example.com
```

The following components are defined in an SRV resource record:

  ❑ **_ldap._tcp.example.com** Refers to the advertised service (_ldap), the transport protocol (_tcp), and the domain (example.com). In this case, the Lightweight Directory Access Protocol (LDAP) service resolves LDAP queries for the example.com domain.

  ❑ **600** Refers to the Time to Live (TTL), which is the amount of time, in seconds, that the SRV resource record will be cached at a DNS server or DNS client in the resolver cache.

  ❑ **SRV** Indicates that the resource record is a service resource record that specifies the location of a network service.

  ❑ **0 100** Refers to the priority and weight, which allow you to configure preferences for one SRV resource record over another SRV resource record for the same service.

  ❑ **389** References the port upon which the service is listening. In this case, the LDAP service listens on Transmission Control Protocol (TCP) port 389.

  ❑ **dc1.example.com** The network host where the LDAP service resides.

Threats to DNS Servers

Because of Windows 2000's dependence on the DNS name service, DNS servers are targets for attacks. Attackers can pose the following threats to the DNS service:

- Overwriting existing DNS resource records and hijacking sessions

- Acquisition of DNS zone data by performing unauthorized zone transfers

- Exposure of the internal IP addressing scheme to the public network

- Denial-of-service attacks that disable all DNS services

Modification of DNS Records

By supporting dynamic DNS updates, a Windows 2000 DNS server is susceptible to modification of DNS resource records if the security of the DNS server is
not configured correctly. If attackers can modify a DNS resource record at a
DNS server, they can redirect clients to a server impersonating the original
server. Once the resource record is modified at the DNS server, all DNS clients
receive the fraudulent information from the DNS service.

Alternatively, attackers might attempt to pollute the cache of the DNS
server with false DNS information. When a DNS server responds to a DNS
query, it first verifies that the requested DNS name exists in the DNS server's
DNS cache. If the requested DNS resource record exists in the cache, the
response is based upon the cached information. If attackers can modify or
inject information into the DNS server's cache, the DNS server will send the
modified response to the DNS clients, rather than contacting the authoritative
DNS server for the zone.

Zone Transfer of DNS Data by an Unauthorized Server

The DNS zone contains SRV resource records and IP address information that
can provide an attacker with the layout of the network and location of key
Active Directory services. If attackers can obtain the DNS zone data, they can
easily generate a diagram of the network.

The simplest way for attackers to gain the DNS zone data is to request a
zone transfer of the zone data from an existing DNS server. The zone transfer
moves all DNS zone data to the target server.

Exposure of Internal IP Addressing Schemes

When DNS is poorly designed, Active Directory information is published to
DNS zones accessible from the Internet. The Active Directory information is
required only on the private network, where network clients must authenticate
with and connect to Active Directory resources.

> **Tip**   If an external client must connect to Active Directory resources,
> Microsoft recommends you provide external clients access to the pri-
> vate network by deploying the Routing and Remote Access Service
> (RRAS) on a computer hosting virtual private network (VPN) connec-
> tions. By connecting to the private network via a VPN, the client will
> have an IP address on the private network and can securely access
> an internal DNS server.

Denial-of-Service Attacks Against DNS Services

An attacker can prevent access to DNS services on the network by launching a denial-of-service attack against the DNS server. A denial-of-service attack will prevent the DNS server from responding to normal queries. Because of Active Directory's dependence on DNS for name resolution, the removal of the DNS service from the network via a denial-of-service attack will prevent network authentication and the resolution of host names on the network.

Securing DNS Servers

When planning the security of DNS servers, you should prepare for attacks against both DNS clients and DNS servers. Both can lead to clients being directed to unauthorized DNS servers or referenced to incorrect servers via fraudulent DNS resource records. By implementing the following security measures, you can reduce the probability of a successful attack against your DNS server. These measures increase the security of your DNS servers and lessen the chances of a successful attack:

- Implementing Active Directory–integrated zones
- Implementing separate internal and external DNS name servers
- Restricting zone transfers
- Implementing IP Security (IPSec) between DNS clients and servers
- Restricting DNS traffic at the firewall
- Limiting management of DNS
- Protecting the DNS cache

Implementing Active Directory–Integrated Zones

Active Directory–integrated zones store zone information in the domain naming context, rather than in plaintext files on the local file system. An Active Directory–integrated zone implements each resource record as a separate *dnsNode* object in the following Active Directory location:

```
DC=DNSZoneName, CN=MicrosoftDNS, CN=System, DC=DomainDN
```

DNSZoneName is the DNS fully qualified domain name (FQDN) of the DNS zone, and *DomainDN* is the LDAP distinguished name of the Active Directory domain where the DNS zone is stored. For example, the zone named example.com stored in an Active Directory domain named south.example.com would be stored in the following location:

```
DC=example.com, CN=MicrosoftDNS, CN=System, DC=south,DC=example,DC=com
```

The zone information is replicated to all other domain controllers in the domain. This information is accessible to DNS clients if the DNS service is installed at a specific domain controller and if the DNS clients are configured to use that domain controller as a DNS server.

If the zone must be hosted on DNS servers in other domains, the DNS servers in those domains must be configured with secondary zones, with the domain controllers in the initial domain acting as master DNS servers for the zone. Active Directory replication does not provide replication of Active Directory–integrated zones to other domains in the forest.

Because each DNS resource record is stored as a separate *dnsNode* object, each resource record has its own individual DACL. By default, the only security principals with the permission to modify a DNS resource record are members of the local Administrators group, the Domain Admins group, the Enterprise Admins group, the DNSAdmins group, and the Enterprise Domain Controllers group, as well as the computer account that registered the DNS resource record with the DNS zone if you have enabled Secure Dynamic Updates for the zone.

Implementing Separate Internal and External DNS Name Servers

Even if you implement the same DNS namespace on both the private and public networks, you should create separate zones for the internal and external DNS servers. The external DNS servers must contain only externally accessible DNS resource records. The internal DNS servers must contain internally accessible DNS resource records and can contain externally accessible DNS resource records, depending on the namespace implemented for Active Directory and the addressing scheme implemented in the perimeter network (also known as DMZ, demilitarized zone, and screened subnet) of the network. See Figure 15-1 for an example of this DNS configuration.

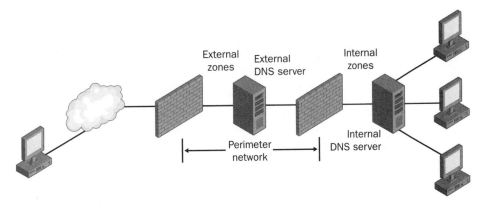

Figure 15-1   A namespace protected by implementing separate external and internal DNS servers

> **Note**   Implementing separate internal and external DNS servers might require you to include external resource records in the internal DNS zone. You need to do this when the Active Directory forest root uses the same DNS domain name as the external network or when you want to reference the externally accessible resources by their true IP addresses in the perimeter network, rather than using the addresses published to the Internet by the firewall protecting the perimeter network.
>
> If the same namespace is used both internally and externally, you cannot use forwarders to resolve the DNS resource records hosted at the external DNS server because the internal DNS server is authoritative for the DNS zone. If the resource record is not found in an authoritative zone, DNS reports that the resource record does not exist and the DNS request will not be forwarded to the configured forwarder.

Another method that attackers can use to obtain DNS zone data is to perform a zone transfer, transferring all DNS resource records from the target DNS zone. Attackers can accomplish this by typing the following command within the Nslookup console:

```
ls -d
```

This command attempts to acquire all DNS resource records for the *DNSDomain* by requesting a zone transfer from the DNS server you connect to via the Nslookup console.

You can block this type of attack by restricting zone transfers in the properties of the DNS zone, as shown in Figure 15-2.

Via the Zone Transfers tab, you can restrict DNS zone transfers to the following:

- **Servers listed on the Name Servers tab**   A zone transfer is possible only from DNS servers listed on the Name Servers tab of the DNS zone properties. If a DNS server requests a zone transfer and a DNS Name Server (NS) resource record does not exist in the DNS zone for the requesting IP address, the zone transfer is blocked. We recommend you use this option when you have numerous DNS servers that might request zone transfers.

- **Specific IP addresses**   A zone transfer is possible only if the requesting DNS server's IP address is included in the list of approved DNS servers. If the requesting IP address is not included in the list, the zone transfer is blocked. We recommend you use this option only when a small number of secondary DNS servers exist for a zone.

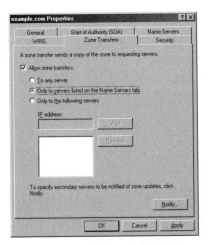

Figure 15-2   Restricting DNS zone transfers for the example.com zone

Implementing IPSec Between DNS Clients and DNS Servers

You can prevent unauthorized DNS clients from requesting DNS information from the internal DNS server by implementing IPSec to authorize connections to the DNS servers. With IPSec, a DNS client must successfully negotiate an IPSec security association (SA) with the DNS server before the DNS client can perform any DNS queries. If the DNS client is unable to establish an IPSec SA, the DNS client is blocked from all communications with the DNS server.

When configuring the IPSec filters for the DNS clients, you can choose from one of two IPSec protocols:

- **Authentication Header (AH)**   Protects the DNS packets by requiring the DNS client to authenticate with DNS servers before communications can be established. AH also protects the DNS queries against modification and proves the source of the DNS queries. AH does not provide any encryption to the transmitted data, making DNS queries and responses subject to network inspection.

- **Encapsulating Security Payload (ESP)**   Protects the DNS packets by encrypting them during the transmission between a DNS server and the DNS clients. In addition to encrypting the data, the ESP protocol signs the data payload, protecting it from modification.

> **Warning**   Be careful when applying IPSec filters to protect network traffic. Ensure that the IPSec filters describe all forms of network traffic in which the client or server participates. If you omit any forms of traffic from the listing of IPSec filters, the client will not be able to transmit data by using those forms. Be sure to include communications with DNS servers, domain controllers, and other essential network services in the IPSec filter listing.

Restricting DNS Traffic at the Firewall

A firewall can be used to restrict and protect the DNS traffic allowed to enter and exit the network. Depending on the network's DNS configuration, consider implementing the following packet filters at your firewall:

■ **Prevent external DNS clients from querying the internal DNS server.**   Ensure that the firewall does not allow connections from the Internet to the DNS server hosting the internal DNS zone data. You must prevent connections from the Internet to the internal DNS server's TCP port 53 (for zone transfers) and User Datagram Protocol (UDP) port 53 (for DNS queries).

■ **Prevent internal DNS clients from directly querying DNS servers on the Internet.**   You can configure the firewall to allow only approved hosts, such as the internal DNS servers, to query DNS servers on the Internet. The actual packet filter configuration will depend on whether you use forwarders or root hints when resolving DNS queries.

If you use forwarders, configure the firewall to allow DNS communications only to TCP port 53 and UDP port 53 of the DNS servers included in the Forwarders tab of the internal DNS servers. This ensures that internal DNS servers can forward DNS requests only to the approved DNS servers. If you use root hints, an internal DNS server can send a DNS query to any DNS server on the Internet, not just the root hint DNS servers. You must configure the firewall to allow all outbound queries sent from the IP addresses of the internal DNS servers sent to TCP port 53 or UDP port 53.

Limiting Management of DNS

Windows 2000 includes a custom domain local group, named DNSAdmins, in each domain in an Active Directory forest. The DNSAdmins group is delegated permission to fully manage DNS, without providing excess permissions to manage other services or objects in Active Directory.

You must ensure that membership in each DNSAdmins group is monitored to verify that unauthorized users or groups are not added. In addition, you should monitor membership in the local Administrators group, the Domain Admins group in each domain, the Enterprise Admins group, and the Enterprise Domain Controllers group. This is because members of these groups also have permissions to modify DNS configuration or Active Directory resource records.

Protecting the DNS Cache

If a DNS server receives a DNS query for a DNS resource record for which the DNS servers is not authoritative, the DNS server will check its DNS cache for a queried entry before it queries other DNS servers to resolve the DNS query. If an attacker is able to add unauthorized entries directly into the cache of the DNS server, he can redirect DNS clients to unauthorized hosts. This process is known as *cache pollution*.

To prevent corruption of the cache on a Windows 2000 DNS server, you can enable the Secure Cache Against Pollution option. This option is enabled in the Advanced tab of a DNS server's property sheet in the DNS console.

When enabled, the Secure Cache Against Pollution option inspects the response from another DNS server to determine whether any referenced names are attempts to pollute the DNS cache. For example, if a query is made for a Mail Exchange (MX) record for example.com and the response includes a referral record for host.contoso.com, the host.contoso.com response would not be cached because it is from a different namespace than was queried. This can result in a valid response not being cached. For example, contoso.com might be hosting the Internet e-mail services for example.com.

Best Practices

- ■ **Use Active Directory–integrated zones with secure dynamic updates.** Active Directory–integrated zones implement all DNS resource records as *dnsNode* objects in Active Directory. The *dnsNode* objects are protected against modification by security principals—not assigned permissions—in the object's DACL. To host Active Directory–integrated zones, the DNS service must be running on a Windows 2000 domain controller. DNS servers installed on Windows 2000 member servers or workgroup members cannot host Active Directory–integrated zones.

- **Implement DNS cache protection at the DNS servers.** Enable the Secure Cache Against Pollution option in the properties of all DNS servers implemented on the network to prevent attackers from adding fraudulent DNS responses to the cache of a DNS server.

- **Restrict membership in the DNSAdmins group.** Members of the DNSAdmins group can modify any DNS resource record hosted at the DNS server and are assigned permission to modify the DNS server's configuration. You should also restrict the membership in all other groups with the necessary permissions to manage DNS. This includes the local Administrators, Enterprise Admins, and Enterprise Domain Controllers groups, as well as the Domain Admins group in the domain where the DNS server's computer account resides.

- **Restrict zone transfers to only authorized DNS servers.** Prevent unauthorized DNS servers or external clients from obtaining all content of the DNS zone by restricting DNS zone transfers either to servers listed on the Name Servers tab of the DNS zone or to IP addresses specified in the DNS zone's properties.

- **Do not expose any Active Directory–related DNS resource records to the Internet.** Ensure that you implement separate zones for internal and external resources. The DNS server hosting the external zone must contain only DNS resource records for externally accessible resources. The IP addressing in this zone must reference the IP addresses exposed to the Internet. Active Directory–related DNS resource records should not be included in this externally accessible DNS zone.

Additional Information

- Microsoft Official Curriculum course 1561, *Designing Microsoft Windows 2000 Directory Services Infrastructure*, Module 2: "Designing an Active Directory Naming Strategy" (*http://www.microsoft.com/traincert/syllabi/1561bfinal.asp*)

- *Microsoft Windows 2000 Server Resource Kit*, Supplement 1: "TCP/IP Core Networking Guide—Introduction to DNS" (Microsoft Press, 2000) (*http://www.microsoft.com/windows2000/techinfo/reskit/en-us/cnet/cncc_dns_wgga.asp*)

- *MCSE Training Kit: Designing Microsoft Windows 2000 Network Security*, Chapter 9: "Designing Microsoft Windows 2000 Services Security" (Microsoft Press, 2001)

- "GSS Algorithm for TSIG (GSS-TSIG)" (*http://www.ietf.org/internet-drafts/draft-ietf-dnsext-gss-tsig-05.txt*)

- RFC 2136: "Dynamic Updates in the Domain Name System (DNS UPDATE)" (*http://www.faqs.org/rfcs/rfc2136.html*)

- RFC 2782: "A DNS RR for Specifying the Location of Services (DNS SRV)" (*http://www.ietf.org/rfc/rfc2782.txt*)

- "IP Security for Local Communication Systems" white paper (*http://www.microsoft.com/technet/security/bestprac/bpent/sec3/ipsecloc.asp*)

- U.S. National Security Agency's "Guide to Securing Microsoft Windows 2000 DNS" (*http://www.nsa.gov/snac/win2k/guides/w2k-6.pdf*)

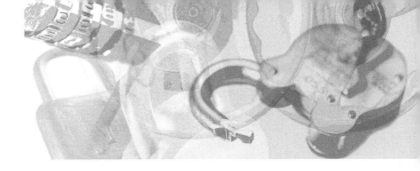

16

Implementing Security for Terminal Services

Terminal Services in Microsoft Windows 2000 permits remote clients to execute programs on a remote server by using the Windows 2000 desktop. When a user connects to a terminal server via a Terminal Services client, keyboard and mouse actions are transmitted from the Terminal Services client to the terminal server. The responses of the terminal server, which appear as changes in the display, are sent back to the Terminal Services client.

All applications execute on the terminal server, and performance is dependent upon the hardware at the terminal server. The Terminal Services client only requires sufficient hardware to run the Terminal Services client.

Terminal Services can be installed on a computer running Windows 2000 Server, Windows 2000 Advanced Server, or Windows 2000 Datacenter Server by using the Add/Remote Windows Components applet in Control Panel. It is also possible to connect to a Microsoft Windows XP client by using a Terminal Services client if the Remote Desktop option is enabled in the Remote tab of the computer's System applet in Control Panel.

> **Note** A Microsoft Windows XP client with the Remote Desktop option enabled can support only a single client connection, regardless of whether the connection is made by the locally logged-on user or by using a Terminal Services client. If a user is logged on at a Windows XP client computer, he is logged off when a Terminal Services client connects. The same is true if a local user logs on while a Terminal Services client is connected.

Threats to Terminal Services

When Terminal Services is installed on a Windows 2000 server, it allows remote computers to connect to the terminal server and launch a remote Windows desktop. When Terminal Services is installed, nonauthorized users can attempt to connect to the terminal server. If not configured for security, Terminal Services on a Windows 2000 server is a security threat. For example, when Terminal Services is installed on a Windows 2000 server, the following vulnerabilities exist:

■ Terminal Services users might be connecting with excess permissions.

■ Firewall security might be bypassed by Internet clients.

■ Terminal Services uses a well-known port.

■ Terminal Services requires the Log On Locally user right.

■ Attackers are provided a full Windows desktop.

Grants Excess Permissions for Users

If Terminal Services is installed with the Permissions Compatible With Terminal Server 4.0 Users, all users will connect with excess permissions. The excess permissions provide all terminal server clients with full access to critical registry locations and file locations on the disk.

When users connect to a terminal server, they are automatically made members of the Terminal Server Users group and will receive all permissions assigned to the Terminal Server Users group. Rather than being assigned individual permissions, Terminal Services users are all assigned the same permissions based upon their membership in the Terminal Server Users group.

Allows Bypass of Firewall Security

If a firewall allows remote clients to connect to a terminal server, the firewall cannot apply additional filters to the protocols and applications running within the Terminal Services session. Even if the firewall applies specific filters—for example, by preventing the use of FTP through the firewall—the Terminal Services client can run an FTP client and transfer data on the network by using the FTP protocol.

The firewall will only allow connections to the terminal server's Transmission Control Protocol (TCP) port 3389. The actual data stream is initiated at the terminal server, not from the terminal server client. The only information transmitted between the terminal server client and the terminal server is mouse input, keyboard input, and display information. Depending on the level of encryption employed, this information is encrypted as it passes through the firewall.

Uses a Well-Known Port

By default, all connections to a terminal server connect to TCP port 3389 on the terminal server. Attackers can perform port scans that determine whether TCP port 3389 is open on a target server. No other ports are used in the connection to the terminal server, making it more difficult to detect a port scan against this single port.

Requires the Log On Locally User Right

To connect to a Windows 2000 terminal server, the user or group that contains the user's account must be assigned the Log On Locally user right. This user right applies to Terminal Services connections and physical connections at the computer hosting Terminal Services. The user right does not differentiate between a Terminal Services connection and a local logon at the terminal server.

Provides an Attacker with a Full Windows Desktop

Terminal Services is the most functional remote connectivity solution. By default, when you connect to a terminal server, you gain total access to the remote terminal server's desktop. This includes all text-based and graphical applications installed on the terminal server, subject to the permissions assigned to the applications.

Securing Terminal Services

Once you have identified the threats facing your Terminal Services deployment, you can take action. The measures you can take include the following:

- Choose the correct Terminal Services mode.

- Restrict which users and groups are assigned the Log On Locally user right.

- Prevent remote control on terminal servers.

- Restrict which applications can be executed.

- Implement strong encryption to data transmitted between the client and server.

- Strengthen the security configuration of the terminal server.

Choosing the Correct Terminal Services Mode

When you install Terminal Services on a Windows 2000 server, you must select between two modes: remote administration mode and application server mode.

Remote Administration Mode

Remote administration mode, by default, allows only members of the local Administrators group to connect by using Terminal Services. Nonmembers cannot connect to the terminal server, and the maximum number of simultaneous connections is two.

Remote administration mode should be implemented when administrators require the ability to remotely manage servers such as domain controllers. Microsoft recommends you implement Terminal Services only in remote administration mode on domain controllers so that nonadministrators are not assigned the Log On Locally user right.

Application Server Mode

Application server mode allows Terminal Services clients to connect to the terminal server and run any installed applications. The only limiting factors to the number of simultaneous connections that can be made are the physical hardware implemented for the terminal server and the number of licenses you have purchased. For example, if the users implement applications that are processor dependent, such as Microsoft Excel, you should allocate 10 MB of RAM for each Terminal Services client session.

Microsoft recommends you implement application server mode on member servers when you want users to run an application remotely. For example, you might consider using Terminal Services to deploy an application with a corporate security policy that does not allow it to be run locally on multiple client computers. Terminal Services allows the application to be run from a single location (at the terminal server), rather than at each of the remote client computers.

You also can use Terminal Services when client computers on your network do not have sufficient hardware to run Windows 2000 Professional or Windows XP Professional. In these cases, clients can connect to a server by using application server mode to gain access to a full Windows 2000 desktop without upgrading the client OS to Windows 2000 Professional or Windows XP Professional.

> **Caution**   Installing applications once Terminal Services is installed in application server mode has its issues. Applications must be installed to allow execution by remote users. We recommend you either run the command Change User/Install in a command prompt before installing applications or install all applications by using the Add New Programs option in the Control Panel's Add/Remove Programs applet.

Restricting Which Users and Groups Have the Log On Locally User Right

The Log On Locally user right is required to connect to a Windows 2000 terminal server. You can restrict which users or groups can connect by using Group Policy to define the users or groups assigned the Log On Locally user right.

To ensure consistent application of the user rights, consider placing all terminal servers in the same OU and defining the user rights in a Group Policy object (GPO) linked to the OU. Ensure that terminal servers are dedicated terminal servers or that they do not host other network services or data that would restrict the assignment of the Log On Locally user right. For example, it is not a good idea to install Terminal Services in application server mode on a domain controller because nonadministrators would require the Log On Locally user right.

Preventing Remote Control on Terminal Servers

Remote control allows administrators to view session actions of a Terminal Services connection. In addition to allowing administrators to view sessions, remote control enables them to perform actions in Terminal Services sessions. These actions are performed in the security context of Terminal Services users, allowing administrators to impersonate users.

You can restrict the use of remote control either in the properties of each user account or in the Terminal Services Configuration console in the properties of the Remote Desktop Protocol—Transmission Control Protocol (RDP-TCP) connection object.

In the properties of a user account, in the Remote Control tab, you can choose whether to enable remote control. If you do not want remote control capabilities for a user's Terminal Services connections, disable the Remote Control check box. If you *do* require remote control capabilities, enable the Enable Remote Control option. In addition, you should enable the Require User's Permission option to prevent an administrator from spying on a Terminal Services user. When you enable remote control, you must decide how an administrator interacts with the Terminal Services user. You can choose between the following options:

- **View The User's Session**   The administrator can only view the user's actions from a remote location.

- **Interact With The Session**   The administrator can take control of the user's session and perform actions on behalf of the user.

> **Warning**   If you allow administrators to interact with the Terminal Services connection, they will be able to perform actions in the security context of the user.

Alternatively, you can override individual user remote control settings by defining the default remote control settings in the Terminal Services Configuration console at the terminal server. Settings defined in the Remote Control tab of the RDP-TCP Properties dialog box override any individual user's remote control settings.

Restricting Which Applications Can Be Executed

Rather than allowing Terminal Services users to connect to any application running on the Windows 2000 terminal server, you can restrict which applications they can execute. You can choose to either restrict users to a single application or create a list of approved applications that can be executed in a Terminal Services session.

Restricting Terminal Services Sessions to a Single Application

In the Terminal Services Configuration console at the terminal server, you can configure Terminal Services to execute a single application rather than launch the Windows desktop. This setting is defined in the Environment tab of the RDP-TCP Properties dialog box. When you enable the option to override settings from the user profile and Client Connection Manager Wizard, you must define which application executable is launched and which folder is the default folder.

When Terminal Services is configured to launch a single application, the application is immediately launched when a user connects to a terminal server. When the user exits the application, the Terminal Services session terminates.

> **Note**   Configuring Terminal Services to launch a single application does not preclude the user from launching another application from within that single application. For example, if you restrict a Terminal Services user to running Microsoft Word, nothing will prevent that user from launching Explorer.exe from a Word macro.

Restricting Terminal Services Sessions to Specified Applications

In most cases, you will want to restrict which applications are available to Terminal Services users. By using the Microsoft Application Security tool (Appsec.exe) from the *Microsoft Windows 2000 Server Resource Kit* (Microsoft Press, 2000), you can control which applications can be executed.

The Appsec.exe tool allows you to designate which executables are available to Terminal Services users when they connect to a terminal server running in application server mode. Each application is referenced by its full path. For example, C:\Program Files\Microsoft Office\Office10\Winword.exe is the default path for Microsoft Word 2002. If you copy the Winword executable to another folder, the Appsec.exe tool blocks its execution.

> **Caution**   The Appsec.exe tool does not perform any hashing functions on the executable. The tool only looks at the full path of the executable to determine whether the application is allowed to run. If attackers are able to overwrite the allowed application, they can run that application in place of the approved application. For example, if attackers overwrite Winword.exe in the path detailed previously with Cmd.exe, they can gain access to a command prompt.

Once the Application Security tool is enabled, nonadministrators are limited to the applications included in the listing. Default applications are included in the Appsec.exe tool. You should review the default applications listed and determine whether you need them in your environment. Administrators of a computer are not affected by the Appsec.exe restrictions and can run any application loaded at the terminal server.

> **More Info** If you implement the Appsec.exe tool, ensure that you also apply the patch discussed in 257980, "Appsec Tool in the Windows 2000 Resource Kit is Missing Critical Files."

Implementing the Strongest Form of Encryption

Terminal Services can implement different levels of encryption to protect data transmitted between the Terminal Services client and the terminal server. The level you select should be based on your company's security policy.

The Terminal Service encryption level is defined in the Terminal Services Configuration console via the General tab of the RDP-TCP properties of the terminal server. You can choose from the following encryption levels:

- **Low encryption** Network traffic is encrypted only when sent from the client to the server. Data is encrypted by using the RC4 encryption algorithm with either a 40-bit key or a 56-bit key. The 40-bit key is required for RDP 4.0 clients. RDP 5.0 clients implement a 56-bit key by default. This encryption format protects passwords input by users but does not protect the screen data returned from the server to the client.

- **Medium encryption** Network traffic is encrypted in both directions as it transmits between the client and server. Data is encrypted by using the RC4 encryption algorithm with either a 40-bit key or a 56-bit key.

- **High encryption** Network traffic is encrypted in both directions as it transmits between the client and server. Data is encrypted by using the RC4 encryption algorithm with a 128-bit key and requires the installation of the Windows 2000 High Encryption Pack at both the client and server. If the High Encryption Pack is not installed, encryption will fall back to the 40-bit or 56-bit key used for medium encryption.

> **More Info** High encryption is limited to countries/regions that the United States does not have an embargo against. For more information on the export of High encryption, see *http://www.microsoft.com/exporting*.

Strengthening the Security Configuration of the Terminal Server

You can increase the default security configuration of the terminal server by installing Terminal Services with the Permissions Compatible With Windows 2000 Users option enabled. The default setting, Permissions Compatible With Terminal Server 4.0 Users, allows users connecting with Terminal Services clients to modify critical registry and file system locations. Access is granted by using the TerminalServerUser account in discretionary access control lists (DACLs).

If you install Terminal Services with Permissions Compatible With Terminal Server 4.0 Users, you can strengthen the security by implementing the Notssid.inf security template. This template reverses weakened security settings and ensures that registry and file system permissions do not refer to the TerminalServerUser account. To implement the Notssid.inf security template, have a local administrator run the following command at the terminal server:

```
secedit /configure /db notssid.sdb /cfg notssid.inf /log notssid.log /verbose
```

This command applies the Notssid.inf security template and records a log file in a file named Notssid.log.

Best Practices

- **Apply the Notssid.inf security template to terminal servers running Permissions Compatible With Terminal Server 4.0 Users.** This security template ensures that excess permissions are not granted to Terminal Services clients. This option might not allow some older applications to execute, so we recommend you upgrade to newer applications that follow the Windows 2000 security model.

- **Use the AppSec tool to limit which applications can be executed.** Appsec.exe allows you to designate which applications are available to nonadministrators in a Terminal Services session. Users are limited to executing the programs listed within the Appsec.exe console.

- **Do not enable remote control.** Remote control allows administrators to view tasks performed by Terminal Services clients. If remote control is configured to allow administrators to interact with the desktop, they can actually perform tasks in the security context of the user, allowing for the impersonation of users.

■ **Do not implement application server mode on domain controllers.** To connect to a terminal server from the network, users must have the Log On Locally user right assigned. If you implement application server mode on a domain controller, nonadministrators must be assigned the Log On Locally user right at the domain controller. Because this user right is typically assigned in Group Policy, it enables users to log on at the console of any domain controller in the domain, greatly reducing security.

■ **Implement the strongest available form of encryption between the Terminal Services client and server.** Ensure that you have installed the High Encryption Pack to allow the implementation of high encryption for Terminal Services.

■ **Choose the correct mode for your Terminal Services deployment.** If remote administration is your only requirement, configure Terminal Services to implement remote administration mode, rather than application server mode. Remote administration mode allows only two simultaneous connections by members of the Administrators group. By default, nonadministrators are blocked from connecting to the terminal server.

■ **Install the latest service pack and security updates.** Ensure that your terminal server is protected by installing the latest service packs and security updates to protect against any known Terminal Services vulnerabilities.

Additional Information

■ U.S. National Security Agency's "Guide to Securing Microsoft Windows 2000 Terminal Services" (*http://www.nsa.gov/snac/win2k/guides/w2k-19.pdf*)

■ *Microsoft Windows 2000 Server Deployment Planning Guide*, Chapter 16, "Deploying Terminal Services" (Microsoft Press, 2002) (*http://www.microsoft.com/technet/prodtechnol/windows2000serv/reskit/deploy/part4/chapt-16.asp*)

■ MCSE Training Kit: *Designing Microsoft Windows 2000 Network Security*, Chapter 9, "Designing Microsoft Windows 2000 Services Security" (Microsoft Press, 2001)

■ "Windows 2000 Terminal Services Capacity and Scaling" (*http://www.microsoft.com/technet/prodtechnol/win2kts/maintain/optimize/w2ktsscl.asp*)

■ 187623: "How to Change Terminal Server's Listening Port"

■ 238965: "Removing Additional Permissions Granted to Terminal Services Users"

■ 247989: "Domain Controllers Require the 'Log on Locally' Group Policy Object for Terminal Services Client Connections"

■ 257980: "Appsec Tool in the Windows 2000 Resource Kit is Missing Critical Files"

■ 260370: "How to Apply Group Policy Objects to Terminal Services Servers"

■ 320181: "How to Use the Application Security Tool to Restrict Access to Programs in Windows 2000 Terminal Services"

> **Note**   The previous six articles can be accessed through the Microsoft Knowledge Base. Go to *http://support.microsoft.com* and enter the article number in the Search The Knowledge Base text box.

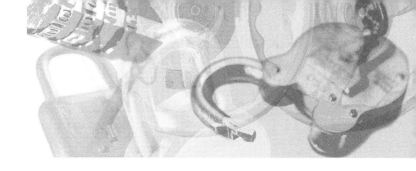

17

Implementing Security for DHCP Servers

Dynamic Host Configuration Protocol (DHCP) eases the deployment of IP addresses to TCP/IP-based network hosts, including client computers and network devices such as TCP/IP-based print servers. A DHCP client acquires an IP address and related TCP/IP configuration information from a DHCP server.

When you implement DHCP on your network, DHCP clients send out broadcast information to User Datagram Protocol (UDP) port 67, requesting TCP/IP configuration information. DHCP servers listen for the DHCP requests and respond with DHCP configuration information. Technically, four packets are exchanged between the DHCP server and the DHCP client during the DHCP lease process:

1. The DHCP client sends a DHCPDISCOVER message that contains the requesting host's Media Access Control (MAC) address and, if the client is a computer, the client computer's name.

2. All DHCP servers that receive the DHCPDISCOVER message and have available addresses for the subnet where the DHCP request was initiated respond with a DHCPOFFER message. The message contains the client's MAC address, an offered IP address and subnet mask, the length of the DHCP lease, and the IP address of the offering DHCP server.

3. The DHCP client responds to the first offer it receives by broadcasting a DHCPREQUEST message. This message includes the IP address of the DHCP server whose offer is accepted so that other DHCP servers will withdraw their offers and return the IP addresses to the available pool of DHCP IP addresses.

4.   The DHCP server issues the address information to the requesting client in a DHCPACK message. The message contains the final lease period for the address, along with other TCP/IP configuration information.

A typical attack against DHCP involves an attempt to prevent an authorized DHCP server from responding to a DHCPDISCOVER message, or it involves modifying a DHCP server to assign incorrect TCP/IP configuration information. This chapter looks at the configuration measures you can take to prevent attacks against DHCP servers.

Threats to DHCP Servers

If attackers are able to compromise a DHCP server on the network, they might disrupt network services, preventing DHCP clients from connecting to network resources. By gaining control of a DHCP server, attackers can configure DHCP clients with fraudulent TCP/IP configuration information, including an invalid default gateway or Domain Name System (DNS) server configuration.

The following threats exist when you implement DHCP on your network:

■   Unauthorized DHCP servers can issue incorrect TCP/IP configuration information to DHCP clients.

■   DHCP servers can overwrite valid DNS resource records with incorrect information.

■   DHCP can create DNS resource records without ownership defined.

■   Unauthorized DHCP clients can obtain IP addresses on the network.

Unauthorized DHCP Servers

If attackers can connect a computer to your company's network, they can launch an unauthorized DHCP server. This DHCP server can provide incorrect IP addressing information to DHCP clients. Microsoft Windows 2000 reduces the possibility of unauthorized Windows 2000–based DHCP servers by requiring that Windows 2000–based DHCP servers be authorized in the Active Directory directory service. Only Windows 2000–based DHCP servers authorized by a member of the Enterprise Admins group can issue IP addresses to DHCP clients.

A Windows 2000 DHCP server uses DHCPINFORM messages to determine whether it is authorized. When a DHCP server starts, the DHCP server queries any domain controller to ensure it is listed as an authorized DHCP server in the Configuration naming context. If the DHCP server is authorized, the DHCP service initializes and provides IP address information to DHCP clients. If the server is not authorized, DHCP services do not initialize. The DHCP service will also start if it determines that Active Directory does not exist on the network, indicating that DHCP servers do not require authorization.

> **Warning**   The DHCPINFORM process does not prevent DHCP servers that do not support DHCPINFORM messages, such as a Microsoft Windows NT 4.0 DHCP server, from issuing addresses on the network.

DHCP Servers Overwriting Valid DNS Resource Records

By default, the DHCP server and the DHCP client split the process of registering DNS resource records with the DNS server. By default, the DHCP server registers and owns the Pointer (PTR) resource records written to the reverse lookup zone at the DNS server. The DHCP client registers its Host (or A) resource record in the forward lookup zone.

If attackers modify the DHCP server's configuration, it is possible for the DHCP server to register and own both resource records. If the DHCP server overwrites the client information, the client can be blocked from updating its IP address information in DNS. The client is blocked because the DNS resource record's discretionary access control list (DACL) allows only the owner of the resource record to modify the resource record when secure dynamic updates are implemented at the DNS server.

> **Note**   This modification is required for pre-Windows 2000 clients that do not support dynamic DNS updates but is not recommended for Windows 2000, Microsoft Windows XP, or other operating systems that support dynamic DNS updates.

DHCP Not Taking Ownership of DNS Resource Records

If a DHCP server is configured as a member of the DNSUpdateProxy group, the DHCP server does not take ownership of the DNS resource records it registers. Although this behavior is desired when a DHCP server registers Host (A) resource records for pre-Windows 2000 client computers, allowing pre-Windows 2000 client computers to take ownership of the A resource record when upgraded to Windows 2000 or Windows XP is not recommended if the DHCP server is also a domain controller.

It also is not desirable for a DHCP server to take ownership of DNS resource records when multiple DHCP servers provide IP addresses for the network. If the DHCP server took ownership of A resource records registered on behalf of a downlevel client, another DHCP server would not be able to overwrite the record if the client acquired its IP address from a different DHCP server.

If the DHCP service runs on a domain controller, membership in the DNSUpdateProxy group results in the DHCP server not taking ownership of *any* DNS resource records it registers with the DNS server. This includes all Service (SRV) resource records registered with DNS. If the DHCP server does not take ownership of the SRV resource records, attackers will be able to modify the SRV resource records, causing DNS clients to connect to incorrect servers.

Unauthorized DHCP Clients

By default, a DHCP server will issue an IP address to any DHCP client that requests one, as long as addresses are available in the *DHCP scope*, which is a pool of IP addresses leased by the DHCP server. This means that any DHCP client can obtain an IP address and TCP/IP configuration information from a DHCP server, even if the DHCP client is not an authorized computer. Once a DHCP client has obtained TCP/IP configuration information, the DHCP client can communicate with any TCP/IP services on the network, including file servers and other Active Directory services on the network.

Securing DHCP Servers

You can take several measures to prevent attacks against DHCP servers and DHCP clients. These measures range from monitoring membership in the DHCP Administrators group to performing specific DHCP service configuration. Specifically, consider the following measures:

- Keep default behavior for name registrations.
- Determine whether to include the DHCP server computer account in the DNSUpdateProxy group.
- Do not install DHCP on domain controllers.
- Review the DHCP database frequently for BAD_ADDRESS entries.
- Limit membership in the DHCP Administrators group.
- Enable DHCP auditing.

Keeping Default Name Registration Behavior

By default, when a DHCP client obtains IP configuration information from a DHCP server, the DHCP server registers the PTR resource record for the client and the client registers its own A resource record. We recommend you maintain this default behavior so that the DHCP server maintains ownership of PTR resource records. You can change this default behavior, but doing so can lead to incorrect DNS information if the client changes subnets and the TCP/IP address configuration information is supplied by a different DHCP server that cannot modify the DNS resource records.

> **Tip**   If a Windows 2000 or Windows XP computer is assigned a static IP address, that computer will use the DHCP Client service to register both its A and PTR resource records. You must not disable the DHCP Client service on computers that are assigned a static TCP/IP configuration.

Determining Whether to Use the DNSUpdateProxy Group

If a computer is a member of the DNSUpdateProxy group, the computer does not take ownership of resource records it registers in DNS. In upgrade scenarios, it is common to configure the DHCP server to register DNS information on behalf of Windows clients that do not support dynamic DNS updates. Including the DHCP server's computer account in the DNSUpdateProxy group ensures that the DHCP server does not take ownership of DNS resource records it updates. This allows the Windows client to take ownership of the A resource record when the OS is upgraded to Windows 2000 or Windows XP.

You should place the DHCP server's computer account in the DNSUpdateProxy group only if you plan to upgrade pre-Windows 2000 computers to Windows 2000 or Windows XP or if you run multiple DHCP servers on the network that might register A and PTR records for the same computers.

Avoiding Installation of DHCP on Domain Controllers

You should not install the DHCP service on Windows 2000 domain controllers, especially if you require that DHCP servers be members of the DNSUpdateProxy group. If the computer account is a member of the DNSUpdateProxy group, the computer will not take ownership of any DNS resource records it registers with DNS. This includes all SRV resource records registered by a Windows 2000 domain controller.

We do not recommend you deploy DHCP services on a domain controller to ensure that the domain controller always has ownership of its A and SRV resource records.

Another Solution for Running DHCP and DNS on Domain Controllers

The risk of running DHCP and DNS on a domain controller is that the DNS registrations are performed in the security context of the domain controller. If you do not include the domain controller's computer account in the DNSUpdateProxy group, all registrations are owned by the domain controller. Members of the Domain Controllers group are assigned Full Control for all DNS zones and resource records, allowing the domain controller to overwrite existing resource records.

If you include the domain controller's computer account in the DNSUpdateProxy group, no ownership is assigned to the resource records registered by the domain controller. This includes both DHCP registrations and the SRV resource records registered by the Netlogon service.

Windows 2000 Service Pack 1 introduces the ability to configure the DHCP service to impersonate another user account when registering DHCP-related DNS resource records. When implemented, all DNS registrations performed by the DHCP service are performed in the security context of this designated user account, rather than using the DHCP server's computer account.

To designate the user account, you must have access to the Netsh.exe tool included in Windows 2000 Support Tools. The process for designating the user account is as follows:

1. Create a user account in the Active Directory Users And Computers console. This user account will be used by the DHCP Server service for all DNS registrations.

2. In a command prompt, use the Netsh.exe tool to designate the user account:

   ```
   Netsh dhcp server set dnscredentials UserName DomainName Password
   ```

Alternatively, you can replace the *Password* option with an asterisk (*) to have the command prompt you for the password assigned to the user account. Once you have typed this command, you must restart the DHCP Server service.

Reviewing DHCP Database for BAD_ADDRESS Entries

If an IP address in the DHCP database is registered to BAD_ADDRESS, it might be in conflict with an address that already resides on the network. This scenario occurs when the DHCP server assigns a DHCP client an IP address that is in use. When a DHCP client receives IP address information from a DHCP server, the DHCP client sends an Address Resolution Protocol (ARP) packet that ensures that the IP address is not in use. If the DHCP client determines that the IP address is in use, the client informs the DHCP server and the DHCP server marks the reservation as a BAD_ADDRESS.

A BAD_ADDRESS lease can take place under different circumstances. If you overlap DHCP scopes between DHCP servers, it is possible for two DHCP servers to issue the same IP address. When a second DHCP server attempts to issue a duplicate IP address, the second DHCP server will register the IP address as a BAD_ADDRESS.

Alternatively, an attacker could assign multiple static IP addresses to her computer. If those addresses are assigned by a DHCP server, DHCP clients determine that the IP addresses are in use and reject the offered DHCP-assigned IP address.

Monitoring Membership in the DHCP Administrators Group

Members of the DHCP Administrators group are delegated permissions to configure a DHCP server. DHCP Administrators can create DHCP scopes, define DHCP configuration options, and create DHCP reservations.

Closely monitor membership in the DHCP Administrators group—as well as membership in the local Administrators group, the Domain Admins group, and the Enterprise Admins group—to determine who has the necessary permissions to manage DHCP services. Membership in these groups allows management of all DHCP servers in the domain.

> **Note**   A member of the DHCP Administrators group cannot authorize a DHCP server in Active Directory. Only members of the Enterprise Admins group can perform this task. You can delegate the right to authorize DHCP servers by following the solution proposed in Knowledge Base article 239004, "How to Allow Non-Root or Enterprise Administrators to Authorize RIS Servers in Active Directory."

Enabling DHCP Auditing

To determine exactly which DHCP clients are connecting to the DHCP server and where BAD_ADDRESS entries originate, enable DHCP auditing at the DHCP server. You can permit DHCP server auditing by enabling the Enable DHCP Auditing Logging option in the properties of the DHCP server in the DHCP console. This option provides daily log files for the DHCP service in the %windir%\system32\dhcp folder. In addition to enabling DHCP auditing in the DHCP console, you can further adjust DHCP auditing by modifying the HKLM\SYSTEM\CurrentControlSet\Services\DhcpServer\Parameters\DhcpLog-FilesMaxSize registry entry, which defines the maximum size of DHCP log files.

Best Practices

- **Do not install a domain controller as a DHCP server.** If you install DHCP on a domain controller, ensure that the DHCP server computer account is *never* added to the DNSUpdateProxy group. Membership in this group prevents the DHCP server from taking ownership of DNS resource records registered by the DHCP server (including SRV resource records) if the DNS service is installed on a domain controller.

- **Do not use DHCP-assigned addresses for servers.** It is preferable to assign static IP addresses to servers and critical workstations to ensure they cannot receive incorrect TCP/IP configuration information from a rogue DHCP server.

- **Monitor membership in the DNSUpdateProxy group.** Unless you are performing computer upgrades or maintaining multiple DHCP servers on the network, the DNSUpdateProxy group should not have any members. Membership in the DNSUpdateProxy group prevents a DHCP server from taking ownership of the resource records it registers with DNS.

- **Monitor membership in the DHCP Administrators group.** Members of the DHCP Administrators group can modify DHCP configuration. Also watch membership in the local Administrators group, the Domain Admins group, and the Enterprise Admins group because these groups have permissions to allow management of the DHCP server.

- **Enable DHCP auditing.** DHCP auditing allows you to track which devices are assigned DHCP addresses and to troubleshoot address conflicts when BAD_ADDRESS entries appear in the DHCP database.

■ **Do not change the default behavior for DNS registration.**   The default behavior for DHCP is that the DHCP server owns the PTR resource records and the DHCP client owns the A resource records. Do not change this behavior unless you require that the DHCP server owns all DNS resource records.

Additional Information

■ U.S. National Security Agency's "Guide to Securing Microsoft Windows 2000 DHCP" (*http://www.nsa.gov/snac/win2k/guides/w2k-18.pdf*)

■ *Microsoft Windows 2000 Server Resource Kit*, Supplement 1, "TCP/IP Core Networking Guide—Dynamic Host Configuration Protocol" (Microsoft Press, 2000) (*http://www.microsoft.com/windows2000/techinfo/reskit/en-us/cnet/cncb_dhc_klom.asp*)

■ RFC 2131: "Dynamic Host Configuration Protocol" (*http://www.ietf.org/rfc/rfc2131.txt*)

■ 239004: "How to Allow Non-Root or Enterprise Administrators to Authorize RIS Servers in Active Directory"

■ 255134: "Installing Dynamic Host Configuration Protocol (DHCP) and Domain Name System (DNS) on a Domain Controller"

> **Note**   The previous two articles can be accessed through the Microsoft Knowledge Base. Go to *http://support.microsoft.com* and enter the article number in the Search The Knowledge Base text box.

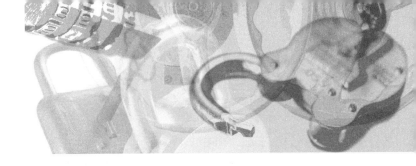

18

Implementing Security for WINS Servers

Windows Internet Name Service (WINS) server provides resolution of computer and group NetBIOS names to IP addresses. The WINS server provides resolution of both computer and group names, such as a workgroup name, to IP addresses. For example, when you log on to the network from a pre–Windows 2000 computer, the computer, by default, will query the WINS server configured in the TCP/IP properties to find a domain controller for network authentication.

NetBIOS names can be broken into two general categories: *unique registrations* and *group registrations*. A unique registration is registered by a single user or computer. By default, if a record exists, that record is not modified. The only time a record is modified is when the current owner cannot be contacted by the WINS server. A group registration is registered by mapping a NetBIOS name to multiple IP addresses. For example, the first 24 domain controllers in a domain will register their IP address in the *Domain*[1C] group NetBIOS name.

The following records are unique registration NetBIOS records you generally will see. Attackers can attempt to hijack these registrations by registering the NetBIOS names with the WINS server, preventing the correct host or user from registering the names, or performing a denial-of-service attack against the registered user or computer, thereby preventing that user or computer from responding to the WINS server verification.

- **Computer[00]**   The Workstation service registration for a computer. Enabled when the Workstation service is enabled.

- **Computer[20]**   The Server service registration for a computer.

- ***Computer*[03]**   The Messenger service registration for a computer account. This service allows NET SEND messages to reach the computer.

- ***User*[03]**   The Messenger service registration for a user account. This service allows NET SEND messages to reach the user.

- ***Domain*[1B]**   The domain master browser registration.

Note   Typically, this NetBIOS name is registered by the domain controller holding the Primary Domain Controller (PDC) Emulator role in a Microsoft Windows 2000 domain or the PDC in a Microsoft Windows NT 4.0 domain. If the PDC is unavailable, another domain controller in the domain will register the *Domain*[1B] registration.

For group registrations, the behavior depends on the specific group record. For example, the *Domain*[1C] record contains the first 24 IP addresses of domain controllers in a domain. Any additional domain controllers will simply add their IP addresses to the current list. Other group registrations might indicate only the domain or workgroup of which a computer is a member (for example, *Domain*[20]).

The Death of NetBIOS

With Windows 2000, NetBIOS is not necessarily required. In fact, you can remove NetBIOS support in the TCP/IP properties of Windows 2000 computers. Rather than connecting to a computer on the NetBIOS port (Transmission Control Protocol port 139), Windows 2000 and Microsoft Windows XP computers can implement file shares by using Common Internet File System (CIFS), an evolution of NetBIOS that does not require NetBIOS implementation. CIFS-compliant applications will connect to TCP port 445, rather than to TCP port 139.

You can remove NetBIOS support from the TCP/IP stack, thereby eliminating the need for WINS servers. Before you perform this task, make sure that no applications or pre–Windows 2000 computers that require NetBIOS remain.

Threats to WINS Servers

A WINS server faces several threats that can result in compromised or unauthorized modifications of records in the WINS server database. These threats include the following:

- Preventing replication between WINS servers
- Registration of false NetBIOS records
- Incorrect registration of WINS records
- Modification of WINS configuration

Preventing Replication Between WINS Servers

The WINS database is a distributed database. Clients register their NetBIOS names with the first WINS servers listed in the client's TCP/IP properties. The WINS servers then replicate their portion of the WINS database with the other WINS servers on the network. If replication is prevented, a WINS client will not be able to reach any NetBIOS clients whose NetBIOS records are missing from their WINS server database. Replication can be prevented by denial-of-service attacks against the WINS server or by compromising the WINS servers, resulting in the modification of the WINS replication settings.

Registration of False NetBIOS Records

A WINS client will register its NetBIOS host and group records with its configured WINS server. If the record already exists in the WINS database, the WINS server will attempt to detect whether the current owner of the record exists on the network. If the previous client cannot be reached, a new client replaces the current record. An attacker can hijack the WINS database record by performing a denial-of-service attack against the current record holder. The denial-of-service attack prevents the previous client from responding to the WINS server's validation request.

Incorrect Registration of WINS Records

An attacker can register a computer record with the same name as a group record. For example, to block authentication with a domain named NWTRADERS, an attacker might attempt to register a host record with the name NWTRADERS. Although the names are technically different (one is a host name and the other is a group name), the existence of the host record will prevent registration of the domain record. This results in authentication failure for clients attempting to connect to the domain record.

Modification of WINS Configuration

If an attacker gains access to the WINS console with the appropriate permissions, she can modify the configuration of the WINS server. The attacker can modify the settings for WINS replication, add static WINS records, or remove valid WINS records and replace them with false WINS records.

Securing WINS Servers

To protect a WINS server against these threats, you must take measures that limit the probability of a successful attack. The following measures can be taken:

- Monitor membership in the WINS Admins group.
- Validate WINS replication configuration.
- Eliminate NetBIOS applications and decommission them.

Monitor Membership in the WINS Admins Group

Members of the WINS Admins group can modify the WINS server's configuration, including replication and the ability to add static WINS records to the WINS database. By restricting membership, you restrict who can make these modifications. Remember that members of the Server Operators and the local Administrators groups at the WINS server can also modify settings. Periodically review the membership of these administrative groups to ensure that members are authorized.

Validate WINS Replication Configuration

Periodically review the WINS replication configuration to make certain that sufficient connectivity exists between the deployed WINS servers. Sufficient connectivity enables full replication of the WINS database between all WINS servers. If a WINS server is removed from the network, it is possible for duplicate WINS records—including false records—to be created in the WINS database.

Eliminate NetBIOS Applications and Decommission Them

Ultimately, attacks against a WINS server can be prevented by eliminating Net-BIOS applications. Upgrade all applications that require NetBIOS to versions that do not.

You can disable NetBIOS on Windows 2000 clients by clicking Disable NetBIOS Over TCP/IP on the WINS tab of Advanced TCP/IP Settings for a network adapter. Alternatively, you can disable NetBIOS under Advanced Scope Options For A DHCP Scope by clicking the Microsoft Disable NetBIOS option under Microsoft Windows 2000 Options For DHCP Clients.

Ensure that NetBIOS is not used on the network before disabling NetBIOS at each Windows 2000–based computer. You can determine whether NetBIOS is required by monitoring the following Performance Monitor counters at each WINS server:

- Windows Internet Name Service Server: Total Number Of Registrations/Sec

- Windows Internet Name Service Server: Queries/Sec

- Windows Internet Name Service Server: Successful Queries/Sec

Remember that if a client computer is configured with a WINS server's IP address, it will send queries to the WINS server.

Best Practices

- **Minimize the number of WINS servers on the network.**   By minimizing the number of WINS servers, you reduce the number of server configurations that must be verified. In addition, minimizing the number of WINS servers lessens the complexity of configuring WINS replication.

- **Manually define WINS replication.**   If you minimize the number of WINS servers, you can manually configure WINS replication partners to ensure that all WINS servers receive all updates to the WINS database, including all updates registered at the other WINS servers.

- **Monitor the membership of all administrative groups.**   The WINS Admins, Administrators, and Server Operators groups have the necessary permissions to modify a WINS server's configuration. Validate the membership of these groups at regular intervals.

- **Apply the latest hotfixes and security patches.** Application of the latest hotfixes and security patches ensures that your WINS servers are protected against any known WINS service attacks.

- **Eliminate NetBIOS applications.** By eliminating NetBIOS-dependent applications, you remove the need for NetBIOS name resolution. Take measures—such as upgrading applications and installing the Microsoft Directory Services client on Microsoft Windows 95, Microsoft Windows 98, Microsoft Windows Me, and Microsoft Windows NT 4.0 clients—to remove their dependency on NetBIOS for network authentication.

Additional Information

- 300603: "How to Use Netsh to Monitor Domain Records"
- 251067: "WINS Registry Parameters for Windows 2000"
- 225130: "Verifying Name Records in WINS in Windows 2000"
- 185786: "Recommended Practices for WINS"

> **Note** The previous four articles can be accessed through the Microsoft Knowledge Base. Go to *http://support.microsoft.com* and enter the article number in the Search The Knowledge Base text box.

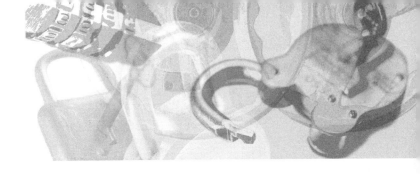

19

Implementing Security for Routing and Remote Access

The Routing and Remote Access Service (RRAS) allows remote computers to connect to corporate networks by using either dial-up connections or virtual private network (VPN) connections. The extension of the corporate network to these remote access clients requires a review on your part to ensure that the security of your network is not weakened when you allow remote access connectivity. Specifically, you must look at how the available components for a remote access solution work together to provide security.

Remote Access Solution Components

Remote access to the corporate network is provided through the interaction of different network services and client software to allow remote clients to connect securely to the corporate network. Remote access solution components include the following:

- Authentication protocols
- VPN protocols
- Client software
- Server services and software

Authentication Protocols

When a remote access client connects to the network, the user authenticates with the remote access server by providing credentials. These credentials can include the user's name, password, and the domain in which their user account exists. When a user connects to a remote access server, authentication is performed by using Point-to-Point Protocol (PPP) authentication methods. The authentication methods supported by RRAS include the following:

- **Password Authentication Protocol (PAP)**   Although supported by almost all dial-up network services, PAP transmits user credentials to the remote access server as plaintext, offering no protection against password determination and replay attacks.

- **Shiva Password Authentication Protocol (SPAP)**   Provides support for Shiva remote access clients. SPAP uses a reversible encryption method called *base64 encoding*, which is stronger than the protection offered by PAP. However, SPAP is still susceptible to replay attacks.

- **Challenge Handshake Authentication Protocol (CHAP)**   Provides a stronger form of authentication by sending a hash of the password and a challenge string to the server. The remote access server identifies the user, obtains the password from the directory, and performs the same hashing algorithm against the password and challenge string. If the results match, the user is authenticated. This form of authentication provides protection against replay attacks.

> **Warning**   CHAP authentication requires that the user's password be stored in a reversibly encrypted format at the domain controller for comparison purposes. This weakens password security at the domain controller and requires stronger physical security of the domain controller. In addition, the password is not stored in a reversibly encrypted format until the next time the user changes the password after this attribute is enabled.

- **Microsoft Challenge Handshake Authentication Protocol (MS-CHAP)**   Differs from CHAP in that the remote access client creates the challenge/response by encrypting the challenge string and MD4 hash version of the user's password. User passwords, by default, are stored in the directory in an MD4 hashed form. Encryption keys for Microsoft Point-to-Point Encryption (MPPE) are derived from the MS-CHAP authentication process. MPPE is used as the encryption algorithm for PPP payloads for dial-up and remote access connections based on Point-to-Point Tunneling Protocol (PPTP).

- **Microsoft Challenge Handshake Authentication Protocol version 2 (MS-CHAPv2)**   When a remote access client authenticates by using MS-CHAPv2, the remote access client sends a challenge/response based on a challenge from the remote access server, and the remote access server sends a challenge/response based on a challenge from the remote access client. This is known as *mutual authentication*. For MS-CHAPv2, the remote access client and remote access server prove to each other that they have knowledge of the user's password. In addition, MS-CHAPv2 derives stronger MPPE encryption keys and uses two different encryption keys: one for sending data and one for receiving data.

- **Extensible Authentication Protocol (EAP)**   Provides an extensible architecture for advanced PPP authentication methods, such as two-factor authentication. EAP-MD5 CHAP is the CHAP authentication method using EAP. EAP-TLS (Extensible Authentication Protocol-Transport Layer Security) is used for public key certificate–based authentication and provides mutual authentication and secured MPPE key exchange between the remote access server and the remote access client.

VPN Protocols

If remote access clients connect to the corporate network by using VPN connections, two protocols are supported:

- **Point-to-Point Tunneling Protocol (PPTP)**   A tunneling protocol supported by all Microsoft operating systems since Microsoft Windows NT 4.0. PPTP uses MPPE to encrypt transmitted data by using a 40-bit, 56-bit, or 128-bit encryption key. PPTP is often used because it supports legacy clients and can cross most network address translation (NAT) devices.

- **Layer Two Tunneling Protocol (L2TP)**   A tunneling protocol natively supported by Microsoft Windows 2000 and Microsoft Windows XP and supported by Microsoft Windows 98, Microsoft Windows Me, and Microsoft Windows NT 4.0 Workstation clients running Microsoft L2TP/IPSec VPN client. L2TP does not provide native encryption but uses IP Security (IPSec) with Encapsulating Security Payload (ESP) in transport node, which implements either Data Encryption Standard (DES) with a 56-bit key or 3DES encryption using three 56-bit keys. Because of IPSec encryption, L2TP/IPSec VPN connections cannot pass through NAT devices.

Note   RRAS in Windows 2000 does not support NAT traversal, but drafts proposing methods for NAT traversal are being evaluated by the Internet Engineering Task Force (IETF). The proposed solutions are implemented by the Microsoft L2TP/IPSec VPN client for Windows 98, Windows Me, and Windows NT 4.0 Workstation. The solution is also implemented in the beta versions of Microsoft Windows Server 2003. Microsoft has plans to implement this solution for Windows 2000 and Windows XP computers functioning as remote access clients.

Client Software

Microsoft operating systems since Windows 95 have supported PPP-based remote access connectivity software, either in the base OS or in software freely distributed from the Microsoft Web site, such as the Microsoft Dial-Up Networking client software. Windows 2000 includes the Connection Manager Administration Kit (CMAK) and the Connection Point Server (CPS) to ease client remote access configuration and deployment.

The CMAK provides the ability to define remote access connectivity software packages that are preconfigured with your company's remote access settings. For example, if your company requires that a client implement the corporate virus detection software for remote connectivity, the CMAK package can be configured to run a preconnection script that ensures that the virus detection software is installed.

CPS provides the ability to download an updated list of ISP dial-in numbers, referred to as the *phone book*, to remote access clients. The phone book provides the latest local access phone numbers for Internet connectivity so that clients always have updated phone book information and do not have to manually input phone numbers for Internet connectivity.

Server Services and Software

Remote access solutions require that services and software be configured at the server to accept remote access connections and, possibly, at servers that reside between the remote access clients and the remote access server if deploying VPN solutions. When deploying remote access solutions, you might need the following services:

■ **Routing and Remote Access Service (RRAS)**   As mentioned earlier, this service allows you to provide both dial-up and VPN connectivity to the corporate network. RRAS can use the Active Directory directory service, the local Security Account Manager (SAM) database of the server, or a centralized account database provided by a Remote Authentication Dial-In User Service (RADIUS) server. To provide additional security to remote access connections, you can define remote access policies that outline constraints and configuration settings that must be implemented before remote client connectivity is allowed.

■ **Internet Authentication Service (IAS)**   This service provides RADIUS authentication for remote access connections. Rather than each server running RRAS to authenticate remote access clients, remote access servers can forward authentication requests to the IAS server by using the RADIUS protocol. In addition to authentication, the IAS server provides centralized accounting and authorization via remote access policies to the remote access servers.

In addition to these services, you can implement Internet Security and Acceleration (ISA) Server as a firewall between the remote clients and the remote access server, or you can actually deploy it on the computer running RRAS. ISA Server provides the ability to filter connections so that authorized VPN protocols are allowed to connect to the remote access server.

Threats to Remote Access Solutions

When you extend network connectivity to remote access clients, several threats exist that can compromise your network's security. These threats exist because the remote clients are no longer directly connected to the corporate network, but they are connected to public networks (phone or Internet) and are connecting to the corporate network over public networks. The threats caused by this extension of the corporate network to remote clients are listed on the following page.

- Authentication interception

- Data interception

- Bypass of the firewall to the private network

- Nonstandardized policy application

- Network perimeter extended to location of dial-in user

- Denial of service caused by password attempts

- Stolen laptops with saved credentials

Authentication Interception

Remote access solutions require users to send authentication credentials to your private network across public networks. Some early remote access authentication protocols do not provide security mechanisms, or they provide weak security for these credentials.

If you use authentication protocols such as PAP, SPAP, or CHAP, be aware that some tools can intercept these authentication streams and determine the password of the authenticating user through inspection or brute force techniques. Likewise, the implementation of CHAP weakens security of a user's password at domain controllers because CHAP requires that the password be stored in a reversibly encrypted format. The interception of the user's password compromises the user's remote access password. Also, in a Windows 2000 network, the remote access password is the user's domain password.

> **Note**   Although the risk of password interception is more likely in a VPN scenario, it is still possible for a dial-in client's password information to be intercepted if the required tapping equipment is attached to the phone system.

Data Interception

When connecting remotely to a corporate network, the protocols you use for authentication and VPNs determine the level of protection against interception. For dial-up connections, encryption of transmitted data is performed only if you use EAP-TLS, MS-CHAP, or MS-CHAPv2 as the authentication protocol. Only these authentication protocols determine encryption keys for MPPE.

For VPN connections, varying strengths of encryption are provided. If you implement PPTP, the highest level of encryption possible is MPPE with 128-bit encryption. PPTP can also implement 40-bit and 56-bit encryption. If you implement L2TP/IPSec as your VPN protocol, IPSec encryption strengths range from 56-bits for DES encryption to three 56-bit keys for 3DES encryption. The stronger the encryption, the less chance you have of data being deciphered.

> **Warning**   The MPPE encryption implemented by dial-up and PPTP connections is based on the user's password. If the user implements a poor password, the MPPE encryption strength is weakened. L2TP's use of IPSec for encryption ensures that the encryption strength is not affected by the user's password strength.

Bypass of the Firewall to the Private Network

If a user's account is provided local administrative access to computers, it is possible for him to install and configure RRAS to accept dial-up connections, thereby bypassing perimeter network security devices such as firewalls.

Establishing unauthorized remote access servers weakens your network's security because doing so enables unauthorized users or attackers to bypass existing perimeter security. In addition, these unauthorized remote access servers do not have the required remote access policy applied and might allow less secure connections.

Nonstandardized Policy Application

If more than one remote access server exists on your network, it is possible that remote access security is being applied in a nonstandard fashion. If the different sets of constraints and policies are applied, connection attempts might yield varied results.

The nonstandardized application of remote access policy can lead to unauthorized connections to the network or, in some cases, connections that do not meet your company's security policy. For example, your company might require that all remote access connections use MS-CHAPv2 or EAP-TLS for authentication. If you do not uniformly mandate that the remote access policy require this authentication for a successful connection attempt, a user might be able to connect by using PAP authentication, which transmits the authentication credentials in cleartext.

Network Perimeter Extended to Location of Dial-In User

When you implement remote access solutions, the perimeter of your company's network is extended to the location of the remote access client. The security of your network is now lowered to the level of security implemented at the remote client. For example, if clients are connect to a remote network that is infected with a new virus, they might become infected and in turn infect your network through their remote access connection. Ensure that all computers that participate on your network—whether attached locally or connecting by remote access solutions—are protected with the latest antivirus software.

Likewise, if clients modify their routing table so that they have routing entries to both the Internet and the company's network through the VPN or dial-up connection, it might be possible for attackers to route information through the remote access client to the corporate network. This modification of the routing table by clients to simultaneously access both the Internet and the intranet is referred to as *split tunneling*.

Denial of Service Caused by Password Attempts

Sometimes taking good security measures can lead to security threats. For example, your company might implement an account policy that locks out a user account after a specified number of incorrect password attempts.

Although this security setting is intended to prevent online dictionary attacks against the user account, it is possible for attackers to use this setting to launch a denial-of-service attack. Rather than attempt to guess a user's password, attackers can use this setting to intentionally lock out the user's account by inputting the required number of incorrect passwords, resulting in the user's account being locked out from all network activities. The user can participate in the network only after her account is unlocked by a user account administrator. The user account is not protected against subsequent attacks because the attacker is not attempting to guess the user's password.

Stolen Laptops with Saved Credentials

Remote users typically use notebook or laptop computers to connect to the corporate office. Because these computers are removed from the corporate offices and are taken to public locations, they are more susceptible to theft. If a laptop is stolen, it is subject to attacks against the local account database if local SAM accounts are used. Likewise, if a user saves his credentials for dial-up or VPN connections, an attacker can simply launch the connection, rather than attempt to guess the user's domain credentials.

Another threat to your remote access security exists if you implement shared secrets, rather than certificates, for IPSec authentication of L2TP/IPSec VPN connections. When you implement a shared secret—as described in 240262, "How to Configure a L2TP/IPSec Connection Using Pre-shared Key Authentication"—all remote access clients use the same shared secret to authenticate with the remote access server for the IPSec security association (SA). If one laptop is compromised, all laptops effectively are compromised and a new shared secret must be deployed. This is because the shared secret is stored in cleartext in the registry of the laptop.

Securing Remote Access Servers

To implement security for remote access servers, you must consider the configuration of servers running RRAS, servers running IAS, and servers running ISA Server. The combination of these servers and services provides the required security for remote access dial-up and VPN connection. Specifically, when designing security for remote access servers, consider taking the following measures:

- Implement RADIUS authentication and accounting.

- Secure RADIUS authentication traffic between the remote access server and the RADIUS server.

- Configure a remote access policy.

- If using L2TP/IPSec, deploy required certificates.

- Restrict which servers can start or stop RRAS.

- Implement remote access account lockout.

Implementing RADIUS Authentication and Accounting

RADIUS authentication and accounting allow for centralized authentication, authorization, and accounting for remote access connectivity. Rather than authentication and authorization being performed at individual remote access servers, connection request messages are sent to the RADIUS server, which is a server running IAS in a Windows 2000 network.

The RADIUS packets are sent to specific ports on the IAS server. Authentication packets are sent to User Datagram Protocol (UDP) port 1812, and the accounting packets are sent to UDP port 1813. The format of the RADIUS packets allows for NAT traversal. This permits you to place the IAS server on the private network behind firewalls, rather than in your network's perimeter network (also known as DMZ, demilitarized zone, or screened subnet). Therefore, the IAS server can connect directly to a domain controller to validate a user's provided credentials and access the user's account properties.

The IAS server then validates the authentication attempt against Active Directory. If the credentials sent to the RADIUS server match the credentials in Active Directory, the authentication succeeds and the RADIUS server tells the remote access server to authenticate the user.

In addition to providing centralized authentication and accounting, IAS provides centralized remote access policy for remote access connection authorization. Rather than having to configure a remote access policy at each remote access server, the remote access policy is configured at the IAS server. The RADIUS clients implicitly trust the answer they receive from the IAS server when a RADIUS connection request response is received. By implementing the remote access policy at a single location, you ensure that the same conditions and policy configuration are applied to each remote access client, no matter which remote access server sends the connection request.

Securing RADIUS Authentication Traffic Between the Remote Access Server and the RADIUS Server

Technicians have raised concerns that RADIUS traffic between the remote access server and the RADIUS server is susceptible to inspection and brute force attacks. To protect against these attacks, you can implement an IPSec policy that requires ESP encryption of RADIUS traffic. This ensures that RADIUS traffic is protected against inspection and brute force attacks. You must ensure that the remote access server and the IAS server are not separated by a NAT device to ensure that IPSec traffic can be transmitted between the two servers.

Configuring a Remote Access Policy

To authorize remote access connections, you must define remote access policy. The remote access policy must be defined at each remote access server (when using Windows authentication) or at the configured IAS server (when using RADIUS authentication). The remote access policy must enforce the company's security policy for remote access connections. Remote connections are secured by configuring conditions and profiles for each remote access policy.

Remote Access Policy Conditions

All remote access connections are evaluated against conditions defined for each remote access policy. If a remote access connection matches these conditions, the connection attempt is either allowed or denied based on the first matching remote access policy (its remote access permissions and profile settings) and the dial-in properties of the user's account.

You can use the following condition attributes to identify a remote access connection attempt:

■ **Called-Station-ID**   The phone number dialed by the remote access client. This condition allows you to apply different remote access policies depending on the phone number the remote client uses.

■ **Calling-Station-ID**   The phone number from which the call originates. This condition allows you to apply remote access policies depending on which phone number originates the connection.

■ **Client-Friendly-Name**   The name of the RADIUS client that forwards the authentication request. This condition allows you to apply differing remote access policies based on the RADIUS client that forwards the request. This condition can be implemented only in a remote access policy defined at an IAS server.

■ **Client-IP-Address**   The IP address of the RADIUS client that sent the authentication request. This condition is used to identify RADIUS clients for VPN authentication requests. This condition can be implemented only in a remote access policy defined at an IAS server.

■ **Client-Vendor**   Identifies the manufacturer of the RADIUS client that forwards the authentication request. This condition allows you to apply manufacturer-specific remote access policies. This condition can be implemented only in a remote access policy defined at an IAS server.

■ **Day And Time Restrictions**   Allows you to restrict connections to specific days of the week or times of day. For example, you can prevent remote connections from being made outside office hours.

■ **Framed Protocol**   Allows you to define which remote access protocols are allowed for connections. For example, you can restrict connections to only Point-to-Point Protocol (PPP) connections, while preventing Serial Line Internet Protocol (SLIP) connections that transmit all data in plaintext.

> **Note**   Although a Windows 2000 server running RRAS cannot accept SLIP connections, an IAS server can authenticate dial-in requests to a non-Microsoft remote access server.

- **NAS-Identifier** Allows you to identify the RADIUS client that forwards the request by comparing the string sent by the RADIUS client to a string defined in the remote access policy.

- **NAS-IP-Address** Allows you to identify the RADIUS client by its IP address. This is useful if you want to apply different remote access policies to a specific VPN server, based on its IP address.

- **NAS-Port-Type** Allows you to identify the medium used by the remote access client. You can indicate dial-up, ISDN, or VPN connections. For wireless communications, you can choose 802.11b connections.

- **Service-Type** Allows you to identify the service requested by the client. For remote access clients, the type of service typically is Framed.

- **Tunnel-Type** Allows you to restrict which protocol a client uses for a VPN connection. You can specify PPTP or L2TP, subject to the existing network infrastructure.

- **Windows-Groups** Allows you to restrict access by Windows 2000 group membership. You can select only Windows 2000 universal groups or global groups.

Remote Access Policy Profiles

Remote access policy allows you to apply additional security that extends beyond condition matching. Once a remote connection attempt matches the conditions of a defined remote access policy, the remote access policy profile is applied to the connection. The remote access policy profile defines what security settings must be implemented by the remote access connections. These profile settings include the following:

- **Dial-In Constraints** Include how long a connection can remain idle before it is disconnected, the maximum time for session lengths, the day and time limitations, the dial-in number constraints, and the dial-in media constraints. Typically, the dial-in constraints ensure that remote access sessions are terminated if left idle for long periods of time and that they take place only during specific times of the day or week.

- **IP Constraints** Allow you to define packet filters that restrict access to the network for the remote access client. These packet filters can limit which protocols can be used by remote access clients.

- **Multilink**   Define whether multilink sessions are allowed and where a client can make multiple remote access connections to the remote access server, thus effectively increasing available bandwidth.

- **Authentication**   Allow you to define which protocols are allowed for a remote access connection. If the remote client is not configured to use the required authentication protocol(s), the connection attempt is terminated.

- **Encryption**   Allow you to define what type of encryption must be applied to the remote access session. You can choose to require no encryption, basic encryption (56-bit keys for DES and 40-bit keys for MPPE), strong encryption (56-bit keys for DES or MPPE), or the strongest encryption (3DES or 128-bit MPPE).

- **Advanced**   Allow you to define advanced RADIUS attributes that are used when remote access connections are using RADIUS authentication.

Deploying Required Certificates for L2TP/IPSec

If you are implementing L2TP/IPSec for VPN connections to the corporate network, you must deploy the necessary certificates to your network's computers and users. Computer certificates are required for IPSec authentication, and User certificates are required for EAP-TLS authentication.

IPSec Certificate Deployment

Computer certificates are required for the authentication of the remote client computer with the remote access server. Computer certificates authenticate the IPSec main mode SA established between the VPN client and the VPN server. The certificate used by the VPN client must chain to a Certification Authority (CA) located in the trusted root store of the VPN server. The certificate used by the VPN server must chain to a CA located in the trusted root store of the VPN client. Although it is possible for the VPN client and server to use certificates from different chains, it is easiest to issue certificates to both the client and the server from CAs in the same chain.

To deploy certificates automatically, you can implement a Windows 2000 enterprise CA that publishes the IPSec or Computer certificate template (for client computers or domain controllers). If an enterprise CA is deployed, you can automatically send the computer certificates to the remote access client computers by using the Automatic Certificate Request Settings Group Policy setting. This setting automatically deploys the defined computer-based certificates to the computer accounts against which the Group Policy object (GPO) is applied.

> **Note**   If you must deploy certificates to nondomain members, you must publish the IPSec (Offline Request) certificate template at the enterprise CA. This template allows nondomain members to enroll the certificate template by using Web-based certificate enrollment. The nondomain members must provide credentials that are assigned the Read and Enroll permissions for the IPSec (Offline Request) certificate template.

Alternatively, if the user is a local administrator, the IPSec certificate can be deployed by using the Certificates Microsoft Management Console (MMC) focused on the local machine or by using the Certificate Web-based enrollment pages.

> **Caution**   Although it is possible to use shared secrets for L2TP/IPSec computer authentication, it is not recommended because doing so weakens remote access computer security. Always use certificate-based authentication for L2TP/IPSec computer authentication. Kerberos authentication for L2TP/IPSec computer authentication is not possible.

User Authentication Certificates

If your remote access solution uses EAP-TLS authentication, regardless of whether you are using dial-up connections, PPTP connections, or L2TP/IPSec connections, you must deploy user authentication certificates to the remote access user and server authentication certificates to either the remote access server or the IAS server. If you are using Windows authentication, the server authentication certificate (either a Computer certificate or a Domain Controller certificate) must be installed on the remote access server. If you are using RADIUS authentication, the server authentication certificate must be installed on the IAS server. These two certificate deployment scenarios are shown in Figure 19-1.

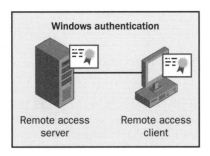

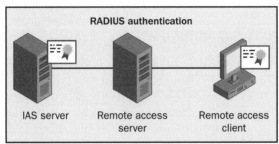

Figure 19-1   The deployment of user authentication certificates, which varies depending on whether you implement RADIUS authentication

The remote access client will require either a Smart Card Logon certificate, which is recommended, or a User certificate that is stored in the user's certificate store. This proves the user's identify for the remote access connection.

Restricting Which Servers Can Run RRAS

To prevent unauthorized connections to the network, not only must you implement remote access policy to define the allowed remote access connections, you also must prevent users from running unauthorized remote access servers. You can accomplish this by ensuring that all servers and computers in the domain are members of the local domain or forest you are running in your company. If the computers are members of the domain, you can utilize Group Policy to ensure that only authorized remote access servers can start RRAS. The start state of any Windows 2000 service is defined in the following Group Policy location: Computer Configuration\Windows Settings\Security Settings\System Services. For each service listed in the details pane, you can define the default start state of the service as well as permissions defining which users or security groups can start, pause, or stop the service.

To ensure that only approved remote access servers can start RRAS, verify that all approved remote access servers are placed in a common OU or OU structure in which a GPO is linked. The GPO should set RRAS as an automatic startup mode and allow only Administrators or the System account to change the startup mode for the service.

For all other computers, configure the default domain policy to disable RRAS. To prevent RRAS from ever being started, do not assign any security groups other than the System account and local Administrators group the permission to start, stop, or pause the service.

Implementing Remote Access Account Lockout

To prevent online dictionary attacks against a user's password, you can enable remote access account lockout, which denies remote access to user accounts but does not lock out user accounts for local network activities. If attackers attempt an online dictionary attack, the account is blocked from further remote access attempts when the remote access account lockout threshold is reached.

You activate remote access account lockout by enabling two registry entries at the server that performs remote access authentication. If using Windows authentication, the registry settings are defined at each remote access server. If using RADIUS authentication, the registry settings must be defined at the IAS server.

These are the registry settings that enable remote access account lockout:

- **HKEY_LOCAL_MACHINE\SYSTEM\CurrentControlSet\Services \RemoteAccess\Parameters\AccountLockout\MaxDenials** Must be set to the required maximum attempts before remote access is prevented. If the counter exceeds the configured value, remote access is prevented for the account, until the reset time. A successful authentication resets a failed attempt's counter for each account.

- **HKEY_LOCAL_MACHINE\SYSTEM\CurrentControlSet\Services \RemoteAccess\Parameters\AccountLockout\ResetTime** Defines the interval, in minutes, when the failed attempts counter is reset to 0. The default for this value is 2880 minutes (48 hours).

Securing Remote Access Clients

In addition to securing the remote access server, you must implement security measures at client computers. These security measures ensure that the client is configured with the required security settings for remotely accessing your corporate network. The measures that you can implement at the remote access client include the following:

- Configuring the CMAK packages.

- Implementing strong authentication.

- Deploying required certificates.

Configuring the CMAK Packages

The CMAK allows you to create Connection Manager packages that are preconfigured with your company's required security settings. In addition to choosing the type of authentication and encryption strength used by remote clients, the CMAK allows you to define other options, such as preventing a user's password from being saved or removing specific tabs from the Properties dialog box of the dial-up or VPN connection.

Implementing Strong Authentication

To ensure that user credentials cannot be determined from intercepted traffic, you should implement the strongest form of authentication available. Microsoft recommends using MS-CHAPv2 only for password-based authentication and using EAP-TLS only for certificate-based authentication. This is because these forms of authentication mutually authenticate both the remote client and the remote access server.

> **Note**   If you use the CMAK to create the remote client connection packages, you can specify within the package that only MS-CHAPv2 and EAP-TLS authentication are supported.

Deploying Required Certificates

The remote client will require certificates if either of the following conditions exist:

- The remote client connects by using an L2TP/IPSec connection. L2TP/IPSec requires that an IPSec or Computer certificate be installed at the remote access client.

■   The remote client authenticates with the remote access server by
     using EAP-TLS authentication. In this case, the user must have a cer-
     tificate that includes the Client Authentication OID in the Extended
     Key Usage attribute of the certificate. This OID indicates that the cer-
     tificate can be used for client authentication. The certificate can be
     stored in either the user's profile or on a physical device, such as a
     smart card.

> **Note**   It is always recommended you use a smart card rather
> than a certificate stored in the user's profile because a smart
> card is a form of two-factor authentication. To compromise a
> smart card, attackers must obtain both the smart card and the
> personal identification number (PIN) that protects the private
> key stored on the smart card. For a certificate stored in the
> user's profile, the attacker can access the private key material
> if they can compromise the user's password.

Best Practices

■   **Allow only MS-CHAPv2 or EAP-TLS for remote client
     authentication.**   Only these forms of authentication provide maxi-
     mum protection of user credentials as well as mutual authentication
     of the remote client and the remote access server.

■   **Implement RADIUS authentication for all remote access
     authentication.**   By implementing RADIUS authentication, you
     ensure that remote access policy is applied centrally from the IAS
     server, rather than by each remote access server.

■   **Ensure that the latest service packs or the Windows 2000 High
     Encryption Pack are applied to all remote access servers, IAS
     servers, and remote access clients.**   This guarantees that the
     strongest forms of encryption are used for VPN connections. For
     PPTP connections, accept only connections that implement 128-bit
     MPPE encryption. For L2TP/IPSec connections, accept only connec-
     tions that implement ESP with 3DES encryption.

■   **If implementing L2TP/IPSec as your VPN protocol, use certificates to authenticate the remote access client computer and the remote access server.** Using preshared keys for IPSec authentication of L2TP/IPSec connections is considered a security weakness and should be avoided.

■   **Create remote access client packages by using the CMAK.** The CMAK packages ensure that the correct configuration is implemented and enforced at remote client computers.

■   **Create separate remote access policies for each remote access solution.** Ensure that remote access policies are ordered correctly at the remote access server or the IAS server so that the correct remote access policy is applied for each type of connection attempt.

■   **Implement remote access account lockout.** This prevents online dictionary attacks against a user's password.

■   **Prevent RRAS from starting on nonauthorized computers in the domain.** You can do so by defining System Services policies. Allow only the local Administrators and the System account on approved remote access servers to start, stop, or pause the service.

Additional Information

■   MCSE Training Kit: *Designing Microsoft Windows 2000 Network Security*, Chapter 13, "Securing Access for Remote Users and Networks" (Microsoft Press, 2002)

■   "Deploying Remote Access Clients Using Connection Manager" white paper (*http://www.microsoft.com/technet/prodtechnol/ WindowsNetServer/Evaluate/CPP/Reskit/NetSvc/RKDnsCM.asp*)

■   "Administrator's Guide to Microsoft L2TP/IPSec VPN Client" white paper (*http://www.microsoft.com/technet/itsolutions/network/maintain/ security/VPNClntA.asp*)

■   "Virtual Private Networking with Windows 2000: Deploying Remote Access VPNs" white paper (*http://www.microsoft.com/ technet/itsolutions/network/deploy/depovg/vpndeply.asp*)

- "Internet Authentication Service for Windows 2000" white paper (*http://www.microsoft.com/technet/prodtechnol/windows2000serv/ evaluate/featfunc/ias.asp*)

- "Planning Your Remote Access Solution" (*http://www.microsoft.com/ technet/itsolutions/network/deploy/projplan/planning.asp*)

- RFC 2637: "Point-to-Point Tunneling Protocol (PPTP)" (*http:// www.ietf.org/rfc/rfc2637.txt?number=2637*)

- RFC 2661: "Layer Two Tunneling Protocol 'L2TP'" (*http:// www.ietf.org/rfc/rfc2661.txt?number=2661*)

- RFC 2809: "Implementation of L2TP Compulsory Tunneling via RADIUS" (*http://www.ietf.org/rfc/rfc2809.txt?number=2809*)

- RFC 2865: "Remote Authentication Dial In User Service (RADIUS)" (*http://www.ietf.org/rfc/rfc2865.txt?number=2865*)

- RFC 2866: "RADIUS Accounting" (*http://www.ietf.org/rfc/ rfc2866.txt?number=2866*)

- IPsec-NAT Compatibility Requirements (*http://www.ietf.org/ internet-drafts/draft-ietf-ipsec-nat-reqts-02.txt*)

- 240262: "How to Configure a L2TP/IPSec Connection Using Pre-shared Key Authentication"

Note The previous article can be accessed through the Microsoft Knowledge Base. Go to *http://support.microsoft.com* and enter the article number in the Search The Knowledge Base text box.

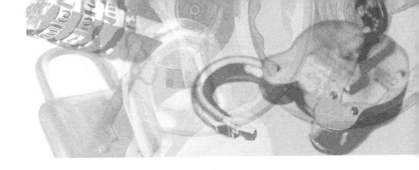

20

Implementing Security for Certificate Services

The installation of Certificate Services allows you to configure a Certification Authority (CA) in a Microsoft network that issues digital certificates to users and computers. Certificate Services is the core component of the Windows 2000 Public Key Infrastructure (PKI).

Windows 2000 Certificate Services allows for the installation of two types of CAs: *standalone CAs* and *enterprise CAs*. A standalone CA is typically used for offline CAs (CAs that are removed from the network to increase security). An enterprise CA is typically used to issue certificates to users and computers.

Threats to Certificate Services

When you deploy Certificate Services, threats exist to CAs on the network. These include the following:

- Compromise of a CA's key pair
- Attacks against servers hosting certificate revocation lists (CRLs) and CA certificates
- Attempts to modify the CA configuration
- Attempts to modify certificate template permissions
- Attacks that disable CRL checking
- Addition of nontrusted CAs to the trusted root CA store
- Issuance of fraudulent certificates
- Publication of false certificates to the Active Directory directory service

Compromise of a CA's Key Pair

If attackers can gain access to a CA's private key, they can build a replica of the CA and issue network-valid certificates. You must protect all the CA's private and public key pairs so that attackers cannot gain access. The keys can be protected by monitoring membership in groups that have access to the private key material and implementing hardware solutions that remove the private key material from the physical computer hosting Certificate Services.

Attacks Against Servers Hosting CRLs and CA Certificates

If an application or service performs CRL checking, the application or service must validate the certificate to ensure that the certificate is not revoked. If an attacker can prevent access to the servers hosting the CRLs or CA certificates, a client will not be able to validate presented certificates. If an application cannot determine the revocation status of a presented certificate, the application might prevent access to the user or computer presenting the certificate.

Attempts to Modify the CA Configuration

If an attacker can gain local administrator access to the computer running Certificate Services, the attacker can modify the CA configuration. This modification can include altering URLs for CRL publication, revoking legitimate certificates, and issuing certificates to nonvalid computers or users.

Attempts to Modify Certificate Template Permissions

If attackers gain Enterprise Admins level access, they can modify certificate template permissions in the CN=Certificate Templates, CN=Public Key Services, CN=Services, CN=Configuration, CN=*ForestName* container (where *ForestName* is the LDAP distinguished name of the forest root domain). Modifying permissions might enable an attacker to enroll a certificate that provides excess permissions (such as an Enrollment Agent certificate), thereby permitting the attacker to request certificates on behalf of other users.

Attacks that Disable CRL Checking

Attackers might attempt to turn off revocation checking for an application. If CRL checking is turned off, the application does not determine whether a presented certificate is revoked. A certificate revocation invalidates the certificate before its validity period has expired. Common reasons for revoking a certificate include compromised private keys and terminated users.

Addition of Nontrusted CAs to the Trusted Root CA Store

If attackers can publish a nontrusted CA certificate to the trusted root store, all certificates that chain to that trusted root CA certificate are considered trusted. A certificate that chains to a trusted root CA certificate is trusted for any and all purposes, thereby allowing attackers to create their own trusted certificates. Alternatively, if attackers can create a certificate trust list (CTL)—a list of CA certificates that are not issued by your company's CA hierarchy but are trusted for specific purposes and periods of time—they can use a certificate issued by CAs on your network.

Issuance of Fraudulent Certificates

Before the creation of the 329115 hotfix, "Certificate Validation Flaw Might Permit Identity Spoofing," it was technically possible for attackers to sign certificates with their own user certificates. This created a false certificate chain that included a certificate that was not issued by a CA in the CA hierarchy but was still trusted. This type of attack worked because Windows 2000 did not enforce basic constraints. Basic constraints ensure that only CAs can issue certificates and prevent a user or computer certificate from signing another user or computer certificate.

Publication of False Certificates to Active Directory

If an attacker gains administrative access to a user account in Active Directory, the attacker can add a certificate to the properties of the user's account. The attacker can use this certificate to authenticate as that user without providing a password. If an attacker holds the private key associated with the certificate, he can perform any action permitted for that user.

Securing Certificate Services

To prevent the likelihood of these threats, you can take the following measures:

- Implement physical security measures.
- Implement logical security measures.
- Modify CRL and CA certificate publication points.
- Enable CRL checking in all applications.
- Manage permissions of certificate templates.

Implementing Physical Security Measures

Physical security measures prevent attackers from gaining physical access to the computer running Certificate Services. When an attacker gains physical access to a computer, any number of attacks can take place. Physical security measures can include the following:

■ Creating a three-tier hierarchy that deploys the root CA and the second-level CAs (also referred to as *policy CAs*) as offline CAs. An offline CA is removed from the network and is turned on only to issue new CA certificates and to publish updated CRLs.

■ Deploying hardware-based key modules, such as hardware storage modules, for the generation and protection of the CA key pair and for the signing of all issued certificates.

■ Removing offline CAs from the network and storing them in physically secure locations, such as vaults, safes, or secured server rooms, based on your company's security policy.

Implementing Logical Security Measures

In addition to physical security measures, modifying the configuration of Certificate Services can increase the security of a CA. Logical security measures can include these:

■ Restricting membership in the local Administrators group at the CA. Only local administrators can modify CA configuration by default.

■ Modifying permissions of the %systemroot%\system32\Certsrv folder so that Administrators and System have Full Control permissions and Authenticated Users have Read & Execute, List Folder Contents, and Read permissions.

■ Modifying the permissions to the %systemroot%\system32\Certlog folder so that Administrators, System, and Enterprise Admins have Full Control permissions.

■ Assigning the Administrators, System, and Enterprise Admins security principals Full Control permissions if a shared folder location is specified in the configuration of the CA for the CertEnroll share.

■ Monitoring the membership of the Cert Publishers group in each domain. Membership in the Cert Publishers group allows member CA computer accounts to publish certificates in user objects. Only members of the Cert Publishers group have this permission.

> **Tip**   The Cert Publishers group is a global group. If multiple domains exist in your forest, a CA in one domain cannot publish certificates to user account objects in other domains. You can change this behavior by modifying permissions in Active Directory, as described in 281271, "Windows 2000 Certification Authority Configuration to Publish Certificates in Active Directory of Trusted Domain." This Knowledge Base article recommends creating a custom universal group that contains the Cert Publishers group from each domain in the forest, as well as assigning required permissions to the universal group.

Modifying CRL and CA Certificate Publication Points

Publish CRLs and Authority Information Access (AIA) to locations accessible by all users. The certificate chaining engine must have access to the CRL and CA certificate for each CA in the certificate chain. If any CA in the certificate chain's CRL or CA certificate is not available, the chaining engine will prevent that certificate from being used if certificate revocation is enabled.

Enabling CRL Checking in All Applications

When you enable CRL checking in all applications, you ensure that every presented certificate is validated. Doing so confirms that the certificate has not been revoked, is time valid, and meets any constraints defined for the application. If an application does not perform CRL checking, it is possible for an attacker to use a certificate that was revoked for authentication or encryption purposes.

Managing Permissions of Certificate Templates

You can modify the default permissions for any certificate template so that only specific security groups have the necessary Read and Enroll permissions. If the permissions of a certificate template are modified, attackers could acquire a certificate with special privileges, such as an Enrollment Agent certificate that allows the subject to request certificates on behalf of other users.

Best Practices

- **Increase the security of root CA computers.**   You can do this by deploying offline CAs and, if possible, by deploying offline policy CAs, depending on your company's security policy.

- **Implement a hardware storage module.**   You should do this only if your company's security policy requires strong protection of CA key pairs.

- **Ensure that CRLs and CA certificates are published to accessible locations.**   The certificate chaining engine must have access to all CRLs and CA certificates in the certificate chain to validate a presented certificate. If any certificate or CRL is unavailable, its status cannot be determined.

- **Enable CRL checking in all applications.**   CRL checking ensures that a presented certificate passes validation tests for approval. If the certificate fails any tests, it is considered invalid.

- **Apply the latest service packs and hotfixes to CAs.**   This way, you ensure that the CA is protected against known vulnerabilities.

Additional Information

- Microsoft Official Curriculum course 2150: *Designing a Secure Microsoft Windows 2000 Network*, Module 14, "Designing a Public Key Infrastructure" (*http://www.microsoft.com/traincert/syllabi/2150afinal.asp*)

- "Troubleshooting Certificate Status and Revocation" white paper (*http://www.microsoft.com/technet/prodtechnol/WinXPPro/support/tshtcrl.asp*)

- "Certificate Authority Root Key Protection: Recommended Practices" security assurance white paper from Deloitte & Touche (*http://www.chrysalis-its.com/news/library/industry_white_papers/dt-wp.pdf*)

- "Deploying Certificate Services on Windows 2000 and Windows Server 2003 with the Chrysalis-ITS Luna CA3 Hardware Security Module" white paper (*http://www.microsoft.com/windows2000/techinfo/planning/chrysalis.asp*)

- "Windows 2000 Server and PKI: Using the nCipher Hardware Security Module" white paper (*http://www.microsoft.com/windows2000/techinfo/administration/security/win2kpki.asp*)

- "An Introduction to the Windows 2000 Public Key Infrastructure" white paper (*http://www.microsoft.com/windows2000/techinfo/howitworks/security/pkiintro.asp*)

- "Microsoft Windows 2000 Public Key Infrastructure" white paper (*http://www.microsoft.com/windows2000/techinfo/planning/security/pki.asp*)

- *Microsoft Windows 2000 Security Technical Reference*, Chapter 6, "Cryptography and Microsoft Public Key Infrastructure" (Microsoft Press, 2000) (*http://www.microsoft.com/windows2000/technologies/security/redir-crypto.asp*)

- 329115: "Certificate Validation Flaw Might Permit Identity Spoofing"

- 281271: "Windows 2000 Certification Authority Configuration to Publish Certificates in Active Directory of Trusted Domain"

> **Note**   The previous two articles can be accessed through the Microsoft Knowledge Base. Go to *http://support.microsoft.com* and enter the article number in the Search The Knowledge Base text box.

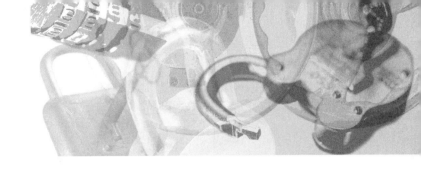

21

Implementing Security for Microsoft IIS 5.0

Microsoft Internet Information Services (IIS) 5.0 is included with the Microsoft Windows 2000 operating system. IIS provides you with the ability to host Web and FTP sites on a Windows 2000 server. When implementing a Web server or an FTP server, you must install the latest service packs and security patches to ensure your server is protected. In addition, you must implement measures to increase baseline security of the Web server. The measures you can take to secure IIS include the following:

■ **Implement Windows 2000 security.** The Web or FTP server you deploy must run on a Windows 2000 server that is properly configured for security. You must configure user accounts, the file system, and the registry to implement baseline security required for Internet services.

■ **Configure IIS security.** The Internet Services Manager console allows you to implement an IIS-specific security configuration to ensure that the maximum level of security is implemented for your Web server. This includes defining authentication and Web site permissions and securing communication channels.

■ **Implement IIS security tools.** Microsoft provides two tools that you can use to configure the security of an IIS server. The IIS Lockdown tool and the URLScan filter increase IIS server security by removing or disabling unnecessary services, restricting which scripts are allowed to execute, and removing unnecessary IIS server components.

■ **Configure the FTP service.**   If you implement an FTP server, you must configure IIS to increase FTP service security. This includes limiting authentication to anonymous access and configuring an FTP folder structure to reduce attacks against the disk system.

Implementing Windows 2000 Security

When implementing an IIS server, you must first ensure that the Windows 2000 server hosting the IIS service is secure. Measures you can take include the following:

■ Minimize services.

■ Define the user account for anonymous access.

■ Secure the file system.

■ Apply specific registry settings.

Minimizing Services

At a minimum, an IIS server requires that you configure the following services to start automatically:

■ **IISAdmin**   Allows administration of the Web server

■ **World Wide Web Publishing Service**   Enables the World Wide Web (WWW) Publishing service on the IIS server

You might have to enable additional Internet-based services if they are required on your IIS server. These services are enabled in the Add/Remove Programs applet in the Control Panel by adjusting the properties of IIS. These services include the following:

■ **FTP Publishing Service**   Enables the IIS server to function as an FTP server

■ **Network News Transport Protocol (NNTP)**   Enables the IIS server to host NNTP newsgroups

■ **Simple Mail Transfer Protocol (SMTP)**   Enables the IIS server to send and receive e-mail as an SMTP server

In addition to these services, you should configure baseline security services as recommended in the Windows 2000 Security Operations Guide.

> **More Info**   For more information on recommended baseline services configuration, see Chapter 8, "Securing Services."

Defining User Accounts

For anonymous access to the Web server, IIS provides a user account, IUSR_*ComputerName*, where *ComputerName* is the NetBIOS name of the member server. By default, all anonymous Web access is performed in the security context of the IUSR_*ComputerName* account. When created, the IUSR_*ComputerName* account is configured as a member of the local Guests group on the member server.

> **Warning**   If you install IIS on a domain controller, the IUSR_*WebServerName* user account is assigned excess privileges. Any user account created in the Active Directory directory service is automatically assigned membership in the Domain Users global group. Membership in this group results in the IUSR_*WebServerName* user account having the same permissions as the Users domain local group. To rectify this security issue, add the IUSR_*WebServerName* user account to the membership of the Domain Guests global group, change the primary group for the user account to the Domain Guests global group, and delete the membership in the Domain Users global group. You must designate a new primary group before you can delete the Domain Users group's membership.

You should implement a custom account for anonymous access to the Web server. Rather than maintain default memberships, create a custom local group or domain local group. By creating a custom group, you can assign all anonymous permissions to that group, rather than assigning permissions to the Everyone group or to the Guests group.

> **Tip**   If you implement a custom IIS anonymous account, disable the IUSR_*ComputerName* account to prevent attackers from using this account to attempt network connections.

You must assign specific account options and user rights to the anonymous Web access account. These custom settings include the following:

- **Account options**   The custom user account must have the User Cannot Change Password and Password Never Expires options enabled.

- **User rights**   You must assign the custom user account the Log On Locally user right.

In addition to these custom settings, you must configure IIS to manage the user account's password. This is accomplished by enabling the Allow IIS To Control Password check box in the properties of the IIS anonymous user account.

Securing the File System

To allow configuration of local file system security, all volumes that host Web content should be formatted by using the NTFS file system. In addition to using NTFS, you should consider hosting all Web content on a volume separate from the OS to prevent attackers from performing *directory traversal attacks* to gain access to OS files.

In a directory traversal attack, an attacker attempts to navigate to a location on the file system not published by the Web server. For example, the default path for the Web server root is %systemdrive%\Inetpub\WWWroot. An attacker might attempt to gain access to the command shell by using the URL *http://../../windir/system32/cmd.exe*.

In addition to storing all Web content on a separate drive, you should create a folder structure that separates available content by type to allow specific permissions for the assignment of file types. For example, you can create the folder structure shown in Figure 21-1 to separate content into the categories of executables, scripts, include files, images, and static Web pages.

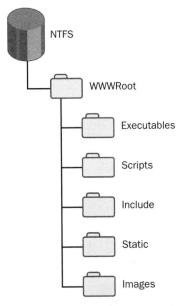

Figure 21-1   Dividing Web content into separate folders

Once you create the required folder structure, you can apply discretionary access control lists (DACLs) specific to the Web content type, as shown in Table 21-1. The AnonWebAccess group is a custom local group created at the Web server that contains only the custom anonymous IIS user account.

Table 21-1   Securing Web Content by Content Type

Content Type	Recommended DACL Settings
Executables (.exe, .dll, .cmd, and .pl)	AnonWebAccess (Execute)
	Administrators (Full Control)
	System (Full Control)
Scripts (.asp)	AnonWebAccess (Execute)
	Administrators (Full Control)
	System (Full Control)
Server-side includes (.inc, .shtm, and .shtml)	AnonWebAccess (Execute)
	Administrators (Full Control)
	System (Full Control)

(continued)

Table 21-1 Securing Web Content by Content Type *(continued)*

Content Type	Recommended DACL Settings
Images (.jpg, .gif)	AnonWebAccess (Read)
	Administrators (Full Control)
	System (Full Control)
Static content (.htm, .html)	AnonWebAccess (Read)
	Administrators (Full Control)
	System (Full Control)

Applying Specific Registry Settings

Web servers are frequently targets of denial-of-service attacks. You can help protect a Web server against a synchronization (SYN) attack by enabling the SynAttackProtect registry value:

```
HKLM\System\CurrentControlSet\Services\Tcpip\Parameters\SynAttackProtect
```

This REG_DWORD registry value protects against SYN attacks by adjusting the retransmission of SYN acknowledgment packets. These are the allowed values for the registry value:

- **0**   Provides typical protection against SYN attacks

- **1**   Adjusts the retransmission of SYN acknowledgments. This setting causes responses to time out faster if a SYN attack is detected

- **2**   Adds delays to connection indications and times out Transmission Control Protocol (TCP) connection requests at a faster rate if a SYN attack is detected

A computer detects a SYN attack by inspecting three other registry values in the Tcpip/parameters registry key:

- **TCPMaxPortsExhausted**   Determines how many connection requests the system refuses before initiating SYN attack protection. This should be set to a value of 2 or greater.

- **TCPMaxHalfOpen**   Determines how many connections the server maintains in the half-open state before TCP/IP initiates SYN attack protection. A half-open state occurs when a client starts a TCP/IP three-way handshake but does not respond to the server's synchronization request. This should be set to a value of 2 or greater.

■ **TCPMaxHalfOpenRetried** Determines how many connections the server maintains in the half-open state even after a connection request is retransmitted. This should be set to a value of 2 or greater.

Configuring IIS Security

Within the Internet Services Manager console, you can configure additional security for IIS by modifying the Web server's Master Properties and properties of individual Web sites, virtual directories, and Web content. The properties that affect the security include the following:

■ Authentication

■ Web site permissions

■ Communication channels

Authentication

IIS provides different methods for authenticating users when they connect to a Web site hosted by the Web server. The method you choose depends on the type of data stored on the Web site, as well as your network environment. The network environment includes the domain membership of the Web server and the Web browser implemented by Web clients.

Configuring Authentication Methods

IIS authentication methods can be configured in two locations. The first location is in the properties of the Master Properties for the WWW Service. Master Properties affect default settings for all future Web sites installed at the Web server. The following steps explain how to configure IIS authentication methods via Master Properties:

1. From Administrative Tools, open the Internet Services Manager.

2. In the console tree, right-click *ComputerName* (which is the NetBIOS name of the Web server) and then click Properties.

3. In the Master Properties section of the *ComputerName* Properties dialog box, select WWW Service from the Master Properties drop-down list. Then click Edit.

4. In the Anonymous Access And Authentication Control section of the Directory Security tab in the WWW Service Master Properties For *ComputerName* dialog box, click Edit.

5. In the Authentication Methods dialog box (shown in Figure 21-2), enable all required authentication methods and click OK.

Figure 21-2 Defining authentication methods allowed for a Web site

You can also configure authentication methods for each Web site. Individual Web site properties take precedence over those of the Master Properties. To modify authentication methods for a specific Web site or a virtual directory within a Web site, you must edit authentication methods within the Directory Security tab of the Web site's or the virtual directory's properties.

Choosing Authentication Methods

The following methods are available for authenticating users as they connect to a Web site or virtual directory:

- Anonymous authentication
- Basic authentication
- Digest authentication
- Integrated Windows authentication
- Certificate-based authentication

Anonymous Authentication   Anonymous authentication allows users to access a Web site without providing a user name and password for credentials. The Web site implements a predefined user account and password for the connection. By default, a local user account is created when IIS is installed. The name of this account is IUSR_*ComputerName* and is a member of the local Guests group account.

You can increase anonymous user account security by creating a custom user account and custom group for all security assignments. The user account's password must be controlled by IIS to ensure the password is changed when required. By using a custom group, you assign all anonymous permissions for the Web site directly to the custom group, while prohibiting the application of other permissions to the Web site's anonymous user account. If you implement a custom IIS anonymous user account, you must assign the user account the Log On Locally user right either in the local security policy of the Web server or at the OU where the computer account for the Web server exists.

Basic Authentication   Basic authentication is supported by most Web browsers. Basic authentication allows a user to provide credentials when requested by a Web site. The security issue with basic authentication is that the user's account and password are sent to the Web server in an unencrypted format that uses base64 encoding, meaning that the user's credentials are susceptible to inspection.

> **Note**   You can increase the security of basic authentication by implementing Secure Sockets Layer (SSL) to encrypt all data sent to the Web site. The user's credentials are then encrypted as they are transmitted from the Web client to the Web server.

Digest Authentication   Digest authentication increases the security of the user's credentials by not sending the user's password over the network. Instead, the user's password and other information about the account are used to create a hash that is sent to the Web server. The Web server compares this hash with Active Directory's version of the hash. If the two hash versions match, the user is considered authenticated.

Digest authentication requires that the Store Password Using Reversible Encryption option is enabled at the user account. This option stores the user's password hash in Active Directory, but the setting does not take effect until the next time the user changes her password. The password's reversibly encrypted format is stored when the user's password is set.

> **Note** Although digest authentication increases the security of trans-
> mitted credentials, it *lessens* the security of Active Directory. Because
> of the weakened password storage required by digest authentication,
> you must ensure that the domain controller is physically secure.

Integrated Windows Authentication   Integrated Windows authentication uses NT
LAN Manager (NTLM) or Kerberos v5 to authenticate a Web client with a Web
server. The user name and password are not sent across the network, protecting
against credential interception. Integrated Windows authentication requires that
the Web client use the Microsoft Internet Explorer Web browser because other
browsers do not support this form of authentication.

Certificate-Based Authentication   Windows 2000 allows User certificates to be
used for user account authentication. If you want to enforce certificate-based
authentication, User certificates must have the Client Authentication Extended
Key Usage (EKU) attribute to allow certificate-based authentication and the
Web server must have a Web Server certificate installed.

When a user connects to a Web server, he is prompted to select an authentication certificate. The user's certificate is sent to the Web server, which associates the presented certificate to a user account either in the local Security
Accounts Manager (SAM) database of the Web server or in Active Directory. The
certificate is mapped to a user account either in the IIS console or in Active
Directory if the Enable The Windows Directory Service Mapper option is
enabled in the Web site's Properties page. The public key associated with the
certificate is retrieved from IIS or Active Directory, depending on the mapping,
and is then used to encrypt authentication data. Only the holder of the certificate's private key can decrypt the authentication data.

You enforce certificate-based authentication by performing two steps:

1. Enforce client-based certificates in the Web site's Properties page. In
   the Secure Communications dialog box, you can require client certificates by enabling SSL for the Web site and clicking the Require Client Certificates option button, as shown in Figure 21-3.

2. Remove all other forms of authentication from the properties of the
   Web site. If you clear all the authentication method check boxes
   shown in Figure 21-2, you prevent all forms of authentication other

than certificate-based authentication. This prevents IIS from presenting alternate authentication forms if the certificate-based authentication fails.

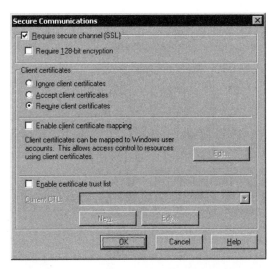

Figure 21-3   Configuring the Web site to require client certificate-based authentication

Web Site Permissions

The Internet Services Manager console allows you to define permissions for a Web site or virtual directory. These permissions are separate from NTFS permissions applied to the actual Web content folder.

If NTFS permissions and Web site permissions are in conflict, the more restrictive permissions are applied. For example, if NTFS permissions allow a user to modify the contents of a folder but the Web permissions grant only Read permissions, the user is assigned Read permissions.

You define the permissions for a Web site in the Home Directory tab of a Web site's property pages, as shown in Figure 21-4. When defining a Web site's permissions, you can apply any combination of the following permissions:

■   **Script Source Access**   Allows users of the Web site or virtual directory to access the source code for a Web site, including Microsoft Active Server Pages (ASP) applications, if the Read or Write permissions are also defined for the Web site or virtual directory. This permission is available for Web sites, virtual directories, and individual files.

- **Read** Allows users of the Web site to read Web content posted at the Web site and to navigate between pages on the Web site. This permission is available for Web sites, virtual directories, and individual files.

- **Write** Allows users to upload files to the Web site or the Web site's specific upload folder. This permission also allows a user to modify the contents of a Write-enabled file at the Web server. This permission is available for Web sites, virtual directories, and individual files. Write permissions are available only to Web browsers that support the HTTP 1.1 protocol standard PUT feature.

- **Directory Browsing** Allows users to view hypertext listings of all files and subdirectories within a Web site folder or a virtual directory, if a default document is not located in the folder or virtual directory. Virtual directories will not appear in the hypertext listing. The user must know the virtual directory's alias or must click a link that refers her to the virtual directory. This permission is available only for Web sites and virtual directories.

Figure 21-4 Defining permissions for a Web site

Communication Channels

Additional security can be provided for connections to the Web server by implementing SSL encryption between the Web server and Web clients. SSL is enabled by installing a Web Server certificate at the Web server. Specifically, the Web Server certificate must have the following attributes:

■   The certificate must chain to a trusted root authority. The root Certification Authority (CA) in the certificate chain must be included in the trusted root store of all clients that connect to the SSL-protected Web server.

■   The installed certificate must have a Server Authentication object ID (OID) in the EKU attribute of the certificate. The Server Authentication OID (1.3.6.1.5.5.7.3.1) indicates that the Web Server certificate can be used to authenticate the Web server's identity and can also be used to encrypt session data between the Web server and Web clients.

■   The subject of the certificate must match the Domain Name System (DNS) name used to access the Web site. For example, if the Web site is accessed by connecting to *http://www.example.com*, the subject of the Web Server certificate must be *www.example.com*.

> **Caution**   A common mistake administrators make when requesting a Web Server certificate is to request the certificate with the Web server's NetBIOS name as the subject, rather than the Web site's DNS name as the subject. If you do not use the Web site's DNS name as the subject, a user connecting to the Web site will receive a warning that the Web site's certificate name does not match the name of the Web site.

Enabling SSL

To enable SSL, you must install a Web Server certificate at the Web server. You can install a Web Server certificate by running the Web Server Certificate Wizard:

1.   From Administrative Tools, open the Internet Service Manager console.

2.   In the console tree, expand the NetBIOS name of the Web server, right-click Default Web Site, and click Properties.

3.   In the Default Web Site Properties dialog box, click Server Certificate on the Directory Security tab.

4.   In the Welcome To The Web Server Certificate Wizard page, click Next.

5.   On the Server Certificate page, click Create A New Certificate and then click Next.

6. On the Delayed Or Immediate Request page, perform one of the following and then click Next:

   ❑ If submitting the request to an online enterprise CA on the local network, click Send The Request Immediately To An Online Certification Authority.

   ❑ If submitting the request to a commercial CA such as VeriSign, click Prepare The Request Now, But Send It Later. This will create a PKCS#10 certificate request format file.

7. On the Name And Security Settings page, type a name for the Web site, define the bit length for the certificate encryption key, and click Next.

8. On the Organization Information page, type the organization and OU names and click Next.

9. On the Your Site's Common Name page, type the DNS fully qualified domain name (FQDN) of your Web server and click Next.

10. On the Geographical Information page, identify the Country/Region, State/Province, and City/Locality for your Web server, and click Next.

11. If you select Send The Request Immediately To An Online Certification Authority, the Choose A Certification Authority page appears. You must select an enterprise CA from the drop-down list and click Next. If you select Prepare The Request Now, But Send It Later, the Certificate Request File Name page appears. You must type the file name for the certificate request and click Next.

12. A summary page will appear that displays the naming information provided to the Web Server Certificate Request Wizard. Verify the information and click Next.

13. On the Completing The Web Server Certificate Request Wizard page, click Finish.

If you request the Web Server certificate from a commercial CA, you must submit the certificate request file to the commercial CA. Once you receive the certificate from the commercial CA, you must install it at the Web server. The Web Server certificate is installed by using the following process:

1. From Administrative Tools, open the Internet Service Manager console.

2. In the console tree, expand the NetBIOS name of the Web server, right-click Default Web Site, and click Properties.

3. In the Default Web Site Properties dialog box, click Server Certificate on the Directory Security tab.

4. In the Welcome To The Web Server Certificate Wizard page, click Next.

5. On the Pending Certificate Request page, click Process The Pending Request And Install The Certificate and then click Next.

6. On the Process A Pending Request page, provide the full path to the certificate file returned to you from the commercial CA and click Next.

7. On the Certificate Summary page, ensure that the information provided in the certificate is correct and click Next.

8. On the Completing The Web Server Certificate Request Wizard page, click Finish.

Configuring SSL

Once you have completed the installation of the Web Server certificate, you are ready to configure SSL options for the Web server. SSL configuration options are defined by clicking the Edit button in the Secure Communications section of a Web site or a virtual directory's Directory Security tab. The options that can be defined for SSL include the following:

■ **Choose where to implement SSL encryption.**   You can choose to enable SSL encryption for a Web site, virtual directory, or specific file at a Web site. You enable SSL by clicking the Require Secure Channel (SSL) check box. We recommend that you provide the encryption for either the entire Web site or a specific virtual directory to ensure the security of all data sent to and from a specific Web application.

■ **Enforce 128-bit encryption.**   This encryption level increases the encryption strength for data transmitted to and from an SSL-protected Web site. If you enable this option, all Web browsers must support 128-bit encryption. If a Web browser does not have the High Encryption Pack installed or a service pack that enables strong encryption, connection attempts to the SSL-protected Web site will fail.

■ **Define client certificate requirements.**   Once a Web Server certificate is installed at the Web server, you can enable certificate-based authentication. The user authenticates with the Web site by presenting a certificate from his certificate store. The Web server will associate (or map) the certificate to a user account. The possession of the private key associated with the certificate proves the user's identity.

When enabled, you can choose to either accept or require client certificates for authentication.

- **Enable client certificate mapping.**   If you enable the mapping of certificates to user accounts, you must enable client certificate mapping. This option allows mappings defined in Active Directory or IIS.

- **Enable certificate trust lists.**   A certificate trust list defines trust for external CAs. You can limit which external certificates are trusted by determining the accepted enhanced key usages and validity periods for external certificates, as well as identifying trusted CAs.

In addition to these settings, you can define the SSL listening port for the Web site or virtual directory. By default, the Web SSL listening port is TCP port 443, but you can configure a custom SSL listening port. This is required when a Web server hosts multiple SSL-protected Web sites.

Using Tools to Secure IIS

Two tools are available to secure an IIS server: the IIS Lockdown tool and the URLScan filter. These tools remove known weaknesses in the IIS configuration and provide filters to prevent known attacks against the IIS server.

The IIS Lockdown Tool

By default, Windows 2000 includes the installation of IIS. The IIS Lockdown tool allows you to secure IIS configuration without removing and reinstalling the service. The IIS Lockdown tool can be run by an administrator or can be scripted to allow the unattended application of IIS Lockdown settings to an IIS server. The installation of the tool is broken down into security configuration sections:

- Selecting a server template

- Configuring Internet services

- Enabling script maps

- Applying additional security

Selecting a Server Template

The Select Server Template page provides a list of predefined IIS configuration templates. Each template contains IIS settings designed for the software in the IIS Server template name. By selecting a server template from the list, the IIS Lockdown tool will apply the necessary settings to secure IIS in that environment.

When you select a server template, you can view the specific settings by enabling the View Template Settings check box. This option allows you to review the configured settings and apply any modifications necessary for your IIS environment.

Creating a Custom Server Template

You can create custom server templates in the IISlockd.ini file for use with the IIS Lockdown tool. All custom server templates appear in the IIS Lockdown tool as available templates. You can create a custom server template by editing the IISlockd.ini file to include your custom settings.

The first step is to include pointers to your custom server template section. You must declare your custom template in either the *ServerTypesNT4*, the *ServerTypes*, or *UnattendedServerType* lines in the *[Info]* section, as shown next. In this case, *CustomTemplate* is available for both manual and unattended installations.

```
[Info]
ServerTypesNT4=sbs4.5,exchange5.5,frontpage,proxy,staticweb,dynamicweb,
    other,iis_uninstalled
ServerTypes=CustomTemplate,sbs2000,exchange5.5,exchange2k,
    sharepoint_portal,frontpage,biztalk,commerce,proxy,staticweb,
    dynamicweb,other,iis_uninstalled
UnattendedServerType=CustomTemplate
Unattended=TRUE
Undo=FALSE
```

Once you define the pointers, you must create a section based on the referral in the *[Info]* section that details the settings for the custom server template. The following example ensures that

■ Only the Web service is installed. All other services are disabled, rather than uninstalled.

■ Only ASPs are enabled.

■ Anonymous rights for running system utilities and viewing content are enabled.

■ IIS Samples, IIS scripts, the Microsoft Advanced Data Connector (MSADC) virtual directory, the IIS Administration virtual directory, and the IIS Help virtual directory are removed from the IIS server.

(continued)

Creating a Custom Server Template *(continued)*

■ URLScan is enabled and the URLScan.ini file is stored in the %windir%\system32\Inetsrv\URLscan folder.

These settings are all defined in the *[CustomTemplate]* section, which enforces the previous settings and is shown next. The section name is based on the tag assigned to the section in the *[Info]* section shown earlier.

```
[CustomTemplate]
label="A Custom Server Template"
Enable_iis_http=TRUE
Enable_iis_ftp= FALSE
Enable_iis_smtp= FALSE
Enable_iis_nntp= FALSE
Enable_asp= TRUE
Enable_index_server_web_interface= FALSE
Enable_server_side_includes= FALSE
Enable_internet_data_connector= FALSE
Enable_internet_printing= FALSE
Enable_HTR_scripting= FALSE
Enable_webDAV= FALSE
Disable_Anonymous_user_system_utility_execute_rights= TRUE
Disable_Anonymous_user_content_directory_write_rights= TRUE
Remove_iissamples_virtual_directory=TRUE
Remove_scripts_directory=TRUE
Remove_MSADC_virtual_directory=TRUE
Remove_iisadmin_virtual_directory=TRUE
Remove_iishelp_virtual_directory=TRUE
UrlScan_Install=ENABLED
UrlScan_IniFileLocation=%Windir%\System32\Inetsrv\Urlscan
AdvancedSetup =
UninstallServices=FALSE
```

Configuring Internet Services

If you enable the View Template Settings check box or choose to configure the other server template, you can configure which Internet services are available at the IIS server. You can select whether each service is enabled or disabled, as shown in Figure 21-5.

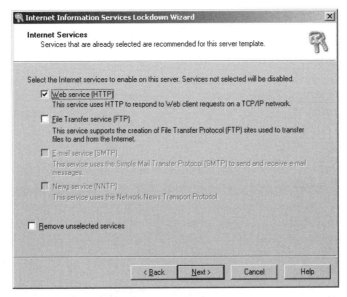

Figure 21-5   Defining the startup state for IIS

An enabled service is indicated by a selected check box. A disabled service is indicated by an unselected check box. If a service is grayed out, it is not installed on the IIS server.

You can also remove unselected services by enabling the Remove Unselected Services check box. This option removes any unselected services, rather than leaving the services disabled.

> **Caution**   We recommend you leave services disabled. Many applications depend on dynamic-link libraries (DLLs) enabled by IIS. If a service is disabled, the DLLs remain available for other applications. If the service is removed, some applications will reinstall and enable IIS to gain access to the required DLLs.

Enabling Script Maps

IIS can limit what scripts can be executed on an IIS server by defining script maps. Script maps associate script files, such as ASP pages, with a specific scripting engine for processing. Script maps are implemented by using Internet Server Application Programming Interface (ISAPI).

In the Script Maps page, you can enable and disable predefined script maps. If a script map is disabled, the default script map is replaced with a script that causes the server to respond with a "HTTP 404—File not found" error. The following script maps can be enabled or disabled:

■   **Active Server Pages (.asp)**   This technology enables the creation of dynamic Web pages. When a user connects to an ASP page, the server executes the ASP script at the server and generates an HTML page. The resultant HTML page is returned to the user who connected to the ASP page.

■   **Index Server Web Interface (.idq)**   These scripts allow an administrator to remotely manage Index Server services from the Web. The scripts also allow a user to create custom Web-based queries against an Index Server. If you do not require these features, you can disable this script map.

> **Note**   Disabling the .idq script mapping does not prevent your Web site from allowing standard Web-based searches that utilize Index Server.

■   **Server-Side Includes (.shtml, .shtm, .stm)**   These scripts enable a Web server to add text, graphics, or application information to a Web page before it is sent to a user.

■   **Internet Data Connector (.idc)**   These scripts allow queries to be sent to backend databases and then display the results in an HTML-formatted page.

■   **HTR Scripting (.htr)**   These scripts are similar to ASP scripts. HTR scripts are commonly used for allowing logon passwords to be changed via a Web server. For example, Microsoft Outlook Web Access (OWA) uses HTR scripts to enable users to change their passwords from the OWA Web site.

■   **Internet Printing (.printer)**   These scripts allow you to send and manage print jobs sent from the Internet to your network's TCP/IP-based printers.

You must determine whether each script map is required for your IIS environment. Some script maps (such as server-side includes and .idc scripts) can be updated to use ASP pages.

Applying Additional Security

The Additional Security page allows you to implement extra measures for your IIS server, as shown in Figure 21-6.

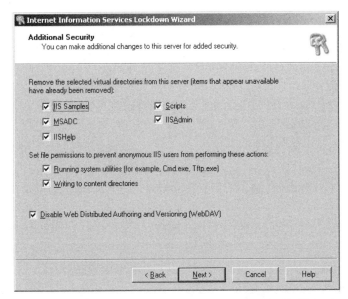

Figure 21-6   Defining additional security settings in the IIS Lockdown tool

The extra measures that you can take include the following:

■ **Remove Selected Virtual Directories.**   IIS automatically installs with several virtual directories that provide access to IIS Samples, MSADC, IIS Help files, sample scripts, and the Web-based IIS Administration pages. You can choose to remove each of these from the IIS server.

■ **Define Permissions For Anonymous Users.**   You can configure IIS to prevent anonymous Web users from executing system utilities such as the command prompt or Trivial File Transfer Protocol (TFTP). Also, you can prevent anonymous users from uploading data to content directories.

■ **Disable Web-Based Distributed Authoring And Versioning (WebDAV).**   This option allows you to prevent the creation of Web folders on the IIS server. Web folders allow a share to be published as a virtual directory with directory browsing enabled. In addition, a drive letter can be mapped to the WebDAV folder. This option must not be enabled at a Microsoft Exchange 2000 server because WebDAV is used for the mail store drive.

URLScan

URLScan is an ISAPI filter that screens and analyzes HTTP requests as Microsoft IIS receives them. The URLScan filter will apply settings based on the IIS Server template selected in the IIS Lockdown tool.

The URLScan Filter

As mentioned in the description of the IIS Lockdown tool, URLScan is an ISAPI filter that screens and analyzes inbound HTTP requests as IIS receives them. The URLScan filter will apply settings based on the IIS Server template selected in the IIS Lockdown tool. This ISAPI filter can be installed on IIS. If you install the Internet Security and Acceleration (ISA) Server Feature Pack, the ISAPI filter can be installed on an ISA server that protects multiple IIS servers.

URLScan analyzes all incoming HTTP requests against a URLScan filter configuration file to determine whether the request should be allowed. If the request is allowed, the Web server responds with the requested resource. If the request is denied, the Web server sends an "Object not found" response to the client, rather than sending details about why the request is denied.

Installing URLScan

URLScan can be automatically installed when you run the IIS Lockdown tool or manually installed by modifying the properties of the IIS server. When you install the IIS Lockdown tool, you have the option to install URLScan. In this case, the URLScan filter is configured to match the server environment selected in the IIS Lockdown tool. After you complete installation, you can manually modify the configuration of the URLScan.ini file to customize Web server security.

Configuring URLScan

The URLScan ISAPI filter screens incoming HTTP requests and blocks requests based on the configuration of the URLScan.ini file. By default, this file is stored in the %systemroot%\system32\Inetsrv\URLScan folder and must reside in the same folder as URLScan.dll if you modify the default storage location.

Note   You must restart the WWW Publishing service to enable any configuration changes in the URLScan.ini file.

The URLScan.ini file consists of seven sections:

- **Options**   Allows the definition of default security options for the URLScan ISAPI filter.

- **AllowVerbs**   Defines which HTTP verbs or methods are allowed in HTTP requests.

- **DenyVerbs**   Defines which HTTP verbs or methods are explicitly not allowed in HTTP requests.

- **DenyHeaders**   Defines which HTTP request headers are explicitly not allowed in HTTP requests.

- **AllowExtensions**   Defines a list of file extensions that are allowed in HTTP URL requests.

- **DenyExtensions**   Defines a list of file extensions that are explicitly not allowed in HTTP URL requests.

- **RequestLimits**   Defines and enforces limits on the size for each part of an HTTP request that reaches the Web server. All sizes are defined in bytes. The RequestLimits section is recognized only when running URLScan version 2.5 or later.

Options Section   The Options section defines the main options for the URLScan filter. It also designates which additional sections are used while processing incoming HTTP requests. You can define the following options:

- **UseAllowVerbs**   If set to a value of 1, URLScan reads the Allow-Verbs section of URLScan.ini and rejects any request that does not contain an HTTP verb included in the AllowVerbs section. If set to 0, URLScan reads the DenyVerbs section of URLScan.ini and rejects any request that contains a listed HTTP verb. The default value is 1.

- **UseAllowExtensions**   If set to a value of 1, URLScan allows only HTTP requests for files whose extensions are included in the AllowExtensions section of URLScan.ini. If set to 0, URLScan reads the DenyExtensions section of URLScan.ini and rejects any HTTP requests for files with an extension included in the DenyExtensions list. The default value is 0.

- **NormalizeURLBeforeScan**   If set to a value of 1, URLScan analyzes the requested URL after IIS decodes and normalizes the URL. If set to 0, URLScan analyzes the raw URL sent by the Web client. The default value is 1.

> **Note** We do not recommend setting the *NormalizeURLBe-foreScan* option to a value of 0. This is because doing so exposes the IIS server to canonicalization attacks that bypass proper analysis of the URL extensions and gain permissions to certain types of files hosted on a Web server that are file types implemented through ISAPI extensions.

- **VerifyNormalization** If set to a value of 1, URLScan verifies normalization of the URL. This action will defend against canonicalization attacks that attempt to conceal the true URL requested. For example, the string %252e is an example of a double-encoded string for the "." character. The %25 decodes to a "%" character, and the resulting %2e decodes to the "." character. If set to 0, this test is not performed by URLScan. The default value is 1.

- **AllowHighBitCharacters** If set to a value of 1, URLScan allows any characters outside the ASCII character set to exist in the URL. If set to 0, URLScan rejects any request in which the URL contains a character outside the ASCII character set. Although this feature can protect against Unicode attacks, it can lead to the rejection of valid URLs if you implement URLs with Unicode characters. The default value is 0.

- **AllowDotInPath** If set to a value of 0, URLScan rejects any requests containing multiple instances of the dot (".") character in a URL. If set to 1, URLScan does not perform this test. URLScan assumes that an extension is the part of the URL beginning after the last dot in the string and ending at the first question mark, the first slash character after the dot, or the end of the string. The default value is 0.

- **RemoveServerHeader** If set to a value of 1, URLScan removes the server header on all responses. If set to 0, URLScan does not perform this action. The default value is 0.

> **Note** This option prevents only one method of determining that the Web server is an IIS server. Many other ways of determining whether the Web server is running IIS exist.

- **EnableLogging**   If set to a value of 1, URLScan logs its actions into the URLScan.log file that is in the same directory as the URLScan.dll file. If set to 0, logging is disabled. The default value is 1.

- **LoggingDirectory**   Allows you to specify a custom folder in which to store the URLScan log file. The folder must be a local folder, such as C:\Logfiles. If this option is not specified, URLScan creates the log file in the same folder as the URLScan.dll file. This option is available only in URLScan version 2.5 and later.

- **LogLongURLs**   If set to a value of 1, URLScan will log up to 128 KB per request. If set to 0, URLScan will log the first 1024 bytes of the request. The default value is 0. This option is available only in URLScan version 2.5 and later.

- **PerProcessLogging**   If set to a value of 1, URLScan appends the process ID of the IIS process hosting URLScan.dll to the log file's name. If set to 0, all processes are logged into the same log file, which is named URLScan.log. The default value is 0.

- **AlternateServerName**   Allows you to create a different string that is presented in the server header. This setting is ignored if the RemoveServerHeader option is set to a value of 1. By default, the AlternateServerName is a null value.

- **AllowLateScanning**   If set to a value of 1, URLScan registers as a low-priority filter. This allows other ISAPI filters to modify the URL before it is analyzed by URLScan. If set to 0, URLScan registers as a high-priority filter. The default value is 0.

> **Note**   If you implement both Microsoft FrontPage Server Extensions and URLScan, you must set the AllowLateScanning option to a value of 1. In addition, URLScan must be placed after FrontPage Server Extensions on the filter load list.

- **PerDayLogging**   If set to a value of 1, URLScan creates a new log file each day and adds a date to the log file name. If a day passes with no URLScan activity, no log is created for that day. If set to 0, URLScan opens a single file called URLScan.log. The default value is 1.

■ **RejectResponseURL**   Allows you to define a response URL string that is returned to a Web client when URLScan rejects an HTTP request. In the RejectResponseURL string, you can use the following variables to tailor a response:

❑ **HTTP_URLSCAN_STATUS_HEADER**   Provides the reason why the HTTP request is rejected

❑ **HTTP_URLSCAN_ORIGINAL_VERB**   Provides the verb given in the original HTTP request

❑ **HTTP_URLSCAN_ORIGINAL_URL**   Provides the rejected URL requested in the original HTTP request

> **Note**   You can place URLScan into a logging-only mode by setting RejectResponseURL to a value of /~*. With this setting, URLScan performs all configured scanning and logs the results but still allows IIS to serve the rejected page. This mode allows you to test URLScan.ini settings without actually rejecting any requests.

■ **UseFastPathReject**   If set to a value of 1, URLScan ignores the RejectResponseURL and returns a short "HTTP 404—File not found" response to the client when an HTTP request is rejected. If set to 0, the RejectResponseURL option is used to create the rejection response. The default value is 0.

AllowVerbs Section   The AllowVerbs section contains a list of HTTP verbs that are allowed in HTTP requests. If the UseAllowVerbs option is set to 1, URLScan rejects any HTTP requests containing a verb not explicitly listed. The entries in this section are case sensitive.

DenyVerbs Section   The DenyVerbs section contains a list of HTTP verbs that are explicitly not allowed in HTTP requests. If the UseAllowVerbs option is set to 0, URLScan rejects any HTTP requests that contain a listed verb. The entries in this section are case insensitive.

DenyHeaders Section   The DenyHeaders section contains a list of request headers. Any HTTP requests that contain a request header listed in this section are rejected. The entries in this section are case insensitive.

AllowExtensions Section   The AllowExtensions section contains a list of allowed file extensions. If the UseAllowExtensions option is set to a value of 1, any request containing a URL with an extension not listed is rejected. You can specify URLs that do not have an extension by adding an extension represented by a dot and no trailing characters.

DenyExtensions Section   The DenyExtensions section contains a list of disallowed file extensions. If the UseAllowExtensions option is set to 0, any request containing a URL with an extension in the listing is rejected. The entries in this section are case insensitive.

RequestLimits Section   This section allows you to enforce limits on the size of an HTTP request. The size definitions can be defined for each section of an HTTP request. The size restrictions are defined in the following three entries:

- **MaxAllowedContentLength**   Enforces a maximum value for the content length. MaxAllowedContentLength does not actually prevent the server from accepting more data than the amount that this value is set to if the action is performed by using a chunk transfer, in which the data is broken into separate chunks, transferred, and then reassembled. The default value is roughly 2 GB.

- **MaxURL**   Restricts the length of the requested URL, not the length of the query string. The value of this registry will vary depending on how you install URLScan. If you manually extract URLScan.dll, the default setting is 260 bytes. If you install URLScan by installing the IIS Lockdown tool, the default setting is 16 KB.

- **MaxQueryString**   Restricts the length of the query string. The value is defined in bytes, with a default value of 4 KB.

In addition to these settings, you can create custom limitations by request header type by creating an entry based on the header name and adding the prefix "Max-". For example, to limit the length of the "Content-Type" header to 200 bytes, you can add the entry "Max-Content-Type=200" in the RequestLimits section.

URLScan Logging

If URLScan denies a Web request, it will log the action into the %systemroot%\system32\inetsrv\urlscan\URLScan.log file. The log file will include the reason for the denial and additional information about the request:

- **The complete URL requested**   Details whether a false URL was requested or whether an attacker attempted to gain access to a non-published folder by using a directory traversal attack.

- **IP address of the source of the request**   Helps determine the origin of the attack. Remember that the IP address can also be the IP address of a network address translation (NAT) device, a proxy server address, or a spoofed IP address.

> **Note**   If the IP address is a spoofed IP address, you will not be able to determine the true IP address that initiated the request. The IP address recorded in the URLScan log file is the spoofed IP address, not the true IP address of the remote client.

Configuring the FTP Service

In addition to providing Web server functionality to Windows 2000, IIS provides an FTP service. This service, if implemented, must be secured to ensure that the server hosting the FTP service is not compromised.

FTP allows users to transfer files to and from an FTP server. If you must implement FTP on your network, consider the following security guidelines:

- **Implement only anonymous access.**   Like most Internet-based protocols, the FTP protocol does not provide any security mechanisms for user credentials. User credentials are passed in cleartext and can lead to the compromise of a user's domain credentials. You can configure the FTP service to allow only anonymous connections to prevent credential interception.

> **Warning**   Configuring FTP to allow only anonymous connections does not prevent a user from inputting his user name and password in an FTP session. It only prevents those credentials from being accepted by the FTP server.

- **Prevent Write access to the FTP server.**   Disabling Write access prevents users from uploading information to the FTP server. If you require the ability to upload files to the FTP server, consider creating a separate folder in the FTP site that allows only uploads. This is configured by assigning only Write permissions to the folder.

■ **Implement a custom anonymous user account.**   The account defined for the Web service can be implemented as the anonymous user account for the FTP service. NTFS permissions can be assigned to a custom local group at the FTP server that contains only the custom anonymous user account.

■ **Implement the FTP home folder on a different volume than the OS.**   As with the Web service, it is recommended you create a folder structure for the FTP service that resides on a different volume than the OS. This involves changing the default folder from the default of %systemdrive%\Inetpub\Ftproot.

■ **Enable logging.**   Enable logging of the FTP service so that all connections to the FTP server are recorded to FTP audit logs. This allows you to review all connections to the FTP server.

Best Practices

■ **Ensure that the base OS is secure.**   The OS must be secure on a Windows 2000 server hosting the IIS service. If the OS—including its services, user accounts, files system, or registry—is not secure, IIS is susceptible to all vulnerabilities caused by the poor OS security configuration.

■ **Implement the strongest form of user authentication supported by users connecting to an IIS server.**   Weak authentication configuration can lead to the compromise of a user's domain account and password. By enforcing strong authentication methods—be they integrated Windows or certificate–based methods—you provide the strongest protection of user credentials.

■ **Assign the minimum required permissions for Web sites.** Implement a combination of NTFS and Web site permissions that provide the minimum permissions required to access a Web site. Do not assign excess permissions because this reduces the overall security of the Web site

■ **Implement SSL for Web sites or virtual directories that provide access to nonpublic data.**   SSL ensures that all data transmitted between the Web browser and the IIS server is encrypted. SSL also protects weaker forms of authentication, such as basic authentication, by encrypting the weaker credential information as it is sent to the Web server.

■ **Implement Microsoft security tools to lock down the IIS server.** Implement the IIS Lockdown tool and the URLScan filter to configure IIS services, enable script maps, and apply additional security to an IIS server.

Additional Information

■ *Security Operations Guide for Windows 2000 Server*, Chapter 4, "Securing Servers Based on Role" (*http://www.microsoft.com/technet/security/prodtech/windows/windows2000/staysecure/secops04.asp*)

■ *MCSE Training Kit: Designing Microsoft Windows 2000 Network Security*, Chapter 14, "Securing an Extranet" (Microsoft Press, 2001)

■ IIS Security Planning tool (*http://www.microsoft.com/downloads/release.asp?ReleaseID=24973*)

■ IIS Lockdown tool (*http://www.microsoft.com/technet/security/tools/tools/locktool.asp*)

■ URLScan security tool (*http://www.microsoft.com/technet/security/tools/tools/URLScan.asp*)

■ Secure Internet Information Services 5 Checklist (*http://www.microsoft.com/technet/security/tools/chklist/iis5chk.asp*)

■ IIS 5.0 Baseline Security Checklist (*http://www.microsoft.com/technet/security/tools/chklist/iis5cl.asp*)

■ Microsoft Windows 2000 Advanced Documentation: "Mapping Certificates to User Accounts" (*http://www.microsoft.com/windows2000/en/advanced/help/sag_CS_CertMapAccounts.htm*)

■ U.S. National Security Agency's "Guide to the Secure Configuration and Administration of Microsoft Internet Information Services 5.0" (*http://www.nsa.gov/snac/win2k/guides/w2k-14.pdf*)

■ 315669: "How to Harden the TCP/IP Stack Against Denial of Service Attacks in Windows 2000"

■ 309677: "Known Issues and Fine Tuning When You Use the IIS Lockdown Wizard in an Exchange 2000 Environment"

■ 309675: "IIS Lockdown Tool Affects SharePoint Portal Server"

Note   The previous three articles can be accessed through the Microsoft Knowledge Base. Go to *http://support.microsoft.com* and enter the article number in the Search The Knowledge Base text box.

Part V

Managing
Security Updates

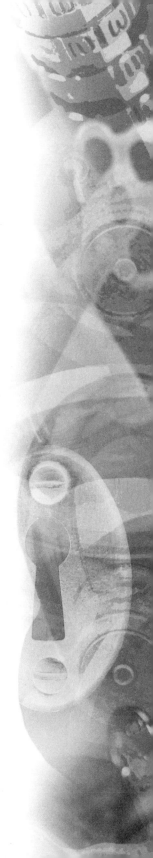

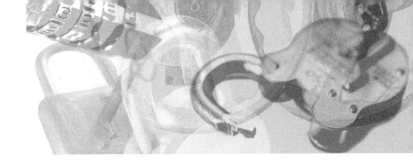

22

Patch Management

Patch management is required in a Microsoft network because software is not bug-free. Hotfixes and patches must be periodically applied to the Microsoft Windows NT 4.0, Microsoft Windows 2000, and Microsoft Windows XP operating systems to address security and functionality issues. Typically, hotfixes are developed to resolve one of the following issues:

- **Testing for all the design possibilities is difficult.** As network designs become more complex, it is increasingly problematic to test every use of a Windows OS component during initial testing and development of the OS by Microsoft.

- **More legacy versions must be supported.** Although Windows XP is Microsoft's latest client OS, not all customers will deploy it immediately. Customers will continue to use their common base operating systems, and these versions must be patched to protect against newer vulnerabilities.

- **Customers demand higher quality.** The quality bar rises as customers' network infrastructures change. More companies are connected to the Internet and are vulnerable to Internet attacks. This awareness drives higher the quality requirements for Internet-related components of Windows 2000.

- **Critical security issues must be fixed before the next product release.** Many issues cannot wait for a new version of the product to ship. Security issues, memory leaks, and other problems must be addressed immediately, especially if the vulnerabilities can lead to the compromise of a Windows 2000–based computer.

This chapter examines the following topics:

- **Types of patches**   Not all patches are the same. This section looks at hotfix formats and how Microsoft rates security patches.

- **Development of a hotfix**   The development cycle of a hotfix illustrates what happens after a security vulnerability or bug is reported to Microsoft, before the hotfix is released to the public.

- **Patch management in six steps**   The last section of this chapter proposes a methodology for patch management that will allow you to successfully deploy patches.

Types of Patches

Microsoft releases patches to provide updates to the Windows OS and Microsoft applications. These patches fix known problems, or bugs, in an OS or application and are shipped in three formats:

- **Hotfixes**   These updates address a single problem or bug encountered by a customer. They are developed in a short period of time and are released with less testing than other update types. Some hotfixes are referred to as *security fixes*. Security fixes differ from hotfixes in that the issues related to hotfixes are identified by the Microsoft Security Response Center (MSRC), rather than identified by Microsoft Product Support Services (PSS). Hotfixes are sometimes referred to as *Quick Fix Engineering (QFE) fixes*.

- **Roll-ups**   As the name suggest, a roll-up fix combines the updates of several hotfixes into a single update file. Roll-up fixes are run through more testing than single hotfixes but are released more frequently than service packs (discussed next).

- **Service packs**   At fairly regular intervals, Microsoft produces a collection of all hotfixes released since the OS's or application's release, including hotfixes released in previous service pack versions. These collections include fixes not previously released and occasionally introduce new functionality. Service packs undergo extensive testing before their release to ensure no deployment issues exist. Microsoft might issue several beta releases of a service pack before it is ready for the public.

> **Note**   Microsoft strives to not release new functionality in service packs. Instead, a new class of update to the OS or application, known as a *feature pack*, now exists. A feature pack extends the functionality of the OS or application by adding new features, options, or functionality.

When a security fix is released, MSRC issues a security bulletin that identifies the addressed vulnerability. In addition, a severity rating is applied to the security bulletin. If a security fix is a roll-up fix, the highest security rating of the individual hotfixes in the roll-up is applied.

This is the ratings system implemented by the MSRC in November 2002:

- **Critical**   A vulnerability that might allow the propagation of an Internet worm without user action. You should always apply critical rating updates after testing.

- **Important**   A vulnerability that might compromise the confidentiality, integrity, or availability of user data, as well as the integrity or availability of processing resources. You should always apply important rating updates after testing.

- **Moderate**   A vulnerability that might be mitigated by good security measures, such as implementing a security baseline configuration or performing regular network auditing. This rating can also be applied to vulnerabilities that are difficult to exploit. You should evaluate a moderate update to determine whether the vulnerability addressed is relevant to your company before testing and deployment.

- **Low**   A vulnerability that is extremely difficult to exploit or whose impact is minimal. You should determine whether a low rating update is necessary before testing and deployment.

> **Note**   Many exploits that affect networks are based on previously known vulnerabilities. For example, the Code Red and Nimda worm virus attacks of early 2002 took advantage of known application vulnerabilities. However, if you had already applied the previously released updates to your OS and applications, your computers were not vulnerable to these attacks.

Development of a Hotfix

Once product support or the MSRC identifies the need for a hotfix, the development process begins. This process differs between operating systems and applications, but the same general method is used:

1. The vulnerability identified by MSRC or the bug identified by product support is escalated to the Microsoft sustained engineering team.

2. The sustained engineering team investigates the bug and assigns it to a developer. The developer might be on the sustained engineering team or might be the core team developer responsible for the OS or application component.

3. The developer creates an initial hotfix. This hotfix addresses the vulnerability or bug but does not undergo testing other than that performed by the developer. This version of the hotfix is referred to as a *private*.

4. The private is sent to the customer who reported the problem to MSRC or to product support. The customer deploys the private to determine whether it corrects the problem.

5. If the customer reports that the bug is fixed, the sustained engineering team registers the bug against the next version of the OS or application. This ensures that the next release does not include the same bug.

6. The private is provided to the core team developer responsible for the OS or application component affected by the vulnerability. The developer reviews the hotfix to ensure no other issues exist.

7. When the developer completes her analysis, the hotfix is submitted to the build lab, which creates the hotfix and runs it through several build verification tests.

8. The hotfix is then passed through testers. The testers ensure that the hotfix works as expected. Because of time constraints, testing is not as extensive as the testing performed on service packs.

9. Localization teams review the hotfix to determine whether localized versions are required for different language versions of the OS or application. If required, localized versions are developed.

10. The completed hotfix is released to customers. If the hotfix is deemed a security update, Microsoft releases a related security bulletin that applies a vulnerability rating and provides further descriptions of the vulnerability.

Patch Management in Six Steps

Microsoft recommends a six-step process for patch management. This process ensures that you apply the patches in a organized way that prevents other applications on the network from failing. This is the recommended six-step process for patch management:

1. **Notification**   You must be aware of new security updates or service packs to ensure that the updates or service packs are installed in a timely manner.

2. **Assessment**   You must identify which computers on the network require the security update or service pack.

3. **Obtainment**   You must acquire the security update or service pack installation files from Microsoft.

4. **Testing**   You must test the security updates or service pack before you apply them to all affected computers on your network to ensure that undesired effects do not occur.

5. **Deployment**   You must deploy the security updates or service pack to the affected computers in a timely manner, taking advantage of tools to assist in the deployment.

6. **Validation**   You must ensure that the security updates or service pack are successfully installed on all affected computers.

Step 1. Notification

The first step in patch management is being aware of when Microsoft releases security patches. When a security patch is released, Microsoft issues a security bulletin that details the vulnerability fixed by the security patch as well as a vulnerability rating so that you can assess whether to deploy the security patch immediately after testing.

One way to stay on top of releases is to subscribe to the Microsoft Security Notification Service, which you access at *http://register.microsoft.com/subscription/subscribeme.asp?ID=135*. The notification service sends you an e-mail when a new security bulletin is released.

> **Note**   All e-mails from the Microsoft Security Notification Service are signed with a Pretty Good Privacy (PGP) key. The Microsoft PGP key is available at *http://www.microsoft.com/technet/security/MSRC.asc*. You can verify Microsoft's PGP key by inspecting its fingerprint, which is 5E39 0633 D6B3 9788 F776 D980 AB7A 9432.

In addition to the Microsoft Security Notification Service, several other notification services can inform you when new security issues arise for Windows NT 4.0, Windows 2000, and Windows XP:

- **NTBugtraq**   The *http://www.ntbugtraq.com* Web site, hosted by Russ Cooper, maintains a mailing list that discusses security bugs and exploits in Microsoft Windows NT 4.0, Windows 2000, and Windows XP.

- **Computer Emergency Response Team (CERT) Advisory Mailing List**   CERT maintains its own mailing list that notifies participants when computer-related security problems arise. You can subscribe to the CERT Advisory Mailing List at *http://www.cert.org/contact_cert/certmaillist.html*.

Step 2. Assessment

Once you identify the release of a security patch, you must determine whether the vulnerability affects your company and whether your computers require the patch. As mentioned earlier, you can utilize the Microsoft security bulletin rating system to assist in this decision. If a security bulletin is rated as critical or important, you should consider immediately applying the patch once you have tested it.

After testing, you must identify which computers require patch application. In many ways, this is the most difficult part of patch management. Keeping manual records of which patches and service packs are applied to every network computer is not possible if you have a large number of computers. Sometimes just determining which OS a computer is running is a challenge, never mind which service packs and security patches are applied.

Keeping an inventory of your systems assists you in planning patch deployment. By categorizing your computer systems, you can quickly identify how many computers are affected by a reported vulnerability. For example, if Microsoft releases a new security bulletin relating to a bug in Microsoft

Exchange 2000 Server, it will be useful to know how many instances of Exchange 2000 Server are on the network, as well as their physical location and which service packs and hotfixes are current.

By utilizing software, such as Microsoft's Systems Management Server (SMS), you can create a detailed inventory of network computers. The inventory information should help you determine which service packs and hotfixes are applied to each computer.

> **More Info**   For detailed information on the SMS Software Update Services Feature Pack, see the "SMS Software Update Services Feature Pack" section in Chapter 23, "Using Patch Management Tools."

Based on the inventory, you can categorize computers into common collections for deploying service packs and hotfixes. For example, creating a collection of all Windows 2000–based computers will assist in the deployment of the latest Windows 2000 Service Pack.

Step 3. Obtainment

Once you identify the computers you must patch, you must obtain the patches or service pack files. The online location you choose to download from will depend on several factors, including which application or OS is affected by the patch, whether all network computers are connected to the Internet, and whether you have a service pack or hotfix deployment solution in operation.

The following locations are available for downloading service packs and hotfixes:

■   Microsoft Windows Update

■   Microsoft Office Product Updates

■   Microsoft Download Center

Windows Update

Windows Update is available for the download and application of Windows 2000 security updates, hotfixes, and service packs. In addition to downloading and installing patches, you can also use the Windows Update Catalog to download patches for future application. The Windows Update Catalog provides a searchable collection of updates that can be installed on Windows-based computers across your home network or corporate network. The Windows Update

Catalog allows you to download service packs, security updates, and driver updates without installing them on the local computer. Instead, the files are downloaded into a folder containing instructions for future installations.

Enabling the Windows Update Catalog By default, the Windows Update Catalog is not enabled when you connect to the Windows Update Web site (*http:// windowsupdate.microsoft.com*). To enable the Windows Update Catalog, you must use the following procedure:

1. Open Microsoft Internet Explorer.

2. Open *http://windowsupdate.microsoft.com*.

3. In the left-hand pane of the Microsoft Windows Update site, click Personalize Windows Update.

4. In the details pane, enable the Display The Link To The Windows Update Catalog Under See Also check box.

5. In the details pane, click the Save Settings button.

This procedure will add a link to the Windows Update Catalog in the left-hand pane of the Microsoft Windows Update site, under the heading of See Also.

Using the Windows Update Catalog The Windows Update Catalog allows you to find patches for Microsoft Windows operating systems and hardware device drivers. You can download updates for specific operating systems, including the following:

■ The 64-bit version of the Windows Server 2003 family

■ Windows Server 2003 family

■ The 64-bit version of Windows XP

■ Windows XP family

■ Windows 2000 family

■ Windows Me

■ Windows 98

In addition to selecting the OS version, you can choose to download localized versions of the updates by indicating the preferred language for the updates. You can search for updates based on the date they were posted to the Windows Update Web site, on the keywords in the update descriptions, and by the type of update (such as critical updates, service packs, and recommended updates).

As mentioned, you can also use the Windows Update Catalog to download updated device drivers. You can select these device drivers based upon the type of hardware. For example, you can select network drivers by manufacturer, OS, language, date posted, and specific keywords.

Once you select the desired OS and device driver updates, you can download updates to your download basket. The Windows Update Catalog allows you to designate a local folder for downloads. The files are stored in the folder structure shown in Figure 22-1.

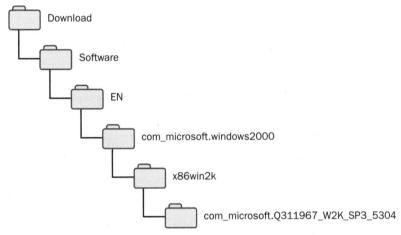

Figure 22-1   The folder structure created for the Windows Update Catalog

The folder structure created by the Windows Update Catalog depends upon whether you download a Windows OS or device driver update. Below the folder you select as the download location—in this example, \Download— the Windows Update Catalog creates one of two folders. For OS updates, a folder named Software is created, as shown in Figure 22-1. For device driver updates, a folder named Drivers is created.

Below this top-level folder, the next level of folders is based on the language selected. As Figure 22-1 shows, the English (EN) version of the update was downloaded. The next two levels of folders designate the update's OS version. The example shown in Figure 22-1 is a Windows 2000 update designated by two folders: com_microsoft.windows2000 and x86win2k.

The final folder designates the actual downloaded update. The update's name indicates the related Microsoft Knowledge Base article, the update's intended OS, the update's service pack version, and a unique identifier number. As shown in Figure 22-1, the update relates to 311967, "Unchecked Buffer in the Multiple UNC Provider." The update is intended for Windows 2000 computers and is included in Windows 2000 Service Pack 3. If the update is an updated device driver, the final folder's name is assigned by the updated device driver's manufacturer.

Microsoft Office Product Updates

The Microsoft Office Product Updates provides updates, add-ins, extras, converters, and viewers for Microsoft Office 97, Office 98, Office 2000, and Office 2002. The updates can be selected by individual Office software components or by the entire Office suite.

To download Microsoft Office updates to your computer, use the following procedure:

1. Open Internet Explorer.

2. Open *http://office.microsoft.com/ProductUpdates/default.aspx.*

3. Select the Office product and version updates you want to download.

4. Select whether to download updates, add-ins and extras, or converters and viewers for the selected Office component.

5. Select the individual updates from the list of available downloads.

> **Note**   You also have the option to view downloads from other providers. The Microsoft Office Product Updates site also displays a list of third-party updates for the Office suite components.

The Microsoft Office Product Updates site does not download the update files into any specific folder structure. You must designate a custom location for the download.

Microsoft Download Center

The Microsoft Download Center (*www.microsoft.com/downloads/*) allows you to search for other software and updates from Microsoft. As with the Microsoft Office Product Updates, you must manually designate a download location.

The following update categories are available from the Microsoft Download Center:

- **Games**   Includes trial versions and updates for games from Microsoft.

- **Microsoft DirectX**   Includes updates and the latest versions of DirectX. DirectX provides innovations in graphics, sound, music, and 3-D animation for gaming and graphics.

- **Internet**   Includes updates for all Internet-based applications, such as Windows Messenger and Internet Explorer.

- **Windows (security and updates)**   Includes security updates for any components of Windows. This includes service packs, Internet Explorer updates, and security updates.

- **Windows Media**   Includes updates and codecs for Windows Media Player for various operating systems.

- **Drivers**   Includes updated drivers for Microsoft hardware, as well as updates for common OS components, such as Microsoft Data Access Components (MDAC).

- **Office and home applications**   Includes updates for Microsoft Office and other home applications, such as Microsoft MapPoint.

- **Mobile devices**   Includes updates for the Palm PC, Microsoft ActiveSync, and Windows CE.

- **Macintosh and other platforms**   Includes updates of software for Macintosh, Solaris, and Unix computers.

- **Server applications**   Includes updates for Microsoft BackOffice components, such as Microsoft SQL Server, Microsoft Exchange Server, Microsoft Systems Management Server (SMS), and Microsoft SharePoint Portal Server.

- **System management tools**   Includes updates for Windows management, including Windows Installer, the Internet Information Services (IIS) Lockdown Tool, and Sysprep.

- **Development resources**   Includes updates for Microsoft Visual Basic, the Microsoft .NET Framework, and Microsoft Visual Studio.

Each download category presents a list of the five most popular downloads. You can also search for a download by specific products, technologies, and keywords.

Step 4. Testing

In an enterprise network, you cannot take the risk of deploying service packs or hotfixes without testing them in your environment. Testing ensures that the application of a service pack or hotfix does not create any undesired side effects.

To ensure that the testing is valid, consider implementing the following measures:

■   **Deploy a test network.**   A test network contains computers with the standard configuration used on your network. This ensures that a hotfix or service pack will not cause issues with other applications installed on a standard desktop computer.

■   **Implement a pilot project.**   Service packs should be tested by a subset of your network computers. The subset will determine whether the service pack causes any issues on the corporate network for the affected computers.

> **Note**   Typically, you should perform pilot projects only for service packs, not for hotfixes or security roll-ups.

Once this initial testing is completed, you can start the deployment of the service pack or hotfix to all affected computers.

Step 5. Deployment

Once you download and test the necessary hotfixes or service pack, you must install them on the affected computers. As mentioned earlier, you can determine the affected computers on your network by reviewing your computer inventory. The method you use to deploy a hotfix or service pack will depend on whether your company uses manual or automated distribution.

> **More Info**   This chapter discusses only the manual deployment of service packs or hotfixes. For detailed information on automating service pack or hotfix distribution, see Chapter 23.

Installing Service Packs

The latest Windows 2000 Service Pack can be downloaded from *http://www.microsoft.com/windows2000/downloads/servicepacks*. This site lists all available Windows 2000 service packs, including the latest version.

Once you choose the latest version of the Windows 2000 Service Pack, you must decide whether to download the Express Installation or Network Installation version. Express Installation detects the target computer's system components and then downloads the required components. For example, if the computer is running Windows 2000 Professional, updates exclusively for Windows 2000 Server are not downloaded. The Network Installation download includes all updated files for Windows 2000 Professional, Windows 2000 Server, and Windows 2000 Advanced Server. This version is recommended for multiple network updates.

To install the latest service pack by using Express Installation, use the following process:

1. In Internet Explorer, open *http://www.microsoft.com/windows2000/downloads/servicepacks*.

2. In the list of service packs, click the link for the most recent Windows 2000 Service Pack.

3. To download the latest version of the Windows 2000 Service Pack, click the Download link.

> **Note**   You can also order the latest Windows 2000 Service Pack on CD.

4. In the ensuing Web page, choose the language version of the service pack and click Go.

5. To install a Windows 2000 Service Pack by using Express Installation, click the Express Installation link. If you want to download the Network Installation version of the service pack, click the Network Installation link. If you click the Express Installation link, a minimal installation file is downloaded to the local computer. This launches the Windows 2000 Service Pack Setup Wizard.

6. On the Welcome To The Windows 2000 Service Pack Setup Wizard page, click Next.

7. On the License Agreement page, read the agreement and click I Agree and then click Next.

8. In the Select Options dialog box, click Archive Files and then click Next.

9. When the installation is complete, click Restart Now.

> **Note** This option archives all replaced files in the %windir%\$NTServicePackUninstall$ folder, allowing you to uninstall the service pack if post-installation issues arise. The installation then proceeds with an inspection of the current configuration to determine which files are required for the service pack installation.

Other Methods of Installing a Service Pack

If you download the Network Installation version of a service pack, you can extract the service pack files from the downloaded executable by running **w2ksp#.exe -x** (where # is the service pack version number). Once you extract the service pack files, you can run *download folder***i386\Update\Update.exe** to install. If you have not extracted the service pack files, run *download folder***w2ksp#.exe** (where # is the service pack version number).

Alternatively, you can use the packaged *download folder***i386\Update\Update.msi** file to deploy the service pack to Windows 2000 computer accounts in a software installation Group Policy object (GPO). By assigning the Update.msi package to a GPO applied to an OU with computer accounts, you can deploy the service pack through Group Policy.

Installing Hotfixes

All Windows 2000 hotfixes—whether released prior to or since Windows 2000 Service Pack 3—are packaged in a format that automatically installs the service pack when you run the downloaded hotfix executable. The executable automatically extracts all files related to the hotfix and installs them. The following two subsections discuss the manual installation of hotfixes to computers.

Installing Hotfixes Released Prior to Windows 2000 Service Pack 3   Hotfixes released prior to Windows 2000 Service Pack 3 are installed by using Hotfixe.exe. When you install a hotfix, you can use several command-line switches to customize installation. The available command-line switches for hotfixes released prior to Windows 2000 Service Pack 3 include:

- **/f** Causes all other programs to quit when the computer is shut down.

- **/l** Displays a list of all hotfixes currently installed on the computer.

- **/m** Performs an unattended hotfix installation.

- **/n** Prevents the computer from archiving previous versions of files replaced by the hotfix. (This switch prevents the uninstallation of the hotfix.)

- **/q** Performs the installation in quiet mode. (Quiet mode does not require user interaction.)

- **/y** Uninstalls the hotfix. (This option must be used with /m or /q.)

- **/z** Prevents the computer from restarting after installation.

When performing an unattended hotfix installation, you typically use the following command line:

```
Hotfix.exe /m /q /z
```

This command line allows the installation of multiple hotfixes in a single batch file.

> **Warning**   Hotfix.exe does not perform version control when you install multiple hotfixes. If you create a batch process that installs multiple hotfixes, you must ensure that the last line of the batch file is QChain.exe. QChain.exe ensures that if a file is modified by multiple hotfixes, the most recent version is maintained when the computer restarts. For more information on QChain.exe, see 296861, "Use QChain.exe to Install Multiple Hotfixes with Only One Reboot."

Installing Hotfixes Released Since Windows 2000 Service Pack 3   Hotfixes released after Windows 2000 Service Pack 3 are installed by using the Update.exe program. The Update.exe program includes the QChain.exe functionality, eliminating the need to run QChain.exe if multiple hotfixes are installed by a batch-file method. Update.exe is also used as the hotfix installation method for Windows XP hotfixes.

The following command-line switches are available when you install a hotfix released since Windows 2000 Service Pack 3:

- **-u** Performs the installation in unattended mode.

- **-f** Forces all other programs to quit when the computer shuts down.

- **-n** Prevents the archiving of previous versions of files replaced by the hotfix. (This switch prevents the uninstallation of the hotfix.)

- **-o** Overwrites original equipment manufacturer (OEM) files without prompting.

- **-z** Prevents the computer from restarting after the hotfix installation. (This option allows the application of multiple hotfixes without rebooting.)

- **-q** Performs an unattended installation but does not show the user interface during the installation process.

- **-l** Lists all hotfixes currently installed on the computer.

Step 6. Validation

Once you complete the hotfix installation, verify that it was installed successfully. Numerous methods to determine whether a hotfix is correctly applied to a computer exist, including the following:

- **Inspect the file system.** When a hotfix is installed so that the previous versions of replaced files are archived, the archived files are stored in the %windir%\\$NTUninstallQ######$ folder, where ###### is the related Microsoft Knowledge Base article number. If the folder exists, you can assume the hotfix was applied correctly. Be aware that this does not prevent the updated version from being replaced by an incorrect version at a later time, especially with hotfixes released prior to Service Pack 3 that do not have QChain.exe functionality.

- **Inspect the registry.** When a hotfix is successfully installed, the installation program registers the hotfix in the HKLM\Software\Microsoft\Windows NT\CurrentVersion\Hotfix\Q###### registry key, where ###### is the related Microsoft Knowledge Base article. As with inspecting the file system, examining the registry does not detect whether updated files are later replaced.

■ **Use hotfix diagnosis tools.**   To inspect the system for currently applied hotfixes and determine which hotfixes are required for your computer, you can use hotfix diagnosis tools, such as the Microsoft Baseline Security Analyzer command-line version executable Mbsacli.exe, Shavlik's hotfix network checker HfNetChk.exe (found at *http://www.shavlik.com*), and those found on the Microsoft Windows Update Web site (*http://windowsupdate.microsoft.com*). These tools can determine whether the hotfix needs reapplication by inspecting the checksums on the updated files.

> **More Info**   For more information on using these patch management tools, see Chapter 23.

Best Practices

■ **Subscribe to security update and service pack notification services.**   Notification services assist you in identifying recently released security updates and service packs, allowing you to deploy the updates or service packs in a timely manner.

■ **Assess your network to determine which computers require the security update or service pack.**   A security update or service pack might not be applicable to all computers on your network. You must identify which computers will require the update or service pack.

■ **Obtain security update or service pack installation files from download locations.**   Depending on which OS or application is affected by the security update or service pack, you must connect to the appropriate Web site to download the installation files.

■ **Test the security update or service pack on test computers before performing a full deployment.**   By performing a pilot deployment, you identify any issues that might arise with the security update or service pack installation. This prevents the security update or service pack installation from causing undesired side effects on the target computers or network.

■ **Use the appropriate tools to deploy the security update or service pack.**   The tools that you choose for deploying security update or service pack will determine the administrative effort required for the deployment.

■ **Validate the installation of the security update or service pack.** Once you complete the installation of the security update or service pack, you must ensure that the security update or service pack is installed correctly on the target computers.

Additional Information

■ Microsoft Security Notification Service (*http://www.microsoft.com/technet/security/bulletin/notify.asp*)

■ Microsoft TechNet Security Web site (*http://www.microsoft.com/technet/security/default.asp*)

■ "Managing Security Hotfixes" article from the July 2002 issue of *Windows & .NET Magazine* (*http://www.microsoft.com/technet/security/tips/sechotfx.asp*)

■ *Security Operations Guide for Windows 2000 Server*, Chapter 5, "Patch Management" (*http://www.microsoft.com/technet/security/prodtech/windows/windows2000/staysecure/secops05.asp*)

■ NTBugtraq Web site (*http://www.ntbugtraq.com*)

■ 262841, "Windows 2000 Hotfix.exe Program Description and Command-Line Switches"

■ 296861, "Use QChain.exe to Install Multiple Hotfixes with Only One Reboot"

> **Note** The previous two articles can be accessed through the Microsoft Knowledge Base. Go to *http://support.microsoft.com* and enter the article number in the Search The Knowledge Base text box.

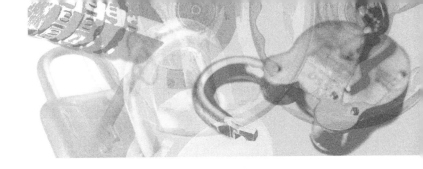

23

Using Patch Management Tools

Several tools allow you to apply Microsoft Windows patches and determine patch deployment status. This chapter looks at available patch management tools, describes how they operate, and provides recommendations on when to utilize each of them.

Currently, several organizations manually distribute service packs and security updates. Although you can script update deployments, you often end up falling behind in security update distribution, leaving your computers vulnerable. In addition, when manually installing security updates, it is possible to overwrite an updated executable or dynamic-link library (DLL) file with an older version if the security updates are not applied in the correct order.

Using the QChain Tool

The QChain tool allows you to install multiple security updates without having to reboot between installations. The QChain tool evaluates the drivers, DLLs, and executable files updated by each security update and ensures that only the most recent versions of the files are maintained after reboot.

To use the QChain tool, you must create a batch file for the security update installation. The batch file looks something like the sample shown on the following page.

(continued)

Using the QChain Tool   *(continued)*

```
@echo off
setlocal
set PATHTOFIXES=c:\patches
%PATHTOFIXES%\Q123456_w2k_sp2_x86.exe -z -m
%PATHTOFIXES%\Q123321_w2k_sp2_x86.exe -z -m
%PATHTOFIXES%\Q123789_w2k_sp2_x86.exe -z -m
%PATHTOFIXES%\qchain.exe
```

The batch file installs each security update with the -z switch to prevent reboots after each security update installation and uses the -m switch to enable unattended installs. Once all updates are installed, the QChain tool is executed to ensure that only the most current versions of updated files are maintained.

QChain is not required if you are deploying security updates to Microsoft Windows XP or Microsoft Windows 2000 computers with Service Pack 3 or later because QChain functionality is built into these versions.

To reduce the cost of deploying security updates and patches, many companies use tools to automatically deploy security updates. Microsoft's current roster of security patch management tools includes the following:

- Windows Update

- Automatic Updates

- Microsoft Software Update Services (SUS)

- Microsoft Baseline Security Analyzer (MBSA)

- Microsoft Systems Management Server (SMS) Software Update Services Feature Pack

You must understand that the catalog used by these tools determines which security patches are installed on target computers and, more importantly, which security patches are required by the target computer.

The Security Patch Bulletin Catalog

All the available patch management tools discussed in this chapter utilize the Security Patch Bulletin Catalog (MSSecure.xml) to determine which security updates are installed and which are required on target computers. Every time a patch management tool is executed, it automatically downloads the latest version of MSSecure.xml to ensure that you check for the application of the latest security bulletins.

> **Note**   If you implement a custom tool for managing software patches or if you must execute a patch management tool from a computer not connected to the Internet, you can download, to another computer, the latest version of the Security Patch Bulletin Catalog in the cabinet (.cab) file format from *http://www.microsoft.com/technet/security/search/ mssecure.cab*. The cabinet format is digitally signed by Microsoft to identify whether it is modified, and it provides proof that you have the legitimate version of the latest security patch bulletin catalog.

The following code sample shows the entry for MS02-010, a security patch that protects against a buffer overflow attack against Microsoft Commerce Server 2000. The MSSecure.xml file contains a section named <Bulletins> that provides all available bulletins included in the file:

```
<Bulletin BulletinID="MS02-010" BulletinLocationID="73" FAQLocationID="73"
    FAQPageName="FQ02-010" Title="Unchecked Buffer in ISAPI Filter Could
    Allow Commerce Server Compromise" DatePosted="2002/02/21"
    DateRevised="2002/02/21" Supported="Yes" Summary="A security
    vulnerability results because AuthFilter contains an unchecked buffer
    in a section of code that handles certain types of authentication
    requests. An attacker who provided authentication data that overran the
    buffer could cause the Commerce Server process to fail, or could run
    code in the security context of the Commerce Server process. The
    process runs with LocalSystem privileges, so exploiting the
    vulnerability would give the attacker complete control of the server."
    Issue="" ImpactSeverityID="0" PreReqSeverityID="0" MitigationSeverityID="0"
    PopularitySeverityID="0">
    <BulletinComments />
    <QNumbers>
        <QNumber QNumber="Q317615" />
    </QNumbers>
    <Patches>
        <Patch PatchName="tempcs" PatchLocationID="73" SBID="0"
            SQNumber="Q317615" NoReboot="0">
            <PatchComments />
            <AffectedProduct ProductID="127" FixedInSP="0">
                <AffectedServicePack ServicePackID="168" />
            </AffectedProduct>
        </Patch>
    </Patches>
</Bulletin>
```

> **Note**   We do not expect you to memorize the syntax of the MSSecure.xml file. This example is provided to allow you to see what information is provided in the file for patch tools to determine whether a security update is applied on a target computer.

The <Bulletin BulletinID="MS02-010"> line provides detailed information on the security bulletin related to the MS02-010 security patch. The line includes a summary of the security vulnerability as well as the ratings of the security bulletin. The line also includes the BulletinLocationID and FAQLocationID references, which indicate where the security bulletin can be acquired. These two location IDs reference location ID "73", which is detailed in a later section of the MSSecure.xml file:

```
<Locations>
    <Location LocationID="73"
        Path="http://www.microsoft.com/technet/security/bulletin"
        AbsolutePath="False" />
</Locations>
```

The <QNumbers> section details the Microsoft Knowledge Base article or articles detailing the security vulnerability. In this case, the security vulnerability is detailed in 317615, "Unchecked Buffer in ISAPI Filter May Allow Commerce Server Compromise."

The <Patches> section details specific patches required to protect against a security vulnerability. The <Patches> section includes information on the affected products (in this case, ProductID="127") and the affected service pack level (ServicePackID="168".) These two numbers also reference sections appearing later in the MSSecure.xml file:

```
<Products>
    <Product ProductID="127" Name="Commerce Server 2000"
        MinimumSupportedServicePackID="167" CurrentServicePackID="168"
        CurrentVersion="">
        <ProductFamilies />
        <AvailableSPs>
            <AvailableSP ServicePackID="167" />
            <AvailableSP ServicePackID="168" />
        </AvailableSPs>
    </Product>
</Products>
```

As with most security patches, the MS02-010 security patch is dependent upon the service pack level at the target computer. In the <Bulletins> section, the MS02-010 security update entry indicates that the affected ServicePackID is "168". In the <Products> section, the entry for Commerce Server 2000 indicates that two ServicePackIDs are available: "167" and "168". The actual names of these service pack levels are detailed in the <ServicePacks> section of the MSSecure.xml file:

```
<ServicePacks>
    <ServicePack ServicePackID="167" Name="Commerce Server 2000 Gold"
        URL="" ReleaseDate="" />
    <ServicePack ServicePackID="168" Name="Commerce Server 2000 SP2" URL=""
        ReleaseDate="" />
</ServicePacks>
```

Based on this information, you can see that the MS02-010 security update requires the application of Commerce Server 2000 Service Pack 2.

> **Note**   Once a security patch is released, it can be updated later. The <Bulletin> line includes information on the date the security patch was released as well as the date it was revised, if revision was required. Typically, the summary of the bulletin is updated to reflect which modifications were performed to the security patch.

Windows Update

Microsoft Windows Update is a Web-based application that enables you to determine whether new updates are required for your computer. You can use Windows Update by connecting to the Windows Update Web site at *http://windowsupdate.microsoft.com*.

Windows Update can determine necessary security updates and service packs for the following Windows operating systems:

- Microsoft Windows 98
- Microsoft Windows 98 Second Edition
- Microsoft Windows 2000 Professional

- Microsoft Windows 2000 Server

- Microsoft Windows 2000 Advanced Server

- Microsoft Windows Me

- Microsoft Windows XP

- Microsoft Windows Server 2003 family

To use the Windows Update site, the following requirements must be met:

- **Microsoft Internet Explorer must enable cookies.** The Windows Update site uses cookies to track and record security patch installation data. Windows Update identifies your computer by generating a globally unique identifier (GUID), which is stored in a cookie. The cookie contains the following information to identify your computer:

  - ❑ The OS version for determining security patches related to your OS and service pack level

  - ❑ The Internet Explorer version for determining Internet Explorer version-specific updates

  - ❑ The version number for other software that can be updated by Windows Update, including Windows Media Player and Microsoft SQL Server

  - ❑ The Plug and Play identification numbers of hardware devices to identify required hardware device driver updates

  - ❑ The region and language settings to determine whether a localized version of a security patch must be installed

- **Internet Explorer must allow Microsoft ActiveX controls.** The Windows Update site downloads an ActiveX control to determine which security patches are required by your computer. To enable the download of the ActiveX control, the security settings for the Internet zone in Internet Explorer must be set to Medium or lower.

- **The person running the ActiveX control must be a member of the local Administrators group.** Only members of the local Administrators group have the necessary permissions to scan the file system and registry to determine whether a security update is installed. In addition, only members of the local Administrators group have the necessary permissions to install security updates.

To use Windows Update to scan for required security updates and other patches for your OS and applications, following these steps:

1. Ensure that you are logged on as a local administrator. As we mentioned, only members of the local Administrators group have permissions to download and install updates from the Windows Update site.

2. Open Microsoft Internet Explorer and connect to *http://windowsupdate. microsoft.com*. You must use Internet Explorer because the Windows Update site uses an ActiveX control to determine which updates your computer requires. If prompted, click Yes to download the latest version of the Windows Update ActiveX control.

3. In the Welcome To Windows Update page, click Scan For Updates. Based on your OS and current updates, the Windows Update site will determine which updates are required.

4. In the Pick Updates To Install page, click Review And Install Updates. This option will allow you to pick exactly which updates to apply during this connection to the Windows Update site.

5. In the Total Selected Updates page, critical updates are automatically populated in the selected updates list. Some updates might require separate installation, so be sure to scan the list of proposed updates. You can remove individual updates by clicking the Remove button. You can add Windows 2000 or driver updates to the list by clicking Windows 2000 or Driver Updates in the left-hand pane and clicking the Add button for individual updates in the details pane (as shown in Figure 23-1).

6. Once you have selected all updates to apply to your computer, click Review And Install Updates.

7. In the Total Selected Updates page, click Install Now.

8. In the Microsoft Windows Update—Web Page Dialog box, read the Windows Update license agreement and click Accept to accept it. The selected updates are installed from the Windows Update site. Once the download is complete, the installation proceeds.

9. When all updates are installed, a listing will appear indicating which updates were successfully installed and which, if any, were not. Once you review the list, you typically must restart the computer by clicking OK in the Microsoft Internet Explorer dialog box.

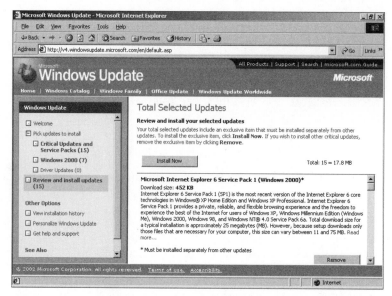

Figure 23-1   Choosing which critical updates, Windows 2000 updates, or driver updates are applied to a computer

Automatic Updates

In Windows XP and on computers running Windows 2000 with Service Pack 3, you can take advantage of Automatic Updates to apply security updates. In Windows XP, Automatic Updates is configured in the property pages of the Control Panel's System applet. On Windows 2000–based computers, the application of Service Pack 3 adds the Automatic Updates applet to the Control Panel, as shown in Figure 23-2.

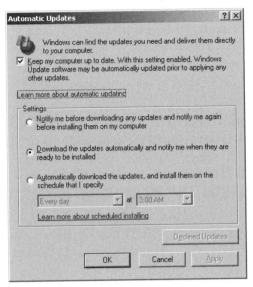

Figure 23-2   Scheduling the download and application of Windows
updates by using Automatic Updates

The Automatic Updates application simplifies the maintenance of Windows 2000 and Windows XP updates by connecting to the Windows Update site and determining whether your computer requires any updates. Specifically, you can configure the following options:

■   Enable or disable Automatic Updates. You can choose whether to keep your computer's updates current by using Automatic Updates.

■   **Define how Automatic Updates are applied.**   You can choose from three options:

  ❏   **Notify Me Before Downloading Any Updates And Notify Me Again Before Installing Them On My Computer**   Notifies you before downloading an update application. This option allows you to choose when to download updates as well as which updates to apply once the downloads are complete.

❑ **Download The Updates Automatically And Notify Me When They Are Ready To Be Installed**   Automatically downloads required updates as background tasks. When updates are downloaded, you are notified that they are ready to be installed. This provides you with the opportunity to review updates and choose which ones to apply.

❑ **Automatically Download The Updates And Install Them On The Schedule That I Specify**   Automates the download and application of updates. Updates are installed based on the schedule configured in the Automatic Updates applet.

As with all Windows updates, the computer might require a restart to finish the update application. If you are currently logged on to the computer, you will be notified of the pending restart and provided with the option of delaying the restart.

Microsoft Software Update Services

Microsoft Software Update Services (SUS) leverages the Windows Update and Automatic Updates technology to allow a company to choose which updates to apply. Rather than connecting to the Windows Update site for the download of security patches and Windows updates, clients connect to an internal SUS server that issues only approved updates.

How SUS Works

Microsoft SUS depends on the interaction of the Microsoft SUS server and Microsoft SUS clients. The following process is used to deploy security updates via SUS:

1. The SUS server is configured to synchronize its available updates with either the Windows Update site or with another SUS server on the corporate network. The synchronization can be scheduled or initiated manually by the SUS administrator.

2. The SUS administrator reviews the list of available updates at the SUS server and approves the updates for distribution. Updates should be approved only after being tested on network computers.

3. SUS clients connect to the SUS server and download any approved updates but do not download installed updates. Depending on the SUS client configuration, updates either are installed automatically or require a member of the local Administrators group to initiate installation.

4. SUS clients send information to a configured SUS statistics server. This information details whether the updates were successfully applied to the client computer.

> **Note**   SUS can be used only for the application of updates to the Windows OS and supported applications. You cannot deploy service packs by using SUS.

Configuring the SUS Server

To configure the computer designated as the SUS server, you must first install the SUS server software. The SUS server software is a free download available at *http://www.microsoft.com/Windows2000/downloads/recommended/susserver/*.

Installing the SUS Server Software

Once you download the SUSSetup.msi file, you must ensure that the SUS server has the minimally required software. The SUS server application is a Web-based application and requires Internet Explorer 5.5 or later, in addition to the following Microsoft Internet Information Services (IIS) components for installation:

- Common Files
- Internet Information Services Snap-In
- World Wide Web Service

> **Warning**   The SUS server cannot be installed on a domain controller. This requirement prevents the installation of an SUS server in a Microsoft Small Business Server (SBS) environment.

Once the SUS server has the required IIS components as well as the latest service packs and updates, you can install the software there by using the following process:

1. At the SUS server, double-click the SUSSetup.msi file.

2. On the Welcome screen, click Next.

3. Read and accept the End User License Agreement (EULA) and click Next.

4. In the Installation Type page, click Typical and then click Next.

5. Record the URL that SUS clients must connect to when interacting with the SUS server and click Install.

6. The SUS server setup then executes the IIS Lockdown tool. The IIS Lockdown tool removes the IIS Administration Web site and templates from the SUS server, disables all scripting mappings except for Microsoft Active Server Pages (ASP), disables Web-Based Distributed Authoring and Versioning (WebDAV), and prevents the anonymous Web user account from executing system utilities and writing Web content. The scripting mappings are enforced by the URLScan Internet Server Application Programming Interface (ISAPI) filter.

7. The installation completes and provides a URL for the SUS Administration Web pages.

Defining SUS Server Options

Once you install the SUS server, the best practice is to configure its options. You can define the server's options by connecting to the SUS Administration Web page at *http://SUSServerFQDN/susadmin* (where *SUSServerFQDN* is the fully qualified domain name of the SUS server) and then clicking the Set Options link. The Set Options Web page allows you to define the following options for the SUS server:

- **Proxy server configuration**   If the SUS server is on a network protected by a Microsoft Internet Security and Acceleration (ISA) Server or another vendor's proxy server, you must designate the proxy server configuration information. This can include the name, the listening port, and any required credential information for the proxy server.

- **SUS server name**   This is the name that SUS clients use when connecting to the SUS server. We recommend you use a Domain Name System (DNS) name rather than a NetBIOS name so that DNS is used to resolve the SUS server name—rather than Windows Internet Name Service (WINS).

- **Master server**   You can designate whether the SUS server synchronizes its content with the Microsoft Windows Update server or connects to another SUS server on your network.

- **Approval settings**   You can choose to approve all updates automatically or manually.

- **Storage and locale information**   You can choose to store updates on the SUS server's local file system or to connect to the Windows Update server for the download of all updates. In addition, you can choose which locales to download updates for, such as English, Arabic, or Japanese.

Synchronizing the SUS Server

Installing SUS server software adds the Software Update Services Synchronization Service. This service allows the SUS server to synchronize update content with either the Microsoft Windows Update Web site or with another SUS server in your company.

To modify synchronization settings for an SUS server, you must perform the following procedure:

1. Connect to the SUS Administration Web page at *http://SUSServerFQDN/ susadmin* (where *SUSServerFQDN* is the fully qualified domain name of the SUS server).

2. Click the Synchronize Server link.

3. If you want to perform a manual synchronization of the SUS server, click Synchronize Now. If you want to schedule standard synchronization times for the SUS server, click Synchronization Schedule.

4. In the Schedule Synchronization dialog box (see Figure 23-3), specify the time for the scheduled update, whether you want to synchronize daily or weekly, and how to many times to retry a synchronization in the event of a failure. Once you configure your required settings, click OK.

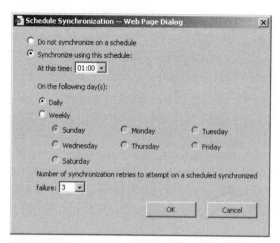

Figure 23-3   Defining the synchronization schedule for the SUS server

Approving Updates

Once you synchronize the SUS server, you must define which updates are approved for distribution to SUS clients. When you click the Approve Updates link in the SUS Administration Web site, you are presented with all the available updates.

After testing the updates on your network—either by testing the update distribution on a pilot network or performing a test on your computer—you must select all updates you want to distribute to SUS clients in the listing and click the Approve button.

Warning   You cannot select which SUS clients will receive a security update. All SUS clients that connect to your SUS server will receive the security update if they are running software that requires it. If you want to apply a security update to a subset of clients, you must use an alternate solution such as Microsoft Systems Management Server (SMS), as described later in this chapter.

Configuring the SUS Clients

SUS requires that client computers have the Automatic Updates client loaded. As mentioned earlier in this chapter, the Automatic Updates client is automatically installed on Windows 2000–based computers with Service Pack 3 and on

Windows XP–based computers. If you are running Windows 2000–based computers that do not have Service Pack 3 or a later version, you can download the SUS client software from *http://www.microsoft.com/windows2000/downloads/ recommended/susclient/.*

Configuration in an Active Directory Environment

Once you deploy the Automatic Update client, you can configure it by using Group Policy. The Automatic Update client settings are included in the Wuau.adm policy template, which is automatically added to the %systemroot%\inf folder when you apply Service Pack 3 to a computer running the Windows 2000 operating system. The inclusion of the policy template adds Administrative Templates settings for Windows Update, as shown in Figure 23-4.

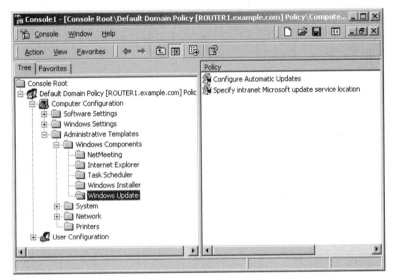

Figure 23-4   Configuring Windows Update settings in Group Policy

Once you have added the Wuau.adm policy template, you can configure two settings to assist with your SUS deployment:

- **Configure Automatic Updates**   Allows you to specify the Automatic Update client settings. As mentioned earlier, we recommend you automatically download updates from the SUS server and schedule the install.

- **Specify Intranet Microsoft Update Service Location**   Allows you to designate an SUS server as the update service for detecting updates, rather than using the default Microsoft Windows Update servers. In addition, you can designate an internal server to which statistics for Windows Update are sent. The statistics server must be running IIS. The statistics sent to the server will be stored in the IIS logs.

Configuration in a Non–Active Directory Environment

In a non–Active Directory environment, you can designate SUS client settings by editing the registry. Registry updates can be applied by manually editing the registry or deploying registry keys.

To define Automatic Update settings, you must add the following registry values to the HKLM\Software\Policies\Microsoft\Windows\WindowsUpdate\AU registry key:

- **NoAutoUpdate (Reg_DWORD)**   Allows you to enable (0) or disable (1) Automatic Updates. If not specified, the default value is Enable (0).

- **AUOptions (Reg_DWORD)**   Defines how updates are downloaded and installed. You can choose to be notified for both downloads and installations (2), automatically perform downloads and be notified for installations (3), or automatically perform downloads and installations using a predefined schedule (4).

- **ScheduledInstallDay (Reg_DWORD)**   Defines the days on which the scheduled installation of Automatic Updates takes place. You can specify that the installation occur every day (0) or on a specific day between Sunday (1) and Saturday (7).

- **ScheduledInstallTime (Reg_DWORD)**   Defines the hour the scheduled installation of Automatic Updates takes place. Values ranging from 0 to 23 are based on the 24-hour day.

- **UseWUServer (Reg_DWORD)**   Indicates whether the Automatic Update client will contact an SUS server, rather than contacting the Windows Update site. A value of 1 indicates that updates will be determined by connecting to an SUS server.

If you enable the SUS client to contact an SUS server, you must designate a server to act as the SUS server, and you must designate where statistics information will be sent. These statistics are stored in the HKLM\Software\Policies\Microsoft\Windows\WindowsUpdate registry key:

- **WUServer (Reg_SZ)**   This defines the URL of the SUS server. To designate the SUS server in the example.com domain as the SUS server, you would enter a value of **http://sus.example.com**, for example.

- **WUStatusServer (Reg_SZ)**   This defines the URL for the SUS statistics server. As with WUServer, you must enter the value in a URL format.

Microsoft Baseline Security Analyzer

The Microsoft Baseline Security Analyzer (MBSA) is a tool that can determine which critical updates are installed on a target computer, as well as which security updates are required. MBSA allows you to target the current computer, a remote computer, a specified list of computers, a range of IP addresses, or all computers in a designated domain. The tool will scan computers for an update status based on a downloaded XML catalog file and will report the status in output files or to the screen.

MBSA allows scanning for common security misconfiguration errors on target computers. MBSA reports only on the current status of the computer and does not provide you with any distribution functionality. Once a computer is analyzed, other tools must be used to deploy the missing service packs and updates. Otherwise, the missing service packs and updates must be manually downloaded and installed.

> **Note**   To run MBSA, a user must be a local administrator on the target computer. This prevents attackers from using MBSA to scan a remote computer to determine potential weaknesses.

MBSA version 1.1 scans for the latest service packs and security updates for the following products:

- Microsoft Windows NT 4.0, Windows 2000, and Windows XP

- IIS 4.0 and IIS 5.0

- SQL Server 7 and SQL Server 2000 (including Microsoft Data Engine)

- Internet Explorer 5.01 or later

- Windows Media Player 6.4 or later

- Microsoft Exchange Server 5.5 and Exchange 2000 Server (including Exchange Admin Tools)

> **Note**   In addition to scanning for service pack and security updates, MBSA scans for common security-related configuration issues and stores the results of the scans in XML format files. However, MBSA does not scan for security configuration issues for Exchange Server or for Windows Media Player. For these products, the MBSA only scans for security updates.

What About HfNetChk?

MBSA version 1.1 includes the same functionality provided by Shavlik's hotfix network checker (HfNetChk) tool, meaning that Microsoft no longer provides updates to the HfNetChk tool. You can still download and use the HfNetChk tool from the Shavlik Web site to scan for security updates. The functionality is the same as MBSA's command-line version. Because Microsoft no longer provides updates to the HfNetChk tool, we recommend you visit the Shavlik Web site for updates.

In addition, Shavlik produces a full-feature version of the tool, known as HfNetChkpro, which provides a GUI interface and allows the distribution and installation of missing security updates after the initial scan. For more information on Shavlik tools for security updates, see *http://www.shavlik.com*.

Scanning for Updates in the GUI Mode

By default, MBSA runs in a GUI mode that allows you to define scanning options and view the results of the security scan in the MBSA window. The security update scan performed by MBSA only scans and reports on updates designated as critical security updates by the Windows Update site.

> **Note**   If you enable the option to use an SUS server, MBSA does not download the updates from the SUS server. Instead, MBSA will report only updates approved at the SUS server in its XML report for the target computer.

When scanning for security updates, perform the following procedure:

1. Open MBSA.

2. Choose whether to scan a single computer or multiple computers.

3. To scan for security updates only, designate your target computer or computers as shown in Figure 23-5, enable the Check For Security Updates option, and click Start Scan.

4. When the scan is complete, you can view an XML file for each computer. For each computer, the output will report any missing security updates for Windows, IIS, Windows Media Player, Exchange Server, and SQL Server, as well as give a security assessment rating for the target computer.

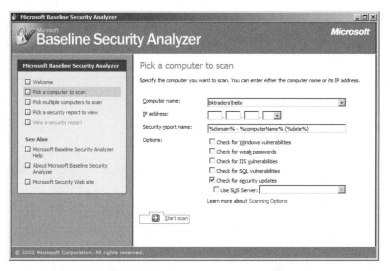

Figure 23-5   Scanning for security updates with MBSA

Security scan reports are stored in the %userprofile%\SecurityScans folder at the computer where MBSA is executed. The reports are in an XML format and are best viewed in the MBSA interface.

More Info   For details on using MBSA for performing security audits, see Chapter 24, "Using Security Assessment Tools."

Scanning for Updates with the Command-Line Version of MBSA

MBSA includes a command-line version executable, Mbsacli.exe, which can perform scans for security updates and service packs. Version 1.1 of the Mbsacli.exe utility can perform the same tests performed by Shavlik's HfNetChk.exe utility.

When you execute Mbsacli.exe with the /hf switch, indicating an HfNetChk -style scan, all security-related updates are included in the scan and the resulting reports. The results of the Mbsacli.exe scan are displayed in the command window, rather than in XML files.

When scanning for security updates with the Mbsacli.exe /hf command, you can use the following parameters:

- **-h *hostname***   Scans the computer designated by the NetBIOS computer name. If not included, the local host is scanned. Multiple computers can be scanned by separating each host name with a comma.

- **-fh *filename***   Scans the computer names specified in the named text file. The text file must contain one computer name per line, with a maximum of 256 names.

- **-i *xxx.xxx.xxx.xxx***   Scans the designated IP address. You can designate multiple IP addresses by separating each entry with a comma.

- **-fip *filename***   Scans the IP addresses designated in the named text file. The text file must contain one IP address per line, with a maximum of 256 IP addresses.

- **-r *xxx.xxx.xxx.xxx–xxx.xxx.xxx.xxx***   Specifies a range of IP addresses to be scanned.

- **-d *domainname***   Specifies that all computer accounts in the designated domain name are to be scanned.

- **-b**   Scans only for critical updates, rather than for all security updates. This parameter produces the same list of required updates as the graphical version of MBSA.

- **-s 1**   Suppresses NOTE messages. NOTE messages do not include an installable executable but provide a detailed procedure that must be performed to prevent the security vulnerability associated with the update.

- **-s 2**   Suppresses WARNING messages. WARNING messages do not prescribe remedies to prevent vulnerabilities. They simply state that the usage of the specific service is considered a security weakness.

- **-nosum**   Specifies that the computer should not perform checksum validation for the security update files.

- **-z**   Specifies that the computer should not perform registry checks.

- **-v**   Displays verbose details when a security update is determined to be missing. This is useful when you receive NOTE or WARNING messages.

- **-f** *filename*   Specifies the name of a file in which to store the results.

- **-u** *username*   Specifies the user name to use when scanning a local or remote computer or groups of computers.

- **-p** *password*   Specifies the password to use when scanning a local or remote computer or groups of computers. You must use this switch with the user name switch. Note that this password is not sent over the network in cleartext. Instead, Mbsacli.exe implements NT LAN Manager (NTLM) authentication.

- **-x** *XMLfile*   Specifies an XML data source for the security scan. If not specified, the latest version of MSSecure.xml is downloaded from the Microsoft Web site.

More Info   For a complete listing of the parameters available when running Mbsacli.exe /hf, see 303215 "Microsoft Network Security Hotfix Checker (HfNetChk.exe) Tool Is Available."

SMS Software Update Services Feature Pack

The SMS Software Update Services Feature Pack provides the ability to determine the security update status for SMS clients and distribute and install the necessary updates to them. In addition, the feature pack provides reporting tools that allow the creation of detailed reports outlining your company's security update distribution.

The SMS Software Update Services Feature Pack provides stronger management capabilities than any of the other patch management solutions because it allows you to target specific computers within the company for security updates. Likewise, by leveraging the capabilities of SMS 2.0, you can perform the following:

- **Identify all computers on the network.**   SMS inventory capabilities allow you to identify all computers connected to the corporate network, identify installed applications, and determine current security updates.

- **Schedule the deployment of security updates.**   SMS software can distribute identified security updates to SMS clients during non-peak hours.

- **Enable status reporting.**   SMS queries can determine the progress of security update distribution to identify computers that have not yet received and installed critical updates.

- **Enable local distribution of updates.**   SMS allows security updates to be replicated to multiple software distribution servers. This allows clients to connect to local or nearby software distribution servers for security update installations.

- **Enable support for more operating systems.**   All SMS clients—not just Windows 2000–based and Windows XP–based computers—can receive security updates by using the SMS Software Update Services Feature Pack.

The SMS Software Update Services Feature Pack is comprised of four tools for the distribution of security and Microsoft Office software updates:

- **Security Update Inventory tool**   Creates an inventory of security updates for each SMS client computer. The inventory identifies current and missing security updates for each computer and stores the results in the SMS inventory. The Security Update Inventory tool is comprised of three components:

    - **Security Update Inventory Installer**   Runs on the SMS site server and builds the packages, collections, and advertisements to deploy other SMS tool components to SMS clients.

    - **Security Update Inventory tool**   Uses MSSecure.xml and MBSA to carry out security scans of SMS client computers for installed or required security updates. The resulting data is converted into SMS inventory data.

❑ **Security Update Sync tool**   Runs on a single computer with Internet access. This computer checks with the Windows Update Web site to download the latest MSSecure.xml file.

■ **Microsoft Office Inventory tool**   Creates an inventory of installed and required Microsoft Office updates for SMS client computers. The Microsoft Office Inventory tool consists of three components:

❑ **Office Update Inventory Installer**   Runs on the SMS site server and builds the necessary packages, collections, and advertisements to deploy the other components required for Microsoft Office updates.

❑ **Office Update Inventory tool**   Performs scans of SMS client computers for installed or required office updates. The collected information is stored as SMS inventory data.

❑ **Office Update Sync tool**   Runs on a single, Internet-accessible computer. This tool downloads the latest Office Update Inventory tool and Office Update inventory database and uses SMS distribution points to deploy the latest versions to SMS client computers.

■ **Distribute Software Updates Wizard**   Performs the software and security update distribution tasks in the SMS environment. The wizard consists of three components:

❑ **Distribute Software Updates Wizard Installer**   Runs on the SMS site server and installs the Distribute Software Updates Wizard component.

❑ **Distribute Software Updates Wizard**   Analyzes the Microsoft Office update status for all SMS client computers based on the SMS inventory information. Once the status is determined, the wizard allows you to review and authorize updates for distribution, download updates, create packages and advertisements for each update, distribute advertisements to SMS clients, and deploy the Software Updates Installation Wizard (discussed next).

❑ **Software Updates Installation Wizard**   Evaluates advertised software updates against current updates on the client computer to ensure that only required updates are installed at the SMS client computer.

- **SMS Web Reporting tool**   Provides the ability to create and view reports based on the inventory information collected by the software inventory tools. You can track the deployment of individual updates as well as the update status of a specific computer or group of computers. When this tool is used with the Web Report add-in for Software Updates, the software update inventory information can be viewed with a Web browser.

Best Practices

- **If you manually install multiple security updates on target computers, use the QChain tool.**   Doing so ensures that the most current version of any DLL or executable is retained. If the OS is either Windows XP or Windows 2000 with Service Pack 3 or later, QChain is not required because the QChain functionality is built in.

- **You must be a member of the local Administrators group of the computer to install any detected updates.**   The Windows Update Web site requires that you have this membership.

- **Configure the Automatic Updates client to implement the desired installation method.**   By doing so, you ensure that your organization's updates are downloaded and installed regularly.

- **Windows Update is appropriate only for scanning a single computer or a small group of computers.**   The scan can only be performed against the current computer.

- **MBSA allows for the diagnosis of security update status only.**   It does not provide any distribution methods.

- **Use the command-line version of MBSA to script security update reporting.**   The Mbsacli.exe tool allows you to create scripts that scan a single computer, an IP range, or an entire domain for security update status.

- **SUS can be used only to distribute security updates, not service packs.**   You must use methods such as Microsoft SMS, scripts, or Group Policy to automatically distribute service packs.

- **Use the SMS Software Update Services Feature Pack to deploy software patches to a subset of computers on your network.**   Only the SMS Software Update Services Feature Pack allows you to define specific targets for software patch deployment, allowing you to pick and choose targets for patch deployment.

■ **Both SUS and the SMS Software Update Services Feature Pack provide reporting on the status of software patch deployment.** Because of the data stored in SMS inventory, the SMS Software Update Services Feature Pack can produce more detailed reports.

■ **SUS can only support up to 15,000 client computers.** If you must support more than 5000 computers, consider using the SMS Software Update Services Feature Pack or other third-party security update deployment software.

Additional Information

■ Microsoft Software Update Services Web site (*http://www.microsoft.com/windows2000/windowsupdate/sus/default.asp*)

■ Software Update Services Flash Demo (*http://www.microsoft.com/windows2000/windowsupdate/sus/flashpage.asp*)

■ Software Update Services Overview" white paper (*http://www.microsoft.com/windows2000/windowsupdate/sus/susoverview.asp*)

■ Software Update Services Deployment" white paper (*http://www.microsoft.com/windows2000/windowsupdate/sus/susdeployment.asp*)

■ SMS Software Update Services Feature Pack (*http://www.microsoft.com/SMServer/downloads/20/featurepacks/suspack/default.asp*)

■ SMS Software Update Services Deployment Guide (*http://www.microsoft.com/technet/prodtechnol/sms/deploy/confeat/smsfpdep.asp*)

■ Microsoft Baseline Security Analyzer home page (*http://www.microsoft.com/technet/security/tools/Tools/MBSAhome.asp*)

■ Shavlik Technologies (*http://www.shavlik.com*)

■ Microsoft Windows Update Web site (*http://windowsupdate.microsoft.com*)

■ 303215: "Microsoft Network Security Hotfix Checker (HfNetChk.exe) Tool Is Available"

- 320454: "Microsoft Baseline Security Analyzer (MBSA) Version 1.1 Is Available"

- 296861: "Use QChain.exe to Install Multiple Hotfixes with Only One Reboot"

> **Note**   The previous three articles can be accessed through the Microsoft Knowledge Base. Go to *http://support.microsoft.com* and enter the article number in the Search The Knowledge Base text box.

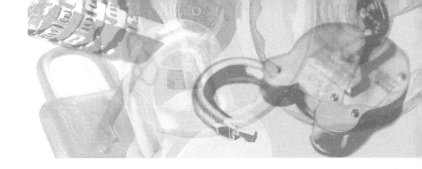

24

Using Security Assessment Tools

Once you have implemented a security baseline configuration on your Microsoft Windows 2000 computers, you should periodically review the security configuration by using security assessment tools. These tools allow an administrator to perform two separate yet related tasks:

- **Identify when computers deviate from the established security baseline.** Security assessment tools can identify when a computer's configuration has been modified, which would result in weaker overall security of the host.

- **Identify new risks to computers.** Assessment software can scan for newly discovered vulnerabilities by detecting whether recent hotfixes have been applied or by determining that recommended security configurations have not been implemented on scanned hosts.

This chapter discusses how to implement security assessment tools to perform these tasks.

Assessing Security Configuration

Windows 2000 and Windows XP allow you to define security configuration settings in security templates. These templates contain security configuration settings for a computer account, either by applying the security template settings to the local computer directly or by importing them into a Group Policy object (GPO). Importing the security template into a GPO linked to the OU where the computer account is located ensures consistent application of security template settings to all computers affected by the GPO.

Security templates applied by using a GPO can be affected by other GPOs and the local security policy applied to the computer account. Local policies and GPOs are processed in the following order:

1. Any local security policies defined for the local computer.

2. Any GPOs defined for the site where the computer is located.

3. Any GPOs defined for the domain in which the computer account exists.

4. Any GPOs defined in the OU in which the computer account exists. GPOs are applied based on where they exist in the OU structure, with the GPOs applied at the OU where the computer account resides located last.

> **Note** If multiple GPOs are defined at a Group Policy container, GPOs are applied based on their order in the site's Group Policy tab. The GPO at the top of the list is applied last, ensuring that if conflicts exist, the GPO at the top takes precedence.

In addition to the default Group Policy inheritance model, the Resultant Set of Policies (RSoP)—the effective policies applied to the computer or user after all local policies and group policies are applied—can be affected by the No Override and Block Policy Inheritance settings at the Group Policy container.

To determine whether security policy matches the security template, you can use one of two tools to analyze the computer's security configuration:

- The Security Configuration and Analysis console
- The Secedit command-line utility

The Security Configuration and Analysis Console

You can use the Security Configuration and Analysis console to determine whether the RSoPs applied to a computer differ from those defined in a security template.

When performing a security analysis, you import the security settings defined in one or more security templates into an analysis database. When you import the security templates, you can merge the template settings and create a composite security template. The order in which you import the security templates is important. As with GPOs, the settings of the last imported security template take precedence if settings in different security templates conflict.

> **More Info**   For information on creating custom security templates to enforce security settings, see Chapter 11, "Configuring Security Templates."

To analyze current security settings of a local computer by using the Security Configuration and Analysis console, follow these steps:

1. Open a blank MMC and add the Security Configuration and Analysis console.

2. In the console tree, right-click Security Configuration And Analysis and click Open Database.

3. In Open Database, create a new database by entering a name in the File Name field. Then click Open.

4. In the Import Template window, select the security template that defines the required settings for the computer and click Open.

5. In the details pane, right-click Security Configuration And Analysis and click Analyze Computer Now.

6. In the error log file path, click OK to create a log file in the default location.

When the analysis is complete, the Security Configuration and Analysis console displays the results, as shown in Figure 24-1.

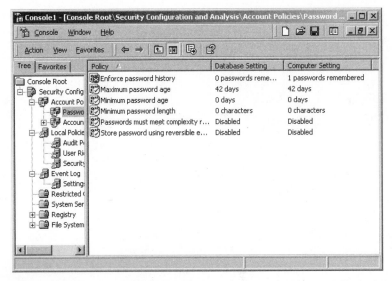

Figure 24-1 Analysis results of the Security Configuration and Analysis console

The console uses the icons shown in Table 24-1 to describe how well the security template settings are enforced at the analyzed computer.

Table 24-1 Using the Output of the Security Configuration and Analysis Console

Icon	Description
Red X	The entry is defined in the analysis database and on the system, but the security setting values do not match.
Green check	The entry is defined in the analysis database and on the system, and the setting values match.
Question mark	The entry is not defined in the analysis database and therefore is not analyzed. This occurs when a setting is not defined in the analysis database or when the user running the analysis does not have sufficient permissions.
Exclamation point	This item is defined in the analysis database but does not exist on the actual system.
No highlight	The item is not defined in the analysis database or on the system.

> **Warning**   A red X does not necessarily indicate a security configuration weakness. The actual system can be configured more securely than the security level indicated by settings of the security template. For example, in Figure 24-1, the Enforce Password History setting indicates a mismatch between the security template and the actual computer configuration. In the security template, no passwords are kept in the password history, whereas the computer's current configuration does not allow a password to be reused when a user must change his password.

The Secedit.exe Command-Line Utility

The Secedit.exe utility includes all the analysis functionality of the Security Configuration and Analysis console. To use the Secedit utility to analyze whether a computer implements the security settings defined in a security template, use the following syntax:

```
secedit /analyze /db DBFileName /CFG SecurityTemplate /log LogPath /verbose
```

This command is comprised of the following parts:

- **/analyze**   Indicates that Secedit will compare the current security settings of the local computer against the security settings defined in *SecurityTemplate*.

- **/db *DBFileName***   Determines the analysis database file into which the *SecurityTemplate* settings are imported. You must indicate the full path to the security analysis database.

- **/cfg *SecurityTemplate***   Indicates one or more security template files to import into the security analysis database. You must indicate the full path to the security template file or files. This option is not required if the security analysis database exists and the desired security template is already imported.

- **/log *LogPath***   Provides the path to the folder where the log file is generated for security analysis.

- **/verbose**   Enables verbose output during the security analysis.

Once the Secedit command process is complete, you can view the results in the Security Configuration and Analysis console by opening the database file referenced in the Secedit command in the Security Configuration and Analysis console.

Performing Security Assessments

In addition to comparing the security configuration of your Windows computers with the baseline security settings defined in security templates, you should assess your computers for common security misconfigurations. You can use different tools for security assessments, including the following:

■   **Microsoft Baseline Security Analyzer (MBSA)**   Analyzes common security misconfigurations.

■   **Third-party security tools**   Tools such as the Internet Security Systems (ISS) Security Scanner or the eEye Retina Network Security Scanner can detect common vulnerabilities.

■   **Port scanners**   Determine which available server ports are exposed to the Internet.

Microsoft Baseline Security Analyzer

The MBSA tool allows you to assess the security configuration of one or more Windows-based computers. MBSA performs two major tasks:

■   Scans for missing service packs and security updates. MBSA uses Shavlik HfNetChk version 3.81 to determine which hotfixes and service packs are not applied to a target computer. The MBSA tool can also filter the list of missing updates and service packs based on approved updates configured at a Microsoft Software Update Services (SUS) server.

> **More Info**   For more information on using the Mbsacli.exe command-line tool to determine which service packs and security updates are applied, please see Chapter 23, "Using Patch Management Tools."

■   Scans the Windows OS, Microsoft Internet Information Services (IIS), Microsoft SQL Server, desktop applications, Windows Media Player, and Microsoft Exchange Server for common security misconfigurations.

Tests Performed

The MBSA tool can be executed from both a GUI and from the command line. Both versions of MBSA perform the tests outlined in this section.

Security Update Checks   MBSA performs checks for security updates and service packs released for the following Windows operating systems, Windows components, and applications:

- Microsoft Windows NT 4.0

- Microsoft Windows 2000

- Microsoft Windows XP

- Microsoft Internet Explorer version 5.01 and later

- Windows Media Player 6.4 and later

- IIS 4.0 and 5.0

- SQL Server 7.0 and SQL Server 2000

- Exchange Server 5.5 and Exchange 2000 Server

Windows OS Tests   MBSA will perform various OS security checks for Windows NT 4.0, Windows 2000, and Windows XP target computers. The specific tests include the following:

- **Administrators group membership**   MBSA identifies and lists all members of the local Administrators group. If more than two accounts are detected, MBSA reports a potential vulnerability.

- **Auditing**   MBSA determines whether auditing is enabled at the target computer. The tool does not look for specific audit settings—it only ensures that some form of auditing is enabled.

- **Auto Logon feature**   MBSA reports whether Auto Logon is enabled at a target computer. If Auto Logon is enabled, MBSA determines how user credentials are stored. If user credentials are stored in an encrypted format in the registry, the tool reports the enabling of Auto Logon as a potential vulnerability. If user credentials are stored in plaintext, the tool reports a high-level vulnerability.

- **Unnecessary services**   You can configure MBSA to scan for specific services by editing the %Systemdrive%\Program Files\Microsoft Baseline Security Analyzer\Services.txt file. MBSA will scan the target computer to determine whether any of the listed services are enabled on the target computer.

> **Note**   When adding service names to the Services.txt file,
> you must use the registry-based name of the service. You can
> find the registry-based name for each service in the properties
> of the specific service in the Services console. For example,
> the registry-based name for the World Wide Web Publishing
> service is W3SVC.

- **Domain controller identification**   MBSA identifies whether a target computer is functioning as a domain controller. This allows the scanner to identify nonauthorized domain controllers and further inspect which vulnerabilities are found at the domain controller.

- **File system**   MBSA identifies whether all the target computer's volumes use the NTFS file system. Only the NTFS file system allows for local file security by implementing discretionary access control lists (DACLs) for each file and folder on the disk volume.

> **Note**   To determine whether a remote computer implements
> the NTFS file system, the default administrative shares must be
> enabled on the target computer. For example, the C drive must
> be shared as C$.

- **Guest account**   MBSA identifies whether the Guest account is enabled on the target computer. An enabled Guest account can allow remote users to access the computer without providing credentials and will be reported as a vulnerability.

- **Local account passwords**   All passwords in the local account database are scanned to determine whether they are weak. MBSA will scan for blank passwords, passwords that match the user's account name, passwords that match the computer name, and commonly used passwords such as **password**, **admin**, or **administrator**.

- **Password expiration**   MBSA determines whether local accounts are configured with nonexpiring passwords.

- **RestrictAnonymous registry key**   MBSA determines whether the target computer restricts anonymous connections. You can allow all anonymous connections (which has an associated value of 0), prevent anonymous connections from enumerating Security Accounts Manager (SAM) accounts and names (which has an associated value of 1), or prevent all access without explicit anonymous permissions (which has an associated value of 2).

Warning   If you configure the RestrictAnonymous registry key to prevent all access without explicit anonymous permissions at a Windows 2000 domain controller, you can prevent downlevel computers from connecting to the domain controller. Downlevel members of the domain cannot set up a Netlogon secure channel for authentication, downlevel domain controllers in trusting domains cannot set up a Netlogon secure channel to allow interdomain authentication, the Browser service cannot retrieve domain and server lists from computers, Windows NT users cannot change an expired password, and Macintosh users can never change their passwords.

- **Enumerate shares**   MBSA reports all shares on the target computer. This includes both manually created shares and administrative shares. For each share, the detected share and NTFS permissions are reported.

IIS Tests   If any IIS components are installed on the target computer, MBSA performs a series of tests to detect common IIS security misconfigurations. These tests include the following:

- **IIS Lockdown tool**   MBSA determines whether the IIS Lockdown tool is used to secure the target computer.

- **Determining whether the target computer is a domain controller**   The existence of the IIS service on a domain controller is considered a high-level vulnerability, unless the target computer is a Microsoft Small Business Server (SBS).

- **IIS logging**   MBSA determines whether IIS logging is enabled on the target computer. IIS logging provides detailed information about each connection attempt to Web sites hosted on the IIS computer. The test also ensures that the World Wide Web Consortium (W3C) extended log file format is implemented.

- **IIS parent paths**   MBSA determines whether the ASPEnableParent-Paths setting is enabled on the target computer. If enabled, this setting allows attackers to use the ".."syntax in URLs, permitting them to access files not available, by default, from the Web service. (The ".." syntax attempts to access files and folders in the parent folder of the current folder.)

- **Virtual directories**   MBSA scans for Microsoft Advanced Data Connector (MSADC) and Scripts virtual directories. These directories contain sample scripts that attackers can use to compromise IIS. The tool also looks for the IISadmpwd virtual directory on IIS 4.0 target servers. This virtual directory allows users to change their Windows passwords from a Web site.

> **More Info**   Virtual directories can be removed by running the IIS Lockdown tool. For more information on the IIS Lockdown tool, please see Chapter 21, "Implementing Security for Microsoft IIS 5.0."

- **IIS sample applications**   MBSA determines whether the default IIS sample applications are installed on the target server. The sample applications provide script samples that attackers can use to compromise the target server. These sample applications can be removed by running the IIS Lockdown tool against the IIS server.

Microsoft SQL Server Checks   MBSA scans for SQL Server security configuration issues if SQL Server is detected on a target computer. SQL Server tests are run against each SQL Server instance found on the computer. The specific tests include the following:

- **Sysadmin membership**   MBSA scans the target server to identify all members of the Sysadmin role on the server running SQL Server. MBSA also determines whether the local Administrators group is assigned the Sysadmin role.

- **CmdExec rights**   MBSA ensures that only members of the Sysadmin role are assigned the CmdExec right.

- **SQL Server local account password checks**   MBSA determines whether any SQL Server accounts implement poor passwords. In addition to the checks performed for Windows OS passwords, the password check looks for a password of **SA**. The password check will also report any locked out or disabled SQL Server accounts.

- **SQL Server authentication mode**   MBSA reports whether the server running SQL Server is configured to implement Windows authentication mode or mixed mode. When Windows authentication mode is implemented, the instance of SQL Server depends on Windows authentication for all user authentication. In mixed mode, users might be authenticated by using Windows authentication or by the server running SQL Server. If authenticated by the server running SQL Server, the users' account and password pairs are maintained within the SQL Server system tables.

- **SQL Server directory permissions**   MBSA verifies that only the SQL Server service account and members of the target computer's local Administrators group have access to the following folders within the %Systemdrive%\Program Files folder:

    - Microsoft SQL Server\MSSQL$InstanceName\Binn

    - Microsoft SQL Server\MSSQL$InstanceName\Data

    - Microsoft SQL Server\MSSQL\Binn

    - Microsoft SQL Server\MSSQL\Data

- **SA password protection**   MBSA determines whether the **SA** password or SQL Server service account and password are stored in plaintext in the Setup.iss, Sqlsp.log, or Sqlstp.log files found in the %Windir%\Temp and %Temp% folders.

- **SQL Server guest account**   MBSA determines whether the Guest account is assigned access to any databases other than Master, Tempdb, and Msdb. All databases that enable Guest access are included in the security report.

- **SQL Server registry key permissions**   MBSA ensures that the Everyone group is assigned only Read permissions for the HKLM\Software\Microsoft\Microsoft SQL Server and HKLM\Software\Microsoft\MSSQLServer registry keys.

- **Service account check**   MBSA determines whether the SQL Server service account is a member of the local Administrators group or is assigned membership in the domain's Administrators or Domain Admins groups.

> **Note** If you receive a "No permission to access database" error message when scanning a server running SQL Server, the account used to execute MBSA does not have sufficient permissions for the Master database on the target SQL Server computer.

Desktop Application Checks MBSA also checks for security issues with commonly used desktop applications. Specifically, MBSA scans for the following:

- **Internet Explorer security zones** MBSA scans all defined Internet Explorer security zones and identifies zones not defined at the recommended level. We recommend you implement Medium security for the Local Intranet, Trusted Sites, and Internet zones and High security for the Restricted Sites zone.

> **Note** A custom level might be reported as a false positive by MBSA. MBSA does not evaluate individual settings within a custom security level to determine whether security meets or exceeds recommended settings.

- **Microsoft Office macro settings** MBSA issues a warning if the macro security is not at the recommended level for Office applications. You should implement High macro security for Microsoft Word, Microsoft Outlook, and Microsoft PowerPoint, and Medium macro security for Microsoft Excel.

- **Microsoft Outlook security zones** MBSA issues a warning if the Outlook security zone is not set to the recommended security level. The same recommendations for the Internet Explorer security zones apply to Outlook.

Requirements for Running MBSA

The requirements for running MBSA vary, depending on the type of scan you are performing and whether you are scanning the local computer or performing a scan against remote computers. To perform a security assessment of the local computer, the following requirements must be met:

■   The user must be a local Administrator of the target computer.

■   The computer must be running Windows 2000 or Windows XP.

■   The computer must have Internet Explorer 5.01 or later.

> **Note**   Alternatively, you can use an older version of Internet Explorer or a different Web browser if you have an XML parser installed. You can download a stand-alone version of the Microsoft XML Parser (MSXML) from *http://msdn.microsoft.com/downloads/sample.asp?url=/msdn-files/027/001/772/msdncompositedoc.xml.*

Additional requirements exist when you perform a scan of a remote computer:

■   The user must be a member of the local Administrators group on all target computers.

■   To allow remote IIS scanning, IIS Common Files must be installed on the computer running MBSA.

■   The Workstation service and the Client for Microsoft Networks must be installed.

Requirements also exist for the target computers of the MBSA scan. The remote computer must meet the following requirements:

■   The remote computer must be running Windows NT 4.0 Service Pack 4 or later, Windows 2000, or Windows XP.

■   The remote computer must have the Workstation, Server, and Remote Registry services running. In addition, File And Print Sharing must be enabled.

■   The remote computer must be running Internet Explorer 5.01 or later.

■   To inspect for IIS vulnerabilities, the target computer must be running IIS 4.0 or IIS 5.0.

■   To inspect for SQL Server vulnerabilities, the target computer must be running SQL Server 7.0 or SQL Server 2000.

■   To inspect for desktop application vulnerabilities, the target computer must be running applications from Microsoft Office 2000 or Microsoft Office XP.

Performing Graphical MBSA Assessments

The primary reason for utilizing MBSA is to run security assessments from the GUI. To perform a scan against a single computer, the following procedure can be used:

1.   On the desktop, double-click the Microsoft Baseline Security Analyzer shortcut. By default, the MBSA icon is automatically placed on the desktop upon installation.

2.   On the Welcome To The Microsoft Baseline Security Analyzer screen, click Scan A Computer.

3.   On the Pick A Computer To Scan page, you must indicate the computer name or the IP address of the computer, a name for the resulting XML report, and the specific security tests to perform, as shown in Figure 24-2.

4.   Once the options are defined, click the Start Scan link. When the scan is complete, the results of the current scan are shown in the details pane and will include an overall security assessment.

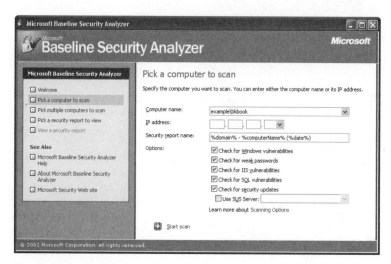

Figure 24-2   Defining scanning options for a single computer

You can choose to scan all computers in a specific domain or all computers within a specific IP subnet. The following procedure is used to scan multiple computers:

1. On the desktop, double-click the Microsoft Baseline Security Analyzer shortcut.

2. On the Welcome To The Microsoft Baseline Security Analyzer screen, click Scan More Than One Computer.

3. On the Pick Multiple Computers To Scan page, you must indicate either the domain or the IP address range to scan, a name format for the resulting XML reports, and the specific tests to perform, as shown in Figure 24-3.

4. When all options are defined, click the Start Scan link.

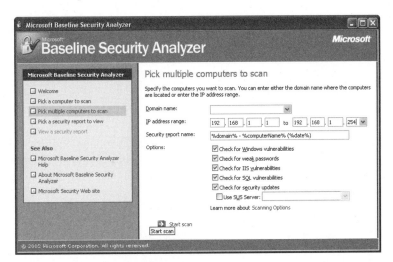

Figure 24-3   Defining scanning options for a multiple computer scan

Once you complete either a single-computer or multiple-computer scan, the resulting reports are stored in XML format in the %UserProfile%\Security-Scans folder, where UserProfile is the full path of the user's profile folder. These reports are best viewed in the MBSA console by clicking the View Existing Security Reports link on the Welcome page.

> **Note**   If a scan is performed against an entire domain or IP subnet, an individual report is produced for each detected computer.

Performing Text-Based MBSA Assessments

To perform a text-based MBSA assessment, you must use the text-based version of MBSA, Mbsacli.exe. This version of MBSA performs security assessments of either a single computer or multiple computers from a command prompt. The results are stored in XML format output files that can be viewed in the graphical version of the MBSA.

The command-line options for Mbsacli.exe include the following:

- **/c** *domain\computer* Performs a security assessment of the designated computer.

- **/I** *xx.xx.xx.xx* Performs a security assessment of the computer at the designated IP address.

- **/r** *xx.xx.xx.xx–yy.yy.yy.yy* Performs security assessments of all computers with IP addresses in the designated range.

- **/d** *domain* Performs security assessments of all computers in the designated domain.

- **/n** *options* Bypasses the designated scanning options. Options include IIS, OS, Password, SQL, or Updates.

> **Note** To bypass multiple tests, you can identify the test names in a single option. For example, to bypass IIS and SQL tests, you would use **/n IIS+SQL**.

- **/sus** SusServer Filters security updates so that only security updates approved at the designated SUS server are displayed.

- **/s** Suppresses output for scan options. If you designate /s 1, all security update check notes are suppressed. If you designate /s 2, both security update check notes and warnings are suppressed.

- **/nosum** Bypasses testing of file checksums when determining whether a security update is installed on the target computer or computers.

- **/o** Defines the format of the output XML file name. You can use a combination of %*domain*%, %*computername*%, and %*date*% when designating the format. The default format name is %*domain*% - %*computername*% (%*date*%).

> **Note**   If no options are provided when running Mbsacli.exe, a security assessment of the local computer is performed, using all default options.

For a complete listing of all Mbsacli.exe command-line switches, see the MBSA Help file, available from the Welcome screen of the MBSA graphical tool.

> **More Info**   For details on using the Mbsacli.exe text-based tool to scan for security updates by using a HfNetChk-style scan, see the "Scanning for Updates with the Command-Line Version of MBSA" section in Chapter 23.

Third-Party Tools

Third-party tools also perform network security assessments. These tools offer downloadable updates for new security issues and provide more tests than those currently offered by MBSA.

You might consider using the following tools to perform security assessments:

- **ISS Security Scanner**   Scans for security vulnerabilities and configuration issues on the local computer. This tool also records baseline settings for the registry, file system, currently running services, processes, existing users, existing groups, and existing file shares. This baseline allows you to determine whether files are modified by viruses. A trial version of the ISS Security Scanner is included in the *Microsoft Windows 2000 Server Resource Kit* (Microsoft Press, 2000) in the \apps\systemscanner folder.

> **Warning**   The application of a service pack or security update can lead to false positives for file and registry modification. Any time you apply a service pack or security update, you should reset the security baseline in the tool.

- **ISS Internet Scanner**   The ISS Internet Scanner allows you to scan remote computers for security policy compliance. Within the IIS Internet Scanner, you can reflect your company's security policies by defining custom scan policies. These scan policies define the baseline security requirements for your company and indicate which vulnerability checks are included in a scan session. Once you define a scan policy, you can implement the scan against one or more hosts on the network, depending on your ISS Internet Scanner license.

> **Note**   An evaluation version of the ISS Internet Scanner can be obtained at *http://www.iss.net/download/*.

- **eEye Retina Network Security Scanner**   The eEye Retina scanner is a network security scanner that allows the creation of custom scanning policies. These policies define which ports are scanned and which security audits are performed during a security assessment. The report generated by the Retina scanner includes audit results, open port analysis, detected services, share enumeration, and user account enumeration. You can download a free 15-day evaluation version of the eEye Retina scanner at *http://www.eeye.com/html/Products/Retina/Download.html*.

Port Scanning

Another common security assessment task is to determine which ports are open to the Internet. Attackers can use port information to determine which services are accessible from the Internet. A port scanner inspects a target computer on the network and probes each port to determine whether the target computer is listening for connections on the scanner ports. A port scanner also identifies which ports are available to the scanner.

As part of your network security assessment, you should periodically perform external scans of your network to ensure that only authorized ports are exposed to the Internet. For example, if you perform a scan against the IP address of your company's Web server, the only ports open should be the ports for HTTP on TCP port 80 and for Secure Sockets Layer–protected HTTP on TCP port 443. Assuming you are not running any other services on the Web server, no other ports should be visible.

Common Windows Ports

When you perform a port scan, the main goal is to identify all open ports on the target computer. Ideally, if the computer is exposed to the Internet, the only exposed ports will be those the firewall publishes to the Internet.

When performing port scans, it is useful to identify common ports used by Windows and Windows services. Some of the more common ports on Windows 2000 Servers are listed in Table 24-2.

The ports listed in Table 24-2 are the listening ports at a server. Typically, a client computer will use a random Transmission Control Protocol (TCP) or User Datagram Protocol (UDP) port above port 1023 when connecting to the server's listening port.

Table 24-2   Common Windows Ports

Port	Application
TCP port 20	FTP data
TCP port 21	FTP control
TCP port 23	Telnet
TCP port 25	Simple Mail Transfer Protocol (SMTP)
TCP port 53	Domain Name System (DNS) zone transfer
UDP port 53	DNS name resolution
UDP port 67	Dynamic Host Configuration Protocol (DHCP) server
UDP port 68	DHCP client
TCP port 80	HTTP
TCP port 88/UDP port 88	Kerberos authentication
TCP port 110	Post Office Protocol version 3 (POP3)
TCP port 119	Network News Transfer Protocol (NNTP)
UDP port 123	Network Time Protocol (NTP)
TCP port 135/UDP port 135	Microsoft remote procedure calls (RPCs)
UDP port 137	NetBIOS Name Service
UDP port 138	NetBIOS Datagram Service
TCP port 139	NetBIOS Session Service
TCP port 143	Internet Message Access Protocol (IMAP) version 4
UDP port 161	Simple Network Management Protocol (SNMP)
UDP port 162	SNMP traps
TCP port 389/UDP port 389	Lightweight Directory Access Protocol (LDAP)

(continued)

Table 24-2 Common Windows Ports   *(continued)*

Port	Application
TCP port 443	Hyper Text Transfer Protocol with Secure Sockets Layer (HTTPS)
TCP port 445/UDP port 445	Microsoft Common Internet File System (CIFS)
TCP port 464/UDP port 464	Kerberos password
UDP port 500	Internet Key Exchange (IKE) for IP Security (IPSec)
TCP port 563	NNTP with Secure Sockets Layer (SSL)
TCP port 636	LDAP with SSL (LDAPS)
TCP port 993	IMAP4 SSL
TCP port 995	POP3 SSL
TCP port 1433	SQL Server
UDP port 1701	Layer Two Tunneling Protocol (L2TP)
TCP port 1723	Point-to-Point Tunneling Protocol (PPTP)
UDP port 1812	Remote Authentication Dial-In User Service (RADIUS) authentication
UDP port 1813	RADIUS accounting
UDP port 2504	Microsoft Network Load Balancing (NLB) service remote control
TCP port 3268	LDAP Global Catalog
TCP port 3269	LDAP Global Catalog with SSL
TCP port 8080	Microsoft Internet Security and Acceleration (ISA) Server proxy port

> **More Info**   For a complete listing of assigned port numbers, see the Internet Assigned Numbers Authority (IANA) Web site at *http://www.iana.org/assignments/port-numbers*.

Determining Open Ports on the Local Computer

On the local computer, you can use the Netstat.exe command-line tool to show all open TCP and UDP ports. To show all open ports on the current computer, you can use the following Netstat command syntax:

```
Netstat -a -n
```

The -a indicates that all TCP and UDP listening ports are enumerated. The -n forces the output to show the actual open port numbers, rather than translating the port numbers to protocol names from the %swindir%\system32\drivers\etc\services file.

> **Note**   If you are running Netstat on a Windows XP–based computer, you can also use the -o switch, which shows the process that is listening on each open port. This can help identify rogue applications on the local computer.

Determining Open Ports on a Remote Computer

When performing security assessments, you can use a port scanner from the Internet to ensure that only required ports are open on an externally accessible server, such as a Web server.

To perform the port scan, you must acquire a port scanner from a third-party source, such as the Prosolve WinScan 2.0. In its most basic form, a port scanner will scan a designated computer to determine which ports are open on the target computer.

> **Note**   Depending on the manufacturer, a port scanner might also attempt attacks that target known vulnerabilities with open ports. For example, if TCP port 139 (the NetBIOS Session Service) is detected by the port scan, a port scanner might attempt to enumerate shares on the target server.

To scan a computer with Prosolve Winscan 2.0, use the following procedure:

1. From the Start menu, point to Programs, point to Prosolve, point to WinScan 2.0, and then click Winscan 2.0. (See Figure 24-4.)

2. In the Target section of the Winscan window, enter the Host/IP and Netmask for the port scan.

3. In the Operation section of the Winscan window, click Scan.

4. In the Port Range section, enter the Start and End port numbers for the scan.

5. In the Options section, enable both the TCP and UDP options. You can increase the speed of the scan by disabling the Prescan option.

6. Click Start Scan to start the port scan of the target computer.

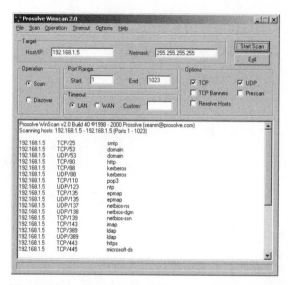

Figure 24-4   The Prosolve Winscan 2.0 port scanner

Note   Other freeware port scanners are available on the Internet. These include the Foundstone SuperScan v3.0 utility (*http://www.foundstone.com/knowledge/scanning.html*) and Portqry.exe (*http://www.microsoft.com/downloads/release.asp? ReleaseID=37344*), a command-line port scanner from Microsoft.

Best Practices

■   **Define baseline security settings in security templates.**   By defining baseline security settings in security templates, you ensure that the required security settings can be reproduced on additional computers. Security templates also document the required security settings.

- **Implement separate security templates for each computer configuration deployed on your network.** For example, a Microsoft SQL Server security template will contain security settings specific to instances of SQL Server deployed on the network.

- **Use GPOs to ensure consistent application of security templates.** By importing the security template settings into a GPO, you ensure that the security settings are consistently applied to the target computers and you prevent modification of the settings in the local security policy of a target computer.

- **Review security configuration of computers.** Periodically, you should use tools such the Security Configuration and Analysis console or the Secedit.exe utility to ensure that the security settings defined at a target computer do not differ from the security template defined for that computer configuration.

- **Perform regular security assessments of the computers on your network.** Security assessments identify common security misconfigurations and security patches or updates that must be applied to the target computer. You can choose from Microsoft-specific tools such as the MBSA tool or third-party tools such as the eEye Retina Network Security Scanner and the ISS Internet Scanner.

- **Identify all open ports on computers exposed to the Internet.** An attacker will typically scan an Internet-exposed computer to identify which ports are open and exposed to the Internet. By performing port scans from both the Internet and the local computer, you can ensure that only desired ports are exposed to the Internet. For example, a Web server should expose only TCP port 80 and TCP port 443 to the Internet. All other ports should not be accessible to the Internet.

Additional Information

- *Microsoft Windows 2000 Server Resource Kit*, Supplement 1, "Internet Information Services Resource Guide" (*http://www.microsoft.com/windows2000/techinfo/reskit/en-us/w2rkbook/iis.asp*)

- Microsoft Baseline Security Analyzer (*http://www.microsoft.com/technet/security/tools/Tools/MBSAhome.asp*)

- Shavlik Technologies (*http://www.shavlik.com*)

- eEye Retina Network Security Scanner evaluation version (*http:// www.eeye.com/html/Products/Retina/Download.html*)

- ISS Internet Scanner evaluation version (*http://www.iss.net/ products_services/enterprise_protection/vulnerability_assessment/ scanner_internet.php*)

- Foundstone SuperScan v3.0 (*http://www.foundstone.com/knowledge/ scanning.html*)

- Prosolve Winscan 2.0 (*http://www.prosolve.com/software*)

- Microsoft Portqry.exe command-line port scanner (*http:// www.microsoft.com/downloads/release.asp?ReleaseID=37344*)

- Security Configuration Tool Set (*http://www.microsoft.com/ windows2000/techinfo/howitworks/security/sctoolset.asp*)

- "Step-by-Step Guide to Using the Security Configuration Tool Set" (*http://www.microsoft.com/windows2000/techinfo/planning/ security/secconfsteps.asp*)

- IANA port number assignments (*http://www.iana.org/assignments/ port-numbers*)

- 246261: "How to Use the RestrictAnonymous Registry Value in Windows 2000"

Note   The previous article can be accessed through the Microsoft Knowledge Base. Go to *http://support.microsoft.com* and enter the article number in the Search The Knowledge Base text box.

Part VI

Planning and Performing Security Assessments and Incident Responses

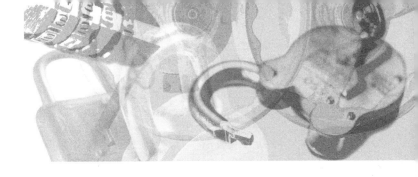

25

Assessing the Security of a Network

By now, you have vigilantly implemented security measures and deployed security updates. But how do you know if your network is really secure? If you have not yet asked yourself this question, now is a good time to do so. Security trickles down through organizations, from executives to IT managers, and eventually to you, the network administrator. Unlike many IT implementations, where clear, tangible indicators of success exist and direct proof of this question can be delivered, no network is 100 percent secure.

For example, if you deploy a Dynamic Host Configuration Protocol (DHCP) infrastructure, you can see when it is functioning properly. If the DHCP infrastructure is not functioning properly, users will be quick to recognize the symptoms and notify the help desk. Similarly, over time, you can prove the success of the DHCP infrastructure through the number of support incidents received by the help desk and the uptime of the DHCP services.

Often the first indicator of a security malfunction is the compromise of the network. Even good security can become susceptible to compromise when a new vulnerability is exposed or a tool is published to exploit a previously little-known, difficult-to-execute vulnerability. In truth, at any point in time, your organization is secure *only to the best of your knowledge*. By conducting security assessments, you can provide executives and managers with some evidence of how secure the network is, as well as give yourself some peace of mind.

Types of Security Assessments

Your organization can use different types of security assessments to verify its level of security on network resources. You must choose the method that best suits the requirements of your situation. Each type of security assessment requires that the people conducting the assessment have different skills. Consequently, you must be sure that the people—whether they are employees or outsourced security experts—have extensive experience with the type of assessment you are interested in.

Vulnerability Scanning

Vulnerability scanning is the most basic type of security assessment. Vulnerability scanning assesses a network for potential security weaknesses. Most commercial vulnerability scanning software packages do the following:

- **Enumerate computers, operating systems, and applications.** Vulnerability scanning software searches network segments for IP-enabled devices, including computers and network devices. It also identifies the configuration of the devices, including the OS version running on computers or devices, IP protocols and Transmission Control Protocol/User Datagram Protocol (TCP/UDP) ports that are listening, and applications installed on computers.

- **Identify common security mistakes.** Such software scans for common security mistakes, such as accounts that have weak passwords, files and folders with weak permissions, default services and applications that might need to be uninstalled, and mistakes in the security configuration of common applications.

- **Search for computers with known vulnerabilities.** Vulnerability scanning software scans computers for publicly reported vulnerabilities in operating systems and applications. Most vulnerability scanning software packages scan computers against the Common Vulnerabilities and Exposures (CVE) index and security bulletins from software vendors. The CVE is a vendor-neutral listing of reported security vulnerabilities in major operating systems and applications and is maintained at *http://cve.mitre.org*.

- **Test for exposure to common attacks.** Such software tests computer and network devices to see whether they are vulnerable to common attacks, such as the enumeration of security-related information and denial-of-service attacks.

Vulnerability scanning is effective in assessing a common weakness discovered on a network that has not been previously scanned and when verifying that security policy is being implemented on software configuration. Because vulnerability scanning reports can expose weaknesses in arcane areas of applications and frequently include many false positives, network administrators who analyze vulnerability scan results must have sufficient knowledge and experience with the operating systems, network devices, and applications being scanned and their role in the network.

For example, a vulnerability scan of a server running Microsoft Windows 2000 might reveal that global system objects and process tracking are not audited. An inexperienced administrator who has no knowledge of the functionality of global system objects and process tracking might see this report and decide to enable auditing on these two things, reasoning that auditing is a recommended security measure. In reality, enabling auditing on global system objects and process tracking does little to augment an organization's security and will almost certainly result in filling up the event log.

Caution   Vulnerability scanning software is limited to what it can detect at any one point in time. As with antivirus software, which requires that the signature file be updated when new viruses are discovered, vulnerability scanning software must be updated when new vulnerabilities are discovered and improvements are made to the software being scanned. Thus, the vulnerability software is only as effective as the maintenance performed on it by the software vendor and by the administrator who uses it. Vulnerability scanning software itself is not immune to software engineering flaws that might lead it to miss or misreport serious vulnerabilities.

The Microsoft Baseline Security Analyzer (MBSA) is an example of a vulnerability scanning application. The MBSA can scan computers that are running Microsoft Windows NT 4.0, Microsoft Windows 2000, and Microsoft Windows XP, as well as applications such as Microsoft Internet Information Services (IIS) and Microsoft SQL Server. The MBSA scans for the installation of security updates and service packs, common vulnerabilities such as weak passwords, and security best practices such as checking to see whether auditing is enabled.

> **More Info**   For detailed information on MBSA, see Chapter 24, "Using Security Assessment Tools," in this book.

Penetration Testing

Penetration testing, often called *pen testing*, is a much more sophisticated type of security assessment than vulnerability scanning. Unlike vulnerability scanning, which generally only examines the security of individual computers, network devices, or applications, penetration testing assesses the security of the network as a whole. Similarly, penetration testing can help educate network administrators, IT managers, and executives about the potential consequences of a real attacker breaking into the network. Penetration testing also will reveal these security weaknesses missed by vulnerability scanning:

■ **How vulnerabilities are exploited**   A penetration test not only will point out vulnerabilities, it also will document how the weaknesses can be exploited and how several minor vulnerabilities can link those exploited vulnerabilities and, in combination with them, compromise a computer or network. Most networks inevitably will have vulnerabilities you will not be able to resolve because of business or technical reasons. By knowing how these vulnerabilities can be exploited, you might be able to take other types of security measures to prevent them from compromising the network—without disrupting business continuity.

■ **Weakness in people and processes**   Because vulnerability scanning is based on software, it cannot assess security that is not related to technology. Both people and processes can be the source of security vulnerabilities just as easily as technology can. A penetration test might reveal that employees routinely allow people without identification to enter company facilities where they would have physical access to computers. Similarly, a penetration test might reveal process problems, such as not applying security updates until a week after they are released, which would give attackers a seven-day window to strike known vulnerabilities on servers.

Because a penetration tester is differentiated from an attacker only by his intent and lack of malice, you must use caution when allowing employees or external experts to conduct penetration tests. Penetration testing that is not completed professionally can result in the loss of services and disruption of business continuity.

> **Caution**   Before conducting any type of penetration testing, you must get written approval from management. This approval should include a clear description of what will be tested and when the testing will take place. Because of the nature of penetration testing, failure to obtain this approval might result in committing computer crime, despite your best intentions.

IT Security Audit

IT security auditing differs greatly from vulnerability scanning and penetration testing. IT security audits generally focus on the people and processes used to design, implement, and manage security on a network. In an IT security audit, the auditor and your organization's security policies and procedures use a baseline. IT security audits should be initiated by IT management. Conducting IT security audits is beyond the scope of this book.

> **More Info**   The National Institute of Standards and Technology (NIST) has created an IT security audit manual and associated toolset to conduct the audit. You can download the manual and toolset from the NIST Automated Security Self-Evaluated Tool (ASSET) Web site at *http://csrc.nist.gov/asset/*.

How to Conduct Security Assessments

Conducting a security audit might help you answer the question, "How do I know if my network is really secure?" However, it will not improve the security of your network. Regardless of the type of security assessment that your organization undertakes, you can help increase the security of your network by implementing your security assessment in these three phases:

- Planning a security assessment
- Conducting a security assessment
- Resolving issues discovered during the security assessment

Planning a Security Assessment

The success of a security assessment is largely determined before the actual assessment begins: in the planning phase. Like most IT projects, the major cause of failure for security assessments is poor planning. To avoid this common pitfall, you can create project vision and scope documents.

Creating a Project Vision

The project vision for your security assessment should precisely describe the reason you are conducting the security assessment, the type of security assessment that will be done, the milestones for completing the project, and the project goals. Other items that the project vision commonly contains include the proposed budget for the project, explanations of project team roles and responsibilities, and metrics that can be used to determine the success of the security assessment.

The project vision document will help ensure that everyone working on the project understands the project goals and how the project will accomplish them. It is essential that you obtain executive sponsorship on the vision for the security assessment. Without executive sponsorship, the project will suffer from a lack of prioritization on the part of middle management and consequently might not receive the necessary budget.

Creating a Project Scope

The project scope for your security assessment details what you will be assessing the security of, what tools will be used, what methodology will be employed, and the time constraints of the project. The scope also defines what tasks are beyond the parameters of the project. For example, you might create a project scope for a two-week penetration test on a Web server, specifying that only publicly available tools will be used to attack a given Web server but prohibiting testers from using denial-of-service attacks or disrupting the services that the Web server provides.

Conducting a Security Assessment

Although it is obvious that you must document the results of a security assessment, the fact that you must document the procedures used in a security assessment might not be obvious. Unfortunately, well-organized and detailed documentation often is not created during IT projects, including security assessments, because it is somewhat time-consuming and often falls outside the skill set of administrators. Regardless of the type of security assessment that your organization plans to undertake, you must diligently document the procedures used during the security assessment to ensure that the result of the assessment can be used to augment the security of the network.

Documenting the methodology used during the security assessment will ensure that the results can be independently reviewed and reproduced if necessary. This documentation includes the tools used during the assessment and operating conditions and the assumptions made by the people conducting the assessment.

With vulnerability scanning, the methodology used might impact the result of the test. For example, vulnerability scanning software that runs under the security context of the domain administrator will yield different results than if it were run under the security context of an authenticated user or a nonauthenticated user. Similarly, different vulnerability scanning software packages assess security differently and have unique features, which both can influence the result of the assessment.

For penetration tests, detailed documentation of the methodology that was used during the test—regardless of whether it was successful in compromising the network—can be reviewed to find areas where your organization must make changes to secure the network. For example, knowing that a penetration tester compromised a domain controller does little to help you secure your network. However, knowing that a penetration tester was able to break into a file server by enumerating account information on local accounts through a null connection to the IPC$ share and discovering that the password for a local service account was contained in the description of the account can help you make the necessary changes to secure your network.

For IT security audits, documenting the methodology and tools used to perform the audit is essential. After the items found deficient in the audit have been resolved, or at some scheduled point in the future, the audit can be repeated in the same manner to assess the progress made since the previous audit. Because organizations frequently use progress made since prior audit findings as metrics to judge their relative success, maintaining such documentation is crucial.

Resolving Issues Discovered During the Security Assessment

After the security assessment is complete, the work of securing the network begins. You will need to analyze the results of the security assessment and determine which methods you can take to address the deficiencies discovered. The first step is to prioritize the deficiencies according to their impact on your organization. The following list details how you should prioritize such impacts:

1. **Human safety** Although not all organizations will have security vulnerabilities that, if exploited, could lead to the loss of life or otherwise jeopardize human safety, such vulnerabilities should always be given the highest priority.

2. **Destruction of data** The next priority should be given to the destruction of data, especially when it results in total data loss. At any given point in time, data that has not been backed up to remote storage exists. If an attacker can gain access to this data, it probably cannot be restored. For some organizations, losing even a day's worth of data would be devastating.

3. **Disclosure of confidential information** Confidential data includes customer information, employee information, business plans, financial information, and trade secrets. The disclosure of this information can cause loss of customer confidence, litigation against the organization, loss of competitive advantage, and loss of intellectual property.

4. **Loss of services** A denial-of-service attack causes organizations or their customers to lose the use of IT services. The impact of a denial-of-service attack depends on the nature of your organization's business. For example, the loss of IT services impacts a business-to-consumer (B2C) Web site or an ISP much more that it does a software vendor.

5. **Annoyances** The least critical category of impact is that of attack vulnerabilities, which, if exploited, result in the minor disruption of business continuity, leading to nothing more than mere annoyances. For example, attacks that require a user to reboot her computer—such as attacks that flood a user's computer with NetBIOS messages sent to the console—will cause a minor disruption of business services and be a general annoyance to the user but will have no lasting consequences.

After you have prioritized the security issues discovered in the security assessment, you should incorporate them into your organization's risk management plan or at least apply them to the process your organization normally uses to mitigate security risks.

> **More Info**   See Chapter 1, "Key Principles of Security," for more information about managing risk.

Conducting Penetration Tests

Not all network administrators think like attackers or have the skill set required to break into networks. Conducting penetration tests requires you to think like an attacker. Additionally, you will need to have experience identifying weaknesses in network security, experience with tools that are used to compromise networks, and at least a basic level of expertise with one or more programming languages. If you are not confident in your abilities to think like an attacker, you should consider enlisting the help of another administrator or a consultant who is.

For a penetration test to be useful to your organization for more than just proving that weaknesses in security exist, you must carefully document your actions. The first step in conducting a penetration test is to create a methodology that you will follow when attempting to break into the network. This methodology will help ensure that you complete all the attacks that you have outlined, budget your time appropriately, and establish a foundation for creating documentation on the results of the penetration test.

> **Caution**   Conducting penetration testing on networks without explicit written permission from the target organization is a computer crime in many parts of the world. Do not conduct penetration tests on any network, even that of your own organization, unless you have this permission.

The objective of the penetration test is to compromise the intended target or application. To accomplish this goal, a patient attacker will stick to a well-defined methodology. For example, if you are conducting a penetration test, you might want to follow these steps:

1. Gather information.

2. Research vulnerabilities.

3. Compromise the target application or network.

Step 1. Gathering Information

Like an attacker, at first you might have little to no knowledge about your target network. But by the end of this step, you will have constructed a detailed road-map of the network that you can use to break into the network in an organized manner. The goal of performing this step is to gather as much information as possible about the target network through publicly available sources. This will give you an indication of how large the target might be, how many potential entry points exist, and which security mechanisms exist to thwart the attack.

Gathering information, often called *footprinting*, requires you to be patient, detail oriented, and resourceful. During this step, you should gather the following types of information:

■ Basic information about the target

■ Domain Name System (DNS) domain name and IP address information

■ Information about hosts on publicly available networks

Obtaining Basic Information About the Target

All information about the target and subsidiaries of the target is useful, including Web sites and other IT services offered by the target, contact information for the target, organizational structure, and names of employees. You can get most of this information on the Internet simply by searching the target organization's Web site and querying search engines by using the name of the target.

Basic information about the company will reveal details that might be used to generate passwords, points of entry into the target's network—including physical buildings and logical entry points such as phone numbers and names of key employees—that can be used in social engineering attacks, and a general understanding of the technical sophistication of the target. (For more on social engineering, see the sidebar on the next page.) For example, you can query Internet search engines on the name of the target and the strings "password for" and "ftp". Surprisingly, with a little fine-tuning, this tactic will unearth the logins to FTP servers used by many large organizations.

Social Engineering

Sometimes the easiest way to get information about a network or break into that network is to ask. As strange as it sounds, employees have been known to wittingly or unwittingly reveal important information about their company. For the attacker, it is about asking the right questions to the right person with the right tone. This exploitation of trust is called *social engineering*.

For example, an attacker might find the telephone number for the company switchboard operator and ask to be transferred to the help desk. Because the call is transferred rather than directly dialed, the call identification will appear to the help desk as though it originated internally. The attacker might then explain that he is a new employee and is very afraid of computers. The attacker might continue by saying he is not sure what his account name is and how long his password needs to be. After the help desk administrator patiently explains how account names are generated and the organization's password policy, the attacker might explain—while complimenting the help desk administrator on how smart she is and how well she explained the account and password problem—that his boss told him his account was enabled for remote access but that he lost the information about which server to connect to.

By the end of the conversation, the attacker will have a good idea of how hard breaking into the network by logging on with a valid user's credentials might be. The attacker can use the names of employees he has gathered from the Web site and information learned from the help desk about the password policy to attempt to log on to the remote access server by using passwords that users are likely to pick. Meanwhile, the help desk administrator will end the conversation feeling as though she did a great job in assisting a user who really needed help.

An attacker might even gain access directly to the network simply by asking. In July 2002, a student at the University of Delaware was caught changing her grades in the school's database system by calling the university's help desk and pretending to be her professors. In all cases, she reportedly stated that she had forgotten her password and asked to have it reset, and in all cases, the help desk obliged.

Social engineering is difficult for networks to defend against, especially if network administrators and other employees in key positions (such as administrative assistants) do not know that they might be the target of such attacks. Consequently, security awareness training is essential for everyone in the company.

Using DNS Domain Name and IP Address Information

By using information about the target network stored in DNS servers, you can begin to create a diagram of the target organization's network. You can analyze DNS zones for the target organization to obtain information, including the server host names, services offered by certain servers, IP addresses of servers, and contact information for members of the IT staff.

By analyzing DNS records, you also can get a pretty good idea about the location of the servers and the OS or applications that are being run on the server. For example, you might be able to deduce that a computer with the host name SFO04E2K that is registered with a Mail Exchange (MX) record is a server running Windows 2000 and Microsoft Exchange 2000 Server and is located in San Francisco, or that a network device named cis2500dt2 is a Cisco Systems 2500 series router directly connected to the target's ISP. One of the first things that attackers do is create a network diagram with information gained from analyzing DNS zones.

The IP address information about the target—gained from the DNS zone, American Registry of Internet Numbers (ARIN), and other sources—can be scanned with port-scanning software to further develop your network diagram. Attackers have been known to use publicly available sources to create better network diagrams on the target network than the target network's administrators have.

Enumerating Information About Hosts on Publicly Available Networks

After gathering the IP addresses used by the target network, an attacker can begin the process of profiling the network to find possible points of entry. The attacker does this by enumerating information about hosts that are exposed to the Internet by the target organization. To accomplish this, you can use port-scanning software to scan hosts for listening TCP/UDP ports and IP protocols. Port scans will reveal information about hosts such as the OS running on the host and the services running on the host.

You can use port scanning to determine how router and firewall IP filters are configured. An effective attacker will be able to produce a network diagram for all publicly accessible screened subnets and a reasonably complete listing of the types of traffic allowed in and out of the network.

An attacker also can use software to crawl the target organization's public Web sites and FTP sites. Often, organizations have information that is not intended for public use posted on their public Web sites or FTP sites but not listed in these sites' directory structures. Similarly, information that would be useful for breaking into the network might be embedded in the code that the Web pages are written in. For example, a developer might have placed a note to himself about a test login ID and password in the comments of an HTML page or might have used static login information for connections to a server running SQL Server. After downloading the Web pages or FTP files to a local computer, an attacker can run a program such as Grep to search for text strings in the files.

Step 2. Researching Vulnerabilities

After the attacker has completed gathering information about the target network and has created a list of operating systems, network devices, and applications running on the network (including information about how they are configured), her next step is to research their vulnerabilities. Aside from weak passwords and servers with no access control, the easiest way to break into a network is to exploit known vulnerabilities to the hardware and software used by the target organization.

Simple methods of compromising the security of computers, network devices, and applications might already exist. So before you spend any time attempting to break into your networks—using elaborate techniques that might reveal your existence—do your homework. Researching vulnerabilities when acting as an attacker is not any different from the research that you must do as a network administrator. Use the following resources for your sleuthing:

- **Hardware and software vendor Web sites**   The most obvious place to look for vulnerabilities in hardware or software is the vendor's Web site. In general, you can find product documentation that describes the default security of the hardware or software, knowledge base articles that describe how security works on the hardware or software, and security bulletins that describe known vulnerabilities in the vendor's products.

- **Security-related Web sites and newsgroups**   Numerous Web sites for security professionals discuss security and security weaknesses. You can often use this information to break into networks too. For example, the Web site *http://www.netstumbler.com* has extensive information about wireless network security. Another good Web site is *http://www.securityfocus.com*, from which a mailing list called Bugtraq is operated. Bugtraq contains discussions about the latest security vulnerabilities in hardware and software.

- **Web sites run by attackers**   Web sites run by attackers often contain detailed information and tools that be used to break into networks. If you are not familiar with breaking into networks, you can learn a lot about how attackers compromise networks by browsing these Web sites. As with all information, the content of these sites can be used for good purposes and malicious ones. Because in some countries possessing tools that are used to break into computer networks is against the law, you should be careful about downloading tools from these Web sites. Check your local computer crime laws first. Furthermore, many of the applications that can be downloaded from these Web sites have to be modified and are Trojan horse applications themselves.

Step 3. Compromising the Target Application or Network

After you have gathered information about the target network and fully researched potential avenues of attack, you can begin the process of attempting to compromise the network. In general, the compromise of a network starts with the compromise of a single host. Many ways to compromise a network exist, and without knowing the details of a specific scenario, it is difficult to prescribe a precise set of actions. However, when compromising a network, attackers will attempt to accomplish several tasks, including these:

1. **Get passwords.**   The first thing that an attacker will do is copy the passwords or password databases from the compromised host to a computer controlled by the attacker. If the compromised host is a member server running Windows 2000, the attacker will retrieve the password hashes from the Security Accounts Manager (SAM) database, the local security authority (LSA) secrets, and the passwords stored by Microsoft Internet Explorer autocomplete. Immediately after obtaining the password hashes, the attacker will begin an offline attack on them.

2. **Gather information.**   After the attacker gains access to a host inside the target's network—whether in a screened subnet or in the internal network—the attacker gains a new source of information about the network. Consequently, the attacker returns to step 1 in this methodology and begins gathering basic information about the network from the inside.

3. **Elevate their privileges.**   After an attacker has initially penetrated the network, one of her first goals is to gain access to or create elevated security credentials. Once an attacker has Administrator or System privileges on a computer or network device, little can be done to prevent her from doing whatever she wants to that computer or device. Similarly, if an attacker can obtain control over a domain administrator account, the attacker functionally controls the entire network.

4. **Leverage the compromised host.**   Once under the control of the attacker, a compromised host becomes a platform for attacking other computers on the network from the inside. The attacker might also use the host as a zombie system to attack another network.

5. **Replace files.**   An attacker might want to either ensure that she can continue to access the compromised computer or gather information from users of the computer. To accomplish this, the attacker can install a backdoor application or keystroke logging software to record the keystrokes of locally logged on users, including their passwords.

Important   During a penetration test, you should compromise the network only in ways agreed to by the target organization ahead of time. You should not disrupt business continuity when performing a penetration test.

Best Practices

■ **Use security assessments to evaluate the security of your network.**   Security assessments will help answer the question, "How do I know that my network is really secure?" You can also track progress toward improving the security of your network by repeating a security assessment after you have addressed the weaknesses discovered in the initial security assessment.

■ **Choose the appropriate type of security assessment for your business or technical requirements.**   The security assessments discussed in this chapter are very different: each attempts to assess different areas of security, requires special areas of expertise, and calls for different levels of investment from your organization. To ensure that the security audit you perform meets the needs of your organization, choose the appropriate security assessment. For example, conducting a vulnerability scan probably will not reveal issues with IT security policies and procedures, just as an IT security audit probably will not reveal that weak passwords are used on servers.

- **Take time to carefully plan your security assessment project.** As with most IT projects, the major reason that security assessments fail is poor planning. To avoid this pitfall, take time during the planning stage to create a project vision and a scope to guide the security assessment. Do not conduct a security assessment without executive sponsorship.

- **Document in detail the methodology used to conduct the security assessment.**   To ensure that the security assessment results can be independently reviewed and reproduced if necessary, carefully document the methodology used to conduct the security assessment.

Additional Information

- The MBSA Web site (*http://www.microsoft.com/technet/security/tools/Tools/MBSAhome.asp*)

- Automated Security Self-Evaluation Tool (ASSET) on the National Institute of Standards and Technology (NIST) Web site (*http://csrc.nist.gov/asset/*)

- *Hacking Exposed: Windows 2000* (McGraw-Hill Osborne, 2001)

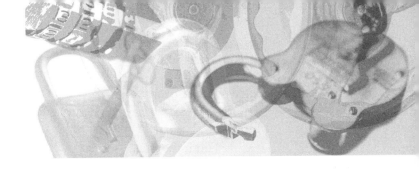

26

Planning for Incident Response

Even if your network has solid protections in place, a determined attacker might be able to penetrate your defenses if given sufficient time. By understanding the baseline of your network and its "normal" behavior, monitoring audits and other logs to see activity in real time, and maintaining an inquisitive skepticism, you can build a solid incident response framework.

In this chapter, we will look at incident response as a component of the often used Protect→Detect→Respond model. The model is iterative: protect against the threats you can, detect those threats you have not prevented against, respond to any threats you detect, improve your processes and defenses based on what you have learned, and then repeat the sequence.

Creating an Incident Response Team

The first step in creating a successful incident response process is to identify and enlist the necessary staffing resources. Although it is not essential that these staff members devote all of their time to incident response, defining an incident response team and the capacity in which they will act prevents any uncertainty from occurring during an incident response. Even if you have personnel who devote all of their time to incident response, taking the time now to define the employees who will assist that core group (to provide either specialized skills or additional manpower) will save time during a large-scale response. Furthermore, the members of the incident response team will be in the best position to create, maintain, and update the processes and guidelines associated with incident response.

Obtaining an Executive Sponsor

Before selecting a team, you must obtain an executive sponsor for your incident response efforts. The sponsor should likely be the CEO or one of her direct reports, though this can differ based on the structure and size of your organization. You need the executive sponsor to help remove obstacles associated with implementing the policies that support your incident response work. You will also need the sponsor any time a policy must be enforced by a member of your organization who is reluctant to do so for fear of retribution. Metaphorically speaking, your sponsor is the edge of your sword. Although the sponsor does not need to be Chief Security Officer by title, this will likely one of her roles.

Your sponsor will need to be kept aware of the activities of the incident response team. She will likely want some form of tangible reporting on the successes and challenges of the incident response team, as well as the details of any incident, so that she can educate other members of senior management on the importance of security to your organization. Coupling such reporting with an accurate assessment of risk and exposure can be a powerful tool during budget discussions and one that affects the incident response team's long-term potential for success.

Identifying the Stakeholders

After a sponsor is in place, you must identify all stakeholders so that they can be included in policy discussions. Although senior IT staff will likely perform most core activities during an incident response, other individuals will need to be involved to ensure that the response is optimally successful from an overall business perspective.

As just implied, the members of the incident response team will not be limited to technical staff. Although senior members representing each technical specialty (operating systems, networks, databases, development, and so on) will certainly rank among the team's core members, the team also needs to include key representatives from all the company's major lines of business. These business leaders will ensure that an incident response protects the most essential assets of their work, intrudes minimally on specific initiatives they might have under way, and hopefully protects their ability to be successful as a business unit and contribute to the company's overall success.

The team will also need supporting members from various administration groups such as helpdesk, internal communications, HR, and the legal department to ensure that labor laws continue to be observed and that the company minimizes liability during any incident response activities. The internal communications and helpdesk representatives will help facilitate communications with end users when such communications are required. The HR representative will be responsible for answering questions about overtime compensation, non-standard working hours, union requirements, and the like. Regardless of whether the legal representative is internal or external to your organization, he must be familiar with the concepts of expectation of privacy, evidentiary procedure, and downstream liability as well as the laws used in prosecuting computer crime—not only in your company's local jurisdiction but also worldwide. Rounding out the team will be members of your public relations department, who will be responsible for the communications described later in this chapter in the section "Creating a Communications Plan".

When not responding to incidents, team members can still conduct a wide variety of security-related activities. Some of these activities require additional planning and executive sponsorship, and all of them will benefit from a prescribed format that stems from process discussions about forming the incident response team. These activities include the following:

- Staying up-to-date on patches issued by vendors

- Staying up-to-date on industry trends by reading various online lists and IT trade periodicals

- Conducting security awareness activities to inform all staff how they contribute to the security of the organization

- Reviewing and testing new security products

- Analyzing publicly available information about the organization

- Baselining systems and reviewing related logs

- Performing an architectural review of the company's networks from a security perspective

- Testing restoration of systems from backup media

- Auditing systems to ensure compliance to policy

- Performing approved penetration testing of key systems

All these activities contribute in some manner to the incident response capability of your organization.

Choosing a Team Leader

Once the members of the team are in place, the team needs a leader. The team leader will be responsible for the actions of the entire incident response team and will coordinate those actions as well as sessions on the lessons learned during the response process. These sessions should follow each incident response. In addition, such sessions should be conducted periodically throughout the year (for example, every six months). The team leader will use the lessons learned to make policy update recommendations.

The role of the team leader differs from that of the incident response leader. Each incident will require a leader who will direct the response activities. All communications regarding the incident's progress should flow through this incident response leader to ensure that no duplication of efforts occurs and that the response team is optimally effective in its activities. The incident response leader is similar to a project manager in this respect.

Table 26-1 outlines the activities and roles of a typical incident response team.

Table 26-1 Incident Response Team Activities and Roles

Activities	Basic Permissions				
	Incident Lead	IT Contact	Legal Representative	Public Relations Representative	Line of Business Management
Performs initial assessment	Owner	Advises	None	None	None
Provides initial response	Owner	Implements	Informed	Informed	Informed
Collects forensic evidence	Implements	Advises	Owner	None	None
Implements temporary fix	Owner	Implements	Informed	Informed	Advises
Sends communication	Advises	Advises	Advises	Implements	Owner
Checks with local law enforcement	Updater	Informed	Implements	Informed	Owner
Implements permanent fix	Owner	Implements	Informed	Informed	Informed
Determines financial impact on business	Updater	Informed	Advises	Informed	Owner
Determines impact on brand or goodwill	Informed	Informed	Advises	Owner	Advises

Defining Incident Response Policy

Once the members of the incident response team have been identified, they should convene to build an incident response process and a supporting policy. Some of the related policies might already be in place in your organization, but the team will need to review how each of these policies relates to incident response and recommend changes that support incident response activities. The team must also formalize the approach to take should responding to an incident become necessary.

Categorizing Types of Incidents

Up to this point, we have been using the term *incident* in a generic manner. An incident is an occurrence that creates some level of crisis and requires action to reduce or eliminate the risk caused. Possible incidents, or threats, range from computer intrusion, denial of service, virus infestation, and inappropriate access to events that normally call for disaster recovery measures, such as power outages and other forms of force majeure.

Because of the wide range of incident types, it is helpful to define policies and procedures for each type of incident. Steps appropriate to foiling an attacker might not work as well when dealing with a citywide blackout or an insider viewing the salary details of the rest of the company's employees. By categorizing each type of threat and defining both proactive and reactive responses to them, your team can eliminate much of the ambiguity that occurs when executing a response.

Whether the occurrences your incident response team responds to are accidental, malicious, or happenstance, the team members will require guidance on the response techniques expected of them. Such techniques must be defined in advance so that valuable response time is not wasted defining them during the crisis. As part of the overall incident response policy and process, a number of difficult decisions must be made and documented in advance of any incident. Doing so ensures that the roles and responsibilities of any given team member are not called into question during an incident response and that the boundaries of the activities that can be conducted without seeking additional approval are clear.

> **Tip** Ensure that the incident response team's escalation path, priorities, process, and constraints are clearly defined and documented before an incident occurs. Failing to do so will likely result in wasted time during critical periods of the incident response as team members try to define their roles and responsibilities on the spot or locate members of management team for additional approval or instruction.

Outlining Proactive and Reactive Responses

Once you have detailed the different types of threats, you should examine the methods needed to exploit each of them. Once you have developed a list of methods, you should go through the list methodically to define the proactive and reactive approaches your team will take for each incident type.

From a proactive standpoint, you should predict the following:

- The possible damage your organization can incur

- Any potential vulnerabilities in your network

- The security measures and controls needed to minimize those vulnerabilities

- The contingency plans needed should your protective measures fail

From a reactive standpoint, you will need to determine the following:

- The amount of damage inflicted and its cause

- How to prevent additional damage from occurring

- How to repair the damage that has been done

- How you will document and learn from the experience

- How to implement any contingency plans necessitated by the event

Determining Whether to Prosecute the Attacker

When defining procedures for a reactive response, you need to make a number of difficult decisions. Though primarily business decisions, these decisions will have a dramatic effect on the tasks your team members perform. One example of how business requirements can impact an investigation is the decision to prosecute an attacker. If your organization intends to prosecute the offender, the proper collection of evidence will often take precedence over the restoration of service. For instance, if a system will be used as evidence in a court of law, that system must not be modified at all, from the moment the incident occurred until the court date—which makes securing the system and restoring service problematic.

We will discuss specific investigative techniques in more detail in Chapter 27, "Responding to Security Incidents," but this example illustrates some of the challenging decisions the incident response team must make. By making such difficult decisions proactively during your incident response planning stage— rather than reactively making them during an incident response—you buy your-self a great deal of time to discuss the relative merits of each approach. Of course, this also allows for the possibility of "analysis paralysis", where an extended discussion is the only thing that gets accomplished. Be wary of that outcome in your response planning meetings.

A corollary issue to deciding whether to pursue a law enforcement solu-tion (rather than simply restoring service) is the likelihood that such prosecu-tion will bring media attention to your organization. Weigh carefully the impact that this could have on your company's reputation and brand image. Although a positive outcome is possible when pursuing law enforcement, your team's handling and communication of the incident will play a significant role in shap-ing the outcome. We will discuss this in greater detail in the "Creating a Com-munications Plan" section of this chapter.

Deciding Whether to Stop the Attack

Another frequent challenge faced by incident response teams is whether to stop the attack or collect additional information about its root cause. Although pre-venting the spread of an attack or virus might seem like the obvious choice, tip-ping off an attacker that you are onto him could have devastating results—for example, if the attacker decides to wipe out the entire system in an effort to reduce his risk of being caught. By disconnecting a computer from network to preserve its state for further examination, you could be alerting the attacker that you have discovered his presence. This could result in the attacker attempting to compromise other computers on your network that have not yet been com-promised or immediately initiating destructive methods on other computers he has already compromised to prevent collection of evidence that could be used to track him. In a similar vein, deciding to watch the attacker and gain more information about the extent of control he has over systems in your network and the techniques being employed to expand influence could open your firm to downstream liability if your network becomes a launching point for an attack against another network.

Constructing Policies to Support Incident Response

The incident response team cannot be successful if the rest of the organization is not prepared to properly support the team's activities. The most effective way to drive behavior that will support the team is to codify these behaviors into policies and guidelines and use them to direct the organization as a whole. When crafting these policies, be sure to consider how staff will receive them. If the policies are written in a dictatorial manner, they might lack effectiveness because of people's inherent resistance to change. If, however, they are written as thoughtful explanations—outlining not only the *what* but also the *why*, they will be better received and more diligently followed.

That latter point is critical: the best policies are useless if they are not observed. Again, owing to people's resistance to change, the best policies will be those that stand the test of time rather than those continuously rewritten and distributed. A policy should be written in a manner that will not require frequent revision. Lasting policies describe the needs of the business and the direction that must be taken to support those needs—not the specific steps to be taken. Lasting policies are the *what* and the *why*, but they are not the *how*.

Acceptable Use Policy

A primary policy supporting incident response is the acceptable use policy (AUP). This policy reduces overall risk by providing guidance to staff about the appropriate use of the company's network (and by extension, the types of activities that are higher risk and therefore not appropriate). In addition, this policy provides a method for paring down the potential traffic types to allow for easier baselining of network traffic.

The AUP should also contain language that covers the employees' rights and privacy, in addition to their responsibilities. Although your legal counsel should be involved in crafting this policy, you should consider a couple of key points. First, clarify the company's stance on personal privacy. Is personal use of company resources allowed and, if so, to what extent? Many companies recognize that their staff can make reasonable judgments about when their use of company resources is excessive and use a self-managed approach; others are more strict in their guidelines. Second, note that this portion of the policy should indicate that e-mail is considered a corporate resource that should not be misused and—under the course of normal security operations—can be monitored.

Clarifying that the possibility of monitoring exists can eliminate the expectation of privacy on the part of employees. Privacy expectations can dramatically impede an investigation. If an expectation of privacy exists, it might not be possible to review e-mail records or, in some cases, to utilize network monitoring software. Furthermore, if your organization uses encryption, a user's unwillingness to share her encryption keys because of privacy concerns could further complicate the investigation. Again, consult with your legal counsel if you have questions on this topic, and note that privacy laws vary by jurisdiction.

Access Policy

Another important policy involves access. This policy will define the conditions under which connections to other networks (such as the Internet, your business partners' networks, and so on) can be implemented. The policy should also clarify which groups in your organization can provide the best security practices for ensuring that such connections are deployed and managed appropriately. Access policy should do the following:

- Include language discussing guest or vendor access to the company network

- Detail the circumstances under which such access is and is not allowed

- List the appropriate contacts for any questions or comments

Availability Guidelines

Guidelines for availability are another area to address in incident response policy. Specifically, you need to clarify how availability might be affected during an incident response and during security-related maintenance. By clearly stating that security is a priority for your organization, you support the needs of your team during the inevitability of being forced to take a system or network connection offline to defend your environment. This can help to ensure that incident response needs are not immediately subordinated by uptime requirements. In addition, you send a message on the importance of security to the firm—which can be a component of a larger security awareness campaign.

Classification Policies

Defining who should be granted access to which type of information and how broadly that information can be shared is another critical component of ensuring the protection of your company's assets. Classifying data into different sensitivity layers provides guidance to staff on the circulation restrictions of any given document and helps to protect against inappropriate leaks. Examples of classification schemes include "unlabeled, secret, top secret, eyes only" and "public, internal only, internal-restricted viewing, highly sensitive." You must choose labeling that is appropriate to your business rather than blindly copying from another organization's classification policy. You need to do a business analysis of the types of information your company creates and work with your business managers to identify the minimum appropriate levels of confidentiality.

Password Policy

Because one goal of the incident response process is the elimination of incidents throughout the organization, you should consider providing further guidance to all staff on how they contribute to the overall security of the company. Because every employee is a link in your firm's security chain, ensuring that steps are taken to eliminate weak links can be just as important as the work that is done after a breach occurs.

One common place where weak links exist is in an organization's password policy. The password policy will indicate choices the organization has made about authentication. This policy is not limited to text-based passwords—it includes other forms of authentication, such as smart cards, biometrics, and tokens. Beyond simply covering the requirements of each authentication type, your organization's password policy should differentiate specific access types that require specific authentication factors. Policy might be different for service accounts, user accounts, administrator accounts, remote access accounts, and so on.

When addressing each access scenario—local area network, VPN, wireless, etc.—take into account the specific business requirements and the security threats that type of access involves. The password policy should also discuss the following:

- Whether it is appropriate for individuals to share credential information and under which circumstances

- The process for granting and receiving assistance on password resets that protect against social engineering (For more information on social engineering, see the sidebar on page 555 of Chapter 25, "Social Engineering.")

- Standard considerations for the duration of password life

- The complexity requirements for passwords

- The number of failed logons allowed before lockout

> **More Info**   See Chapter 3, "Securing User Accounts and Passwords," for more information on configuring password policies.

Security Reporting Policy

Policy relating to security reporting is often overlooked, but it plays a critical role in the speed of your incident response. You will need to describe the types of potential threats clearly enough so that all staff can understand those risks and identify when one of those risks is being realized. Security reporting policy will also clarify who should be contacted if a potential compromise to your organization's security is occurring, what information needs to be provided, whether the contact is anonymous, and how information about the incident is collected.

Putting It All Together

Finally, you need to craft an incident response policy that describes how each of these pieces fits together to support your incident response efforts. The overall incident response policy will also detail issues that must be addressed during an incident response that might differ from normal, day-to-day operations. Items such as monitoring, availability, chain of command, and other components of the investigation are essential here. In addition, this blanket policy must include a discussion of the consequences associated with impeding the investigation or performing a policy violation that leads to a security incident.

Creating a Communications Plan

A communications plan is the framework for how information about your organization is shared among those who need it. This plan will be different during an incident than during normal day-to-day operations. Communications techniques and content will also differ depending on whether the audience is internal or external. Determining communications policies that deal with incident response likely will represent some of the most difficult decisions a company must make. Err on the side of disseminating too much or the wrong pieces of information and you run the risk of negatively impacting the perception of your organization—or worse—clouding key information, thereby causing the intended recipient to miss it. And providing too little information can cause unfounded speculation or prevent an active participant from taking a specific appropriate action.

Preincident Internal Communications

Internal communications begin the first time a potential employee contacts your firm and continue until the end of that employee's affiliation with your organization. It is critical that all communications are positioned appropriately to support business requirements—especially those involving security. Coordination with your HR, public relations, and legal teams will be essential for successfully creating a proper framework for communications.

New Employee Orientation

Some of the most important communications within your organization will be with new hires. Orientation sessions need to acquaint new employees with all the policies described in the "Defining Incident Response Policy" section of this chapter—as well as why these policies are important. Each employee must understand his role in the security of the organization, know the steps required to protect company assets, know where to seek additional information or report a circumstance that warrants investigation, and anticipate the result—both to the organization and himself—should he fail to observe policies. These orientation discussions afford you the greatest opportunity to gain a new employee's acceptance of these security concepts. Information imparted during these initial meetings can shape every workplace decision an employee makes from that point on.

Security Refresher Courses

As a supplement to the new hire training, an organization should consider security refresher courses. These courses should do the following:

- Occur regularly throughout an employee's career

- Recertify that employees understand what is expected of them

- Update employees on any changes to policy for which they might not have been notified

- Provide employees with a forum to obtain clarification on any security topic

- Reinforce the importance of security to the firm

Holding short trainings annually (or more frequently) or in conjunction with major events such as a reorganization or proposed merger is a good approach.

Additional Training

Certain groups in your organization might require additional training on concepts specific to their job function. For example, anyone developing software that is used internally or becomes part of a shipping product should be trained in how to write, test, and manage their code with security as a driving factor. Because such training would not be useful to every member of the organization, it should be provided separately from other new hire training so that it does not dilute other important messages.

Awareness Campaigns

Rounding out preincident internal communications is the concept of awareness campaigns. An awareness campaign can take many forms. Regardless of the methods employed, the goals of such a campaign are to change specific, undesirable behavior centered around security and to reinforce the importance of security to all staff. Awareness campaigns are most successful when they are least intrusive. For example, you should not send out daily, multiple-page memos on security because, over time, people will stop reading them. Awareness activities should be simple, should be easy to consume, and should contain the minimum verbiage required to make their point.

Examples of awareness activities include the following:

- Posters of the *Loose lips sink ships* variety

- Targeted e-mails reminding employees of a specific policy

- A one-line sidebar in a company newsletter

- Wallet cards with a short list of tips telling individuals how they can improve the overall security of the organization

- Distribution of critical phone numbers and e-mail addresses

- Any other form of information sharing that is easily assimilated by its audience

The key is to impart a message that employees can quickly absorb before making a conscious decision about whether the information is important to them (especially because you have already determined that the information *is* important to them). Behaviors to target with these awareness campaigns are those most likely to lead to a security incident but that cannot be easily mitigated by technology. For example, you no doubt want your employees to create passwords that are hard to crack and to not allow tailgaters to follow them into company buildings secured by a card key or similar system.

Communication During an Incident

Communication is not limited to disclosure and reinforcement of policy. During an incident, communication is a crucial component of response activity—one that can cause the overall success or failure of the incident response team.

Communication Among Response Team Members

During the course of an incident, a number of types of communication must be executed effectively for the team to succeed. The first of these is communication among team members. Although it seems obvious, this is an area often overlooked during an investigation. This is because everyone is operating in a time-sensitive, reactive mode. In other words, providing status reports and sharing intelligence gathered might not be the primary concern.

However, during a crisis, communication needs to be a primary concern of response team members. The incident response leader needs to have a complete understanding of all aspects of the investigation at all times, to ensure that the direction she provides to the team represents the best possible course of action. If the incident response leader does not have complete information, she likely will make less-than-optimal decisions and provide inappropriate guidance, both of which can have a negative impact on the speed or capability of team members. All information must flow through the incident response leader. The leader, in turn, will provide summaries to the team, along with any necessary analysis and instruction.

Communication among team members can be made more difficult by the nature of a specific incident. For example, if the incident is a denial-of-service attack against your e-mail servers or a worm that forces you to close down your routers or key systems to prevent its spread, communicating by e-mail might not be possible. Or, if a natural disaster occurs at night, other communications media might be impacted. Identifying all possible occurrences ahead of time and crafting a clear, easy-to-follow communications plan can mean the difference between a successful and failed incident response.

The communications plan should include both a primary and secondary form of communication as well as details on what to do when communication using either of those methods is not possible. The plan should also outline the chain of command in the event of an incident so that team members know what to do—and who to contact—should a key member of the team be unreachable.

Another team communication concern is that an intruder could be monitoring specific communications channels. If the e-mail system has been compromised, the attacker could be reading the e-mail of administrators involved in the investigation. If the voice mail system has been compromised, the intruder could be eavesdropping on those communications as well. Furthermore, Trojan horse applications can enable the microphone or Web cam of an infected computer system, thereby capturing information and activity conducted nearby. An attacker who can leverage your communications channels can easily gain the upper hand.

Frequently, investigation communications will extend beyond the technical members of the incident response team. In such cases, the incident response leader will also act as the liaison to the business managers likely to be impacted the most. Business managers whose workflow is impacted, who are at risk of sensitive information being leaked, or who might be at risk of missing internal or external deadlines as a result of the incident and its investigation become ad-hoc members of the incident response team. These managers will provide guidance to the incident leader on how to choose the best course of action—in other words, how to choose the "least bad" outcome, or the outcome that is least detrimental to the organization as a whole. Such choices are about mapping business need to technical implementation.

Communication with Law Enforcement Agencies

Communications with law enforcement agencies are also important in the early stages of an incident investigation. Before an incident occurs, you will have determined the circumstances under which you need to involve specific law enforcement agencies, and you will have established appropriate contact processes for each agency. By communicating with those channels early in an incident investigation, you bring additional resources to the response and ensure that evidentiary procedure is adhered to. You also ensure that any steps taken do not interfere with later prosecution.

Companywide Communication

At various points during an investigation, it might be prudent to engage in companywide communication on the status of the investigation or remediative work. Such communication can minimize speculation and drive specific supporting behaviors. In the latter capacity, companywide communication is similar to an awareness campaign.

Companywide communication is very sensitive when conducted during an investigation. Whether an attack is internal or external, broad communications can tip off the attacker on the success or lack of success of the investigative process. The most appropriate communications in this scenario are brief, concise, and easily assimilated, without providing any specifics on the incident. For example,

> "We are experiencing intermittent outages of various network resources, the appropriate personnel are working on correcting the problem, and we hope to have service restored quickly. If you have an immediate concern, please contact the service desk."

would likely be more effective than

> "We are collecting evidence on an attacker who has compromised at least seven systems in our e-business unit, and the FBI will be shutting systems down intermittently to collect forensic images before the attacker has a chance to cover his tracks."

Basically, you are keeping your cards close to your vest.

Companywide communication can also include a wrap-up message at the close of the investigation on lessons learned and next steps to be taken. For example,

> "Our security team, during a routine analysis of our network, has identified and removed several unapproved network services. Specific policy requires that all network services be approved by the Director of IT and implemented through our normal change control process. Because of the potential security implications, we will be forcing a password reset for all users over the next three days."

Contacting the Attacker

One particularly sensitive area is communicating with the attacker. Depending on the specifics of the case, contacting the attacker might be a valuable component of the investigation. For example, if the attacker is trying to extort money or other gains from your firm, contact with the attacker could buy you valuable investigation time (by stalling the attacker) and stave off further intrusion. Of course, the opposite is also possible. Contacting the attacker could cause her to take additional action, such as formatting all your network systems to cover her tracks because she knows she has been discovered.

If law enforcement agencies are involved, they likely will have more experience dealing with these issues than your response team—so you should defer to their judgment of these agencies. Of course, prudence dictates a careful evaluation of the capability of these agencies before deferring to them. You will find a wide range of capabilities and technical sophistication, depending on whether you are dealing with local or federal investigators and on the frequency with which an agency handles computer crime investigations. You might also want to involve your legal counsel because contact with an attacker could have an impact on any prosecution attempt.

Finally, you will want to evaluate the risk created by making contact with an attacker before deciding to do so. Profiling the attacker's behavior is a critical element in deciding this. Each of these questions can help you develop a fair amount of insight about the attacker's probable next moves:

- Does the attacker seem to be after something specific, or simply snooping around?

- Has the intrusion gone on for months, or did it begin recently?

- Was the attack method exceptionally crafty, or did your firm get caught with its defenses down by not being up to date with vendor-released patches?

■   If the attacker has made contact with you, what can your response team infer about his education or locale based on the phrasing used in that contact?

■   Is it possible to use this contact with the attacker to collect additional information that law enforcement authorities can use to locate him?

Once you have determined that the risk of contacting the attacker is appropriate, consider your goals for the communication and the method by which you will make contact. If the attacker's intrusions typically occur during certain hours of the day or night, it might be prudent to time your contact at the beginning of that window. If the attacker has not contacted your organization directly, you should determine the best way of contacting her. It is unlikely that the attacker will have left her home telephone number on any given compromised system.

Finally, make certain that the goal of your contact is clear: Are you trying to slow the intruder's attacks? Gain additional evidence against the attacker? Find out the extent of her intrusions? Ask her nicely to go away? Something else? Each answer might point toward a specific method of communication and the framework for the conversation, including whether you use a medium you can log and trace.

Dealing with the Press

When wider knowledge of a security breach exists, it is possible that the event will garner the attention of the press. In such cases, you must brief your public relations staff on the incident and prepare them to respond to inquiries. Contact with the press should be reserved for duly appointed individuals within your organization that you trust to represent the information in an appropriate manner. All other staff members should be trained to direct press inquiries to the appropriate resources.

When speaking to the press, your public relations representatives should adhere to several core principles:

■   Be precise in your use of language. Say exactly what you intend to say in short, complete sentences that cannot be misinterpreted or taken out of context.

■   Stick to the facts, and do not let emotion play into the discussion. Similarly, avoid speculation about the root cause or parties involved or their motives unless you have sufficient evidence to that effect.

■ When being interviewed, ensure that with every answer you bring the conversation back to a point that you want to make.

■ Keep the technical detail low enough that you do not inadvertently invite additional attacks and that you do not exceed the understanding of the interviewer.

■ If you are working with law enforcement officials, ensure that any information, documents, photos, or other materials provided to the press does not impair the investigation or decrease the likelihood of successful prosecution.

■ Ensure you are prepared with answers to the most likely questions. Do not go into any interview situation before you are ready.

■ Recognize that, in many cases, your tone and manner say as much as your words.

■ Do not allow media attention to interfere with the investigation.

In some cases, it might be appropriate to provide a press release about the incident. This might seem contrary to conventional wisdom about how best to protect your company's image and brand, but in some cases, it can be a valuable step. Specifically, releasing your own press announcement allows you to provide an appropriate context for the event and highlight important points you feel need to be made clear. For example, you might want to stress that even though a security breach occurred, no source code in a specific Web service or product was compromised.

Best Practices

■ **Employ diligent planning to alleviate uncertainty when responding to incidents.** Because time is of the essence when handling incidents, it is critical to do as much work up front as possible. This work includes the following:

❑ Implementing preventative measures described throughout this book

❑ Implementing policies that support incident response

❑ Training all staff in their role in security

❑ Selecting the people who will be involved in incident response and designating the roles each will play

❑   Collecting and maintaining incident handling guidelines

❑   Assembling a comprehensive and accurate contact sheet

In addition, difficult scenarios should be discussed by the incident response team and management to establish boundaries and pre-define response goals. Team members and management should also discuss and agree upon aspects of involving the media and law enforcement agencies in an incident investigation. The more decisions you make up front, the easier incident response will be.

■   **Remember that executive sponsorship is essential.** Your sponsor will be able to make changes required to create the policies needed to support incident response. He also will be able to provide budget for training, staffing levels, and tools. For the most effective relationship with your sponsor, your team leader will must be able to understand and communicate the core business issues to the sponsor and to present complex issues in a logical, concise manner.

■   **Formalize your incident response team.** By formalizing the team—even in cases where incident response is not the team's core activity—you will dramatically improve response times and capability while minimizing uncertainty and power struggles.

■   **Utilize the best resources.** Make certain that the leader for each incident response is the most technically appropriate person for that type of incident. It does not make sense to use a senior Microsoft Windows technician for a mainframe issue. Nor does it makes sense to use an infrastructure engineer whose focus is routers and switches as leader on an intrusion in a database system.

Additional Information

■   RFC 2196: "Site Security Handbook" (*http://www.ietf.org/rfc/rfc2196.txt*)

■   RFC 2350: "Expectations for Computer Security Incident Response" (*http://www.ietf.org/rfc/rfc2350.txt*)

■   MOF Resource Library (*http://microsoft.com/technet/itsolutions/tandp/opex/mofrl/default.asp*)

■   Microsoft Solution for Securing Windows 2000 Server (*http://www.microsoft.com/technet/security/prodtech/Windows/SecWin2k/default.asp*)

- *The Cuckoo's Egg: Tracking a Spy Through the Maze of Computer Espionage* (Pocket Books, 2000)

- *Incident Response—Investigating Computer Crime* (Osborne, 2001)

- *Incident Response—A Strategic Guide to Handling System and Network Security Breaches* (New Riders, 2002)

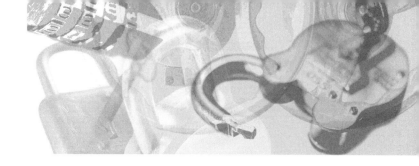

27

Responding to Security Incidents

As a network administrator, you must be able to recognize when a security incident is under way. Unfortunately, not all attacks are obvious. Recognizing that the network is under attack early is essential for protecting information or computers that have not yet been compromised. The detection of security incidents centers on investigating events that fall outside of the normal behavior of the network or computers on the network. Consequently, the key to detecting security events is to have a clear understanding of the baseline network operation. Creating a baseline for the computers and network components includes cataloging applications and services that should be running, documenting appropriate user rights and group membership, and supporting these lists with solid change control processes that update them when an approved alteration occurs.

> **More Info** For more information on creating a performance baseline, see Chapter 27, "Overview of Performance Monitoring," of the *Microsoft Windows 2000 Professional Resource Kit* (Microsoft Press, 2000).

For example, suppose an organization has implemented a host-based and network-based intrusion detection system (IDS) and analyzes the log files from the IDS software regularly. The regular analysis shows a normal spike occurring in reported connection attempts every night at 1:00 A.M.; the rest of the time, the attempted attacks are recorded at a consistent level. If the organization encounters a dramatic spike in the number of attempted attacks at 4:00 A.M., the network administrator could conclude that the organization is under a coordinated attack. Without the baseline log files for comparison, the attempted attacks might easily be dismissed as unremarkable port-scanning activity. Similarly, without the baseline, the normal spike in attacks at 1:00 A.M. might appear as a coordinated attack against the organization. Both cases illustrate the importance of having a baseline record of normal behavior.

Once you have established a baseline of behavior, you can monitor the network for sudden variations from the baseline, including short-term spikes and longer-term, more gradual increases. You should investigate all these variations. In most cases, you will find no attack in progress. In some cases, you will find an incident in progress and will be able to take action before the attacker can steal or destroy information or otherwise damage the network. The earlier you detect an anomaly and investigate it, the greater your likelihood of minimizing damage to the network.

Common Indicators of Security Incidents

Several types of events are common indicators of security incidents. You should pay particular attention to these types of events. Although after investigation, most of these events will prove harmless, some will warrant closer investigation and possibly trigger your organization's incident response plan.

Internet Port Scans

The most common indicator of a security incident is the scanning of Transmission Control Protocol (TCP) and User Datagram Protocol (UDP) ports from the Internet. Because port scanning can be a prelude to more serious penetration attempts, you should keep track of the amount and type of port scans your network receives. Variations in the number of scans or the sophistication of the scans used against your network can be an early indicator of a possible attack.

Given the frequency of port scans, you should closely monitor log files, either manually or through a log collection and correlation system. You can use a variety of tools to monitor event log files, including products such as Microsoft Operations Manager or tools that come at no cost, such as Event Comb and Dumpel.exe. (EventcombMT.exe is located in the Tools\EventComb folder on the CD that accompanies this book. Dumpel.exe is located in the Tools folder on the CD that accompanies this book.)

> **More Info**   See Chapter 12, "Auditing Microsoft Windows Security Events," in this book for detailed information on configuring auditing in Microsoft Windows 2000 and Microsoft Windows XP.

If an attacker succeeds in penetrating your defenses, one common approach she might take is to attempt to cover her tracks by erasing or modifying the event logs. Because of this, you must stay current with your logs either by exporting them to a well-secured network location (or to write-once media) or by analyzing them in real time.

The act of clearing the security event log creates an event 517. The presence of that event and the lack of events in a log that should be populated can indicate that a successful attack has occurred and evidence has been manipulated. Because attack tools that allow for the manipulation of the event log now exist, your optimal goal will be to remove logs from a given system in real time and store them in a protected data store. These principles also apply to logs other than the event logs.

You should also monitor the logs files listed in Table 27-1, as well as any other log files that seem applicable based on the details of the specific incident. Consider implementing a process to collect these log files on a daily basis and placing them in a secure, central location.

Table 27-1   Log Files of Interest to an Incident Response Team

Log File	Default Location	Description
URLScan log	%windir%\system32\ inetsrv\urlscan	The URLScan log file details why rejected requests were rejected (which specific rule in the URLScan.ini triggered the rejection) as well as the time and date, the URL in question, and the IP address of the requestor. The logging functionality for URLScan allows you to toggle logging on or off (the default is on) and allows for separate logs on a per-process or per-day basis.
Domain Name System (DNS) log	%windir%\system32\ DNS\DnsEvent.Evt	The DNS event log file can be used to identify any inappropriate DNS activity, such as unauthorized zone transfers, which can be a precursor to an attack on the network.

(continued)

Table 27-1   Log Files of Interest to an Incident Response Team   *(continued)*

Log File	Default Location	Description
Microsoft Internet Information Services (IIS) log	By default, when you install IIS 4.0, 5.0, or 5.1, the IIS logs are created in C:\%windir%\ system32\ LogFiles\W3SVC# (where # is the Web site number). To find the log file location, examine the properties of the Web site in the Internet Services Manager (ISM).	IIS extends beyond the scope of the event-logging or performance-monitoring features of Windows. The logs can include information such as who has visited your Web site, what the visitor viewed, and when the information was viewed last. You can monitor attempts, either successful or unsuccessful, to access your Web sites, virtual folders, or files. This includes events such as reading the file or writing to the file. You can choose which events you want to audit for any site, virtual folder, or file. By regularly reviewing these files, you can detect areas of your server or your sites that might be subject to attacks or other security problems. You can enable logging for individual Web sites and choose the log format. When logging is enabled, it is enabled for all the site's folders, but you can disable it for specific directories. Inspect the IIS logs for suspicious Web server activities, including (but not limited to) the following: ■ Multiple unsuccessful commands trying to run executable files or scripts. (Closely monitor the Scripts folder.) ■ Excessive unsuccessful attempts from a single IP address, with the possible intention of increasing network traffic and denying access to other users. ■ Unsuccessful attempts to access and modify .bat or .cmd files. ■ Unauthorized attempts to upload files and executable files to a folder that contains execute permissions by using HTTP PUT or POST methods.
Internet Authentication Service (IAS) log	%windir%\system32\ LogFiles\Iaslog.log	The IAS log contains listings of both successful and rejected authentication requests. This can help you determine baseline patterns for Remote Access Service (RAS) users, as well as identify anomalous activity and rejected authentication attempts, which might indicate an attack in progress.

Table 27-1   Log Files of Interest to an Incident Response Team   *(continued)*

Log File	Default Location	Description
Internet Connection Firewall (ICF) log	Windows XP or later: %windir%\ pfirewall.log	On network connections protected by ICF, the ICF logs can be configured to show successful and unsuccessful connections to that network interface, including the date and time, IP address, and ports utilized.
Dr. Watson log	%AllUsersProfile%\ Documents\ DrWatson\ Drwtsn32.log	The Dr. Watson log records process information for the processes that are running when an application crashes. If an application crashes, it might be possible to see information about the processes running at the time of the crash to help determine whether the cause was related to an attack.
IDS log	Varies based on the IDS use	IDS systems create log files that can provide a great deal of information about what is happening at the network layer of the computer. Some IDS systems incorporate a GUI and search capability to correlate large volumes of detailed information quickly.

Inability to Access Network Resources

Another indication that an incident has occurred is the sudden inability to access a network resource or a degraded response from that resource under otherwise normal conditions. If a system suddenly reboots, an application hangs unexpectedly, a system undergoes a routing change, or a modification to DNS occurs, clients might not be able to access network resources. Some or all of these events might occur in the event of an intrusion, depending on the attacker's approach. Investigate such outages to determine whether they were caused by an intruder.

Excessive CPU Utilization

Similarly, higher than normal CPU or network utilization can indicate rogue processes that might be indicators of an attack. It is normal for a system's processor to jump to 100 percent utilization periodically, or for high network traffic to be seen during a large file transfer to or from a file server. However, when a system that normally averages 40 percent CPU utilization operates at an average of 70 percent CPU utilization, or when large quantities of data travel to or from a server that normally does not generate such traffic, some form of attack might be in progress.

Although most processes being executed on a computer running Windows 2000 or Windows XP will be displayed in the Task Manager, if an attacker has compromised the computer, it will be possible to execute processes that are hidden from the Task Manager. You should be careful about how you use computers that might have been compromised. For example, an attacker might have installed keystroke logging software that is responsible for the excess CPU utilization. Thus, when you log on to the computer to investigate this issue, the attacker could intercept your account logon name and password.

Irregular Service Operations

Other variances from baseline behavior that might require investigation relate to system services. Services that should be running but are paused or stopped, services that are new to the system, and services that should be running but are missing can all indicate that an attacker has made modifications to your system to suit his needs. Tools such as SvcMon.exe—which first shipped with *Microsoft Windows 2000 Server Resource Kit* (Microsoft Press, 2000)—can monitor local or remote systems to detect changes in state of the various services on a system that you select by using the SMConfig.exe tool. Should a service stop or start, the tool will notify the administrator by e-mail and log the event.

Irregular File System Activity

Indicators of an attack at the file system level can include missing files or folders or a noticeable decrease in the available space on a system. Missing files can result from the attacker modifying your system because she wants more space or the attacker covering her tracks. A decrease in disk space can occur because the attacker is using your system for Internet Relay Chat (IRC) or file storage, or because she has copied tools to that system to extend her attack to other systems in your environment. Other file system changes, such as changes to the datestamp on system files or to the MD5 hash of system files, can be an indicator of an intrusion. Attackers will often replace executables with Trojan horse versions of the same program that can either help hide their presence or provide them with additional levels of access.

> **On the CD**   You can use the file integrity verification tool Fciv.exe, which is located in the Tools\Fciv folder that accompanies this book, to create and verify hash signatures of files.

The presence of new drivers also can point to an attack. You can monitor the drivers on a system by using the Drivers.exe tool, which is included in the Tools folder on the CD that ships with this book. This tool displays all installed device drivers on the computer on which the tool is executed. The output of the tool includes the driver's file name, the size of the driver on disk, and the date that the driver was linked. The link date can be used to identify any newly installed drivers. If an updated driver was not recently installed, this can indicate a replaced driver on the part of an attacker.

Permissions Changes

Changes to user permissions, group membership, or other security policy are also common attack indicators. If a user is granted permissions outside your change control process or if an account is added to a more privileged group, an attacker might be trying to access resources he currently cannot access. An example of this is the Nimda worm, which adds the Guest account to the Administrators group. Other changes along this vein include changes to Group Policy objects (GPOs) and auditing changes. If any of these events occur outside planned operations, we recommend you conduct an investigation. Event IDs 608–612 and 624–643 can denote such improper changes.

Analyzing a Security Incident

Once an incident has been identified—regardless of who identifies it—the information needs to be communicated to the incident response team. Following that communication, a number of steps must be taken by the response team. The approach taken will differ depending on the specifics of the incident, but the underlying intent remains the same. These are the steps:

1. Determine the cause.

2. Prevent further exploitation of the attack vector.

3. Avoid escalation and further incidents.

4. Assess the impact and damage of the incident.

5. Restore the computers' services.

6. Update policies and procedures as needed, based on the lessons learned from the security incident.

7. Find out who launched the attack (if appropriate and possible) and take business-appropriate action.

> **More Info** For more information on incident response teams and plans, see Chapter 26, "Planning for Incident Response."

Determining the Cause

At the outset of the investigation, the incident response team will need to determine the cause of the behavior, which software might be involved, how the software has been compromised, and the scope of the compromise. If hostile code is involved, the team should assess the capability and propagation methods of that code. Frequently, such analysis assistance can be obtained on the Web site of your antivirus software vendor.

> **Tip** Microsoft provides a free support hotline for viruses, worms, and similar attacks. The U.S. telephone number for this hotline is 1-866-PC SAFETY. Customers with a Premier Support agreement have additional support options and should contact their technical account manager. For international support, see *http://support.microsoft.com/ common/international.aspx?gssnb=1.*

Preventing Further Exploitation

Following the initial analysis, the team should take steps to prevent further exploitation of this type of attack. See the "Conducting Security Investigations" section later in this chapter for important considerations for this stage of your response. This stage can involve many different approaches, including applying an already existing patch for a particular vulnerability to all at-risk systems, modifying the network topology, temporarily suspending a service or application, and performing user awareness activities. The specific response will vary based on the details of the incident.

Avoiding Escalation and Further Incidents

The next step in an incident response is to avoid escalation of the existing incident and further incidents. This is a large concern when an attacker has interactive access to one or more of your systems. Shutting down the attacker's session might result in new and potentially more destructive attacks. This can also be an issue with automated attacks, such as the Nimda and Code Red worms. In those cases, the escalation is the spread of the worm or an attacker taking advantage of your vulnerable state to launch new attacks on your network.

Restoring Service

Restoration of service occurs next, once the scope and damage of the incident are fully understood. Service must be restored in a secure manner or workarounds must be put in place to enable the business activities requiring those services. Systems not being used as evidence in an attack investigation need to be brought back online without reintroducing a security threat to the network.

One of the most difficult decisions a response team can face is determining the appropriate course of action to restore a system to service after it has been compromised. Although immediate restoration of service is laudable and appears to be in the best interest of the firm, it often is a poor choice. For example, if an attacker compromises one of your servers and you decide to secure the system as it stands and bring it back online, several events can happen:

The process of securing the system could overwrite evidence, making it difficult or impossible to determine the source of the attack.

More importantly, short of comparing known good file hashes for every file on the system, you cannot know whether the compromise extends beyond the elements you have identified. Too often an attacker will enter your system by exploiting one avenue and then expand her influence by installing additional software tools or Trojan horse applications. In such cases, the system might seem to be behaving normally, when instead, it is camouflaging its own improper behavior.

Although you have identified one intrusion, others that you are unaware of might exist. The system fell to one attacker, and it is folly to think that such a system could not be hosting others with ill will.

The process of taking a system offline; verifying the checksum of every file on the system against a known good baseline (using trusted executables from your forensics workstation or tools CD); reviewing and understanding every .ini file, registry entry, setting, and service; and correcting anything found to be out of line takes considerably more time than simply rebuilding the system from known clean media, securing the system before it is brought online, and restoring service on the rebuilt system. Having spare hardware can enable you to preserve evidence by restoring affected services to different equipment, thereby leaving the impacted systems untouched. Also, if your organization has automated a process for installing the OS, you can create a single installation media that incorporates the latest service packs and hotfixes. By incorporating security updates into the media used to install the OS, a process often called *slipstreaming*, you can decrease the time it takes to recover the computer's services.

Once you have the situation under control, you should assess the impact and damage the event has caused. To better allocate resources for securing the network, you should determine the costs associated with the loss of productivity because of the security incident and the costs of recovering the disrupted services.

Incorporating Lessons Learned into Policy

Every incident is a learning experience. Your incident response team will learn about new techniques and tools as a result of the security breach, and your organization will learn where its policies and procedures might not sufficiently address risks to your environment. At this stage, it is essential to hold an incident debriefing and examine the lessons learned from the experience. Look at the cause of the event and how it could have been prevented. If your policy does not address the behavior or processes that allowed the incident to occur, look at what revisions might be necessary. If your policy does support such preventative behavior or processes, look to where the policy broke down and see what you can learn from that.

Tracking the Attacker

After you have incorporated the lessons learned into your operations, determine whether it is appropriate to track the intruder. Using the information collected from your investigation (logs, packet traces, timestamps, process lists, methods, and so on), you can trace the attacker's steps to determine his origin. To do so, use the data shown in your logs to determine the owner of the IP address or domain. You can trace the IP address or domain used by the attacker by performing a whois search at *http://www.arin.net*, *http://www.samspade.org*, or another site that provides the whois search capability.

Although possible, more extensive tracing of attackers might be illegal in some countries. You should discuss this issue with your organization's IT management and legal representatives before taking any action. Based on your detective work, you might find an individual working alone, a corporation, or a government at the other end of the attack. Or you might hit a dead end and find that intervening network providers are unable or unwilling to cooperate without a subpoena. Knowing this type of information can help you to determine whether your team is able to undertake this aspect of the incident response themselves or if additional assistance is required.

Conducting Security Investigations

Another challenging aspect of incident response is conducting the investigation itself. Although other stages of incident response have their own issues, the process used in the investigation can expand or inhibit the capability of the response team. Unskilled investigators will often damage critical evidence that could lead to discovery of the attacker, or they will otherwise hinder the team. Similarly, approaches that could yield additional information might be overlooked. For these reasons, the team should practice their response techniques before they are needed so that these techniques are already fine-tuned when an actual incident occurs.

Involving Law Enforcement

Many times, incident response involves making the least bad choice rather than making optimal choices. At no point is this more true than when you must decide whether to involve law enforcement authorities. Your organization should decide whether to involve law enforcement officials before a security incident occurs to ensure that the proper evidence collection techniques are used.

One consideration about involving law enforcement is that it will likely slow the restoration of network services. Also, if your organization does chose to work with law enforcement officials, there is a strong chance that the security incident will become public record and damage the reputation of your organization. If your organization does decide that it might want to prosecute attackers if an incident occurs, you should work with local or regional law enforcement agencies in advance to determine how to engage law enforcement and receive training in forensic investigation methods.

Conducting the Investigation

In cases where an incident response might ultimately include taking the attacker to court, it is imperative that you perform all your operations with the knowledge that they will contribute—positively or negatively—to the proceedings. The rule of thumb is to always follow the principle of best evidence while conducting the investigation. Criminal investigations involve something known as *chain of custody*, where specific processes for collecting evidence are required. Such processes vary by jurisdiction. If these processes are not followed, the chain is considered "broken" and the evidence might not be admitted into court or could be picked apart by opposing counsel. (We will discuss chain of custody and collecting evidence in more detail momentarily.)

Although your legal counsel can provide more details on the topic of evidence handling, some general principles exist. First, ensure that your handling and collection of information is beyond reproach and will stand up to the closest scrutiny. If you collect such incontrovertible evidence to prove, beyond the shadow of a doubt, a particular detail, be assured that the opposing counsel will not try to refute the evidence. Instead, the opposing counsel will attempt to undermine the credibility of the collectors and your incident response process—to inject doubt into the proceedings.

With this in mind, ensuring precision in your investigative work is key, as is validating sources and details. Ensure that no possible questions can be raised about each of the investigative activities your team performs. Document in as much detail as possible all the actions of every member of the investigative team throughout the course of the investigation. If not documented, even the seemingly mundane details, such as a time difference between the computer BIOS and the OS, can cause a great deal of heartache in court. Your documentation should include the time and date on the system—including the time zone, the name of the person conducting the action, details of the steps taken and their results, the timestamp following the steps taken, the signature of the investigator, and a signature of a skilled witness.

> **Note** In addition to helping prove the quality of evidence in your own legal jurisdiction, if you find yourself working with law enforcement authorities in another region or country, such documentation can clarify the steps taken to protect evidence from tampering and damage should that jurisdiction's rules of evidence differ from those of your own jurisdiction.

Limiting Investigative Work to Backup Media

Because the act of inspecting files on a live system can modify last modified times and access times of individual files, thus eliminating potential evidence, you should conduct investigative work only on copies of the original media. These must be byte-level copies because *slack space*—the space between files—on drives can contain significant quantities of evidence that should be retained.

A number of tools can be used to make a forensic image of the drive, including SafeBack from NTI (*http://www.forensics-intl.com/safeback.html*).

Ensure that the receiving media has not been previously used because previous data on the target drive can lead to incorrect assumptions during the investigation. Furthermore, the target media must have the same or similar hardware geometry. If a receiving drive has a dramatically different number of cylinders or sectors, evidence can be lost during the transfer. If time permits, you might want to make additional, second-generation copies from the first set of copies. This guarantees that you have an unmodified first-generation copy at all times should one be needed for additional avenues of investigation. An illustration of this method is in Figure 27-1.

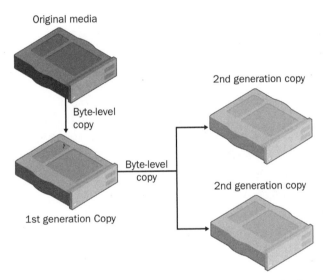

Figure 27-1   Preserving evidence by making forensically-sound backups of the original media and working copies from the first-generation backup

Treatment of the original media, which is now your evidence copy, must also be handled properly throughout the investigation. You must be able to account for the original media's whereabouts at all times, identify who has access to it at any given point, and pinpoint when possession of the evidence changed—along with the reason for any change. This is the chain of custody process we referred to earlier. To protect the chain of custody, place the media in a secure location that a minimum number of people have access to and require that all access be logged. Store the logs in such a way that no question about whether they have been altered can arise. These logs should contain the time, date, and circumstance under which the evidence changes hands, and they should document each person who takes possession of this evidence.

Collecting Evidence

If you decide to pursue a law enforcement solution, the agency you work with will have additional recommendations about the steps to take to preserve evidence and conduct the investigation. This is because the methods you use to collect one type of evidence can obscure or destroy the collection of another type. You should not begin collecting information about an attack until you have a good understanding of the type of attack that is occurring—without this understanding, you risk tipping off an intruder or destroying evidence

When you begin collecting information about an attack, you might not know exactly what you are looking for. Even if you think you know, you might be wrong: as mentioned earlier, the attack might have occurred on more levels than you are aware of. With this in mind, a keen-eyed investigator—with journal in hand—will look at every potential clue to determine what occurred and the extent of any damages.

Two primary types of data exist on a computer system: *volatile data* and *nonvolatile data*. Simply put, volatile data is data that will disappear if the system loses power, and nonvolatile data is the data that persists after power is restored. Because many attacks leave only remnants in the form of volatile data, it is essential that you collect as much of this data as possible (without causing additional damage) before shutting down the system.

Volatile Data

Volatile data includes information about the following:

- The processes that are running, suspended, or disabled

- The network connections that are open

- All recently executed programs

- The dynamic contents within the registry

- The contents of the Address Resolution Protocol (ARP) cache and of the rest of memory

- The pagefile (if it has been set to wipe itself clean upon shutdown)

- Any backup media inserted into the local system (because running processes might cause a backup to initiate and overwrite the contents of the media)

- The accounts that have sessions logged on (either locally or remotely)

- How long the system has been running since the last reboot

- The ports that are open and the applications listening on those open ports

When capturing this information, keep in mind that it might not be possible to trust the executables on the machine you are cataloging because an attacker might have modified them with one or more Trojan horses. Because it is easy to overwrite or otherwise destroy forensic information, you should conduct this type of investigation only if you have received training or are working with more experienced administrators. To properly evaluate the forensic evidence, you must know what the state of the computer would be under normal conditions. For example, it is very difficult to look at a list of processes running on a computer and determine which normally execute on the computer and which are malicious. As mentioned previously, understanding the baseline operation of the computers on your network is essential during an investigation.

> **Tip**   As you collect information, you also must ensure that you are capturing the time at which the collection occurs. Looking at your watch and noting it in your journal does not suffice because the system time might differ. A good rule of thumb is to note both the clock time and the system time in your journal before and after each command.

Nonvolatile Data

Nonvolatile data is also important to the investigation. The primary difference between volatile and nonvolatile data is when and how they can be collected. As mentioned, nonvolatile information persists after a system shutdown. Therefore, assuming no processes are running that will eliminate the evidence when the system is stopped, you can collect this information after the system is taken offline—ideally from a forensically sound backup of the media (described in the previous section).

Nonvolatile information includes the following:

- The contents of the registry
- Event logs and other log files
- Service startup configurations
- The access and modification times of files
- Recently deleted files
- The slack space between the end of a file and the end of the cluster

> **Tip**   Because normal activity that occurs when starting up a system can change the access and modification times of a large number of files—as well as causing processes set to run at startup to overwrite slack space or change other elements of the OS configuration—we suggest you conduct analysis of these aspects offline.

Data Collection Tools

Incident response teams should be familiar with the wide variety of tools that are available for collecting data, along with their capabilities, strengths, and weaknesses. Practicing working with these tools before they are needed in an incident response will help investigators hone their skills. This can help reduce the number of steps required to collect the necessary information and prevent other evidence from being destroyed in the process—which, as we mentioned, is a large factor in determining the success of the investigation. Table 27-2 shows some of the tools available for gathering data in an incident investigation and where you obtain them.

Table 27-2   Tools for Gathering Information

Data Type	Command or Tool
Processes running	Task Manager or the command-line tools TList (Windows 2000) and Tasklist (Windows XP), which are both available in default installations of Windows 2000 and Windows XP
	PsTools from Sysinternals at *http://www.systeminternals.com*
	Fport from Foundstone at *http://www.foundstone.com*
Current system activity	Filemon and Regmon from Sysinternals at *http://www.systeminternals.com*
Services and drivers	SC.exe, Slist.exe, and Drivers.exe, found in the Tools folder on the CD included with this book
	Net Start and Reg.exe, which are both available in default installations of Windows 2000 and Windows XP
New files	Dir /q /-c /o:d /t:a /s > *filename*.txt, which is available in default installations of Windows 2000 and Windows XP
	Forensic Toolkit from Foundstone at *http://www.foundstone.com*
Memory contents	CheckSym.exe, found in the Tools\CheckSym folder on the CD included with this book

Table 27-2   Tools for Gathering Information   *(continued)*

Data Type	Command or Tool
Registry	Reg.exe, which is available in default installations of Windows 2000 and Windows XP
	Regdmp.exe, found in theTools folder on the CD included with this book
Permissions	Xcacls.exe, Xcacls.vbs, and Subinacl.exe, which are found on the CD included with this book. (Xcacls.exe and Subinacls.exe are in the Tools folder; Xcacls.vbs is in the Tools\Scripts\XCACLS VBS folder.)
Current network connections	Netstat.exe -ano and Nbtstat.exe, which are available in default installations of Windows 2000 and Windows XP (the -o switch for Netstat.exe works in Windows XP only)
	Fport from Foundstone at *http://www.foundstone.com*
Network IP routes	Netstat.exe -r and Route Print, which are available in default installations of Windows 2000 and Windows XP
Shares information	Net Share, which is available in default installations of Windows 2000 and Windows XP
	Srvcheck.exe, found in the Tools folder on the CD included with this book
	DumpSec from SomarSoft at *http://www.somarsoft.com*
	Vadump.exe, found in the Tools folder on the CD included with this book
Scheduled tasks	At and Run registry keys, which are available in default installations of Windows 2000 and Windows XP
Slack space	Tools such as EnCase (*http://www.guidancesoftware.com/*), NTI (*http://www.forensics-intl.com/tools.html*), WinHex (*http://www.sf-soft.de*), Norton Utilites Disk Editor (*http://www.sf-soft.de*)

The capabilities of tools listed in Table 27-2 vary widely. Not every tool will be valuable in every instance. In some cases, combining the output of multiple tools will be necessary to gain information that is useful to the investigation—for example, when collecting information on running processes. Although it is useful to collect a list of the processes running, it is even more useful to combine that information with information on open network sessions. This combination can help you, as the investigator, ferret out abnormal system behavior.

You can extend the usefulness of this combination of data when comparing the results with a known good baseline. For example, if you are concerned about changes to the files that are listed in your services list, you can use a tool such as Tripwire (*http://www.tripwire.com*) to compare hashes of all system files to see whether any have changed. Alternately, you can use a command such as

```
dir /q /-c /o:d /t:a /s > filename.txt
```

to output a complete, recursive file listing of all files on the system sorted in date order to the Filename.txt file. To perform the same type of activity with the registry, you can leverage the Reg.exe tool and its /query and /compare switches. To review permissions, you can utilize Xcacls.exe, Xcacls.vbs, or Subinacl.exe.

> **Note**   As many of the examples discussed in this section illustrate, if you want to be effective, you must collect a fair amount of data long before an incident occurs. In cases where you have not performed this preparatory activity, you might be able to obtain enough information from similarly configured systems for comparison. Keep in mind that if those other systems have also been compromised, the information you collect might be useless at best, or it might lead you to believe that no compromise has occurred.

Once volatile data has been collected, you must preserve the state of the original media either for evidence or for additional investigation by making one or more backup copies, as mentioned earlier. When making copies of the drives, it is not enough to simply copy files. Additional evidence can be found in the space between files—the slack space—in the form of previously deleted (but not yet overwritten) files. Additional evidence can also be found in the space between the end of a file and the end of the sector where the tail end of that file resides. Because of this, the backup needs to be a byte-level backup of the entire drive. Best results will be obtained by matching the original drive as closely as possible in terms of its geometry. The drive must not have been previously used because remnants of that earlier use could contaminate evidence and impede the investigation. A number of tools exist for performing a sector-by-sector copy of a hard drive, including SafeBack from NTI (*http://www.forensics-intl.com/safeback.html*), Norton Ghost from Symantec (only when using the -IR switch, and found at *http://www.symantec.com/sabu/ghost/ghost_personal/*), EnCase (*http://www.guidancesoftware.com/*), and dd, a tool for forensically-sound backups.

> **Note**   RAID arrays pose a challenge to the forensic recovery process because data often spans multiple drives and slack space is quickly overwritten by other data as the RAID array is optimized. It can be difficult, if not impossible, to extract data from the slack space on a RAID volume.

Performing Network Monitoring

If the information described throughout this section does not provide you with sufficient guidance, you might want to perform full network monitoring and inspect traffic on the network. By analyzing which systems are talking to each other as well as the contents of those communications, you can gain a great deal of information about an attack in progress. However, the analysis of masses of raw data can be very time-consuming.

Besides taking into account the tedium of network monitoring, you must consider the issue of privacy. If an investigator reads all data passing on the wire, she likely will review user data and thereby violate the privacy of those users. This is a larger issue for some law enforcement personnel who might be legally barred from this type of monitoring to prevent the possibility of inadvertent privacy violation.

Because privacy violation is a complex legal issue that varies among jurisdictions, we recommend you discuss this topic with your organization's legal counsel. Even in cases where full packet details cannot be reviewed because of privacy concerns, it is possible to gain useful information by analyzing transactional data contained in packet headers. Knowing which systems are talking to each other, which protocols are being used, whether the traffic is encrypted, and the volume of the traffic flow can allow an investigator to make inferences that can help with future investigative tasks.

> **More Info**   See Part VII of this book, "Applying Key Principles of Privacy," for more information about privacy issues.

Implementing Countermeasures to a Security Incident

Once the cause of the incident has been identified, you should close off any entry vector the attacker has utilized. In essence, you have identified a specific threat through risk analysis and you should now mitigate that risk. This simple description applies regardless of whether the threat is a denial-of-service condition, a malicious attacker who has installed Trojan horse applications on a server, a curious employee viewing files to which he should not have access, or any of the other myriad security risks networks face today. Although the response will differ depending on the threat, the goal is to eliminate the risk and continue with normal operations.

When implementing countermeasures to an attack, you must consider the benefit produced by the countermeasure and the effects on business continuity. For example, the decision to disconnect an organization's connection to the Internet or its network connection to a business partner might cause the company loss of productivity, but if the alternative promises to cost more than this disruption, the alternative is not preferable. Such decisions should be made only by senior-level management. Other types of countermeasures have less drastic business consequences and can be more easily implemented.

For example, if upon reflection, you realize that a firewall was configured in a manner that is too permissive, the application of stricter settings is needed. If the method of attack exploits a known vulnerability for which a security update exists, you should test and apply the security update to all computers that have not yet had the update applied. If a user's password was compromised, that password should be changed immediately and all of that user's sessions should be terminated. If an account with administrative credentials has been compromised, all passwords throughout the organization might need to be reset.

Assessing the Scope of an Attack

The risk assessment for the particular attack will dictate the specific countermeasures required. If you cannot discern the full scope of an intrusion, more drastic measures might need to be taken than if you had noticed the attack early and are aware of its full scope. Given the nature of computer security, it is much more likely that the former will be the case. That said, a more conservative response is typically preferable to one that is permissive. This is because implementing a solution that lacks the necessary protections is no better than performing no countermeasures at all.

This is most clearly illustrated by a system-level compromise—one in which an attacker has gained high levels of privilege on one or more systems and might have utilized those privileges. Because an administrative user can do anything on the systems over which she has authority, an attacker who raises his privileges to that level can do the same. The attacker could add accounts to the system or domain, add privileges to existing accounts, add accounts to privileged groups, replace system files with Trojan horse applications, modify the core of the OS to mask his continued presence, or perform any other task that an administrator can.

The industry consensus on the best practice for recovering from such a situation is to rebuild any system that has endured a system-level compromise, unless you are 100 percent certain that no additional damage has been done. Even restoring the system from backup might not resolve the issues created by the attacker because you might not have detected the attack until after the backup in question took place. The only way to be certain that the system has been restored is to rebuild it by using trusted media that employs secure build processes that protect the system from compromise until it has been secured.

> **Tip**   Building a system on an isolated network can protect the computer from being compromised by viruses or attackers that have penetrated the network before the system is secured.

Weighing Tradeoffs

As you implement countermeasures, be cognizant of the tradeoffs that might be involved. For example, by disconnecting a computer from the network to preserve its state for further examination, you could alert the attacker to the fact that you have discovered his presence. This could result in the attacker attempting to compromise other computers on your network that have not yet been comprised, or it could result in the attacker immediately initiating destructive methods on other computers he has already compromised to prevent you from collecting evidence that might be used to track him. However, allowing the attacker to continue unimpeded can cause further damage to your organization's network or computers. Consider the possible reactions an attacker might have to the countermeasures you put in place before you deploy them.

The implementation of countermeasures is more complex when the intruder is internal. In such situations, the incident response team must be careful not to alert the intruder that the team is aware of his activities so that further damage can be prevented. This situation is made even worse if the attacker is a trusted member of the response team. As a response team member, he will be aware of many or all details of the investigation and could change his attack posture to defeat the efforts of the response team. Or the attacker could go dormant to make it appear that attacks have ceased, in order to protect himself from being discovered.

> **Caution** If you believe that the intruder is an employee of your orga-
> nization, you should involve the HR department as soon as possible to
> avoid violating the employee rights of the suspect.

Recovering Services After a Security Incident

Once the incident has been controlled and countermeasures are in place against
that type of attack, you should begin looking at the restoration of normal operations. Services that have been closed down will be reopened, network connections that have been rerouted will be restored, and systems that have been
compromised will be rebuilt and brought online. Of course, it might not be prudent to return to normal operations all at once. For example, if you have terminated all external access to your network as a countermeasure to an attack in
progress, turning on every service at once might not be the best course of action.

If all services that have been shut down are brought online at once, it
might not be possible to monitor them adequately and ensure that no additional
compromise is attempted. The result can be as bad or even worse than the original incident if your countermeasures fail and the attacker regains her foothold
on your network. In such a case, the stakes will be higher for the attacker: she
might have concerns about covering her tracks to escape retribution for her
actions, or her pride might be wounded, or both things might be case. In other
words, you should consider an attacker in this position much more dangerous.

You should also be concerned with existing client sessions on any backup
servers. If a secondary server is brought back online, either because it was
taken offline for evidence or because it had been compromised and was later
rebuilt, you need to be aware of the user experience of those accessing such
a secondary system. Building a duplicate system with the same name can cause
numerous network problems that can result in poor user experience (or
worse) for that system's users. Instead, plan and implement a graceful transi-
tion that follows operational best practices, such as those described in
Microsoft Operations Framework (MOF) under Release Management (*http://
www.microsoft.com/technet/itsolutions/msm/smf/SMFRELMG.asp*). By applying
a project management mindset to service restoration, you can avoid many
potentially devastating problems.

Conducting a Security Incident Post Mortem

Because of the iterative nature of security, you need to ensure that your response team and organization learn from any incident that occurs, and you must incorporate those lessons into future protective measures and their supporting processes. Following each security issue, you should hold a debriefing session. In that session, all the participants and key stakeholders should discuss the specifics of the incident, including the following:

- What went right

- What could have gone more smoothly

- Measures that could have prevented the incident

- What the organization needs to do to ensure that this type of incident is not repeated

- How much the security incident has cost the organization

During the post mortem review, you should determine changes that will need to be made to your organization's security policies and procedures, and you might need to implement new security measures to prevent such an incident from recurring or similar incidents from happening. You should assign a single person responsibility for recording this information and ensuring its follow-up. If these changes will impact business continuity, you should conduct a risk analysis to determine the appropriate solution.

The results of the debriefing should be fully documented and distributed on a need-to-know basis. Often, it makes sense to have two versions of the write-up—one that is couched in business terms and is appropriate for business managers, and another that delves into technical detail and is appropriate for the IT teams that will be implementing changes to the environment.

Best Practices

- **Clearly establish and enforce all policies and procedures.** Many security incidents are accidentally created by IT personnel who have not followed or understood change management procedures or have improperly configured security devices, such as firewalls and authentication systems. Your policies and procedures should be thoroughly tested to ensure that they are practical, clear, and provide the appropriate level of security.

- **Provide comprehensive training on tools to your incident response team.** Ensure that you provide training to your Computer Security and Incident Response Team (CSIRT) on the use and location of tools that will be used during an incident response. Consider providing portable computers preconfigured with these tools to ensure that no time is wasted installing and configuring tools when responding to an incident. These systems and the associated tools must be properly protected when not in use.

- **Verify your backup and restore procedures.** Be aware of where backups are maintained, who can access them, and your procedures for data restoration and system recovery. Make sure that you regularly verify backups and media by selectively restoring data. Ensure that your backup retention policy supports incident response by including trusted copies of incident response tools and process documents in any offsite backup.

- **Assemble all relevant communication information.** Ensure that you have contact names and phone numbers for people within your organization that need to be notified (including members of the CSIRT, those responsible for supporting all your systems, and those in charge of media relations). You will also need details for contacting your ISP and local and national law enforcement agencies. Consider contacting local law enforcement agencies before an incident happens to ensure you understand proper procedures for communicating incidents and collecting evidence.

- **Always conduct post mortem reviews of security incidents.** Make sure to hold a session to discuss what can be learned from each incident and incorporate those lessons into your organization's policies, procedures, build process, and network design. Given the amount of effort typically associated with responding to an incident, missing out on this potential benefit would be a shame.

Additional Information

- RFC 2196: "Site Security Handbook" (*http://www.ietf.org/rfc/rfc2196.txt*)

- RFC 2350: "Expectations for Computer Security Incident Response" (*http://www.ietf.org/rfc/rfc2350.txt*)

- ISO 17799: "Code of Practice for Information Security Management" (*http://www.iso-17799.com/*)

- Microsoft Operations Framework (MOF) Resource Library (*http://microsoft.com/technet/itsolutions/tandp/opex/mofrl/default.asp*)

- Forum of Incident Response Security Teams Web site (*http://www.first.org*)

- "Steps for Recovering from a UNIX or NT System Compromise" white paper from the CERT Coordination Center at Carnegie Mellon University (*http://www.cert.org/tech_tips/root_compromise.html*)

- Microsoft Solution for Securing Windows 2000 Server (*http://www.microsoft.com/technet/security/prodtech/Windows/SecWin2k/default.asp*)

- *The Cuckoo's Egg: Tracking a Spy Through the Maze of Computer Espionage* (Pocket Books, 2000)

- *Incident Response: Investigating Computer Crime* (Osborne, 2001)

- *Incident Response: A Strategic Guide to Handling System and Network Security Breaches* (New Riders, 2002)

- *Network Intrusion Detection, Third Edition* (New Riders, 2002)

- 296085: "How to Use SQL Server to Analyze Web Logs"

- 313064: "Monitor Web Server Performance by Using Counter Logs in System Monitor in IIS"

- 326444: "How to Configure the URLScan Tool"

- 300390: "How to Enable IIS Logging Site Activity in Windows 2000"

> **Note**   The previous four articles can be accessed through the Microsoft Knowledge Base. Go to *http://support.microsoft.com* and enter the article number in the Search The Knowledge Base text box.

Part VII

Applying Key Principles of Privacy

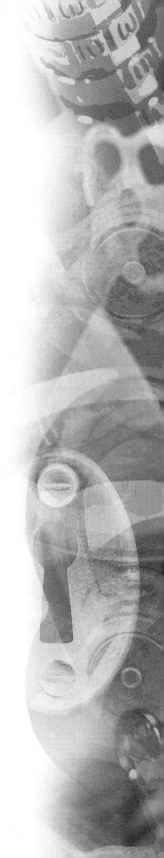

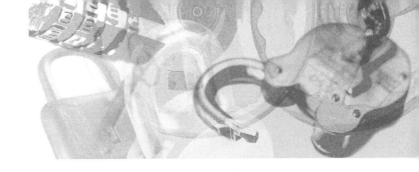

28

Understanding the Importance of Privacy

Until now, this book has focused on security. However, a book on securing your network would be incomplete without a section on protecting the privacy of the data that your company collects. Many companies collect information about their customers, but doing so carries a lot of responsibility. Protecting your customers' privacy will go a long way toward winning their trust. Today, consumer trust in companies protecting their privacy is at an all-time low. According to a survey by UCO Software, Inc. released November 7, 2001, in 2001 online and offline retailers lost $6.2 billion in sales because of privacy issues. (See *http://www.cyberdialogue.com/news/releases/2001/11-07-uco-retail.html* for more information.) In addition, according to a survey by Culnan-Milne, that same year, 64 percent of consumers reported leaving a Web site they had been browsing because of privacy reasons. (See *http://www.ftc.gov/bcp/workshops/glb/supporting/culnan-milne.pdf* for more information.) This mistrust has negatively impacted both Internet commerce and traditional retail sales. One bad experience with a Web site can diminish a user's desire to do business with any site or traditional retailer.

Consumers are more closely scrutinizing how companies handle personal information. Your company probably stores data for employees, customers, partners, and business entities. You will need to set up policies for handling information from each of these groups. In addition, depending on the type of data or the age of the person from which you are collecting data, you will need to comply with specific regulations such as HIPAA, GLBA, and COPPA, which are described later in this chapter. Neglecting to do so can cause you to lose business and lead to unwanted legal entanglements.

Whether your company is in the service, manufacturing, or retail industry, your total revenues will be affected by how much your customers trust you. Think about the companies that you refuse to do business with simply because you do not trust them. Perhaps you refuse to shop online because you do not trust a Web site to safeguard your personal information. It is your job to avoid becoming one of those companies.

You have probably received literature in the mail from companies with which you do business informing you of their privacy policy. Your company should also have a privacy policy and an infrastructure in place to guarantee it. This chapter, Chapter 29, "Defining Privacy for the Corporate Web Site," and Chapter 30, "Deploying Privacy in the Enterprise," will describe the various intricacies of privacy and the measures you can take to help build a sound privacy infrastructure for your enterprise.

Defining Privacy

Privacy can be defined as *freedom from the intrusion of others in one's personal life or affairs*. Within your enterprise, ensuring privacy will mean complying with the wishes of a person or organization when it comes to their privacy preferences. This can include protecting sensitive information and activities. For example, online shoppers want their credit card information protected as well as the type of purchases they are making. While many individuals will want to protect their personal information, many companies will want to protect their intellectual property.

Sensitive information is any information about a person that could be used to embarrass or discriminate against him or her. Examples of sensitive information include a person's race, age, sex, sexual orientation, religion, ethnicity, national origin, political stance, medical history, and professional or social associations.

As mentioned earlier, you will probably store personal information for individuals and organizations that have different types of relationships with your company. You also may store confidential information about your own company, such as the number of widgets the company has sold. Your company needs to have a strategy in place for ensuring the privacy of sensitive information no matter where it originates. Once you have this strategy in place, you will be on the road to building better customer trust.

Privacy vs. Security

These are the simplified definitions of security and privacy with regard to protecting sensitive information:

- **Security**   The protection of sensitive information from individuals that do not have the appropriate level of access

- **Privacy**   Complying with the preferences of a person or organization when handling their data

Access to sensitive information should not simply be viewed as allowed or disallowed. Even Read, Write, and Delete access to data should not be applied in a blanket fashion. For example, if you are storing customer contact information and you have a staff of people who spend all their time calling customers, you do not need to give that staff access to your customers' e-mail and home addresses. Your company should consider implementing task-based or role-based security that not only restricts the records to which your employees have access but the fields within those records.

The practice of complying with a person's privacy is more complex than you might think. For instance, suppose that you have a business relationship with some customers and you have agreed to send them e-mail messages to keep them updated on certain products. Does that mean that other members of your department can send those customers e-mail messages too? Can you send those customers e-mail messages about product plans that fall outside the parameters of your business relationship? Can you include those customers in your e-mail marketing campaigns? Can you call them on the phone at their home or office unexpectedly? Are you allowed to share their information with other departments in your company or outside business partners?

You should understand your customers' preferences for each of these situations and ensure that your employees understand your company's policy for respecting these preferences. Your customers should also be clear about how you will use their personal information. By not taking these factors into account, you risk ruining your company's image and affecting its overall success.

Protecting Consumers from Inappropriate Contact and Tracking

Privacy is often viewed as safeguarding how personally identifiable information is handled. However, privacy does not end there. A person's privacy has to do with more than how you use his data—it includes how you interact with him. For instance, inappropriate contact and tracking can be viewed as an invasion of privacy.

Inappropriate Contact

Consider the random spam you receive every day in your Inbox and the telemarketing calls you receive in the evening when you get home from work. These disruptions can be irritating. However, if the contact is expected or welcome, you usually will not be bothered by it.

If during your initial contact with a customer—be it in person or via a Web form—you inform her that you want to send a short e-mail once a month to update her on a product or service special and you give her the opportunity to agree to or decline this contact, your future e-mails will rarely be viewed as an irritant. Future phone contact can be set up the same way. Construct a contact agreement with your customers and stick to it. This type of policy should be included in your corporate privacy strategy and adopted by all your employees.

Inappropriate Tracking

If you have a Web site that uses cookies or some other mechanism to track visitors' browsing habits, this should be clearly stated in your privacy policy. Your company should not track users in a unique fashion without their consent. Furthermore, you should not force your site's visitors to accept cookies unless doing so benefits them in some way. Cookies can help visitors by remembering preferences and selections making it easier for them to navigate your Web site. Anonymous or aggregate tracking of visitors to your Web site is OK. Tracking users to complete their online transactions is also fine, but even then, you should notify users about what you are doing.

Why is tracking the browsing habits of your users more harmful than you might think? Suppose that you visit New York City and as you walk around Manhattan, you notice someone following you and taking notes. You confront the person and he tells you he wants to ensure that you find the items you need easily while shopping in Manhattan. You ask the person to stop following you, but he either ignores you or asks you to leave Manhattan. How would that make you feel? Tracking a user on your Web site is similar to having a stranger look over your shoulder while you surf the Web.

The Roots of Privacy Legislation

Before the computer age, individuals viewed protecting their privacy as avoiding Peeping Toms and keeping the government from tapping their phone lines. The invention of the computer not only enabled companies and governments to collect endless amounts of information about people, it allowed them to share and even sell this information. Few safeguards on this personal data, leaving it open to abuse by those handling it as well as outside attackers. In the 1980s, numerous countries, regions, and organizations started creating guidelines and legislation to stop the improper flow of personal information. This section will look at some of the advances made in privacy protection during the past two decades.

Organisation for Economic Co-operation and Development

The Organisation for Economic Co-operation and Development (OECD), found on the Web at *http://www.oecd.org*, is comprised of 30 member countries and 70 nonmember countries. The OECD's purpose is to discuss, develop, and refine economic and social policies. When many of its member countries were first considering privacy legislation, the OECD was concerned that the creation of such disparate privacy regulations would impede the flow of personal data among countries. To avoid this problem, the OECD adopted the Guidelines on the Protection of Privacy and Transborder Flows of Personal Data in September 1980. Most of the privacy legislation that exists today is based on these guidelines. The guidelines consist of the following principles:

- **Collection Limitation Principle**   Limits on the collection of personal data should exist, and this collection should be obtained in a lawful and fair way with the knowledge and consent of the data owner, where appropriate.

- **Data Quality Principle**   Personal data should be relevant to the purposes for which they will be used and should be accurate, complete, and current.

- **Purpose Specification Principle**   The purpose for which the data is being collected should be specified, and changes to this purpose should be compatible with the original purpose. For example, if a Web site selling music initially tracked tape sales to determine the most popular artist, it later can switch to tracking CD sales to determine the top-selling artist.

- **Use Limitation Principle**   Personal data should not be disclosed or otherwise used for purposes other that those specified in the previous principle. However, this data can be disclosed or used for other purposes with the consent of the data owner or legal authorities.

- **Security Safeguards Principle**   Personal data should be protected by reasonable security safeguards against risks such as loss, unauthorized access, destruction, use, modification, and disclosure.

- **Openness Principle**   Organizations should maintain a general policy of being forthcoming about their personal data collection practices and policies. An organization should be willing to specify the type of personal data it is storing and what it intends to use that data for.

- **Individual Participation Principle** An individual should have the right to confirm that an organization is maintaining data on him and should be allowed to erase, rectify, complete, or amend the data. Access to the data should be straightforward and inexpensive.

- **Accountability Principle** An organization collecting personal data must be accountable for providing measures that comply with the previous principles in this list.

Privacy Legislation in the United States

In the United States, privacy awareness with regard to personal data was born in 1973, when the Department of Health, Education, and Welfare published the report "Records, Computers, and the Rights of Citizens," which discussed the protection of personal information on computer systems. Between 1973 and 1998, several other U.S. organizations published reports on the treatment of personal information. In 1998, the Federal Trade Commission created their Fair Information Practices to combine these various papers into a set of core principles. The principles are as follows:

- **Notice/Awareness** Informs users about the data an organization is collecting and how it is being used

- **Choice/Consent** Gives users the ability to choose the data about them that is collected and how it is used

- **Access/Participation** Permits users to see the information about them that was collected and to change the information as appropriate

- **Integrity/Security** Protects user data that is collected from unauthorized access or changes made without the user's consent

- **Enforcement/Redress** Gives users a way to submit complaints to companies that collect their data

Unfortunately, companies were not compelled to comply with these principles. However, consumers were able to use these principles to bring lawsuits against companies who violated their privacy. This basically meant that, under the Fair Information Practices, companies could do whatever they wanted with consumers' personal data, as long as they were not caught. The U.S. Department of Commerce's creation of the Safe Harbor Principles changed all that.

The Safe Harbor Principles

Many guidelines on privacy were written in the United States before the country's creation of the Safe Harbor Principles in 1998. However, as with the Fair Information Practices, none of these guidelines had any real influence on the way companies did business in the United States. The European Union (EU) Directives on data protection changed all that. If U.S. companies wanted to continue to do business with EU companies, they had to show that they were serious about privacy protection. To ensure the continued flow of information from companies in the EU to U.S. companies, the U.S. Department of Commerce created the Safe Harbor Principles.

The Safe Harbor Principles are, in effect, the U.S. version of the EU Directives. In addition, these principles marked the beginning of the adoption of effective privacy policies in the United States. By complying with the Safe Harbor Principles, U.S. companies could continue to work with EU companies. This means abiding by the seven tenets of the Safe Harbor Principles, which specify how personal information should be handled. To view the full set of requirements for acceptance into safe harbor, visit *http://www.export.gov/safeharbor/ sh_overview.html*. The seven tenets of safe harbor are described next.

Notice   Notice means informing users about the type of information you are collecting, why you are collecting it, how long you will keep it, who will have access to it, which third parties you will share the information with, how users can access and then change or delete their data, and who they can contact if they feel that these commitments were broken.

As a company, this means that you need to create a privacy policy that covers how your employees will handle this personal information, and you must ensure that your employees adhere to this policy. Your policy should be compiled into a privacy statement and posted on your Web site in a conspicuous manner. Ensure that the document is clearly visible and easy to understand.

To view Microsoft's privacy statement, visit *http://www.microsoft.com/info/ privacy.htm*. For assistance in creating a privacy statement, use the Privacy Statement Generator, located at *http://cs3-hq.oecd.org/scripts/pwv3/pwhome.htm*.

Choice   Choice means giving your customers an opportunity to tell you how they want their data handled before you collect it and to change their selection later if they want. Giving users a choice is not just about determining how your company will handle sensitive information; it also means specifying the method your company can use to contact a user. For example, can you contact users via e-mail, phone, or postal mail? Can you send users product materials, sales specials, and third-party materials, and can you include them in your marketing campaigns? Choice also governs how you record a user's browsing habits at your Web site.

Think about how you feel when you receive a sales call on the telephone during your favorite TV show or when you receive lots of random e-mail messages about improving your physical appearance. You do not want your customers to think negatively of your company when you contact them, so make sure your contact with them is expected.

You should give users *opt-in* and *opt-out* choices for how their data will be used. Opt-in means the user has to implicitly agree for their data to be used for a specific purpose. Opt-out means that the user has to indicate that they do not want their data used for a specific purpose. The determination for sensitive user information should be opt-in. When a user gives permission for their information to be used, for any secondary uses of their data, or for your company to share their personal information with third parties, the user should have the ability to opt-out of this use of her data.

Onward Transfer   Onward transfer refers to sharing a user's information with a business partner or other third party. For example, suppose that you sell bedroom furniture and you often team with a company that makes linen. After selling a bed to a customer, the linen company might want to send the customer a special offer on sheets. So you give the linen manufacturer your customer's contact information as a service to them. As innocent as this might sound, it should not happen without the customer's approval.

It is acceptable for you to share your customer information with a vendor who works with your company on a particular project, as long as that information sharing is based on the agreement you made with your customers and as long as the vendor agrees to comply with your company's privacy policy and abides by the Safe Harbor Principles. For example, if your customers agree to let you send them product materials, you are allowed to share your customers' address information with a company you hire to mail the material to your customers.

Security   Sensitive customer information should be protected to ensure that only individuals with a valid reason can access the data and that the data is protected from alteration, misuse, destruction, or loss. Such security measures should not only include applying password protection; they should also include encrypting data while it is transmitted or stored. Network and database administrators should not have access to sensitive information unless they need to this information to perform their job duties. Invest in making the ability to steal information difficult. For example, encrypt the storage of data and audit each access of the data. Employees that have access to your customers' data must abide by the corporate privacy policy specifying how the data is handled.

Data Integrity   Data integrity governs the quality of information that is being stored. It starts with collecting only the minimum amount of information you need to provide the service that you are offering to your customers. If you do not need a customer's cell phone number, do not collect it. When you transfer customer information to vendors, do not send the entire customer record. Transfer only the information that the vendor needs to perform the task they were hired to do.

Maintaining data integrity also involves ensuring that the information that you collect is current, complete, and accurate before you use it. Information that does not meet these requirements should be recollected or purged from the system.

Access   Customers from whom you collect information should be able to verify and update their information in an easy and inexpensive fashion. When your company no longer needs the information, users should be able to have their information removed from your storage systems. You can enable a user to directly access his information via an online form, indirectly access it via e-mail, or access it by contacting a company representative over the phone. In any of these cases, the user's identity should be verified before you permit him to read or modify his data.

Enforcement   Your customers should have some recourse if they feel their privacy rights have been abused. The privacy policy on your Web site should include an e-mail address or point to an online form that customers can use to contact your company about privacy abuses. Your company should also look into joining one of several online privacy compliance organizations. For more information on self-regulation and a list of online privacy compliance programs, visit the U.S. Federal Trade Commission's Self-Regulation and Privacy Online page at *http://www.ftc.gov/os/1999/9907/pt071399.btm*.

Other U.S. Privacy Legislation

Several other pieces of U.S. privacy legislation have been introduced to protect a specific aspect of a person's privacy or a specific type of data. We discuss some of these pieces of legislation in the remainder of this section. When storing customer information, someone from your organization's privacy department should review the type of information that you are storing, from whom you are collecting the information, and by what means you are collecting this data to ensure that you are abiding by the various privacy statutes. Once again, when it comes to practices that could affect your company's revenues or image, be proactive.

Children's Online Privacy Protection Act (COPPA)   This act prohibits the collection or transfer of information from individuals that are 13 years of age or younger without their parents' permission. If your Web site knowingly collects information from children under the age of 13 or allows them to post personal information about themselves via chat rooms, e-mail, or other means, this act applies to you. COPPA is relevant to companies that operate sites that either target children or have knowledge that certain users are under the age of 13. When collecting information in person, verify the person's age. When collecting the information online, include a warning and have the user validate that they have their parents' permission before collecting any data. In either case, the Web site should record the user's age for future reference, in case employees need to contact that user—for example, to renew her membership.

Computer Fraud and Abuse Act (CFAA)   This act prohibits anyone from having physical or electronic access to any computer for any reason without permission from the user. No information can be read from, added to, modified on, or deleted from a user's computer without her permission. This act covers computers that are owned by individuals, not companies. A company always has the right to access its computers, even if an employee is storing personal information on it. Before downloading information or software to a user's computer or obtaining any information from a user's computer, get that user's permission.

Gramm-Leach-Bliley Act (GLBA)   This act governs the handling of financial information. Always inform a user in detail why you are collecting his financial data. Financial information is any descriptive information about a user's finances or any data that can be used to retrieve financial information—for example, a person's salary or checking account number. The control and transmission of this information should be covered by strict corporate policies.

Health Insurance Portability and Accountability Act (HIPAA)   This act governs the handling of medical information. Always inform a user in detail why you are collecting her medical information. Medical information is any descriptive information about a user's health or any information that can be used to retrieve a user's medical history—for example, a person's medical condition or health insurance number. The control and transmission of this information should be covered by strict corporate policies.

Privacy Legislation in Canada

In the 1980s, each of the Canadian provinces began to pass its own privacy legislation that applied to government agencies and regulated organizations. Quebec was the only province to pass privacy laws to protect the private sector, passing Bill 68, or the Act Respecting the Protection of Personal Information in the Private Sector, in 1994. In response to the EU Directives, the Canadian Standards Association (CSA) created the Model Code for the Protection of Personal Information (*http://www.csa.ca/standards/privacy/code/Default.asp*). A summary of the code's principles follows:

- **Accountability**   An organization is responsible for personal information under its control and should designate someone who is accountable for the organization's compliance with the following principles.

- **Identifying Purposes**   The purposes for which personal information is collected must be identified by the organization before or while the information is collected.

- **Consent**   The knowledge and consent of the user are required for the collection, use, or disclosure of personal information, except where inappropriate.

- **Limiting Collection**   The organization should only collect personal information necessary for the purposes it originally specified. Information must be collected by fair and lawful means.

- **Limiting Use, Disclosure, and Retention**   Personal information must not be used or disclosed for purposes other than those for which it was collected, except with the consent of the user or as required by law. Personal information should be retained only as long as necessary for the fulfillment of those purposes.

- **Accuracy**   Personal information must be as accurate, complete, and up to date as the project at hand requires.

- **Safeguards**   Personal information should be protected by security safeguards appropriate to the sensitivity of the data.

- **Openness**   An organization should make readily available to users specific information about its policies and practices relating to the management of personal information.

- **Individual Access**   Upon request, a user must be informed of the existence, use, and disclosure of his personal information and must be given access to that information. A user should be able to challenge the accuracy and completeness of the information and have it amended as appropriate.

- **Challenging Compliance**   A user must be able to challenge an organization's compliance with these principles. To do so, user must have access to the organization employee accountable for the organization's compliance.

Canada's privacy code was the basis for their Personal Information Protection and Electronic Documents Act, or PIPEDA (*http://www.privcom.gc.ca/legislation/02_06_01_01_e.asp*). This law was enacted in January 2001 and brings Canada into compliance with the EU Directives.

Privacy Legislation in Europe

In 1981, the Council of Europe introduced the Convention for the Protection of Individuals with Regard to Automatic Processing of Personal Data, also known as Convention 108. This resolution, along with the OECD guidelines, influenced many European countries to adopt privacy legislation. However, years later, several countries still had not moved to pass similar legislation. In July 1998, the European Union ratified the EU Directives on data protection in an effort to prevent the improper collection and use of personal data in EU countries. This directive compelled EU countries that had not yet done so to enact privacy legislation.

Today, Europe has some of the toughest privacy laws in the world. In general, European companies are forbidden to use someone's personal data for any reason unless a law indicates that it is OK to do so. This is contrary to privacy law in the United States.

One of the important provisions of the EU Directives forbids the transfer of personal information from any EU country to a country outside the EU that does not conform to a set of principles similar to the EU Directives. This could cause a major problem for companies in countries outside Europe that want to do business with EU countries. In fact, this was a major motivator for privacy legislation in the United States and other countries throughout the world.

Privacy Legislation in Asia

Asia as a whole is not as far along in regards to privacy legislation. However, the creation of the OECD guidelines has encouraged several pieces of legislation, as listed here. (See *http://www.pco.org.hk/english/infocentre/speech_19970917.html* for more information.)

- **Japan**   The Act for Protection of Computer Processed Personal Data Held by Administrative Organs (enacted December 1988)

- **Hong Kong SAR**   The Personal Data (Privacy) Ordinance (enacted September 1995)

- **Taiwan**   Law Governing Protection of Personal Data Processed by Computers (enacted July 1995)

Privacy Legislation in Australia

Australia's Privacy Act (*http://www.privacy.gov.au/act/index.html#2.12*) was passed by the Australian Parliament in 1988. This act is Australia's implementation of the OECD guidelines. The act consists of 11 principles that were meant to protect personal information being held by the federal government and its agencies. A summary of the principles follows:

- **Principle 1**   Manner and purpose of collection of personal information

- **Principle 2**   Solicitation of personal information from individuals concerned

- **Principle 3**   Solicitation of personal information generally

- **Principle 4**   Storage and security of personal information

- **Principle 5**   Information relating to records kept by the record keeper

- **Principle 6**   Access to records containing personal information

- **Principle 7**   Alteration of records containing personal information

- **Principle 8**   Record keeper to check accuracy of personal information before its use

- **Principle 9**   Personal information to be used only for relevant purposes

- **Principle 10**   Limits on use of personal information

- **Principle 11**   Limits on disclosure of personal information

In December 2000, Australia's parliament passed the Privacy Amendment Act 2000, which extends coverage of the Australian privacy act to most private sector organizations.

Formulating an Enterprise Privacy Strategy

Building a privacy vision and an execution strategy for an enterprise is a full-time job and a serious undertaking. Privacy should not be treated as an afterthought, a part-time job, or a short-term project for an organization. Even if your company is not collecting any type of sensitive information, your customers will want to understand your company's position on privacy.

Creating a Privacy Organization

Many consumers are aware of the importance of privacy today. However, many companies are not prepared to respond to consumer privacy concerns in an effective manner. Often a group within a company will respond to a privacy issue autonomously without consulting with company executives or their legal department. Sometimes multiple people from a company will attempt to respond to the same issue without coordination. This can lead to conflicting and sometimes incorrect messages being given to customers. A group within a company should not assume the task of providing the corporate position on privacy issues. This can cause negative press coverage and damage a company's image, which can result in a loss of sales.

The privacy strategy for a company should come from the executive ranks and should be adopted by all groups within a company. In small organizations, the Chief Information Officer (CIO), Chief Operations Officer (COO), Chief Technology Officer (CTO), or another executive can take this on as part of her role. This executive might have to rely more heavily on industry experts for guidance to make up for her lack of experience in the privacy arena. Larger organizations should hire a Chief Privacy Officer (CPO) who is familiar with privacy practices and legislation. The CPO would work with the legal and public relations departments to create a corporate privacy strategy.

Figure 28-1 shows an example of an organizational structure for a privacy department. The CPO reports to a corporate executive and works closely with the public relations and legal departments. The CPO might also be in charge of a corporate privacy group.

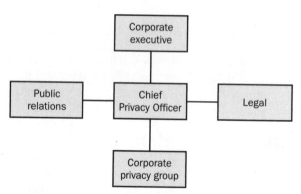

Figure 28-1   A corporate privacy team

The Role of the Chief Privacy Officer

The CPO is the person ultimately responsible for developing a privacy strategy for the company and disseminating it to all employees. He should ensure that all privacy issues are brought to his attention. In addition, all responses to issues should be reviewed by the virtual privacy team, which should include representatives from the legal and public relations departments and a privacy advocate from every major group in the company.

To be effective, the CPO needs to have a good understanding of how the company operates. He should know what data is collected by the company and how it is used. The CPO should work closely with the marketing and Internet teams because they are the departments that normally use customer information the most.

To stay current with privacy trends, the CPO will need to subscribe to trade journals, work with government agencies, participate in privacy organizations, and meet with CPOs from other companies. A list of privacy organizations can be found at *http://www.epic.org/privacy/privacy_resources_faq.html*. One good way to determine how well your company is doing with regard to privacy awareness is to compare your company's privacy position to the positions of your competitors. Another good measure of how aware your company is of privacy issues is to track the number of privacy complaints that the company receives.

The Role of the Privacy Advocate

The privacy advocate (PA) is an individual who works within a particular group at a company and is responsible for the implementation of the privacy plan for the group. The PA works closely with the CPO to understand the privacy strategy for the company and determines how that strategy will apply to her group. Within the group, the PA assists with privacy training, creating a privacy policy, resolving privacy issues, and ensuring the group's compliance with corporate privacy policy.

In a small company, the PA might be a member of the corporate privacy group and might be responsible for a certain number of groups within the company. In large companies, each group should have their own PA. Figure 28-2 shows an example of how this could be structured.

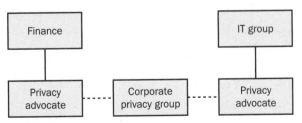

Figure 28-2   Privacy advocate relationships with the corporate privacy group

Assigning a Managing Privacy Advocate

Large departments might have several PAs that work with or for a managing privacy advocate in the department, who in turn works with the CPO as a traditional PA would. The managing privacy advocate is responsible for the privacy plan for the department and works with the various PAs in the department to execute the plan.

Responding to Privacy Issues

If your company is collecting personal information, has a Web site that tracks visitors' browsing habits, or sends e-mail messages to individuals outside the company, you will eventually run into privacy issues. These issues can arise in the form of news articles, e-mails from angry customers, a complaint filed at a privacy organization such as TRUSTe, or litigation. When these issues arise, you need to respond quickly and effectively. The best way to do this is to have a plan in place for handling privacy issues.

Employees in your company should not try to respond to privacy issues without working with the corporate privacy group on an appropriate response. Letting teams handle privacy issues on their own can result in incorrect, insensitive, incomplete, or libelous responses to customer complaints. You should not place individual teams in the position of representing the privacy policy for the company. Always get the corporate privacy group involved in resolving privacy issues. Employees in your company should be trained to have the corporate privacy group involved as soon as possible when a privacy issue occurs.

To prevent your organization's privacy issues from being highlighted by the media, or to prevent your customers from contacting an outside organization for resolution (such as the U.S. Federal Trade Commission or TRUSTe), make it easy for consumers to contact your company. Provide an e-mail address as part of the privacy statement on your Web site, and include contact information in privacy statements that you send to your customers via e-mail or postal mail.

Building a Privacy Response Center

To establish a centralized and formalized way of handling privacy issues, companies should create their own privacy response center (PRC). Set up a PRC as the first line of defense for all privacy issues for your company. The PRC should be staffed by key privacy personnel, including public relations, legal, and privacy representatives as well as representatives from groups that are prone to privacy issues. Information for all privacy issues should be stored in a central database system. A bug tracking system would work well for this purpose. The tracking system should have the ability to attach documents and store links to Web pages and file shares. A PRC can provide the following benefits:

- Centralized processing of issues

- Reduction in the duplicate processing of issues

- Faster processing of repeat issues

- Easier reporting and trend analysis

- Ability to link to department databases

Figure 28-3 shows a sample workflow for a PRC. The response desk for the PRC might receive word of a privacy issue from many sources. As mentioned, information about each issue that comes in should be placed into a tracking database. If a complaint comes in from an individual, a response should be sent to him as soon as possible to show that his issue is important and being processed. Try not to use auto-responders for this purpose. The owner should investigate the issue and propose a resolution. The resolution might require a change in policy, application, Web page, or other resource. The owner should work with the PRC team to draft an appropriate response to the originator of the issue. A representative from your company should then make sure that the response is delivered to the originator of the issue. Each step of this issue resolution should be noted in the tracking database.

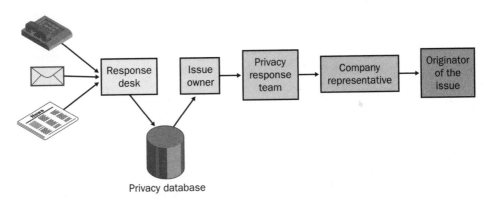

Privacy database

Figure 28-3   The workflow for a privacy response center

Best Practices

- **Assign a Chief Privacy Officer for your organization.**   The CPO will add credibility to your privacy policy and provide an effective response to privacy issues that might arise for your company.

- **Assign a privacy advocate on each of your teams.**   In large companies, privacy advocates make the job of the CPO easier.

■ **Stay current with privacy legislation.** Privacy legislation changes often. Privacy legislation in other countries can also affect you. Staying current with these changes will help keep your company out of trouble.

■ **Define a privacy policy for your company and apply it to your practices.** Your privacy policy will act as a guideline for your employees. Without it, your employees are bound to make mistakes.

■ **Get involved with privacy organizations.** Privacy organizations can provide you with ideas on how to become a more privacy-aware company and to create a privacy policy for your company. Avoid reinventing the wheel.

■ **Set up a privacy response center.** A privacy response center can help your company respond to privacy issues in a consistent and efficient manner. Establishing a PRC will be invaluable for large companies.

Additional Information

■ European Union directive for data protection (*http://www.cdt.org/privacy/eudirective/EU_directive_.html*)

■ U.S. Federal Trade Commission's Self-Regulation and Privacy Online page (*http://www.ftc.gov/os/1999/9907/pt071399.htm*)

■ U.S. Electronic Privacy Information Center (EPIC) Online Guide to Privacy Resources (*http://www.epic.org/privacy/privacy_resources_faq.html*)

■ U.S. Children's Online Privacy Protection Act of 1998 (*http://www.ftc.gov/opa/1999/9910/childfinal.htm*)

■ U.S. Computer Fraud and Abuse Act (*http://www4.law.cornell.edu/uscode/18/1030.html*)

■ U.S. Fair Information Practice Principles of 1998 (*http://www.ftc.gov/reports/privacy3/fairinfo.htm*)

■ U.S. Gramm-Leach-Bliley Act of 1999 (*http://www.senate.gov/~banking/conf*)

■ U.S. Health Insurance Portability and Accountability Act of 1996 (*http://cms.hhs.gov/hipaa*)

- Organisation of Economic Co-operation and Development (OECD) (*http://www.oecd.org*)

- "Records, Computers, and the Rights of Citizens" July 1973 U.S. report (*http://aspe.hhs.gov/datacncl/1973privacy/tocprefacemembers.htm*)

- U.S. Department of Commerce Safe Harbor Principles (*http://www.export.gov/safeharbor*)

- The U.S. Privacy Act of 1974 (*http://www.usdoj.gov/foia/privstat.htm*)

- Privacy Exchange's privacy surveys (*http://www.privacyexchange.org/iss/surveys/surveys.html*)

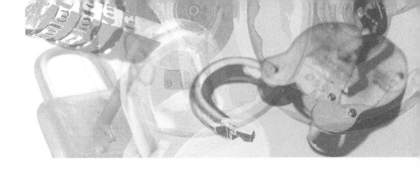

29

Defining Privacy for the Corporate Web Site

The first contact a customer has with a company often is made via that company's Web site. This contact should be as inviting as possible. Your Web site should convey an element of comfort. You often will not get a second chance to earn your customers' trust, so take every opportunity to win their confidence from the get-go. Providing a privacy statement on your Web site to express your company's position on customer privacy is key to instilling confidence in visitors to your site. This chapter will examine how you can define privacy for your Web site and outline some considerations to keep in mind when collecting personal data on your Web site.

Many Web sites collect information from their visitors so that these visitors can access special content on the site, the site can add these visitors to a membership plan, and the company can attempt to sell goods and services to visitors at a later date. If you are collecting information from your site's users, you need to explain why you are collecting this information. The explanation should be part of a privacy statement that is clearly visible and simple to understand.

When collecting information, collect only the information that you need. Ensure that the transmission and storage of this data is secure. Encrypt the data to make it difficult for database administrators and attackers to access it. Do not share this information with third parties unless doing so is necessary to provide the services that you have offered to your customers.

Defining a Privacy Statement

A privacy statement is an essential document for your Web site. It informs visitors to your site that you are concerned about their privacy and are willing to tell them how you are handling their data. Visit several Web sites—especially the Web sites of your competitors—and view their privacy statements. Check for their Platform for Privacy Preferences Project (P3P) integration. (We will describe P3P later in the chapter.) The discussions that follow provide step-by-step guidelines on how to create a privacy statement.

Anatomy of a Privacy Statement

Several major sections should exist in a privacy statement. Of course, the structure of different privacy statements will vary based on their audience, the product or service represented, and the type of data collected.

Introduction

Usually a privacy statement will begin with a sentence or two about your company's commitment to protecting its customers' privacy. For example:

> At [company], we are committed to protecting your privacy.

The privacy statement should then identify the specific site, service, or product the statement covers:

> This privacy statement explains data collection and use practices of [insert name of site, service, or product]; it does not apply to other online or offline company sites, products, or services.

Also, a privacy statement must have language that clearly establishes that by using the site, service, or product, the user consents to the relevant data collection and use. Place language similar to the following near the top of the privacy statement—for example, at the end of the introductory paragraph:

> By using this site, you consent to the data practices described in this statement.

Note   Include similar language in your site's user interface where data is collected, near the Submit button.

Details About the Personal Information Collected

Because this section of the privacy statement specifically describes the information the site or service collects, it will vary significantly from statement to statement. Still, it is among the most important sections of the privacy statement.

This section requires a clear and detailed statement outlining the data that is being collected. Although the focus is on personal information, the statement should also briefly describe any other data collection, including unique identifiers or globally unique identifiers (GUIDs), IP addresses, site or product usage data, and machine data. The statement should disclose whether any of this data will be tied to the user's personal data or whether this other data will remain anonymous.

If the privacy statement is for a Web site that uses cookies, clear GIFs, and/or similar tracking technologies, the statement must disclose this fact and clearly explain how these technologies are used. We will give an example of how cookies can be described later in this section.

How the Personal Information Will Be Used

This section should describe how a customer's personal data will be used in relation to the product or service provided on the Web site. This section should explain why the information described in the previous section is being collected. Although the description should be as specific as possible, some general statements about usage are often included in this section. For example, although this likely would not suffice as a complete description of the site's use of the information collected from customers, some or all of the following language might be appropriate:

> The personal information we collect will be used to provide the service(s) or carry out the transaction(s) you have requested or authorized. This may include using the personal information to provide you with important information about the product or service that you are using, including critical updates and notifications; to improve the product or service; and to provide you with more effective customer service. We also use the information we collect to make the site or service easier to use by eliminating the need for you to repeatedly enter the same information or by customizing the site or service to your particular preferences or interests.

Your privacy statement should also convey that you do not consider your company's subsidiaries and controlled affiliates to be third parties for the purpose of data transfers, and that data therefore might be shared within your subsidiaries and affiliates. This is important because in large companies, you might have integrated data systems in which it is impossible to keep subsidiaries from accessing data. One way to convey this is to include language such as the following.

> Except as otherwise described in this statement, personal information you provide on this site will not be shared outside of [company] and its controlled subsidiaries and affiliates without your permission.

Some groups at your company on occasion might contract with one or more third-party agents to provide some back-end service in the operation of your site or some aspect of the service you are offering the customer. And sometimes these third-party agents need to obtain access to customer information to provide this service. Thus, the privacy statement should disclose the use of such agents:

> We occasionally hire other companies to provide limited services on our behalf, such as handling the processing and delivery of mailings, providing customer support, or performing statistical analysis of our services. We will provide those companies only the personal information they need to deliver that service. These companies are required to maintain the confidentiality of that information and are prohibited from using that information for any other purpose.

Your company might be forced to disclose personal customer information without providing notice to customers and without the consent of the customer if required by law. Thus, the privacy statement should have a disclaimer such as the following:

> [Company] may access and/or disclose personal information if required to do so by law or in the good faith belief that such action is necessary to conform to the edicts of the law or comply with legal process served on our company or the site; protect and defend the rights or property of our company and its family of Web sites; or act in urgent circumstances to protect the personal safety of our employees, users, or the public.

Finally, the privacy laws of some countries have restrictions regarding the transfer of customer data outside those countries' borders. One way to permit international transfers of data is to show that the user consented to the transfer. Having a notice in the privacy statement that the data will be stored in the United States is not a complete remedy for this issue, but it is nevertheless important. Additionally, the privacy statement should indicate whether your company is a participant in the US-EU Safe Harbor Agreement. For example:

> Personal information collected on this site may be stored and processed in the United States or any other country in which our company or its affiliates, subsidiaries, or agents maintain facilities, and by

using this site, you consent to any such transfer of information outside of your country. Our company abides by the safe harbor framework as set forth by the U.S. Department of Commerce regarding the collection, use, and retention of data from the European Union.

The Choices Available to Users

A fundamental privacy requirement of a Web site is that users must be given a choice regarding any secondary uses or transfers of personal information about them. The privacy statement must describe the ways users can exercise these choices. One common choice mechanism is a setting on the page where users submit personal information giving them the opportunity to consent to secondary marketing uses of their data. Another choice mechanism might be a central location on the site where users can go to enter or update their preferences on the use of their personal data.

> **More Info**   For more on choice mechanisms for Web site users, see the discussion of opt-in and opt-out choices in the section titled "The Safe Harbor Principles" in Chapter 28, "Understanding the Importance of Privacy."

Additionally, it is a good idea to specify that the choices users make about the use of the data they submitted via your site might not affect the use of any data they provided to your company in other contexts. For example:

> Please be aware that this privacy statement and the choices you make on this site will not necessarily apply to personal information you may have provided to [company] in the context of other, separately operated company products or services.

How Users Can Access Their Personal Information

Another fundamental privacy principle is that users must have the ability to access the personal information about them being stored by your company and be able to correct, amend, or delete any information that is inaccurate. Thus, the privacy statement must address how users can obtain such access.

Statement on Security

The privacy statement should include a description of the security measures that will be taken to protect users' personal information. For example:

[Company] is committed to protecting the security of your personal information. We use a variety of security technologies and procedures to help protect your personal information from unauthorized access, use, or disclosure. For example, we store your personal information on computer servers that are located in controlled facilities and have restricted access. Additionally, when we transmit sensitive personal information (such as a credit card number) over the Internet, we protect it through the use of encryption techniques, such as the Secure Sockets Layer (SSL) protocol.

Changes to the Privacy Statement

Include a short section in your site's privacy statement that explains how readers can learn about updates made to the statement:

We may occasionally update this privacy statement. When we do, we will also revise the "last updated" date at the top of the privacy statement. For material changes to this privacy statement, we will notify you either by placing a prominent notice on the home page of our Web site or by directly sending you a notification. We encourage you to periodically review this privacy statement to stay informed about how we are protecting the personal information we collect. Your continued use of the service constitutes your agreement to this privacy statement and any updates to it.

The Remedy Available to Users

If a privacy statement is for a Web site that is a licensee of a third-party privacy organization, the statement should describe the enforcement (or remedy) process available through that organization. (We will discuss using third-party privacy organizations in a moment, when we look at the TRUSTe organization.) At a minimum, the remedy section of the privacy statement must include contact information for users who want to provide feedback on the statement. For example:

[Company] welcomes your comments regarding this privacy statement. If you believe that our company has not adhered to this statement, please contact us by e-mail or postal mail, and we will use commercially reasonable efforts to promptly determine and remedy the problem.

[Company address]

Click here to send e-mail.

To find contact details for one of our subsidiaries or affiliates in your country or region, see the [Contact Us/Affiliates/Subsidiaries] page of our Web site [Web site name].

You will need to set up a mail stop and an e-mail address that will route customer questions or comments to the person in your organization who handles privacy inquiries. For more on this topic, see the "Formulating an Enterprise Privacy Strategy" section in Chapter 28.

Key Privacy Statement Considerations

Some Web sites will be involved in special programs or have special features, including the following:

- Enlisting a third-party privacy organization such as TRUSTe
- Using Microsoft .NET Passport as an authentication mechanism
- Collecting personal information from children
- Using cookies, clear GIFs, or similar technologies

Gaining Approval from TRUSTe

When creating a privacy statement for a Web site, you might want to consider having an evaluation by TRUSTe, an independent, nonprofit organization that promotes the use of fair information practices on the Internet. If approved by TRUSTe, the privacy statement should contain language such as the following:

TRUSTe Certification

[Company] is a licensee of the TRUSTe Privacy Program. TRUSTe is an independent, nonprofit organization whose mission is to build trust and confidence in the Internet by promoting the use of fair information practices. Because [site or company name] wants to demonstrate its commitment to your privacy, we have agreed to publish our information practices and have our privacy practices reviewed for compliance by TRUSTe.

If you have questions regarding this statement, you should first contact our company using the contact information at the bottom of this Statement. If you do not receive acknowledgment of your inquiry or your inquiry has not been satisfactorily addressed, you should then contact TRUSTe at their Web site, *http://www.truste.org/users/ users_watchdog.html*. TRUSTe will serve as a liaison with [site or company name] to resolve your concerns.

Using .NET Passport as an Authentication Mechanism

If your Web site uses .NET Passport as an authentication tool, the privacy statement should have a short explanation of .NET Passport, with a link to the full .NET Passport privacy statement (*http://www.passport.com/Consumer/Privacy-Policy.asp*). For example:

This Web site uses the .NET Passport service. When you sign in to this site using .NET Passport, you will be asked to provide your e-mail address and a password. This same .NET Passport sign-in allows you to access many other participating .NET Passport Web sites. To learn more about the .NET Passport service and how .NET Passport uses and protects your personal information, please read the .NET Passport privacy statement at *http://www.passport.com/Consumer/PrivacyPolicy.asp*.

Collecting Personal Information from Children

Web sites that collect information from children under the age of 13 must abide by the Children's Online Privacy Protection Act (COPPA). If your site is likely to be subject to COPPA, the privacy statement should have some specific language on children's privacy and the COPPA compliance mechanism that the site uses.

Using Cookies, Clear GIFs, or Similar Technologies

If you are creating a privacy statement for a Web site that uses cookies, clear GIFs, or similar tracking technologies, the privacy statement must disclose this fact and give a clear explanation of how these technologies are used. (A clear GIF, also known as a *Web beacon*, is an image usually no larger than 1 pixel by 1 pixel that you place on a Web page or in an e-mail message to monitor the behavior of a user visiting your Web site or sending an e-mail message.) This description in the privacy statement should disclose whether data collected via these means is in any way linked to personally identifiable information (as opposed to anonymous customization or tracking). Following the description of how cookies are used on the site, it is a good idea to provide a brief description of what cookies are and how users can decline them. For example:

A cookie is a small text file that is placed on your hard disk by a Web page server. Cookies cannot be used to run programs or deliver viruses to your computer. Cookies are uniquely assigned to you and can be read only by a Web server in the domain that issued the cookie to you.

One of the primary purposes of cookies is to provide a convenience feature to save you time. For example, if you personalize a Web page or navigate within a site, a cookie helps the site to recall your specific information on subsequent visits. This simplifies the process of delivering relevant content, eases site navigation, and so on. When you return to the Web site, the information you previously provided can be retrieved, so you can easily use the site's features that you customized.

You have the ability to accept or decline cookies. Most Web browsers automatically accept cookies, but you can usually modify your browser setting to decline cookies if you prefer. If you choose to decline cookies, you may not be able to fully experience the interactive features of this or other Web sites you visit.

Other Rules for Creating and Posting a Privacy Statement

This section describes some extra tips to guide you through the creation of a comprehensive privacy statement.

Tagging Collected Data

Always make sure that your back-end systems can support every claim you make in your privacy statement. It is critical that you fully understand where the data flows. You must make sure that the data is adequately tagged so that its use will be limited to the purposes stated in the privacy statement and the choices exercised by the user. These tags must remain with the data if it is transferred to other storage systems, and you must make sure that these storage systems can recognize and comply with the use restrictions the tags reflect.

Additionally, you must make sure that a mechanism is in place that allows users to access and correct data as described in the privacy statement. You also must make sure that adequate security measures are in place to protect the data. For example, you could use access controls or encryption to accomplish this.

Ensuring Consistency Between Your Statement and Other Web Pages

Always make sure that your Web site's privacy statement is consistent with any claims you make in the forms that collect data or in any other pages of your site. For example, if the form says something along the lines of, "Please fill out this form so that we can contact you about updates to this site/product," you have told the user why the data is being collected and how it will be used. Therefore, you should not have a different or additional use of personal data listed in the site's privacy statement.

Ensuring a Consistent P3P Implementation

The Platform for Privacy Preferences Project, or P3P, was defined by the World Wide Web Consortium (W3C) to warn users when a Web site they are visiting has questionable privacy practices or no privacy statement whatsoever. A Web site's P3P implementation consists of three versions of a company's privacy statement: the full statement, the XML version of the statement, and the P3P compact policy. These pieces should be consistent with one another and should be modified at the same time. For more information on P3P, see the next section.

Using a Unique Privacy Statement for Each Product and Service

This consideration specifically applies to large Web sites or companies with multiple Web sites. Avoid labeling your privacy statement the *corporate privacy statement*. It is difficult to maintain a single privacy statement for all your sites. This is because no privacy statement can be that all-encompassing and because individual company branches or sites might change policies without the others knowing. Furthermore, you should never give the impression that your privacy statement extends beyond the specific products or services for which it was written.

Making Privacy Statements Easy to Find

Always make a Web site's privacy statement or its link to the privacy statement clear and conspicuous. The link to the privacy statement should be included in the standard footer along with the copyright notice and the terms of use that appear on all pages of the Web site. At a minimum, the link must appear on the home page and on any page that collects information from the user or the user's machine, including passive collection through the use of cookies or clear GIFs.

Additionally, on Web pages or screens where the user is asked to submit personal information, the privacy statement link should be elevated and made more prominent. For example, above the Submit button, you should have text that tells users that the information they submit is subject to the [company/ product name] privacy statement. This text should also state that by submitting this information, users agree to the terms of the privacy statement, including any updates. Moreover, this text should provide a link to the privacy statement.

Conducting a Formal Review

In the United States, your company can be held liable by the U.S. Federal Trade Commission (FTC) or your customers for the content of your privacy statement. In addition, a poorly worded privacy statement can cause users to avoid your site. Therefore, do not release privacy statements before they are reviewed. Always have your legal department and corporate privacy group review each privacy statement.

Platform for Privacy Preferences Project

The Platform for Privacy Preferences Project, or P3P, was defined by the World Wide Web Consortium (W3C). P3P permits Web sites to define their privacy statements by using XML and predefined codes known as the *P3P compact policy*. This combination of XML and the compact policy can be read by browsers such as Microsoft Internet Explorer 6, which now include the P3P capability. P3P-aware browsers can warn users when a Web site they are visiting has questionable privacy practices or no privacy statement what-soever. By using P3P to define your privacy statement, you ensure that visitors to your site easily understand your company's position on privacy and how your site will handle their personal data. If you do not implement P3P for your Web site, visitors might be reluctant to remain at or return to your site.

P3P Integration for Internet Explorer 6

One new feature of Internet Explorer 6 is its ability to interpret the P3P privacy policy of a Web site. Based on its interpretation of your Web site's P3P privacy policy, Internet Explorer 6 will block, restrict, or accept a cookie that your site attempts to send out. A cookie can be blocked or restricted when the privacy setting in Internet Explorer 6 is inconsistent with the privacy policy for a Web site or when a Web site does not have P3P integration at all. Restricting a cookie means that it will be available only for the current session and will not be stored on your computer. Blocked cookies are neither stored nor used during the session. If a cookie is blocked or restricted, Internet Explorer 6 will display the icon shown in Figure 29-1 in the lower right-hand corner of the browser window.

Figure 29-1   Internet Explorer 6 P3P warning icon

This is not what you want you want visitors to your Web site to see. You should work to keep this icon from being displayed when the privacy setting for Internet Explorer 6 is set to Medium, which is the default setting. The Medium setting indicates that when a user visits a Web site, first-party cookies will be restricted and third-party cookies will be blocked when the Web site uses personally identifiable information (PII) without the user's consent or when the site has not implemented P3P. (First-party cookies are cookies placed by a Web site that a user is visiting. Third-party cookies are cookies placed by a Web site other than the one a user is visiting, which is something banner ads typically do.) PII is any information about a user that can be used to identify or locate him. A user's name, address, and phone number are considered PII. An IP address, a GUID, or an account ID can be considered PII when they can be correlated with a user's PII.

> **Note**   Internet Explorer 6 performs a P3P interpretation of sites only within the Internet, Trusted sites, and Restricted sites zones, not the Local Intranet zone.

By double-clicking the P3P warning icon, you can see whether a cookie was blocked or restricted. Figure 29-2 shows an example of a dialog box that might be displayed after you click this icon.

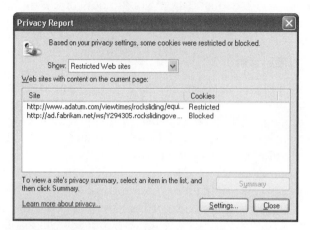

Figure 29-2   Privacy report from a site with a blocked cookie

Viewing a Site's Privacy Statement

Internet Explorer 6 can be used to view a Web site's privacy statement if the site has implemented P3P. By selecting Privacy Report from the View menu, you will see the translated version of the site's XML privacy statement. Figure 29-3 shows the privacy statement from the Microsoft Web site.

Figure 29-3   Summary of the privacy statement from the Microsoft.com site

By clicking the Here link, you can access the site's full privacy statement. Notice that the TRUSTe logo is visible, which can be an added comfort for visitors to your site.

Internet Explorer 6 Privacy Settings

The Internet Explorer 6 browser has several dialog boxes that permit you to control cookies by way of the privacy settings you select. Figure 29-4 shows a diagram of the Privacy tab on the Internet Properties dialog box, which can be accessed by selecting the Tools menu and then clicking Internet Options.

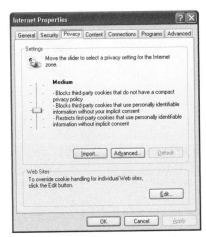

Figure 29-4   Internet Explorer 6 Internet Properties dialog box, with the Privacy tab selected

You can override the handling of cookies based on their type by selecting the Advanced button in the Privacy tab of the Internet Properties dialog box. Figure 29-5 shows the dialog box that is displayed when the Advanced button is selected.

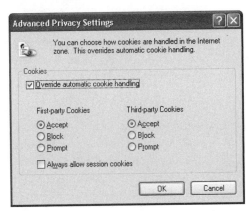

Figure 29-5   Internet Explorer 6 Advanced Privacy Settings dialog box

You can override the handling of cookies for a specific Web site by selecting the Edit button on the Internet Properties dialog box. Figure 29-6 shows the dialog box that is displayed when the Edit button is selected.

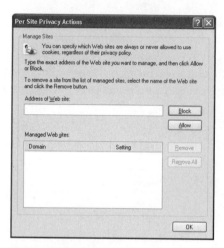

Figure 29-6 Internet Explorer 6 Per Site Privacy Actions dialog box

Implementing P3P for Your Web Site

Implementing P3P requires you to create four pieces of content. Except for the full privacy statement, each of these pieces of content is based on the P3P specification shown at *http://www.w3.org/p3p/*. The first piece of content is the reference file, which is an XML file that is used to point to the XML version of your privacy statement. This file should be named P3p.xml and stored in W3C directory beneath the root of your Web site. For example, the Microsoft.com P3P reference file follows and can be found at *http://www.microsoft.com/w3c/p3p.xml*.

```
<?xml version="1.0" ?>
<META xmlns="http://www.w3.org/2000/12/P3Pv1">
    <POLICY-REFERENCES>
        <POLICY-REF about="http://www.microsoft.com/w3c/p3policy.xml">
            <INCLUDE>/*</INCLUDE>
        </POLICY-REF>
    </POLICY-REFERENCES>
</META>
```

The second piece of content is the XML version of your privacy statement. This file describes the data that is collected and how it is used. It represents the condensed form of your full privacy statement. This file also points to the full version of the privacy statement. The name and placement of this file is not fixed. The location of the file needs to be indicated in the reference file. This is the file that is processed by the Internet Explorer 6 Privacy Report dialog box. The XML version of the privacy statement for Microsoft.com can be found at *http://www.microsoft.com/w3c/p3policy.xml.*

The third piece of content is the full privacy statement, which is pointed to by the XML privacy statement. The full privacy statement should indicate in simple language your company's privacy policy. See "Defining a Privacy Statement" earlier in the chapter for more information on how to create a privacy statement. The full privacy statement for Microsoft.com can be viewed at *http://www.microsoft.com/info/privacy.htm.*

The fourth piece of content is the P3P compact policy, which is the compact representation of the XML privacy statement. The values for the XML tags of the XML privacy statement are converted to codes. These codes are placed into the header of HTTP responses.

Establishing Corporationwide Policy Settings

Within your corporation, you will want to ensure that your employees understand the risks of visiting certain Web sites when the tables are turned and they step into the role of Web site user. You might want to distribute a list of restricted sites for employees to enter into their privacy settings for Internet Explorer 6. You might also want employees to choose a privacy setting above Medium to help protect them from dishonest Web sites. In either case, your employees should be trained on the privacy settings for Internet Explorer 6.

Specific information about the privacy features of Internet Explorer 6 can be found at *http://msdn.microsoft.com/library/en-us/dnpriv/html/ie6privacyfeature.asp* and in Chapter 10, "Securing Microsoft Internet Explorer 6 and Microsoft Office XP," in this book.

Best Practices

- **Create a privacy statement for each of your Web sites.**   Today, visitors to a Web site expect that site to display a privacy statement. Doing so is an easy way for your company to tell visitors to your site which data about them you are collecting and how you will handle and use it.

- **Integrate P3P into your company's Web sites**   Adding P3P integration to your Web site will help prevent P3P-aware browsers from providing false warnings about the privacy compliance of your Web site.

- **Train your employees on the P3P features of browsers.**   Understanding the warning icons and how to adjust a browser's privacy settings will help you and your employees avoid Web sites whose privacy practices differ from your preferences.

Additional Information

- *Web Privacy with P3P* (O'Reilly & Associates, 2002)

- W3C Platform for Privacy Preferences Project (*http://www.w3.org/p3p*)

- "Privacy in Internet Explorer 6" white paper (*http://msdn.microsoft.com/library/en-us/dnpriv/html/ie6privacyfeature.asp*)

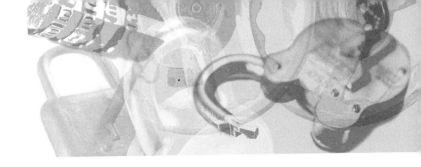

30

Deploying Privacy in the Enterprise

Your company's privacy strategy should play a major role in purchasing or creating applications, building Web sites, and formulating company policy. You have an obligation to protect the privacy of your customers and partners. Keep them in mind as you expand your business and review your business plans. Integrate privacy into your mission to make your company more profitable, and you will be much closer to success than you might think. The journey to becoming a privacy-aware company does not end with the vision. A privacy policy must be woven into the very fabric of what the company stands for. Let your employees know that building customer trust is a major goal for the company and that getting serious about privacy is an integral part of realizing this goal.

Selecting Applications Based on Their Privacy Features

When selecting applications for purchase or building applications to be used internally, be cognizant of their privacy features. Using applications with privacy features makes it easier to protect your customers' personal information. Applications should have privacy settings that permit users to indicate whether they can be contacted and, if so, how they can be contacted. These settings should also permit users to indicate how their data can be used. For example, a customer or business partner should be able to indicate whether her data can be shared among different groups within your company or with third parties. Also, look for applications that have an unsubscribe feature that users can access from the Web.

Finally, look for applications that come with a privacy statement or that permit the inclusion of your privacy statement. This will allow employees of your company who use the application to easily see the guidelines for handling the data they are collecting.

Protecting the Privacy of Your Employees

Employees in the United States unfortunately do not have many rights with regard to their privacy within the company they work for. Because a company owns the computers, phone systems, and network infrastructure that its employees use, the company has the right to take reasonable measures to protect its physical and intellectual property.

As a U.S. company, you have a lot of freedom when it comes to monitoring your employees' actions; however, you should use this power sparingly. For example, recently, in a hospital in the western United States, employees were forced to wear devices that tracked them during work hours. This was done to decrease the response time for nurses and doctors by making them easier to find. Ironically, morale dropped and productivity decreased. In some instances, employees destroyed the devices or refused to wear them.

Companies should work to protect the privacy of their employees. For instance, every company must make an effort to protect its employees' financial and health information. Strict guidelines should be established and enforced to prevent the release of this information to unauthorized people. You should let your employees know that you will work to protect their privacy whenever feasible. Employees should be made aware of any company policies on monitoring their activities or sharing their personal information.

Protecting the Privacy of Your Customers and Business Partners

Customers want to feel comfortable when sharing their contact information with your company. When customers ask you how you will protect their personal data, you should be able to offer an answer that instills confidence in your company's ability to protect access to and use of their data. Showing customers your company's security and privacy policy in writing is the best way to set their minds at ease.

Storing Customer Data Securely

Security is a big part of protecting a customer's personal information. This book has already covered a number of security techniques; however, it will be helpful here to reiterate a few tips on using security to protect a user's data:

- Use physical security to protect the computers that hold sensitive data.

- Use encryption to protect the transfer of data between computer systems and to store data.

- Set the appropriate level of application and file security to prevent unwanted access to information.

- Use the principle of least privilege. In other words, all users and administrators should receive only those network permissions and rights they need to do their job.

Collecting Customer Data and Privacy Preferences

When collecting contact information from your customers, you should offer them a way to enter their privacy preferences. Web sites should include privacy settings on the same form where their data is collected. If your customers are sending their information to you via e-mail, provide them with a template to fill out that includes privacy fields or send them such a template in an acknowledgment e-mail message. Mark a customer's record as incomplete until you receive his response, or set his preferences to the most restrictive values by default. A customer's privacy preferences should be stored along with his contact information. When sending customer contact information to another group with your company or to a third party, include the customer's privacy preferences.

Controlling the Handling of Customer Data

Your customers' privacy preferences will be useless unless you have a policy in place to help your employees understand the guidelines for handling customer information. As part of your company's new employee orientation, you should train employees on the proper handling of customer data.

Applications that collect data from customers should have a privacy menu that points to the company's privacy policy. The first time that the application is run, customers should be forced to accept the terms of the privacy policy. Furthermore, before employees can access customer data via the company's intranet, those employees should be required to read a privacy policy page and accept its conditions.

Creating a Centralized Contact System

Managing customer contact information throughout a company can be a daunting task, especially at large companies where each department might have its own contact system. In addition, employees might have their own private contact databases, separate from their department's contact database. Department and employee databases often will be inconsistent, and they probably will not contain any of the customers' privacy preferences.

So what happens when a customer demands that your company stop sending him e-mail messages or when he wants to update his contact information? How do you manage this information across multiple databases? Centralizing your contact system is the only way your company can respond to these requests in a practical manner.

By creating a single contact database, your company can be more effective in executing its marketing campaigns and more responsive to a customer's privacy needs. Some software companies, Microsoft included, sell contact solutions that enable the centralized storage of customers' contact information and privacy preferences. Your company can also build its own contact system. The remainder of this section examines how to implement a solution by using Microsoft Windows 2000 Active Directory directory service or by using a database.

Using Active Directory to Build a Contact System

In many enterprises, Active Directory is used to manage the corporate network and its resources. Contacts are one of the resources (objects) that Active Directory can manage. These contacts can be used to manage your customer contact list. The built-in security of Active Directory will permit you to restrict access to only those employees who have a relationship with your customers.

The only thing missing from Active Directory is the ability to track a user's privacy preferences. Fortunately, the schema for Active Directory can be easily extended to add attributes to accommodate these preference values.

> **More Info**   For more information on Active Directory, see Chapter 4, "Securing Active Directory Objects and Attributes" of this book. For information on extending the Active Directory schema, visit *http://msdn.microsoft.com/library/en-us/netdir/ad/extending_the_schema.asp*.

Figure 30-1 shows an example of an implementation using Active Directory in a small company. In this example, all the customer contact information is stored in Active Directory, and the schema has been extended to permit the storage of privacy preferences. The privacy flags represent the extended data that is added to the directory.

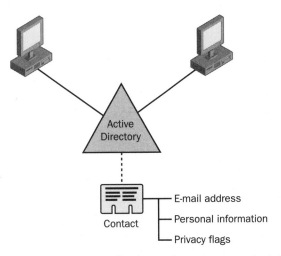

Figure 30-1   A small company's customer contact database

Larger companies might have multiple groups that store the same contact information about a customer in their local database, along with customer information specific to their group. Figure 30-2 provides an example of this. In this example, a user's e-mail address is used to correlate the data in Active Directory with the data in the particular local database.

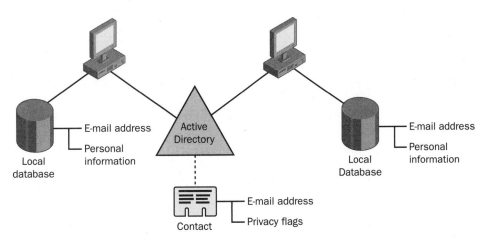

Figure 30-2   A larger company's customer contact database

Using a Database to Build a Contact System

Many companies use databases to store contact information. A database can be used to store contact information and user privacy preferences in the same way Active Directory is used to accomplish these tasks. Be sure to place adequate protections on each table, not only to prevent unauthorized access, but also to isolate access to the group's data to group administrators.

A small company might store its customers' contact and privacy information in a single table. In the following example, the user information and privacy preferences are stored in the same database table:

E-mail	Name	Address	email_ok	mail_ok	phone_ok	marketing_ok
joe@microsoft.com	Joe	101 Main Street	Y	Y	Y	N

If your company has multiple groups that store information about the same customer, you might want to store customers' personal data in one table and their privacy preferences in another table. This will permit customers to specify explicit privacy settings for each group within your company storing personal information about them. The tables that follow show an example this. These two tables use an assigned ID as the common key that connects them:

ID	E-mail	Name	Address
123	joe@microsoft.com	Joe Worden	101 Main Street

ID	Department	email_ok	mail_ok	phone_ok	marketing_ok
123	Marketing	Y	Y	Y	Y
123	Sales	Y	Y	N	N

Best Practices

- **When purchasing applications, select those that have privacy features.**   Applications with privacy features make it easier to protect the privacy of your employees and customers. Adding these features after installation can sometimes be difficult.

- **When storing contact information, include your customers' privacy preferences.**   Storing your customers' privacy preferences with their data makes it easier for your employees to comply with these preferences.

■   **Use a centralized contact database for your company.** By using a centralized database, you can access your customers' privacy preferences and their personal data from one location.

Additional Information

■   White paper on extending the Active Directory schema (*http:// msdn.microsoft.com/library/en-us/netdir/ad/extending_the_schema.asp*)

Index

Numbers and Symbols
3DES algorithm, 157, 235, 236

A
abstract classes, 85
acceptable use policy (AUP), 568–69
acceptance, as risk management strategy, 6
access
  controlling in role-based security structure, 64–67
  defining policies to support incident response, 569
  role of DACLs in controlling, 90
Access, as safe harbor tenet, 617
access control entries (ACEs)
  adding to organizational units, 93–94
  as DACL elements, 87–88, 136
  explicit deny and allow, 90, 140–41
  generic deny and allow, 87, 88, 89, 136
  inherited deny and allow, 90, 141
  object-specific, 88, 89, 90, 93–94
access control lists (ACLs). *See also* discretionary access
    control lists; system access control lists
  laptops and, 343
  moving or copying files and folders, results, 142–43
access tokens
  list of contents, 36–37
  overview, 36
  role in access control, 90
account logon events, 310–14
account management events, 315–17
Account Operators group, 61, 62
account SIDs, in access tokens, 36
accounts. *See also* administrative accounts;
    Administrator account; user accounts
  Active Directory and, 364–65
  configuring security options, 38–42
  defining security policies, 269, 270–73
  Kerberos policy settings, 272–73
  list of common logon events, 313–14
  list of common management events, 316–17
  list of security template settings, 271–73
  lockout policy settings, 272
  making secure, 33–49
  password policy settings, 271

ACEs. *See* access control entries
Acldiag.exe program, 95
ACLs. *See* access control lists
Active Directory
  auditing changes to directory service access, 317–18
  autonomy of authority, 115–16
  best practices, 96–97, 128–30
  configuring default DACLs on objects and attributes
    from command line, 94–96
  configuring default DACLs on objects and attributes
    using MMC, 91–93
  data administrators, 116, 123, 127–28
  delegating authority, 126–28
  designing DNS to support, 123–26
  designing domains, 121–23
  designing forests, 116–21
  DNS resource records and, 373
  domain-level password policies, 43–49
  integrated zones, 126
  isolation of authority, 115–16
  object attributes, 84
  object classes, 84–85
  protecting built-in groups and user accounts, 364–66
  protecting stored passwords, 360–61
  role in creating customer contact systems, 648–49
  schema control, 117–18
  schema overview, 83–86
  schema security, 86
  securing communications, 366–69
  securing individual user accounts, 38–40
  securing objects and attributes, 91–96
  service administrators, 116, 122, 127
  service administrators vs. data administrators, 116
  Service (SRV) resource records, 374, 375
  threats to security, 358
Active Directory Services Interface (ADSI), 94, 95
active security systems, for laptops, 340
Active Server Pages (ASP), 459, 460
ActiveX controls
  configuring in Internet Explorer, 252–54
  configuring in Office XP, 263–65
  Windows Update and, 498
activism, as attacker motive, 25

Ben Smith

Ben Smith is a senior security strategist at Microsoft, where he works on developing the company's long-term security strategy. Prior to joining the Microsoft Security Strategies team, he was the lead subject matter expert on security for Microsoft Training & Certification. In addition to being a featured speaker at IT industry conferences, Ben recently consulted with the U.S. National Science Foundation on creating methods for preparing a cyber security workforce. Ben is also the chair of the vendor-neutral security certification, CompTIA Security+. He is a Microsoft Certified Systems Engineer (MCSE), Microsoft Certified Trainer (MCT), Certified Information Systems Security Professional (CISSP), and a Cisco Certified Network Associate (CCNA). Ben lives near Redmond, Washington, with his wife Beth Boatright.

Brian Komar

Brian Komar is the owner and principal consultant for Komar Consulting, Inc., a consulting firm specializing in network security and Public Key Infrastructure (PKI). Brian partners with Microsoft on several ventures, which include developing security-related courseware for Microsoft Training & Certification, authoring material for Microsoft Prescriptive Architecture Guides, and writing PKI white papers for the Microsoft Security team. Brian is a frequent speaker at IT industry conferences such as Microsoft Tech Ed, MCP TechMentor, and Windows & .NET Magazine Connections. Brian lives in Winnipeg, Canada, with his wife Krista Kunz.

JC Cannon

JC Cannon is a Privacy Manager in the Corporate Privacy group at Microsoft. He works as a technical strategist for the team, focusing on ways to apply technology to applications that will give consumers better control over their privacy and enable developers to create privacy-aware applications. Prior to this role, JC was a program manager for Active Directory directory service for more than two years, where he worked with developers and independent software vendors on integration strategies for Active Directory and applications. He has written several white papers, which are posted on MSDN, and has given presentations on Active Directory integration techniques at the major Microsoft conferences.

Jeff Williams

Jeff Williams is a security operations consultant in the Microsoft Services for the Enterprise organization at Microsoft. In this role, he provides consulting and training on security to the company's largest customers, including delivering security vulnerability assessments, performing design reviews, and providing prescriptive guidance on a wide variety of topics. Before joining Microsoft, Jeff served as a technical project manager and senior network architect for an international financial services firm. Jeff earned his Masters of Business Administration in Technology Management (MBA/TM) at the University of Phoenix, where he has also served as an adjunct professor. Jeff is the author of A Guide to Windows NT Server 4.0 in the Enterprise (Course Technologies, 1998) and NT Server 4 in the Enterprise Exam Prep (Exam: 70-068) (Coriolis, 1998) and he writes the quarterly column "IT Pragmatics" for The Public Manager. Jeff and his wife Amanda live in Seattle, where they have just celebrated the birth of their son, Alexander.

The Lock

The **lock** is a mechanical device used for fastening doors, chests, and lids, consisting essentially of a bolt guarded by a mechanism released by a combination or a **key**—a small, shaped cut of metal used to move or release a bolt or catch in the lock. The so-called pin-tumbler cylinder lock, or Yale lock, introduced about 1860 by the American inventor Linus Yale, was the first device to employ a small, flat key in place of a large, cumbersome one. The Yale lock consists essentially of a cylindrical plug placed in an outer barrel. The plug is rotated by a key and in turn moves the bolt of the lock by means of a cam. In order to rotate the plug, the inserted key must raise five pins of different sizes into corresponding holes in the plug. Five similar pins are contained in the upper part of each of the holes. If the pins are not raised to the circumference of the plug, the plug cannot be turned.*

At Microsoft Press, we use tools to illustrate our books for software developers and IT professionals. Tools very simply and powerfully symbolize human inventiveness. They're a metaphor for people extending their capabilities, precision, and reach. From simple calipers and pliers to digital micrometers and lasers, these stylized illustrations give each book a visual identity, and a personality to the series. With tools and knowledge, there's no limit to creativity and innovation. Our tagline says it all: *the tools you need to put technology to work*.

*__Microsoft ® Encarta ® Reference Library 2002.__ © 1993-2001 Microsoft Corporation. All rights reserved.

The manuscript for this book was prepared and galleyed using Microsoft Word. Pages were composed by Microsoft Press using Adobe FrameMaker+SGML for Windows, with text in Garamond and display type in Helvetica Condensed. Composed pages were delivered to the printer as electronic prepress files.

Cover Designer:	Methodologie, Inc.
Interior Graphic Designer:	James D. Kramer
Principal Compositor:	Dan Latimer
Interior Artist:	Joel Panchot
Copy Editor:	Michelle Goodman
Proofreader:	nSight, Inc.
Indexer:	Julie Kawabata

Inside *security information* you can trust

Microsoft® Windows® Security Resource Kit
ISBN 0-7356-1868-2   Suggested Retail Price: $59.99 U.S., $86.99 Canada

Comprehensive security information and tools, straight from the Microsoft product groups. This official RESOURCE KIT delivers comprehensive operations and deployment information that information security professionals can put to work right away. The authors—members of Microsoft's security teams—describe how to plan and implement a comprehensive security strategy, assess security threats and vulnerabilities, configure system security, and more. The kit also provides must-have security tools, checklists, templates, and other on-the-job resources on CD-ROM and on the Web.

Microsoft Encyclopedia of Security
ISBN 0-7356-1877-1   Suggested Retail Price: $49.99 U.S., $72.99 Canada

The essential, one-of-a-kind security reference for computer professionals at all levels. This encyclopedia delivers 2000+ entries detailing the latest security-related issues, technologies, standards, products, and services. It covers the Microsoft Windows platform as well as open-source technologies and the platforms and products of other major vendors. You get clear, concise explanations and case scenarios that deftly take you from concept to real-world application—ideal for everyone from computer science students up to systems engineers, developers, and managers.

Microsoft Windows Server 2003 Security Administrator's Companion
ISBN 0-7356-1574-8   Suggested Retail Price: $49.99 U.S., $72.99 Canada

The in-depth, practical guide to deploying and maintaining Windows Server 2003 in a secure environment. Learn how to use all the powerful security features in the latest network operating system with this in-depth, authoritative technical reference—written by a security expert on the Microsoft Windows Server 2003 security team. Explore physical security issues, internal security policies, and public and shared key cryptography, and then drill down into the specifics of the key security features of Windows Server 2003.

Microsoft Internet Information Services Security Technical Reference
ISBN 0-7356-1572-1   Suggested Retail Price: $49.99 U.S., $72.99 Canada

The definitive guide for developers and administrators who need to understand how to securely manage networked systems based on IIS. This book presents obvious, avoidable mistakes and known security vulnerabilities in Internet Information Services (IIS)—priceless, intimate facts about the underlying causes of past security issues—while showing the best ways to fix them. The expert author, who has used IIS since the first version, also discusses real-world best practices for developing software and managing systems and networks with IIS.

To learn more about Microsoft Press® products for IT professionals, please visit:

microsoft.com/mspress/IT

Microsoft Press products are available worldwide wherever quality computer books are sold. For more information, contact your book or computer retailer, software reseller, or local Microsoft Sales Office, or visit our Web site at **microsoft.com/mspress**. To locate your nearest source for Microsoft Press products, or to order directly, call 1-800-MSPRESS in the United States. (In Canada, call 1-800-268-2222.)

Complete planning and migration information
for Microsoft Windows Server 2003

Introducing Microsoft® Windows® Server 2003
ISBN 0-7356-1570-5

Plan your deployment with this first look at Windows Server 2003, the successor to the Windows 2000 Server network operating system. A first look at the Windows Server 2003 network operating system, this book is ideal for IT professionals engaged in planning and deployment. It provides a comprehensive overview of the powerful new operating system and what's different about it—including new XML Web services and components, security, networking, Active Directory® directory service, Microsoft Internet Information Services, Microsoft SharePoint™ Team Services, support for IPv6, and more. This book has all the initial planning information and tools IT professionals need, whether they're upgrading from Microsoft Windows NT® or Windows 2000.

Migrating from Microsoft Windows NT Server 4.0 to Microsoft Windows Server 2003
ISBN 0-7356-1940-9

In-depth technical information for upgrading Windows NT 4.0–based systems to Windows Server 2003 from those who know the technology best. Get essential information for upgrading and migrating Windows-based servers, direct from the experts who know the technology best—the Microsoft Windows Server product team. This book gives IT professionals the information and resources they need to effectively migrate file servers, print servers, domain controllers, network infrastructure servers, Web servers, database servers, and other application servers. The book includes practical information and tips for planning server migrations; consolidating servers; resolving hardware, network, and application compatibility issues; configuring servers for high availability and security; migrating domains and domain accounts; transferring and updating account settings and policies; piloting, testing, and rolling out servers; and preparing to automate server administration.

To learn more about the full line of Microsoft Press® products for IT professionals, please visit:

microsoft.com/mspress/IT

Microsoft Press products are available worldwide wherever quality computer books are sold. For more information, contact your book or computer retailer, software reseller, or local Microsoft Sales Office, or visit our Web site at **microsoft.com/mspress**. To locate your nearest source for Microsoft Press products, or to order directly, call 1-800-MSPRESS in the United States. (In Canada, call 1-800-268-2222.)

The practical, portable guides to
Microsoft Windows Server 2003

Microsoft® Windows® Server 2003 Admin Pocket Consultant
ISBN 0-7356-1354-0

The practical, portable guide to Windows Server 2003. Here's the practical, pocket-sized reference for IT professionals who support Windows Server 2003. Designed for quick referencing, it covers all the essentials for performing everyday system-administration tasks. Topics covered include managing workstations and servers, using Active Directory® services, creating and administering user and group accounts, managing files and directories, data security and auditing, data back-up and recovery, administration with TCP/IP, WINS, and DNS, and more.

Microsoft IIS 6.0 Administrator's Pocket Consultant
ISBN 0-7356-1560-8

The practical, portable guide to IIS 6.0. Here's the eminently practical, pocket-sized reference for IT and Web professionals who work with Internet Information Services (IIS) 6.0. Designed for quick referencing and compulsively readable, this portable guide covers all the basics needed for everyday tasks. Topics include Web administration fundamentals, Web server administration, essential services administration, and performance, optimization, and maintenance. It's the fast-answers guide that helps users consistently save time and energy as they administer IIS 6.0.

To learn more about the full line of Microsoft Press® products for IT professionals, please visit:

microsoft.com/mspress/IT

Microsoft Press products are available worldwide wherever quality computer books are sold. For more information, contact your book or computer retailer, software reseller, or local Microsoft Sales Office, or visit our Web site at **microsoft.com/mspress.** To locate your nearest source for Microsoft Press products, or to order directly, call 1-800-MSPRESS in the United States. (In Canada, call 1-800-268-2222.)

Microsoft *Press*

Official Microsoft study guides *for the skills you need on the job—and on the exams.*

MCSA Self-Paced Training Kit: Microsoft® Windows® 2000 Core Requirements, Exams 70-210, 70-215, 70-216, and 70-218, Second Edition
ISBN 0-7356-1808-9

MCSE Self-Paced Training Kit: Microsoft Windows 2000 Core Requirements, Second Edition, Exams 70-210, 70-215, 70-216, and 70-217
ISBN 0-7356-1771-6

The **Microsoft Certified Systems Administrator (MCSA)** certification is designed for professionals who implement, manage, and troubleshoot existing network and system environments based on the Microsoft Windows 2000 and Windows .NET Server platforms. Whether you are seeking a new job as a systems administrator or already have experience in the field, MCSA certification will help advance your career by ensuring you have the skills to successfully implement and manage systems based on Microsoft technology. The **Microsoft Certified Systems Engineer (MCSE)** credential is the premier certification for professionals who analyze the business requirements and design and implement the infrastructure for business solutions based on the Microsoft Windows operating system and Microsoft Servers software. Master the skills tested on the MCSA and MCSE certification exams—and, more critically, on your job—with these official book-and-CD self-study TRAINING KITS. They're designed to teach you everything you need to know to plan, deploy, and support Windows 2000–based desktop, enterprise server, and network environments. They also give you CD-based testing tools to measure your progress and sharpen your test-taking skills. Best of all, you drive the instruction—working through the lessons and skill-building exercises on your own time, at your own pace. It's learning you can really put to work!

To learn more about the full line of Microsoft Press® certification products, please visit us at:

microsoft.com/mspress/certification

Microsoft Press products are available worldwide wherever quality computer books are sold. For more information, contact your book or computer retailer, software reseller, or local Microsoft Sales Office, or visit our Web site at **microsoft.com/mspress**. To locate your nearest source for Microsoft Press products, or to order directly, call 1-800-MSPRESS in the United States. (In Canada, call 1-800-268-2222.)

Get a **Free**
*e-mail newsletter, updates,
special offers, links to related books,
and more when you*

register on line!

Register your Microsoft Press® title on our Web site and you'll get
a FREE subscription to our e-mail newsletter, *Microsoft Press Book
Connections.* You'll find out about newly released and upcoming books
and learning tools, online events, software downloads, special offers
and coupons for Microsoft Press customers, and information about
major Microsoft® product releases. You can also read useful additional
information about all the titles we publish, such as detailed book
descriptions, tables of contents and indexes, sample chapters, links to
related books and book series, author biographies, and reviews by other
customers.

Registration is easy. Just visit this Web page and fill in your information:

http://www.microsoft.com/mspress/register

Microsoft®

Proof of Purchase

Use this page as proof of purchase if participating in a promotion or rebate offer on
this title. Proof of purchase must be used in conjunction with other proof(s) of
payment such as your dated sales receipt—see offer details.

Microsoft® Windows® Security Resource Kit
0-7356-1868-2

CUSTOMER NAME

Microsoft Press, PO Box 97017, Redmond, WA 98073-9830

END-USER LICENSE AGREEMENT
MICROSOFT SOFTWARE: Resource Kit CD

IMPORTANT—READ CAREFULLY: This Microsoft End-User License Agreement ("EULA") is a legal agreement between you (either an individual or a single entity) and Microsoft Corporation for the Microsoft software product identified above, which includes computer software and may include associated media, printed materials, and "online" or electronic documentation (**"SOFTWARE PRODUCT"**). This EULA constitutes the entire agreement between you and Microsoft with respect to this subject matter and supercedes all prior and contemporaneous agreements and/or communications. **By installing, copying, or otherwise using the SOFTWARE PRODUCT, you agree to be bound by the terms of this EULA. If you do not agree to the terms of this EULA, do not install or use the SOFTWARE PRODUCT; you may, however, return it to your place of purchase for a full refund.**

1. **GRANT OF LICENSE.** Microsoft grants you the following rights provided that you comply with all terms and conditions of this EULA:
   - **Software Product.** You may install and use one copy of the SOFTWARE PRODUCT on a single computer. The primary user of the computer on which the SOFTWARE PRODUCT is installed may make a second copy for his or her exclusive use on a portable computer.
   - **Storage/Network Use.** You may also store or install a copy of the SOFTWARE PRODUCT on a storage device, such as a network server, used only to install or run the SOFTWARE PRODUCT on your other computers over an internal network; however, you must acquire and dedicate a license for each separate computer on which the SOFTWARE PRODUCT is installed or run from the storage device. A license for the SOFTWARE PRODUCT may not be shared or used concurrently on different computers.
   - **License Pak.** If you have acquired this EULA in a Microsoft License Pak, you may make the number of additional copies of the computer software portion of the SOFTWARE PRODUCT authorized on the printed copy of this EULA, and you may use each copy in the manner specified above. You are also entitled to make a corresponding number of secondary copies for portable computer use as specified above.

2. **DESCRIPTION OF OTHER RIGHTS AND LIMITATIONS.**
   - **Separation of Components.** The SOFTWARE PRODUCT is licensed as a single product. Its component parts may not be separated for use.
   - **Support Services.** Microsoft may, but is not obligated to, provide you with support services related to the SOFTWARE PRODUCT ("Support Services"). Use of Support Services is governed by the Microsoft policies and programs described in the user manual, in "on-line" documentation, and/or in other Microsoft-provided materials. Any supplemental software code provided to you as part of the Support Services shall be considered part of the SOFTWARE PRODUCT and subject to the terms and conditions of this EULA. With respect to technical information you provide to Microsoft as part of the Support Services, Microsoft may use such information for its business purposes, including for product support and development. Microsoft will not utilize such technical information in a form that personally identifies you.

3. **RESERVATION OF RIGHTS AND OWNERSHIP.** Microsoft reserves all rights not expressly granted to you in this EULA. The SOFTWARE PRODUCT is protected by copyright and other intellectual property laws and treaties. Microsoft or its suppliers own the title, copyright, and other intellectual property rights in the SOFTWARE PRODUCT. **The SOFTWARE PRODUCT is licensed, not sold.**

4. **LIMITATIONS ON REVERSE ENGINEERING, DECOMPILATION, AND DISASSEMBLY.** You may not reverse engineer, decompile, or disassemble the SOFTWARE PRODUCT, except and only to the extent that such activity is expressly permitted by applicable law notwithstanding this limitation.

5. **NO RENTAL/COMMERCIAL HOSTING.** You may not rent, lease, lend or provide commercial hosting services with the SOFTWARE PRODUCT.

6. **CONSENT TO USE OF DATA.** You agree that Microsoft and its affiliates may collect and use technical information gathered as part of the product support services provided to you, if any, related to the SOFTWARE PRODUCT. Microsoft may use this information solely to improve our products or to provide customized services or technologies to you and will not disclose this information in a form that personally identifies you.

7. **INTELLECTUAL PROPERTY RIGHTS.** All title and intellectual property rights in and to the SOFTWARE PRODUCT (including but not limited to any images, photographs, animations, video, audio, music, text, and "applets" incorporated into the SOFTWARE PRODUCT) and any copies of the SOFTWARE PRODUCT that you are expressly permitted to make herein, are owned by Microsoft or its suppliers. All title and intellectual property rights in and to the content which may be accessed through use of the Product are the property of the respective content owner and may be protected by applicable copyright or other intellectual property laws and treaties. This Agreement grants you no rights to use such content. If the SOFTWARE PRODUCT contains documentation which is provided only in electronic form, recipient may print one copy of such electronic documentation. You may not copy the printed materials accompanying the SOFTWARE PRODUCT.

8. **U.S. GOVERNMENT LICENSE RIGHTS.** All Software provided to the U.S. Government pursuant to solicitations issued on or after December 1, 1995 is provided with the commercial license rights and restrictions described elsewhere herein. All Software provided to the U.S. Government pursuant to solicitations issued prior to December 1, 1995 is provided with "Restricted Rights" as provided for in FAR, 48 CFR 52.227-14 (JUNE 1987) or DFAR, 48 CFR 252.227-7013 (OCT 1988), as applicable.

9. **EXPORT RESTRICTIONS.** You acknowledge that the SOFTWARE PRODUCT is subject to U.S. export jurisdiction. You agree to comply with all applicable international laws that apply to the SOFTWARE PRODUCT, including the U.S. Export Administration Regulations, as well as end-user, end-use, and destination restrictions issued by U.S. and other governments. For additional information see http://www.microsoft.com/exporting.

10. **LINKS TO THIRD PARTY SITES.** You may link to third party sites through the use of the SOFTWARE PRODUCT. The third party sites are not under the control of Microsoft, and Microsoft is not responsible for the contents of any third party sites, any links contained in third party sites, or any changes or updates to third party sites. Microsoft is not responsible for webcasting or any other form of transmission received from any third party sites. Microsoft is providing these links to third party sites to you only as a convenience, and the inclusion of any link does not imply an endorsement by Microsoft of the third party site.

11. **ADDITIONAL SOFTWARE/SERVICES.** This EULA applies to updates, supplements, add-on components, or Internet-based services components, of the SOFTWARE PRODUCT that Microsoft may provide to you or make available to you after the date you obtain your initial copy of the SOFTWARE PRODUCT, unless we provide other terms along with the update, supplement, add-on component, or Internet-based services component. Microsoft reserves the right to discontinue any Internet-based services provided to you or made available to you through the use of the SOFTWARE PRODUCT.

12. **TERMINATION.** Without prejudice to any other rights, Microsoft may terminate this EULA if you fail to comply with the terms and conditions of this EULA. In such event, you must destroy all copies of the SOFTWARE PRODUCT and all of its component parts.

13. **NOT FOR RESALE SOFTWARE.** SOFTWARE PRODUCT identified as "Not For Resale" or "NFR," may not be sold or otherwise transferred for value, or used for any purpose other than demonstration, test or evaluation.

14. **SOFTWARE PRODUCT TRANSFER.** The initial user of the SOFTWARE PRODUCT may make a one-time permanent transfer of this EULA and the SOFTWARE PRODUCT to another end user, provided the initial user retains no copies of the SOFTWARE PRODUCT. This transfer must include all of the SOFTWARE PRODUCT (including all component parts, the media and printed materials, any upgrades, this EULA, and, if applicable, the Certificate of Authenticity). The transfer may not be an indirect transfer, such as a consignment. Prior to the transfer, the end user receiving the SOFTWARE PRODUCT must agree to all the EULA terms.

15. **DISCLAIMER OF WARRANTIES. TO THE MAXIMUM EXTENT PERMITTED BY APPLICABLE LAW, MICROSOFT AND ITS SUPPLIERS PROVIDE THE SOFTWARE PRODUCT AND SUPPORT SERVICES (IF ANY)** *AS IS AND WITH ALL FAULTS*, **AND HEREBY DISCLAIM ALL OTHER WARRANTIES AND CONDITIONS, WHETHER EXPRESS, IMPLIED OR STATUTORY, INCLUDING, BUT NOT LIMITED TO, ANY (IF ANY) IMPLIED WARRANTIES, DUTIES OR CONDITIONS OF MERCHANTABILITY, OF FITNESS FOR A PARTICULAR PURPOSE, OF RELIABILITY OR AVAILABILITY, OF ACCURACY OR COMPLETENESS OF RESPONSES, OF RESULTS, OF WORKMANLIKE EFFORT, OF LACK OF VIRUSES, AND OF LACK OF NEGLIGENCE, ALL WITH REGARD TO THE SOFTWARE PRODUCT, AND THE PROVISION OF OR FAILURE TO PROVIDE SUPPORT OR OTHER SERVICES, INFORMA-TION, SOFTWARE, AND RELATED CONTENT THROUGH THE SOFTWARE PRODUCT OR OTHERWISE ARISING OUT OF THE USE OF THE SOFTWARE. ALSO, THERE IS NO WARRANTY OR CONDITION OF TITLE, QUIET ENJOYMENT, QUIET POSSESSION, CORRESPONDENCE TO DESCRIPTION OR NON-INFRINGEMENT WITH REGARD TO THE SOFTWARE PRODUCT.**

16. **EXCLUSION OF INCIDENTAL, CONSEQUENTIAL AND CERTAIN OTHER DAMAGES.** TO THE MAXIMUM EXTENT PERMITTED BY APPLICABLE LAW, IN NO EVENT SHALL MICROSOFT OR ITS SUPPLIERS BE LIABLE FOR ANY SPECIAL, INCIDENTAL, PUNITIVE, INDIRECT, OR CONSEQUENTIAL DAMAGES WHATSOEVER (INCLUDING, BUT NOT LIMITED TO, DAMAGES FOR LOSS OF PROFITS OR CONFIDENTIAL OR OTHER INFORMATION, FOR BUSINESS INTERRUPTION, FOR PERSONAL INJURY, FOR LOSS OF PRIVACY, FOR FAILURE TO MEET ANY DUTY INCLUDING OF GOOD FAITH OR OF REASONABLE CARE, FOR NEGLIGENCE, AND FOR ANY OTHER PECUNIARY OR OTHER LOSS WHATSOVER) ARISING OUT OF OR IN ANY WAY RELATED TO THE USE OF OR INABILITY TO USE THE SOFTWARE PRODUCT, THE PROVISION OF OR FAILURE TO PROVIDE SUPPORT OR OTHER SERVICES, INFORMATION, SOFT-WARE, AND RELATED CONTENT THROUGH THE SOFTWARE PRODUCT OR OTHERWISE ARISING OUT OF THE USE OF THE SOFTWARE PRODUCT, OR OTHERWISE UNDER OR IN CONNECTION WITH ANY PROVISION OF THIS EULA, EVEN IN THE EVENT OF THE FAULT, TORT, (INCLUDING NEGLIGENCE), MISREPRESENTATION, STRICT LIABILITY, BREACH OF CONTRACT, OR BREACH OF WARRANTY OF MICROSOFT OR ANY SUPPLIER, AND EVEN IF MICROSOFT OR ANY SUPPLIER HAS BEEN ADVISED OF THE POSSIBILITY OF SUCH DAMAGES.

17. **LIMITATION OF LIABILITY AND REMEDIES.** NOTWITHSTANDING ANY DAMAGES THAT YOU MIGHT INCUR FOR ANY REASON WHATSOEVER (INCLUDING, WITHOUT LIMITATION, ALL DAMAGES REFERENCED HEREIN AND ALL DIRECT OR GENERAL DAMAGES IN CONTRACT OR ANYTHING ELSE), THE ENTIRE LIABILITY OF MICROSOFT AND ANY OF ITS SUPPLIERS UNDER ANY PROVISION OF THIS EULA AND YOUR EXCLUSIVE REMEDY HEREUNDER SHALL BE LIMITED TO THE GREATER OF THE ACTUAL DAMAGES YOU INCUR IN REASONABLE RELIANCE ON THE SOFTWARE PRODUCT UP TO THE AMOUNT ACTUALLY PAID BY YOU FOR THE SOFTWARE PRODUCT OR FIVE DOLLARS (US$5.00). THE FOREGOING LIMITATIONS, EXCLUSIONS AND DISCLAIMERS (INCLUDING SECTIONS 15 AND 16 ABOVE) SHALL APPLY TO THE MAXIMUM EXTENT PERMITTED BY APPLICABLE LAW, EVEN IF ANY REMEDY FAILS ITS ESSENTIAL PURPOSE.

18. **APPLICABLE LAW.** If you acquired this Software in the United States, this EULA is governed by the laws of the State of Washington. If you acquired this Software in Canada, unless expressly prohibited by local law, this EULA is governed by the laws in force in the Province of Ontario, Canada; and, in respect of any dispute which may arise hereunder, you consent to the jurisdiction of the federal and provincial courts sitting in Toronto, Ontario. If you acquired this Software in the European Union, Iceland, Norway, or Switzerland, then local law applies. If you acquired this Software in any other country, then local law may apply.

19. **ENTIRE AGREEMENT; SEVERABILITY.** This EULA (including any addendum or amendment to this EULA which is included with the Software) are the entire agreement between you and Microsoft relating to the Software and the support services (if any) and they supersede all prior or contemporaneous oral or written communications, proposals and representations with respect to the Software

or any other subject matter covered by this EULA. To the extent the terms of any Microsoft policies or programs for support services conflict with the terms of this EULA, the terms of this EULA shall control. If any provision of this EULA is held to be void, invalid, unenforceable or illegal, the other provisions shall continue in full force and effect.

Should you have any questions concerning this EULA, or if you desire to contact Microsoft for any reason, please use the address information enclosed in this SOFTWARE PRODUCT to contact the Microsoft subsidiary serving your country or visit Microsoft on the World Wide Web at *http://www.microsoft.com*.

Si vous avez acquis votre produit Microsoft au CANADA, la garantie limitée suivante s'applique :

DÉNI DE GARANTIES. **DANS LA MESURE MAXIMALE PERMISE PAR LES LOIS APPLICABLES, LE LOGICIEL ET LES SERVICES DE SOUTIEN TECHNIQUE (LE CAS ÉCHÉANT) SONT FOURNIS *TELS QUELS ET AVEC TOUS LES DÉFAUTS* PAR MICROSOFT ET SES FOURNISSEURS, LESQUELS PAR LES PRÉSENTES DÉNIENT TOUTES AUTRES GARANTIES ET CONDITIONS EXPRESSES, IMPLICITES OU EN VERTU DE LA LOI, NOTAMMENT, MAIS SANS LIMITATION, (LE CAS ÉCHÉANT) LES GARANTIES, DEVOIRS OU CONDITIONS IMPLICITES DE QUALITÉ MARCHANDE, D'ADAPTATION À UNE FIN PARTICULIÈRE, DE FIABILITÉ OU DE DISPONIBILITÉ, D'EXACTITUDE OU D'EXHAUSTIVITÉ DES RÉPONSES, DES RÉSULTATS, DES EFFORTS DÉPLOYÉS SELON LES RÈGLES DE L'ART, D'ABSENCE DE VIRUS ET D'ABSENCE DE NÉGLIGENCE, LE TOUT À L'ÉGARD DU LOGICIEL ET DE LA PRESTATION OU DE L'OMISSION DE LA PRESTATION DES SERVICES DE SOUTIEN TECHNIQUE OU À L'ÉGARD DE LA FOURNITURE OU DE L'OMISSION DE LA FOURNITURE DE TOUS AUTRES SERVICES, RENSEIGNEMENTS, LOGICIELS, ET CONTENU QUI S'Y RAPPORTE GRÂCE AU LOGICIEL OU PROVENANT AUTREMENT DE L'UTILISATION DU LOGICIEL . PAR AILLEURS, IL N'Y A AUCUNE GARANTIE OU CONDITION QUANT AU TITRE DE PROPRIÉTÉ, À LA JOUISSANCE OU LA POSSESSION PAISIBLE, À LA CONCORDANCE À UNE DESCRIPTION NI QUANT À UNE ABSENCE DE CONTREFAÇON CONCERNANT LE LOGICIEL.**

EXCLUSION DES DOMMAGES ACCESSOIRES, INDIRECTS ET DE CERTAINS AUTRES DOMMAGES. **DANS LA MESURE MAXIMALE PERMISE PAR LES LOIS APPLICABLES, EN AUCUN CAS MICROSOFT OU SES FOURNISSEURS NE SERONT RESPONSABLES DES DOMMAGES SPÉCIAUX, CONSÉCUTIFS, ACCESSOIRES OU INDIRECTS DE QUELQUE NATURE QUE CE SOIT (NOTAMMENT, LES DOMMAGES À L'ÉGARD DU MANQUE À GAGNER OU DE LA DIVULGATION DE RENSEIGNEMENTS CONFIDENTIELS OU AUTRES, DE LA PERTE D'EXPLOITATION, DE BLESSURES CORPORELLES, DE LA VIOLATION DE LA VIE PRIVÉE, DE L'OMISSION DE REMPLIR TOUT DEVOIR, Y COMPRIS D'AGIR DE BONNE FOI OU D'EXERCER UN SOIN RAISONNABLE, DE LA NÉGLIGENCE ET DE TOUTE AUTRE PERTE PÉCUNIAIRE OU AUTRE PERTE DE QUELQUE NATURE QUE CE SOIT) SE RAPPORTANT DE QUELQUE MANIÈRE QUE CE SOIT À L'UTILISATION DU LOGICIEL OU À L'INCAPACITÉ DE S'EN SERVIR, À LA PRESTATION OU À L'OMISSION DE LA PRESTATION DE SERVICES DE SOUTIEN TECHNIQUE OU À LA FOURNITURE OU À L'OMISSION DE LA FOURNITURE DE TOUS AUTRES SERVICES, RENSEIGNEMENTS, LOGICIELS, ET CONTENU QUI S'Y RAPPORTE GRÂCE AU LOGICIEL OU PROVENANT AUTREMENT DE L'UTILISATION DU LOGICIEL OU AUTREMENT AUX TERMES DE TOUTE DISPOSITION DE LA PRÉSENTE CONVENTION OU RELATIVEMENT À UNE TELLE DISPOSITION, MÊME EN CAS DE FAUTE, DE DÉLIT CIVIL (Y COMPRIS LA NÉGLIGENCE), DE RESPONSABILITÉ STRICTE, DE VIOLATION DE CONTRAT OU DE VIOLATION DE GARANTIE DE MICROSOFT OU DE TOUT FOURNISSEUR ET MÊME SI MICROSOFT OU TOUT FOURNISSEUR A ÉTÉ AVISÉ DE LA POSSIBILITÉ DE TELS DOMMAGES.**

LIMITATION DE RESPONSABILITÉ ET RECOURS. **MALGRÉ LES DOMMAGES QUE VOUS PUISSIEZ SUBIR POUR QUELQUE MOTIF QUE CE SOIT (NOTAMMENT, MAIS SANS LIMITATION, TOUS LES DOMMAGES SUSMENTIONNÉS ET TOUS LES DOMMAGES DIRECTS OU GÉNÉRAUX OU AUTRES), LA SEULE RESPONSABILITÉ DE MICROSOFT ET DE L'UN OU L'AUTRE DE SES FOURNISSEURS AUX TERMES DE TOUTE DISPOSITION DE LA PRÉSENTE CONVENTION ET VOTRE RECOURS EXCLUSIF À L'ÉGARD DE TOUT CE QUI PRÉCÈDE SE LIMITE AU PLUS ÉLEVÉ ENTRE LES MONTANTS SUIVANTS : LE MONTANT QUE VOUS AVEZ RÉELLEMENT PAYÉ POUR LE LOGICIEL OU 5,00 $US. LES LIMITES, EXCLUSIONS ET DÉNIS QUI PRÉCÈDENT (Y COMPRIS LES CLAUSES CI-DESSUS), S'APPLIQUENT DANS LA MESURE MAXIMALE PERMISE PAR LES LOIS APPLICABLES, MÊME SI TOUT RECOURS N'ATTEINT PAS SON BUT ESSENTIEL.**

À moins que cela ne soit prohibé par le droit local applicable, la présente Convention est régie par les lois de la province d'Ontario, Canada. Vous consentez à la compétence des tribunaux fédéraux et provinciaux siégeant à Toronto, dans la province d'Ontario.

Au cas où vous auriez des questions concernant cette licence ou que vous désiriez vous mettre en rapport avec Microsoft pour quelque raison que ce soit, veuillez utiliser l'information contenue dans le Logiciel pour contacter la filiale de Microsoft desservant votre pays, ou visitez Microsoft sur le World Wide Web à *http://www.microsoft.com*.

System Requirements

System Requirements for Tools and Scripts

To use the tools included on the companion CD, you'll need the following:

- Microsoft Windows 2000 or Microsoft Windows XP

> **Note** The *Microsoft Windows Security Resource Kit* companion CD includes a variety of tools and scripts. Many of these tools are from the *Microsoft Windows 2000 Server Resource Kit*, Supplement One, and were only tested in the Windows 2000 environment. For any additional information on tool requirements, consult the documentation included with each tool. Some of the tool documentation requires Microsoft Word or Word Viewer or Microsoft Excel or Excel Viewer. Word Viewer and Excel Viewer have been included on the CD-ROM.

Recommended System Requirements for eBook

The following system configuration is recommended for the best viewing experience of Microsoft Press eBooks:

- Microsoft Windows 98, Microsoft Windows 2000, or Microsoft Windows XP
- Pentium II (or similar) with 266 MHz or higher processor
- 64 MB RAM
- 8X CD-ROM drive or faster
- 800x600 with high color (16-bit) display settings
- Microsoft Internet Explorer 5.01 or later (Internet Explorer 6 SP1 is included on the CD)